TAKING SIDES

Clashing Views in

Abnormal Psychology

SEVENTH EDITION

Selected, Edited, and with Introductions by

Richard P. Halgin
University of Massachusetts–Amherst

Mc
Graw
Hill

Connect
Learn
Succeed™

The McGraw·Hill Companies

TAKING SIDES: ABNORMAL PSYCHOLOGY, SEVENTH EDITION

Published by McGraw-Hill, a business unit of The McGraw-Hill Companies, Inc., 1221 Avenue of
the Americas, New York, NY 10020. Copyright © 2013 by The McGraw-Hill Companies, Inc. All
rights reserved. Previous edition(s) © 2011, 2009, 2007, and 2005. No part of this publication
may be reproduced or distributed in any form or by any means, or stored in a database or
retrieval system, without the prior written consent of The McGraw-Hill Companies, Inc.,
including, but not limited to, in any network or other electronic storage or transmission, or
broadcast for distance learning.

Some ancillaries, including electronic and print components, may not be available to customers
outside the United States.

Taking Sides® is a registered trademark of the McGraw-Hill Companies, Inc.
Taking Sides is published by the **Contemporary Learning Series** group within the McGraw-Hill
Higher Education division.

1 2 3 4 5 6 7 8 9 0 DOC/DOC 1 0 9 8 7 6 5 4 3 2

MHID: 0-07-805050-2
ISBN: 978-0-07-805050-3
ISSN: 1527-604X (print)
ISSN: 2157-9725

Managing Editor: *Larry Loeppke*
Senior Developmental Editor: *Jade Benedict*
Permissions Coordinator: *DeAnna Dausener*
Senior Marketing Communications Specialist: *Nathan Edwards*
Senior Project Manager: *Jessica Portz*
Cover Graphics: *Studio Montage, St. Louis, Mo.*
Buyer: *Jennifer Pickel*
Media Project Manager: *Sridevi Palani*

Compositor: MPS Limited
Cover Image: Lisa Zador/Getty Images

Library of Congress Cataloging-in-Publication Data

Main entry under title:
    Taking sides: clashing views in abnormal psychology/selected, edited, and with introductions
    by Richard P. Halgin. —7th ed.

    Includes bibliographical references.
    1. Psychology, Pathological. I. Halgin, Richard P. *comp.*
                              616.89

Editors/Academic Advisory Board

Members of the Academic Advisory Board are instrumental in the final selection of articles for each edition of TAKING SIDES. Their review of articles for content, level, and appropriateness provides critical direction to the editors and staff. We think that you will find their careful consideration well reflected in this volume.

TAKING SIDES: Clashing Views in ABNORMAL PSYCHOLOGY
Seventh Edition

EDITORS

Richard P. Halgin
University of Massachusetts–Amherst

ACADEMIC ADVISORY BOARD MEMBERS

Preface

The field of abnormal psychology is inherently controversial because we lack a clear delineation between normal and abnormal behavior. Most phenomena in the realm of abnormal psychology fall along continua; the point on a continuum at which behavior moves from being considered "normal" to being considered "abnormal" varies considerably and is influenced by a number of factors. Consider the example of an active boy's behavior. His running around impulsively and shouting out aimless comments would be viewed as normal behavior on a playground but abnormal behavior in a quiet classroom. In a classroom setting, his behavior might be referred to as impulsive and hyperactive, possibly prompting his teacher to refer him to a mental health professional for therapy and medication to help him settle down and pay attention. Although such referrals are commonplace in American schools, some people contend that we pathologize the normal behavior of children when we view their high levels of energy as mental disorders. This is but one of the debates about which you will read in this book, and it is a good example of the kind of controversy found in the field of mental health.

There are many complex issues that arise in the field of abnormal psychology; in this book you will read about 18 controversial matters with which mental health experts struggle. Unit 1 looks at psychological conditions and treatments about which there has been vehement disagreement in recent years, with some experts expressing intense skepticism about the validity of specific clinical problems and interventions that have been in the spotlight. Unit 2 looks at the trend toward biological interventions for an array of psychological problems and mental disorders. Unit 3 explores pertinent social issues that interface with the field of abnormal psychology, particularly debates about ethical and legal issues that pertain to the field of mental health.

Most students who enroll in a course in abnormal psychology begin the semester with the belief that they will be learning about problems that affect "other people," rather than themselves. In a short period of time, however, they come to realize that they are reading about conditions that have much more personal salience than they had anticipated. Sooner or later, they recognize conditions that they or someone close to them has experienced, and their interest in the topic intensifies. In all likelihood, you will have a similar reaction as you read this book. To capture the essence of each debate, you will find it helpful to connect yourself in a personal way to the issue under consideration; you might imagine yourself dealing with the issue personally, or as the relative of a client with the particular problem, or even as a professional trying to provide mental health assistance.

Plan of the book To assist you in understanding the significance of each issue, every issue begins with an enumeration of five learning outcomes which will help you focus on the important lessons contained in the readings. You will then be provided with a thoughtful summary of the major points raised in each reading, with particular attention to the contrasting arguments on each side of the debate. Each issue concludes with a set of questions entitled "Exploring the Issue" which will guide you in the process of critical thinking and reflection. Next comes the section entitled "Is There Common Ground?" which considers shared concerns that emerged from both sides of the controversy. Additional resources are then provided so that you can delve more deeply into the topic in scholarly readings and relevant websites. At the back of the book is a listing of all the *Contributors to This Volume* with a brief biographical sketch of each of the prominent figures whose views are debated here.

Changes to this edition   This seventh edition of *Taking Sides: Clashing Views in Abnormal Psychology* includes some important changes from the sixth edition. This edition includes eight new sets of topics, containing a total of 16 new articles, plus an updated reading for the chapter on ADHD (Issue 1). The eight new topics address provocative debates which have emerged in recent years. "Is Posttraumatic Stress Disorder (PTSD) Overdiagnosed and Ovetreated?" (Issue 2) addresses a condition that has become increasingly common as a result of the wars in Iraq and Afghanistan. "Do We Still Need Psychiatrists?" (Issue 5) raises the question about the extent to which psychiatrists may be overstepping boundaries by engaging in diagnostic mislabeling and mistreatment. "Should 'Smart Drugs' Be Used to Enhance Cognitive Functioning?" (Issue 6) is a topic that will be of interest to many college students looking for any means available to help them excel academically. "Should Memory-Dampening Drugs Be Used to Prevent and Treat Trauma in Combat Soldiers?" (Issue 7) addresses the thorny topic of whether it is advisable to suppress the experience of trauma resulting from combat. "Does Research Confirm That Violent Video Games Are Harmful to Minors?" (Issue 9) discusses the legal arguments relating to research on the possible detrimental psychological effects of violent video games on minors. "Should Individuals with Anorexia Nervosa Have the Right to Refuse Life-Sustaining Treatment?" (Issue 13) discusses the extent to which personal autonomy should be respected even in situations involving life-threatening self-starvation. "Is Excessive Use of Facebook a Form of Narcissism?" (Issue 18) questions whether the personality trait of narcissism correlates with excessive use of social network systems such as Facebook.

A word to the instructor   An *Instructor's Resource Guide with Test Questions* (multiple-choice and essay) is available through the publisher for the instructor using *Taking Sides* in the classroom. Instructors will also find a general guidebook, *Using Taking Sides in the Classroom*, which discusses methods and techniques for integrating the pro-con approach into any classroom setting. Online versions of all of these resources, as well as correspondence service for *Taking Sides* adopters, can be found on the "instructor" link of the book's website at www.mhhe.com/cls.

While article references have not been included in the printed book in order to limit book size, all references for articles appearing in *Taking Sides:*

Clashing Views in Abnormal Psychology, 7/e are available on the "student" link of the book's website at www.mhhe.com/cls.

Acknowledgments   Very special gratitude goes to the research assistants who contributed to the preparation of this volume by conducting bibliographic research and editing the issues. Special thanks to Conor Allen, who served as senior editorial assistant in preparing the manuscript for publication and developing the material for several chapters. Also invaluable were the contributions of Cassandra Treat and Wilton Dadmun, who provided creative ideas and conducted careful research throughout the project. Special gratitude also goes to the research assistants whose contributions to previous editions continue to be evident in the seventh edition: Rebecca Gray, Ilana Klarman, Alexander Miller, and Eric Nguyen.

Thanks also to Jade Benedict and the staff at McGraw-Hill Contemporary Learning Series, who have contributed in countless ways in making this volume as vibrant and effective as possible.

Richard P. Halgin
University of Massachusetts–Amherst

*To my wonderful wife, Lucille, whose love
and support provide me with immeasurable
amounts of energy, and to our children,
Daniel and Kerry, whose values
and achievements have been
inspiring.*

The Educational Experience of Disciplinary Controversy*

BRENT D. SLIFE
Brigham Young University

As a long-time user of the *Taking Sides* books, I have seen first-hand their educational impact on students. A student we will call "Brittany" is a prime example. Until her role in a *Taking Sides* panel discussion, she had not participated once in class discussions. It is probably fair to say that she was sleepwalking through the course. However, once she was assigned to a "side" of the panel discussion, she vigorously pitched in "to do battle," as she put it, with the opposing team. She described a "kind of energy" as she and the rest of her team prepared for the upcoming debate. In fact, she found herself and her teammates "talking trash" good-naturedly with the opposing team before the actual discussion, despite her usual reserve. Because she wanted to win, she "drilled down" and even did extra research.

The panel discussion itself, she reported, was exhilarating, but what I noticed afterward was probably the most intriguing. Not only did she participate in class more frequently, taking more risks in class discussions because she knew her teammates would support her, she also found herself having a position from which to see other positions in the discipline. Somehow, as she explained, her advocating a particular position on the panel, even though she knew I had arbitrarily assigned it, gave her a stake in other discussions and a perspective from which to contribute to them. Brittany's experience nicely illustrates the unique educational impact of the *Taking Sides* series.

Taking Sides is designed quite intentionally to shore up some of the weaknesses of many contemporary educational settings. The unique energy that Brittany experienced is a result of *Taking Sides* specific focus on the controversial side of academic disciplines. For several good reasons instructors and textbooks have traditionally focused almost exclusively on the more factual or settled aspects of their disciplines. This focus has led, in turn, to educational strategies that can rob the subject matter of its vitality.

Taking Sides, on the other hand, is uniquely structured to highlight the more issue-oriented aspects of a discipline, allowing students to care about and even invest in the subject matter as did Brittany. Involvement can spur a deeper understanding of the topic and help students to appreciate how knowledge advancement is sometimes driven by passionate positions. This focus has led, in turn, to educational strategies that can rob the subject matter of its vitality.

---

*The full text of this essay and references are available online at: http://highered .mcgraw-hill.com/sites/0076667771/information_center_view0/

Including the Controversial

A case could be made that a complete understanding of any discipline includes its controversies. Controversies may not be considered "knowledge" per se, depending on the discipline, but there is surely no doubt that they are part of the process of advancing knowledge. The conflicts generated among disciplinary leaders often produce problem-solving energy, if not disciplinary passions. In fact, they can drive entire disciplinary conferences and whole programs of investigation. In this sense, disciplinary controversies are not just "error" or an indication of the absence of knowledge; they can be viewed as a positive part of the discipline, a generator of disciplinary vigor if not purpose.

If this is true, then de-emphasizing the controversial elements of a discipline is de-emphasizing a vital part of the discipline itself. Students may learn accepted aspects of the discipline, but they may not learn, at least directly, the disputed aspects. This de-emphasis may not only produce an incomplete or inaccurate sense of the discipline, but it may also mislead the student to understand the field as more sterile, less emotional, and less "messy" than it truly is. The more rational, factual side is clearly important, perhaps even the more important. The question, however, is: do these more settled and perhaps rational aspects of the discipline have to monopolize courses for beginning students?

Another way to put the question might be: couldn't some portion of the course be devoted to the more controversial, thus allowing the student to engage the field in a more emotional manner? In some sense, the more settled and accepted the information is, the less students can feel they are truly participating in the disciplinary enterprise. After all, this information is already decided; there is no room for involvement in developing and "owning" the information. Students may even assume they will be punished for challenging the disciplinary status quo.

Specific Educational Benefits

Engaging the Discipline. When controversy is placed in the foreground of an educational experience, it gives disciplinary novices (students) permission to participate in and perhaps even form their own positions on some of the issues in the field. After all, some issues have not been addressed; some problems have not been solved. As Brittany put it, she was ready to "do battle" with the alternative position, even though she was quite aware of the arbitrariness of her own positional assignment. She was aware that something was at stake; something was to be decided.

In other words, it is the very *lack* of resolution in a controversy that invites students to make sense of the issues themselves and perhaps even venture their own thoughts. Obviously, students should be encouraged to be humble about these positions, understanding that their perspective is fledgling, but even novice positions can facilitate greater engagement with the materials. In a sense, the controversy, and thus a vital part of the discipline, becomes their own, as the example of Brittany illustrates. She not only "owned" a disciplinary position, she used it as a conceptual bridge to engage other settled and unsettled aspects of the discipline.

Appreciating the Messy. Students can also experience the messiness of disciplines using *Taking Sides.* I use the term "messiness" because conventional texts are notorious for representing the field too neatly and too logically, as if there were no human involvement. If disciplines are more than their settled aspects, there are also unsettled elements, including poorly defined terms and inadequately understood concepts, which also need to be appreciated. This messiness is what led Brittany to "drill down" and do "extra research" in her preparation for her panel discussion. She knew that some of the basic terms and understandings were at play.

Good conventional texts may attempt to include these unsettled aspects, but they typically do so in a deceptively logical fashion, as though the controversy is solely rational. This presentation may not only distort these aspects of the discipline but also deliver merely a secondhand report. By contrast, *Taking Sides* books—in pitting two authors against one another—facilitate an *experience* with actual published authorities, who are struggling with the issues from completely different perspectives. In reading both articles, students cannot help but struggle *with* the authors. They do not need to be *told* that the terms of the debate are problematic; the students *experience* these terms as problematic when they attempt to understand what is at stake in the authors' positions.

Preventing Premature Closure. The *Taking Sides* structure also serves to prevent students from prematurely closing controversies. Premature closure can occur by underestimating the controversy's depth or deciding it without a proper appreciation for the issues involved. *Taking Sides* prevents this prematurity by helping the student to experience how two reasonable and highly educated people can so thoroughly disagree. In other words, premature closure is discouraged because real experts are countering each other, sometimes point by point.

A student would almost have to ignore one side of the controversy, one of the experts, to prematurely close the issue. Brittany, for example, reported that she became "absolutely convinced" of the validity of the first authors' position, only to have the second reading put this position into question! Obviously, if the issue could be closed or settled so easily, presumably the experts or leaders of the discipline would have done so already. Controversies are controversies because they are *deeply* problematic, so it is important for the student to appreciate this, and thus have a more profound understanding of the disciplinary meanings involved.

Rehabilitating the Dialectic. One of the truly unique benefits of the *Taking Sides* experience is its rehabilitation of the age-old educational tradition of the dialectic. Since at least the time of Socrates, educators have understood that a *full* understanding of any disciplinary meaning, explanation, or bit of information requires not only knowing what this meaning or information is but also knowing what it isn't. The dialectic, in this sense, is the educational relation of a concept to its alternative (see Rychlak, 2003). As dialectician Joseph Rychlak (1991) explains, all meanings "reach beyond themselves" and are thus clarified and have implications beyond their synonyms. It may be trivial to note, for example, that one cannot fully comprehend what "up" means without understanding what "down" means. However, this dialectic is not trivial when the meanings are disciplinary, such as when the political science student realizes that justice is incomprehensible without some apprehension of the meaning of injustice.

One of the more fascinating educational moments, when using *Taking Sides* books, occurs when students recognize that they cannot properly understand even one side of the controversy without taking into account another side. Brittany described learning very quickly that she clarified and even became aware of important aspects of her own position only *after* she understood the alternative to her position. This dialectical awareness is also pivotal to truly critical thinking.

Facilitating Critical Thinking. I say "truly" critical thinking because critical thinking has sometimes been confused with rigorous thinking (see Slife et al., 2005). Rigorous thinking is the application of rigorous reasoning or analytical thinking to a particular problem, which is surely an important skill in most any field. Still, it is not truly *critical* thinking until one has an alternative perspective from which to criticize a perspective. Recall that Brittany did not participate in class until she developed a perspective to view other perspectives. In other words, one must have a (critical) perspective "outside of" or alternative to the perspective being critiqued. Otherwise, one is "inside" the perspective being critiqued and cannot "see" it as a whole.

As many recent educational formulations of critical thinking attest, this approach means that critical thinkers should develop at least a dialectic of perspectives (one plus an alternative). That is to say, they should have an awareness of their own perspective as *facilitated* by an understanding of at least one alternative perspective. Without an alternative, students assume either they have no position or their position is the *only* one possible. A point of comparison, on the other hand, prevents the reification of one's perspective and allows students to have a perspective on their perspectives. A clear strength of the *Taking Sides'* juxtaposition of alternative perspectives is that it facilitates this kind of critical thinking.

These five benefits—engaging the discipline, appreciating the messy, preventing premature closure, rehabilitating the dialectic, and facilitating critical thinking—are probably not exclusive to controversy. However, they are, I would contend, a relatively unique *package* of educational advantages that students can gain with the inclusion of a *Taking Sides* approach in the classroom. Controversy, of course, is rarely helpful on its own; settled information and sound reasoning must buttress and perhaps even ground controversy. Otherwise, it is more heat than light. Even so, an *exclusive* focus on the settled and more cognitive aspects can deprive students of the vitality of a discipline and prevent the ownership of information that is so important to real learning.

Contents In Brief

Contents

Dr. Stephen Joseph argues that since the development of posttraumatic stress disorder (PTSD) as a diagnosis, the definition of trauma has been altered from its 1980 definition in *DSM-III,* and has been applied so loosely that everyday experiences can now be considered traumatic. The Department of Veterans Affairs (VA) states that PTSD can develop in any individuals who have gone through a life-threatening event that caused them to fear for their lives, see horrible things, and feel helpless. The VA urges therapists to help individuals with PTSD identify what triggers their stressful memories, find ways to cope with intense feelings about the past, become aware of their feelings and reactions in order to change their reactions, and raise their self-esteem.

The Traditional Values Coalition argues that gender-variant people are psychologically disturbed individuals who need professional help, and that their condition should be viewed as a mental disorder. Kelley Winters asserts that the GID diagnosis imposes the stigma of mental illness upon people who meet no scientific definition of mental disorder.

Psychologists Grant J. Devilly and Peter Cotton assert that critical incident stress debriefing (CISD) is poorly defined and has been shown to do more harm than good. They propose alternative approaches for responding to trauma survivors, which they consider more effective. Jeffrey T. Mitchell of the International Critical Incident Stress Foundation (ICISF) argues that Devilly and Cotton have misrepresented important information about psychological debriefing and have confused several aspects of this system of responding to trauma survivors.

Psychiatrist Steven Moffic states that psychiatrists play critically important roles in the field of mental health care because they are extensively trained and well-versed in understanding the functioning of the human body and the treatment of mental disorders. He urges psychiatrists to accept constructive criticism and to take steps to move forward in developing innovative intervention models such as collaborating on-site with primary care physicians in offering integrated care. Psychiatrist Steven Balt believes that psychiatrists have overstepped the boundaries of their position, and doing so has often led to mislabeling and mistreating countless people. He contends that much of what psychiatrists do is pseudoscience, but that most people nevertheless buy into the psychiatric model. He argues that psychiatrists, with their years of scientific education, can use their influence to change the current state of affairs in the field of mental health.

Professor Barbara J. Sahakian and Dr. Sharon Morein-Zamir note that cognitive enhancing medications provide considerable benefits to individuals with cognitive disabilities, and can also serve as "smart drugs" for healthy individuals for the purpose of cognitive enhancement. While more research is needed into the long-term effects of these drugs on healthy individuals, responsible use of these drugs is recommended in order to gain maximum benefits with minimal harm to the individual and to society as a whole. Attorney and Professor Helia Garrido Hull explains that the use of cognitive enhancing drugs by healthy individuals can have a negative impact on individuals with disabilities. The use of such drugs in competitive environments such as classrooms creates an imbalance between students without cognitive disabilities and those with disabilities for whom the drugs were originally intended. She asserts that the government has a responsibility to enforce the law in order to maintain the integrity of decades of legal precedent intended to protect individuals with disabilities from becoming disadvantaged again. Although many of these drugs are listed as controlled substances, their use without a prescription has become widespread and viewed as morally acceptable.

Research scientist Elise Donovan states that an alarming and rising number of soldiers are returning from combat suffering from PTSD, and that medications such as the beta-blocker propranolol can alleviate their symptoms. Propranolol, she argues, will help soldiers with PTSD who have essentially lost "their sense of self" reintegrate into society. Because the drug causes memory dampening, rather than memory loss, it will create an opportunity for veterans to better cope with everyday life upon returning from combat. She believes that symptoms and consequential behaviors associated with PTSD (i.e., suicide, domestic abuse, alcohol or drug abuse) will be greatly reduced in PTSD patients who take propranolol. Dr. Donovan also states that use of propranolol will foster an experience of posttraumatic growth. The President's Council on Bioethics, chaired by Dr. Leon Kass, criticizes the use of memory-dampening drugs to treat the symptoms of trauma by asking, "What kind of society are we likely to have when the powers to control memory, mood, and mental life through drugs reach their full maturity?" The Council asserts that identities are formed by what people do and what they undergo or suffer. Escaping painful memories would necessarily result in a change in the identity of who the person is, as well as the person's perception and understanding of significant life events.

In the NIDA publication, the argument is made that addiction is indeed a disease, and that scientific information is available about the nature, prevention, and treatment of this disease. Psychiatrist Sally Satel and psychologist Scott O. Lilienfeld object to the brain disease characterization of drug addiction, asserting that addiction is an activity whose course can be altered by its foreseeable consequences.

UNIT 3   SOCIAL, ETHICAL, AND LEGAL ISSUES   197

California State Senator Leland Yee and Attorney Steven F. Gruel (Counsel of Record for the professional associations in pediatrics and psychology) contend that substantial research shows that violent video games can cause psychological or neurological harm to minors. Studies have shown that, in addition to fostering aggressive thought and behavior, ultra-violent video games can lead to reduced activity in the frontal lobes of the brain as well as behavioral problems such as antisocial behavior and poor school performance. Senator Yee and Attorney Gruel believe that the government has a duty to protect children, and that the First Amendment of the U.S. Constitution, with regard to free speech, should not be used to place at risk immature children who cannot discern the difference between fantasy and reality. Attorney Patricia A. Millett (Counsel of Record for the amicus curiae submitted on behalf of the Entertainment Merchants Association) argues that there is insufficient evidence to show that violent video games can cause psychological or neurological harm to minors. Attorney Millett claims that the various studies cited in the opposing amicus curiae are either flawed or have been discredited. She also asserts that studies have shown no compelling causal connections between playing violent video games and aggressive or antisocial behavior in youths.

Professor of law Arnold H. Loewy views the issue of virtual child pornography from a legal perspective, asserting that such material is a form of free speech that ought to be constitutionally protected. He also contends that legalizing virtual child pornography would reduce the extent to which real children would be exploited. Authors Diana E. H. Russell and Natalie J. Purcell express vehement objections to any forms of pornography involving images of children, asserting that Internet users with no previous sexual interest in children may find themselves drawn into a world in which the societal prohibition against adult–child sex is undermined.

The American Psychological Association, the American Psychiatric Association, and the National Alliance on Mental Illness collaborated in the preparation of an *amici curiae* brief pertaining to the case of Scott Panetti, who was sentenced to death for murder. In this brief, The argument is made that mentally ill convicts should not be executed if their disability significantly impairs their capacity to understand the nature and purpose of their punishment or to appreciate why the punishment is being imposed on them. In his position as Attorney General of Texas, Greg Abbott argued the case of "*Scott Louis Panetti, Petitioner v. Nathaniel Quarterman, Director, Texas Department of Criminal Justice, Correctional Institutions Division, Respondent.*" Attorney General Abbott asserts that punishment for murder does not depend on the rational understanding of the convicted individual, but rather on the convict's moral culpability at the time the crime was committed.

The APA Task Force (TFMHA) reviewed the empirical literature and concluded that for women who have an unplanned pregnancy, the risk of mental health problems is no greater than the risk for women who deliver an unplanned pregnancy. Professor Priscilla K. Coleman contends that the TFMHA analysis of the evidence reflects politically motivated bias in the selection of studies, analysis of the literature, and the conclusions derived.

Dr. Campbell and Dr. Aulisio argue that anorexia patients should be allowed to refuse treatment so long as they are competent and capable of understanding the implications of their actions. Drs. Tan, Stewart, Fitzpatrick, and Hope assert that anorexia nervosa profoundly affects individuals with this condition in a variety of ways which could make them incompetent.

Laurie Ahern and Eric Rosenthal, writing on behalf of Mental Disability Rights International (MDRI), characterize the intentional infliction of pain at JRC as human rights abuses. Psychologist Matthew Israel, director of the Judge Rotenberg Center (JRC), responds to the MDRI with insistence that JRC is using behavioral methods to save individuals from their treatment-resistant, life-threatening disorders.

Psychologists Mark Costanzo, Ellen Gerrity, and M. Brinton Lykes assert that the involvement of psychologists in enhanced interrogations is a violation of fundamental ethical principles. Psychologist and intelligence expert Kirk M. Hubbard asserts that psychologists can assist in developing effective, lawful ways to obtain actionable intelligence in fighting terrorism and can bring a wealth of knowledge to the administration of interrogations.

Authors Tim Bayne and Neil Levy argue that people with body integrity identity disorder are in emotional pain because of their experience of incongruity between their body image and their actual body. Such individuals should be accorded with their prerogative to have a healthy limb amputated. Author Wesley J. Smith objects to the notion of acquiescing to the wishes for healthy limb amputation in people whom he views as severely mentally disturbed. Smith asserts that these people need treatment, not amputation.

Attorney Samuel J. Brakel and psychiatrist John M. Davis assert that society has a responsibility to take care of seriously mentally ill individuals who are incapable of making an informed decision about their need for care and treatment. Attorney James B. Gottstein contends that forced treatment of mentally ill citizens represents a curtailment of liberty which leads many people down a road of permanent disability and poverty.

Communication Professor Christopher J. Carpenter asserts that there is a relationship between the frequency of Facebook use and narcissistic traits. While maintaining that Facebook provides opportunities for positive social interaction, Professor Carpenter argues that some users abuse the affordances and behave in anti-social ways on Facebook. Looking at two characteristics of narcissism, "grandiose exhibitionism" (GE) and "entitlement/exploitativeness" (EE), GE is related to extensive self-presentation to as large an audience as possible via status updates, photos, and acquiring large numbers of friends. EE is related to anti-social behaviors such as retaliating against negative comments, reading others' status updates for references to self, and seeking more social support than one provides. Communication Professors Bruce C. McKinney, Lynne Kelly, and Robert L. Duran argue that narcissism is unrelated to the frequency of using Facebook to post about oneself (i.e., status updates and photos), although it is related to number of Facebook friends. They conclude, however, that Facebook is not dominated by narcissistic Millennials, but by people who are oriented toward openness with regard to their daily lives, and who believe that it is appropriate and enjoyable to share information with a wide circle of friends.

Correlation Guide

The *Taking Sides* series presents current issues in a debate-style format designed to stimulate student interest and develop critical thinking skills. Each issue is thoughtfully framed with an issue summary, an issue introduction, and challenge questions. The pro and con essays—selected for their liveliness and substance—represent the arguments of leading scholars and commentators in their fields.

Taking Sides: Clashing Views in Abnormal Psychology, 7/e is an easy-to-use reader that presents issues on important topics such as *Posttraumatic Stress Disorder, cognitive enhancing medications,* and *forced treatment.* For more information on *Taking Sides* and other *McGraw-Hill Contemporary Learning Series* titles, visit www.mhhe.com/cls.

This convenient guide matches the issues in **Taking Sides: Clashing Views in Abnormal Psychology, 7/e** with the corresponding chapters in two of our best-selling McGraw-Hill Abnormal Psychology textbooks by Whitborne/Halgin and Nolen-Hoeksema.

Taking Sides: Abnormal Psychology, 7/e	Abnormal Psychology, 7/e by Whitborne/Halgin	Abnormal Psychology Media and Research Update, 5/e by Nolen-Hoeksema
Issue 1: Is Attention-Deficit/Hyperactivity Disorder (ADHD) a Real Disorder?	**Chapter 11:** Development-Related Disorders	**Chapter 10:** Childhood Disorders
Issue 2: Is Posttraumatic Stress Disorder (PTSD) Over-diagnosed and Overtreated?	**Chapter 6:** Somatoform Disorders, Psychological Factors Affecting Medical Conditions, and Dissociative Disorders	**Chapter 5:** Anxiety Disorders **Chapter 7:** Mood Disorders and Suicide
Issue 3: Is Gender Identity Disorder a Mental Illness?	**Chapter 2:** Classification and Treatment Plans **Chapter 7:** Sexual Disorders	**Chapter 9:** Personality Disorders **Chapter 10:** Childhood Disorders **Chapter 13:** Sexual Disorders
Issue 4: Is Psychological Debriefing a Harmful Intervention for Survivors of Trauma?	**Chapter 2:** Classification and Treatment Plans	**Chapter 2:** Theories and Treatment of Abnormality **Chapter 5:** Anxiety Disorders
Issue 5: Do We Still Need Psychiatrists?	**Chapter 1:** Overview to Understanding Abnormal Behavior	**Chapter 2:** Theories and Treatment of Abnormality
Issue 6: Should "Smart Drugs" Be Used to Enhance Cognitive Functioning?	**Chapter 11:** Development-Related Disorders **Chapter 12:** Aging-Related and Cognitive Disorders	**Chapter 4:** The Research Endeavor
Issue 7: Should Memory-dampening Drugs Be Used to Prevent and Treat Trauma in Combat Soldiers?	**Chapter 2** Classification and Treatment Plans	**Chapter 2:** Theories and Treatment of Abnormality **Chapter 5:** Anxiety Disorders **Chapter 7:** Mood Disorders and Suicide

(Continued)

Taking Sides: Abnormal Psychology, 7/e	Abnormal Psychology, 7/e by Whitborne/Halgin	Abnormal Psychology Media and Research Update, 5/e by Nolen-Hoeksema
Issue 8: Is Addiction a Brain Disease?	**Chapter 13:** Substance-Related Disorders	**Chapter 14:** Substance-Related Disorders
Issue 9: Does Research Confirm That Violent Video Games Are Harmful to Minors?	**Chapter 11:** Development-Related Disorders **Chapter 15:** Ethical and Legal Issues	**Chapter 4:** The Research Endeavor
Issue 10: Would Legalization of Virtual Child Pornography Reduce Sexual Exploitation of Children?	**Chapter 7:** Sexual Disorders	**Chapter 13:** Sexual Disorders
Issue 11: Must Mentally Ill Murderers Have a Rational Understanding of Why They Are Being Sentenced to Death?	**Chapter 15:** Ethical and Legal Issues	**Chapter 8:** Schizophrenia **Chapter 16:** Mental Health and the Law
Issue 12: Does Research Confirm That Abortion Is a Psychologically Benign Experience?	**Chapter 3:** Assessment **Chapter 8:** Mood Disorders	**Chapter 2:** Theories and Treatment of Abnormality **Chapter 4:** The Research Endeavor
Issue 13: Should Individuals with Anorexia Nervosa Have the Right to Refuse Life-sustaining Treatment?	**Chapter 14:** Eating Disorders and Impulse-Control Disorders **Chapter 15:** Ethical and Legal Issues	**Chapter 12:** Eating Disorders
Issue 14: Is the Use of Aversive Treatment an Inhumane Intervention for Psychologically Disordered Individuals?	**Chapter 2:** Classification and Treatment Plans **Chapter 15:** Ethical and Legal Issues	**Chapter 2:** Theories and Treatment of Abnormality
Issue 15: Is It Unethical for Psychologists to Be Involved in Coercive Interrogations?	**Chapter 15:** Ethical and Legal Issues	**Chapter 16:** Mental Health and the Law
Issue 16: Is It Ethical to Support the Wish for Healthy Limb Amputation in People with Body Integrity Identity Disorder (BIID)?	**Chapter 6:** Somatoform Disorders, Psychological Factors Affecting Medical Conditions, and Dissociative Disorders **Chapter 15:** Ethical and Legal Issues	**Chapter 6:** Somatoform and Dissociative Disorders **Chapter 16:** Mental Health and the Law
Issue 17: Is Forced Treatment of Seriously Mentally Ill Individuals Justifiable?	**Chapter 2:** Classification and Treatment Plans **Chapter 15:** Ethical and Legal Issues	**Chapter 2:** Theories and Treatment of Abnormality **Chapter 4:** The Research Endeavor **Chapter 15:** Health Psychology **Chapter 16:** Mental Health and the Law
Issue 18. Is Excessive Use of Facebook a Form of Narcissism?	**Chapter 3:** Assessment **Chapter 10:** Personality Disorders **Chapter 14:** Eating Disorders and Impulse-Control Disorders	**Chapter 9:** Personality Disorders

Topic Guide

This topic guide suggests how the selections in this book relate to the subjects covered in your course. You may want to use the topics listed on these pages to search the web more easily. On the following pages a number of websites have been gathered specifically for this book. They are arranged to reflect the units of this Taking Sides reader. You can link to these sites by going to www.mhhe.com/cls.

All issues, and their articles that relate to each topic are listed below the bold-faced term.

Abortion

12. Does Research Confirm That Abortion Is a Psychologically Benign Experience?

Addiction

8. Is Addiction a Brain Disease?

Anorexia Nervosa

13. Should Individuals with Anorexia Nervosa Have the Right to Refuse Life-Sustaining Treatment?

Attention Deficit/Hyperactivity Disorder (ADHD)

1. Is Attention-Deficit/Hyperactivity Disorder (ADHD) a Real Disorder?

Cognition

6. Should "Smart Drugs" Be Used to Enhance Cognitive Functioning?

Deviant Behavior

9. Does Research Confirm That Violent Video Games Are Harmful to Minors?
10. Would Legalization of Virtual Child Pornography Reduce Sexual Exploitation of Children?

Ethics

15. Is it Unethical for Psychologists to Be Involved in Coercive Interrogations?
16. Is It Ethical to Support the Wish for Healthy Limb Amputation in People with Body Integrity Identity Disorder (BIID)?

Interrogations

15. Is It Unethical for Psychologists to Be Involved in Coercive Interrogations?

Intervention

4. Is Psychological Debriefing a Harmful Intervention for Survivors of Trauma?

Media

9. Does Research Confirm That Violent Video Games Are Harmful to Minors?
18. Is Excessive Use of Facebook a Form of Narcissism?

Medication

6. Should "Smart Drugs" Be Used to Enhance Cognitive Functioning?
7. Should Memory-Dampening Drugs Be Used to Prevent and Treat Trauma in Combat Soldiers?

Introduction

What's "Abnormal" about Abnormal Psychology?

Richard P. Halgin

The field of abnormal psychology lends itself well to a discussion of controversial issues because of the inherent difficulty involved in defining the concept of "abnormal." The definition of abnormality is contingent on a myriad of influences that include cultural, historical, geographical, societal, interpersonal, and intrapersonal factors. What is considered everyday behavior in one culture might be regarded as bizarre in another. What was acceptable at one point in time might seem absurd in contemporary society. What seems customary in one region, even in one section of a large city, might be viewed as outrageous elsewhere. Even on a very personal level, one person's typical style of emotional expression might be experienced by another person as odd and disruptive. This introductory essay looks at some of the complex issues involved in defining and understanding abnormality and, in doing so, will set the stage for the controversial issues that follow. With this theoretical foundation, you will be better equipped to tackle the thorny issues in this volume and to develop an approach for reaching your own conclusions about these controversies.

Defining Abnormality

One of the best ways to begin a discussion of the complexity of defining abnormality is by considering our own behavior. Think about an outlandish costume that you wore to a Halloween party and the fun you had engaging in this completely normal behavior. Now imagine wearing the same costume to class the following day, and think about the reactions you would have received. What seemed so normal on the evening of October 31 would have been considered bizarre on the morning of November 1. Only a day later, in a different context, you would have been regarded as abnormal, and your behavior would have been viewed as both disturbed and disturbing. Consider another example: Recall a time in which you were intensely emotional, perhaps weeping profusely at a funeral. If you were to display similar emotionality a few days later in a class discussion, your behavior would cause considerable stir, and your classmates would be taken aback by the intensity of your emotions. Now consider a common behavior that is completely acceptable and expected in American culture, such as shaking a person's hand upon meeting. Did you know that in some cultures such behavior is regarded as rude and unacceptable? These simple examples highlight the ways in which the concept of "normal" is contingent on many factors. Because of the wide variability in definitions of what is abnormal, psychologists have spelled out criteria that can be used in determining abnormal human behavior. These criteria fall into four categories: distress, impairment, risk to self or other people, and socially and culturally unacceptable behavior.

Distress

I begin with the most personal criterion of abnormality because the experience of inner emotional distress is a universal phenomenon and a powerful way in which every person at some point in life feels different from everyone around them. Distress, the experience of emotional pain, is experienced in many ways, such as depression, anxiety, and cognitive confusion. When people feel any of these responses to an extreme degree, they feel abnormal, and they typically look for ways to alleviate their feelings of inner pain. Some of the issues in this book illustrate the various ways in which different people respond to similar life events. For example, following the devastating events of September 11, the Asian tsunami, and Hurricane Katrina, many mental health professionals were called upon to intervene with the survivors of these life-threatening traumas. Although providing a therapeutic response in the form of psychological debriefing might seem beneficial, some critics argue that such efforts might make a difficult emotional situation even worse (Issue 4). In recent years efforts have been made to find medications that alleviate the memories associated with the experience of a trauma; Issue 7 addresses the possible benefits as well as the disadvantages of dampening memories of a traumatic experience.

Impairment

People who are intensely distressed are likely to find it difficult to fulfill the everyday responsibilities of life. When people are very depressed or anxious, they typically have a difficult time concentrating on their studies, attending to their work responsibilities, or even interacting with other people. Impairment involves a reduction in a person's ability to function at an optimal or even an average level. Although distress and impairment often go hand in hand, they do not always; a person can be seriously impaired but feel no particular distress. This is often the case with substance abuse, in which people are incapable of the basic tasks of physical coordination and cognitive clarity but feel euphoric. Some of the debates in this book address the issue of impairment and the difficulty in assessing the extent to which people are impaired. For example, Issue 8 focuses on the question of whether addiction is a brain disease. This issue has relevance to issues about the extent to which drug-addicted individuals are capable, physiologically and psychologically, of controlling their self-destructive addictive behaviors.

Risk to Self or Others

Sometimes people act in ways that cause risk to themselves or others. In this context, risk refers to danger or threat to the well-being of a person. In the case of suicide or self-mutilating behavior, the personal risk is evident. In the case of outwardly directed violence, rape, or even emotional exploitation, the risk is to other people. Although the issue of risk to self or others might not seem controversial on the surface, there are many facets of risk that provoke debate. For example, does an individual have the right to engage in self-injurious, perhaps even life-ending, behavior, or does society have a right, even a responsibility, to intervene? As addressed in Issues 13 and 17, do individuals who are at risk of harming other people (i.e., by means of violence) or themselves (i.e., self-starvation) have the right to refuse intervention, or do health professionals have a responsibility to prevent such individuals from engaging in such potentially dangerous behavior? To what extremes should clinicians go in order to behaviorally control the self-injurious, and potentially fatal, behaviors of severely disturbed children and adults? Issue 15 addresses the question of whether harsh aversive treatments are forms of torture or lifesaving interventions. Other potentially harmful behaviors are also discussed, such as pornography involving images of children (Issue 10). Although no reasonable person would defend real child pornography, some argue that virtual images generated by computers are not only legally permissible, but could reduce the victimization of real children by the pornography industry. Critics of that stance argue that pornography involving children, whether virtual or not, increases the likelihood of real-life victimization.

Socially and Culturally Unacceptable Behavior

Another criterion for defining abnormality pertains to the social or cultural context in which behavior occurs. In some instances, behavior that is regarded as odd within a given culture, society, or subgroup is common elsewhere. For example, some people from Mediterranean cultures believe in a phenomenon called *mal de ojo*, or "evil eye," in which the ill will of one person can negatively affect another. According to this belief, receiving the evil eye from a person can cause a range of disturbing physical and emotional symptoms; consequently, individuals in these cultures often take steps to ward off the power of another person's evil eye. Such beliefs might be regarded as strangely superstitious, almost delusional, in American culture, but they are considered common elsewhere. Even more subtle contexts can influence the extent to which a behavior is defined as abnormal, as illustrated by the example of the Halloween costume mentioned previously. This book features issues related to social and cultural variables, such as whether violent video games promote violent behavior in young people (Issue 9). Some people in society view gender-variant behavior as abnormal. At one extreme are those who consider gender identity disorder a mental illness, and at the other end are those who consider such a perspective to represent a stigmatization of mental illness on people who meet no scientific definition of mental disorder (Issue 3).

What Causes Abnormality?

In trying to understand why people act and feel in ways that are regarded as abnormal, social scientists consider three dimensions: biological, psychological, and sociocultural. Rather than viewing these dimensions as independent, however, experts discuss the relative contribution of each dimension in influencing human behavior, and they use the term *biopsychosocial* to capture these intertwining forces. In the context of abnormality, the biopsychosocial conceptualization of human behavior conveys the sense that abnormal behavior arises from a complex set of determinants in the body, the mind, and the social context.

Biological Causes

During the past several decades scientists have made tremendous progress in discovering ways in which human behavior is influenced by a range of biological variables. In the realm of abnormal psychology, the contributions of the biological sciences have been especially impressive, as researchers have developed increasing understanding of the ways in which abnormal behavior is determined by bodily physiology and genetic makeup. As is the case with many medical disorders, various mental disorders, such as depression, run in families. Mental health researchers have made great efforts to understand why certain mental illnesses are passed from one generation to another and also to understand why certain disorders are not inherited even in identical twin pairs when one of the twins has the condition and the other does not.

In addition to understanding the role of genetics, mental health experts also consider the ways in which physical functioning can cause or aggravate the experience of psychological symptoms. Experts know that many medical conditions can cause a person to feel or act in ways that are abnormal. For example, a medical abnormality in the thyroid gland can cause wide variations in mood and emotionality. Brain damage resulting from a head trauma, even a slight one, can result in bizarre behavior and intense emotionality. Similarly, the use of drugs or alcohol can cause people to act in extreme ways that neither they nor those who know them well would have ever imagined (Issue 8). Even exposure to environmental stimuli, such as toxic substances or allergens, can cause people to experience disturbing emotional changes and to act in odd or bizarre ways. Several issues in this book explore conditions in which biology plays a prominent causative role. For example, attention deficit/hyperactivity disorder (ADHD) is regarded as a disorder of the brain that interferes with a person's ability to pay attention or to control behavior (see Issue 1).

Psychological Causes

Biology does not tell the entire story about the causes of mental disorders; many forms of emotional disturbance arise as a result of troubling life experiences. The experiences of life, even seemingly insignificant ones, can leave lasting marks on a person. In cases in which an experience involves trauma, such as rape or abuse, the impact can be emotionally disruptive throughout life, affecting a person's thoughts, behaviors, and even dreams (Issues 2 and 7).

In trying to understand the psychological causes of abnormality, social scientists and mental health clinicians consider a person's experiences. Not only do they focus on interpersonal interactions with other people that may have left a mark, but they also consider the inner life of the individual—thoughts and feelings that may cause distress or impairment. Some conditions arise from distorted perceptions and faulty ways of thinking. For example, highly sensitive people may misconstrue innocent comments by acquaintances that cause obsessional worry about being disliked or demeaned. As a result, these people may respond to their acquaintances in hostile ways that perpetuate interpersonal difficulties and inner distress.

Sociocultural Causes

The term *sociocultural* refers to the various circles of social influence in the lives of people. The most immediate circle is composed of people with whom we interact in our immediate environment; for college students, this includes roommates, classmates, and coworkers. Moving beyond the immediate circle are people who inhabit the extended circle of relationships, such as family members back home or friends from high school. A third circle is composed of the people in our environments with whom we interact minimally and rarely by name, such as residents of our community or campus, whose stan-dards, expectations, and behaviors influence our lives. A fourth circle is the much wider culture in which people live, such as American society.

Abnormal behavior can emerge from experiences in any of these social contexts. Troubled relationships with a roommate or family member can cause intense emotional distress. Involvement in an abusive relationship may initiate an interpersonal style in which the abused person becomes repeatedly caught up with people who are hurtful or damaging. Political turmoil, even on a relatively local level, can evoke emotions ranging from intense anxiety to incapacitating fear.

This book discusses several conditions in which sociocultural factors are significant. For example, Issue 9 discusses the ways in which exposure to media violence may promote aggressive behavior, and Issue 10 addresses the ways in which pornography, even in virtual form, may contribute to the victimization of children.

The Biopsychosocial Perspective

From the discussion so far, it should be evident that most aspects of human behavior are determined by a complex of causes involving an interaction of biological, psychological, and sociocultural factors. As you read about the clinical conditions and mental disorders discussed in this book, it will be useful for you to keep the biopsychosocial perspective in mind, even in those discussions in which the authors seem narrowly focused. For example, a condition may be put forth as being biologically caused, leading the reader to believe that other influences play little or no role. Another condition may be presented as being so psychologically based that it is difficult to fathom the role that biology might play in causing or aggravating the condition. Other issues may be discussed almost exclusively in sociocultural terms, with minimal attention to the roles of biological and psychological factors. An intelligent discussion in the field of abnormal psychology is one that explores the relative importance of biological, psychological, and sociocultural influences. Such a discussion should avoid reductionistic thinking and simplistic explanations for complex human problems.

Why We View Behavior as "Abnormal"

In addition to understanding how to define abnormality and what causes abnormal behavior, it is important to understand how members of society view people who are abnormal and how this view affects people with emotional problems and mental disorders. Many people in our society discriminate against and reject mentally disturbed people. In so doing, they aggravate one of the most profound aspects of dealing with mental disorder—the experience of stigma. A stigma is a label that causes certain people to be regarded as different and defective and to be set apart from mainstream members of society. Today, several decades after sociologist Erving Goffman brought the phenomenon of stigma to public attention, there is ample evidence in American society that people with mental disorders are regarded as different and are often deprived of the basic human right to respectful treatment.

It is common for people with serious psychological disorders, especially those who have been hospitalized, to experience profound and long-lasting emotional and social effects. People who suffer from serious psychological problems tend to think less of themselves because of these experiences, and they often come to believe many of the myths about themselves that are perpetuated in a society that lacks understanding about the nature of mental illness and psychological problems.

Although tremendous efforts have been undertaken to humanize the experiences of people with psychological problems and mental disorders, deeply rooted societal reactions still present obstacles for many emotionally distressed people. Controversies continue to rage about the systems of diagnosis and assessment used by mental health professionals, about the validity of certain clinical conditions, and about the efficacy of various psychotherapeutic and medical interventions. As you read both sides of the debates in this book, it is important that you keep in mind the strong personal beliefs that influence, and possibly bias, the statements of each writer and to consider the ways in which various societal forces are intertwined with the comments of the author.

The most powerful force within the field of mental health during the twentieth century was the medical model, upon which many forms of intervention are based. This book frequently mentions a system of diagnosis developed by the American Psychiatric Association that has been revised several times during the past 50 years. This system is published in a book called the *Diagnostic and Statistical Manual of Mental Disorders*. The most recent version is the fifth edition, which is abbreviated *DSM-5*. In this medical model diagnostic system, mental disorders are construed as diseases that require treatment. There are both advantages and disadvantages to this approach.

Not only does *DSM-5* rely on the medical model, but it also uses a categorical approach for most conditions. A categorical approach assumes that disorders and diseases fall into distinct categories. For example, the medical disease pneumonia is a condition that fits into a category of diseases involving the respiratory system. In corresponding fashion, conditions involving depression fit into a category of depressive disorders, and conditions involving anxiety fit into a category of anxiety disorders. However, there are limitations to the categorical approach. For one thing, psychological disorders are not neatly separable from each other or from normal functioning. For example, where is the dividing line between normal sadness and clinical depression? Furthermore, many disorders seem linked to each other in fundamental ways. In a state of agitated depression, for example, an individual suffers from both anxiety and saddened mood. The editors of *DSM-5* struggled with the limitations of the categorical approach and made some changes from previous *DSM* editions. For example, for the diagnosis of personality disorders, a hybrid dimensional-categorical model is used for assessing personality disorder. Thus, levels of personality functioning are based on the severity of disturbances in self (e.g., identity and self-directedness) and interpersonal functioning (e.g., empathy and intimacy). The diagnosis of narcissistic personality disorder continues to be included in the *DSM,* and reflects an interpersonal style that has captured considerable attention in the new media age in which self-promotion has become easier than ever due to social network services such as Facebook (Issue 18).

Several of the conditions and interventions discussed in this book have been debated for years. As you read about these issues, it will be helpful for you to keep in mind the context in which these debates have arisen. Some debates arise because of turf battles between professions. For example, psychiatrists may be more inclined to endorse the diagnostic system of the American Psychiatric Association (*DSM-5*) and to support biological explanations and somatic interventions for mental disorders. Psychologists, on the other hand, may urge mental health professionals to take a broader point of view and to proceed more cautiously in turning to biological explanations and causes.

The Influence of Theoretical Perspective on the Choice of Intervention

Although impressive advances have been achieved in determining why people develop various mental disorders, understanding how best to treat their conditions remains limited and also powerfully influenced by the ideological biases of many clinicians and researchers. For much of the twentieth century, various interventions emerged from markedly different schools of thought, each approach being tied to one of the three major realms—biological, psychological, or sociocultural. But how are biological, psychological, and sociocultural frameworks used in determining choice of intervention?

Within the biological perspective, disturbances in emotions, behavior, and cognitive processes are viewed as being caused by abnormalities in the functioning of the body, such as the brain and nervous system or the endocrine system. Treatments involve a range of somatic therapies, the most common of which is medication, the most extreme of which involves psychosurgery. Several issues in this book focus on debates about reliance on biological explanations and interventions, such as the issue on ADHD (Issue 1), and the issues on medications (Issues 5–8, and 17).

The realm of psychological theories contains numerous approaches, although three schools of thought emerged as most prominent during the second half of the twentieth century: psychodynamic, humanistic, and behavioral. Proponents of the psychodynamic perspective emphasize unconscious determinants of behavior and recommend the use of techniques involving exploration of the developmental causes of behavior and the interpretation of unconscious influences on thoughts, feelings, and behavior.

At the core of the humanistic perspective is the belief that human motivation is based on an inherent tendency to strive for self-fulfillment and meaning in life. Humanistic therapists use a client-centered approach in which they strive to treat clients with unconditional positive regard and empathy. Mental health professionals are called upon to act in ways that are more client-centered as they deal with issues pertaining to gender identity (Issue 3), trauma (Issues 2 and 7), or abortion (Issue 12).

According to the behavioral perspective, abnormality is caused by faulty learning experiences, with a subset of behavioral theory focusing on cognitive functions such as maladaptive thought processes. Because behaviorists and cognitive theorists believe that disturbance results from faulty learning or distorted thinking, intervention focuses on teaching clients more adaptive ways of thinking and behaving. Some of the discussions in this book focus on the ways in which behavioral and cognitive approaches might be preferable to medical approaches to conditions such as ADHD (Issue 1), and the use of aversive techniques for treating self-injurious individuals (Issue 14).

Clinicians working within sociocultural models emphasize the ways that individuals are influenced by people, social institutions, and social forces. According to this viewpoint, psychological problems can emerge from social contexts ranging from the family to society. In a corresponding vein, treatments are determined by the nature of the group. Thus, problems rooted within family systems would be treated with family therapy; societal problems caused by discrimination or inadequate care of the mentally ill would be dealt with through enactment of social policy initiatives. Several issues in this volume touch upon sociocultural influences, such as the effects of pornography (Issue 10), and how best to respond to survivors of life-threatening trauma (Issues 2, 4, and 7).

Keeping the Issues in Perspective

In evaluating the content of the writings in this book, it is important to keep in mind who the writers are and what their agendas might be. Most of the contributors are distinguished figures in the fields of mental health, ethics, and law. They are regarded as clear and influential thinkers who have important messages to convey. However, it would be naive to think that any writer, particularly when addressing a controversial topic, is free of bias.

It is best to read each issue with an understanding of the forces that might influence the development of a particular bias. For example, as physicians, psychiatrists have been trained in the medical model, with its focus on biological causes for problems and somatic interventions. Nonphysician mental health professionals may be more inclined to focus on interpersonal and intrapersonal causes and interventions. Lawyers and ethicists are more likely to be further removed from questions of etiology, focusing instead on what they believe is justified according to the law or right according to ethical standards (Issues 9–11 and 14–16).

As you read about the issues facing mental health clinicians and researchers, you are certain to be struck by the challenges that these professionals face. You may also be struck by the powerful emotion expressed by the authors who discuss their views on topics in this field. Because psychological stresses and problems are an inherent part of human existence, many discussions about abnormal psychology are emotionally charged. At some point in life, most people have a brush with serious emotional problems, either directly or indirectly. This is a frightening prospect for many people, one that engenders worried expectations and intense reactions. By acknowledging our vulnerability to disruptive emotional experiences, however, we can think about the ways in which we would want clinicians to treat us. As you read the issues in this book, place yourself in the position of an individual in the process of being assessed, diagnosed, and treated for an emotional difficulty or mental disorder.

Before you take a side in each debate, consider how the issue might be personally relevant to you at some point in life. You may be surprised to discover that you respond in different ways to issues that might have special salience to yourself, as opposed to random people somewhere else. By imagining yourself being personally affected by a professional's controversial opinion regarding one or more of the debates in this book, you will find yourself immersed in the discussions about issues for which there is no clear right or wrong.

Internet References . . .

Coalition Against Institutionalized Child Abuse (CAICA)

CAICA is an informational and educational website that provides news articles and reports regarding children and teens abused, neglected, and who have died in residential treatment settings.

www.caica.org/

The World Professional Association for Transgender Health, Inc.

This website offers information on understanding and treating gender identity disorders, along with the organization's compiled standards of care for the medical, psychological, and surgical management of gender identity disorders.

www.wpath.org/

Treatment Advocacy Center

A national nonprofit organization dedicated to eliminating barriers to the timely and effective treatment of severe mental illnesses.

http://psychlaws.blogspot.com/

National Eating Disorders Association (NEDA)

NEDA is committed to providing education, resources, and support to people affected by eating disorders.

www.nationaleatingdisorders.org/

The Recovered Memory Project

This project collects and disseminates information relevant to the debate over whether traumatic events can be forgotten and then remembered later in life.

www.brown.edu/Departments/Taubman_Center/Recovmem/

Centers for Disease Control and Prevention (CDC)—ADHD Web Page

The CDC maintains a Web page containing a wealth of information about diagnosis, treatment, and research pertaining to ADHD.

www.cdc.gov/ncbddd/adhd/

National Institute on Drug Abuse (NIDA)—MDMA (Ecstasy) Web Page

NIDA maintains a Web page containing information about the effects of MDMA on the brain, and research that is being conducted on this drug.

www.nida.nih.gov/Infofacts/ecstasy.html

National Center for PTSD

This website is sponsored by the U.S. Department of Veterans Affairs for the purpose of advancing science and promoting understanding of traumatic stress.

www.ptsd.va.gov/

Psychological Conditions and Treatments

*A*t the heart of abnormal psychology are the psychological conditions and mental disorders for which people seek psychological treatment. At the center of many debates regarding psychiatric diagnosis is
the Diagnostic and Statistical Manual of Mental Disorders, *Fifth Edition* (DSM-5), *published in May 2013. Most psychological conditions
included in DSM-5 are widely recognized as psychological disorders, but
some conditions engender considerable debate. Although symptoms of
debilitating depression or disabling anxiety warrant a psychiatric diagnosis, critics have raised issues about the validity of some diagnoses and
have questioned the extent to which some conditions are overdiagnosed,
and consequently overtreated. For example, are attentional difficulties
and high levels of activity reflective of a mental disorder (i.e., ADHD) or
reflections of typical childhood behavior, albeit at the far end of the normal spectrum? Taking the challenge even further are those who criticize
the pathologizing of children with diagnoses such as disruptive mood
dysregulation disorder, a label that will likely lead to pharmacological
treatment of the children so diagnosed. Moving to a later developmental
age, debates have arisen about whether posttraumatic stress disorder is
being overdiagnosed, and consequently overtreated. One particular intervention, critical incident stress debriefing, for survivors of trauma has
been particularly scrutinized in terms of appropriateness and effectiveness. On a different topic, there is debate about whether gender variant
conditions are mental disorders or simply less common presentations of
human identity. In the issues that follow, you will read selections addressing various viewpoints about diagnoses and appropriate interventions.*

- Is Attention-Deficit/Hyperactivity Disorder (ADHD) a Real Disorder?
- Is Posttraumatic Stress Disorder (PTSD) Overdiagnosed and Overtreated?
- Is Gender Identity Disorder a Mental Illness?
- Is Psychological Debriefing a Harmful Intervention for Survivors of Trauma?

ISSUE 1

Is Attention-Deficit/Hyperactivity Disorder (ADHD) a Real Disorder?

YES: National Institute of Mental Health (NIMH), from *Attention Deficit Hyperactivity Disorder* (NIH Publication No. 08-3572). (National Institute of Mental Health, National Institutes of Health, U.S. Department of Health and Human Services 2012, May 22), www.nimh.nih.gov/health/publications/attention-deficit-hyperactivitydisorder/index.shtml

NO: Rogers H. Wright, from "Attention Deficit Hyperactivity Disorder: What It Is and What It Is Not," in Rogers H. Wright and Nicholas A. Cummings, eds., *Destructive Trends in Mental Health: The Well-Intentioned Path to Harm* (Routledge, 2005)

Learning Outcomes

After reading this issue, you should be able to:

- Understand the diagnostic criteria generally associated with the *DSM* diagnosis of ADHD.
- Discuss the scientifically supported theories about the causes of ADHD, as well as the etiological theories that have been discredited.
- Understand the kinds of medications most commonly used to treat ADHD, as well as the side effects and risks associated with these medications.
- Evaluate the argument that ADHD is a "fad diagnosis" which is used as an excuse by some people for the misbehavior of their child, or an excuse for their personal difficulties with organization and follow-through.
- Discuss the benefits of accurate diagnosis, as well as the risks of inappropriate diagnosis of ADHD.

ISSUE SUMMARY

YES: The National Institute of Mental Health concurs with the *Diagnostic and Statistical Manual of Mental Disorders* in viewing ADHD as a valid disorder that warrants thoughtful diagnosis and effective intervention.

NO: Psychologist Rogers H. Wright argues that ADHD has vague diagnostic criteria that lead to overdiagnosis and overmedication of an excessive number of people.

$\mathbf{A}$nyone who has set foot in an American classroom has observed a range of children whose behaviors and compliance span a relatively wide continuum. At one end are well-behaved children who listen attentively to their teachers, cooperate, and follow instructions. At the other end are children who seem to be completely out of control. They show a constellation of behaviors characterized by inattention and/or hyperactivity. These children are referred to by teachers and special educators as having attention-deficit/hyperactivity disorder (ADHD), as described in the *Diagnostic and Statistical Manual of Mental Disorders*, Fifth Edition *(DSM-5)*. According to *DSM-5*, their inattention is evidenced by a range of behaviors such as the following: They fail to attend to details or they make careless mistakes; they have difficulty sustaining attention in tasks or play; they often seem like they're not listening when spoken to; they have difficulty organizing tasks and activities; they often avoid, dislike, or resist tasks that require sustained mental effort; they often lose things; they are easily distracted; and they are often forgetful in daily activities. *DSM-5* also enumerates a range of behaviors that characterize hyperactivity. Hyperactive individuals often fidget, tap, or squirm; they often leave their seats when expected to sit; they run about or climb in inappropriate situations; they are often unable to play or engage quietly in leisure activities; they seem to be "on the go" and acting as if "driven by a motor"; they often talk excessively; they may blurt out or complete the sentences of others; they may have difficulty waiting their turn; and they often interrupt others. In the ADHD diagnostic group, individuals can be classified as having a predominantly hyperactive, or inattentive, or combined presentation of symptoms.

A few decades ago, these hyperactive and impulsive children might have been labeled as having "minimal brain dysfunction," a label that suggested that an underlying neurological problem was the basis for their disruptive behavior. As times have changed, so have the labels, such that the terms *ADHD* and *ADD* (attention deficit disorder, a label in popular usage) have become commonplace, not only in describing many children, but also in describing many adults.

In the first reading, the National Institute of Mental Health (NIMH) views ADHD as a very real disorder, referring to this condition as "one of the most common childhood disorders" which can continue through adolescence and adulthood. In discussing ADHD, NIMH approaches the discussion from a medical model vantage point, noting that "like many other illnesses" ADHD probably results from a combination of factors, with many studies suggesting that genes play a large role, and some studies also pointing to the contributing role of toxic environmental factors.

According to NIMH, ADHD symptoms usually appear early in life, between the ages of 3 and 6. Parents may notice that their child loses interest sooner than other children or seems constantly out of control. Although no single test is used to diagnose ADHD, health professionals can gather information about the child's behavior and environment in an effort to rule out competing diagnostic hypotheses.

NIMH discusses various treatment options for individuals with ADHD. Medications in the form of stimulants are the most common medications used, although as NIMH notes, some of these medications can have significant side effects such as decreased appetite, sleep problems, and in some rare cases alarming effects including suicidal thoughts. Psychotherapeutic interventions include behavioral therapy to help the individual organize tasks, complete schoolwork, work through emotionally difficult events, and develop better social skills.

NIMH states that some children with ADHD continue to have this condition as adults. It is also stated that many adults who have DHD do not know it; they just feel that it is impossible to get organized, stick to a job, or remember appointments. The simple tasks of daily life such as getting up on time, preparing to leave for work, getting to the job on time, and being productive prove to be challenging for them. As is the case with children, these individuals are likely to have a history of failure at school, problems at work, or difficulties in relationships. Adults with ADHD, according to NIMH, may benefit from cognitive behavioral therapy in which they work to change their poor self-image, give more effort to thinking before acting, and resist taking unnecessary risks.

In the second selection, Rogers H. Wright asserts that ADHD is a fad diagnosis, which does not exist, as was the case with a former fad label, "minimal brain syndrome." This more recent fad diagnosis, Dr. Wright contends, has moved beyond the confines of childhood and adolescence, and is now a diagnosis that has invaded adulthood as well.

Dr. Wright points out that the diagnostic criteria for the "so-called" disorder include symptoms that normal children and adults experience on a day-to-day basis. Hyperactivity and distractibility are behaviors that are most commonly symptoms of excessive fatigue or stress, rather than signs of a psychological disorder. He acknowledges that there are some extreme cases for which a comprehensive evaluation by several specialists might provide evidence of neurological involvement; in such cases, if medication is indicated, it would be of a type quite different from what is so widely prescribed to people with the condition known as ADHD.

Dr. Wright argues that a major disservice caused by the elevation of nonspecific symptoms, and then diagnoses of ADHD, is that we lump together individuals with very different needs and problems, and then attempt to treat the problems with a single entity, resulting in a one-pill-fits-all response. Treatment interventions focused primarily on medication, and based on such ethereal and universal symptoms, promise an instant "cure" for a patient who now does not have to confront possible unhappiness or stress. Whether or not someone has ADHD is a judgment that is best made only after exhaustive study by pediatrics, psychology, neurology, and perhaps, last of all, psychiatry, which so often seems too eager to overmedicate.

Attention Deficit Hyperactivity Disorder

What Is Attention Deficit Hyperactivity Disorder?

Attention deficit hyperactivity disorder (ADHD) is one of the most common childhood disorders and can continue through adolescence and adulthood. Symptoms include difficulty staying focused and paying attention, difficulty controlling behavior, and hyperactivity (over-activity). ADHD has three subtypes:[1]

- **Predominantly hyperactive-impulsive**
  - Most symptoms (six or more) are in the hyperactivity-impulsivity categories.
  - Fewer than six symptoms of inattention are present, although inattention may still be present to some degree.

- **Predominantly inattentive**
  - The majority of symptoms (six or more) are in the inattention category and fewer than six symptoms of hyperactivity-impulsivity are present, although hyperactivity-impulsivity may still be present to some degree.
  - Children with this subtype are less likely to act out or have difficulties getting along with other children. They may sit quietly, but they are not paying attention to what they are doing. Therefore, the child may be overlooked, and parents and teachers may not notice that he or she has ADHD.

- **Combined hyperactive-impulsive and inattentive**
  - Six or more symptoms of inattention and six or more symptoms of hyperactivity-impulsivity are present.
  - Most children have the combined type of ADHD.

Treatments can relieve many of the disorder's symptoms, but there is no cure. With treatment, most people with ADHD can be successful in school and lead productive lives. Researchers are developing more effective treatments

National Institute of Mental Health, 2008.

and interventions, and using new tools such as brain imaging, to better understand ADHD and to find more effective ways to treat and prevent it.

What Causes ADHD?

Scientists are not sure what causes ADHD, although many studies suggest that genes play a large role. Like many other illnesses, ADHD probably results from a combination of factors. In addition to genetics, researchers are looking at possible environmental factors, and are studying how brain injuries, nutrition, and the social environment might contribute to ADHD.

Genes. Inherited from our parents, genes are the "blueprints" for who we are. Results from several international studies of twins show that ADHD often runs in families. Researchers are looking at several genes that may make people more likely to develop the disorder.[2,3] Knowing the genes involved may one day help researchers prevent the disorder before symptoms develop. Learning about specific genes could also lead to better treatments. Children with ADHD who carry a particular version of a certain gene have thinner brain tissue in the areas of the brain associated with attention. This NIMH research showed that the difference was not permanent, however, and as children with this gene grew up, the brain developed to a normal level of thickness. Their ADHD symptoms also improved.[4]

Environmental factors. Studies suggest a potential link between cigarette smoking and alcohol use during pregnancy and ADHD in children.[5,6] In addition, preschoolers who are exposed to high levels of lead, which can sometimes be found in plumbing fixtures or paint in old buildings, may have a higher risk of developing ADHD.[7]

Brain injuries. Children who have suffered a brain injury may show some behaviors similar to those of ADHD. However, only a small percentage of children with ADHD have suffered a traumatic brain injury.

Sugar. The idea that refined sugar causes ADHD or makes symptoms worse is popular, but more research discounts this theory than supports it. In one study, researchers gave children foods containing either sugar or a sugar substitute every other day. The children who received sugar showed no different behavior or learning capabilities than those who received the sugar substitute.[8] Another study in which children were given higher than average amounts of sugar or sugar substitutes showed similar results.[9]

In another study, children who were considered sugar-sensitive by their mothers were given the sugar substitute aspartame, also known as Nutrasweet. Although *all* the children got aspartame, half their mothers were told their children were given sugar, and the other half were told their children were given aspartame. The mothers who thought their children had gotten sugar rated them as more hyperactive than the other children and were more critical of their behavior, compared to mothers who *thought* their children received aspartame.[10]

Food additives. Recent British research indicates a possible link between consumption of certain food additives like artificial colors or preservatives, and an increase in activity.[11] Research is under way to confirm the findings and to learn more about how food additives may affect hyperactivity.

How Is ADHD Diagnosed?

Children mature at different rates and have different personalities, temperaments, and energy levels. Most children get distracted, act impulsively, and struggle to concentrate at one time or another. Sometimes, these normal factors may be mistaken for ADHD. ADHD symptoms usually appear early in life, often between the ages of 3 and 6, and because symptoms vary from person to person, the disorder can be hard to diagnose. Parents may first notice that their child loses interest in things sooner than other children, or seems constantly "out of control." Often, teachers notice the symptoms first, when a child has trouble following rules, or frequently "spaces out" in the classroom or on the playground.

No single test can diagnose a child as having ADHD. Instead, a licensed health professional needs to gather information about the child, and his or her behavior and environment. A family may want to first talk with the child's pediatrician. Some pediatricians can assess the child themselves, but many will refer the family to a mental health specialist with experience in childhood mental disorders such as ADHD. The pediatrician or mental health specialist will first try to rule out other possibilities for the symptoms. For example, certain situations, events, or health conditions may cause temporary behaviors in a child that seem like ADHD. Between them, the referring pediatrician and specialist will determine if a child:

- Is experiencing undetected seizures that could be associated with other medical conditions
- Has a middle ear infection that is causing hearing problems
- Has any undetected hearing or vision problems
- Has any medical problems that affect thinking and behavior
- Has any learning disabilities
- Has anxiety or depression, or other psychiatric problems that might cause ADHD-like symptoms
- Has been affected by a significant and sudden change, such as the death of a family member, a divorce, or parent's job loss.

A specialist will also check school and medical records for clues, to see if the child's home or school settings appear unusually stressful or disrupted, and gather information from the child's parents and teachers. Coaches, babysitters, and other adults who know the child well also may be consulted. The specialist also will ask:

- Are the behaviors excessive and long-term, and do they affect all aspects of the child's life?
- Do they happen more often in this child compared with the child's peers?
- Are the behaviors a continuous problem or a response to a temporary situation?
- Do the behaviors occur in several settings or only in one place, such as the playground, classroom, or home?

The specialist pays close attention to the child's behavior during different situations. Some situations are highly structured, some have less structure.

Others would require the child to keep paying attention. Most children with ADHD are better able to control their behaviors in situations where they are getting individual attention and when they are free to focus on enjoyable activities. These types of situations are less important in the assessment. A child also may be evaluated to see how he or she acts in social situations, and may be given tests of intellectual ability and academic achievement to see if he or she has a learning disability.

Finally, if after gathering all this information the child meets the criteria for ADHD, he or she will be diagnosed with the disorder.

How Is ADHD Treated?

Currently available treatments focus on reducing the symptoms of ADHD and improving functioning. Treatments include medication, various types of psychotherapy, education or training, or a combination of treatments.

Medications

The most common type of medication used for treating ADHD is called a "stimulant." Although it may seem unusual to treat ADHD with a medication considered a stimulant, it actually has a calming effect on children with ADHD. Many types of stimulant medications are available. A few other ADHD medications are non-stimulants and work differently than stimulants. For many children, ADHD medications reduce hyperactivity and impulsivity and improve their ability to focus, work, and learn. Medication also may improve physical coordination.

However, a one-size-fits-all approach does not apply for all children with ADHD. What works for one child might not work for another. One child might have side effects with a certain medication, while another child may not. Sometimes several different medications or dosages must be tried before finding one that works for a particular child. Any child taking medications must be monitored closely and carefully by caregivers and doctors.

Stimulant medications come in different forms, such as a pill, capsule, liquid, or skin patch. Some medications also come in short-acting, long-acting, or extended release varieties. In each of these varieties, the active ingredient is the same, but it is released differently in the body. Long-acting or extended release forms often allow a child to take the medication just once a day before school, so they don't have to make a daily trip to the school nurse for another dose. Parents and doctors should decide together which medication is best for the child and whether the child needs medication only for school hours or for evenings and weekends, too.

What are the Side Effects of Stimulant Medications?
The most commonly reported side effects are decreased appetite, sleep problems, anxiety, and irritability. Some children also report mild stomachaches or headaches. Most side effects are minor and disappear over time or if the dosage level is lowered.

- **Decreased appetite.** Be sure your child eats healthy meals. If this side effect does not go away, talk to your child's doctor. Also talk to the doctor if you have concerns about your child's growth or weight gain while he or she is taking this medication.

- **Sleep problems.** If a child cannot fall asleep, the doctor may prescribe a lower dose of the medication or a shorter-acting form. The doctor might also suggest giving the medication earlier in the day, or stopping the afternoon or evening dose. Adding a prescription for a low dose of an antidepressant or a blood pressure medication called clonidine sometimes helps with sleep problems. A consistent sleep routine that includes relaxing elements like warm milk, soft music, or quiet activities in dim light, may also help.

- **Less common side effects.** A few children develop sudden, repetitive movements or sounds called tics. These tics may or may not be noticeable. Changing the medication dosage may make tics go away. Some children also may have a personality change, such as appearing "flat" or without emotion. **Talk with your child's doctor if you see any of these side effects.**

Are Stimulant Medications Safe?

Under medical supervision, stimulant medications are considered safe. Stimulants do not make children with ADHD feel high, although some kids report feeling slightly different or "funny." Although some parents worry that stimulant medications may lead to substance abuse or dependence, there is little evidence of this.

FDA Warning on Possible Rare Side Effects

In 2007, the FDA required that all makers of ADHD medications develop Patient Medication Guides that contain information about the risks associated with the medications. The guides must alert patients that the medications may lead to possible cardiovascular (heart and blood) or psychiatric problems. The agency undertook this precaution when a review of data found that ADHD patients with existing heart conditions had a slightly higher risk of strokes, heart attacks, and/or sudden death when taking the medications.

The review also found a slight increased risk, about 1 in 1,000, for medication-related psychiatric problems, such as hearing voices, having hallucinations, becoming suspicious for no reason, or becoming manic (an overly high mood), even in patients without a history of psychiatric problems. The FDA recommends that any treatment plan for ADHD include an initial health history, including family history, and examination for existing cardiovascular and psychiatric problems.

One ADHD medication, the non-stimulant atomoxetine (Strattera), carries another warning. Studies show that children and teenagers who take atomoxetine are more likely to have suicidal thoughts than children and teenagers with ADHD who do not take it. **If your child is taking atomoxetine, watch his or her behavior carefully. A child may develop serious symptoms suddenly, so it is important to pay attention to your child's behavior every day.** Ask other people who spend a lot of time with your child to tell you if they notice changes in your child's behavior. Call a doctor right away if your child shows any unusual behavior. While taking atomoxetine, your child should see a doctor often, especially at the beginning of treatment, and be sure that your child keeps all appointments with his or her doctor.

Do Medications Cure ADHD?

Current medications do not cure ADHD. Rather, they control the symptoms for as long as they are taken. Medications can help a child pay attention and complete schoolwork. It is not clear, however, whether medications can help children learn or improve their academic skills. Adding behavioral therapy, counseling, and practical support can help children with ADHD and their families to better cope with everyday problems. Research funded by the National Institute of Mental Health (NIMH) has shown that medication works best when treatment is regularly monitored by the prescribing doctor and the dose is adjusted based on the child's needs.[12]

Psychotherapy

Different types of psychotherapy are used for ADHD. Behavioral therapy aims to help a child change his or her behavior. It might involve practical assistance, such as help organizing tasks or completing schoolwork, or working through emotionally difficult events. Behavioral therapy also teaches a child how to monitor his or her own behavior. Learning to give oneself praise or rewards for acting in a desired way, such as controlling anger or thinking before acting, is another goal of behavioral therapy. Parents and teachers also can give positive or negative feedback for certain behaviors. In addition, clear rules, chore lists, and other structured routines can help a child control his or her behavior.

Therapists may teach children social skills, such as how to wait their turn, share toys, ask for help, or respond to teasing. Learning to read facial expressions and the tone of voice in others, and how to respond appropriately can also be part of social skills training.

How Can Parents Help?

Children with ADHD need guidance and understanding from their parents and teachers to reach their full potential and to succeed in school. Before a child is diagnosed, frustration, blame, and anger may have built up within a family. Parents and children may need special help to overcome bad feelings. Mental health professionals can educate parents about ADHD and how it impacts a family. They also will help the child and his or her parents develop new skills, attitudes, and ways of relating to each other.

Parenting skills training helps parents learn how to use a system of rewards and consequences to change a child's behavior. Parents are taught to give immediate and positive feedback for behaviors they want to encourage, and ignore or redirect behaviors they want to discourage. In some cases, the use of "time-outs" may be used when the child's behavior gets out of control. In a time-out, the child is removed from the upsetting situation and sits alone for a short time to calm down.

Parents are also encouraged to share a pleasant or relaxing activity with the child, to notice and point out what the child does well, and to praise the child's strengths and abilities. They may also learn to structure situations in more positive ways. For example, they may restrict the number of playmates to one or two, so that their child does not become overstimulated. Or, if the child has trouble completing tasks, parents can help their child divide large tasks into smaller, more manageable steps. Also, parents may benefit from learning stress-management techniques to increase their own ability to deal with frustration, so that they can respond calmly to their child's behavior.

Sometimes, the whole family may need therapy. Therapists can help family members find better ways to handle disruptive behaviors and to encourage behavior changes. Finally, support groups help parents and families connect with others who have similar problems and concerns. Groups often meet regularly to share frustrations and successes, to exchange information about recommended specialists and strategies, and to talk with experts.

Can Adults Have ADHD?

Some children with ADHD continue to have it as adults. And many adults who have the disorder don't know it. They may feel that it is impossible to get organized, stick to a job, or remember and keep appointments. Daily tasks such as getting up in the morning, preparing to leave the house for work, arriving at work on time, and being productive on the job can be especially challenging for adults with ADHD.

These adults may have a history of failure at school, problems at work, or difficult or failed relationships. Many have had multiple traffic accidents. Like teens, adults with ADHD may seem restless and may try to do several things at once, most of them unsuccessfully. They also tend to prefer "quick fixes," rather than taking the steps needed to achieve greater rewards.

How Is ADHD Diagnosed in Adults?

Like children, adults who suspect they have ADHD should be evaluated by a licensed mental health professional. But the professional may need to consider a wider range of symptoms when assessing adults for ADHD because their symptoms tend to be more varied and possibly not as clear cut as symptoms seen in children.

To be diagnosed with the condition, an adult must have ADHD symptoms that began in childhood and continued throughout adulthood.[13] Health professionals use certain rating scales to determine if an adult meets the diagnostic criteria for ADHD. The mental health professional also will look at the person's history of childhood behavior and school experiences, and will interview spouses or partners, parents, close friends, and other associates. The person will also undergo a physical exam and various psychological tests.

For some adults, a diagnosis of ADHD can bring a sense of relief. Adults who have had the disorder since childhood, but who have not been diagnosed, may have developed negative feelings about themselves over the years. Receiving a diagnosis allows them to understand the reasons for their problems, and treatment will allow them to deal with their problems more effectively.

How Is ADHD Treated in Adults?

Much like children with the disorder, adults with ADHD are treated with medication, psychotherapy, or a combination of treatments.

Medications. ADHD medications, including extended-release forms, often are prescribed for adults with ADHD, but not all of these medications are approved for adults.[14] However, those not approved for adults still may be prescribed by a doctor on an "off-label" basis. Although not FDA-approved specifically for the treatment of ADHD, antidepressants are sometimes used to treat adults with ADHD. Older antidepressants, called tricyclics, sometimes are used because they, like stimulants, affect the brain chemicals norepinephrine and dopamine. A newer antidepressant, venlafaxine (Effexor), also may be prescribed for its effect on the brain chemical norepinephrine. And in recent clinical trials, the antidepressant bupropion (Wellbutrin), which affects the brain chemical dopamine, showed benefits for adults with ADHD.[15] Adult prescriptions for stimulants and other medications require special considerations. For example, adults often require other medications for physical problems, such as diabetes or high blood pressure, or for anxiety and depression. Some of these medications may interact badly with stimulants. An adult with ADHD should discuss potential medication options with his or her doctor. These and other issues must be taken into account when a medication is prescribed.

Education and psychotherapy. A professional counselor or therapist can help an adult with ADHD learn how to organize his or her life with tools such as a large calendar or date book, lists, reminder notes, and by assigning a special place for keys, bills, and paperwork. Large tasks can be broken down into more manageable, smaller steps so that completing each part of the task provides a sense of accomplishment.

Psychotherapy, including cognitive behavioral therapy, also can help change one's poor self-image by examining the experiences that produced it. The therapist encourages the adult with ADHD to adjust to the life changes that come with treatment, such as thinking before acting, or resisting the urge to take unnecessary risks.

References

1 DSM-IV-TR workgroup. *The Diagnostic and Statistical Manual of Mental Disorders,* Fourth Edition, Text Revision. Washington, DC: American Psychiatric Association.

2 Faraone SV, Perlis RH, Doyle AE, Smoller JW, Goralnick JJ, Holmgren MA, Sklar P. Molecular genetics of attention-deficit/hyperactivity disorder. *Biological Psychiatry,* 2005; 57:1313–1323.

3 Khan SA, Faraone SV. The genetics of attention-deficit/hyperactivity disorder: A literature review of 2005. *Current Psychiatry Reports,* 2006 Oct; 8:393–397.

4 Shaw P, Gornick M, Lerch J, Addington A, Seal J, Greenstein D, Sharp W, Evans A, Giedd JN, Castellanos FX, Rapoport JL. Polymorphisms of the dopamine D4 receptor, clinical outcome and cortical structure in attention-deficit/hyperactivity disorder. *Archives of General Psychiatry,* 2007 Aug; 64(8):921–931.

5   Linnet KM, Dalsgaard S, Obel C, Wisborg K, Henriksen TB, Rodriguez A, Kotimaa A, Moilanen I, Thomsen PH, Olsen J, Jarvelin MR. Maternal lifestyle factors in pregnancy risk of attention-deficit/hyperactivity disorder and associated behaviors: review of the current evidence. *American Journal of Psychiatry,* 2003 Jun; 160(6):1028–1040.

6   Mick E, Biederman J, Faraone SV, Sayer J, Kleinman S. Case-control study of attention-deficit hyperactivity disorder and maternal smoking, alcohol use, and drug use during pregnancy. *Journal of the American Academy of Child and Adolescent Psychiatry,* 2002 Apr; 41(4):378–385.

7   Braun J, Kahn RS, Froehlich T, Auinger P, Lanphear BP. Exposures to environmental toxicants and attention-deficit/hyperactivity disorder in U.S. children. *Environmental Health Perspectives,* 2006 Dec; 114(12):1904–1909.

8   Wolraich M, Milich R, Stumbo P, Schultz F. The effects of sucrose ingestion on the behavior of hyperactive boys. *Pediatrics,* 1985 Apr; 106(4):657–682.

9   Wolraich ML, Lindgren SD, Stumbo PJ, Stegink LD, Appelbaum MI, Kiritsy MC. Effects of diets high in sucrose or aspartame on the behavior and cognitive performance of children. *New England Journal of Medicine,* 1994 Feb 3; 330(5):301–307.

10 Hoover DW, Milich R. Effects of sugar ingestion expectancies on mother-child interaction. *Journal of Abnormal Child Psychology,* 1994; 22:501–515.

11 McCann D, Barrett A, Cooper A, Crumpler D, Dalen L, Grimshaw K, Kitchin E, Lok E, Porteous L, Prince E, Sonuga-Barke E, Warner JO. Stevenson J. Food additives and hyperactive behaviour in 3-year-old and 8/9-year-old children in the community: a randomised, double-blinded, placebo-controlled trial. *Lancet,* 2007 Nov 3; 370(9598):1560–1567.

12 The MTA Cooperative Group. A 14-month randomized clinical trial of treatment strategies for attention-deficit hyperactivity disorder. *Archives of General Psychiatry,* 1999; 56:1073–1086.

13 Wilens TE, Biederman J, Spencer TJ. Attention deficit/hyperactivity disorder across the lifespan. *Annual Review of Medicine,* 2002; 53:113–131.

14 Coghill D, Seth S. Osmotic, controlled-release methylphenidate for the treatment of attention-deficit/hyperactivity disorder. *Expert Opinions in Pharmacotherapy,* 2006 Oct; 7(15):2119–2138.

15 Wilens TE, Haight BR, Horrigan JP, Hudziak JJ, Rosenthal NE, Connor DF, Hampton KD, Richard NE, Modell JG. Bupropion XL in adults with attention-deficit/hyperactivity disorder: a randomized, placebo-controlled study. *Biological Psychiatry,* 2005 Apr 1; 57(7):793–801.

Attention Deficit Hyperactivity Disorder: What It Is and What It Is Not

It is almost axiomatic in the mental health field that fads will occur in the "diagnosis" and treatment of various types of behavioral aberrations, some of which border on being mere discomforts. Although the same faddism exists to some degree in physical medicine, its appearance is not nearly as blatant, perhaps in part because physical medicine is more soundly grounded in the physical sciences than are diagnoses in the mental health field. These fads spill over into the general culture, where direct marketing often takes place. One has to spend only a brief period in front of a television set during prime time to discover ADHD (Attention Deficit Hyperactivity Disorder), SAD (Social Anxiety Disorder), or IBS (Irritable Bowl Syndrome). Even when purporting to be informational, these are more or less disguised commercials, inasmuch as they posit a cure that varies with the drug manufacturer sponsoring the television ad.

The other certainty is that these "diagnoses" will fall from usage as other fads emerge, as was the case a decade or so ago with the disappearance of a once-common designation for what is now sometimes called ADHD. That passing fad was known as minimal brain syndrome (MBS) and/or food disorder (ostensibly from red dye or other food additives). From this author's perspective, these fad "diagnoses" don't really exist. Other writers in this volume (e.g., Cummings, Rosemond, and Wright) have commented on the slipperiness of these "diagnoses"—that is, the elevation of a symptom and/or its description to the level of a disorder or syndrome—and the concomitant tendency to over-medicate for these nonexistent maladies.

Children and ADHD

Certainly, there are deficiencies of attention and hyperactivity, but such behavioral aberrancies are most often indicative of a transitory state or condition within the organism. They are not in and of themselves indicative of a "disorder." Every parent has noticed, particularly with younger children, that toward the end of an especially exciting and fatiguing day children are literally "ricocheting off the walls." Although this behavior may in the broadest sense be classifiable as hyperactivity, it is generally pathognomonic of nothing more than excessive fatigue, for which the treatment of choice is a good night's sleep. Distractibility (attention deficit) is a frequent concomitant of excessive fatigue, particularly with children under five years of age and can even be seen in adults if fatigue levels are extreme or if stress is prolonged. However, such "symptoms" in these contexts do not rise to the level of a treatable disorder.

Conversely, when distractibility and/or hyperactivity characterize the child's everyday behavior (especially if accompanied by factors such as delayed development, learning difficulties, impaired motor skills, and impaired judgment), they may be indicative of either a neurological disorder or of developing emotional difficulties. However, after nearly fifty years of diagnosing and treating several thousand such problems, it is my considered judgment that the distractibility and hyperactivity seen in such children is not the same as the distractibility and hyperactivity in children currently diagnosed as having ADHD. Furthermore, the hyperactivity/distractibility seen in the non-ADHD children described above is qualitatively and quantitatively different, depending on whether it is caused by incipient emotional maldevelopment (functional; i.e., nonorganic) or whether it is due to neurological involvement.

It is also notable that most children whose distractibility and/or hyperactivity is occasioned by emotional distress do not show either the kind or degree of learning disability, delayed genetic development, poor judgment, and impaired motor skills that are seen in children whose "distractibility/hyperactivity" is occasioned by neurological involvement. Only in children with the severest forms of emotional disturbance does one see the kind of developmental delays and impaired behavioral controls that are more reflective of neurological involvement (or what was known as MBS until the ADHD fad took hold). Differentiating the child with actual neurological involvement from the child that has emotionally based distractibility is neither simple nor easy to do, especially if the behavioral (as opposed to neurological) involvement is severe.

A major and profound disservice occasioned by the current fad of elevating nonspecific symptoms such as anxiety and hyperactivity to the level of a syndrome or disorder and then diagnosing ADD/ADHD is that we lump together individuals with very different needs and very different problems. We then attempt to treat the problem(s) with a single entity, resulting in a one-pill-fits-all response. It is also unfortunately the case that many mental health providers (e.g., child psychiatrists, child psychologists, child social workers), as well as many general care practitioners (e.g., pediatricians and internists), are not competent to make such discriminations alone. Therefore, it follows that such practitioners are not trained and equipped to provide ongoing care, even when an appropriate diagnosis has been made.

To add to an already complicated situation, the symptom picture in children tends to change with time and maturation. Children with neurological involvement typically tend to improve spontaneously over time, so that the symptoms of distractibility and hyperactivity often represent diminished components in the clinical picture. Conversely, children whose distractibility and hyperactivity are emotionally determined typically have symptoms that tend to intensify or be accompanied/replaced by even more dramatic indices of emotional distress.

Management of Children Exhibiting "ADHD" According to Etiology

It is apparent that somewhat superficially similar presenting complaints (i.e., distractibility and hyperactivity) may reflect two very different causative factors, and that the successful treatment and management of the complaint should vary according to the underlying causation. Neurological damage can stem from a number of causative factors during pregnancy or the birth process, and a successful remedial program may require the combined knowledge of the child's pediatrician, a neuropsychologist specializing in the diagnosis and treatment of children, and a child neurologist. In these cases, appropriate medication for the child is often very helpful.

Psychotherapy for the child (particularly younger children) is, in this writer's experience, largely a waste of time. On the other hand, remedial training in visual perception, motor activities, visual–motor integration, spatial relations, numerical skills, and reading and writing may be crucial in alleviating or at least diminishing the impact of symptoms. Deficits in these skills can be major contributors to the hyperactivity and distractibility so frequently identified with such children. Counseling and psychotherapeutic work with the parents is very important and should always be a part of an integrated therapeutic program. Such children need to be followed by an attending pediatrician, a child neurologist, a child neuropsychologist, and an educational therapist, bearing in mind that treatment needs change throughout the span of remediation. For example, medication levels and regimens may need to be adjusted, and training programs will constantly need to be revised or elaborated.

It is also noteworthy that so-called tranquilizing medication with these children typically produces an adverse effect. This writer remembers a situation that occurred early in his practice, a case he has used repeatedly to alert fledgling clinicians to the importance of a comprehensive initial evaluation and ongoing supervision in the development of neurologically involved children.

John, a two-and-a-half-year-old boy, was referred by his pediatrician for evaluation of extreme hyperactivity, distractibility, and mild developmental delay. The psychological evaluation elicited evidence of visual perceptual impairment in a context of impaired visual motor integration, a finding suggestive of an irritative focus in the parietal-occipital areas of the brain. This finding was later corroborated by a child neurologist, and John was placed on dilantin and phenobarbital. A developmental training program was instituted, and the parents began participation in a group specifically designed for the parents of brain-injured children. Over the next couple of years, the patient's progress was excellent, and his development and learning difficulties were singularly diminished. The parents were comfortable with John's progress and with their ability to manage it, so they decided to have a long-wanted additional child. In the meantime, the father's work necessitated moving to another location, leading to a change of obstetrician and pediatrician.

The second pregnancy proceeded uneventfully and eventuated in the birth of a second boy. Shortly after the mother returned home with the new infant, John began to regress, exhibiting a number of prior symptoms such as hyperactivity and distractibility as well as problems in behavioral control. The new pediatrician referred the family to a child psychiatrist, who promptly placed John on a tranquilizer. Shortly thereafter, John's academic performance began to deteriorate dramatically, and his school counseled the parents about the possibility that he had been promoted too rapidly and "could not handle work at this grade level."

At this point, the parents again contacted this writer, primarily out of concern for John's diminished academic performance. Because it had been more than two years since John had been formally evaluated, I advised the parents that another comprehensive evaluation was indicated. The parents agreed, and a full diagnostic battery was administered to John, the results of which were then compared to his prior performance. It immediately became apparent that he was not functioning at grade level, and that the overall level of his functioning had deteriorated dramatically.

In his initial evaluation, John's functional level had been in the Bright Normal range (i.e., overall IQ of 110 to 119), whereas his current functioning placed him at the Borderline Mentally Retarded level (IQ below 60). The history revealed nothing of significance other than the behavioral regression after the birth of the sibling and the introduction of the new medication. I advised the parents that I thought the child was being erroneously medicated, with consequent diminution of his intellectual efficiency, and that the supposition could be tested by asking the attending child psychiatrist to diminish John's medication to see if the child's performance improved.

The attending child psychiatrist was quite upset by the recommendations and the implications thereof and threatened to sue me for "practicing medicine without a license." I informed the physician that I was not practicing medicine but rather neuropsychology, along with deductive reasoning known as "common sense," which we could test by appropriately reducing John's dosage level for a month and then retesting him. Faced with the alternative of a legal action for slander or libel for having accused this neuropsychologist of a felony, the child psychiatrist agreed.

Upon retesting a month later, the child's performance level had returned to Bright Normal, and his academic performance and behavior in school had improved dramatically. By this time approximately six to eight months had elapsed since the birth of the sibling, and John had become accustomed to his new brother. All concerned agreed that the medication had not been helpful and that the child should continue for another three to six months without medication. Subsequent contact with the parents some six months later indicated that John was doing well at school. The parents were quite comfortable with the behavioral management skills they had learned, which enabled them to handle a child with an underlying neurological handicap.

As noted earlier, the marked distractibility and/or hyperactivity in children with neurological involvement tends to diminish through adolescence, especially after puberty, as do many of the other symptoms. As a consequence, these children present a very different clinical picture in adolescence and adulthood. Typically, they are characterized by impulsivity, at times poor judgment, and excessive fatigability. It is generally only under the circumstances of extreme fatigue (or other stress) that one will see fairly dramatic degrees of distractibility and hyperactivity. Thus, an appropriate diagnosis leading to productive intervention is difficult to make.

Conversely, children who exhibit the symptoms of distractibility and hyperactivity on an emotional basis typically do not show the diminution of symptomatology with increasing age. In fact, the symptoms may intensify and/or be replaced by even more dramatic symptoms, especially during puberty and adolescence (Myklebust, 1973). It should also be emphasized that the kind of distractibility and hyperactivity exhibited by the emotionally disturbed youngster is very different in quality and quantity from that of a youngster whose hyperactivity and distractibility has a neurological basis (Myklebust, 1973; Ochroch, 1979). Unfortunately, it is also frequently the case that a youngster with a neurological handicap may have significant emotional problems overlaying the basic neurological problems, making diagnosis even more complicated (Small, 1980). But the overriding problem confronting parents today is the misdiagnosis of emotionally based symptoms that brings the recommendation of unwarranted medication.

In the largest study of its kind, Cummings and Wiggins (2001) retrospectively examined the records of 168,113 children and adolescents who had been referred and treated over a four-year period in a national behavioral health provider operating in thirty-nine states. Before beginning treatment, sixty-one percent of the males and twenty-three percent of the females were taking psychotropic medication for ADD/ADHD by a psychiatrist, a pediatrician, or a primary care physician. Most of them lived in a single-parent home and lacked an effective father figure or were subjected to negative and frequently abusive male role models. Behavioral interventions included a compassionate but firm male therapist and the introduction of positive male role models (e.g., fathers, Big Brothers, coaches, Sunday school teachers, etc.) into the child's life. Counseling focused on helping parents understand what constitutes the behavior of a normal boy.

After an average of nearly eleven treatments with the parent and approximately six with the child, the percentage of boys on medication was reduced from sixty-one percent to eleven percent, and the percentage of girls on medication went from twenty-three percent to two percent. These dramatic results occurred despite very strict requirements for discontinuing the medication, which seems to point to an alarming overdiagnosis and overmedication of ADD/ADHD and greater efficacy of behavioral interventions than is generally believed to be the case by the mental health community.

Adult ADHD

The wholesale invasion of ADHD in childhood and adolescence is accompanied by a concurrent explosion of such diagnoses into adulthood. One cannot watch television without being bombarded by the direct marketing that asks: "Do you find it difficult to finish a task at work? Do you frequently find yourself daydreaming or distracted? You may be suffering from ADD. Consult your physician or WebMD." Of course, adult ADD exists; children with real ADD will grow into adulthood. But the symptoms described in this aggressive TV marketing are more reflective of boredom, the mid-day blahs, job dissatisfaction, or stress than a syndrome or disorder requiring treatment.

Unfortunately, treatment interventions focused primarily on medication and based on such ethereal and universal symptoms promise an instant "cure" for the patient who now does not have to confront possible unhappiness or stress. Such simple solutions also find great favor with the insurers and HMOs that look for the cheapest treatment. Persons exhibiting "symptoms" are more likely to benefit from a variety of behavioral interventions ranging from vocational counseling for job dissatisfaction and marital counseling for an unhappy marriage, to psychotherapy for underlying emotional stress, anxiety, or depression. Such interventions tend to be time-consuming and costly, with the consequence that the patients may inadvertently ally themselves with managed care companies devoted to the principle that the least expensive treatment is the treatment of choice.

Distractibility and hyperactivity of the type that we have called the "real ADHD" does exist in adults. However, in general, symptoms are much more subtle and, in many if not most cases, overshadowed by other symptoms. Thus, if mentioned at all, distractibility and hyperactivity are rarely significant presenting complaints. Such things as poor judgment, behavioral difficulties, forgetting, difficulties in reading/calculating, and getting lost are typically preeminent in the adult patient's presenting complaints. These usually become apparent in adulthood after an accident, strokes (CVA), infections of the brain, and other such events. The very drama of the causative factor typically makes the diagnosis apparent, and treatment providers are "tuned in" to anticipate sequellae secondary to neurological damage: intellectual and/or judgmental deficits, behavioral change, impulsivity, and motor impairment.

It should be emphasized that hyperactivity and distractibility, although present, are less dramatic symptoms that are understandably of less concern to the patient. Furthermore, they often diminish rapidly in the first eighteen months following the neurological event. Even then, the major constellation of symptoms may not be sufficiently dramatic to alert attending medical personnel as to the primary cause of the patient's complaints. This is particularly true of contrecoup lesions occurring most frequently in auto accidents.

Although circumstances resulting in contrecoup damage are frequent and often missed, there are also other, even more significant, types of neurological involvement that may also pass unnoticed. These include early-onset Alzheimer's disease beginning at age fifty and cerebral toxicity resulting from inappropriate medication in the elderly, which is usually misdiagnosed as incipient Alzheimer's. Expectation can unfortunately contribute not only to a misdiagnosis, but also failure to order tests that might elicit the underlying condition. In addition, the converse may infrequently occur: Neurological involvement may be anticipated but is not demonstrable and does not exist. Three illustrative cases follow.

Case 1

Bill, a young construction worker, received notice of his imminent induction into the armed services. Right after lunch on a Friday afternoon, a large section of 2 × 4 lumber dropped from the second story of a work site, striking him butt-first in the right anterior temporal region of the head. He was unconscious for a short period of time, quickly recovered consciousness, and showed no apparent ill effects from the blow. He refused hospitalization and was taken by his employer to his home.

On the following Monday, Bill phoned his employer saying that he was still "not feeling too good," and given the imminence of his induction into the Army, he "was just going to goof off" until he was "called up." The employer had no further contact with Bill, who was inducted into the Army, where he almost immediately began to have difficulty, primarily of a behavioral type. Throughout his basic training, he tended to be impulsive and to use poor judgment, and he was constantly getting into fights with his companions. He barely made it through training and was shipped overseas where he was assigned to a unit whose primary duty was guard duty.

Throughout his training and his subsequent duty assignment, Bill was a frequent attendee at sick call with consistent complaints of headache, earning him the reputation of "goof-off." His military career was terminated shortly after an apparently unprovoked attack on the officer in charge of the guard detail to which Bill was assigned. After a short detention in the stockade, he was discharged from the Army. His headaches and impulsivity continued into civilian life and prompted Bill to seek medical assistance through the Veterans Administration. The VA clinic's case study included neurological screening tests that were strongly suggestive of brain involvement. Consequently, he was given a full psychological work-up, which revealed intellectual impairment attendant to temporal lobe damage.

Subsequent neurological and encephalographic studies were consistent with the neuropsychological conclusions, and indicated a major focus in the anterior temporal area of the brain. A careful and detailed history was taken, and the incident of the blow to the head was elicited. This case suggests that even though Bill refused hospitalization, because of the severity of the blow it would have been prudent for the employer to insist on a thorough evaluation.

Case 2

James, a man in his late forties, was the son of a Southern sharecropper. Upon graduation from high school, he attended the Tuskegee Institute for a short period before he was drafted into the armed forces. James had a productive military career and upon his discharge moved to California, got married, and proceeded to raise his family. He had trained himself as a finish carpenter and cabinetmaker. His work was highly regarded, and his annual income was well above the average for his field. One of his three children was a college graduate, a second was well along in college, and the third was graduating from high school. James owned his own home and enjoyed a fine reputation as a contributing citizen of his community.

While at work installing a complicated newel post and banister, James became disoriented and tumbled from a stair landing, falling some five feet, and landing primarily on his head and shoulders but experiencing no apparent loss of consciousness. He was taken to a hospital for evaluation but was released with no significant findings. Almost immediately thereafter, he began to have difficulty at work. He would become disoriented, could not tell left from right, and made frequent mistakes in measuring, sawing, and fitting even simple elements. Before the accident he seldom if ever missed work, but now he became a frequent absentee. The quality of his work deteriorated and his income plummeted. He sought medical advice and was given a small stipend under the Workers Compensation program.

Over several weeks, he demonstrated no progress, and the attending neurologist and neurosurgeon referred him for neuropsychodiagnostic evaluation as a possible malingerer. The neuropsychologist noted that James' current status was completely at odds with his prior history, and not at all consistent with malingering. For example, the evaluation revealed that this highly skilled cabinetmaker, to his embarrassment, could no longer answer the question, "How many inches are there in two and a half feet?" The neuropsychological finding of pervasive occipital-parietal involvement was subsequently corroborated by electroencephalographic study.

Case 3

An airline captain driving along Wilshire Boulevard in Los Angeles lost consciousness when he experienced a spontaneous cerebral hemorrhage. He was immediately taken to a nearby major hospital where he received immediate and continuing care. Subsequently, a subdural hematoma developed, requiring surgical intervention. The captain recovered and showed no clinically significant signs of neurological involvement. An immediate postrecovery issue was the possibility of being returned to flight status. The attending neurosurgeon referred the patient for a comprehensive neuropsychological evaluation that found no indication of residual neurological deficit. Consequently, the neuropsychologist and the attending neurosurgeon recommended return to flight status.

In summary, in none of the foregoing situations was attention deficit or hyperactivity a significant presenting complaint, although the presence of both was clinically demonstrable at various times in the posttraumatic period. Yet the failure to recognize their presence would not have had a negative impact on treatment planning and or management in any of the three cases. Conversely, if excessive focus on the possible "attention deficits and/or hyperactivity disorder" dictated the nature of the therapeutic intervention, a significant disservice to each of these patients would have resulted.

Traditionally when distractibility and/or hyperactivity are prominent parts of the presenting complaint, the mental health provider directs diagnostic energies toward ascertaining the underlying source of these dysphoric experiences. The distractibility and hyperactivity would have been viewed as secondary symptoms to be tolerated, if possible, until the resolution of the underlying problem resulted in their alleviation. In situations where the symptoms were so extreme as to be significantly debilitating, the mental health provider might reluctantly attempt to provide some symptom relief. However, in such cases this was done with the certain knowledge that it was an expedient and was not addressing causation.

Times have changed dramatically, reflecting the interaction of a number of factors such as competition and cost controls. With the emergence of a plethora of mental health service providers, psychiatry opted to "remedicalize," essentially abandoning what it refers to as "talk therapy" in favor of medicating questionable syndromes and disorders. Psychology, pushed by its academic wing, could never decide what level of training was sufficient for independent mental health service delivery (i.e., master's versus doctoral degrees), and graduate-level training programs began to turn out hordes of master's-level providers in counseling, social work, education, and school psychology.

Meanwhile, the inclusion of mental health benefits in prepaid health programs broadened consumption and brought about managed care as a means of reducing consumption of all kinds of health services, including behavioral health services. When the American public's impatience with time-consuming processes is added to managed care's limiting of services in the context of a glut of mental health providers the scene is set for considerable mischief. Add to this brew the fact that psychiatry holds a virtual medication-prescribing monopoly in mental health and that drug manufacturers are constantly developing and marketing new magic pills, it all adds up to an environment that encourages the "discovery" of yet another syndrome or disorder for which treatment is necessary.

Summary

When hyperactivity and/or distractibility is truly one of the presenting symptoms, it is indicative of a complex situation that warrants extensive and thoughtful evaluation, and, more often than not, complex and comprehensive treatment planning from the perspective of a variety of specialists. In situations where the attention deficit and/or hyperactivity reflects problems in parenting, chemotherapeutic intervention for the child is likely to be, at best, no more than palliative and, at worse, may succeed in considerably complicating the situation. In this writer's experience, chemotherapeutic intervention for emotionally disturbed children is a last resort and of minimal value in addressing the overall problem. Psychotherapeutic intervention with the parents, which may or may not include the child, is more often than not the treatment of choice. This is a judgment that is best made only after exhaustive study by pediatrics, psychology, neurology, and perhaps, last of all, psychiatry, which so often seems all too eager to overmedicate. . . .

Where the presenting complaints of hyperactivity and distractibility are in a context of delayed development, excessive fatigability, learning deficits, and other such signs, the complexity of the diagnostic problem is substantially increased. In such circumstances, it is absolutely not in the child's best interest to limit the diagnostic evaluation to a single specialty. With the increasing evidence that neurological involvement can follow any number of prenatal and postnatal exposures, wise and caring parents will insist on a comprehensive evaluation by specialists in pediatrics, child neurology, and child neuropsychology. More often than not, if medication is indicated, it will be of a type quite different than what is used in the management of so-called ADHD.

Furthermore, treatment intervention and case management will likely involve skilled educational training of the specialized type developed for use with the brain-injured child (see Myklebust, 1973, 1978; Ochroch, 1979; Small, 1980, 1982; Strauss & Kephart, 1955). In the case of a friendly pediatrician, a concerned psychologist, or a caring child psychiatrist, any or all attempting unilaterally to diagnose and/or manage the treatment regimen, the concerned and caring parent is well advised to promptly seek additional opinions. For a comprehensive description of the type of evaluation that is most productive in the management of children of this kind, see Small (1982).

EXPLORING THE ISSUE

Is Attention-Deficit/Hyperactivity Disorder (ADHD) a Real Disorder?

Critical Thinking and Reflection

1. To what extent should conditions involving inattention and hyperactivity be regarded as medical, as opposed to emotional, disorders?
2. What are the minimal behavioral criteria that should be met before recommending that an inattentive and easily distracted individual should be prescribed medication?
3. What might motivate some individuals to want to be diagnosed with the ADHD label?
4. How would you go about designing a research study aimed at differentiating normal characteristics such as occasional inattentiveness from diagnosable conditions such as ADHD?
5. A common style in contemporary society is to multitask, in which attention is divided among several simultaneous tasks (e.g., word processing, checking Facebook, talking on the phone). To what extent does multitasking cause people to believe that they have ADHD because they feel unable to process all the information coming their way?

Is There Common Ground?

Dr. Wright concurs with NIMH in recognizing that some people do indeed have deficiencies in attention and struggle with hyperactivity, although he is more inclined to view some experiences as transitory states within the person, rather than representing characteristics of a "disorder" per se. There is also concurrence with the notion that thoughtful assessment is warranted by a professional capable of differentiating normal behavioral characteristics from pathological conditions. NIMH recommends that a licensed health professional should be consulted who can gather information about the child and the environmental influences on the child. Such an evaluation should be conducted in a way that pays attention to the child's behavior in different situations. Dr. Wright points out that the symptom picture in children tends to change with time and maturation, and this fact should be taken into consideration before jumping to a diagnostic conclusion.

Regarding treatment, Dr. Wright recommends that ADHD-like behaviors should be managed on the basis of etiology. He feels that psychotherapy for the child, especially young children, is largely a waste of time; however, he does note that remedial training in various psychomotor skills can be beneficial. Of particular importance is counseling for parents who can obtain guidance and training in the most effective strategies for helping their child gain behavioral control and enhanced attentional skills. NIMH also speaks to parents, pointing out that children with ADHD need guidance and understanding from parents and teachers to reach their full potential. Mental health professionals can educate parents about their child's condition, and help them with skill acquisition, attitudinal change, and improved ways of relating to each other.

Additional Resources

Bruchmüller, K., Margraf, J., & Schneider, S. (2012). Is ADHD diagnosed in accord with diagnostic criteria? Overdiagnosis and influence of client gender on diagnosis. *Journal of Consulting and Clinical Psychology, 80*(1), 128–138. doi:10.1037/a0026582

Centers for Disease Prevention: www.cdc.gov/ncbddd/adhd/

Children and Adults with Attention Deficit/Hyperactivity Disorder (CHADD): www.chadd.org/

Massachusetts General Hospital Pediatric Psychopharmacology Clinical and Research Program: www.massgeneral.org/psychiatry/services/pedipsych_home.aspx

O'Regan, F. (2008). *Understanding AD/HD: Frequently asked questions*. London: Jessica Kingsley Publishers.

Pauc, R. (2006). *The learning disability myth: Understanding and overcoming your child's diagnosis of dyspraxia, Tourette's syndrome of childhood, ADD, ADHD or OCD*. London: Virgin Books.

Phillips, C. B. (2006). Medicine goes to school: Teachers as sickness brokers for ADHD. *PLOS Medicine, 3*(4). Retrieved from http://medicine.plosjournals.org/perlserv/?request=get-document&doi=10.1371%2Fjournal.pmed.0030182.

Zeigler Dendy, C. A. (2006). *Teenagers with ADD and ADHD: A guide for parents and professionals* (2nd ed.). Bethesda, MD: Woodbine House.

ISSUE 2

Is Posttraumatic Stress Disorder (PTSD) Overdiagnosed and Overtreated?

YES: Stephen Joseph, from "Has PTSD Taken Over America?" (2011, November 18), www.psychologytoday.com/blog/what-doesnt-kill-us/201111/ has-ptsd-taken-over-america; "What is Trauma?" (2012, January 5), www.psychologytoday.com/blog/what-doesnt-kill-us/201201/what-is-trauma; "Therapy for Posttraumatic Growth: Car Mechanics and Gardeners" (2011, November 1), www.psychologytoday.com/ blog/what-doesnt-kill-us/201111/therapy-posttraumatic-growth-car-mechanics-and-gardeners; "Changing How We Think About Psychological Trauma" (2011, October 28), www.psychologytoday .com/blog/what-doesnt-kill-us/201110/changing-how-we-think-about-psychological-trauma

NO: U.S. Department of Veteran Affairs, National Center for PTSD, from "What Is PTSD?" (2012, April 25), www.ptsd.va.gov/public/pages/ what-is-ptsd.asp; "How Common Is PTSD?" (2012, April 25), www.ptsd .va.gov/public/pages/how-common-is-ptsd.asp; "Treatment of PTSD" (2012, April 25), www.ptsd.va.gov/public/pages/treatment-ptsd.asp

---

Learning Outcomes

After reading this issue, you should be able to:

- Discuss the symptoms of PTSD and the characteristics of PTSD that distinguish it from expectable stress following exposure to an upsetting experience.
- Critically evaluate the question of whether "trauma" has become too broadly defined, and the diagnosis of PTSD applied too liberally.
- Understand the differences between two treatment approaches to PTSD: an intervention based on facilitating growth and an intervention focused on reforming how one thinks about the traumatic experience.
- Discuss how the criteria for PTSD have evolved over time and consider the forces contributing to changes in this diagnosis.
- Understand the concept of posttraumatic growth.

ISSUE SUMMARY

YES: Dr. Stephen Joseph argues that since the development of post-traumatic stress disorder (PTSD) as a diagnosis, the definition of trauma has been altered from its 1980 definition in *DSM-III*, and has been applied so loosely that everyday experiences can now be considered traumatic.

NO: The Department of Veterans Affairs (VA) states that PTSD can develop in any individuals who have gone through a life-threatening event that caused them to fear for their lives, see horrible things, and feel helpless. The VA urges therapists to help individuals with PTSD identify what triggers their stressful memories, find ways to cope with intense feelings about the past, become aware of their feelings and reactions in order to change their reactions, and raise their self-esteem.

Most people would acknowledge that involvement in the horrors of war leaves an indelible psychological mark on the soldiers who have risked their own lives or witnessed the death and injury of others. Although the experience of life-threatening trauma can take place in any human context, research efforts and clinical intervention have focused primarily on the condition known as posttraumatic stress disorder (PTSD) associated with military combat. In fact, the label PTSD was only added to the *Diagnostic and Statistical Manual of Mental Disorders* in 1980 when *DSM-III* was published by the American Psychiatric Association, in great part due to the growing awareness of the psychological casualties reported by veterans of the Vietnam War. In *DSM-5,* the PTSD diagnosis continues to evolve with the addition of more specificity about operationalizing some of the criteria, and by adding new symptoms (e.g., negative cognitions and mood). Even a new subtype is being added: Posttraumatic Stress Disorder in Preschool Children.

Because of all that was learned from the Vietnam era about PTSD, major efforts were made from the outset of the Afghanistan and Iraq wars on the part of the Department of Defense and the U.S. Department of Veterans Affairs to assess the impact of combat and to develop interventions aimed at reducing long-standing psychological disturbance. The research initiatives of the VA as well as the studies being conducted in other research programs have also made valuable contributions to the literature on PTSD arising from nonmilitary traumas, such as the diagnosis and treatment of people surviving trauma in noncombat situations: the national trauma of the September 11 attacks, the regional traumas caused by natural disasters such as hurricanes and tornadoes, and the personal traumas experienced by people who have been assaulted, raped, abused, or devastated by accident or injury.

Along with the justifiable attention to the nature of trauma and the development of effective interventions for trauma survivors has come some scrutiny, particularly about the possibility that PTSD is being overdiagnosed. More specifically, the question has been proposed about the extent to which individuals who experience distressing and possibly traumatizing experiences are being inappropriately labeled with a psychiatric *disorder,* rather than an expectable response to stress. Are such individuals being led to psychotherapy to treat their *disorder* instead of being given the tools to use their harrowing experience as an opportunity for posttraumatic growth?

Dr. Stephen Joseph challenges us to change how we think of trauma, and he expresses concern that PTSD may be taking over America. In considering the diagnosis of PTSD, he notes that the current definition is far more wide-ranging than that published in 1980 in *DSM-III,* and he asserts that the current definition is fraught with problems. According to Dr. Joseph, it is a normal process following traumatic events to suffer from intrusive thoughts, upsetting memories, and nightmares accompanied by attempts at emotional numbing and problems sleeping, difficulties with concentration, and feelings of being on edge. In this natural response lies the opportunity for personal transformation as the person works through the significance of what has happened and what it means.

Dr. Joseph believes that over the past three decades, the diagnosis of PTSD has undergone "bracket creep" such that the diagnosis of PTSD is now much more common than it would have been 30 years ago. Not only is it more common, it has also become more widely used to describe what previously would have been viewed as normal human distress. The task for therapists, then, is to facilitate posttraumatic growth.

Contrasting with the view of Dr. Joseph is the Department of Veterans Affairs, which has been facing the challenge of responding to the needs of millions of soldiers returning from war and combat. During the first decade of the twenty-first century, the VA has played a tremendously important role in tending to the needs of soldiers returning from combat, particularly those who served in Iraq and Afghanistan. With the numbers of soldiers returning with physical injury and psychological trauma reaching an all-time high, the VA has become a major player in responding to these men and women. Cynics might view the VA as having a vested interest in perpetuating the diagnosis of PTSD so that billions of dollars of funding will continue to be directed to the VA, which is the U.S. government's second largest department (after the Department of Defense). On the other side of that argument, however, is the fact that the budget of the VA is indeed limited, and therefore tremendous effort must be invested in ensuring the validity of every single diagnosis of PTSD among soldiers and veterans, so that financial resources are directed to those individuals whose lives have been so detrimentally affected by trauma.

In the VA's materials, acknowledgment is made of the fact that going through trauma does not mean that a person will develop PTSD. The VA states that although approximately half of all Americans go through some type of trauma, only 7–8 percent of the population develops PTSD. As for the most appropriate response, the VA does not discuss posttraumatic growth, but rather advocates interventions that help traumatized individuals change their cognitions. In cognitive therapy, the therapist helps the client understand how certain thoughts about the trauma cause an increase in stress and a worsening of symptoms. Clients are taught how to identify thoughts about the world and themselves which are causing fear and upset, and to replace these thoughts with more accurate and less distressing thoughts.

YES

Stephen Joseph

Has PTSD Taken Over America?

Last week I was interviewed by Alice Karekezi for Salon.Com. She asked me if I thought PTSD was over diagnosed.

There are actually two questions rolled up into this I think. The first is whether people are being inappropriately diagnosed with PTSD as defined by DSM. The second is whether the concept of PTSD has been over applied.

So, the first question; I think the vast majority of psychologists and psychiatrists are responsible professional people and are using the diagnostic category as it is meant to be used. Overall they are doing what it says on the tin.

It's what it says on the tin I wonder about. To the second question I wonder whether the concept of PTSD has been applied too widely.

It is my view that posttraumatic stress occurs in people following all sorts of threatening events and that these reactions are on a spectrum ranging from mild to severe levels. The job of psychiatric classification is to draw a line somewhere on that spectrum. Above the line, the person is suffering from a disorder, below the line they are not. I'm not saying that this is how it should be, simply that this is what is happening when a diagnosis is made. In my view the line has been drawn in such a way that a clear cut distinction is not made between those who are suffering from PTS and those who are suffering from PTSD.

To me it seems that to suffer from intrusive thoughts, upsetting memories and nightmares accompanied by attempts at avoidance, emotional numbing and problems sleeping, concentrating, and feelings of being on edge and tense, and so on following traumatic events is a normal and natural process—of personal transformation as the person works through the significance of what has happened to them and what it means. As distressing as such an experience may be it is not an illness. As such the term PTS seems appropriate.

The problem is if people who are suffering from PTS are given the diagnosis of PTSD. This happens because the diagnositic criteria do not make a distinction between PTS and PTSD.

So, when does the label PTSD become appropriate? In my view the label PTSD should be applied when it is clear that there is a dysfunction of these normal and natural mental mechanisms such that the person is unable to cognitively-emotionally process their experiences. We know that there are brain correlates but that line of research needs to go further and show that PTSD is a disorder of the brain.

In the context of psychiatric classification I simply think we ought to be cautious with the word disorder and to make sure that it means more than being distressed, different or difficult.

***

What Is Trauma?

Is it time to dump the diagnosis of PTSD?

My dictionary defines trauma as a deeply distressing or disturbing experience. Defined like that the events which can be considered traumatic are wide ranging indeed—from what might be considered the stuff of ordinary life such as divorce, illness, accidents and bereavement to extreme experiences of war, torture, rape and genocide.

Insofar as we adopt this wide ranging definition trauma is the stuff of everyday life.

The American Psychiatric Association's current definition of posttraumatic stress disorder (PTSD), introduced in 1994, states that a person must have experienced or witnessed an event or events that involved actual or threatened death or serious injury, or a threat to the physical integrity of self or others, and which involved fear, helplessness, or horror.

While the American Psychiatric Association's definition is more restrictive than my dictionary definition it is still far more wide ranging than the original 1980 definition of PTSD which stated that an event had to be outside the range of usual human experience. Then, only the most horrific events would qualify.

Looking to the future, debate rages in clinical and scientific circles about whether the next definition of trauma in DSM-V should be more or less restrictive.

Should we go back to something closer to the original idea that a trauma was an experience than when encountered would psychologically overwhelm all who encountered it? Or should we move in the direction of thinking that all life events have the potential to be perceived as traumatic.

Not surprisingly the elastic nature of the concept of trauma over the years has caused a great deal of public confusion.

And the topic of PTSD seems charged with emotion. There are two points of view.

First is the view that PTSD results from a stressor that is so overwhelming that no matter what the person's resources they will develop PTSD. As such the diagnosis of PTSD does not reflect any personal vulnerability.

The second is that people who develop PTSD are vulnerable in some way. As such the diagnosis of PTSD does reflect inner vulnerability. Those who do not develop PTSD are resilient.

And sometimes people who take the former view are dismissive of those who have received a diagnosis of PTSD following more everyday events as if their PTSD is somehow less valid. It is claimed that PTSD is being over-diagnosed.

But the fact is that since the 1994 definition, research has defined PTSD in such a way that trauma is necessary but not always sufficient to produce PTSD—so both these points of view are right.

The current definition has it both ways by understanding PTSD as the outcome of an interaction between trauma intensity and personal vulnerability.

An extreme event may be sufficient to produce PTSD in all who experience it so that personal vulnerability is not a factor. But a less extreme event may only produce PTSD in those who are already vulnerable.

Not surprisingly, in a culture in which mental illness is stigmatized, the issue of whether PTSD is caused by an event or by personal vulnerability is one which is charged with emotion. As the public understanding seems closer to the original definition of PTSD, the current definition is fraught with problems.

***

Changing How We Think About Psychological Trauma

The possibility of posttraumatic growth has become one of the most exciting topics in modern clinical psychology and psychotherapy.

Many commentators have talked about how trauma can be a catalyst to positive psychological change. Often, people's philosophies of life change; perhaps becoming wiser, less materialistic, or more able to live in the present. Their sense of self changes too; perhaps becoming more patient, compassionate or grateful. And people's relationships change; perhaps with a new depth of quality, the ability to make time for others, or becoming more giving.

Certainly, the study of posttraumatic growth is fascinating.

But what I find so compelling about this topic, and what most commentators haven't spotted yet, is that posttraumatic growth turns on its head how we think about psychological trauma.

For the last thirty years, the idea of posttraumatic stress disorder (PTSD) has been the big idea in the field of psychological trauma. But PTSD has increasingly come under fire by its critics.

Critics point to how PTSD has become scientifically meaningless. Psychiatric classification demands that a line is drawn that separates people into two groups: those without the disorder and those with the disorder. The question is where to draw that line.

Since the diagnosis of PTSD was formally introduced in 1980 the line has moved twice—in a manner some authors have referred to as bracket creep—so that the diagnosis of PTSD is now much more common than it would have been thirty years ago.

But not only is it more common, it has also become evident that it is widely used to describe what might previously have been viewed as normal human distress. This can't continue without devaluing the idea of PTSD.

The challenge therefore is for the next edition of the Diagnostic and Statistical Manual (DSM) to demonstrate when these normal processes of posttraumatic stress become disordered, so that the term PTSD is used clearly to describe dysfunction of some mental mechanism.

And it becomes increasingly clear that for most people trauma is simply not an illness.

For many years humanistic psychologists have argued against the illness ideology in psychology with little success. But now it is also becoming obvious to the wider audience that what is needed is a new non-pathological understanding of the normal processes that trauma triggers.

This is the cutting edge of posttraumatic growth research and theory. It is why I think posttraumatic growth is one of the most important topics in contemporary psychology. Posttraumatic growth shows that what we need is neither a negative psychology, nor a positive psychology, but an integrative psychology that understands that trauma and transformation, suffering and joy, go hand in hand.

***

Therapy for Posttraumatic Growth: Car Mechanics and Gardeners

What sort of therapy facilitates posttraumatic growth?

The best starting point is to examine the deep seated philosophical assumptions of therapy.

Therapists often talk about having a toolbox in which they have various exercises, techniques and suggestions that they can pull out in the service of the client. For sure, it is important to have a range of tools, but more important is to understand the job that needs to be done.

Look in a car mechanic's toolbox and you see a particular set of tools. Look in a gardener's toolbox and you see a different set. Each of these workers has a different task in mind.

I choose these two workers deliberately because they represent two different mindsets of the therapy world.

A car breaks down. You look under the hood but you have no idea yourself what the problem is. You need to take it to the appropriate expert mechanic who will then diagnose the problem. The mechanic knows about cars. He knows how they work. He knows what sounds to listen out for that mean something is wrong. He knows what the right levels of fluids should be. After a time the mechanic looks up. He tells you what is wrong and what needs to be done to get the car back into working order. You agree, and the mechanic gets to work.

Therapists who adopt the illness ideology to psychological problems are like the car mechanic. They know what normal functioning is and the different ways a person can be disordered. They listen attentively to what you tell them in order to diagnose the particular disorder that is causing you not to work properly. It's important to get the diagnosis right because only then can they be sure to provide the right treatment to cure the illness. If someone has a stomach upset they need indigestion tablets but if they have a broken leg they need a brace. After all, you wouldn't give indigestion tablets to heal a broken leg! Once the disorder is correctly identified, the right treatment can be provided to get you back to normal.

On the other hand, the gardener adopts the growth ideology. She turns the soil around the new plant making sure that it gets the right nutrients, is not too cold in winter and not too warm in summer, and is getting the right balance of light and shade. With trees whose growth has been stunted by a lack of nutrients, twisted at an angle having strained to get at the sunlight, or damaged in a storm, the gardener sets out to feed the tree, remove the barriers to sunlight, or provide support to grow anew. She trusts in the plant to grow as healthily as it can if all these barriers to growth are removed.

Therapists who are like gardeners don't need to direct growth or define what it will look like, for once the barriers to psychological growth are removed they trust that growth will happen.

Sometimes we need therapists to be like car mechanics and sometimes we need them to be like gardeners. In this sense I would argue that therapy is not so much about what you do as how you do it.

Therapists can make suggestions to their clients, offer advice, provide the opportunity for various exercises and so on, but how any therapist does these things ultimately rests on what they think they are doing—their fundamental assumptions—whether they think of themselves as car mechanics or as gardeners.

Both sets of assumptions have their roles to play in helping people. But we need to know when to be like car mechanics and when to be like gardeners.

To help people suffering from posttraumatic stress disorder (PTSD) it may be that therapists need to be like car mechanics, but to facilitate posttraumatic growth perhaps they need to be more like gardeners.

Is Posttraumatic Stress Disorder Over-Diagnosed and Over-Treated?

What Is PTSD?

Posttraumatic stress disorder (PTSD) is an anxiety disorder that can occur after you have been through a traumatic event. A traumatic event is something horrible and scary that you see or that happens to you. During this type of event, you think that your life or others' lives are in danger. You may feel afraid or feel that you have no control over what is happening.

Anyone who has gone through a life-threatening event can develop PTSD. These events can include:

- Combat or military exposure
- Child sexual or physical abuse
- Terrorist attacks
- Sexual or physical assault
- Serious accidents, such as a car wreck
- Natural disasters, such as a fire, tornado, hurricane, flood, or earthquake

After the event, you may feel scared, confused, or angry. If these feelings don't go away or they get worse, you may have PTSD. These symptoms may disrupt your life, making it hard to continue with your daily activities.

How Does PTSD Develop?

All people with PTSD have lived through a traumatic event that caused them to fear for their lives, see horrible things, and feel helpless. Strong emotions caused by the event create changes in the brain that may result in PTSD.

Most people who go through a traumatic event have some symptoms at the beginning. Yet only some will develop PTSD. It isn't clear why some people develop PTSD and others don't. How likely you are to get PTSD depends on many things:

- How intense the trauma was or how long it lasted
- If you lost someone you were close to or were hurt

- How close you were to the event
- How strong your reaction was
- How much you felt in control of events
- How much help and support you got after the event

Many people who develop PTSD get better at some time. But about 1 out of 3 people with PTSD may continue to have some symptoms. Even if you continue to have symptoms, treatment can help you cope. Your symptoms don't have to interfere with your everyday activities, work, and relationships.

What Are the Symptoms of PTSD?

Symptoms of PTSD can be terrifying. They may disrupt your life and make it hard to continue with your daily activities. It may be hard just to get through the day.

PTSD symptoms usually start soon after the traumatic event, but they may not happen until months or years later. They also may come and go over many years. If the symptoms last longer than 4 weeks, cause you great distress, or interfere with your work or home life, you probably have PTSD.

There are four types of PTSD symptoms:

1. **Reliving the event (also called re-experiencing symptoms)**
   Bad memories of the traumatic event can come back at any time. You may feel the same fear and horror you did when the event took place. You may have nightmares. You even may feel like you're going through the event again. This is called a flashback. Sometimes there is a trigger—a sound or sight that causes you to relive the event. Triggers might include:

   - Hearing a car backfire, which can bring back memories of gunfire and war for a combat Veteran.
   - Seeing a car accident, which can remind a crash survivor of his or her own accident.
   - Seeing a news report of a sexual assault, which may bring back memories of assault for a woman who was raped.

2. **Avoiding situations that remind you of the event**
   You may try to avoid situations or people that trigger memories of the traumatic event. You may even avoid talking or thinking about the event. For example:

   - A person who was in an earthquake may avoid watching television shows or movies in which there are earthquakes.
   - A person who was robbed at gunpoint while ordering at a hamburger drive-in may avoid fast-food restaurants.
   - Some people may keep very busy or avoid seeking help. This keeps them from having to think or talk about the event.

3. **Feeling numb**
   You may find it hard to express your feelings. This is another way to avoid memories.

- You may not have positive or loving feelings toward other people and may stay away from relationships.
- You may not be interested in activities you used to enjoy.
- You may not be able to remember parts of the traumatic event or not be able to talk about them.

4. **Feeling keyed up (also called hyperarousal)**
   You may be jittery, or always alert and on the lookout for danger. This is known as hyperarousal. It can cause you to:

   - Suddenly become angry or irritable
   - Have a hard time sleeping
   - Have trouble concentrating
   - Fear for your safety and always feel on guard
   - Be very startled when something surprises you

What Are Other Common Problems?

People with PTSD may also have other problems. These include:

- Drinking or drug problems
- Feelings of hopelessness, shame, or despair
- Employment problems
- Relationships problems including divorce and violence
- Physical symptoms

Can Children Have PTSD?

Children can have PTSD too. They may have the symptoms described above or other symptoms depending on how old they are. As children get older, their symptoms are more like those of adults. Here are some examples of PTSD symptoms in children:

- Young children may become upset if their parents are not close by, have trouble sleeping, or suddenly have trouble with toilet training or going to the bathroom.
- Children who are in the first few years of elementary school (ages 6 to 9) may act out the trauma through play, drawings, or stories. They may complain of physical problems or become more irritable or aggressive. They also may develop fears and anxiety that don't seem to be caused by the traumatic event.

How Common Is PTSD?

Going through trauma is not rare. About 60% of men and 50% of women experience at least one trauma in their lives. Women are more likely to experience sexual assault and child sexual abuse. Men are more likely to experience accidents, physical assault, combat, disaster, or to witness death or injury.

Going through a trauma doesn't mean you'll get PTSD, though. Although over half of us go through some type of trauma, a much smaller percent develop PTSD.

Here are some facts (based on the U.S.).

- About 7–8% of the population will have PTSD at some point in their lives.
- About 5.2 million adults have PTSD during a given year. This is only a small portion of those who have gone through a trauma.
- Women are more likely than men to develop PTSD. About 10% of women develop PTSD sometime in their lives compared with 5% of men.

Who Is Most Likely to Develop PTSD?

Although most people who go through trauma will not get PTSD, you are more likely to develop PTSD if you:

- Were directly exposed to the trauma as a victim or a witness
- Were seriously hurt during the event
- Went through a trauma that was long-lasting or very severe
- Believed that you were in danger
- Believed that a family member was in danger
- Had a severe reaction during the event, such as crying, shaking, vomiting, or feeling apart from your surroundings
- Felt helpless during the trauma and were not able to help yourself or a loved one.

You are also more likely to develop PTSD if you:

- Had an earlier life-threatening event or trauma, such as being abused as a child
- Have another mental health problem
- Have family members who have had mental health problems
- Have little support from family and friends
- Have recently lost a loved one, especially if it was not expected
- Have had recent, stressful life changes
- Drink a lot of alcohol
- Are a woman
- Are poorly educated
- Are younger

Some groups of people, including blacks and Hispanics, may be more likely than whites to develop PTSD. This may be because these groups are more likely to go through a trauma. For example, in Veterans who survived Vietnam, a larger percent of blacks, Hispanics, and Native Americans were in combat than whites.

Your culture or ethnic group also may affect how you react to trauma. For example, people from groups that are open and willing to talk about problems may be more willing to seek help.

PTSD and the Military

If you are in the military, you may have seen combat. You may have been on missions that exposed you to horrible and life-threatening experiences. You may have been shot at, seen a buddy shot, or seen death. These are types of events that can lead to PTSD.

Experts think PTSD occurs:

- In about 11–20% of Veterans of the Iraq and Afghanistan wars (Operations Iraqi and Enduring Freedom), or in 11–20 Veterans out of 100.
- In as many as 10% of Gulf War (Desert Storm) Veterans, or in 10 Veterans out of 100.
- In about 30% of Vietnam Veterans, or about 30 out of 100 Vietnam Veterans.

Other factors in a combat situation can add more stress to an already stressful situation. This may contribute to PTSD and other mental health problems. These factors include what you do in the war, the politics around the war, where it's fought, and the type of enemy you face.

Another cause of PTSD in the military can be military sexual trauma (MST). This is any sexual harassment or sexual assault that occurs while you are in the military. MST can happen to both men and women and can occur during peacetime, training, or war.

Among Veterans using VA health care, about:

- 23 out of 100 women (23%) reported sexual assault when in the military.
- 55 out of 100 women (55%) and 38 out of 100 men (38%) have experienced sexual harassment when in the military.

Even though military sexual trauma is far more common in women Veterans, over half of all Veterans with military sexual trauma are men. This is because there are many more male Veterans than there are females.

Treatment of PTSD

Today, there are good treatments available for PTSD. When you have PTSD, dealing with the past can be hard. Instead of telling others how you feel, you may keep your feelings bottled up. But talking with a therapist can help you get better.

Cognitive behavioral therapy (CBT) is one type of counseling. It appears to be the most effective type of counseling for PTSD. The VA is providing two forms of cognitive behavioral therapy to Veterans with PTSD: Cognitive Processing Therapy (CPT) and Prolonged Exposure (PE) therapy. To learn more about these types of therapy, see our fact sheets listed on the Treatment page.

There is also a similar kind of therapy called eye movement desensitization and reprocessing (EMDR) that is used for PTSD. Medications have also been shown to be effective. A type of drug known as a selective serotonin reuptake inhibitor (SSRI), which is also used for depression, is effective for PTSD.

Types of Cognitive Behavioral Therapy

What Is Cognitive Therapy?

In cognitive therapy, your therapist helps you understand and change how you think about your trauma and its aftermath. Your goal is to understand how certain thoughts about your trauma cause you stress and make your symptoms worse.

You will learn to identify thoughts about the world and yourself that are making you feel afraid or upset. With the help of your therapist, you will learn to replace these thoughts with more accurate and less distressing thoughts. You will also learn ways to cope with feelings such as anger, guilt, and fear.

After a traumatic event, you might blame yourself for things you couldn't have changed. For example, a soldier may feel guilty about decisions he or she had to make during war. Cognitive therapy, a type of CBT, helps you understand that the traumatic event you lived through was not your fault.

What Is Exposure Therapy?

In exposure therapy your goal is to have less fear about your memories. It is based on the idea that people learn to fear thoughts, feelings, and situations that remind them of a past traumatic event.

By talking about your trauma repeatedly with a therapist, you'll learn to get control of your thoughts and feelings about the trauma. You'll learn that you do not have to be afraid of your memories. This may be hard at first. It might seem strange to think about stressful things on purpose. But you'll feel less overwhelmed over time.

With the help of your therapist, you can change how you react to the stressful memories. Talking in a place where you feel secure makes this easier.

You may focus on memories that are less upsetting before talking about worse ones. This is called "desensitization," and it allows you to deal with bad memories a little bit at a time. Your therapist also may ask you to remember a lot of bad memories at once. This is called "flooding," and it helps you learn not to feel overwhelmed.

You also may practice different ways to relax when you're having a stressful memory. Breathing exercises are sometimes used for this.

What Is EMDR?

Eye movement desensitization and reprocessing (EMDR) is another type of therapy for PTSD. Like other kinds of counseling, it can help change how you react to memories of your trauma.

While thinking of or talking about your memories, you'll focus on other stimuli like eye movements, hand taps, and sounds. For example, your therapist will move his or her hand near your face, and you'll follow this movement with your eyes.

Experts are still learning how EMDR works. Studies have shown that it may help you have fewer PTSD symptoms. But research also suggests that the eye movements are not a necessary part of the treatment.

Medication

Selective serotonin reuptake inhibitors (SSRIs) are a type of antidepressant medicine. These can help you feel less sad and worried. They appear to be helpful, and for some people they are very effective. SSRIs include citalopram (Celexa), fluoxetine (such as Prozac), paroxetine (Paxil), and sertraline (Zoloft).

Chemicals in your brain affect the way you feel. For example, when you have depression you may not have enough of a chemical called serotonin. SSRIs raise the level of serotonin in your brain.

There are other medications that have been used with some success. Talk to your doctor about which medications are right for you.

Other Types of Treatment

Some other kinds of counseling may be helpful in your recovery. However, more evidence is needed to support these types of treatment for PTSD.

Group Therapy

Many people want to talk about their trauma with others who have had similar experiences.

In group therapy, you talk with a group of people who also have been through a trauma and who have PTSD. Sharing your story with others may help you feel more comfortable talking about your trauma. This can help you cope with your symptoms, memories, and other parts of your life.

Group therapy helps you build relationships with others who understand what you've been through. You learn to deal with emotions such as shame, guilt, anger, rage, and fear. Sharing with the group also can help you build self-confidence and trust. You'll learn to focus on your present life, rather than feeling overwhelmed by the past.

Brief Psychodynamic Psychotherapy

In this type of therapy, you learn ways of dealing with emotional conflicts caused by your trauma. This therapy helps you understand how your past affects the way you feel now.

Your therapist can help you:

- Identify what triggers your stressful memories and other symptoms.
- Find ways to cope with intense feelings about the past.
- Become more aware of your thoughts and feelings, so you can change your reactions to them.
- Raise your self-esteem.

Family Therapy

PTSD can affect your whole family. Your kids or your partner may not understand why you get angry sometimes, or why you're under so much stress. They may feel scared, guilty, or even angry about your condition.

Family therapy is a type of counseling that involves your whole family. A therapist helps you and your family to communicate, maintain good relationships, and cope with tough emotions. Your family can learn more about PTSD and how it is treated.

In family therapy, each person can express his or her fears and concerns. It's important to be honest about your feelings and to listen to others. You can talk about your PTSD symptoms and what triggers them. You also can discuss the important parts of your treatment and recovery. By doing this, your family will be better prepared to help you.

You may consider having individual therapy for your PTSD symptoms and family therapy to help you with your relationships.

How Long Does Treatment Last?

CBT treatment for PTSD often lasts for 3 to 6 months. Other types of treatment for PTSD can last longer. If you have other mental health problems as well as PTSD, treatment may last for 1 to 2 years or longer.

What If Someone Has PTSD and Another Disorder? Is the Treatment Different?

It is very common to have PTSD at that same time as another mental health problem. Depression, alcohol or drug abuse problems, panic disorder, and other anxiety disorders often occur along with PTSD. In many cases, the PTSD treatments described above will also help with the other disorders. The best treatment results occur when both PTSD and the other problems are treated together rather than one after the other.

What Will We Work on in Therapy?

When you begin therapy, you and your therapist should decide together what goals you hope to reach in therapy. Not every person with PTSD will have the same treatment goals. For instance, not all people with PTSD are focused on reducing their symptoms.

Some people want to learn the best way to live with their symptoms and how to cope with other problems associated with PTSD. Perhaps you want to feel less guilt and sadness. Perhaps you would like to work on improving your relationships at work, or communicating with your friends and family.

Your therapist should help you decide which of these goals seems most important to you, and he or she should discuss with you which goals might take a long time to achieve.

What Can I Expect from My Therapist?

Your therapist should give you a good explanation for the therapy. You should understand why your therapist is choosing a specific treatment for you, how long they expect the therapy to last, and how they will tell if it is working.

The two of you should agree at the beginning that this plan makes sense for you. You should also agree on what you will do if it does not seem to be working. If you have any questions about the treatment, your therapist should be able to answer them.

You should feel comfortable with your therapist and feel you are working as a team to tackle your problems. It can be difficult to talk about painful situations in your life, or about traumatic experiences that you have had. Feelings that emerge during therapy can be scary and challenging. Talking with your therapist about the process of therapy, and about your hopes and fears in regards to therapy, will help make therapy successful.

If you do not like your therapist or feel that the therapist is not helping you, it might be helpful to talk with another professional. In most cases, you should tell your therapist that you are seeking a second opinion.

EXPLORING THE ISSUE

Is Posttraumatic Stress Disorder (PTSD) Overdiagnosed and Overtreated?

Critical Thinking and Reflection

1. In light of the differing definitions of trauma, how can consensus be reached in determining the definition of a disorder that results from the experience of trauma?
2. What is the dividing line between posttraumatic *stress* and posttraumatic stress *disorder?*
3. Consider the fact that not all people who experience trauma develop PTSD. To what extent might there be personal variables that predispose some people to develop PTSD, and how might researchers determine what these variables are?
4. In what ways could the different therapeutic approaches be integrated, namely an intervention aimed at facilitating posttraumatic growth and an intervention that employs cognitive techniques?
5. *DSM-5* contains a subtype of PTSD called Posttraumatic Stress Disorder in Preschool Children. What are the risks and benefits of such a diagnosis being applied to young children?

Is There Common Ground?

Both sets of articles accept the fact that posttraumatic stress disorder is a debilitating condition experienced by countless numbers of people who have experienced life-threatening or horrifying experiences. Dr. Joseph expresses concern that PTSD is being overdiagnosed. Although the VA does not make this argument so explicitly, the professionals who work in the VA system are committed to precision in diagnosis of PTSD, so that treatments (as well as disability benefits) are adequately provided to those who truly have a disorder and are in dire need of intervention. The wisdom derived from the extensive research conducted by the VA on the nature and treatment of PTSD will prove beneficial to all survivors of trauma, both in the military and in the general public.

Both sets of articles also acknowledge the benefits of obtaining help from professionals to find ways in which the distress resulting from such exposure can be understood and controlled. There also seems to be agreement with the premise that traumatized individuals will benefit from an intervention in which they revise the ways in which they view the traumatic experience and take cognitive control over what can be debilitating symptoms. The VA recommends cognitive therapeutic techniques such as cognitive exposure techniques aimed at reducing the emotional impact of intrusive thoughts and memories. Dr. Joseph recommends an approach, which could also be construed as being cognitively based, in which the trauma survivor views the experience as an opportunity for growth.

Additional Resources

Dobbs, D. (2009, April 13). Soldiers' stress: What doctors get wrong about PTSD. *Scientific American*. Retrieved from www.scientificamerican.com/article.cfm?id=post-traumatic-stress-trap

Joseph, S. (2011). *What doesn't kill us: The new psychology of posttraumatic growth*. New York, NY: Basic Books.

Gateway to Post Traumatic Stress Disorder Information. Retrieved from www.ptsdinfo.org/

Heal My PTSD: Post Traumatic Stress Disorder Symptoms, Treatment, and Support Information. Retrieved from http://healmyptsd.com/

Schiraldi, G. R. (2009). *The post-traumatic stress disorder sourcebook: A guide to healing, recovery, and growth* (2nd ed.). New York, NY: McGraw-Hill Publishing.

ISSUE 3

Is Gender Identity Disorder a Mental Illness?

YES: Traditional Values Coalition, from "A Gender Identity Disorder Goes Mainstream: Cross-Dressers, Transvestites, and Transgenders Become Militants in the Homosexual Revolution" (Traditional Values Coalition)

NO: Kelley Winters, from "Part I: Diagnosis vs. Treatment: The Horns of a False Dilemma" in *GID Reform Weblog* (2008), and from "Part II: Top Ten Problems with the GID Diagnosis" in *GID Reform Weblog* (July 1, 2008/July 16, 2008)

Learning Outcomes

After reading this issue, you should be able to:

- Discuss the *DSM* diagnostic criteria for Gender Dysphoria (GD) in Adults and Adolescents.
- Critically evaluate the justification for including the diagnosis of GD in the *Diagnostic and Statistical Manual of Mental Disorders*.
- Understand the ways in which a diagnostic label can cause gender-variant people to feel stigmatized.
- Evaluate the extent to which the political ideologies play a role in the definition of what constitutes a mental disorder.
- Assess the extent to which the change in *DSM* terminology from "Gender Identity Disorder" to "Gender Dysphoria" represents significant change in thinking about gender-variant conditions.

ISSUE SUMMARY

YES: The Traditional Values Coalition argues that gender-variant people are psychologically disturbed individuals who need professional help, and that their condition should be viewed as a mental disorder.

NO: Kelley Winters asserts that the GID diagnosis imposes the stigma of mental illness upon people who meet no scientific definition of mental disorder.

For decades vehement debates have raged about what is normal and what is abnormal when it comes to human sexual behavior. For much of the twentieth century, homosexuality was regarded as a mental disorder and was listed in the *Diagnostic and Statistical Manual of Mental Disorders* (*DSM*). In 1973, following great controversy and upheaval within the American Psychiatric Association, homosexuality was deleted from the list of mental disorders. Similar controversy emerged about the inclusion of Gender Identity Disorder (GID) in *DSM-IV*. In response to that debate, *DSM-5* has modified the diagnosis by referring to "Gender Dysphoria" (GD). Regardless of the specific terminology, the debate continues about the inclusion of a gender-variant condition in a diagnostic manual of mental disorders. Even though the articles selected for this issue use the term GID, most of the arguments for and against pathologizing gender variance apply. In fact, some people would argue that the diagnostic label should not have been changed from GID to GD, thus making the articles in this issue relevant, even though the official terminology has changed in *DSM-5*.

DSM-5 contains two diagnoses in this category: (1) Gender Dysphoria in Children, and (2) Gender Dysphoria in Adolescents and Adults. Criteria for the adolescent/adult condition include a marked incongruence between one's experienced/expressed gender and assigned gender, as evidenced by two of the following: (1) a marked incongruence between one's experienced/expressed gender and primary and/or secondary sex characteristics; (2) a strong desire to get rid of one's primary and/or secondary sex characteristics; (3) a strong desire for the primary and/or secondary sex characteristics of the other gender; (4) a strong desire to be of the other gender; and (5) a strong conviction that one has the typical feelings and reactions of the other gender. In addition, the individual experiences significant distress or impairment, or a significantly increased risk of suffering distress or disability. Subtypes include (1) GD with a disorder of sex development and (2) GD without a disorder of sex development. The diagnosis of GD can be further specified as post-transition for individuals who have transitioned to full-time living in the desired gender, and who have undergone or are undergoing at least one cross-sex medical procedure or treatment regimen (i.e., regular cross-sex hormone treatment or gender reassignment surgery, e.g., penectomy, vaginoplasty in a born male, mastectomy, phalloplasty in a born female).

Those who argue that such gender variance should be viewed as a mental disorder, such as members of the Traditional Values Coalition, assert that transgender people are psychologically disturbed individuals who need professional help, rather than societal approval or affirmation. They contend that maleness and femaleness are unchangeable because they exist in a person's DNA; surgical efforts to change a person's sex result in little other than bodily mutilation. According to the Coalition, a man who has his sex organ removed and takes hormone treatments to grow female breasts is still genetically a male. He is simply a mutilated man, not a woman. This fiction, however, is being perpetrated by a perverted sexual ideology—not by biological facts or science. Homosexuals and their transgender allies believe that "gender" is a cultural invention, not a biological reality. Gender-confused individuals need long-term counseling, not approval for what is clearly a mental disturbance.

In a two-part publication, Kelley Winters argues that diagnosing gender variance as a mental disorder has imposed the stigma of mental illness and sexual deviance upon people who meet no scientific definition of mental disorder. Because of this stigmatization, many gender-variant people fear losing their families, homes, jobs, civil liberties, and access to medical care. Such diagnostic labels, Winters argues, imply that the inner identities of gender-variant individuals are not legitimate, but represent perversion, delusion, or immature development. Those who support such labeling do not acknowledge the existence of many healthy, well-adjusted transsexual and gender-variant people or justify why they are labeled as mentally ill. Identification with the "other sex," meaning other than assigned birth sex, is described as symptomatic regardless of an individual's satisfaction and happiness with that identification. The *DSM* diagnosis of gender-variant conditions undermines and even contradicts social transition and the medical necessity of hormonal and surgical treatments that relieve the distress of gender dysphoria, defined here as a persistent distress with one's current or anticipated physical sexual characteristics or current ascribed gender role. Furthermore, the *DSM* diagnosis fails to distinguish the intrinsic distress of gender dysphoria from that caused by external societal intolerance.

A Gender Identity Disorder Goes Mainstream: Cross-Dressers, Transvestites, and Transgenders Become Militants in the Homosexual Revolution

Lesbian, Gay, Bisexual, and Transgender (LGBT) activists are working to add "sexual orientation," "gender," and "gender identity" to federal legislation. If this legislation is passed, cross-dressers, transsexuals, and drag queens will have federally protected minority status equal to minority groups.

What Is a Transgender?

The term Transgender is an umbrella term coined by transgender activists to describe the following individuals: heterosexual cross-dressers, homosexual transvestites or drag queens, and transsexuals (individuals undergoing so-called sex change operations) and she-males.

Some of these individuals live their lives as she-males with both female and male sexual characteristics. These are deeply troubled individuals who need professional help, not societal approval or affirmation.

A History Lesson: Gender Bill of Rights?

In Houston, in August 1993, at a meeting of the Second International Conference on Transgender Law and Employment Policy, transgender activists passed the "International Gender Bill of Rights."

Here is the text of the Gender Bill of Rights:

> All human beings carry within themselves an ever-unfolding idea of who they are and what they are capable of achieving. The individual's sense of self is not determined by chromosomal sex, genitalia, assigned birth sex, or initial gender role. Thus the individual's identity and capabilities cannot be circumscribed by what society deems to be masculine or feminine behavior.

It is fundamental that individuals have the right to define, and to redefine as their lives unfold, their own gender identity, without regard to chromosomal sex, genitalia, assigned birth sex, or initial gender role.

The Right to Free Expression of Gender Identity—Given the right to define one's own gender identity, all human beings have the corresponding right to free expression of their self-defined gender identity.

The Right to Control and Change One's Own Body—All human beings have the right to control their bodies, which includes the right to change their bodies cosmetically, chemically, or surgically, so as to express a self-defined gender identity.

The Right to Competent Medical and Professional Care—Given the individual right to define one's gender identity, and the right to change one's own body as a means of expressing a self-defined gender identity, no individual should be denied access to competent medical or other professional care on the basis of chromosomal sex, genitalia, assigned birth sex, or initial gender role.

The Right to Freedom from Psychiatric Diagnosis or Treatment—Given the right to define one's own gender identity, individuals should not be subject to psychiatric diagnosis or treatment solely on the basis of their gender identity or role.

The Right to Sexual Expression—Given the right to a self-define gender identity, every consenting adult has a corresponding right to free sexual expression.

The Right to Form Committed, Loving Relationships and Enter into Marital Contracts—Given that all human beings have the right to free expression of a self-defined gender identity, and the right to sexual expression as a form of gender expression, all human beings have a corresponding right to form committed, loving relationships with one another and to enter into marital contracts, regardless of either partner's chromosomal sex, genitalia, assigned birth sex, or initial gender role.

The Right to Conceive or Adopt Children; the Right to Nurture and Have Custody of Children and Exercise of Parental Rights—Given the individual's right to form a committed, loving relationship with another, and to enter into marital contracts with another, together with the right to sexual expression of one's gender identity, all individuals have a corresponding right to conceive or adopt children, to nurture children and to have custody of children, and to exercise parental rights with respect to children, natural or adopted, without regard to chromosomal sex, genitalia, assigned birth sex, or initial gender role.

Transgenders Are Mentally Disordered

The American Psychiatric Association (APA) still lists transsexualism and transvestism as paraphilias or mental disorders in the *Diagnostic and Statistical Manual (DSM-IV-TR)*. However, homosexual groups such as the Human Rights Campaign (HRC) and GenderPac are pushing hard to have this classification removed from the *DSM*. The objective is to normalize a mental disorder in the same way that homosexuality was normalized in 1973 when psychiatrists removed this sexual dysfunction from the *DSM*. In fact, when the

APA met in May 2003 in San Francisco, Dr. Charles Moser with the Institute for Advanced Study of Human Sexuality argued that sadomasochism, trans-sexualism/transvestism, and even bestiality (sex with animals) should be removed from the *DSM*. According to Moser, psychiatry no longer has a "base line" to judge what constitutes normal behavior, so these categories should be removed.

Media Is Aiding Transgender Movement

Hollywood and the liberal media are doing their part to normalize this serious mental illness. In 2001, for example, the Los Angeles Times published "Era of the Gender Crosser," that portrayed transgendered individuals as a misunder-stood and persecuted minority. According to author Mary McNamara, indi-viduals who believe they are the opposite sex should be treated as if they have a medical condition, not a mental condition.

The Discovery Health Channel repeatedly runs "What Sex Am I?" which questions the reality of male and female.

Hollywood is pushing the transgender agenda in various ways. HBO ran "Normal," in March 2003. This show described a middle-aged married man who decided he was really a woman and sought a sex change. Networks are also running "Brandon Teena," about a poor sexually confused girl who dressed like a boy. She was eventually murdered by two angry young men when they discovered who she was. Teena Brandon has become a martyr for the transgender cause.

The latest martyr for transgender activists is a boy named Justin Zapata, who dressed like a girl and called himself "Angie."

Justin was brutally murdered in 2008 by a Mexican gang member who briefly "dated" Justin until he found out that "Angie" was actually an 18-year-old boy. The gang member has been sentenced to life in prison without parole—plus an extra sentence for committing a "hate crime" against Zapata.

Hollywood, which is dominated in many areas by homosexual activists, will continue to introduced transgender themes into its movies and TV shows.

Transgender activists are also receiving help from journalists. The National Lesbian and Gay Journalists Association, for example, has distributed to media outlets a "Stylebook Supplement." It encourages journalists to cater to the transgender agenda by referring to transgendered persons by their self-identification, not their actual birth sex.

Psychiatrists and Pediatricians Are Pushing Transgender Confusion on Kids

The transgender movement is also being helped by psychiatrists and pediatri-cians who are pushing the view that children should be free to choose their own "genders."

In May 2006, the Pediatric Academic Societies held a conference in San Francisco to promote this bizarre viewpoint.

A member of the National Association for Research and Therapy of Homosexuality (NARTH) was an eyewitness at this conference and described what occurred at this conference.

Two of the attendees were Irene N. Sills and Arlene Istar Lev. They presented a paper titled, "Gender-Variant Youth—The Role Of The Pediatrician." They outlined a "non-pathological model for transgender expression" designed to "help identify the gender-variant child as one who simply marches to the beat of a different drummer."

Pro-transgender activists like these are referring to children with serious Gender Identity Disorders as merely "gender variant."

Some pro-transgender pediatricians are actually injecting preteens with hormones to keep them from developing into adult males or females—until these kids "decide" what sex they wish to be.

This is child abuse, yet the transgender agenda is well-advanced in academia and in the medical and mental health professions.

No One Can Change Their Sex

The reality is that no person can actually change into a different sex. Maleness and femaleness are in the DNA and are unchangeable. A man who has his sex organ removed and takes hormone treatments to grow female breasts is still genetically a male. He is simply a mutilated man, not a woman. This fiction, however, is being perpetrated by a perverted sexual ideology—not by biological facts or science.

Homosexual groups such as the Human Rights Campaign and the National Gay and Lesbian Task Force have provided transgender activists with credibility and political power as they pursue their agenda.

The transgender movement's philosophy is based on the writings of several transsexuals. Among them are Nancy Nangeroni, founder of the International Foundation for Gender Education, Martine Rothblatt, and Marxist radical Leslie Feinberg, author of *Transgender Warrior*, and an editor with the Workers World Party, a Communist splinter group that aligns itself with North Korea.

Nancy Nangeroni claims that Western Civilization is "sick" because it pathologizes any person who wants a sex change operation. Martine Rothblatt is author of *The Apartheid of Sex: A Manifesto on the Freedom of Gender*. According to Rothblatt, our culture's practice of dividing people into two sexes is as evil as racial apartheid. He argues that there are actually several sexes, not just male and female. Those who oppose transgenderism are "transphobic" and intolerant.

The Human Rights Campaign, one of the most aggressive homosexual groups in the United States, is allied with transgender activists and has actually developed workplace guidelines for how businesses should handle men and women who are undergoing sex change operations.

In addition, Parents and Friends of Lesbians and Gays (PFLAG) has a special Transgender Special Outreach Network, which includes coordinators in more than 170 chapters. It also distributed 12,000 copies of "Our Trans Children" to schools and to parents of these sexually confused children.

The leading transgender group is GenderPac, headed by male-to-female transgender Riki Wilchins. He is author of *READ MY LIPS: Sexual Subversion & the End of Gender.* Wilchins works closely with the NGLTF to get the APA to remove transsexualism as a mental disorder. Patricia Ireland, former head of the YWCA, is a member of the board of GenderPac and helps lobby Congress for passage of legislation protecting the "gender identity" of individuals in the workplace and in our culture.

Be Whatever You Wish

Homosexuals and their transgender allies believe that "gender" is a cultural invention, not a biological reality. According to these activists, a person can self-identify and be whatever he or she wishes to be sexually. One pro-transgender activist, Professor Anne Fausto-Sterling, for example, has said that "Complete maleness and complete femaleness represent the extreme ends of a spectrum of possible body types."

Fausto-Sterling published "The Five Sexes: Why Male and Female Are Not Enough," in The Sciences, March/April 1993. In fact, many of these sexually confused individuals decide that they wish to be neither male nor female, but to exist as she-males with female sexual characteristics from the waist up and male sexual characteristics from the waist down.

One of these individuals actually set up a web site to describe herself. Della Grace on her web site "Body Politic," says she is a she-male and former lesbian photographer and visual artist. Grace says she willingly purchased a "one-way ticket" to "no man's land," to inhabit the "nether world" where she is neither male nor female. She calls herself a "pansexual, which means I don't discriminate on the basis of gender or species." She also describes herself as a "gender variant" mutant who has decided against being male or female.

Deconstructing Male and Female

The NARTH has published numerous articles on various Gender Identity Disorders. One is by Dale O'Leary, author of *The Gender Agenda.* In the NARTH paper, "Destabilizing The Categories Of Sex And Gender," O'Leary notes: Patients who suffer from the belief that they are men trapped in the bodies of women (or women trapped in the bodies of men) need real help. . . . The promotion of 'sex changes,' and the normalizing of severe Gender Identity Disorders by radical feminists, pro-same-sex attraction disorder activists, and sexual revolutionaries is part of their larger agenda—namely, the destabilization of the categories of sex and gender."

O'Leary notes that radicals and medical professionals who promote sex change operations are operating under the delusion that one's gender is changeable. One cannot change into a different sex. It is genetically and medically impossible. Gender-confused individuals need long-term counseling, not approval for what is clearly a mental disturbance.

Dr. Martin Silverman, a member of NARTH, has written extensively on Gender Identity Disorders. In a NARTH paper, "Gender Identity Disorder In

Boys: A Complemental Series?" he notes that a boy who has developed a Gender Identity Disorder, such as homosexuality or transvestism, typically comes from a home where the mother is smothering in her love and where the father is passive and feels powerless to overcome his wife's dominance in the family. NARTH has more information on this disorder on its web site: www.narth.com.

What Can Be Done?

If the transgender movement is not already active in your community, it will be. Wherever there are homosexual activist groups, you will find transgendered individuals working alongside them to establish policies and recruitment programs in public schools and to change laws to redefine what it means to be male or female. Here are some suggestions for action:

Monitor city and state legislative proposals that contain the word "gender" in them. Gender is code for cross-dressers, transvestites, and transsexuals. Inform your local politicians of this cultural agenda so they will recognize it when activists attempt to push through legislation.

Oppose Gay Straight Alliance clubs on school campuses. These are recruitment programs to lure children into sexually destructive lifestyles.

These GLSEN-sponsored groups are now promoting cross-dressing for children.

Use TVC, NARTH, and other materials in fighting homosexual/ transgenderism.

 **NO**

Part I: Diagnosis vs. Treatment: The Horns of a False Dilemma

The transgender community has been divided by fear that we must choose between access to corrective hormonal and surgical procedures to support transition and the stigma of mental illness imposed by the current diagnosis of Gender Identity Disorder (GID).[1] This schism has allowed little dialogue and no progress on GID reform in nearly three decades. However, the GID diagnosis has failed our community on both points. Transsexual individuals are poorly served by a diagnosis that both stigmatizes us as mentally deficient and sexually deviant *and at the same time* undermines the legitimacy of social transition and medical procedures that are often dismissed as "elective," "cosmetic," or as reinforcing mental disorder.

Gender Identity Disorder in the *Diagnostic and Statistical Manual of Mental Disorders*[2] has imposed stigma of mental illness and sexual deviance upon people who meet no scientific definition of mental disorder.[3] It does not acknowledge the existence of many healthy, well-adjusted transsexual, and gender variant people or justify why we are labeled as mentally ill.

I have heard countless narratives of suffering inflicted by the stereotype of mental illness and "disordered" gender identity, and I have experienced it myself. We lose our families, our children, our homes, jobs, civil liberties, access to medical care, and our physical safety. With each heartbreak, we're almost invariably told the same thing—that we're "nuts," that our identities and affirmed roles are madness and deviance. The following statement by Dr. Robert Spitzer at the 1973 annual meeting of the American Psychiatric Association remains as true today for transgender people as it was for gay and lesbian people then:

> "In the past, homosexuals have been denied civil rights in many areas of life on the ground that because they suffer from a 'mental illness' the burden of proof is on them to demonstrate their competence, reliability, or mental stability."[4]

The current GID diagnosis places a similar burden of proof upon gender variant individuals to prove our competence, with consequences of social stigma and denied civil rights. It harms those it was intended to help. For example,

> "Transsexuals suffer from 'mental pathologies,' are ineligible for admission to Roman Catholic religious orders and should be expelled if they

have already entered the priesthood or religious life," the Vatican says in new directives."[5]

Simultaneously, GID in the DSM-IV-TR undermines and even contradicts social transition and the medical necessity of hormonal and surgical treatments that relieve the distress of gender dysphoria, defined here as a persistent distress with one's current or anticipated physical sexual characteristics or current ascribed gender role.[6] For example, Paul McHugh, M.D., former psychiatrist-in-chief at Johns Hopkins Hospital, used GID diagnosis as a key reason to eliminate gender confirming surgeries there:

> "I concluded that to provide a surgical alteration to the body of these unfortunate people was to collaborate with a mental disorder rather than to treat it."[7]

Dr. Paul Fedoroff of the Centre for Addiction and Mental Health (formerly the Clarke Institute of Psychiatry) cited the psychiatric diagnosis to urge elimination of gender confirming surgeries in Ontario in 2000,

> "TS [transsexualism, in reference to the GID diagnosis] is also unique for being the only psychiatric disorder in which the defining symptom is facilitated, rather than ameliorated, by the 'treatment.' . . . It is the only psychiatric disorder in which no attempt is made to alter the presenting core symptom."[8]

Paradoxically, the GID diagnosis has been defended as necessary for access to hormonal and surgical transition procedures. It is required by Standards of Care of the World Professional Association for Transgender Health,[9] and GID is cited in legal actions to gain access to these procedures. Attorney Shannon Minter, head counsel for the National Center for Lesbian Rights, was quoted in *The Advocate*,

> "'When we go to court to advocate for transsexual people to get medical treatment in a whole variety of circumstances, from kids in foster care to prisoners on Medicaid,' the GID diagnosis is used to show that treatment is medically necessary."[10]

Dr. Nick Gorton echoed long-standing fears that access to hormonal and surgical procedures would be lost if the GID were removed entirely,

> "Loss of the DSM diagnostic category for GID will endanger the access to care, psychological well being, and in some cases, the very life of countless disenfranchised transgender people who are dependent on the medical and psychiatric justification for access to care."[11]

Gender dysphoric transpeople have therefore assumed that we must suffer degradation and stigma by the current GID diagnosis or forfeit lifesaving medical transition procedures. But has our community been impaled on the horns of a false dilemma?

Are hormonal and surgical procedures available to transitioning individuals because of the current diagnosis of "disordered" gender identity or in spite of it? Because the GID criteria and supporting text are tailored to contradict transition and pathologize birth-role nonconformity[3], affirming and tolerant professionals are burdened to reconstrue GID in more positive and supportive way for transitioning clients. For example, last month the American Medical Association passed a historic resolution, "Removing Financial Barriers to Care for Transgender Patients." It reinterpreted GID to emphasize distress and de-emphasize difference:

> ". . . a persistent discomfort with one's assigned sex and with one's primary and secondary sex characteristics, which causes intense emotional pain and suffering."[12]

The AMA statement is perhaps a model for what the GID diagnosis should become.

The current GID diagnosis and its doctrine of "disordered" gender identity have failed the transcommunity on both issues of harmful psychosexual stigma *and* barriers to medical care access. The DSM-V Sexual and Gender Identity Disorders work group has an opportunity to correct both failures with new diagnostic nomenclature based on scientific standards of distress and impairment rather than intolerance of social role nonconformity and difference from assigned birth sex.

Part I Notes

1. This essay is expanded from K. Winters, "Harm Reduction for Gender Disorders in the DSM-V," Philadelphia Trans Health Conference, May 2008.
2. American Psychiatric Association, *Diagnostic and Statistical Manual of Mental Disorders,* Fourth Edition, Text Revision, Washington, D.C., 2000.
3. K. Winters, "Gender Dissonance: Diagnostic Reform of Gender Identity Disorder for Adults," *Sexual and Gender Diagnoses of the Diagnostic and Statistical Manual* (DSM), Ed. Dan Karasic, MD, and Jack Drescher, MD, Haworth Press, 2005; co-published in *Journal of Psychology & Human Sexuality,* vol. 17 issue 3, pp. 71–89, 2005.
4. R. Spitzer, "A Proposal About Homosexuality and the APA Nomenclature: Homosexuality as an Irregular Form of Sexual Behavior and Sexual Orientation Disturbance as a Psychiatric Disorder," *American Journal of Psychiatry,* Vol. 130, No. 11, November 1973, p. 1216.
5. N. Winfield, Associated Press, "Vatican Denounces Transsexuals," *Newsday,* Jan 2003.
6. Working definition of Gender Dysphoria by Dr. Randall Ehrbar and I following our panel presentations at the 2007 convention of the American Psychological Association. It is defined in glossary of the DSM-IV-TR as "A persistent aversion toward some of all of those physical characteristics or social roles that connote one's own biological sex." (p. 823)
7. P. McHugh, "Surgical Sex," *First Things* 147:34–38, http://www.firstthings.com/ftissues/ft0411/articles/mchugh.htm, 2004.

8. J. Fedoroff, "The Case Against Publicly Funded Transsexual Surgery," *Psychiatry Rounds,* Vol. 4, Issue 2, April 2000.

9. World Professional Association for Transgender Health (formerly HBIGDA), "Standards of Care for The Hormonal and Surgical Sex Reassignment of Gender Dysphoric Persons," http://wpath.org/Documents2/socv6.pdf, 2001.

10. S. Rochman, "What's Up, Doc?" *The Advocate,* http://www.advocate.com/issue_story_ektid50125.asp, Nov 2007.

11. R.N. Gorton, "Transgender as Mental Illness: Nosology, Social Justice, and the Tarnished Golden Mean," www.Nickgorton.org/misc/work/private_research/transgender_as_mental_illness.pdf, 2006.

12. American Medical Association, "Resolution 122, Removing Financial Barriers to Care for Transgender Patients," http://www.ama-assn.org/ama1/pub/upload/mm/16/a08_hod_resolutions.pdf, June 2008.

Part II: Top Ten Problems with the GID Diagnosis

What are the problems with the Gender Identity Disorder diagnosis in the *Diagnostic and Statistical Manual of Mental Disorders* (DSM)[1]? How are overarching issues of psychiatric stigma and access to medical transition procedures related to specific flaws in the diagnostic criteria[2] and supporting text? The philosopher Jiddu Krishnamurti said

> If we can really understand the problem, the answer will come out of it, because the answer is not separate from the problem.[3]

This is my personal list of the most egregious problems with the current Gender Identity Disorder diagnosis. While far from comprehensive, it is perhaps a starting point for dialogue about how harm reduction of gender nomenclature might be possible in the DSM-V.

1. **Focus of pathology on nonconformity to assigned birth sex in disregard to the definition of mental disorder, which comprises distress and impairment.**
   Recent revisions of the DSM increasingly target gender identity and expression that differ from natal or assigned sex as disordered. The current diagnostic criteria for GID in the DSM-IV-TR are preoccupied with social gender role nonconformity, especially for children. Identification with the "other sex," meaning other than assigned birth sex, is described as symptomatic regardless of our satisfaction and happiness with that identification [p. 581].

2. **Stigma of mental illness upon emotions and expressions that are ordinary or even exemplary for nontransgender children, adolescents and adults.**

   Criterion A for Gender Identity Disorder highlights a desire to be treated as, or "frequently passing as," our affirmed gender as pathological. For children, criteria A and B stress ordinary masculine or feminine expression in clothing, play, games, toys, and fantasy as symptoms of mental "disturbance" [p. 581]. The supporting text disparages innocent childhood play as disorder, including Barbie dolls, playing house, Batman and "rough-and-tumble" activity, if they violate stereotypes of assigned birth sex [pp. 576–577]. Incredulously, knitting is implicated as a focus of sexual perversion for adult transwomen in the supporting text [p. 579].

3. **Lacks clarity on gender dysphoria, defined here as clinically significant distress with physical sex characteristics or ascribed gender role.**[4]

   The distress of gender dysphoria that necessitates medical intervention is inadequately described in criterion B of the GID diagnosis in the DSM-IV-TR as "discomfort" or "inappropriateness." For children, this often-debilitating pain is obfuscated in the diagnostic criterion, which emphasizes nonconformity to gender stereotypes of assigned birth sex rather than clinically significant distress. Adolescents and adults who believe that we were "born in the wrong sex" meet criterion B on the basis of their belief, even if our gender dysphoria has been relieved by transition or related medical procedures [p. 581].

4. **Contradicts transition and access to hormonal and surgical treatments, which are well proven to relieve distress of gender dysphoria.**

   Social role transition, living and passing in our affirmed gender roles, and desiring congruent anatomic sex characteristics are listed as "manifestation" of mental pathology in criterion A of Gender Identity Disorder. Requests for hormonal or surgical treatment to relieve gender dysphoria are disparaged as "preoccupation" in criterion B and supporting text rather than medical necessity [p. 581]. Evidence of medical transition treatment, such as breast development for transwomen or chest reconstruction for transmen, is described in a negative context as "associated features and disorders" of mental illness in the supporting text [p. 579].

5. **Encourages gender-conversion therapies, intended to change or shame one's gender identity or expression.**

   The DSM is intended as a diagnostic guide without specific treatment recommendations [p. xxxvii]. Nevertheless, the current GID diagnostic criteria are biased to favor punitive gender-conversion "therapies." For example, gender variant youth, adolescents or adults who have been shamed into the closet, forced into concealing our inner gender identities, no longer meet the diagnostic criteria of Gender Identity Disorder and are emancipated from a label of mental illness.

6. **Misleading title of "Gender Identity Disorder," suggesting that gender identity is itself disordered or deficient.**

   The name, Gender Identity Disorder, implies "disordered" gender identity—that the inner identities of gender variant individuals are not legitimate but represent perversion, delusion or immature development. In other words, the current GID diagnosis in the DSM-IV-TR implies that transwomen are nothing more than mentally ill or confused "men" and vice versa for transmen.[5]

7. **Maligning terminology, including "autogynephilia," which disrespects transitioned individuals with inappropriate pronouns and labels.**

   Maligning language labels gender variant people by our assigned birth sex in disregard of our gender identity. In other words, affirmed or transitioned transwomen are demeaned as "he" and transmen as "she." It appears throughout the diagnostic criteria and supporting text of the GID diagnosis in the current DSM-IV-TR, where affirmed roles are termed "other sex" [p. 581], transsexual women are called "males" and "he" [p. 577], and transsexual men as "females" [p. 579]. Such demeaning terms deny our social legitimacy and empower defamatory social stereotypes like "a man in a dress," in the press, the courts, our workplace, and our families.

8. **False positive diagnosis of those who are no longer gender dysphoric after transition and of gender nonconforming children who were never gender dysphoric.**

   There is no exit clause in the diagnostic criteria for individuals whose gender dysphoria has been relieved by transition, hormones or surgical treatments, regardless of how happy or well adjusted with our affirmed gender roles. The diagnosis is implied "to have a chronic course" for adults [p. 580], despite transition status or absence of distress. Children may be diagnosed with Gender Identity Disorder, solely on the basis of gender role nonconformity, without evidence of gender dysphoria. Criterion A requires only four of five listed attributes, and four of those describe violation of gender stereotypes of assigned birth sex, The fifth, describing unhappiness with birth sex, is not required to meet criterion A. Criterion B may be met by "aversion toward rough-and-tumble play and rejection of male stereotypical toys . . ." for natal boys and "aversion toward normative feminine clothing" for natal girls [p. 581].

9. **Conflation of impairment caused by prejudice with distress intrinsic to gender dysphoria.**

   Criterion D of the GID diagnosis, the clinical significance criterion [p. 581], was intended to require clinically significant distress or impairment to meet the accepted definition of mental disorder [p. xxxi]. Unfortunately, it fails to distinguish intrinsic distress of gender dysphoria from that caused by external societal intolerance. Lacking clarity in criterion D, prejudice, and discrimination can be misconstrued as psychological impairment for gender variant individuals who are not distressed by our physical sex characteristics or ascribed gender roles.

10. **Placement in the class of sexual disorders.**
In 1994, Gender Identity Disorders were moved from the class of "Disorders Usually First Evident in Infancy, Childhood or Adolescence," to the section of sexual disorders in the DSM-IV, renamed "Sexual and Gender Identity Disorders".[6] This reinforces stereotypes of sexual deviance for gender variant people.

The DSM-V Task Force has an opportunity to address these shortcomings in the current GID diagnosis. I hope that this list can help provide a way to evaluate proposals for less harmful diagnostic nomenclature in the fifth edition of the DSM.

Part II Notes

1. American Psychiatric Association, *Diagnostic and Statistical Manual of Mental Disorders,* Fourth Edition, Text Revision, Washington, D.C., 2000, pp. 576–582.

2. DSM-IV-TR Diagnostic criteria for Gender Identity Disorder of Adults and Adolescents are available online at http://www.gidreform.org/gid30285.html and for children at http://www.gidreform.org/gid3026.html

3. "Krishnamurti Quotes," http://www.krishnamurti.org.au/articles/krishnamurti_quotes.htm

4. Working definition of Gender Dysphoria by Dr. Randall Ehrbar and I, following our panel presentations at the 2007 convention of the American Psychological Association. It is defined in glossary of the DSM-IV-TR as "A persistent aversion toward some of all of those physical characteristics or social roles that connote one's own biological sex." (p. 823)

5. K. Winters, "Gender Dissonance: Diagnostic Reform of Gender Identity Disorder for Adults," *Sexual and Gender Diagnoses of the Diagnostic and Statistical Manual (DSM),* Ed. Dan Karasic, MD. and Jack Drescher, MD., Haworth Press, 2005; co-published in *Journal of Psychology & Human Sexuality,* vol. 17, issue 3, pp. 71–89, 2005.

6. American Psychiatric Association, *Diagnostic and Statistical Manual of Mental Disorders,* Fourth Edition, 1994.

EXPLORING THE ISSUE

Is Gender Identity Disorder a Mental Illness?

Critical Thinking and Reflection

1. To what extent should the mental health profession be concerned about personal issues of gender identity, particularly in people who do not view themselves as psychologically disturbed?
2. With the diagnosis of Gender Dysphoria being included in *DSM-5*, the assumption would be that this is a "treatable condition." What kind of "treatment" should be recommended?
3. How would you go about designing a research study of the psychological difficulties experienced by gender variant individuals?
4. If you were designing an educational program to inform the public about gender variant individuals, what message would you want to convey?
5. *DSM-5* includes the diagnosis of Gender Dysphoria in Children. What issues should be considered before assigning this diagnosis to a child?

Is There Common Ground?

Although it is difficult to find areas of agreement between the Traditional Values Coalition and Kelley Winters, there does seem to be agreement about the powerful role of psychiatric diagnosis in our society. The Coalition views gender variant people as deeply troubled people who are psychologically disturbed and in need of professional help. The Coalition sees efforts of various lobbying groups as sharing the objective to "normalize a mental disorder in the same way that homosexuality was normalized in 1973 when psychiatrists removed this sexual dysfunction [sic] from *DSM*."

Kelley Winters also takes note of the pathologizing of gender variant conditions, although their inclusion in the *DSM* is viewed as imposing the stigma of mental illness and sexual deviance upon people who meet no scientific definition of mental disorder. Thus, it seems that in their divergence, both parties in this debate seem to be challenging the very definition of what constitutes a mental disorder. Even the *DSM-5* relabeling of gender variance in terms of "Gender Dysphoria" raises questions about what aspects of gender variance make such conditions mental disorders per se.

Additional Resources

A transgendered psychology-professor's perspective on life, the psychology of gender, & "gender identity disorder." Retrieved from www.genderpsychology.org

Ault, A., & Brzuzy, S. (2009). Removing gender identity disorder from the Diagnostic and Statistical Manual of Mental Disorders: A call for action. *Social Work, 54*(2), 187–189.

Bottorff, J. L., Oliffe, J. L., & Kelly, M. (2012). The gender(s) in the room. *Qualitative Health Research, 22*(4), 435–440.

Bursztyn, A. M. (2011). *Childhood psychological disorders: Current controversies.* Santa Barbara, CA: Praeger/ABC-CLIO.

Dragowski, E. A., Scharrón-del Río, M. R., & Sandigorsk, A. L. (2011). Debates surrounding childhood gender identity disorder. In A. M. Bursztyn (Ed.), *Childhood psychological disorders: Current controversies* (pp. 167–186). Santa Barbara, CA: Praeger/ABC-CLIO.

Hill, D., Rozanski, C., Carfagnini, J., & Willoughby, B. (2007). Gender identity disorders in childhood and adolescence: A critical inquiry. *International Journal of Sexual Health, 19*(1), 57–75.

Lawrence, A. A. (2008). Gender identity disorder in adults: Diagnosis and treatment. In D. L. Rowland & L. Incrocci (Eds.), *Handbook of sexual and gender identity disorders* (pp. 423–456). Hoboken, NJ: John Wiley & Sons, Inc.

Singh, D. (2008). *Psychometric assessment of gender identity/gender dysphoria and recalled sex-typed behaviour in childhood: A comparison of adolescents and adults with gender identity disorder and clinical controls.* Toronto: University of Toronto.

Singh, D., Deogracias, J., Johnson, L., Bradley, S., Kibblewhite, S., Owen-Anderson, A., et al. (2010). The gender identity/gender dysphoria questionnaire for adolescents and adults: Further validity evidence. *The Journal of Sex Research, 47*(1), 49–58.

The World Professional Association for Transgender Health, Inc. Retrieved from www.wpath.org/

Winters, K. (2009). *Gender madness in American psychiatry: Essays from the struggle for dignity.* BookSurge Publishing.

Zucker, K., & Lawrence, A. (2009). Epidemiology of gender identity disorder: Recommendations for the standards of care of the World Professional Association for Transgender Health. *International Journal of Transgenderism, 11*(1), 8–18.

Zucker, K. J., Bradley, S. J., Owen-Anderson, A., Kibblewhite, S. J., Wood, H., Singh, D., & Choi, K. (2012). Demographics, behavior problems, and psychosexual characteristics of adolescents with gender identity disorder or transvestic fetishism. *Journal of Sex & Marital Therapy, 38*(2), 151–189.

Zucker, K. J., & Cohen-Kettenis, P. T. (2008). Gender identity disorder in children and adolescents. In D. L. Rowland & L. Incrocci (Eds.): *Handbook of sexual and gender identity disorders* (pp. 376–422). Hoboken, NJ: John Wiley & Sons, Inc.

ISSUE 4

Is Psychological Debriefing a Harmful Intervention for Survivors of Trauma?

YES: Grant J. Devilly and Peter Cotton, from "Psychological Debriefing and the Workplace: Defining a Concept, Controversies and Guidelines for Intervention," *Australian Psychologist* (July 2003)

NO: Jeffrey T. Mitchell, from "A Response to the Devilly and Cotton Article, 'Psychological Debriefing and the Workplace . . . ,'" *Australian Psychologist* (March 2004)

Learning Outcomes

After reading this issue, you should be able to:

- Understand the concept and procedures of critical incident stress debriefing (CISD).
- Critically evaluate the benefits and risks associated with CISD.
- Discuss the different ways in which people experience trauma, and how mental health professionals should provide an individualized intervention that is responsive to each individual's experience of the trauma.
- Consider research methods for studying the effectiveness of debriefing protocols.
- Discuss the various components that should be included in a debriefing protocol.

ISSUE SUMMARY

YES: Psychologists Grant J. Devilly and Peter Cotton assert that critical incident stress debriefing (CISD) is poorly defined and has been shown to do more harm than good. They propose alternative approaches for responding to trauma survivors, which they consider more effective.

NO: Jeffrey T. Mitchell of the International Critical Incident Stress Foundation (ICISF) argues that Devilly and Cotton have misrepresented important information about psychological debriefing and have confused several aspects of this system of responding to trauma survivors.

Immediately following the September 11 terrorist attacks, thousands of well-meaning people descended upon Ground Zero in New York with the intention of consoling and aiding the survivors of that harrowing trauma. Some of these helpers had the goal in mind of offering their "debriefing" services to traumatized individuals who had just barely escaped death. Psychological debriefing is an intervention process in which survivors are urged to recount and relive the incident in order to avoid long-term consequences and traumatic stress responses. Experts in the field of psychology and crisis intervention, however, debate the efficacy of psychological debriefing and, more specifically, critical incident stress debriefing (CISD). While some professionals insist that CISD can be greatly beneficial, others contend that this approach can do more harm than good.

Grant J. Devilly and Peter Cotton assert that CISD and critical incident stress management (CISM) are poorly defined responses to traumatized individuals, which at their worst are noxious and at their best are ineffective. They cite examples of research suggesting that generic psychological debriefing has almost no effect on trauma victims and that CISD can actually provoke more negative symptoms in those who undergo the debriefing.

Drs. Devilly and Cotton contend that the philosophy and techniques associated with psychological debriefing represent little more than "emotional first aid" for survivors of life-threatening trauma. Good intentions and the passion to help following a trauma may result in paradoxical effects, particularly if the tools being used to aid are cursorily understood and dogmatically applied, and if the providers of such interventions ignore peer-reviewed research relevant to their work.

According to Drs. Devilly and Cotton, expert consensus and meta-analytic reviews suggest that CISD is possibly noxious, that generic psychological debriefing is probably ineffective, and that more emphasis should be placed on screening and providing of early intervention to those who go on to develop pathological reactions. They are critical of what they view as the indistinguishable nature of CISD and CISM, stating that they are unsure whether CISD is one component of CISM, or if CISD and CISM are equivalent, or whether CISM has a definite procedure. These authors contend that debriefing is widely and routinely practiced and is increasingly turned to as a first resort when disasters strike. Following harrowing experiences, psychological debriefing providers frequently advise organizations to use their services, asserting a number of claims about the effectiveness of their debriefing protocols.

Jeffrey T. Mitchell criticizes the article by Devilly and Cotton, arguing that they have not done adequate research and contends that they make several glaring errors, including the erroneous presentation of CISD and CISM as synonymous. Mitchell explains that CISD is a seven-step, small-group crisis intervention process, while CISM is a comprehensive, systematic, and multicomponent system. Mitchell also asserts that the research studies upon which Devilly and Cotton rest their aguments involve instances in which the specifics of CISD are not properly applied, and do not reflect the true efficacy of stress debriefing.

Dr. Mitchell affirms that crisis intervention is not intended to be a substitute for psychotherapy, but rather an effective provision of support following life-threatening trauma. He asserts that there is ample justification for having unequivocal confidence in the group CISD process when it is properly applied according to acceptable standards of practice, and by people who have been properly trained in applying the model.

Dr. Mitchell objects to the characterization by Devilly and Cotton of CISD as "possibly noxious," noting that the studies they cite in support of their comment never actually evaluated CISD processes that were provided by properly trained personnel adhering to acceptable standards of care. The most prominent of the many glaring errors of Devilly and Cotton is the treatment of a specific, structured, seven-step, small-group crisis intervention process called CISD as if it were one and the same as a comprehensive, systematic, and multicomponent program called CISM. Dr. Mitchell also disagrees with his opponent's assertion that psychological debriefing is the first resort when disasters strike. In fact, debriefings are not recommended for several weeks or longer after a disaster. The only people who would resort first to debriefing after a disaster are those who are untrained and unaware of what is needed before debriefing is initiated.

POINT

- The philosophy and techniques associated with psychological debriefing represent little more than "emotional first aid" for survivors of life-threatening trauma.

- Good intentions and the passion to help following a trauma may result in paradoxical effects, particularly if the tools being used to aid are cursorily understood, dogmatically applied, and the peer-reviewed research literature is ignored.

- Current expert consensus and meta-analytic reviews suggest that CISD is possibly noxious, that generic psychological debriefing is probably inert, and that more emphasis should be placed on the screening for, and providing, early intervention to those who go on to develop pathological reactions.

- It appears that CISD and CISM are indistinguishable. We can only conclude

COUNTERPOINT

- Crisis intervention is not intended to be a substitute for psychotherapy, but rather an effective provision of support following life-threatening trauma.

- There is ample justification for having unequivocal confidence in the group CISD process when it is properly applied according to acceptable standards of practice, and by people who have been properly trained in applying the model.

- Devilly and Cotton cannot legitimately state that "CISD is possibly noxious." The studies they use to support this comment never actually evaluated CISD processes that were provided by properly trained personnel adhering to acceptable standards of care.

- The most prominent of the many glaring errors of Devilly and Cotton is the that CISD may or may not be one component of CISM, or CISD may be equivalent to CISM, and CISM may or may not have a definite procedure.

treatment of a specific, structured, seven-step, small-group crisis intervention process called CISD as if it were one and the same as a comprehensive, systematic, and multicomponent program called CISM.

- Debriefing is widely and routinely practiced and is increasingly turned to as a first resort when disasters strike. Following harrowing experiences, psychological debriefing providers frequently advise organizations to use their services, asserting a number of claims about the effectiveness of debriefing.

- Although Devilly and Cotton assert that psychological debriefing is the first resort when disasters strike, in fact, debriefings are not recommended for several weeks or longer after a disaster. The only people who would resort first to debriefing after a disaster are those who are untrained and apparently unaware of what is needed before debriefing.

YES

**Grant J. Devilly and
Peter Cotton**

Psychological Debriefing and the Workplace: Defining a Concept, Controversies and Guidelines for Intervention

Critical incident stress debriefing (CISD), a specific form of psychological debriefing, has gained widespread acceptance and implementation in the few short years since it was first proposed (Mitchell, 1983). However, there has been recent doubt cast on this practice and confusion regarding the terminology used. This article explores the claims frequently made by proponents regarding its use, counterclaims of ineffectiveness by its detractors, and general consensus regarding its specific use and the use of more generic psychological debriefing. We conclude that the recently introduced critical incident stress management (CISM) and its proposed progenitor, CISD, are currently poorly defined and relatively indistinct in the treatment-outcome literature and should be treated similarly. Current expert consensus and meta-analytic reviews suggest that CISD is possibly noxious, generic psychological debriefing is probably inert and that more emphasis should be placed on screening for, and providing, early intervention to those who go on to develop pathological reactions. A set of generic guide lines for the minimisation and management of workplace traumatic stress responses is also proposed.

During times of organisational upheaval and personal and interpersonal crisis, organisations frequently access the services of psychologists to help mitigate the long-term consequences of these occurrences. Indeed, the provision of "debriefing" services to organisations is now a multi-million dollar industry. For example, after the tragedy of the World Trade Centre terrorist attacks in New York (2001) newspaper articles reported that thousands of "debriefers" attended the area, advocating and offering debriefing services (Kadet, 2002). This also involved many of the organisations associated with the World Trade Center being contacted and offered such debriefing services. The primary aims of this article are to evaluate the need for "psychological debriefing," to define the terms currently being used and to determine whether such an intervention is useful or can, in

From *Australian Psychologist*, vol. 38, no. 2, July 2003, pp. 144–150. Copyright © 2003 by Taylor & Francis Journals. Reprinted by permission.

fact, be counterproductive. Our secondary goal is to extrapolate from what we do know from the literature and provide some general guidelines for organisations and psychologists, based on our current state of knowledge.

Psychological debriefing has been recently placed under the scientific microscope (van Emmerik, Kamphuis, Hulsbosch, & Emmelkamp, 2002), and it has been argued that good intentions and the passion to help following a trauma may carry with it paradoxical effects, particularly if the tools being used to aid are cursorily understood, dogmatically applied and the peer-reviewed research literature left untouched (Gist & Devilry, 2002). Yet debriefing is widely and routinely practised and appears to be increasingly turned-to as a first resort when disasters strike. Following harrowing experiences psychological debriefing providers frequently advise organisations to utilise their services, asserting a number of claims about the effectiveness of debriefing. The rationale typically includes the following:

- Debriefing will be seen as a gesture of support by the employer, concerned with the psychological welfare of their employees.
- Psychological debriefing will help mitigate long-term poor functioning, which otherwise is "likely" to occur and is a "foreseeable" consequence of the event.
- This will, therefore, also protect the organisation from litigation for not fulfilling their workplace, health and safety obligations.
- And, lastly, with employees less likely to suffer long-term psychological consequences following the debriefing, the workforce will be healthier— and a healthy workforce is a more productive workforce.

With these claims in mind, it is fitting that we present working definition of our terms. Frequently, and particularly in applied contexts, terms are being used without operational definitions and are often used interchangeably. This makes inspecting the evidence behind the claims a murky and very difficult task.

Definitions

"Psychological debriefing" is a generic term that has been suitably equated with "emotional first-aid" following trauma. To our knowledge the term was first referenced in the Australian literature by Raphael (1984) who noted that some psychological debriefing programs "usually involved the rapid mobilisation of skilled staff to interview and work with the victims to assist them with the psychological response to the disaster and its aftermath, frequently in direct outreach to the disaster sites and the victims' homes" (p. 303). More recently, in a meta-analytic review of psychological debriefing (PD), Rose, Wessely and Bisson (2001) defined PD as "any brief psychological intervention that involves some reworking/reliving/recollection of the trauma and subsequent emotional reactions." However, for the sake of being comprehensive, yet not at the price of specificity, Devilly, Gist, and Cotton (2002) describe PD as:

> . . . the generic term for immediate interventions following trauma (usually within 3 days) that seek to relieve stress with the hopeful intent of

mitigating or preventing long term pathology . . . [and that . . . PD relies predominantly on ventilation/catharsis, normalisation of distress, and psycho-education regarding presumed symptoms] (p. 4).

This is to be contrasted with the proprietary-based term critical incident stress debriefing (and, more recently, critical incident stress management). This is a specific variety of PD, frequently utilised with groups, and developed by Mitchell (1983) as a structured approach with seven aspects. These steps include:

1. the introductory phase (where the rules, process and goals are outlined)
2. the fact phase (serial clarification of what the participants saw, did, heard etc.)
3. the thoughts phase (what the participants' first thoughts were/are following the event)
4. the reaction phase (exploration of individuals emotional reactions)
5. the symptoms phase (global assessment of physical or psychological symptoms)
6. the teaching/information phase (educating the participants about possible, common, or even "likely" stress responses)
7. the re-entry phase (referral information provided for future follow-up).

More recently, and with evidence against the use of CISD becoming more and more convincing, Everly and Mitchell (1999) proposed that CISD had been superseded by Critical Incident Stress Management (CISM), and these authors have since offered two reviews of CISM (Everly, Flannery, & Mitchell, 2000; Everly, Flannery, & Eyler, 2002). But what is CISM and does it significantly and operationally differ from CISD?

A review of the CISM literature offered by Everly et al. (2000) described it as "a new generation of intervention technologies" (p. 23) and, in keeping with a 7-step formula, offered the following definition:

CISM represents seven core integrated elements: (a) pre-crisis preparation (both individual and organisational); (b) large scale demobilisation procedures for use after mass disasters; (c) individual acute crisis counselling; (d) brief small group discussions, called defusings, designed to assist in acute symptom reduction; (e) longer small group discussions, called Critical Incident Stress Debriefing (CISD), designed to assist in achieving a sense of psychological closure post-crisis and/or facilitate the referral process; (f) family crisis intervention techniques; and (g) follow-up procedures, and/or referral for psychological assessment or treatment (p. 24).

It would seem, therefore, that by 2000 CISD had been somewhat redefined and incorporated into a larger and more encompassing approach, although it should be stressed that there is no empirical support for any of the newly proposed steps. However, of interest in the review is that in support of CISM, studies which used only CISD were cited. It, therefore, begs the question of whether CISD and CISM are distinguishable.

In fact, in supporting the use of CISM, one of the studies Everly et al. (2000) cite is an Australian report (Leeman-Conley, 1990). This study details a management-wide intervention for dealing with trauma following violent bank hold-ups in the Commonwealth Banking Corporation. However, the term CISM is never referred to in this study, the procedure appears to differ significantly from that outlined by Everly et al. (2000), and outcome was assessed by comparing compensation costs and absenteeism in the year following the introduction of the intervention to the previous year's costs (i.e., not a randomised trial and open to untold influence from many other organisational and non-specific changes that may have occurred, e.g., improved security, improved health plans, fewer hold-ups, change in seasonal illnesses, changes in absenteeism practices).

By 2002, Everly et al. describe CISM as "an integrated multicomponent crisis intervention system" (p. 171, Everly et al., 2002). It is unclear exactly how to interpret this, but the authors claim that CISD "was designed to be only one component of a comprehensive multicomponent crisis intervention program referred to as Critical Incident Stress Management" (p. 174) and then cite Everly and Mitchell (1999) in support of this. It is difficult to see how this can be the case since the term CISM did not even enter the debriefing lexicon until the mid-1990s and CISD was advocated as a method for mitigating the effects of trauma back in the early 1980s (Mitchell, 1983).

The review by Everly et al. (2002) of CISM also needs further analysis. Firstly, the authors claimed that "CISD was never designed to be implemented as a single intervention outside of the multicomponent CISM program" (p. 174) and provide a 1999 reference to support this. As alluded to above, there appears to be an element of historical revisionism characterising this account, which is further weakened through citing such recent references. Notwithstanding, there are three further factors which are of even greater concern.

First, no operational definition of the facets integral to CISM, and necessary or sufficient to qualify as CISM, were incorporated into the review. Rather, studies were included which were "purporting to specifically assess interventions consistent with the CISM formulation" (p. 177). Second, of the eight studies that met this criteria, six were studies by the directors of the International Critical Incident Stress Foundation (ICISF) who are also the originators of CISD/M. This is important because meta-analyses typically draw on a range of studies delivering conclusions that are less likely to be disproportionately weighted by methodological weaknesses and/or researcher allegiance. Out of the two studies by other authors, one (Busuttil et al., 1995) had incorporated PD within a group therapy program aimed at *treating* posttraumatic stress disorder (PTSD) and no explicit mention of CISM is made, and the other (Richards, 1999) was a presentation at an ICISF conference and, therefore, not easily accessible for review.

Third, the authors of this review included into the same analysis studies using different domains of outcome measurement. Some of the studies were termed "Assault Staff Action Programs" and the outcome measure was the number of times staff (psychiatric hospital staff or community care staff) were assaulted following the intervention compared to before the intervention.

Other studies utilised diagnostic interviews/psychometric assessment of distress levels of workers with PTSD and traumatic reactions. As mentioned, some of the studies were aimed at treating *trauma reactions* (and sometimes many months following the trauma; Busuttil et al., 1995; Mitchell, Schiller, Eyler, & Everly, 1999) and others were aimed at mitigating further distress or number of assaults (Flannery Hanson, Penk, Flannery, & Gallagher, 1995; Flannery et al., 1998; Flannery Penk, & Corrigan, 1999; Flannery, Anderson, Marks, & Uzoma, 2000). Such a fundamental methodological flaw undermines the validity of any conclusions based on the meta-analysis of this group of studies.

For now, we can only conclude that CISD may or may not be one component of CISM, or CISD may be equivalent to CISM, and CISM may or may not have a definite procedure. Until the necessary and sufficient conditions for what counts as CISD and/or CISM are clarified CISM must be regarded as an unfalsifiable intervention system, and the two terms should for now be treated synonymously.

More broadly, it is important to differentiate debriefing from early intervention. Devilly (2002) suggested that early intervention "is the provision of what could be called 'restorative treatment' to individuals who *request* psychological help following crime/trauma and have a *clinically significant* presentation" (p. 4). The notion here is that whilst the individuals report pathological functioning (2 days to 4 weeks following the event), the goal of early intervention is to prevent long-term, psychological and functional impairment. Interventions at this level are goal orientated, explicit and evidence based. Such an example would be interventions for Acute Stress Disorder (ASD). Untreated, about 80% of individuals with ASD go on to develop PTSD by 6 months, and 75% maintain this presentation up to 2 years later (Bryant & Harvey, 2000). However, cognitive-behavioural treatments (CBT) based upon exposure principles have demonstrated efficacy to the point where only 8% at post-treatment (17% at 6 months) meet the criteria for PTSD, which is contrasted to supportive counselling strategies which show that 83% at posttreatment (and 67% at 6 months) meet criteria for PTSD (Foa, Hearst-Ikeda, & Perry, 1995; Bryant, Harvey, Dang, Sackville, & Basten, 1998; Bryant, Sackville, Dang, Moulds, & Guthrie, 1999). Likewise, CBT treatment for PTSD has shown exceptional efficacy with between 80% [and] 90% of those treated no longer meeting criteria at post-treatment and maintaining this presentation to 3 months and even 12 months follow-up (e.g., Devilly & Spence, 1999; Foa et al., 1999; Foa, Rothbaum, Riggs, & Murdoch, 1991). Current research in this paradigm is now focussing on improving the attrition rates during treatment and factors associated with treatment tolerance (see Devilly & Foa, 2001, and Tarrier, 2001, for a discussion of measurement issues relating to this and Foa, Zoellner, Feeny, Hembree, & Alvarez-Conrad, 2002, for a discussion of predictors of attrition during exposure therapy).

It should be clear that the basis of the distinction between CISD and early intervention goals appears to be that while the former aims to mitigate short- and long-term negative reactions through preventative intervention immediately following an event, the latter aims to actively treat pathology with the goal of restoring the individual to pre-trauma functioning.

Consensus: Mitigation of Long-Term Poor Functioning?

At the beginning of this article, we outlined some arguments frequently posited by those promoting the use of PD. Perhaps the most important of these from a psychologist's perspective is the promise that psychological debriefing will help mitigate poor long-term functioning, which otherwise may occur, or even worse is "likely" to occur, and is a "foreseeable" consequence of the event.

Turning to the second half of this statement first, while it can be convincingly argued that there is the *possibility* of poor long-term functioning following a trauma, this is not equivalent to claiming that it is *likely and foreseeable*. In the Australian National Morbidity Study, Creamer, Burgess, and McFarlane (2001) found an estimated 12-month, PTSD prevalence rate of 1.3% in the community, with 64.6% of males and 49.5% of females having ever experienced at least one traumatic event. However, of those who had experienced any trauma, 1.9% of men and 2.9% of women met criteria for PTSD over the previous 12 months. Notwithstanding specific categories of trauma, such as rape, which evidences a *12-month* PTSD prevalence rate of 9.2% in women (Creamer et al., 2001), lifetime prevalence rates of PTSD for the whole community is estimated at 7.8% (10.4% for women, 5.0% for men; Kessler, Sonnega, Bromet, Hughes, & Nelson, 1995). Hence, in the light of this epidemiological evidence, it is specious to assert that PTSD is likely and foreseeable following exposure to a specific stressful event.

Further, PTSD is not the only, or even the most likely pathological outcome from experiencing traumatic events. Studies have demonstrated that a history of trauma is in itself a risk factor for depression (Zlotnick, Warshaw, Shea, & Keller, 1997) with one study (Lopez, Piffaut, & Seguin, 1992) reporting that 71% of raped women suffered from major depression whilst 37.5% developed chronic PTSD that lasted from 1 to 3 years. Given that proponents of CISD have claimed that it aims to mitigate long-term distress, one needs to also investigate whether it has demonstrated potency in domains other than PTSD.

As part of the Cochrane Collaboration, Rose et al. (2001) conducted a meta-analytic review of the psychological debriefing literature. Their inclusion criteria were that the studies utilised psychological debriefing (which employed normalisation and ventilation), was administered as a single session within one month of the trauma, and relied upon a randomised design. This elicited only eight studies in all, two of which had uninterpretable statistics (Bunn & Clarke, 1979; Bordrow & Porritt, 1979). Unfortunately, the randomisation requirement, though scientifically rigorous and laudable, also meant that no group-based interventions were included in the review. This is problematic because group-based debriefing is the usual method of delivery for this type of intervention. Nevertheless, of the six studies that were interpretable, all either found no benefit of PD or—and worryingly—that PD increased the likelihood of developing PTSD compared to no intervention. Rose et al. (2001) concluded that compulsory debriefings should cease immediately and that resources would be better utilised by focusing on those individuals who develop recognisable disorders.

The thrust of this sentiment is shared in a recent meta-analysis by van Emmerik et al. (2002). These authors likewise conducted a literature search to find studies which had used debriefing within 1 month following a trauma, and where symptoms were assessed pre- and post-debriefing using psychometrically acceptable assessment instruments. Seven studies met their criteria, five of which used CISD as one intervention, six used no-intervention control conditions, and three used conditions of other PD interventions (i.e., "30-minute counselling," "education," and "historical group debriefing"). The results suggested that while people have a disposition to improve over time when they received no intervention (on both measures of PTSD and other trauma-related domains), if they received non-CISD based interventions this made no significant difference to the outcome. However, those who received CISD did not improve over time on either PTSD symptoms or on other symptom dimensions. In summary, these authors found that while some generic PD made no significant difference to long-term outcome, CISD would seem to *hinder* recovery.

These findings and conclusions contrast dramatically with the review of CISD/CISM by Everly et al. (2000) and a statistical meta-analysis by Everly and Boyle (1997). The meta-analytic review stated that it only included studies that explicitly used CISD and group debriefings. They concluded that CISD achieved a treatment effect size of Cohen's $d = 0.86$ (i.e., a large, positive effect). However, when one looks at the studies included, it is interesting to note that not one of them was included in either of the reviews outlined above (Rose et al., 2001; van Emmerik et al., 2002). It should also be stressed that none of the studies used a randomised, controlled design and some of the studies were unavailable for inspection. Furthermore, of those that were available, Devilly et al. (2002) were unable to equate the reported effect size in Everly and Boyle (1997) with the original data presented in two of the available three articles. Additionally, if CISD was never designed to be used as a stand-alone intervention, but rather as one aspect of a "multicomponent CISM program" (Everly et al., 2002), then it is puzzling why a meta-analysis of CISD was performed and acts as the bedrock to base claims for CISD/M effectiveness.

For now, one can only conclude that there has never been a randomly controlled trial of group CISD/M and, therefore, its effectiveness has not been demonstrated. On the other hand, a consensus of randomised controlled trials suggests that individual debriefings using the CISD/M system are noxious, and that generic PD has little or no prophylactic effect.

One anomaly characterising PD, though, is the replicated finding that people typically report high satisfaction ratings following involvement in PD (e.g., Matthews, 1998; Robinson & Mitchell, 1993). However, it has been argued that while this is one outcome domain, it is not necessarily the best upon which to make decisions regarding treatment implementation (Devilly, 2002). Additionally, Hart and Cotton (2003) have suggested an alternative explanation in terms of the possible impact of PD not on employee distress levels but on employee positive affective responses. In other words, PD may be more of a "morale maintenance" intervention qua gesture of employer support, rather than a clinical intervention influencing distress and clinical symptomatology. This line of enquiry is promising and warrants further investigation.

Of further interest are the findings that those who are offered PD yet decline to be involved are the most likely to be unaffected by the event in the long term (Matthews, 1998), and those who are most distressed by the event are the very same people who are most likely to be adversely affected by debriefing (Mayou, Ehlers, & Hobbs, 2000). Such results do not make good bed-fellows with enforced practice following employee exposure to a major stressor.

Protection from Litigation

As mentioned above, an argument is frequently made for PD that reminds organisations that they have obligations under workplace health and safety commitments to provide for their staff when traumatic incidents occur in the workplace. Putting aside possible issues related to "terminology slippage" and the definition of what could count as a traumatic event—which has been and is still an issue of great debate (e.g., see Bryant, 1996, and Dobson & Marshall, 1998)—the basis of this claim needs to be scrutinised. Perhaps the most famous case in Australia is that of *Howell v. the State Rail Authority of New South Wales* (1997; S6/1997). On 4th December 1992, a female suicided by jumping in front of a train, the result of which was that some 42 different body parts lay on the track and surrounding area. A rail worker (Mr Howell) was called from a nearby station to secure the scene while emergency service workers were called for, and during this time he witnessed the horrendous outcome of the suicide. A psychologist, contracted by the rail authority to follow-up on their worker, telephoned Mr Howell at home later that night and asked whether he would like to speak about how the event had affected him. Mr Howell reported that he did not wish to do so and the psychologist arranged to follow-up again a few days later. On the second contact, Mr Howell again refused help and the psychologist submitted a report and remit for payment to the rail authority. In a case which came to a close in 1997, Mr Howell sued the rail authority for breach of duty, having developed PTSD as a result of the incident. Mr Howell was first awarded $514,000 ($130,000 damages for non-economic loss, $115,000 for past economic loss, $200,000 for future economic loss, $15,000 for superannuation loss, $16,000 in past medical expenses, $18,000 for future medical costs, and $20,000 relating to topping-up received workers compensation). However, after various presentations and appeals, this sum was eventually increased to $750,000.

Naturally, such a hefty award has made many employers anxious to mitigate the effects of trauma that occur in the workplace. Indeed, a cursory search of Australian websites quickly demonstrates how this case is currently being used as a reason why debriefing should always be advocated, particularly by the providers of Employee Assistance Programs. Furthermore, in answer to Bledsoe (2002) who warns of possible liability *for providing* debriefing, the ICISF recently used this decision as further evidence for the use of CISD (Robinson, 2002). However, this decision needs to be inspected more closely.

First, it was implicitly accepted by the trial judge that debriefing would have improved the status of Mr Howell and acted as a mitigating force in long-term pathology. In light of hindsight and the more recent evidence, as cited above, such a decision would now seem ill-advised. Secondly, the rail authority handbook stipulated that Critical Incident Stress Debriefing (note that CISD was used and not generic PD) be provided in such cases within 48 hours. The fact that this was not followed leant heavily on the decision that the authority had breached their duty and acted negligently. Naturally, such practices need to be amended in keeping with the first point above. Thirdly, the trial judge decided that the psychologist either knew or should have known that "by 12.30 p.m. on Saturday 5 December 1992 . . . that the plaintiff was showing signs of Post-traumatic Stress Disorder." This is indeed a bold claim and in direct contradiction to research evidence and our current method of classification. Acute Stress Disorder (outlined above), as a method of early detection for PTSD, is sensitive but not specific as it currently stands (Harvey & Bryant, 1998) and even then cannot be diagnosed until at least 2 days following the event. However, and of further interest to psychologists, was the judge's explicitly declared low opinion of the psychologist. The judge decided that this psychologist was negligent in not conducting a face-to-face interview with Mr Howell and had:

> . . . seriously suggested in an initial report to the Railways that he had, in fact, had interviews, which would infer that he had conducted face to face interviews with the plaintiff at least on 7 December and 9 December . . . and [therefore] that there had been a misreporting by the psychologist as to what he had done.

It is thought that such a disparaged view of a psychologist may have tempered the final decision and detracted from the substantive point of whether the debriefing would have actually helped or not.

In an appeal that challenged this implicit assumption of debriefing as effective, the awarded sum was actually further increased to $750,000. However, it appears that this was mainly because it was testified by a prominent psychiatrist that had ASD been diagnosed, then early intervention could have been instituted based upon CBT procedures, which would increase the likelihood of recovery. This is a different argument to looking at debriefing effectiveness and appropriateness. Furthermore, this argument appears to be utilising information that was not available to either the organisation or the psychological community in 1992.

In fact, in light of the available evidence it is, in our opinion, more likely that at some point in the future a company may be litigated against where they compel employees to attend CISD rather than omit to provide it. This opinion is being taken more seriously in the literature (e.g., Bledsoe, 2002; in press), and one can only sympathise with organisations who must feel that they are trapped between a rock and a very hard place. Irrespective of vulnerability to litigation, expert traumatic stress panels have warned against such well-intentioned care and, for example, after the World Trade Centre Terrorist attack on 11th September 2001, a letter signed by 14 eminent psychologists from around the world appeared in the *New York Times* and the American Psychiatric Association's newsletter, *The Monitor,* (Herbert et al., 2001) warning of the dangers of "debriefers" flocking to the area. In fact, this practice of armies of debriefers descending upon war-torn or devastated parts of the world has received the moniker, somewhat cynically, of "Trauma Tourism" (Gist & Lubin, 1999).

A Healthy Workforce Is a Productive Workforce

A review of the organisational behaviour and work psychology literature suggests that limited progress has been made in linking workplace-oriented clinical interventions to organisational performance outcomes (Hart & Cooper, 2001; Wright & Cropanzano, 2000). However, there are indications that increasing employee-positive affective responses contributes towards increasing discretionary performance (Borman & Motowildo, 1993) as well as reducing absenteeism (George, 1989, 1996) and workers compensation costs (Hart & Cotton, 2003).

Accordingly, a healthy workforce may well be a more productive workforce, but the most reliable method of avoiding a sick workforce after a traumatic event is still open to debate. Nevertheless, given our current state of knowledge, it is possible to delineate some general guidelines to be used in organisational practice.

General Guidelines

Below we have outlined a very brief summary of suggested intervention principles:

Organisational policy.   An organisation's critical incident management policy should be regularly updated and be consistent with developments in the research literature. To facilitate this, an organisation might contract a recognised expert in this field to review their policy documentation.

Facilitate access to immediate practical and social support.   It is not possible to specify all the kinds of practical support that are viable in all situations. For example, following mass trauma events, such as bushfires and floods, governments provide facilities such as access to information, places of safety, bedding, food and sanitation. Organisations after events, such as a workplace fatality, may provide such facilities as help with funeral arrangements, transport for work colleagues, and general changes in workplace conditions that may facilitate a sense that the employer cares about their plight. This may include making available a "veteran" in their area of work who has a wealth of experience and is willing to talk to those who witnessed the event or are concerned regarding how to cope. This use of a respected veteran that workers know and trust is discussed in greater detail by Bledsoe (in press) and Devilly et al. (2002). Contact from the exposed individuals' immediate manager to express concern and support is also helpful, as is the availability of contact with peers. The type of social support referred to here is the (non-clinical) everyday expression of care and listening to the individual's concerns.

Offer access to employee assistance services for those who request it.   In Australia, organisations have a non-delegable duty of care in relation to workplace health. Providing access to appropriately qualified mental health service providers, for *face-to-face* emotional support and follow-up, also provides an important gesture of employer support. Additionally, accessing employee assistance programs provides an opportunity to screen for individuals who may go on to develop post-trauma reactions. The provision of "comfort" *may* also appease general and non-diagnosable distress. However, at this point it should not be regarded as a clinical intervention, but more as a socially supportive intervention and an opportunity to screen for individuals who may require more substantive support and treatment.

Provide factual information and normalise reactions (not "symptoms"). Without doubt, most frequently the first need of victims of crime or surviving members of a trauma (or related family and friends) is the need for information. This information can include the need to know who has been hurt, how far investigative processes have progressed, which documentation should be completed and when, and how to access facilities. At a national level, this need is frequently met by the use of a well-informed telephone help-line, and at an organisational level this can be accomplished by regular, frequent and official meetings with all those involved.

Some authors recommend educating the client at various points about reactions to stressors (e.g., Litz, Gray, Bryant, & Adler, 2002) and others suggest that psycho-education regarding possible reactions should be done as a matter of course (e.g., Mitchell, 1983). However, we have argued elsewhere (Devilly et al., 2002) that this may in fact be counterproductive and may actually prime participating individuals to develop the very problems we wish them to avoid. However, educating people about *possible* reactions is very different to normalising problems that they report to be *already* experiencing. The latter is the more appropriate focus in post-incident follow-up. In the past, however, such intervention has been mandatory and did not take into account individual coping styles and reflect the wishes of the individuals involved. We suggest that this form of intervention can be conducted in either a group meeting or on an individual basis. The point, however, is that the delivery not be compulsory.

Terminology slippage.   Frequently the types of "critical events" that psychologists are brought in to provide services for are not of a "traumatic" nature. "Debriefing" following, for example, workplace bullying or in reaction to a member of a team being dismissed, has become increasingly frequent and the terminology used during these interventions are often inappropriate. It is our view that the available evidence suggests that in these cases the responsible course is to recommend referral to a specialist in organisational psychology and, frequently, an expert in organisational change or mediation.

Promote proactive problem-solving.   Proactivity increases a sense of mastery over situations and increases a sense of self-efficacy It is suggested that employees be encouraged to devise coping strategies that make sense to their specific situation. No specific coping strategies should be mandated (apart from discouraging counter-productive coping strategies such as increased alcohol consumption).

Monitor staff to identify at-risk individuals.   Following the provision of "comfort" and the facilitation of immediate needs being met, a follow-up for individuals of between 4 days and 2 weeks subsequent to the incident would offer the appropriate window of opportunity to screen for symptoms of depression, excessive arousal, avoidance behaviours, intrusive phenomena and dissociation.

Monitoring can be conducted collaboratively between employee assistance providers, managers and Human Resource professionals. The psychologist or EAP provider can consult with workplace personnel, to support them in identifying possible at-risk individuals, who can then be specifically followed up.

Provide access to early intervention for individuals who report enduring distress.   Access to early intervention psychological treatment has been shown to mitigate long-term pathology. More specifically these interventions are specific and structured, and rely on cognitive-behavioural strategies, and predominantly on exposure treatment. These interventions should not be confounded with more generic supportive counselling which has no demonstrated impact on the course of post-traumatic incident recovery. Moreover, the effective delivery of these interventions requires specialised clinical training. Given the wide range of training and skill levels characterising employee assistance professionals, it is important for an organisation to ensure that any contracted Employee Assistance Providers possess the relevant specialist skills in this area. We note that in our own profession, a wide range of interventions are currently advocated, and not all of these are evidenced-based. Reliance on anecdotal reports or personal commitment to support the application of an intervention is inappropriate. Given that we know that early intervention cognitive-behavioural based interventions have demonstrated effectiveness, we suggest that we are now entering a time where serious ethical concerns may arise in circumstances where exposed individuals are initially offered other types of interventions.

Ensure appropriate organisational liaison and feedback occurs.   This may also require that the psychologist feedback to the organisation ideas, concepts and remedies [are] suggested by the employees. However, caution should be taken during this process to ensure that the psychologist does not actively collude with any dissatisfaction with the organisation that may be expressed by the workers, but rather acts as a facilitative conduit between the organisational floor and management. It is important that service providers avoid confounding post-incident distress with any pre-existing industrial discontent. In effect, the service provider should carefully balance "dual-client" considerations and not become an advocate for the individual and should carefully differentiate incident-related concerns from other industrial preoccupations.

The above guidelines should not be seen as prescriptive but rather suggestive of approaches that may act as a template to be adapted to the specific needs of the organisation and event.

Conclusion

What we hope to have highlighted in this paper is that claims of CISD/M being able to mitigate long-term pathology are not proven and this intervention system may, in fact, result in paradoxical outcomes. Specifically, this appears to be the case for individual CISD. To our knowledge, there are currently no randomised group debriefing studies in existence and hence the efficacy of such approaches is unproven. We also conclude that CISD and CISM, as terms currently used in the research literature, have not been sufficiently differentiated to be used independently. Further, it is our opinion that research and practice in this area of psychological debriefing (or "psychological first-aid"), if not in its embryonic stage, has yet to reach adolescence.

All references for articles included in *Taking Sides: Clashing Views in Abnormal Psychology, 7/e* can be found on the Web at www.mhhe.com/cls.

Jeffrey T. Mitchell  **NO**

A Response to the Devilly and Cotton Article, "Psychological Debriefing and the Workplace . . ."

"**P**sychological Debriefing and the Workplace: Defining a Concept, Controversies and Guidelines for Intervention" appeared in *Australian Psychologist, 38*(2), 144–150. The article is replete with inaccuracies, misinterpretations and distortions. Furthermore, it gives the impression that both peer and editorial review processes were inadequate.

The most prominent of the many glaring errors in the article is the treatment of a specific, structured, 7-step, small group crisis intervention process called the Critical Incident Stress Debriefing (CISD) as if it were one and the same as a comprehensive, systematic and multicomponent program called Critical Incident Stress Management (CISM).

The CISM program includes many tactics and techniques, but it is not limited to:

- crisis assessment services and strategic planning programs
- family support services
- individual, peer-provided crisis intervention services
- pre-crisis education programs
- large group crisis interventions
- the provision of food and fluids to work crews
- rotation and resting of work crews
- advice to command staff and supervisors
- small group crisis interventions
- follow-up services and referral services
- post-crisis education
- and many other services

The authors demonstrate a drastic lack of familiarity with the literature in the field of CISM. There is a substantial body of CISM literature not referred to by the authors. Even a cursory reading of these many publications would certainly have clarified the definitions in the CISM field and most likely would have eliminated the need for this confusing and inaccurate article.

The conclusion that a specific, 7-step group crisis intervention tool is equivalent to an entire multifaceted program defies logic and reason. Likewise,

From *Australian Psychologist,* vol. 39, no. 1, March 2004, pp. 24–28. Copyright © 2004 by Taylor & Francis Journals. Reprinted by permission.

equating a broad spectrum of different crisis intervention tools and psychological counselling techniques, as if they were one and the same, is not only imprecise, it is clinically and academically illegitimate.

Crisis intervention is a support service, not psychotherapy or a substitute for psychotherapy. It is an opportunity for assessment to see if people need additional services including referrals for therapy such as cognitive-behavioral therapy. Comparing supportive "psychological first aid" with psychotherapy is a misguided endeavour which creates further confusion. Therapy does not substitute for crisis intervention. Likewise, crisis intervention does not substitute for psychotherapy.

On page 145, there is a colossal misrepresentation of the facts. Devilly and Cotton say, "More recently, and with evidence against the use of CISD becoming more and more convincing, Everly and Mitchell (1999) proposed that CISD has been superceded by Critical Incident Stress Management (CISM)." The statement is very far from the truth.

In 1983, I wrote the first article ever written on Critical Incident Stress Debriefing ("When Disaster Strikes . . . The Critical Incident Stress Debriefing Process," *Journal of Emergency Medical Services, 13*(11), 36–39). I stated then, "There are many methods to deal with a stress response syndrome" (p. 37). The following items were listed as part of a comprehensive systematic and multicomponent program:

- ". . . strenuous physical exercise . . .
- . . . special relaxation programs . . .
- . . . individual or group meetings . . .
- . . . assessment by the facilitator of the intensity of the stress response in the workers . . .
- . . . support and reassurance from the facilitator . . .
- . . . information is provided . . .
- . . . a plan of further action may be designed . . .
- . . . referrals, if necessary, are made . . .
- The initial defusing . . .
- The *Formal CISD* . . .
- . . . *Follow-up. . . .*" (pp. 37–38)

Keep in mind that in the "When Disaster Strikes . . ." article the concepts were new, the thought processes were new and the wording may not have been perfect. A core of systematic interventions was present, however, and the specific CISD group process (then known at the "formal CISD") was not thought of as a stand-alone intervention.

As in any field of human endeavour, imperfect initial efforts go through refinements and elaborations over time. More clearly defined systems and specific procedures emerge. This dynamic growth certainly occurred in the CISM field.

Shortly after the first article was published, it was recognised that "CISD" was being used as an umbrella term to cover the entire field as well as a label for a specific group crisis intervention process. The dual use of the term "CISD" was confusing. The error was corrected in numerous publications subsequent to the 1983 article. For example, the first issue of *Life Net,* the official publication of the International Critical Incident Stress Foundation, referred to "Critical Incident Stress Management Teams" (1990, pp. 1–2). In the same issue, the use of the term "Critical Incident Stress Management (CISM) teams" was encouraged in an article entitled "CISM vs. CISD" (p. 5). Subsequent issues of *Life Net* contained articles that suggested a clarification and proper utilisation of the terms Critical Incident Stress Management (CISM) for the field and Critical Incident Stress Debriefing (CISD), previously known as the "formal CISD," for the specific group process. In 1998, the following quote appeared on the International Critical Incident Stress Foundation's website and in several of its training workbooks:

> Admittedly, some of the confusion surrounding this point was engendered by virtue of the fact that in the earlier expositions, the term CISD was used to denote the generic and overarching umbrella program/ system, while the term "formal CISD" was used to denote the specific 7-phase group discussion process. The term CISM was later used to replace the generic CISD and serve as the overarching umbrella program/ system . . . (Everly & Mitchell, 1997)

Again in 2001 the correction was made:

> Originally Mitchell (1983) used the term Critical Incident Stress Debriefing, or CISD, as an overarching label to refer to a strategic multi-componential approach to crisis intervention. . . . As can be imagined, the author's use of the term CISD to denote both the entire strategic approach to crisis intervention and the "formal" 6-phase small group discussion process that was part of it, led to significant confusion, which persists even today. In a direct effort to undo the confusion created by the dual usage of the term CISD and, more importantly, by the inferred, but erroneous, tacit endorsement of CISD (the small group discussion) as a stand-alone crisis intervention, the use of the term Critical Incident Stress Debriefing as the label for the cumulative strategic crisis intervention system was abandoned in favor of the term Critical Incident Stress Management. (Everly, Flannery, Eyler, & Mitchell, 2001)

Let me be perfectly clear, the change in terminology described in the paragraphs above had nothing to do with Devilly and Cotton's suggestion that "mounting evidence" against the use of CISD caused the change. In fact, we still have unequivocal confidence in the group CISD process when it is properly applied according to acceptable standards of practice and by people who have been properly trained in applying the model. Their perception of the reason for the change is, therefore, grossly mistaken.

On page 147 of their article, the authors make reference to an Australian legal case *(Howell v. the State Rail Authority of New South Wales, 1997)* and then state ". . . the ICISF recently used this decision as further evidence for the use of CISD." *This is a blatant misrepresentation of the facts.* ICISF *did not* and *would not* use such a case to support the utilisation of the group crisis intervention process known as CISD. First of all, ICISF is not a source of legal guidance.

Second, ICISF is not knowledgeable about the case and would not choose to use it in recommending any kind of service. Third, the case was about an individual and ICISF would never recommend that a CISD be provided to an individual because the CISD is a group process. In any case, my personal opinion on the little I know of that particular legal case is that the CISD would, by commonly accepted standards of practice, have been the wrong intervention to apply.

It is troubling to see a disregard for studies that evaluate CISM and present positive results just because those studies do not refer to the "brand name" of CISM. Such is the case when the authors discuss Dr Raymond Flannery's studies. The authors say that his work is not about CISM because he calls his program the "Assaulted Staff Action Program (ASAP)." One does not have to look very far to see the misinformation that those authors are distributing. On the back cover of Dr Flannery's 1998 book, *The Assaulted Staff Action Program: Coping with the Psychological Aftermath of Violence,* he states "ASAP is a Critical Incident Stress Management approach that includes individual crisis counseling, group debriefings, an employee victims' support group, employee victim family outreach, and professional referrals, when needed." On page 37 of his book, Flannery states:

> It was clear to me that no one intervention, no matter how effective in its own right, could address the differing needs of the employee victims in this facility. These differing situations suggested the need for a CISM approach (Everly & Mitchell, 1997), and led to my developing the *Assaulted Staff Action Program* (ASAP). (Flannery, 1998, p. 37)

Flannery defines his *Assaulted Staff Action Program* as ". . . a voluntary, systemwide, peer help, CISM crisis intervention program for employee victims of patient assault" (1999, pp. 103–108).

Furthermore, Devilly and Cotton say that Dr Flannery used the wrong dependent variable and that he only reports on violence reduction which is not a goal of CISM. They simply skip the other findings that Dr Flannery reports. Those findings demonstrate the effectiveness of his ASAP program which he clearly states is a CISM program. Take a look at what Dr Flannery actually says:

> ASAP, the most widely researched program of its kind in the world, is associated with providing needed support to employee victims and with sharp reductions in the frequency of violence in many of the facilities, where it is fielded. ASAP programs pay for themselves by means of sustained productivity, less medical and legal expense and reduced human suffering.

Again, this quote is on the back cover of his ASAP book. A reading of his actual articles will reveal greater details on the findings this eminent Harvard researcher and clinician has discovered which clearly demonstrate that CISM, even if called by another name, is a successful crisis intervention program.

The point about misinterpretation of Flannery's work has been made. However, I have found no less than eight other articles in peer reviewed journals in which he carefully defines CISM and then directly links CISM and his

ASAP program (Flannery, 2001). Again Devilly and Cotton have demonstrated a significant lack of familiarity with the literature in the CISM field.

The authors cannot legitimately state that "CISD is possibly noxious" as they do in the first paragraph of their article (p. 144). The studies they use to support this comment never actually evaluated CISD processes that were provided by properly trained personnel who adhered to acceptable standards of care. In fact, there has never been a negative outcome study of the actual CISD when properly trained personnel adhered to the commonly accepted standards of practice that are used by 700 CISM teams in 28 countries around the world.

The majority of criticisms against debriefing have been levelled at a process called "single session debriefing" which *in no way resembles* the specific group crisis intervention process of CISD. This is so even in light of the fact that some of studies evaluating the single session debriefing erroneously use the term "CISD." The studies were not measuring the same things. Yet the authors glibly intermingle the terms throughout the article as if they were one and the same. ICISF has never recommended the single session debriefings. They are considered a clear violation of the standards of CISM practice. It should be noted that no other organisation which provides crisis services has ever recommended the "single session debriefings." That includes the International Red Cross, the American Red Cross, the National Organisation of Victim Assistance, the American Academy of Experts in Traumatic Stress, the Salvation Army or the Association of Traumatic Stress Specialists. When primary victims are receiving truncated, poorly designed and badly executed services that call themselves "debriefings," "psychological debriefings," or "CISD," but do not follow the standards of care in the CISM field, it is of no surprise that they would generate negative outcomes. But the authors cannot, with legitimacy, say that those studies are evaluating the same things as a study on the specific group crisis process of CISD.

As a point of fact, the negative outcome studies represent a hodgepodge of different types of interventions which do not equate to the actual CISD but which loosely use the terminology "CISD." Each of those studies is seriously flawed. Such a prejudicial statement about CISD being possibly noxious so early on in an article without substantiating evidence implies an author bias. It is suggested that the readers of this response review the "Crisis Intervention and CISM Research Summary" which appears on the International Critical Incident Stress Foundation website. . . . That article outlines both sides of the controversy and counteracts the unsubstantiated comments of the authors of the article under discussion here.

On page 144, Devilly and Cotton state that psychological debriefing is "first resort when disasters strike." The only people who would resort first to debriefing after a disaster are those who are untrained and apparently unaware that many other things need to be done before a debriefing is provided. Debriefings are not recommended for several weeks or longer after a disaster. The reader should be aware that disaster response is only a tiny percentage of the activity of a CISM team. Most of the Devilly and Cotton argument against CISM seems to be focused on disaster response. At least that is the most sensational (and erroneous) material they bring out in their article.

In proportion to stress management education, individual peer support, family support, defusings, referrals, planning, protocol development, consultation with administration and supervisor staff, and responses to daily small scale emergencies, the number of times that CISM services are used at a disaster is rather small.

Likewise, the number of small group, 7-phase CISD processes actually utilised by any CISM team is minute. The proportion of one-on-one peer support services to CISDs is about 1000 to 1. We have witnessed among the many CISM teams a decline in the number of CISDs when stress education, defusing services and one-on-one crisis intervention services are pursued by CISM teams. Much of that work is provided by trained para-professionals called "peer support personnel."

I would question whether administrations of emergency services organisations are willing to substitute expensive therapy programs run exclusively by mental health professionals when trained peer support personnel have been very successful running these programs for nearly 30 years. My personal experience and that of the nearly 7000 members of the International Critical Incident Stress Foundation which includes over 2500 mental health professionals, is that peer support personnel are absolutely vital to the success of a CISM program and mental health professionals are usually kept at an arm's length from the operations personnel even when they are known and trusted people who have provided valuable services in the past.

The following items are of further concern within the Devilly and Cotton article:

- Paragraph number 2 on page 144 is sensational but not backed up by the actual numbers. The term "multimillion dollar industry" is very questionable. ICISF coordinates over 700 CISM teams and they almost all offer their services free of charge and largely on a "by request" basis. The average call out for a team is less than once a month. No fees are charged for services provided to emergency services personnel. So where is the "multimillion dollar industry?"
- Reports about the World Trade Center that thousands of "'debriefers' attended the area, advocating and offering debriefing services" (p. 144) are greatly exaggerated. First, who were they? Did they come in under some official body designated to provide disaster support services or by themselves? If they came in by themselves, then why would Devilly and Cotton attempt to lay the blame for this abnormal and inappropriate response in the CISM camp? Second, what did they offer? Third, what is the definition of a "debriefing"? It seems that many unauthorised people may have offered a plethora of good and bad services. But these people were not functioning under auspices of a CISM team or any official disaster response organisation such as the Red Cross and the field of CISM should not be blamed for their poor behavior.
- At *the request* of the New York Police Department, ICISF coordinated a response of 1500 CISM trained police officers, police psychologists and police chaplains. It took over *a year and a half* to cycle these people through New York. They went in 7 to 12 at a time, depending on specific

local needs and they stayed for a 7-day commitment. Critical Incident Stress Debriefings (specific, 7-stage, group process provided by a trained team of personnel and following well publicised standards of practice) were rarely held. They were only provided when homogeneous groups with roughly equal exposure to specific traumatic events were finished with their long-term disaster assignments. For some that was months after the event. The greatest emphasis in New York was on individual crisis intervention support. Does this organised, appropriate, free of charge, and requested level of support need to be painted with the same brush that Devilly and Cotton use to condemn the thousands who descended like an army of "trauma tourists" on New York City? Professional articles should, in my opinion, stick to verifiable facts and not degenerate into name calling and fantastic, but unsubstantiated rhetoric.

- On page 145, the authors state that two of the authors of some of the studies in one of the meta-analyses are "directors" of the International Critical Incident Stress Foundation. *That is not the truth.* Dr Everly and I are not the directors of ICISF. Please, let's everyone stick to the facts. The innuendo, of course, is that the authors of the meta-analyses cannot be trusted because they developed the program. It disregards their professional credentials and status and their actual qualifications to evaluate material with which they are most familiar. That is a rather bizarre position to hold and it smacks of an ad hominem argument.

- Toward the end of the article, they describe a program that offers many of the same types of services that a CISM program offers. I must ask "Why is their program any more acceptable than a program that has been functioning well for nearly 30 years?" It appears inappropriate to criticise one program only to offer a similar program with the exception that theirs is based in psychotherapy and mental health professional control instead of crisis intervention with peer support personnel in control. If the Devilly and Cotton are recommending a therapy program, such as cognitive-behavioral therapy, that is just fine. It would appear to me that they would make better progress by extolling the benefits of their program without trying to diminish the value of another program. Should their program not stand on its own without attacking another?

Scientific articles should serve to clear up confusion and misunderstandings. The Devilly and Cotton article, unfortunately, only adds to the cacophony of misinformation about crisis intervention and the field of Critical Incident Stress Management.

All references for articles included in *Taking Sides: Clashing Views in Abnormal Psychology, 7/e* **can be found on the Web at www.mhhe.com/cls.**

EXPLORING THE ISSUE

Is Psychological Debriefing a Harmful Intervention for Survivors of Trauma?

Critical Thinking and Reflection

1. Mitchell claims that only untrained people would resort to psychological debriefing as a first resort after a disaster. Why is it important to wait as long as several weeks or months before using psychological debriefing services?
2. Imagine that you are a clinician who is treating a person who has survived a life-threatening trauma. How would you go about assessing the extent to which you would have the client relive the details of the trauma?
3. If you were a researcher interested in studying the extent to which psychological debriefing helps or harms survivors of trauma, how would you go about studying this question?
4. Some would argue that following the experience of trauma, it makes more sense to try to avoid recollections of the harrowing event. What arguments would support this viewpoint, and how realistic is it to put such troubling memories out of mind?
5. The positions regarding psychological debriefing taken by the authors in the two pieces you read are quite vehement. What are your thoughts about the reasons such strong viewpoints are expressed on this topic?

Is There Common Ground?

A traumatic experience is a disastrous or extremely painful event that has severe psychological and physiological effects. Each traumatic event takes its toll in human suffering, and survivors strive to find ways to cope with painful memories and emotionally disruptive experiences that ensue. In reading the two articles in this issue, you can see how professionals take differing views of the best ways to intervene with individuals who have been traumatized, and at what point intervention is most effective. One form of intervention is critical incident stress debriefing, which Dr. Mitchell has developed over the course of the past few decades, as a response to people in the throes of emotional havoc resulting from the experience of trauma. Dr. Mitchell recognizes the limitations of his approach, noting that crisis intervention is not intended to be a substitute for psychotherapy, but rather an effort to provide support following life-threatening trauma.

Drs. Devilly and Cotton are not in disagreement about the need for traumatized individuals to obtain help for their symptoms. Furthermore, they understand that good intentions and the passion to help trauma survivors provide the rationale for reaching out to these individuals in a timely manner. That being said, they advocate for the implementation of thoughtful techniques that provide support and promote problem-solving. Much of their disagreement with Dr. Mitchell seems to focus on differences in terminology. The ultimate goal of both parties, however, is to help those in crisis get back on their feet. The particular techniques implemented should be based upon evidence-based research.

Additional Resources

Adler, A. B., Bliese, P. D., McGurk, D., Hoge, C. W., & Castro, C. (2011). Battlemind debriefing and battlemind training as early interventions with soldiers returning from Iraq: Randomization by platoon. *Sport, Exercise, and Performance Psychology*, 166–183. doi:10.1037/2157-3905.1.S.66

American Academy of Experts in Traumatic Stress. Retrieved from www.aaets.org/article54.htm

Doka, K. J. (2003). *Living with grief: Coping with public tragedy.* New York, NY: Brunner-Routledge.

Dyregrov, A., & Regel, S. (2012). Early interventions following exposure to traumatic events: Implications for practice from recent research. *Journal of Loss and Trauma: International Perspectives on Stress & Coping, 17(3).*

Freeman, C., & Graham, P. (2012). The role and nature of early intervention: The Edinburgh Psychological First Aid and Early Intervention programs. In R. Hughes, A. Kinder, & C. L. Cooper (Eds.), *International handbook of workplace trauma support.* Oxford, UK: Wiley-Blackwell. doi:10.1002/9781119943242.ch11

International Critical Incident Stress Foundation. Retrieved from www.icisf.org/

Johnson, S. L. (2009). *Therapist's guide to posttraumatic stress disorder intervention.* San Diego, CA: Elsevier.

Mitchell, J. T., & Everly, G. S. (2001). *Critical incident stress debriefing: An operations manual for CISD, defusing and other group crisis intervention services.* Ellicott, MD: Chevron Publishing Company.

Phillips, B. D. (2009). *Disaster recovery.* Boca Raton, FL: Auerbach.

Precin, P. (Ed.) (2004). *Surviving 9/11: Impact and experiences of occupational therapy practitioners.* Binghamton, NY: The Haworth Press.

Thompson, R. (2004). *Crisis intervention and crisis management: Strategies that work in schools and communities.* New York, NY: Brunner-Routledge.

Internet References . . .

National Institute on Drug Abuse

This website, home to the NIDA, contains a wealth of information on topics related to drugs in society. The website contains wide range of information for young people, parents and teachers, health professionals, and researchers. Detailed information is provided about the most commonly abused drugs in society.

www.nida.nih.gov/

Baldwin Research Institute

The website for the Baldwin Research Institute contains articles and links pertinent to the proposition that addiction is not a brain disease, but rather a choice. The website has links to sites aimed at helping people recover from substance addiction, as well as information about the "Baldwin Research Project," an initiative to disprove that addiction is a brain disease.

www.baldwinresearch.com/

The Center for Anxiety and Traumatic Stress Disorders, Massachusetts General Hospital

The CATSD at Massachusetts General Hospital conducts state-of-the-art research aimed at improving the standard of care for people suffering from anxiety disorders such at PTSD.

www2.massgeneral.org/allpsych/anxiety/

VA-Yale Clinical Neurosciences PTSD Research Program

The VA-Yale program investigates the neurobiology of traumatic stress, PTSD, and resilience to stress. The program aims to develop new biological approaches for the treatment of trauma-related disorders.

www.psychiatry.yale.edu/research/programs/clinical_people/ptsd.aspx

Clinical and Research Programs in Pediatric Psychiatry and Adult ADHD at Massachusetts General Hospital

This Web site provides information about current research and clinical endeavors pertaining to pharmacological interventions for children and adults with ADHD.

www2.massgeneral.org/allpsych/pedipsych/home.html

The Mayo Clinic

The Mayo Clinic provides extensive information about diagnosis, treatment, and research pertaining to many psychological disorders including ADHD.

www.mayoclinic.com/health/adhd/ds00275/dsection=treatments-and-drugs

The Prescribing Psychologists Information Page

This website provides information about education, training, and legislation related to prescription privileges for psychologists.

www.prescribingpsychologist.com

The Trend Toward Biological Interventions

*A**lthough the medical model has been prominent in the field of mental health for the past century, in recent years the trend toward biological explanations and interventions for psychological problems has become increasingly evident. For example, debate has intensified about the extent to which drug addiction should be viewed as a disease of the brain or a maladaptive behavior pattern under volitional control. The field of psychopharmacology has mushroomed to such an extent that billions of dollars are spent each year on medications for a wide array of emotional and behavioral problems. Medications are being tried in ways that would have been regarded as quite unlikely only a decade ago, as is the case in the use of drugs to dampen memories of a traumatic experience such as combat, or the case of "smart drugs" being used to enhance cognitive functioning in normal individuals. Major proponents of the medical model are the psychiatrists who belong to the association that publishes the* Diagnostic and Statistical Manual of Mental Disorders, *Fifth Edition (DSM-5). Critics, including some psychiatrists, believe that some psychiatrists have overstepped the boundaries of their position by mislabeling and mistreating countless people by virtue of their rigid adherence to the medical model.*

- Do We Still Need Psychiatrists?

- Should "Smart Drugs" Be Used to Enhance Cognitive Functioning?

- Should Memory-Dampening Drugs Be Used to Prevent and Treat Trauma in Combat Soldiers?

- Is Addiction a Brain Disease?

ISSUE 5

Do We Still Need Psychiatrists?

YES: **Steven Moffic**, from "Why We Still Need Psychiatrists!" (2012, April 12), www.madinamerica.com/2012/04/why-we-still-need-psychiatrists/

NO: **Steven Balt**, from "Yes, We Still Need Psychiatrists, but for What?" (2012, April 15), http://thoughtbroadcast.com/2012/04/15/yes-we-still-need-psychiatrists-but-for-what/

Learning Outcomes

After reading this issue, you should be able to:

- Critically evaluate the influence of psychiatrists on society, and discuss what steps they can take to move beyond traditional methods of providing mental health care.
- Evaluate the advantages and disadvantages of the model in which a single provider prescribes medication and also conducts psychotherapy, as opposed to a model in which a psychiatrist prescribes the medication, but psychotherapy is provided by another mental health professional.
- Consider the influence of pharmaceutical companies that provide "education" to psychiatrists about the effectiveness of their products. To what extent should this influence be monitored by the government?
- Discuss the communication skills that psychiatrists and other mental health professionals should be expected to have, and the ways in which these skills should be evaluated during the years of training.
- Address the criticism that psychiatry has built a scientific façade for a profession that is not really based on rigorous science.

ISSUE SUMMARY

YES: Psychiatrist Steven Moffic states that psychiatrists play critically important roles in the field of mental health care because they are extensively trained and well-versed in understanding the functioning of the human body and the treatment of mental disorders. He urges psychiatrists to accept constructive criticism and to take steps to move forward in developing innovative intervention models such as collaborating on-site with primary care physicians in offering integrated care.

NO: Psychiatrist Steven Balt believes that psychiatrists have overstepped the boundaries of their position, and doing so has often led to mislabeling and mistreating countless people. He contends that much of what psychiatrists do is pseudoscience, but that most people nevertheless buy into the psychiatric model. He argues that psychiatrists, with their years of scientific education, can use their influence to change the current state of affairs in the field of mental health.

For the past half century, a certain tension has existed between the professions of psychiatry and clinical psychology. Psychiatrists, who are physicians, have been trained in the medical model. Although many psychiatrists conduct psychotherapy, their training has been heavily influenced by four years of broad medical training followed by residency training in psychiatry, which usually takes place in a medical center. By contrast, clinical psychologists earn a doctorate in psychology, either at a university or at a professional school of psychology, and are generally more influenced by psychological theories and interventions. Because clinical psychologists (and professionals in several other mental health disciplines) do not prescribe medication, they often work collaboratively with psychiatrists or primary care physicians when treating patients needing psychotropic medication. In fact, in recent years, an increasing number of prescriptions for these medications have been provided by primary care physicians. The benefit of this trend is the fact that such medications are more readily available, and in a context that some patients view as less stigmatizing than that of a mental health provider's office. The disadvantage, however, is that primary care physicians are not as likely as psychiatrists to have specialized knowledge about these medications, and may therefore be less attuned to the benefits and risks of the meds they prescribe.

The influence of psychiatry as a profession has been especially marked in the realm of psychiatric diagnosis. The American Psychiatric Association publishes the *Diagnostic and Statistical Manual of Mental Disorders,* the most recent edition being *DSM-5.* The *DSM* is widely used by mental health professionals for diagnosing patients and for justifying health insurance coverage for treatment of these conditions. All editions of the *DSM* have generated considerable controversy over issues of what constitutes a disease, illness, or disorder. Despite its limitations, *DSM* serves an important function in promoting a common language for characterizing various psychological conditions, although some critics assert that its influence is too great, and that the research underlying the determination of diagnoses is flawed.

The influence of clinical psychology has been especially notable in the development and promotion of evidence-based interventions. Evidence-based practice refers to clinical decision making that integrates the best available research evidence and clinical expertise in the context of the cultural background, preferences, and characteristics of the patient. Because psychologists undergo extensive graduate training in research methods, their expertise is often tapped for research on diagnosis and treatment.

Because of their medical training, psychiatrists would presumably have a distinct professional advantage in terms of their understanding the various ways in which bodily functioning is related to psychological disturbance. They would also presumably have an advanced understanding of somatic interventions ranging from medication to brain procedures such as electroconvulsive therapy and deep brain stimulation. With such sophisticated knowledge, psychiatrists are in a position to have tremendous influence on the patients they treat, and by consequence on their loved ones, the community, and society as a whole. Yet the question arises about the extent of their positive influence, and whether psychiatry in its current form is as good as it can be. Stated in a more extreme form, the question can be asked whether we still need psychiatrists.

Psychiatrist Steven Moffic argues that we do indeed need psychiatrists, but perhaps the profession needs to redefine itself in ways that are more responsive to the needs of contemporary society. He urges his colleagues to listen to criticism, and begin to take steps forward along new paths of service provision. For example, he urges more collaboration between psychiatrists and primary care physicians at the point of service—the medical offices to which patients turn for help with physical as well as emotional symptoms. In such a setting, the best potential exists for making accurate diagnoses and decisions about interventions.

Dr. Moffic contends that psychiatrists have a lengthy and comprehensive medical education and are therefore best equipped to attend to abnormal bodily functioning that might affect emotional experiences (e.g., an underactive thyroid or a brain tumor that could be related to a person's experience of anxiety, depression, or psychotic symptoms). Dr. Moffic states that, because psychiatrists can provide both psychotherapy and medication, their services can be more cost-effective than is the case in which *two* professionals treat a patient.

Psychiatrist Steven Balt does not advocate an end to the profession of psychiatry but rather urges significant changes in the ways in which psychiatrists go about their work. Dr. Balt believes that psychiatry has overstepped its bounds, and has mislabeled and mistreated countless numbers of people. He even muses about the innumerable times he has been asked to prescribe a medication that would have dubious therapeutic value for the patient. The implication is that for some prescribers it would be easier to write the prescription than to engage the patient in a dialogue about the pros and cons of the medication option. Rather than pointing the finger of responsibility solely at psychiatrists, Dr. Balt takes a broader view, and urges his colleagues to challenge the "disability" system that makes people "too demoralized to give a damn."

Dr. Balt views the process of bringing about change an uphill battle, which is made particularly difficult because psychiatrists tenaciously hold onto a status quo, which for some is foisted upon them by their employers (e.g., hospitals, clinics). Dr. Balt recommends that psychiatrists develop a new mindset in which they are taught to *interact* more and intervene less. He is critical of the scientific façade that psychiatry has built on the basis of scant scientific evidence in order to keep itself relevant. With attention to effective communication, psychiatrists can explain to their patients how they can overcome their "illnesses" and help patients realize that some of their complaints are not actually illnesses in the first place.

Concurring with Dr. Moffic, Dr. Balt appreciates the extensive medical training of psychiatrists, but urges them to use their unique position to change the state of affairs. Thus, the question at hand is less about whether we need psychiatrists at all, but whether we need or want the kind of services offered by many psychiatrists at the present time. Psychiatrists have a special opportunity to use their sophisticated understanding of bodily systems to develop and refine comprehensive integrative interventions in which they effectively treat the whole person.

Why We Still Need Psychiatrists!

"It is really quite incredible to me that some . . . are willing to denigrate the 8 years of training that it takes to become sophisticated about pathophysiology of the whole body, understand the intricate play of medical and mental problems and really master complex diagnosis, pharmacotherapy, and psychotherapy, as I feel I did in my training."

—A psychiatrist colleague, personal e-mail communication, 4/2/12

This blog, and many to follow, will try to analyze why we are in this "incredible" state of affairs and what to do about it.

The Siege on Psychiatrists

In many ways, this situation has been building over many years. We can start with the middle of the last century, when psychologists and social workers started to provide more and more of the psychotherapy that psychiatrists like Freud had developed. And, wouldn't you know it, and just as Freud had predicted, not only have their results have been pretty good, but they helped develop more evidence-based psychotherapies like Cognitive-Behavioral Therapy. So, it turned out we don't really need psychiatrists to purely do psychotherapy, do we?

Then, around 1990, the promising new wave of psychopharmacology provided a new direction for psychiatrists. In fact, with Prozac for clinical depression, it all seemed so easy and safe that primary care physicians soon became the major prescribers of psychiatric medications. Just pop a pill like you might a daily vitamin. Patients seemed to like that, too, as it seemed less stigmatizing to go to your general doctor instead of a "shrink."

More recently, the book by Robert Whitaker, *Anatomy of an Epidemic,* strongly suggested that we may have been led down a path mined with unexpected risks for long-term use of most of these new medications. Convincing evidence, which seemed to fit my own personal experience, was presented

Moffic, Steven. From *Mad in America*, April 12, 2012, pp. 1–4. Copyright © 2012 by Steve Moffic. Reprinted by permission.

about how some of our "thought leaders" in psychiatry may have been swayed by pay from the pharmaceutical companies.

To top this all off, a colleague just advertised two jobs for a psychiatrist and/or nurse practitioner, as if there wasn't any difference between the two professions. Similarly, not a week goes by that I don't have a patient ask what the difference is between a psychiatrist and a psychologist. Hint (if you don't know the answer): psychologists cannot yet generally prescribe medication. Adding to this confusion, although anyone with a Ph.D. in any field can call themselves a "doctor," only psychiatrists are medical doctors specializing in mental disorders. Besides confusing psychiatrists with psychologists, "psychiatry" is often confused with all mental healthcare. Technically speaking, "psychiatry" should just refer to what psychiatrists do.

Outside of our profession, scientologists have led an anti-psychiatry movement for decades. More gently and helpfully, many of our patients have formed a consumer movement to achieve more of a voice and remind us that recovery is more than just taking a medication.

We psychiatrists also do not get paid nowadays nearly as much as one may imagine. How about $25 from Medicare or Medicaid to do a medication review for the most seriously symptomatic, a reimbursement which doesn't compare well to what many plumbers make.

Psychiatric Advances and Retreats

Fortunately, our current state of affairs hasn't always been the case, otherwise the profession would not have developed and continued to serve a societal need in the first place. A highly selective view of some of psychiatry's glory days, followed by retrenchments, would include the following.

Back in the 1800s, in the early days of state psychiatric hospitals, inmates with mental illness were able to leave jails and prisons to receive "moral treatment" in attractive new facilities. Imagine how proud these early psychiatrists must have been to be able to increase the dignity and safety of these patients. Unfortunately, over time, these state hospitals started to become overpopulated and in need of repair.

Then, the theories of Sigmund Freud seemed to promise a new way to treat mental illness. Just think of what made this so exciting in the early 1900s. The pride and promise to disclose unknown and unconscious conflicts! Unfortunately, though as Freud himself anticipated, the psychotherapies derived from his theories have major limitations, especially for the most seriously mentally ill.

There is more. The promise of mental healthcare for all with the federally-funded community mental health centers, supplanted by cost-cutting for-profit managed care systems. Therapeutic communities and housing led by such psychiatrists as Loren Mosher, only to give way to scores of homeless mentally ill. But you get the picture by now. One wave of promise supplanted by another, and not one way necessarily complementing and being integrated with the other. Two steps forward, then one step back.

Stepping into an integrated Future

Fortunately, all of these prior treatments and settings are alive and partially well in one way or another. And therein lies the hope for the future: integrating the best of the past in new ways. If we accept constructive criticism, we should be poised to take another two steps forward. One of these emerging new paths leads to clinics that integrate psychiatrists on-site with primary care physicians. It is here, given enough time, where there is the best potential to make accurate diagnoses and more carefully prescribe psychiatric medication when it is needed.

Who has the best potential to lead this advance? By now, you should know the answer. It is still only psychiatrists that have the most comprehensive education and training in all aspects of mental health and mental illness. In the loving spirit of Shakespeare, let us count some of the many ways they can add unique value to those in need.

- Psychiatrists, alone among all the mental healthcare professionals, still take some version of the Hippocratic Oath, dedicating ourselves to the patient first and foremost.
- Psychiatrists, alone among mental healthcare professionals, have worn the white coat of medicine, which forever will infuse our professional identity.
- Psychiatrists, alone and unlike any other mental healthcare discipline, have had direct responsibility for life and death decisions in medical school and internship.
- Psychiatrists by far have the longest and most comprehensive education, with at least 8 years of graduate school.
- Psychiatrists have studied the brain extensively, and know why it is the hardest organ to study in the body, let alone how the brain may differ from our "mind" and "spirit."
- Psychiatrists know that deficits in the frontal lobes of the brain can cause a condition called Anosognosia, which leaves many prospective patients unable to even realize and accept that they have a mental problem in the first place.
- Psychiatrists, by our medical school training, are best equipped to make sure that an underactive thyroid gland or brain tumor is not causing one's anxiety, depression, or psychosis.
- Psychiatrists know best that people with psychiatric illness have much poorer overall health than the general population, and why.
- Psychiatrists are leading the way in understanding that disorders like PTSD and Major Depression may turn out to be not just brain diseases, but whole body illnesses.
- Psychiatrists best understand the medical language of other physicians.

Sure, we have "bad apples" among us, just like any other profession. And we, too, are subject to social forces that limit what we can do. Nevertheless, one might heed the advice of another hard-hitting and truth-finding investigative journalist, Mike Wallace, who just recently died. He had a serious suicide attempt and suffered periodic depressions. When asked once what advice he would give others suffering from depression, he simply recommended to find a "good psychiatrist." Note that he did not say, find any psychiatrist. How to find that good psychiatrist will be the subject of future blogs. If you have any recommendations on how to do so, let us know.

[Additional Statements of Dr. Moffic in Response to Posted Comments]

. . . What we do know is that when psychiatrists provide combined psycho-therapy and medication, instead of a patient seeing both a therapist and a psychiatrist, that it is more cost-effective (saves money and is more therapeutic). We do know that in for-proft managed care healthcare systems led by business people, patients get much less care.

I'm with you for having others providing the same services that psychiatrists can for cheaper and less training. That is how I led, and why I was early to advocate for paraprofessionals and peer specialists. But there are some things that psychiatrists should be able to do better, just like one might only go to dermatologists or surgeons. No excuse if that care is not provided humbly, compassionately, and respectfully.

***

. . . I did not write the blog to defend psychiatry and psychiatrists. It was to try to improve what we can do, if that is possible. We indeed may need a paradigm shift, as some have suggested. For that, I appreciate all the comments on what we are doing wrong or where we are wrong about what we are thinking.

Sometimes it is clear we do well. That is why I gave the Mike Wallace example. For whatever information he shared publicly, whoever was his psychiatrist saved his life, a life that he dedicated to finding the truth and exposing fraud to millions on the *60 Minutes* TV show.

I'm all for other ways of helping than medications. Loren Mosher was a friend and colleague and model of a brave psychiatrist, and I know well what happened to him. [Editor's note: Dr. Mosher was an American psychiatrist who spent his career seeking more humane treatment for people with schizophrenia, including a residential treatment model which did not rely on drugs. He was dismissed from NIMH and resigned from the American Psychiatric Association in 1998 as a protest against the influence of psychiatric companies on psychiatric practice.]

***

It is certainly true that medications can do harm, and more than we realized at first. There are also many other things that do mental harm: racism, sexism, trauma (physical, sexual, and mental), substance abuse, environmental pollution, loss of jobs, poverty. . . .

Steven Balt  **NO**

Yes, We Still Need Psychiatrists, but For What?

If anyone's looking for a brief primer on the popular perception of psychiatry and the animosity felt by those who feel hurt or scarred by this (my) profession, a good place to start would be a recent post by Steven Moffic entitled "Why We Still Need Psychiatrists!" on Robert Whitaker's site, Mad in America.

Moffic, a psychiatrist at the Medical College of Wisconsin, is a published author, a regular contributor to *Psychiatric Times*, and a member of the Group for the Advancement of Psychiatry. Whitaker is a journalist best known for his books *Mad in America* and *Anatomy of an Epidemic*, both of which have challenged modern psychiatric practice.

Moffic's thesis is that we still "need" psychiatrists, particularly to help engineer necessary changes in the delivery of psychiatric care (for example, integration of psychiatry into primary care, incorporating therapeutic communities and other psychosocial treatments into the psychiatric mainstream, etc.). He argues that we are the best to do so by virtue of our extensive training, our knowledge of the brain, and our "dedication to the patient."

The reaction by readers was, predictably, swift and furious. While Whitaker's readers are not exactly a representative sample (one reader, for example, commented that "the search for a good psychiatrist can begin in the obituary column"—a comment which was later deleted by Mr Whitaker), their comments—and Moffic's responses—reinforce the idea that, despite our best intentions, psychiatrists arc still *not* on the same page as many of the people we intend to serve.

As I read the comments, I find myself sympathetic to many of Moffic's critics. There's still a lot we don't know about mental illness, and much of what we do might legitimately be called "pseudoscience." However, I am also keenly aware of one uncomfortable fact: For every patient who argues that psychiatric diagnoses are fallacies and that medications "harm" or "kill" people, there are dozens—if not hundreds—of others who not only disagree, but who INSIST that they DO have these disorders and who don't just accept but REQUEST drug treatment.

For instance, consider this response to Moffic's post:

> Stop chemically lobotomizing adults, teens, children, and infants for your imaginary psychiatric "brain diseases." Stop spreading lies to the world about these "chronic" (fake) brain illnesses, telling people they

Reprinted with permission from *The Carlat Psychiatry Report,* Steven Balt, April 12, 2012. www .thecarlatreport.com can only hope to manage them with "appropriate" (as defined by you and yours) "treatments," so that they are made to falsely believe in non-existent illnesses and deficiencies that would have them "disabled" for a lifetime and too demoralized about it to give a damn.

I don't know how Moffic would respond to such criticism. If he's like most psychiatrists I know, he may just shrug it off as a "fringe" argument. But that's a dangerous move, because despite the commenter's tone, his/her arguments are worthy of scientific investigation.

Let's assume this commenter's points are entirely correct. That still doesn't change the fact that lots of people have already "bought in" to the psychiatric model. In my practice, I *routinely* see patients who want to believe that they have a "brain disease." They ask me for the "appropriate treatment"—often a specific medication they've seen on TV, or have taken from a friend, and *don't want* to hear about the side effects or how it's not indicated for their condition. (It takes more energy to say "no" than to say "yes.") They often appreciate the fact that there's a "chemical deficiency" or "imbalance" to explain their behavior or their moods. (Incidentally, family members, the criminal justice system, and countless social service agencies also appreciate this "explanation.") Finally, as I've written about before, many patients don't see "disability" as such a bad thing; in fact, they *actively pursue it*—sometimes even *demanding* this label—despite my attempts to convince them otherwise.

In short, I agree with many of the critics on Whitaker's site—and Whitaker himself—that psychiatry has far overstepped its bounds and has mislabeled and mistreated countless people. (I can't tell you how many times I've been asked to prescribe a drug for which I think to myself "what in the world is this going to do????") But the critics fail to realize is that this "delusion" of psychiatry is not just in psychiatrists' minds. It's part of society. Families, the legal system, Social Security, Medicaid/Medicare, Big Pharma, Madison Avenue, insurance companies, and employers of psychiatrists (and, increasingly, non-psychiatrists) like me—all of them see psychiatry the same way: as a way to label and "pathologize" behaviors that are, oftentimes, only slight variants of "normal" (whatever *that* is) and seek to "treat" them, usually with chemicals.

Any attempt to challenge this status quo (this "shared delusion," as I wrote in my response to Moffic's post) is met with resistance, as illustrated by the case of Loren Mosher, whom Moffic discusses briefly. The influence of the APA and drug companies on popular thought—not to mention legislation and allocation of health-care resources—is far more deeply entrenched than most people realize.

But the good thing is that Moffic's arguments for why we need psychiatrists can just as easily be used as arguments for why psychiatrists *are* uniquely positioned to change this state of affairs. Only psychiatrists—with their years of scientific education—can dig through the muck (as one commenter wrote, "to find nuggets in the sewage") and appropriately evaluate the medical literature. Psychiatrists *should* have a commanding knowledge of the evidence for all sorts of treatments (not just "biological" ones, even though one commenter lamented that she knew more about meds than her psychiatrist!) and argue for their inclusion and reimbursement in the services we provide.

Psychiatrists can (or should) also have the communication skills to explain to patients how they can overcome "illnesses" or, indeed, to educate them that their complaints are not even "illnesses" in the first place. Finally, psychiatrists should command the requisite authority and respect amongst policymakers to challenge the broken "disability" system, a system which, I agree, *does* make people "too demoralized to give a damn."

This is an uphill battle. It's particularly difficult when psychiatrists tenaciously hold on to a status quo which, unfortunately, is also foisted upon them by their employers. (And I fear that Obamacare, should it come to pass, is only going to intensify the overdiagnosis and ultrarapid biological management of patients—more likely by providers with even *less* education than the psychiatrist). But it's a battle we *must* fight, not just for the sake of our jobs, but—as Whitaker's readers emphasize—for the long-term well-being of millions of patients, and, quite possibly, for the well-being of our society as a whole.

[Additional Statements of Dr. Balt in Response to Posted Comments]

It's truly unfortunate that the good psychiatrists I know . . . piece together pathology and psychiatry and human health and disease . . . "with nutrition, lifestyle, sleep modification, exercise, stress reduction, and . . . medication." Even though most psychiatrists would welcome the opportunity to practice in this manner, most of us don't have luxury of time to do so . . . and, moreover, most patients have little *interest* in any of the above.

BTW, before anyone accuses me of "blaming the patient," I would invite you to spend a day trying to talk patients *out of* a non-indicated benzo, stimulant, sleeper, or Seroquel, or an SSRI for "stress."

***

I have worked in three county mental health systems (and three private-practice settings, plus a VA clinic); I have seen, in my own experience, literally hundreds of people who have come to me and who, in my opinion, do not have a clear psychiatric diagnosis (which begs the question: what is a psychiatric diagnosis anyway?) but who insist that they do and, moreover, who demand the same drugs that people on sites like Whitaker's and Surviving Antidepressants regularly denounce. It's a very interesting quandary.

***

[There are] patients who demand medications even when (a) there is no clear evidence of a mental illness (and never was one); (b) other, less dangerous alternatives exist to manage whatever "symptoms" the patient complains about; (c) the natural course of their disorder precludes the need for ongoing medication; and/or (d) the patient has received a full explanation (i.e., informed consent) about potential risks and dangers.

Early in the course of an illness, when symptoms *do* exist to warrant a diagnosis, the risk/benefit ratio often favors the medication. Furthermore, this is the standard of care, so docs like me avoid any malpractice risks by prescribing the drug, regardless of whether we think it's the best option. But as you know, each illness has its own natural course, and symptoms wax and wane. What's appropriate upon initial presentation is often not appropriate later on (which is why I always work out a tentative "taper" or "discontinuation" strategy at the outset with each patient—for *every* drug). Unfortunately, many of our drugs have addictive qualities (or street value), and many patients are too heavily invested in the belief that the drugs "fix them," both of which lead to their demands for more.

***

Regarding involuntary detention/forced treatment. . . . In my experience at three different hospitals, I can say that the vast majority, if not all, patients who were involuntarily hospitalized truly *did* need to be briefly sequestered for the safety of themselves or others (or were obviously disorganized and incapable of managing their own affairs). I don't think many disinterested observers would disagree with that assessment. Now, whether that was due to mental illness is an entirely *different* question. (Most of the time, drug/ETOH intoxication or withdrawal was a major contributor.) As a result, one could argue that forced drugging was unnecessary and inappropriate, and yes, simply "calming down" was often interpreted as "insight" or "acceptance of treatment."

***

. . . I'm reminded about the training program in which I currently work. The first-year residents (whose psychiatry exposure is limited to the inpatient psych units) spend most of their time (a) writing notes . . . , and (b) learning to argue in favor of involuntary detention. Indeed, twice a week at "probable cause" hearings, the residents argue for continued involuntary treatment of their patients in front of a county judge and a patients' rights advocate (who represents the patients). The residents consider it not only a "badge of honor" to "win" their cases, but an important part of their education. More important, in fact, than proper diagnosis and treatment (which, [in my humble opinion], is virtually impossible in the chaotic environment of the inpatient unit.

***

. . . I'm reminded of an exercise I used to give my students (psychiatry trainees): Go into a room with a patient and forget everything you know about the DSM, psychiatric diagnosis, and medications. Instead, talk to the patient as a fellow human being. Get to know him as you would a new acquaintance. Pretend you're meeting him for coffee or at a social gathering. Try to understand the nature of his suffering, but also his personal strengths and ways in which he can use those strengths or develop new ones. Treat him as a teammate or partner, and identify some goals to achieve together. And so on. . . .

Interestingly, when one approaches patients in this nonjudgmental, unbiased way, true mental "illness" (as much as some commenters here may disagree with that term), when it exists, *does* present itself, and often quite convincingly. On the other hand, many patients start to be seen as pretty "normal," with certain quirks or idiosyncrasies, but nothing too foreign or disturbing.

Indeed, the DSM tells us how to think about human behavior; the drug companies tell us precisely which neurotransmitters are responsible for sadness, elation, irritability, and fatigue; and our practice & payment arrangements effectively prevent us from using any other construct with which to understand our patients. But this simple exercise—sort of like trying to write with one's non-dominant hand—sheds a great deal of light on the biases we bring to the everyday practice of psychiatry. Moreover, it shows us how easy it would be to do things differently.

***

. . . If only we were taught to *interact* more and intervene less. Or, better yet, some strategies for effective interaction. Unfortunately, those are hard to define. They also seem to be skills that some people just seem to have from birth and just can't be taught. (Yes, I know about the literature on common factors of good therapists or effective psychotherapies. . . .)

***

. . . [P]sychiatry has built [a] scientific facade (on the basis of very scant evidence) in order to keep itself relevant in modern medicine. In reality, what's truly relevant (at least until we have better "interventions") is not scientific at all. It's what we say and do, and how we do it.

EXPLORING THE ISSUE

Do We Still Need Psychiatrists?

Critical Thinking and Reflection

1. Although some patients may suffer due to mislabeling and a failure to receive appropriate medication from psychiatrists, what aspects of the current psychiatric model are worth saving?
2. What are some of the advantages of integrating psychiatric care with care provided by a primary care physician? Any disadvantages?
3. During the past two decades, pharmaceutical companies have engaged in direct marketing of psychotropic medications for anxiety, depression, and other emotional symptoms. What are some advantages and disadvantages of this marketing?
4. Many psychiatrists limit their practice to prescribing medications, with the expectation that psychotherapy will be provided by another mental health professional. What are the advantages and disadvantages of this model?
5. Psychiatrists are urged to develop more sensitive and effective styles of communicating with their patients. What are some of the characteristics and behaviors that should be expected in a mental health professional?
6. What can psychologists contribute in terms of developing valid and reliable diagnostic procedures as well as effective therapeutic interventions?

Is There Common Ground?

Despite the way that the issue was framed by the authors, neither is proposing an end to the profession of psychiatry. Rather, they are expressing ardent viewpoints with the intention of sparking change and innovation in the field of mental health. Dr. Moffic calls for a paradigm shift, and Dr. Balt contends that psychiatrists are uniquely positioned to change the current state of affairs.

In challenging psychiatrists to change the status quo (and by implication, other mental health professionals as well), a number of issues emerge that warrant consideration. First, there is the question of science. To what extent are psychiatric diagnoses valid and reliable characterizations of the disorders they label? The development of the fifth edition of the *Diagnostic and Statistical Manual of Mental Disorders* (DSM-5) has been fraught with years of controversy and debate about what characterizes various psychological disorders. Not only have battles raged over diagnostic labels, but so also have debates emerged about what treatments are really effective for specific disorders. Psychiatrists can continue collaborating with psychologists and other mental health researchers in conducting research on the many conditions and treatments still needing investigation.

Professionals from all the mental health disciplines have an opportunity to touch the lives of all the patients they treat, to provide guidance to their loved ones, and to play a role of leadership in society. To maximize this potential, specialists from the various disciplines must come together in collaborative efforts that will benefit the lives of all those with whom they interact professionally.

Additional Resources

American Psychiatric Association. Retrieved from www.psychiatry.org/

Carlat, D. J. (2010). *Unhinged: The trouble with psychiatry—A doctor's revelations about a profession in crisis*. New York, NY: Free Press.

The Royal College of Psychiatrists. Retrieved from www.rcpsych.ac.uk/

Soteria: Schizophrenia Without Antipsychotic Drugs & the Legacy of Loren Moser. Retrieved from www.psychiatry.org/

Tryer, P., & Silk, K. R. (2011). *Effective treatment in psychiatry*. Cambridge, UK: Cambridge University Press.

ISSUE 6

Should "Smart Drugs" Be Used to Enhance Cognitive Functioning?

YES: Barbara J. Sahakian and Sharon Morein-Zamir, from "Neuroethical Issues in Cognitive Enhancement," *Journal of Psychopharmacology* (vol. 25, no. 2, 2011). doi:10.1177/0269881109106926

NO: Helia Garrido Hull, from "Regression by Progression: Unleveling the Classroom Playing Field Through Cosmetic Neurology," *University of Hawaii Law Review* (vol. 33, no. 1, 2010)

Learning Outcomes

After reading this issue, you should be able to:

- Understand the appropriate and inappropriate uses of cognitive enhancing drugs.
- Discuss the risks as well as the benefits of cognitive enhancing drugs by healthy individuals without cognitive disabilities.
- Consider the responsibilities of society to limit the unauthorized use of prescription drugs by people who take them without medical oversight.
- Evaluate the extent to which people with legitimate need for cognitive enhancing medications may be placed at a disadvantage if nonimpaired individuals are prescribed "smart drugs" which will give them an even greater advantage in academic performance.
- Discuss whether cognitive enhancing drugs should be classified as controlled substances.

ISSUE SUMMARY

YES: Professor Barbara J. Sahakian and Dr. Sharon Morein-Zamir note that cognitive enhancing medications provide considerable benefits to individuals with cognitive disabilities, and can also serve as "smart drugs" for healthy individuals for the purpose of cognitive enhancement. While more research is needed into the long-term effects of these drugs on healthy individuals, responsible use of these drugs is recommended in order to gain maximum benefits with minimal harm to the individual and to society as a whole.

NO: Attorney and Professor Helia Garrido Hull explains that the use of cognitive enhancing drugs by healthy individuals can have a negative impact on individuals with disabilities. The use of such drugs in competitive environments such as classrooms creates an imbalance between students without cognitive disabilities and those with disabilities for whom the drugs were originally intended. She asserts that the government has a responsibility to enforce the law in order to maintain the integrity of decades of legal precedent intended to protect individuals with disabilities from becoming disadvantaged again. Although many of these drugs are listed as controlled substances, their use without a prescription has become widespread and viewed as morally acceptable.

I n 2012 various articles and news stories appeared in the national media about the shortage of psychostimulant medications such as Adderall (amphetamine-dextroamphetamine) and Ritalin (methylphenidate). These substances fall under federal regulations of the Drug Enforcement Agency (DEA), which oversees issues pertaining to their manufacture and distribution. The DEA tightly regulates the quantity of psychostimulants produced each year based on what is viewed as the country's legitimate need. However, that "need" seems to be rising exponentially each year. For example, in 2010 more than 18 million prescriptions were written for Adderall, but this figure was more than 13 percent higher than the number of prescriptions written the year before. Millions of individuals, including children, adolescents, and adults, rely on these medications to help them deal with their symptoms of attention-deficit/hyperactivity disorder as well as other neuropsychiatric conditions, and some are finding it more and more difficult to find a pharmacy that has inventory of their prescribed medication. These individuals rely on psychostimulant medications to help them control their hyperactivity and/or enhance their concentration and attentional functioning. People with other psychiatric conditions such as chronic psychotic disorders find these medications beneficial because they result in improved cognitive functioning that can be instrumental in living independently. Rather than referring to these medications as psychostimulants, some prefer terms such as cognitive enhancers or "smart drugs" because they have been shown to improve various aspects of cognitive functioning.

A primary reason for the limited availability of psychostimulant medication pertains to the reality of their illicit use. As "controlled substances" they are considered to be habit-forming and therefore likely to be abused. The major question relating to the shortage of these medications pertains to the extent to which these drugs are being used by people without prescriptions. For example, it is common among college students to "borrow" a friend's prescribed psychostimulant medication, particularly during periods of intense study. These drugs have also become increasingly common in the workplace, particularly by those in stressful and competitive jobs. More worrisome, however, are the instances in which these drugs are being illegally diverted in the distribution system and are being sold as recreational drugs.

Because psychostimulant drugs can be addictive, American society takes a relatively strong stance in terms of trying to control the distribution and use of these drugs. However, in recent years, some critics have questioned the wisdom of restricting availability of medications that might be beneficial to many people, and consequently yield considerable advantages to society in terms of increased success in academics, greater productivity in the workplace, and enhanced cognitive functioning in everyday life. Improved performance in all these areas would likely result in greater self-esteem for individuals, and as a result, a happier society.

Those in favor of loosening the grips on the availability of psychostimulant medication argue that these drugs are not all that different from the caffeine consumed daily by most Americans, sometimes in very high quantities and at a cost to physical health and well-being. Instead of drinking a half-dozen cups of coffee or cans of caffeinated soda, why not just take a pill that will help you stay more alert, focus more effectively, and get your work done more efficiently? Would not it be advantageous for surgeons, military personnel, shift workers, and airline pilots to take a prescribed medication to help them do their jobs better?

In addition to the personal and societal benefits of increased productivity and self-esteem, proponents of smart drugs contend that cognitive enhancement could lead to the reduction of unfair disparity in society. For example, individuals with neuropsychiatric disorders, debilitating medical conditions, brain injury, or ADHD could benefit from the use of cognitive enhancing medications which would enable them to function and compete more effectively in society.

Those opposed to the wider use of smart drugs express alarm about this trend, expressing particular concern that, rather than making people smarter, reliance on such drugs may actually reduce creativity, imagination, and motivation. Rather than viewing psychostimulants as smart drugs, critics label these agents as a form of cosmetic neurology. They also attempt to bring the discussion into the realm of a dialogue about ethics, which is called the field of neuroethics. Critics of these agents also take exception to the argument that smart drugs can level the playing field such that individuals with lower intellectual capacity or those from deprived backgrounds will be better able to compete with those not dealing with such deficits. How is the playing field leveled if the non-disadvantaged are taking these same drugs, and therefore leaping proportionally ahead of their less fortunate peers?

The article for the YES position affirms the need for and value of smart drugs. Professor Barbara J. Sahakian and research associate Sharon Morein-Zamir are prominent researchers in the field of brain functioning. While acknowledging some of the risks of smart drugs, they contend that these agents have considerable potential for improving the lives of countless numbers of people, particularly those with serious brain dysfunction. Regarding the wider use of smart drugs in society, they encourage responsible use, and assert that mentally competent adults should be able to engage in cognitive enhancement, and that regulatory agencies should allow this. At the same time, they urge scientists, physicians, and policymakers to ensure easy access to information about the benefits and risks of using these drugs.

The article for the NO position by law professor Helia Garrido Hull opposes the nontherapeutic use of powerful prescription stimulants because of the significant risks involved, and because such use places disabled individuals at a competitive disadvantage in the classroom. In addition to concerns about equity, Professor Helia Garrido Hull also expresses alarm about the potential detrimental effects on individuals who may experience the unwelcome effect of having their creativity sapped.

YES

Barbara J. Sahakian and Sharon Morein-Zamir

Neuroethical Issues in Cognitive Enhancement

Why Are Smart Drugs Needed?

Cognitive-enhancing drugs, also known as smart drugs, are needed to treat cognitive disabilities and improve the quality of life for patients with neuropsychiatric disorders and brain injury. Cognitive-enhancing drugs are used in treating cognitive impairment in disorders such as Alzheimer's disease (AD), schizophrenia and Attention Deficit Hyperactivity Disorder (ADHD). In neurodegenerative diseases, such as AD, cognitive-enhancing drugs are used to slow down or compensate for the decline in cognitive and behavioural functioning that characterizes such disorders. There are currently 700,000 people with dementia in the UK, most of whom have AD. Each year, 39,400 new cases are diagnosed in England and Wales, translating to a new case every 14 minutes. Current costs of long-term care for dementia in the UK are estimated at £4.6 billion, and with an increasing aging population, this estimate is expected to rise to £10.9 billion by the year 2031 (Knapp and Prince, 2007). Likewise, the number of people placed in institutions is expected to rise from 224,000 in 1998 to 365,000 in 2031. Cognitive-enhancing drugs are important in this context as it has been suggested that a treatment that would reduce severe cognitive impairment in older people by just 1% a year would cancel out all estimated increases in the long-term care costs due to the aging population in the UK (Knapp and Prince, 2007).

Cognitive enhancers may be beneficial not just in neurodegenerative disorders but also in neuropsychiatric disorders for which they are not yet routinely prescribed. For instance, though it is common knowledge that people with schizophrenia typically suffer from hallucinations and delusions, it is the long-term cognitive impairments that often impede everyday function and quality of life for many patients. Twenty four million people world wide suffer from schizophrenia (World Health Organization, 2008). In the USA, direct and indirect costs were estimated at over $60 billion in the year 2000 (Wu et al., 2005). It has been suggested that even small improvements in cognitive functions could help patients make the transition to independent living (Davidson and Keefe, 1995).

Sahakian, Barbara J.; Morein-Zamir, Sharon. From *Journal of Psychopharmacology*, vol. 25, no. 2, February 2011, pp. 197–204. Copyright © 2011 by Sage Publications—Journals. Reprinted by permission via Rightslink.

However, it is not only adults suffering from neuropsychiatric disorders that benefit from cognitive-enhancing drugs. ADHD affects 3 to 7% of all children worldwide, and is the most prevalent neuropsychiatric disorder of childhood (American Psychiatric Association, 2000). ADHD is a highly heritable and disabling condition characterized by core cognitive and behavioural symptoms of impulsivity, hyperactivity and/or inattention. It has important implications for education provision, long-term social outcomes and economic impact. For example, long-term studies indicate it is associated with poorer long-term outcomes, including increased educational dropout, job dismissal, criminal activities, substance abuse, other mental illness and increased accident rates (Barkley, 2006). The annual excess cost of ADHD in the USA in 2000 was estimated to be $42.5 billion (Pelham et al., 2007).

Whilst it is pharmacological cognitive enhancers (PCEs) that we will consider in this paper, there are numerous methods of boosting one's brain power. Some additional methods under development are neuroprosthetics for cognition, and transcranial magnetic stimulation. Importantly, there are many others such as education, physical exercise and neurocognitive activation or cognitive training that are commonly being used (Beddington et al., 2008; Hilman et al., 2008; Willis et al., 2006).

Research on Cognitive Enhancers

Despite the fact that much research has been dedicated to the development and understanding of various cognitive enhancers, we still have limited knowledge as to how specific cognitive functions are modulated by neurotransmitters. For example, whilst we know that methylphenidate improves symptoms of ADHD and improves performance on objective behavioural tasks, such as spatial working memory and stop signal, we have yet to determine conclusively whether dopamine, noradrenaline or both neurotransmitters are required for these effects on cognition. Some of the most notable PCEs being explored to assist individuals with neurological or neuropsychiatric disorders with executive function and attention difficulties include methylphenidate, atomoxetine and modafinil (Stahl, 2008). Methylphenidate, also commonly known as Ritalin, increases the synaptic concentration of dopamine and noradrenaline by blocking their reuptake. Atomoxetine (Strattera) on the other hand, is a relatively selective noradrenaline reuptake inhibitor. In the case of modafinil (Provigil), despite considerable research its precise mechanism of action is unclear, although it has been found to exhibit a multitude of effects including potentiation of noradrenaline and, to a degree, dopamine neurotransmission (Volkow et al., 2009), elevation of extracellular glutamate, serotonin and histamine levels, and decreased extracellular GABA (Minzenberg and Carter, 2008). Recent evidence suggests that some of its cognitive effects may be modulated primarily by noradrenaline transporter inhibition (Minzenberg et al., 2008).

An effective method of testing the effects of cognitive enhancers on cognition is by using double-blind placebo-controlled studies where participants undergo a battery of objective cognitive tasks targeted at measuring various facets of cognition, including memory, attention and executive functions. For example, in the CANTAB Spatial Working Memory task (SWM), a number of coloured boxes are shown on the screen (Owen et al., 1990). The aim of this task is that, by touching the boxes and using a process of elimination, the subject should find one blue 'token' in each of a number of boxes. The number of boxes is gradually increased, until it is necessary to search a total of eight boxes. SWM is a test of the subject's ability to retain spatial information and to manipulate remembered items in working memory. It is a self-ordered task, which also assesses heuristic strategy. This test is sensitive to frontal lobe and 'executive' dysfunction (Owen et al., 1990) and is impaired in childhood and adulthood ADHD (Kempton et al., 1999; McLean et al., 2004; Mehta et al., 2004).

It has been demonstrated that methylphenidate improves spatial working memory performance both in young volunteers with ADHD and in adult patients with ADHD, whereby patients make fewer task-related errors when on methylphenidate (Mehta et al., 2004; Turner et al., 2005). The neural substrates mediating SWM task performance have been examined using imaging techniques such as positron emission topography (PET) and indicate that the dorsolateral and mid-ventrolateral prefrontal cortex are particularly recruited (Owen et al., 1996). Studies using PET and contrasting [(11)C] raclopride binding, with the subject on versus off methylphenidate, have further indicated that methylphenidate influences dopaminergic function, particularly in the striatum (Wang et al., 1999). Methylphenidate has been found to improve both performance and efficiency in the spatial working memory neural network involving the dorsolateral prefrontal cortex and posterior parietal cortex in healthy volunteers (Mehta et al., 2000).

Similar studies using the double-blind, randomized placebo-controlled methodology have reported that additional drugs such as modafinil and atomoxetine can improve performance in some tasks of executive functioning. Thus, modafinil has been found to improve spatial planning and response inhibition in ADHD patients, as measured by a variant of the Tower of London task and the stop signal task, respectively (Turner et al., 2004). It has been further demonstrated that modafinil produced improvements in performance in a group of healthy volunteers on tests of spatial planning, response inhibition, visual recognition and short-term memory (Turner et al., 2003). Likewise, administration of an acute dose of atomoxetine has been found not only to improve response inhibition in ADHD patients (Chamberlain et al., 2007), but also in healthy adults (Chamberlain et al., 2006). Using functional Magnetic Resonance Imaging (fMRI), the brain mechanisms by which atomoxetine exerts its effects in healthy volunteers has been examined in a double-blind placebo-controlled study (Chamberlain et al., 2009). Atomoxetine led to increased activation in the right inferior frontal gyrus when participants attempted to inhibit their responses in the stop signal task. Inhibitory motor control has been shown previously to depend, at least in part, on the function of this brain region (Aron et al., 2003).

Such results demonstrate the potential of drugs to enhance certain domains of cognition. At the same time, psychopharmacological research entails the consideration of several complex factors (Morein-Zamir et al., 2008). These include neurotransmitter function at times following an inverted U-shaped curve, with deviations from optimal level in either direction impairing performance (e.g., Ramos and Arnsten, 2007; Tannock et al., 1995). Likewise, different neurotransmitter levels can be found across brain regions, suggesting a complex interplay between baseline levels and drug administration. While some cognitive functions may improve following drug administration, others may worsen, as they depend on different optimum neurotransmitter levels (Cools and Robbins, 2004). These and related findings strongly suggest that drug-induced neurotransmitter increases may improve functioning in some groups but have no effect or even impair performance in others, already at optimum. In accordance, it is not uncommon for PCEs to improve performance primarily or exclusively in individuals with greater impairment (Mehta et al., 2000). With increasing understanding of the brain's neurochemistry, using imaging techniques and animal models, the complex roles of pre-existing baseline levels, drug dosage and individual differences are becoming more apparent (Morein-Zamir et al., 2008).

The Interest in Cognitive Enhancement

There is a clear trend in many western countries towards increasing prescriptions of methylphenidate (Farah, 2005). With the advent of psychiatric medications with greater tolerability and fewer side effects (though see Swanson et al., 2007), these trends are set to continue. However, it is not only those who suffer from neuropsychiatric and neurological disorders who are appearing to use PCEs. The use of stimulants, including methylphenidate and amphetamines, by students has been rising as well. Trends suggest that between 1993 and 2001 there was a clear increase in the life-time and 12-month prevalence rates of non-medical use of prescription drugs in college students (McCabe et al., 2007). In the USA, studies indicate that up to 16% of students on some college campuses use stimulants (Babcock and Byrne, 2000; McCabe et al., 2005), while 8% of university undergraduates report having illegally used prescription stimulants (Teter et al., 2005). Surveys on students indicate that most illicit use of prescription stimulants reported in the past year involve amphetamine-dextroamphetamine combination agents (e.g., Adderall), with higher use amongst Caucasians and Hispanics compared with African-Americans and Asians, and with considerable variations between colleges (Teter et al., 2006). The most commonly reported motives for use were to aid concentration, help study and increase alertness (Teter et al., 2006). There is also a trend for increasingly younger students to use such drugs, with one report indicating that 2.4% of eighth graders (13–14 years old) abused methylphenidate, as did 3.4% of tenth graders and 4.4% of twelfth graders (Johnston et al., 2006; see also McCabe et al., 2004). The trends are also not reserved solely for North America, as prescriptions rates in England of stimulants have been rising steadily from 220,000 in 1998 to 418,300 in 2004 (Niyadurupola, 2007; see also Turner and Sahakian, 2006). Though drugs such as modafinil are prescribed offlabel in North America, they can be freely obtained without prescription via the internet from multiple websites in various countries. In fact, a recent survey identified 159 sites offering drugs for sale, only two of which were regulated, and 85% not requiring a physician's prescription from the patient (Califano, 2008). Another cognitive domain of great interest is memory. Given the aging population in the UK and elsewhere, and the fact that the lifespan of individuals is being extended, it is highly likely that cognitive-enhancing drugs that can improve memory in healthy elderly people will prove to be in demand.

The popular media has reported extensively both on studies finding improved performance in healthy individuals and on the rising use of PCEs in healthy individuals. For example, the results of the study by Turner and colleagues (2003) on modafinil were reported in the media, including papers, magazines and radio. Papers ranging from The Guardian to The New Yorker and Nature, as well as the BBC, have discussed their potential for widespread use (Ghosh, 2007; Maher, 2008; Meikle, 2002; Talbot, 2009). Maintaining an optimum level of alertness, arousal and attention might be expected to prove valuable in a range of work and leisure activities. Indeed, the use of PCEs is not restricted to academia, and American sprinter Kelli White received a two-year ban in 2004 due to the use of modafinil when competing in the world championships and other US nationals.

These trends of growing use are likely set to increase as presently there are also novel cognitive enhancers under development, many of which are aimed at improving memory and learning. For example, ampakines, which work by enhancing the ΛMPA receptor's response to glutamate, improve cognition in healthy aged volunteers (Lynch, 2004). Novel compounds such nicotinic alpha-7 receptor agonists are now in phase 2 of clinical trials in Alzheimer's disease and schizophrenia (e.g., MEM 3454 Memory Pharmaceuticals/Roche; Mazurov et al., 2006).

The Neuroethics of Cognitive Enhancement

The study of cognitive-enhancing drugs, and their influence both on patients with neuropsychiatric and neurological disorders and healthy adults, raises numerous neuroethical issues. Neuroethics is defined as the study of the ethical, legal and social questions that arise when scientific findings about the brain are carried into medical practice, legal interpretations and health and social policy (Marcus, 2004). In response to the advances in cognitive neuroscience and neuropsychiatry and their increasing potential for broader application in the 'real world', and in part to the use of PCEs in healthy individuals, the Neuroethics Society (www.neuroethicssociety.org) was established (Nature Editorial, 2006). Neuroethics is a subfield within the broader domain of bioethics, which encompasses the ethical and moral implications of all biological and medical advances. Neuroethics was established to address the rapid developments within cognitive neuroscience and neuropsychiatry, and addresses findings relating specifically to the sciences of the mind, encompassing the central nervous system and the underlying brain mechanisms of human behaviour.

It is clear that research conducted by neuroscientists is now eliciting pro-found ethical implications: there are a whole range of ethical issues being raised due to neuroethical research from the use of PCEs in healthy individuals to the use of fMRI technology in military, civil and legal domains (Farah et al., 2004). We have advocated elsewhere that these ethical considerations in regard to societal issues should be part of training in neuroscience courses (Sahakian and Morein-Zamir, 2009). Neuroethics instruction to students is important because these future researchers should have some responsibility, as scientists and as members of society, as to the consequences of their research and how it may impact on society. We will now consider the 'rights' and 'wrongs' of cognitive enhancement in healthy people.

There are many potential positive outcomes for the use of cognitive enhancers in healthy adults. In addition to scientific and clinical advances, cognitive enhancement may lead to the removal of unfair disparity in society. Likewise, such drugs may lead to increased performance in both pleasurable and competitive activities. In an attempt to increase discussion on the topic and understand the subjective effects of healthy individuals taking modafinil for cognitive enhancement purposes, Sahakian and Morein-Zamir (2007) interviewed several scientists who have taken modafinil. The subjective effects ranged from moderate to 'mild but very valuable to me,' and the academics interviewed reported varied effects on cognition including global effects on attention, working memory, word finding, improved sustained hard thinking and increases in mental energy. Better performance may in particular be valu-able for individuals working in military roles, as shift workers or in positions that entail responsibility for the safety of many such as air traffic control-lers. The Research and Development organization for the US Department of Defence (DARPA) has stated that

> eliminating the need for sleep during an operation, while maintain-ing the high level of both cognitive and physical performance of the individual, will create a fundamental change in war fighting and force employment. Such capability has the potential to disrupt enemy opera-tions tempo, increase the effectiveness of small footprint military forces and shorten the duration of conflict.
>
> (Moreno, 2004, 2006).

Similar cognitive enhancement effects may seem desirable also in others, such as surgeons. However, long-term studies by the pharmaceutical industry to ensure safety and efficacy in healthy people are still required. Part of ensur-ing the safety of the use of these drugs long-term would be to address their potential for substance abuse, as there is also the potential for abuse of certain PCEs, such as methylphenidate (Bright, 2008).

Indeed, the potential harms of cognitive enhancement in healthy indi-viduals must not be overlooked. Namely, there could be long-term side effects or risks, which would be unacceptable given that this is not medical treatment.

Patients with debilitating symptoms will often tolerate the side effects of drug treatment because improvements in symptoms outweigh the negative aspects, but this is not the case for cognitive enhancers in healthy individuals (Turner and Sahakian, 2006). Safety concerns are particularly pertinent in the developing brain. Administering drugs to children, who are more vulnerable, may elicit additional harms not apparent in adults (Swanson et al., 2007). Clinical monitoring in this group is even more vital than in adults given the necessary prevalent off-label use, at times the potential for abuse, and the lack of clinical trials in this population (Zito et al., 2008). Additional safety concerns include drug–drug interactions and the presence of contraindications, which may become even more challenging with the increasing availability of PCEs via the internet (Sahakian and Morein-Zamir, 2007).

Another concern is the possibility of people being coerced or even forced into taking cognitive enhancers. This may occur explicitly, for example requiring that workers be alert during a night shift; or it may take on more subtle forms, such as providing a competitive environment where incentives are offered for best performance (Farah et al., 2004). In accordance, surveys indicate that the majority of college students overestimate the prevalence of non-medical use of prescription stimulants, leading to misperceived norms which in turn may promote such behaviour (McCabe et al., 2008). This may result in an overworked 24/7 society where people are pressured into working ever longer hours to the detriment of their own and their family's wellbeing. Concerns have also been raised regarding the possibility of greater inequality with the increased use of cognitive enhancers, if access is dependent on wealth (Chatterjee, 2004; Farah et al., 2004). This is true both between individuals (due to socioeconomic status and financial means), and between nations, as has occurred in the past with some medical advances (Ashcroft, 2005). Alternatively, given the likelihood that some PCEs may be affordable, costing about the same as a cup of coffee (Lennard, 2009), they could be adopted in disadvantaged populations, as was the case of mobile phones. Nevertheless, it is uncertain how the allocation and funding of various cognitive enhancers should be controlled and what the decision-making process should be.

This leads to another concern regarding how healthy individuals may obtain PCEs, ensuring both fair and safe access. Presently, in the USA and the UK, drugs such as modafinil, atomoxetine and methylphenidate require a doctor's prescription as these drugs are regulated for administration in psychiatric or medical conditions (Niyadurupola, 2007). Off-label prescriptions, or the prescription of a medication for a condition not described in the approved labelling, are very common and legal (Radley et al., 2006), and there is very limited regulation of off-label drugs with prescriptions, relying largely on the physician's discretion (Hampton, 2007). Hence modafinil, for instance, can be prescribed for people complaining of jetlag (Sahakian and Morein-Zamir, 2007). It is likely that physicians will face increasing pressure to prescribe PCEs to healthy individuals, and those who view the role of medicine as helping patients live better or achieve their goals may be open to considering such requests (Chatterjee, 2004; Greely et al., 2008). It is the physicians' responsibility to detect malingerers, decide whether or not to prescribe drugs for cognitive enhancement off-label, prescribe and monitor appropriately (Hampton, 2007). Otherwise, they risk that patients may decide to approach other doctors or less safe means of obtaining enhancers such as via friends, colleagues or the internet, where little regulation or monitoring is available and safety can be compromised (Califano, 2008; McCabe and Boyd, 2005). In the UK, the Academy of Medical Sciences workgroup specifically identified cognitive enhancers as a topic to be addressed by the Food Standards Agency and the Medicines and Health Care Regulatory Authority (Academy of Medical Sciences, 2008).

Another concern is that the use of cognitive enhancers may be considered cheating, allocating an unfair advantage over others in particular circumstances such as in competitive situations or test taking. Already the popular press has reported the negative opinions of some college students against their peers who use PCEs when studying for exams. Additional concerns pertain to the possibility of being 'overenhanced', for example being plagued by unwanted memories. Likewise, given that the effectiveness of PCEs will likely increase in the future, concerns have been raised over alternations in personhood and the risk of becoming a homogeneous society (President's Council on Bioethics, 2003). Furthermore, our perception of ourselves could change from mechanistic beings, as we may become unable to take credit for our achievements. Additional concerns relate to the fact that PCEs are 'unnatural' and that virtues such as motivation and hard work could become outdated with the expectation that everyone could just 'take a drug' (for additional discussion of these concerns, please see Chatterjee, 2004; Greely et al., 2008; Wolpe, 2002).

Whilst many of the concerns are already very relevant with the increasing off-label and illicit use of PCEs by young people, such drugs are one method by which individuals can perform better and more effectively and so consequently enjoy more achievements and success. However, we would not want to preclude other methods, for example, extra help in the classroom, smaller classes, and a greater consideration for life/work balance (Sahakian and Morein-Zamir, 2007; Turner and Sahakian, 2006). Currently, PCEs (in particular pharmaceuticals such as modafinil, atomoxetine and methylphenidate) have the potential to provide important clinical benefits and further development in this area is worthy of pursuit. Pharmacogenomics will make it possible to target individuals with safe and effective cognitive enhancers. Pharmacogenomics is the discipline behind how genes influence the body's response to drugs, which is important for enhancing the efficacy of individualized treatments and reducing medication side effects (see also Roiser et al. 2005). This raises the possibility in future of allowing PCEs to subsets of people who will experience benefits but will likely not experience the adverse effects. Presently, scientists are working together with social scientists, philosophers, ethicists, policy makers and the general public to actively discuss the ethical and moral consequences of cognitive enhancement (Sahakian and Morein-Zamir, 2007). This will go some way to ensuring that technological advances are put to maximal benefit and minimal harm.

Several position and discussion papers have been featured in scientific journals and in the media discussing PCE in the healthy (Greely et al., 2008;

Maher, 2008; Sahakian and Morein-Zamir, 2007). With the increased aware-ness of the ever-growing popularity of cognitive-enhancing drugs, many sci-entists have expressed positive and negative views on the issue, reflecting the complexity of the debate. Amongst them, Martha Farah of the University of Pennsylvania has commented that 'It would without question improve my quality of life' but also considered that others may wonder whether improv-ing productivity through artificial means would undermine the value of hard work. Likewise, as reported in an article in the Daily Mail, scientists such as Michael Gazzaniga, Director for the SAGE Center for the Study of Mind at the University of California Santa Barbara has stated, 'If we can boost our abilities to make up for the ones Mother Nature didn't give us, what is wrong with that?'. Other scientists view PCEs in the general population negatively, including Eric Kandel from Columbia University who has stated that using drugs to boost exam scores is 'awful'. The drugs 'are designed for people with serious problems who really need help.' Howard Gardner, from Harvard University, has expressed concern that "We have no idea what these drugs do to other forms of intelligence" (e.g., emotional intelligence Burne, 2007). Furthermore, Anjan Chatterjee, from the University of Pennsylvania, has raised the valid argument that 'No one has conducted thorough studies about how brain-boosting drugs would affect healthy people after weeks or months of use.'

The discussion led to Nature conducting an online poll which collected data from 1400 respondents from 60 countries (Maher, 2008). Interestingly, one in five respondents said they had used drugs for non-medical reasons as cognitive enhancers. Of those responding, 52% obtained cognitive-enhancing drugs by prescription, 34% by the internet and 14% by pharmacy. It was unclear whether the prescribed enhancers were diverted from other people's prescrip-tions, prescribed for different purposes or at different doses for the user, although in the UK a greater proportion obtained the drugs over the internet compared with the USA. In another online survey conducted in the USA, friends and peers were identified by the majority of university student respondents as the source of prescription drugs (McCabe and Boyd, 2005). This latter finding dovetails with a recent survey reported in the UK amongst Cambridge University stu-dents (Lennard, 2009). In the Nature poll, the most popular drug reported in the survey was methylphenidate (Ritalin) with 62% of users, 44% reported taking modafinil, and 15% reported taking beta-blockers (but see Teter et al., 2006 for different findings).

The respondents' opinions were also informative, with 96% of all respondents thinking that people with neuropsychiatric disorders should be given cognitive-enhancing drugs. In marked contrast, 86% of respondents thought that healthy children under the age of 16 should be restricted from taking cognitive-enhancing drugs. However, 33% of respondents said they would feel pressure to give cognitive-enhancing drugs to their children if other children at school were taking them. The Cambridge Varsity survey, completed by 1000 students, revealed that 1 in 10 had taken a prescription drug for cog-nitive enhancement (Lennard, 2009). The survey further found large differ-ences between students of the different colleges within the university, as well as between areas of study, with Science and Engineering students being the least likely to take the drugs modafinil, methylphenidate or an amphetamine–dextroamphetamine combination agent (Adderall). This survey complements the attitudes reported in the Nature survey in that a third of respondents said that given the opportunity, they would take a drug to enhance their cognition. Though suggestive, the data above are likely to suffer from selection bias and so should be interpreted with caution.

Conclusions and Outstanding Questions

In summary, we would like to stress that PCEs have considerable potential for improving the lives of individuals with neuropsychiatric and medical disorders, such as AD, schizophrenia, ADHD and those with brain injury. Therefore, PCEs are likely to be developed further and we expect their use to increase. At the same time caution must be exerted, particularly as studies of long-term effects in healthy humans regarding safety and efficacy are urgently required. Moreover, the potential use of PCEs in children with developing brains and the potential for abuse in certain populations must be considered, together with broader societal concerns such as coercion and inequality of access.

Thus, rather than advocate for overall inclusion or exclusion of PCE use in healthy individuals, we would encourage their responsible use. This includes scientists, physicians and policy makers ensuring that easy access to information about the advantages and dangers of using PCEs is available to the public (Sahakian and Morein-Zamir, 2007). Moreover, the public should be encouraged to use other non-pharmacological methods of cognitive enhancement, such as education. Greely and colleagues (2008) recommend that at present policies and limits should be created at the level of professional societies, such as physicians and educators, rather than the law. They further suggest that mentally competent adults should be able to engage in cognitive enhancement using drugs and that regulatory agencies should allow this given the availability of data for safety and efficacy (Greely et al., 2008). However, in order to do this, an evidence-based approach to the assessment of the risks and benefits of cognitive enhancement must be adopted. Additionally, there is a need for large-scale and refined surveys that do not focus necessarily on addiction, and that target populations beyond college students (see also Boyd and McCabe, 2008). However, others propose the formation of new laws and indeed regulatory structures to protect against the potential harms (Fukuyama, 2002).

Careful and critical evaluation of PCEs for the healthy population continues to be a key challenge to policymakers and regulators (Foresight Mental Capital and Wellbeing Project, 2008) This can be viewed within the context of the wider phenomenon of healthy adults taking drugs for other reasons, such as to enhance mood or sleeping habits. The potential for the development of better treatments for the cognitive symptoms in neuropsychiatric disorders and brain injury means that novel PCEs that are safe and effective have the potential to be of significant benefit to such individuals within society. Yet, enforceable policies concerning the use of PCEs to support fairness, protect individuals from coercion and minimize enhancement-related socioeconomic disparities are critical (Greely et al., 2008). This has also been recognized in the Foresight Mental Capital and Wellbeing Report as 'Novel PCEs may prove of great benefit in the future, particularly given the rapidly developing field of pharmacogenomics and the aging population' (Foresight Mental Capital and Wellbeing Project, 2008). Ultimately, we too advocate a rational approach to the use of PCEs in order to gain maximum benefits with minimum harms to the individual and to society as a whole. The use of PCE is relevant to everyone and particularly to members of the psychopharmacology scientific community. We hope that by raising the neuroethical issues accompanying the scientific findings, and presenting some of the social implications already taking place, the reader will consider these issues.

References

Academy of Medical Sciences (2008) *Brain Science, Addiction and Drugs.* Working group report chaired by Professor Sir Gabriel Horn. Foresight Brain Science, Addiction and Drugs Project. London: Office of Science and Technology.

American Psychiatric Association (2000) *Diagnostic and Statistical Manual of Mental Disorders, IV-Text Revision edn.* American Psychiatric Association, American Psychiatric Association.

Aron AR, Fletcher PC, Bullmore ET, Sahakian BJ, Robbins TW (2003) Stop-signal inhibition disrupted by damage to right inferior frontal gyrus in humans. *Nat Neurosci* 6: 115–116.

Ashcroft RE (2005) Access to essential medicines: a Hobbesian social contract approach. *Develop World Bioeth* 5: 121–141.

Babcock Q, Byrne T (2000) Student perceptions of methylphenidate abuse at a public liberal arts college. *J Am Coll Health* 49: 143–145.

Barkley RA (2006) *Attention-Deficit Hyperactivity Disorder: A Handbook for Diagnosis and Treatment,* 3rd edn. New York: The Guilford Press.

Beddington J, Cooper CL, Field J, et al. (2008) The mental wealth of nations. *Nature* 455: 1057–1060.

Boyd CJ, McCabe SE (2008) Coming to terms with the nonmedical use of prescription medications. *Subst Abuse Treat Prev Policy* 3: 22.

Bright GM (2008) Abuse of medications employed for the treatment of ADHD: results from a large-scale community survey. *Medscape Journal of Medicine* 10: 111.

Burne J (2007) Can taking a pill make you brainy? London: Daily Mail, 64–65.

Califano J (2008) *You've got drugs! V: Prescription drug pushers on the Internet.* New York, Columbia University: The National Center on Addiction and Substance Abuse.

Chamberlain SR, Del Campo N, Dowson J, et al. (2007) Atomoxetine improved response inhibition in adults with attention deficit/hyperactivity disorder. *Biol Psychiat* 62: 977–984.

Chamberlain SR, Hampshire A, Muller U, et al. (2009) Atomoxetine modulates right inferior frontal activation during inhibitory control: a pharmacological functional magnetic resonance imaging study. *Biol Psychiat* 65: 550–555.

Chamberlain SR, Muller U, Blackwell AD, Clark L, Robbins TW, Sahakian BJ (2006) Neurochemical modulation of response inhibition and probabilistic learning in humans. *Science* 311: 861–863.

Chatterjee A (2004) Cosmetic neurology: the controversy over enhancing movement, mentation, and mood. *Neurology* 28: 968–974.

Cools R, Robbins TW (2004) Chemistry of the adaptive mind. *Philosophical Transactions. Series A Mathematical Physical and Engineering Sciences* 362: 2871–2888.

Davidson M, Keefe RS (1995) Cognitive impairment as a target for pharmacological treatment in schizophrenia. *Schizophr Res* 17: 123–129.

Farah MJ (2005) Neuroethics: the practical and the philosophical. *Trends Cog Sci* 9: 34–40.

Farah MJ, Illes J, Cook-Deegan R, et al. (2004) Neurocognitive enhancement: what can we do and what should we do? *Nat Rev Neurosci* 5: 421–425.

Foresight Mental Capital and Wellbeing Project (2008) *Final Project Report.* London: The Government Office for Science.

Fukuyama F (2002) *Our Posthuman Future: Consequences of the Biotechnology Revolution.* USA: Farrar, Straus and Giroux.

Ghosh P (2007) Drugs may boost your brain power. London: BBC News.

Greely H, Sahakian B, Harris J, et al. (2008) Towards responsible use of cognitive-enhancing drugs in the healthy. *Nature* 456: 702–705.

Hampton T (2007) Experts weigh in on promotion, prescription of off-label drugs. *J Am Med Assoc* 297: 683–684.

Hilman CH, Erickson KI, Kramer AF (2008) Be smart, exercise your heart: exercise effects on brain and cognition. *Nat Rev Neurosci* 9: 58–65.

Johnston LD, O'Malley PM, Bachman JG, Schulenberg JE (2006) *Monitoring the Future National Results on Adolescent Drug Use: Overview of Key Findings, 2005.* (NIH Publication No. 06-5882). Bethesda, MD: National Institute on Drug Abuse.

Kempton S, Vance A, Maruff P, Luk E, Costin J, Pantelis C (1999) Executive function and attention deficit hyperactivity disorder: stimulant medication and better executive function performance in children. *Psychol Med* 29: 527–538.

Knapp M, Prince M (2007) *Dementia UK: Summary of key findings.* London, UK: Alzheimer's Society, 1–12.

Lennard N (2009) One in ten takes drugs to study. *Varsity* 693: 1. Available at: http://www.varsity.co.uk/home/.

Lynch G (2004) AMPA receptor modulators as cognitive enhancers. *Curr Opin Pharmacol* 4: 4–11.

Maher B (2008) Poll results: look who's doping. *Nature* 452: 674–675.

Marcus SJ (2004) *Neuroethics: Mapping the Field.* Dana Press, New York, NY.

Mazurov A, Hauser T, Miller CH (2006) Selective alpha7 nicotinic acetylcholine receptor ligands. *Curr Med Chem* 13: 1567–1584.

McCabe SE (2008) Misperceptions of non-medical prescription drug use: a web survey of college students. *Addict Behav* 33: 713–724.

McCabe SE, Boyd CJ (2005) Sources of prescription drugs for illicit use. *Addict Behav* 30: 1342–1350.

McCabe SE, Brower KJ, West BT, Nelson TF, Wechsler H (2007) Trends in non-medical use of anabolic steroids by U.S. college students: results from four national surveys. *Drug Alcohol Depen* 90: 243–251.

McCabe SE, Schulenberg JE, Johnston LD, O'Malley PM, Bachman JG, Kloska DD (2005) Selection and socialization effects of fraternities and sororities on US college student substance use: a multi-cohort national longitudinal study. *Addiction* 100: 512–524.

McCabe SE, Teter CJ, Boyd CJ, Guthrie SK (2004) Prevalence and correlates of illicit methylphenidate use among 8th, 10th, and 12th grade students in the United States, 2001. *J Adolescent Health* 35: 501–504.

McLean A, Dowson J, Toone B, et al. (2004) Characteristic neurocognitive profile associated with adult attention-deficit/hyperactivity disorder. *Psychol Med* 34: 681–92.

Mehta MA, Goodyer IM, Sahakian BJ (2004) Methylphenidate improves working memory and set-shifting in AD/HD: relationships to baseline memory capacity. *J Child Psychol and Psyc* 45:293–305.

Mehta MA, Owen AM, Sahakian BJ, Mavaddat N, Pickard JD, Robbins TW (2000) Methylphenidate enhances working memory by modulating discrete frontal and parietal lobe regions in the human brain. *J Neurosci* 20: RC65.

Meikle J (2002) Scientists wake up to brain stimulant. London: The Guardian.

Minzenberg MJ, Carter CS (2008) Modafinil: a review of neurochemical actions and effects on cognition. *Neuropsychopharmacol* 33: 1477–1502.

Minzenberg MJ, Watrous AJ, Yoon JH, Ursu S, Carter CS (2008) Modafinil shifts human locus coeruleus to low-tonic, high-phasic activity during functional MRI. *Science* 322: 1700–1702.

Morein-Zamir S, Robbins TW, Turner D, and Sahakian, B. J. (2008). State-of-Science Review: SR-E9, Pharmacological Cognitive Enhancement. UK Government Foresight Mental Capital and Mental Wellbeing Project.

Moreno JD (2004) DARPA on your mind. *Cerebrum* 6: 91–99.

Moreno JD (2006) Juicing the brain: research to limit mental fatigue among soldiers may foster controversial ways to enhance any person's brain. *Scientific American Mind* 17: 66–73.

Nature Editorial (2006) Neuroethics needed. *Nature* 441: 907.

Niyadurupola G (2007) *Better Brains. Postnote 285.* London: The Parliamentary Office of Science and Technology.

Owen AM, Downes JJ, Sahakian BJ, Polkey CE, Robbins TW (1990) Planning and spatial working memory following frontal lobe lesions in man. *Neuropsychologia* 28: 1021–1034.

Owen AM, Morris RG, Sahakian BJ, Polkey CE, Robbins TW (1996) Double dissociations of memory and executive functions in working memory tasks following frontal lobe excisions, temporal lobe excisions or amygdalohippocampectomy in man. *Brain* 119: 1597–1615.

Pelham WE, Foster EM, Robb JA (2007) The economic impact of attention-deficit/hyperactivity disorder in children and adolescents. *J Pediatr Psychol* 32: 711–727.

Radley DC, Finkelstein SN, Stafford RS (2006) Off-label prescribing among office-based physicians. *Arch Int Med* 166: 1021–1026.

Ramos BP, Arnsten AF (2007) Adrenergic pharmacology and cognition: focus on the prefrontal cortex. *Pharmacol Therapeut* 113: 523–536.

Roiser JP, Cook LJ, Cooper JD, Rubinsztein DC, Sahakian BJ (2005) Association of a functional polymorphism in the serotonin transporter gene with abnormal emotional processing in ecstasy users. *Am J Psychia* 162: 609–612.

Sahakian B, Morein-Zamir S (2007) Professor's little helper. *Nature* 450: 1157–1159.

Sahakian B, Morein-Zamir S (2009) Neuroscientists need neuroethics teaching. *Science* 325(5937): 147.

Stahl SM (2008) *Stahl's Essential Psychopharmacology*, 3rd edn. Cambridge: Cambridge University Press.

Swanson JM, Elliott GR, Greenhill LL, et al. (2007) Effects of stimulant medication on growth rates across 3 years in the MTA follow-up. *J Am Acad Child Adolesce Psychiatry* 46: 1015–1027.

Tannock R, Schachar R, Logan GD (1995) Methylphenidate and cognitive flexibility: dissociated dose effects in hyperactive children. *J Abnorm Child Psych* 23: 235–266.

Talbot M (2009) Brain gain: the underground world of "neuroenhancing" drugs. New York: The New Yorker.

Teter CJ, McCabe SE, Cranford JA, Boyd CJ, Guthrie SK (2005) Prevalence and motives for illicit use of prescription stimulants in an undergraduate student sample. *J Am Coll Health* 53: 253–262.

Teter CJ, McCabe SE, LaGrange K, Cranford JA, Boyd CJ (2006) Illicit use of specific prescription stimulants among college students: prevalence, motives, and routes of administration. *Pharmacotherapy* 26: 1501–1510.

The President's Council on Bioethics (2003) Beyond Therapy: Biotechnology and the Pursuit of Happiness. Washington, D.C, Washington, D.C. Available at: http://www.bioethics.gov/reports/beyondtherapy/index.html.

Turner DC, Blackwell AD, Dowson JH, McLean A, Sahakian BJ (2005) Neurocognitive effects of methylphenidate in adult attention-deficit/hyperactivity disorder. *Psychopharmacology* 178: 286–295.

Turner DC, Clark L, Dowson J, Robbins TW, Sahakian BJ (2004) Modafinil improves cognition and response inhibition in adult attention-deficit/hyperactivity disorder. *Biol Psychia* 55: 1031–1040.

Turner DC, Robbins TW, Clark L, Aron AR, Dowson J, Sahakian BJ (2003) Cognitive enhancing effects of modafinil in healthy volunteers. *Psychopharmacology* 165: 260–269.

Turner DC, Sahakian BJ (2006) Neuroethics of cognitive enhancement. *BioSocieties* 1: 113–123.

Volkow ND, Fowler JS, Logan J, et al. (2009) Effects of modafinil on dopamine and dopamine transporters in the male human brain: clinical implications. *J Am Med Assoc* 301: 1148–1154.

Wang GJ, Volkow ND, Fowler JS, et al. (1999) Reproducibility of repeated measures of endogenous dopamine competition with [11C]raclopride in the human brain in response to methylphenidate. *J Nucl Med* 40: 1285–1291.

Willis SL, Tennstedt SL, Marsiske M, et al. (2006) Long-term effects of cognitive training on everyday functional outcomes in older adults. *J Am Med Assoc* 296: 2805–2814.

Wolpe PR (2002) Treatment, enhancement, and the ethics of neurotherapeutics. *Brain Cognition* 50: 387–395.

World Health Organization (2008) Available at: http://www.who.int/ mental_health/ management/schizophrenia/en/.

Wu EQ, Birnbaum HG, Shi L, et al. (2005) The economic burden of schizophrenia in the United States in 2002. *J Clin Psych* 66: 1122–1129.

Zito JM, Derivan AT, Kratochvil CJ, Safer DJ, Fegert JM, Greenhill LL (2008) Off-label psychopharmacologic prescribing for children: history supports close clinical monitoring. *Child and Adolescent Psychiatry and Mental Health* 2: 24.

Helia Garrido Hull

 **NO**

Regression by Progression: Unleveling the Classroom Playing Field Through Cosmetic Neurology

"[H]ow much happier that man is who believes his native town to be the world, than he who aspires to become greater than his nature will allow."[1]

Introduction

In the novel *Frankenstein,* Victor Frankenstein exceeds the natural order of reality by creating life and learns to regret his desire to become something greater than his own nature allowed. Although the story is fiction, for many, the desire to exceed their own physical, emotional, or intellectual limitations is very real. Today, medical advances intended to improve the quality of life for those suffering from disease, disorders, or disabilities are routinely employed by healthy individuals to enhance their natural abilities. The illicit use of prescription drugs for non-therapeutic purposes has sparked an ethical debate within the academic and medical communities regarding the propriety of enhancing performance through cosmetic neurology.[2] For some, using prescription drugs for non-therapeutic use is both morally wrong and socially unjustified. As one author opined, "the original purpose of medicine is to heal the sick, not turn healthy people into gods."[3] For others, using prescription drugs to increase attention span, improve learning, or to augment productivity is both morally acceptable and culturally desirable.[4] Nowhere is this more evident than on high school and college campuses throughout the United States, where healthy, intelligent students are increasingly using controlled drugs without prescriptions to enhance academic performance. Lost in this debate, however, is the significant negative impact that illicit use of certain prescription drugs by healthy individuals has on those individuals for whom the drugs were originally intended.

High school and college students across the country are increasingly using methylphenidate and amphetamines to increase cognition, improve grades, and gain a competitive edge over their classmates; they also use these substances recreationally. Both stimulant drugs are prescribed to treat individuals suffering from Attention Deficit Hyperactivity Disorder (ADHD),

Hull, Helia Garrido. From *University of Hawaii Law Review*, vol. 33, 2010, pp. 193–222. Copyright © 2010 by University of Hawaii Law Review. Reprinted by permission.

a psychological disorder that places millions of students at a competitive disadvantage within the learning environment.[5] Due to their high potential for abuse, methylphenidate and amphetamines are listed as controlled substances under U.S. law; therefore, they can only be used legally with a prescription.[6] The non-medical use of either stimulant is a crime punishable by imprisonment and the imposition of substantial monetary fines, but the lack of enforcement coupled with moral acceptance of such use among students has led to an increase in illicit use of each stimulant.[7]

The use of methylphenidate and amphetamines by students without ADHD is both dangerous to the user and unfair to those individuals who require the stimulants to compete with other students in the classroom. When healthy individuals utilize stimulants to enhance their natural cognitive abilities, the gap that use of the medicine was intended to close between students with and without ADHD reemerges. As a result, the classroom playing field once again becomes unlevel, placing certain individuals at a competitive disadvantage while destroying decades of legal precedent intended to protect those individuals from such an imbalance.

This article addresses the increasing use of methylphenidate and amphetamines by high school and college students and argues that states have a responsibility to prevent the uncontrolled, non-therapeutic, and injury-causing use of stimulants by students under their supervision and to protect the rights of individuals with ADHD. [The second section] provides a brief overview of ADHD, the dangers associated with the use of methylphenidate and amphetamines to treat the disorder, and the Food and Drug Administration's response to risks posed by the use of each drug. [The third section] explores the increasing non-medical use of methylphenidate and amphetamines by students across the United States and considers the short-term and long-term implications of such use. [The fourth section] argues that the current regulatory structure is inadequate and negatively impacts students with legitimate medical needs by un-leveling the playing field created by existing laws. [The fifth section] presents recommendations to level the academic playing field.

ADHD: Diagnosis, Regulation, and Risk

Student misconduct in the classroom severely constrains the ability of schools to effectively educate students and has become a common reason for referring students to mental health services.[8] Often, student misconduct is linked to inattention, hyperactivity, or impulsivity that are the hallmarks of ADHD.[9] Once a student is diagnosed with ADHD, teaching strategies, unique learning environments, and adaptive or assistive technologies can be employed to prevent classroom disruptions and assist students with ADHD to compete on a level playing field with their fellow students.[10]

ADHD

ADHD is the current diagnostic label for a developmental disorder that has been known over the last century as "brain-damaged syndrome," "minimal brain dysfunction (MBD)," "hyperkinetic impulsive disorder," or "attention deficit disorder (ADD)."[11] ADHD affects between five to eight percent of school-age children and is the most common reason for referral of children to mental health services.[12] Individuals with ADHD often experience substantial impairment in family, social, and educational functioning.[13] In a classroom environment, individuals with ADHD may have difficulty controlling their behavior and staying focused and may experience periods of hyperactivity.[14] As a result, otherwise simple classroom tasks can become extremely challenging.[15] ADHD symptoms first appear between the ages of three and six, but no single test has proven effective at identifying the disorder.[16] Typically, individuals undergo a battery of tests by physicians and mental health specialists to rule out other possibilities for the symptoms exhibited.[17] Although it is normal for young children to experience periods of inattention, hyperactivity, or impulsivity, children with ADHD exhibit these behaviors more frequently and with greater severity.[18] Thus, ADHD is typically determined upon proof that the child has exhibited such symptoms for at least six months at a degree greater than that expected from children of similar age.[19] Although treatment may temporarily relieve many of the disorder's symptoms to help individuals lead productive lives, no cure exists.[20] ADHD can continue into adulthood.[21] Approximately two to four percent of adults have ADHD.[22] Although diagnostic criteria exist for children, there are currently no age-appropriate diagnostic criteria for adults.[23] Many adult patients are self-referred.[24] Because it is difficult for doctors to accurately diagnose ADHD even in adults, students who understand the testing protocol can easily manipulate the process to obtain a prescription.[25]

Once diagnosed, individuals with ADHD may be treated with one of a number of psychoactive stimulants. However, only two substances are widely utilized by American physicians to treat children: methylphenidate and amphetamines.[26] Stimulants work by increasing dopamine levels in the brain, a chemical associated with pleasure, movement, and attention.[27] These stimulants pass through the blood-brain barrier to affect brain function that manifests in changes in perception, mood, consciousness cognition, and behavior.[28] For individuals with ADHD, the stimulants act to reduce hyperactivity and impulsivity and to improve the individual's ability to focus, work, and learn.[29] Because these medications may pose significant dangers to individuals with cardiovascular (heart and blood) or psychiatric problems, however, physicians should examine individuals diagnosed with ADHD to assess their cardiovascular and psychiatric health and warn them of the dangers associated with using the particular drug.[30]

The use of stimulants has been shown to improve attention span, concentration, compliance, handwriting, fine motor skills, and interactions with other students.[31] Although methylphenidate and amphetamines are effective at treating the symptoms of ADHD, their ability to bring about short-term beneficial changes in consciousness and mood creates a high potential for abuse that can lead to addiction.[32] Congress has addressed this problem by placing strict controls on these and other psychoactive drugs.[33]

Regulation of Psychoactive Drugs

The United Nations Convention on Psychotropic Substances (UNCPS) was signed by the United States on February 21, 1971 and ratified on April 16, 1980. The goal of the Convention is to encourage stricter regulation over the illegal importation, manufacture, distribution, possession, and improper use of controlled substances.[34] The U.S. Drug Enforcement Agency (DEA) was designated as the authority responsible for meeting the United States' obligations under the treaty.[35] However, because the Convention is not self-executing, implementation of its terms required additional action by Congress. Recognizing the "substantial and detrimental effect on the health and general welfare of the American people" caused by such activities, Congress enacted the Controlled Substances Act (CSA) to implement the UNCPS.[36] The Act created five Schedules (classifications) that categorize drugs based on multiple factors including the drug's medical utility and its risk of harm. Schedule I drugs include drugs that have the highest potential for abuse, offer no recognized medical utility, and cannot be used safely.[37] Examples include LSD, PCP, heroin, marijuana, and crack cocaine. Schedule II includes drugs that have a high potential for abuse, the use of which may lead to severe psychological or physical dependence.[38] However, Schedule II drugs do have currently accepted medical use as part of treatment plans.[39] Examples include morphine, cocaine, oxycodone, methylphenidate, and amphetamine mixtures.[40] Drugs listed on Schedules III, IV, and V have decreasing potential for abuse, medical utility, and risk of physical dependence or psychological dependence relative to the drugs and other substances in higher Schedules.[41] The DEA is charged with enforcing the CSA, but the Food and Drug Administration (FDA) also plays a critical role as the primary authority for regulating controlled drugs that are prescribed for therapeutic use.[42]

The CSA created penalties for the unlawful manufacturing, distribution, and dispensing of controlled substances, with penalties that vary based on several factors, including the Schedule of the substance. In 1988, Congress passed the Anti-Drug Abuse Act (ADAA), which imposes penalties on both the seller and the purchaser of the drug.[43] Unless otherwise authorized by law, it is unlawful to knowingly or intentionally distribute a controlled substance.[44] The penalty for such action is imprisonment for up to one year, a minimum fine of $1000, or both.[45] If the distribution is to someone under twenty-one years of age, or occurs within 1000 feet of a private or public school, college, or university, the penalty is twice the maximum punishment normally authorized.[46] It is also unlawful for any person to knowingly or intentionally possess a controlled substance without a valid prescription for the substance.[47] Any individual found to illegally possess such drugs may be imprisoned for up to one year and shall be fined a minimum of $1000.[48] The penalty for such distribution or possession is particularly harsh for students. In addition to the criminal penalties that may be imposed, distributors of controlled substances are ineligible to receive federal benefits for up to five years and possessors are ineligible to receive these benefits for up to one year.[49] This includes student loans and grants.[50] Despite these substantial penalties, students across the country continue to illegally use or distribute methylphenidate and amphetamines. In many cases, individuals who use the drugs illegally are unaware of the risks posed by such use.

Methylphenidate

Methylphenidate shares many of the pharmacological effects of amphetamine, methamphetamine, and cocaine.[51] It is commonly known by a variety of names, including "Diet Coke," "Kiddie Cocaine," "Vitamin R," "Poor Man's Cocaine," "Skittles," and "Smarties."[52] The names reflect the effects that users experience. Both animal and human studies comparing the effects of cocaine with that of methylphenidate showed that subjects could not tell the difference because each produced the same physiologic effects.[53] Methylphenidate acts on the central nervous system (CNS) to reduce symptoms of ADHD by "blocking the neuronal dopamine transporter, and to a lesser extent, norepinephrine."[54] Use of methylphenidate produces "dose-related increases in blood pressure, heart rate, respiration and body temperature, appetite suppression and increased alertness."[55] Chronic use can inhibit growth and result in weight loss.[56] If abused, methylphenidate may cause "excessive CNS stimulation, euphoria, nervousness, irritability," agitation, psychotic episodes, violent behavior, and severe psychological dependence.[57]

Methylphenidate is most commonly marketed under the brand name Ritalin, and its beneficial effects on individuals with ADHD are well documented.[58] The drug's success led to its widespread administration beginning in the 1990s. Between 1990 and 2000, the production of Ritalin increased nearly 500 percent.[59] Today, Ritalin is the most widely prescribed Schedule II stimulant to treat ADHD.[60] According to the United Nations, the United States produces and consumes approximately 75 percent of the world's Ritalin.[61] Although these drugs have helped many individuals with ADHD, their use has become so widespread that questions exist as to whether the drug has been over-prescribed and over-used.[62]

Amphetamines

Amphetamines are potent stimulants that affect the CNS by increasing levels of dopamine and norepinephrine in the brain to produce increased alertness and focus, while decreasing fatigue and hunger.[63] Its actions resemble those of adrenaline, the body's fight or flight hormone.[64] The drug was widely used by soldiers in World War II to combat fatigue and increase alertness on the battlefield. After the war, easy access for the general public led to increased use that culminated in widespread abuse of the drug in the 1960s.[65] In 1971, Congress listed the drug as a Schedule II drug based on its potential for abuse, but it has reemerged as the drug of choice for many students.[66] One of the most common amphetamines used to treat ADHD is marketed under the trade name of Adderall.[67]

Amphetamines act on the brain to "increase alertness, reduce fatigue, heighten concentration, decrease appetite, and enhance physical performance."[68] They may produce a feeling of well-being, euphoria, and loss of inhibitions.[69]

Misuse may result in "seizures, hypertension, tachycardia, hyperthermia, psychosis, hallucinosis, stroke, and fatality."[70]

For individuals with cardiovascular risk factors, amphetamine use is particularly dangerous.[71] Blood pressure may elevate to a point where blood vessels in the brain rupture and cause a stroke.[72] Some individuals, even young athletes, have suffered heart attacks as a result of amphetamine use.[73] In other cases, users may become "extremely paranoid, violent, and out of control."[74] In the United States, Adderall use continues to climb. Between 1990 and 2000, the production for Adderall increased by 2000 percent.[75]

FDA Response to Risk of Methylphenidate and Amphetamine Misuse

In 2005, Canada pulled Adderall off the market, citing reports linking it to twenty deaths between 1999 and 2003.[76] In that same period, twenty-five people died suddenly in the United States and fifty-four others suffered serious, unexplained heart problems while taking ADHD stimulants.[77] The FDA responded by announcing that it found no need to make immediate changes to the marketing or labeling of drugs used to treat ADHD.[78] The FDA noted that most of the victims had existing heart defects that increased the risk for sudden death.[79] It also noted that the overall risk associated with Adderall was only slightly higher than that associated with methylphenidate products used to treat ADHD.[80]

The FDA did acknowledge, however, that use of stimulants presents the potential for rare fatal and nonfatal cardiovascular events.[81] In 2006, the FDA's Drug Safety and Risk Management Advisory Committee voted unanimously to recommend the distribution of Medical Guides to warn of potential cardiovascular risks associated with using ADHD stimulants.[82] The Committee also recommended requiring black box warnings—the strongest warning required by the FDA—to alert users of the significant cardiovascular risks associated with such use.[83] The Committee's decision was based on the proven relationship between elevated blood pressure and cardiovascular risk in adults, and the fact that the number of prescriptions for ADHD increased significantly over the previous fifteen years, including in the adult population.[84] Even those who disagreed with the recommendation noted the need for a broader, more effective means of communicating these risks to patients.[85]

Later that year, the FDA's Pediatric Advisory Committee recommended the implementation of stronger warnings regarding the use of the stimulants in patients with underlying structural cardiovascular defects or cardiomyopathies;[86] however, the Pediatric Advisory Committee opposed requiring a black box warning to the labeling of stimulants.[87] They recommended that the FDA modify information in other sections of the product labeling to address the potential harms.[88] The FDA adopted that recommendation.[89] Product labeling on ADHD stimulants now caution on:

> (1) use in patients with structural cardiac abnormalities or other serious heart problems; (2) the potential for increasing blood pressure and

exacerbating preexisting conditions such as hypertension, heart failure, recent myocardial infarction, or ventricular arrhythmia; (3) the need to conduct a careful history (including assessment for a family history of sudden death or ventricular arrhythmia); (4) a physical examination to assess for the presence of cardiac disease, and further cardiac evaluation if warranted; (5) the potential for causing or exacerbating psychotic, manic, or "aggressive" symptoms or seizures; (6) the potential for growth suppression in continuously medicated youth; and (7) the potential for visual disturbances.[90]

The FDA also directed manufacturers of all drug products approved for the treatment of ADHD to develop Patient Medication Guides to alert patients to potential cardiovascular risks and risks of adverse psychiatric symptoms associated with the use of stimulants.[91] The FDA, however, refused to require pharmaceutical companies to place black box warnings on these drugs as it had done for other dangerous drugs used to treat children and adolescents for depression.[92] Patients, families, and caregivers receive the guides when a medicine is dispensed.[93] The problem with this approach is that its efficacy is based on the assumption that information about the drug's risks is effectively conveyed to the user.

A black box warning is the strongest warning required by the FDA, and it is typically required when (1) "[t]here is an adverse reaction so serious in proportion to the potential benefit from the drug that it is essential that it be considered in assessing the risks and benefits of using a drug," (2) "[t]here is a serious adverse reaction that can be prevented or reduced in frequency or severity by appropriate use of the drug," or (3) where the FDA has approved the drug with restrictions to assure safe use.[94] Although black box warnings are typically mandated based on observed adverse reactions, the FDA has acknowledged that "there are instances when a boxed warning based on an expected adverse reaction would be appropriate."[95]

The FDA's failure to require black box warnings on ADHD stimulants is problematic for several reasons. First, stimulant misuse has increased among school-aged children, and studies show that an increasing number of students obtain the drugs illegally from a friend or acquaintance with a legal prescription.[96] Many students who use the drugs illegally are unaware of the risks associated with taking the drugs.[97] This strongly suggests that the dangers associated with sharing these drugs with others is not being effectively conveyed to those who have a prescription for the drug. Having a black box warning posted on the prescription vial could increase the likelihood that legal users will warn the illegal user of potential serious side effects of non-therapeutic use.

Second, statistically significant increases in heart rate and blood pressure occur in adults treated with stimulant use, and blood pressure is strongly and directly correlated with vascular and overall mortality in adults.[98] Placing a black box warning on the prescription vial could increase awareness of the risks associated with use by individuals with heart conditions and increase the chance that those at serious risk are informed of the dangers. Given the increased distribution of stimulants and the resultant excess supply of the drugs that can be diverted to illegal use, it would be prudent to place additional warnings on stimulants. As the United States becomes more interested in the potential for cognitive enhancement, there is a growing urgency to increase awareness of the harms of illicit stimulant use.

The Decade of the Brain: Better Learning Through Chemistry

Congress declared the 1990s as the "Decade of the Brain" in an effort to increase the scientific study of debilitating neural diseases and conditions that plagued society.[99] The declaration stimulated research that led to breakthroughs in fundamental knowledge on how to treat debilitating neurological disorders and neuropsychiatric diseases.[100] For some, such breakthroughs encouraged the increased acceptance of science as a means to improve the human condition and the expectation that treatments for currently incurable diseases would become available.[101] Moreover, once those cures become available, some individuals with those disorders will seek to do what they wish with their body free from government interference.[102] For others, however, artificial enhancement of humanity through application of human invention is both morally wrong and spiritually corrupt[103] The argument cuts across science, religion and law with no clear answers, and the classroom has emerged as the epicenter of the debate. As the next section reveals, an increasing number of students are turning to stimulants to gain a competitive edge on peers in the classroom.

Illicit Stimulant Use by Students

The United States continues to be the world's largest market for illicit drugs and a major destination of illicit drug consignments.[104] In 2008, an estimated 35.5 million persons in the United States, or 14.2 percent of the population aged twelve or older, reported the use of illicit drugs at one point in their lives.[105] Of these, an estimated 22.2 million persons were classified with substance dependence or abuse.[106] That number is likely to increase, as more than 20 million Americans acknowledged being drug users in 2008.[107] Perhaps more troubling is the increase in abuse of prescription drugs.

In 2008, the number of individuals who abused prescription drugs in the United States exceeded the total number of individuals who abused cocaine, heroin, hallucinogens, and inhalants.[108] Prescription drug abuse now ranks second only to cannabis abuse.[109] Young adults aged eighteen to twenty-five years exhibited twice the level of prescription drug abuse than youth aged twelve to seventeen years, and more than triple the level of abuse among adults aged twenty-six years and older.[110] This trend is likely to continue in the United States because individuals are increasingly turning to prescription drugs to fulfill a need. In 2008, 2.5 million individuals abused prescription drugs for the first time.[111] This is 300,000 more than the number of first-time cannabis users.[112] Of those individuals who used illicit drugs for the first time in 2008, nearly one third (29.6 percent) initiated their use with psychotherapeutics, including pain relievers, tranquilizers, stimulants, and sedatives.[113] Of these, approximately 600,000 individuals initiated their illicit drug use through use of prescription stimulants.[114] More than half of these individuals acknowledged that they received the prescription drugs from friends or relatives for free.[115] Illicit stimulant use begins as early as middle school, extends through high school and college, and continues into the workforce.

Illicit Stimulant Use in Middle School and High School

The misuse and abuse of stimulants used to treat ADHD is common among youth. For example, one study reported that 23.3 percent of middle and high school students taking prescribed stimulants had been solicited to give, sell, or trade their medication to friends.[116] The rate increased as the student moved from middle school to high school.[117] A Wisconsin study reported that of 161 elementary and high school students prescribed the stimulant methylphenidate, 16 percent had been asked to give or sell their medications to others.[118] Another study from Canada reported that of a random sample of middle and high school students who were using legally prescribed stimulants, 14.7 percent gave their medications to others, 7.3 percent sold their medication to others, and 4.3 percent had their medications stolen by others.[119] This early use continues in college.

Illicit Stimulant Use in Post-Secondary Education

In 2008, college-aged students (eighteen to twenty-five years old) had the highest rate (19.6 percent) of illicit drug use among all age groups.[120] In this age group, the use of psychotherapeutics (5.9 percent) was almost four times greater than the use of cocaine (1.5 percent).[121] This data shows that illicit use of prescription stimulants has become a major problem in post-secondary education.[122] In a recent study of 1811 undergraduate students at a large public university, thirty-four of the students questioned admitted to the illegal use of ADHD stimulants.[123] Most of the students questioned acknowledged that they used the drugs during periods of high academic stress because the stimulants increased reading comprehension, interest, cognition, and memory.[124] Furthermore, most students acknowledged that they possessed little knowledge of the drug or its potential to cause harm.[125] In another study of 1550 college students, of those responding who were not diagnosed with ADHD, almost half (43 percent) reported illegally using prescription stimulants.[126] Approximately 16 percent to 29 percent of students with ADHD stimulant prescriptions were asked to give, sell, or trade their medications.[127] Perhaps more troubling, students have acknowledged they find it easy to obtain prescription drugs on campus and that they do not perceive any stigma attached to their use.[128] Rather, many students believe such use is physically harmless, morally acceptable, and even a necessary predicate to success.[129] This perspective has led to an increased illicit use of stimulants in the workforce.

Illicit Stimulant Use in the Workplace

The abuse of drugs has also filtered over into the workforce. In 2008, of the 17.8 million illicit drug users aged eighteen or older, 12.9 million (72.7 percent) were employed either full- or part-time.[130] Today, doctors, lawyers, and other professionals use stimulants such as Ritalin and Adderall to compete in increasingly stressful, competitive work environments.[131] Recent reports suggest the declining economy may be a key factor behind the increasing number of individuals using these inexpensive stimulants.[132]

While stimulants like Ritalin and Adderall increase the user's attention and productivity, they may have the unwelcome effect of sapping the person's creativity. Memory, attention, and creativity represent three different cognitive domains that are interconnected and contribute to the "mental performance" of an individual.[133] As one psychologist noted, individuals taking Ritalin act "like a horse with blinders, plodding along . . . moving forward, getting things done, but . . . less open to inspiration."[134] Many entrepreneurs, performers, politicians, and communicators alike attribute their success to untreated ADHD.[135] Some argue that living with untreated ADHD allows them to think unconventionally and believe that ADHD medications dampen inspiration, leaving them to think like everyone else.[136] This view may have some merit, given that some of the greatest figures in history—including Albert Einstein, Thomas Edison, Salvador Dali, and Winston Churchill—exhibited classic ADHD traits, but were never treated for the disorder.[137]

Although no long-term career studies exist to determine whether stimulants actually dampen creativity and imagination, at least one study has found anecdotal evidence that taking Ritalin renders some children less interested in pursuing creative opportunities.[138] Psychologists have acknowledged that there may be a trade-off between the ability to focus and creativity for individuals using ADHD drugs, where individuals capable of focusing on a single thing while filtering out distractions may be less creative.[139] As Martha Farah, a psychologist and director of the University of Pennsylvania's Center for Cognitive Neuroscience opined, "I'm a little concerned that we could be raising a generation of very focused accountants."[140] Farah, however, also believes cosmetic neurology will be as commonplace as cosmetic surgery, as it may lead to improvements in the world.[141] As another author indicates, despite increased use of stimulants by academics, "so far no one is demanding that asterisks be attached to Nobels, Pulitzers or Lasker awards" like those associated with the possible enhanced performances of professional athletes.[142] The apparent acceptance of cognitive enhancement by professionals in the workplace has raised a number of ethical dilemmas, the answers to which have the potential to change what it means to be successful in or out of the classroom.

The Ethics of Brain Enhancement

The use of ADHD stimulants is just the beginning. Today, scientists are actively investigating memory enhancement drugs to help millions of baby boomers suffering from age-related memory loss. If such a "Viagra for the brain" is discovered, how should it be used?[143] Should it be administered, for example, to the elderly population if it improves their quality of life? No consensus likely exists on this question, given the divergent views on the use of brain enhancers. An affirmative answer would generate important questions and challenge notions about human meaning and its limitations. A negative answer would generate equally important questions about the role of medicine to humanity and challenge notions about the purpose of human intellect. From a purely scientific viewpoint, it makes little sense to wait patiently for evolution to improve brain function. Human intellect has evolved to the point at which it is now capable of creating technology that increases brain capacity.[144] Arguably, using brain enhancement technology to improve the quality of life of modern-day man is no different than the use of rudimentary stone tools by early humans 2.6 million years ago.[145] Such tools were the product of human intellect and dramatically improved early man's quality of life, allowing individuals to perform activities the human body was not equipped to perform.[146] For some, the development of simple tools parallels the development of brain enhancing drugs and represents another step in the evolutionary process that should be embraced. For others, however, the use of technology to enhance natural abilities raises profound questions about the moral status of nature and the proper stance of human beings toward the natural world.[147] Thus, the fundamental question is not whether improvement is possible, but whether humans should aspire to improve their natural state at all.[148]

Much of the debate has focused on the equality of access to enhancers. In 2007, for example, the British Medical Association argued for the equal access to brain enhancement drugs.[149] The authors of that paper acknowledged that equality of opportunity is an explicit goal of the educational system, and requires that individuals are given "the best chance of achieving their full potential and of competing on equal terms with their peers."[150] The best way to achieve this goal, according to the authors, is through selective use of neuroenhancers among individuals with lower intellectual capacity or those who have deprived backgrounds.[151] However, this argument misses the larger problem. From a legal and societal perspective, the question should be whether the use of such brain enhancement drugs by healthy individuals to increase normal abilities is consistent with the goal of leveling the playing field so that *all* students, including those suffering from ADHD, have an equal opportunity to receive an appropriate education.

Unleveling the Playing Field Through Cognitive Enhancement

In 1970, U.S. public schools educated only one in five children with disabilities.[152] In many states, it was illegal for any deaf, blind, emotionally disturbed, or mentally retarded individual to attend public school.[153] That changed after two landmark decisions. In *Pennsylvania Association for Retarded Children v. Commonwealth of Pennsylvania (PARC)*,[154] plaintiffs challenged the constitutionality of state laws that denied mentally retarded children access to a free public education because of their disabilities. *PARC* ended in a consent decree that enjoined the state from denying disabled individuals "access to a free public program of public education and training."[155] In *Mills v. Board of Education of the District of Columbia*,[156] seven children labeled by school personnel as having behavioral problems or mental retardation, or as emotionally disturbed or hyperactive, were denied admission to public school or excluded after admission with no provision for an alternative educational placement or review.[157] The court, relying on a Supreme Court mandate that states provide public education on equal terms, held that the state must provide a free public education to the students.[158]

PARC and *Mills* established that the Equal Protection Clause of the Fourteenth Amendment to the United States Constitution guarantees every child with a disability the right to appropriate public education. In 1975, Congress enacted the Education for All Handicapped Children Act (EHA), to help states protect the educational rights and meet the needs of students with disabilities.[159] The EHA is now codified as the Individuals with Disabilities Education Act (IDEA).[160]

In promulgating the EHA, Congress found that state and local agencies have a responsibility to provide education for all disabled students.[161] Congress also found it in the country's interest for the federal government to assist state and local efforts to provide education for all disabled individuals.[162] The EHA codified existing law by requiring states to provide access for every disabled individual to a Free Appropriate Public Education (FAPE).[163] To be eligible for federal financial assistance under the EHA, states must develop and implement policies assuring access to a FAPE for all children with disabilities.[164] Congress expressly intended that states provide a *full* educational opportunity to ensure that disabled individuals between the ages of three and twenty-one have equal opportunities in the learning environment.[165] Today, challenges to these mandates are brought under the IDEA.

Under the IDEA, a child is considered disabled if that child suffers from "other health impairments . . . [and] by reason thereof, needs special education and related services."[166] Implementing regulations promulgated by the U.S. Department of Education provide:

> *Other health impairment* means having limited strength, vitality, or alertness, including a heightened alertness to environmental stimuli, that results in limited alertness with respect to the educational environment, that
>
> (i) [i]s due to chronic or acute health problems such as . . . attention deficit disorder or attention deficit hyperactivity disorder . . . and
>
> (ii) [a]dversely affects a child's educational performance.[167]

Once a child is evaluated and determined to be learning disabled under the IDEA, states are required to ensure that an individualized education program (IEP) is developed for the student.[168] Academic success is an important factor in determining whether an IEP is reasonably calculated to provide educational benefits.[169] The IEP considers, for example, accommodations provided to the student to help him attain identified academic goals in a regular classroom.[170] Those goals are measured through classroom performance and by state administered standardized test results.[171] Congress added procedural safeguards that permit re-evaluation of state plans to measure their effectiveness in providing a free and appropriate education to all disabled individuals.[172] The Act requires the state or Secretary of Interior to conduct studies, investigations, and evaluations that are necessary to ensure the effective implementation of the Act.[173] Collectively, these provisions were intended to ensure that disabled individuals have a fair chance to compete academically with individuals who do not suffer from a disability.

Studies have demonstrated that the Intelligent Quotients (IQ) of individuals with ADHD are normally distributed and that the academic deficits of ADHD may be a consequence of it rather than a core feature.[174] This suggests that students with ADHD are just as smart and capable as their peers but are hindered by their disorder. Prescription stimulants, therefore, play a critical role in maintaining equality of opportunity. Advances in cognitive neurology, however, threaten to turn back the hands of time and once again place disabled students at a competitive disadvantage in the classroom. The non-therapeutic use of stimulant drugs designed to help disabled individuals compete in the classroom is inconsistent with United States disability policy and must be prevented. Efforts to prevent illicit use in post-secondary education have largely failed; the legal and financial obligations imposed on states related to primary and secondary education, however, offer an effective means to address the problem.

Analysis and Recommendations

The misuse of stimulant drugs is frequently a prelude to chronic abuse or drug dependence.[175] The diversion of prescription drugs for non-therapeutic use begins as early as middle school and continues into high school, college, and the workplace.[176] States have diminishing levels of responsibility and control over students as they progress from primary and secondary education to post-secondary education and into the workforce.[177] As such, states should act early to prevent the illicit drug abuse.

Re-Evaluate Success in the Classroom Under IDEA

Congress exercised its authority under the Spending Clause of the Constitution to enact the IDEA with the express goal of providing a free and appropriate public education to students who are disadvantaged because of a disability.[178] In 2010, the federal government authorized almost $24 billion in funding for the IDEA.[179] To receive federal funds under the IDEA, a state must comply with the extensive goals and procedures set forth in the Act as they apply to state and local educational agencies that accept funds for K-12 programs.[180] Because the IDEA is an entitlement statute, school districts must identify children with disabilities and provide a free and appropriate public education.[181] Unlike other federal disability laws that are designed to ensure equality of access for disabled individuals at all levels, the IDEA was intended to ensure that students are successful in the K-12 system.[182] That success is evaluated in large part on student performance in the classroom and on state-administered standardized tests, where a student's achievement is reflected in relation to how well that student performs relative to other students taking the same test.[183] When healthy individuals use performance enhancing stimulant drugs to perform well on tests, the value of the testing protocol is significantly diminished and test scores may not accurately reflect student achievement.

For many students with debilitating mental or physical disabilities, the IDEA provides help through the provision of educational plans that help modify personal behavior and other aspects of the classroom environment. For students with ADHD, however, the IDEA can do more. Individuals with ADHD are as intelligent as individuals without ADHD, but they require assistance to be successful in the classroom. Like many of their non-disabled peers, students with ADHD are fully capable of performing well in post-secondary education. In fact, individuals with ADHD often move well beyond the basic goals of the IDEA to lead very productive lives. In many ways, the success of students with ADHD reflects the underlying goal of United States disability policy—equality of opportunity through accommodation. Yet, absent change, existing law will act to set back decades of progress in the field of disability law. States must be required to take action to prevent healthy students from using performance enhancing drugs that provide a competitive advantage over individuals with ADHD on standardized tests.

While the IDEA currently does not require states to provide services that maximize each child's potential, it does require states to level the playing field by providing services that are appropriate to ensure the success of the student. For standardized tests, the appropriate environment is one that provides an otherwise capable student with ADHD to compete fairly with students who do not have ADHD. Absent this procedural safeguard, the test scores are rendered meaningless and cannot accurately reflect student progress as required under the IDEA.

In enacting the IDEA, Congress expressly provided for the re-evaluation of state plans to measure their effectiveness in providing appropriate education to all disabled individuals.[184] Given the increasing illicit use of performance enhancing drugs by healthy middle and high school-aged students, the effective implementation of the Act is at risk. As part of any state education plan approved for funding under the IDEA, the state should be required to take appropriate measures to ensure that illicit drug use by healthy students does not detrimentally impact the ability of disabled students to compete in the classroom or on state-administered standardized tests.

Implement Social Norm Educational Programs

Many students who misuse drugs do so because they are unaware of the medical, psychological, and legal consequences of illicit drug use and abuse.[185] One of the most effective ways to address the problem of illicit drug use by students is through targeted educational campaigns that address misconceptions of such use.[186] Through early state-wide intervention, states can counter the potential adverse effects of illicit drug use while promoting student health and protecting the rights of disabled individuals. To be effective, any educational campaign must recognize that illicit stimulant use has become an accepted part of the academic experience for many students.[187] Unlike other forms of drug use, there is little stigma attached to the non-therapeutic use of stimulants. The culture of some schools may actually encourage students to use stimulants.[188] As one student at Columbia University acknowledged, "[a]s a kid, I was made to feel different for taking these drugs . . . [n]ow it's almost cool to take them."[189] Today, students with legal stimulant prescriptions routinely sell or give pills to others, without regard for the consequences of their actions.[190]

The most effective means to prevent illicit stimulant use is to dispel misconceptions students have regarding the drugs. For example, one college used a social norms marketing campaign to target prescription drug misuse in college.[191] Of the students surveyed at the completion of the campaign, 36.6 percent acknowledged that they would be more cautious in using prescription drugs.[192] Other targeted social norms campaigns have documented significant reductions in risky behaviors among students within a few years of the campaign.[193] To effectively address illicit stimulant use, states should implement educational campaigns aimed at addressing both the physiological harm that may occur to individuals who use drugs without a prescription, and the impact illicit drug use has on disabled individuals who require assistance to succeed in the classroom.

Social norm campaigns should elicit student input and use appropriate visual media mat bring credibility to the presentation to improve the likelihood that the message will be received. States must be proactive in addressing student perceptions of stimulant use. Early intervention through education is an essential first step, but states that receive federal funds under the IDEA must also take steps to ensure that student assessment is fair and accurately reflects the performance of disabled students. The state's power to take appropriate steps to protect the health of students and to protect the rights of the disabled is strongest when school authorities act in loco parentis.[194]

Protecting the Rights and Safety of Students

Unemancipated minors are subject to the control of their parents or guardians.[195] Minors placed in private or public schools for their education are subject to the care and control of the teachers and administrators of those schools who stand in loco parentis.[196] The nature of that power is both custodial and tutelary, and it permits school officials a degree of supervision and control that cannot be exercised over adults.[197] Indeed, "a proper educational environment requires close supervision of schoolchildren, as well as the enforcement of rules against conduct that would be perfectly permissible if undertaken by an adult."[198] While schools do not have an absolute duty to protect students from harm in all circumstances, schools do have a responsibility to protect students entrusted to their care from health risks.[199] As the United States Supreme Court has noted, states have a compelling interest in deterring illicit drug use by students in primary and secondary education because "[s]chool years are the time when the physical, psychological and addictive effects of drugs are most severe."[200]

The misuse of stimulants such as Ritalin and Adderall pose significant risk to school-aged students who may not be aware of the strong contraindications to their use. Indeed, the Court itself has noted that amphetamines produce an "'artificially induced heart rate increase, [p]eripheral vasoconstriction, [b]lood pressure increase, and [m]asking of the normal fatigue response,' making them a 'very dangerous drug when used during exercise of any type.'"[201] For students with undiagnosed heart defects, the risk is even greater. Dangerous complications, including death, may result from use of stimulants. Many students overdose as result of misuse and must seek medical intervention.[202]

The Supreme Court has acknowledged that "[t]the effects of drug-infested schools are visited not just upon the users, but upon the entire student body and faculty, as the educational process is disrupted."[203] The illicit use of prescription stimulants by healthy students harms disabled individuals who must use the stimulants to compete in the classroom. Such use interferes with the school's ability to provide an appropriate education to individuals with ADHD and should not be tolerated. When a state accepts funding under the IDEA, it effectively agrees to take all reasonable steps to provide each disabled student with an education that is appropriate for the individual.[204] Illicit stimulant use interferes with that requirement and places students with ADHD at a competitive disadvantage in the classroom, in direct contravention of United States disability policy.

In view of the increased misuse of stimulants among students and the harm it causes to the user and to disabled individuals, state action to protect students from harm is warranted. States must ensure that student assessment accurately and fairly reflects student progress. Since student achievement is largely determined based on the results of standardized tests, states should implement random drug testing procedures prior to administering standardized tests.

Suspicionless drug testing in the middle school and high school environment is constitutional. In *Board of Education of Independent School District No. 92 of Pottawatomie County v. Earls*,[205] high school students challenged the constitutionality of the schools' suspicionless urinalysis drug testing policy. The school district's policy required all middle and high school students to consent to drug testing in order to participate in any competitive extracurricular activity, such as the Academic Team, Future Farmers of America, Future Homemakers of America, band, or choir.[206] The test was designed to detect use of illegal drugs, including amphetamines.[207] After considering the reasonableness of the policy,[208] the privacy interest affected,[209] the character of the intrusion imposed by the policy,[210] and the ability of the policy to meet its stated goals,[211] the Court held that the policy was constitutional.[212]

The Court began its analysis by noting that in the context of safety, a search unsupported by probable cause may be reasonable "when special needs, beyond the normal need for law enforcement, make the warrant and probable-cause requirement impracticable."[213] Special needs inhere in the public school context.[214] The Court placed great emphasis on the fact that the school district's policy was undertaken in furtherance of the district's responsibilities as guardian and tutor of the children entrusted to its care. Thus, the relevant question became whether the policy allowing for suspicionless searches was one that a reasonable guardian and tutor might undertake.[215] The Court found that the policy was reasonable because it was implemented to address the general nationwide epidemic of drug use, and because of the specific evidence of increased drag use in the school district.[216]

In assessing the students' privacy interest, the Court noted that students have a diminished expectation of privacy in public schools where the state is responsible for maintaining discipline, health, and safety.[217] It noted that students are routinely required to submit to physical examinations and vaccinations against disease.[218] Respondents attempted to draw a distinction between individuals engaged in extracurricular athletic activities who had a diminished expectation of privacy under existing law, and individuals engaged in non-athletic extracurricular activities who are not subject to regular physicals and communal undress.[219] The Court disagreed, noting that its prior decision allowing for suspicionless drug testing of high school athletes depended primarily upon the school's custodial responsibility and authority.[220]

Next, the Court considered the character of the intrusion.[221] The Court noted that the degree of the intrusion on privacy associated with sample collection largely depends on the way in which production of the urine sample is monitored.[222] Students were required to fill a sample cup behind closed doors and deliver the sample to an official stationed outside the bathroom.[223] The sample was not released to law enforcement officials, and it was only used to determine eligibility to continue participating in the activity.[224] In view of the non-intrusive mode of collection used by the district, the Court found that the intrusion was negligible.[225]

Finally, the Court considered the nature and immediacy of the government's concerns and the efficacy of the policy in meeting them.[226] The Court noted that "the nationwide drug epidemic makes the war against drugs a pressing concern in every school."[227] The need for state action is magnified, according to the Court, when the threat affects children "for whom [the state] has undertaken a special responsibility of care and direction."[228] The school district's evidence of increased drug use among students, coupled with rising drug use nationwide, convinced the Court that the school district's drug testing policy was a necessary and appropriate means to address the drug problems.

In view of the rising misuse of prescription stimulants by middle and high school students across the country, the substantial risk of harm associated with misuse of stimulants, and the negative impact such use has on the opportunities of disabled individuals to compete in the classroom, it is likely that the United States Supreme Court would uphold any carefully tailored, state-sponsored drug testing of students taking standardized tests. Although standardized tests are not technically extracurricular activities, they are competitive by design and the test results have significant consequences for students intending to continue their education in college. Randomly testing students for illicit use of stimulants to protect students from harm and to preserve the rights of disabled individuals is no less reasonable than testing students involved in Academic Team, Future Farmers of America, Future Homemakers of America, band, choir, or other activities.

Conclusion

Over the last 35 years, the IDEA and other laws have increased educational opportunities for individuals with disabilities and their families.[229] Despite this, a significant threat has emerged that threatens to undo decades of progress. On school campuses across the nation, an increasing number of students illegally use prescription drugs to enhance their natural ability in the classroom. The non-therapeutic use of powerful prescription stimulants poses significant risks for students and places disabled individuals at a competitive disadvantage in the classroom in direct contravention of United States disability policy. Breakthroughs in neuroscience present humanity with a promise and a predicament. Brain enhancement therapeutics has the potential to improve the quality of life for those living with neurological disorders or impairment, and forces humans to address the propriety of artificially elevating human capabilities. The use of stimulants to elevate abilities in the classroom raises difficult questions about nature, science, and fundamental fairness. Given the United States' express goal of providing equal opportunities for disabled individuals, policies and activities directed to the use of enhancement technology must be based on a sound consideration of the impact such use will have on the rights of disabled individuals.

Notes

1. MARY SHELLY, FRANKENSTEIN; OR, THE MODERN PROMETHEUS 47 (Barnes and Noble Books 2003) (rev. ed. 1831).

2. *See generally* Anjan Chatterjee, *Cosmetic Neurology: The Controversy Over Enhancing Movement, Mentation, and Mood,* 63 NEUROLOGY 968, 968 (2004) (defining cosmetic neurology as the use of medicine to artificially improve brain function by modulating motor, cognitive, and affective systems to enhance performance and improve quality of life).

3. Chatterjee, *supra* note 2, at 969 (citing FRANCIS FUKUYAMA, OUR POSTHUMAN FUTURE: CONSEQUENCES OF THE BIOTECHNOLOGY REVOLUTION 208 (2002)).

4. Henry Greely et al., *Towards Responsible Use of Cognitive-Enhancing Drugs by the Healthy,* 456 NATURE 702 (2008), *available at* http://www.nature.com/nature/journal/v456/n7223/full/456702a.html.

5. *Attention Deficit Hyperactivity Disorder (ADHD),* NAT'L INST. OF MENTAL HEALTH, http://www.nimh.nih.gov/health/publications/attention-deficit-hyperactivity-disorder/complete-index.shtml (last visited Sept. 5, 2010) [hereinafter NIMH].

6. 21 C.F.R. §1308.12 (2010).

7. *See* 21 U.S.C. § 841(a)(1) (2006) (imposing penalties for the unauthorized distribution of a controlled substance); *see also* Sean Esteban et al., *Nonmedical Use of Prescription Stimulants Among US College Students: Prevalence and Correlates from a National Survey,* 99 ADDICTION 96 (2005), *available at* http://www.wellcorps.com/files/NonMedicalUseOfPrescriptionStimulants.pdf.

8. *Strategies for Teaching Students With Attention Deficit Disorder,* W. VA. UNIV., http://www.as.wvu.edu/~scidis/add.html (last updated Apr. 10, 2007).

9. *See* NIMH, *supra* note 5.

10. *Strategies for Teaching Students With Attention Deficit Disorder, supra* note 8.

11. *What is ADHD or ADD?*, Nat'l Res. Ctr. on AD/HD, http://www.help4adhd.org/en/about/what (last visited Sept. 5, 2010).

12. *Id.*

13. Am. Med. Ass'n, *Attention Deficit Hyperactivity Disorder,* http://www.ama-assn.org/amal/pub/upload/mm/443/csaphl0a07-fulltext.pdf (last visited Sept. 5, 2010).

14. NIMH, *supra* note 5.

15. *Id.*

16. *Id.*

17. *Id.*

18. American Acad. of Pediatrics, *ADHD and Your School-Aged Child* (Oct. 2001), http://pediatrics.aappublications.org/cgi/data/108/4/1033/DCl/l.

19. *Id.*

20. NIMH, *supra* note 5.

21. *Id.*

22. Nat'l Resource Ctr. on AD/HD, *supra* note 11.

23. ADHD diagnosis in children is based on meeting the criteria of the *Diagnostic and Statistical Manual of Mental Disorders* (DSM-IV-TR). These criteria require evidence of inattention, or hyperactivity and impulsivity, or both.

24. *Adult ADHD: Issues and Answers,* NYU School of Medicine Adult ADHD Newsletter (N.Y.U. Sch. of Med., New York, N.Y.), Spring 2005, *available at* http://webdoc.nyumc.org/nyumc/files/psych/attachments/adult_adhd_l_l.pdf.

25. *Id.* (noting that ADHD can be diagnosed in adults who exhibit criteria used to diagnose children as long as the adult can recollect such symptoms in childhood).

26. *Ritalin Use Among Youth: Examining the Issues and Concerns: Hearing Before the Subcomm. on Early Childhood, Youth and Families of the H. Comm. on Education and the Workforce,* 106th Cong. 12-14, 79-98 (2008) (statement of Terrance W. Woodworth, Deputy Dir., Office of Diversion Control, Drug Enforcement Admin., U.S. Dep't of Justice), *available at* http://www.justice.gov/dea/pubs/cngrtest/ct051600.htm [hereinafter Woodworth Statement].

27. Nat'l Inst. on Drug Abuse, Nat'l Insts. of Health, U.S. Dep't of Health & Human Servs., *NIDA InfoFacts: Stimulant ADHD Medications: Methylphenidate and Amphetamines* (June 2009), *available at* http://drugabuse.gov/pdf/Infofacts/ADHD09.pdf.

28. *Id.*

29. NIMH, *supra* note 5.

30. Victoria L. Vetter et al., *Cardiovascular Monitoring of Children and Adolescents with Heart Disease Receiving Medications for Attention Deficit/Hyperactivity Disorder,* 117 Circulation 2407, 2418 (2008), http://circ.ahajournals.org/cgi/content/full/l17/18/2407 ("The consensus of the committee is that it is reasonable to obtain ECGs as part of the evaluation of children being considered for stimulant drug therapy.").

31. Jay D. Tarnow, *Pharmacological Treatment of Attention Deficit Disorders,* ADHD Self-Mgmt. Ctr. Online, http://www.adhdselfmanagement.com/pharmacological_treatment_add.html (last visited May 24, 2010).

32. *Id.*

33. *See infra* Part II.B.

34. Convention on Psychotropic Substances, E.S.C. Res. 1474 (XLVIII), U.N.Doc. A/RES/1474 (XLVIII) (Mar. 24, 1970).

35. *Continuing Concerns Over Imported Pharmaceuticals: Hearing Before the Subcomm. on Oversight and Investigations of the H. Comm. on Energy and Commerce,* 107th Cong. 37-40 (2001) (statement of Laura M. Nagel, Deputy Assistant Adm'r, Office of Diversion Control, Drug Enforcement Admin.), *available at* http://ftp.resource.org/gpo.gov/hearings/107h/73737.pdf.

36. Controlled Substances Act, Pub. L. No. 91-513, 84 Stat. 1236, 1242 (1970) (codified at 21 U.S.C. §§ 801-904 (2006)).

37. 21 U.S.C. § 812(b)(1) (2006).

38. *Id.* § 812(b)(2).

39. *Id.*

40. *Id.*

41. *Id.* § 812(b)(3)-(5).

42. 21 C.F.R. § 290.1 (2010).

43. Anti-Drug Abuse Act of 1988, Pub. L. No. 100-690, 102 Stat. 4181.

44. 21 U.S.C. § 841(a)(1) (2006).

45. *Id.* § 844(a).

46. *Id.* §§ 859(a), 860(a).

47. *Id.* § 844(a).

48. *Id.*

49. *Id.* § 862(a)(1)(A), (b)(1)(A).

50. *Id.* § 862(d)(1)(A).

51. Drug Enforcement Agency, U.S. Dep't of Justice, Methylphenidate (A Background Paper) (Oct. 1995), *available at* http://www.methylphenidate.net/.

52. Drug Free World, The Truth About Ritalin Abuse (2009), http://www.drugsalvage.com.au/downloads/kiddie_cocaine.pdf.

53. *Id.*

54. Am. Med. Ass'n, *supra* note 13, at 8.

55. Drug Enforcement Agency, *supra* note 51.

56. *Id.*

57. *Id.*

58. *See, e.g., id; see also* Howard Abikoff et al., *Symptomatic Improvement in Children With ADHD Treated With Long-Term Methylphenidate and Multimodal Psychosocial Treatment,* 43 J. Am. Acad. Child & Adolescent Psychiatry 802 (2004) (reporting significant benefits from methylphenidate use in children with ADHD).

59. Woodworth Statement, *supra* note 26, at fig.l.

60. U.N. INT'L NARCOTICS CONTROL BD., REPORT OF THE INTERNATIONAL NARCOTICS CONTROL BOARD FOR 2009, at 13 (Feb. 24, 2010), *available at* http://www.incb.org/pdf/annual-report/2009/en/AR_09_English.pdf.

61. *Id.* at 26.

62. Gene R. Haislip, Deputy Assistant Adm'r, Drug Enforcement Admin., ADD/ADHD Statement of Drug Enforcement Administration, Address at the Conference on Stimulant Use in the Treatment of ADHD (Dec. 10-12,1996), *available at* http://www.add-adhd.org/ritalin.html.

63. Susan Jones et al., *Amphetamine Blocks Long-Term Synaptic Depression in the Ventral Tegmental Area,* 20 J. NEUROSCI. 5575, 5575-80 (2000).

64. Alcoholism & Drug Addiction Research Found., *Amphetamines* (1991), http://www.xs4all.nl/~4david/amphetam.html.

65. Everett H. Ellinwood et al., *Chronic Amphetamine Use and Abuse* (2000), http://www.acnp.org/g4/GN401000166/CH162.htm.

66. Woodworth Statement, *supra* note 26, at fig. 1.

67. Nat'l Inst. on Drug Abuse, *supra* note 27.

68. Patrick G. O'Connor, *Amphetamines, in* THE MERCK MANUAL HOME EDITION (ONLINE VERSION) (last updated Jan. 2009), *available at* http://www.merckmanuals.com/home/sec25/ch312/ch312c.html.

69. *Id.*

70. Neal Handly, *Toxicity, Amphetamine* (last updated Oct. 21, 2009), *available at* http://emedicine.medscape.com/article/812518-overview.

71. O'Connor, *supra* note 68.

72. *Id.*

73. *Id.*

74. *Id.*

75. Woodworth Statement, *supra* note 26, at fig. 1.

76. Matt McMillen, *Adderall: A Stroke of Bad News,* WASH. POST, Feb. 15, 2005, at HE02.

77. Gardiner Harris, *Deaths Cited in Reports on Stimulant Drugs, But Their Cause is Uncertain,* N.Y. TIMES, Feb. 9, 2006, at A19.

78. U.S. Food & Drug Admin., *Statement on Adderall* (Feb. 9, 2005), http://www.fda.gov/NewsEvents/Newsroom/PressAnnouncements/2005/ucml08411.htm.

79. U.S. Food & Drug Admin., *Public Health Advisory for Adderall and Adderall XR* (Feb. 9, 2005), *available at* http://www.fda.gov/Drugs/DrugSafety/PostmarketDrugSafetyInformationforPatientsandProviders/DrugSafetyInformation-forHealthcareProfessionals/PublicHealthAdvisories/ucm051672.htm.

80. *Id.*

81. U.S. Food & Drug Admin., *Drug Safety and Risk Management Advisory Committee Minutes* (Feb. 9, 2006), www.fda.gov/ohrms/dockets/ac/06/minutes/2006-4202MI_FINAL-Minutes.pdf.

82. *Id.* at 4.

83. *Id.*

84. *Id.*

85. *Id.*

86. U.S. Food & Drug Admin., *Minutes of the Pediatric Advisory Committee* 6 (Mar. 22, 2006), http://www.fda.gov/ohrms/dockets/ac/06/minutes/2006-4210m_Minutes%20PAC%20March%2022%202006.pdf.

87. *Id.*

88. *Id.*

89. U.S. Food & Drug Admin., *FDA Directs ADHD Drug Manufacturers to Notify Patients about Cardiovascular Adverse Events and Psychiatric Adverse Events* (Feb. 21, 2007), http://www.fda.gov/NewsEvents/Newsroom/PressAnnouncements/2007/ucml08849.htm.

90. American Med. Ass'n, *supra* note 13, at 12.

91. U.S. Food & Drug Admin., *supra* note 89.

92. *Antidepressant Medications for Children and Adolescents: Information for Parents and Caregivers,* NAT'L INST. ON MENTAL HEALTH (Dec. 3, 2010), http://www.nimh.nih.gov/health/topics/child-and-adolescent-mental-health/antidepressant-medications-for-children-and-adolescents-information-for-parents-and-caregivers.shtml.

93. U.S. Food & Drug Admin., *supra* note 81.

94. *See* U.S. Food & Drug Admin., *Guidance for Industry: Warnings and Precautions, Contraindications, and Boxed Warning Sections of Labeling for Human Prescription Drug and Biological Products—Content and Format* 9 (Jan. 2006), http://www.fda.gov/downloads/Drugs/GuidanceComplianceRegulatoryInformation/Guidances/ucm075096.pdf; *see also* 21 C.F.R. § 314.520 (2010).

95. U.S. Food & Drug Admin., *supra* note 94, at 9.

96. *Id.*

97. Margaret Marrer, Adderall *Use and Abuse: Is Georgetown Part of a Growing Trend?,* GEORGETOWN INDEP. (Jan. 2, 2010), http://www.thegeorgetownindependent.com/2.14589/adderall-use-and-abuse-l.2081595.

98. Joseph Biederman et al., *A Randomized, Placebo-Controlled Trial of OROS-Methylphenidate in Adults With Attention-Deficit/Hyperactivity Disorder,* 59 BIOLOGICAL PSYCHIATRY 829 (2006). *See also* Richard H. Weisler et al., *Long-Term Cardiovascular Effectsof Mixed Amphetamine Salts Extended Release in Adults With ADHD,* 10 CNS SPECTRUMS 35 (2005), *available at* http://www.cnsspectrums.com/aspx/articledetail.aspx?articleid=492 (finding statistically significant increases in blood pressure and heart rate after use of stimulants).

99. *See* Edward G. Jones & Lorne M. Mendell, *Assessing the Decade of the Brain,* 284 SCIENCE 739 (1999).

100. *id.*

101. *Id.*

102. Personal autonomy and the right to privacy is viewed by some as a liberty, protected by the Due Process Clause of the Fourteenth Amendment, that allows the individual to choose what to do with his or her own body free from government restrictions that prevent such action.

103. *See, e.g.*, Benedict Carey, *Smartening Up: Brain Enhancement Is Wrong, Right?*, N.Y. Times, Mar. 9, 2008, at WK1.

104. U.N. Int'l Narcotics Control Bd., *supra* note 60, at 66.

105. *Id.* at 72.

106. Office of Applied Studies, Substance Abuse & Mental Health Servs. Admin., U.S. Dep't of Health & Human Servs., Results from the 2008 National Survey on Drug Use and Health: National Findings (2009), *available at* http://www.oas .samhsa.gov/nsduh/2k8nsduh/2k8Results.pdf.

107. *Id.*

108. U.N. Int'l Narcotics Control Bd., *supra* note 60, at 72.

109. *Id.* at 72-73.

110. *Id.* at 73.

111. *Id.*

112. *Id.* at 73, 74.

113. Office of Applied Studies, *supra* note 106, at 52.

114. *Id.*

115. *Id.* at 30.

116. Sean Esteban McCabe et al., *The Use, Misuse and Diversion of Prescription Stimulants Among Middle and High School Students,* 39 Substance Use & Misuse 1095, 1103 (2004).

117. *Id.*

118. C. J. Musser et al., *Stimulant Use and the Potential for Abuse in Wisconsin as Reported by School Administrators and Longitudinally Followed Children,* J. Developmental & Behavioral Pediatrics 187, 192 (1998).

119. Christine Poulin, *Medical and Nonmedical Stimulant Use Among Adolescents: From Sanctioned to Unsanctioned Use,* 165 Can. Med. Ass'n J. 1039, 1039 (2001).

120. Office of Applied Studies, *supra* note 106, at 2.

121. *Id.*

122. Sean E. McCabe, *Medical Use, Illicit Use and Diversion of Prescription Stimulant Medication,* 38 J. Psychoactive Drugs 45, 45-46 (2006).

123. Alan D. DeSantis et al., *Illicit Use of Prescription ADHD Medications on a College Campus: A Multimethodological Approach,* 57 J. Am. Coll. Health 315, 316 (2008).

124. *Id.*

125. *Id.* at 317.

126. Claire D. Advokat et al., *Licit and Illicit Use of Medications for Attention-Deficit Hyperactivity Disorder in Undergraduate College Students,* 56 J. Am. Coll. Health 601, 602(2008).

127. Timothy E. Wilens et al., Misuse and *Diversion of Stimulants Prescribed for ADHD: A Systematic Review of the Literature,* 47 J. Am. Acad. Child Adolescent Psychiatry 21(2008).

128. DeSantis, *supra* note 123, at 322.

129. *Id.*

130. OFFICE OF APPLIED STUDIES, *supra* note 106, at 2.

131. *Popping Pills a Popular Way to Boost Brain Power,* CBS NEWS (Apr. 25, 2010), http://www.cbsnews.com/stories/2010/04/22/60minutes/main6422159.shtnil.

132. Matt Manning, *Sandusky County Officials: No Decline Seen in Drug Use,* NEWS-MESSENGER (Fremont, Ohio), Aug. 6, 2009 (on file with author) (noting that many new cases of illicit drug use involve the use of less expensive prescription medicines like Adderall and Ritalin).

133. Christina Lanni et al., *Cognition Enhancers Between Treating and Doping the Mind,* 57 PHARMACOLOGICAL RESEARCH 196 (2008).

134. Jeffrey Zaslow, *What if Einstein had Taken Ritalin? ADHD's Impact on Creativity,* WALL ST. J., Feb. 3, 2005, at Dl.

135. *Id.*

136. *Id.*

137. *Id.*

138. *Id.*

139. Margaret Talbot, *Brain Gain: The Underground World of "Neuroenhancing" Drugs,* NEW YORKER, Apr. 27, 2009, *available at* http://www.newyorker.com /reporting/2009/04/27/090427fa_fact_talbot?currentPage=all.

140. *Id.*

141. *Popping Pills a Popular Way to Boost Brain Power, supra* note 131.

142. Carey, *supra* note 103.

143. *See* Pew Forum on Religion & Pub. Life, *The Pursuit of Perfection: A Conversation on the Ethics of Genetic Engineering* (Mar. 31, 2004), *available at* http:// pewforum.org/Science-and-Bioethics/The-Pursuit-of-Perfection-A-Conversation-on-the-Ethics-of-Genetic-Engineering.aspx [hereinafter Pew Forum].

144. Michael S. Gazzaniga, *Smarter on Drugs,* SCI. AM. MIND, Oct. 2005.

145. Sileshi Semaw et al., *2.6-Million-year-old Stone Tools and Associated Bones from OGS-6 and OGS-7, Gona, Afar, Ethiopia,* 45 J. HUM. EVOLUTION 169 (2003).

146. *Id.*

147. Michael J. Sandel, *The Case Against Perfection.* ATL. MONTHLY, Apr. 2004, at 50.

148. *Id.*

149. Med. Ethics Dep't, British Med. Ass'n, *Boosting Your Brainpower: Ethical Aspects of Cognitive Enhancements* 19 (2007), *available at* http://www.bma .org.uk/images/Boosting_brainpower_tcm41-147266.pdf.

150. *Id.*

151. *Id.*

152. OFFICE OF SPECIAL EDUC. PROGRAMS, OFFICE OF SPECIAL EDUC. & REHAB. SERVS., U.S. DEP'T OF EDUC., HISTORY: TWENTY-FIVE YEARS OF PROGRESS IN EDUCATING CHILDREN WITH DISABILITIES THROUGH IDEA (2005), *available at* http://www2.ed.gov/policy/ speced/leg/idea/history.pdf.

153. *Id.*

154. 334 F. Supp. 1257 (E.D. Pa. 1971).

155. *Id.* at 1258.

156. 348 F. Supp. 866 (D.D.C. 1972).

157. *Id.* at 868.

158. *Id.* at 874 (citing Brown v. Bd. of Educ., 347 U.S. 483, 493 (1954)).

159. Education for All Handicapped Children Act of 1975, Pub. L. No. 94-142, 89 Stat. 773.

160. 20 U.S.C. §§ 1400-1482 (2006).

161. *Id.* § 1400(3).

162. *Id.* § 1400(6).

163. *Id.* § 1400(3).

164. *Id.*

165. *Id.* § 1412(a)(1)(A).

166. *Id.* § 1401(3)(A)(i)-(ii).

167. 34 C.F.R. § 300.8(c)(9) (2010).

168. 20 U.S.C. §§ 1412(a)(4), 1414(d)(1)(a) (2006); 34 C.F.R. § 300.347 (2010).

169. 20 U.S.C. §§ 1401(14), 1412(a)(4), 1414(d) (2006).

170. *Id.* § 1414(c)(l)(A)(ii), (d)(l)(A)(i)(II)-(IV).

171. *Id.* § 1412(a)(16)(A).

172. *Id.* § 1418(a).

173. *Id.* § 1418(b).

174. Bonnie J. Kaplan et al., *The IQs of Children with ADHD are Normally Distributed,* 33 J. LEARNING DISABILITIES 410, 425-32 (2000); *see also* T.P. Ho et al., *Situational Versus Pervasive Hyperactivity in a Community Sample,* 26 PSYCHOL. MED. 309 (1996).

175. Donald E. Greydanus, *Stimulant Misuse: Strategies to Manage a Growing Problem* (June 2007), http://www.acha.org/prof_dev/ADHD_docs/ADHD_PDprogram_Article2.pdf.

176. *See generally* NAT'L CTR. ON ADDICTION & SUBSTANCE ABUSE, COLUM.UNIV., NATIONAL SURVEY OF AMERICAN ATTITUDES ON SUBSTANCE ABUSE XV: TEENS AND PARENTS (Aug. 2010), http://www.casacolumbia.org/upload/2010/20100819teensurvey.pdf (discussing the use of prescription drugs for non-therapeutic use by middle and high school students).

177. *See, e.g.,* Guckenberger v. Boston Univ., 974 F. Supp. 106 (D. Mass. 1997) (citing Se. Cmty. Coll. v. Davis, 442 U.S. 397, 401 (1979)) (noting that federal disability laws do not compel educational institutions to make substantial modifications in their program to allow disabled persons to participate).

178. *See* 20 U.S.C. § 1400(d)(1)(A) (2006); *see also* Arlington Cent. Sch. Dist. Bd. of Educ. v. Murphy, 548 U.S. 291 (2006).

179. Office of Special Educ. Programs, U.S. Dep't of Educ., IDEA Regulations: State Funding (2006), http://idea.ed.gov/object/fileDownload/model/TopicalBrief/field/Pdf/file/primary_key/18.

180. *See* 20 U.S.C. §§ 1412-1414 (2006).

181. *Id.*

182. *Id.* §1400(d)(l)(A).

183. For example, Arizona mandates use of a "statewide nationally standardized norm-referenced achievement test in reading, language arts and mathematics[.]" Ariz. Rev. Stat. § 15-741 (West, Westlaw through 2010 legislation).

184. *See* 20 U.S.C. §1418(d)(2)(A)-(C) (2006).

185. *See* DeSantis, *supra* note 123, at 317.

186. *See, e.g.,* Cal. Dep't of Alcohol & Drug Programs, Preventing Prescription Drug Abuse: Colleges (2011), http://www.prescriptiondrugmisuse.org/index.php?page=colleges.

187. *See, e.g.,* Higher Educ. Ctr. for Alcohol & Other Drug Abuse & Violence Prevention, Fraternity and Sorority Members and Alcohol and Other Drug Use (Aug. 2008), http://www.higheredcenter.org/files/product/fact_sheet5.pdf (recommending social norm marketing to combat the widespread drug and alcohol culture on college campuses).

188. Andrew Jacobs, *The Adderall Advantage,* N.Y. Times, July 31, 2005, *available at* http://www.nytimes.com/2005/07/31/education/edlife/jacobs31.html.

189. *Id.*

190. See *id.*

191. *See* Cal. Dep't of Alcohol & Drug Programs, *supra* note 186 (referencing a social norm study conducted by Western Washington University).

192. *Id.*

193. *See generally* Nat'l Social Norms Inst., Univ. of Va., *Articles on the Social Norms Approach—Measuring Misperceptions and Behavior,* http://www.socialnorm.org/ (last visited Sept. 5, 2010) (cataloging studies on social marketing campaigns to students).

194. Vernonia Sch. Dist. 47J v. Acton, 515 U.S. 646, 654 (1995). In *Vernonia,* the Supreme Court noted that during the school day the teacher or school serves "in loco parentis" or "in the place of the parent." *See id.* at 654-55.

195. *Id.* at 654 (citing 59 Am. Jur. 2d *Parent and Child* § 10 (1987)).

196. *Id.*

197. New Jersey v. T.L.O., 469 U.S. 325, 336-337 (1985).

198. *Id.* at 339.

199. *Vernonia,* 515 U.S. at 656 (noting that "[f]or their own good and that of their classmates, public school children are routinely required to submit to various physical examinations, and to be vaccinated against various diseases").

200. *Id.* at 662.

201. *Id.* (quoting Jerald Hawkins, *Drugs and Other Ingesta: Effects on Athletic Performance, in* Herb Appenzeller, Managing Sports and Risk Management Strategies 90, 90-91 (1993)).

202. Beth Beavers, *Campus ADHD Prescription Abuse Increases,* Univ. Daily Kansan, Sept. 2, 2009, *available at* http://www.kansan.com/news/2009/Sep/02/ADHD.

203. *Vernonia,* 515 U.S. at 662.

204. 20 U.S.C. § 1412(a) (2006).

205. 536 U.S. 822 (2002).

206. *Id.* at 826.

207. *Id.*

208. *Id.* at 828-30.

209. *Id.* at 830-31.

210. *Id.* at 832-34.

211. *Id.* at 834-38.

212. *Id.* at 838.

213. *Id.* at 829 (quoting Griffin v. Wisconsin, 483 U.S. 868, 873 (1987)) (internal quotation marks omitted).

214. Vernonia Sch. Dist. 47J v. Acton, 515 U.S. 646, 653 (1995).

215. *Earls*, 536 U.S. at 830.

216. *Id.* at 825.

217. *Id.* at 830.

218. *Id.* at 830-31.

219. *Id.* at 831.

220. *Id.*

221. *Id.* at 832.

222. *Id.*

223. *Id.*

224. *Id.* at 833.

225. *Id.*

226. *Id.* at 834.

227. *Id.*

228. Vernonia Sch. Dist. 47J v. Acton, 515 U.S. 646, 662 (1995).

229. *See, e.g.*, Elementary and Secondary Education Act of 1965, Pub. L. No. 89-10, 79 Stat. 27 (providing grant assistance to help educate children with disabilities); Elementary and Secondary Education Act Amendments of 1965, Pub. L. No. 89-313, 79 Stat. 1158; *see also* Handicapped Children's Early Education Assistance Act of 1968, Pub. L. No. 90-538, 82 Stat. 901 (authorizing support for exemplary early childhood programs); Economic Opportunities Amendments of 1972, Pub. L. No. 92-424, 86 Stat. 688 (authorizing support for increased Head Start enrollment for young children with disabilities).

EXPLORING THE ISSUE

Should "Smart Drugs" Be Used to Enhance Cognitive Functioning?

Critical Thinking and Reflection

1. If researchers determine that there are no dangerous effects of prolonged use of cognitive enhancing drugs, what role should moral considerations play in evaluating the question of widespread availability of these drugs?
2. How would you respond to those who assert that the use of smart drugs by healthy individuals gives them an even greater advantage over cognitively impaired individuals who rely on these drugs to play on an even field?
3. Should the illicit use of drugs such as Ritalin or Adderall be treated as harshly as abuse of drugs such as methamphetamine and heroin?
4. Would you accept a job where the use of cognitive enhancing drugs is recommended or even required? Why or why not?
5. Consider this quotation: "The original purpose of medicine is to heal the sick, not turn healthy people into gods." To what extent do you view the use of smart drugs an attempt to become superhuman?

Is There Common Ground?

In considering the positions taken by the authors of the YES and the NO publications, some points of agreement are evident. There seems to be consensus that psychostimulant medications serve an important role for individuals with various cognitive impairments and neuropsychiatric disorders. Individuals with serious forms of ADHD find that these medications help them control their hyperactivity and assist them in cognitive tasks such as attention and concentration.

The authors of both articles also point out the possible risks of these drugs, and advocate research regarding their long-term effects, with particular attention to issues of safety and efficacy. Especially careful consideration should be given to the use of these drugs with children whose brains are still developing.

Both sides also agree that these drugs should be regulated. The YES authors state that enforceable policies are needed regarding the use of these drugs in order to support fairness, protect individuals from coercion, and minimize enhancement-related socioeconomic disparities. The NO author asserts that, in light of the U.S. goal of providing equal opportunities for the disabled, policies should take into consideration the ways in which enhancement technology will affect the rights of disabled individuals.

Additional Resources

Buccafusco, J. J. (2004). *Cognitive enhancing drugs*. Basel: Birkhäuser.

Buchanan, A. (2011). *Better than human: The promise and perils of enhancing ourselves*. New York, NY: Oxford University Press.

Helpguide.org. Retrieved from www.helpguide.org/mental/adhd_medications.htm

International Neuroethics Society. Retrieved from www.neuroethicssociety.org/

National Institute of Mental Health. Retrieved from www.nimh.nih.gov/health/publications/attention-deficit-hyperactivity-disorder/complete-index.shtml

National Institute on Drug Abuse. Retrieved from www1.drugabuse.gov/drugs-abuse/prescription-medications

ISSUE 7

Should Memory-Dampening Drugs Be Used to Prevent and Treat Trauma in Combat Soldiers?

YES: Elise Donovan, from "Propranolol Use in the Prevention and Treatment of Posttraumatic Stress Disorder in Military Veterans: Forgetting Therapy Revisited," *Perspectives in Biology and Medicine* (vol. 53, no. 1, pp. 61–74, 2010)

NO: The President's Council on Bioethics, from "Happy Souls," in *Beyond Therapy: Biotechnology and the Pursuit of Happiness*, pp. 205–273 (The President's Council on Bioethics, 2003)

Learning Outcomes
After reading this issue, you should be able to: • Evaluate the therapeutic advantages and disadvantages of prescribing memory-dampening drugs to soldiers who have experienced combat-related trauma.   • Understand the three phases of memory (i.e., formation, acquisition, and encoding), and how memory-dampening drugs might be used during each phase.   • Consider the extent to which posttraumatic growth might be limited as a result of taking memory-dampening drugs following the experience of trauma.   • Address the question of whether society has a responsibility to help combat veterans suppress the psychological symptoms arising from the trauma of war.   • Critically evaluate the role of the federal government in formulating bioethical standards such as those pertaining to the use of memory-dampening drugs.

ISSUE SUMMARY

YES: Research scientist Elise Donovan states that an alarming and rising number of soldiers are returning from combat suffering from PTSD, and that medications such as the beta-blocker propranolol can alleviate their symptoms. Propranolol, she argues, will help soldiers with PTSD who have essentially lost "their sense of self" reintegrate into society. Because the drug causes memory dampening, rather than memory loss, it will create an opportunity for veterans to better cope with everyday life upon returning from combat. She believes that symptoms and consequential behaviors associated with PTSD (i.e., suicide, domestic abuse, alcohol or drug abuse) will be greatly reduced in PTSD patients who take propranolol. Dr. Donovan also states that use of propranolol will foster an experience of posttraumatic growth.

NO: The President's Council on Bioethics, chaired by Dr. Leon Kass, criticizes the use of memory-dampening drugs to treat the symptoms of trauma by asking, "What kind of society are we likely to have when the powers to control memory, mood, and mental life through drugs reach their full maturity?" The Council asserts that identities are formed by what people do and what they undergo or suffer. Escaping painful memories would necessarily result in a change in the identity of who the person is, as well as the person's perception and understanding of significant life events.

T raumatic experiences are disastrous or extremely painful events that have severe psychological and physiological effects that can last for years. Trauma survivors experience a constellation of disruptive and possibly disabling symptoms associated with posttraumatic stress disorder. They may re-experience the traumatic event through recurring intrusive recollections, dreams, flashbacks, or physiological reactivity to cues that remind them of the trauma. Because of their heightened sense of vulnerability, trauma survivors avoid stimuli associated with the traumatic event in various ways. They may avoid thoughts, feelings, or conversations associated with the trauma; they may choose to stay away from activities, places, or people that remind them of the event. They may become distant and detached from other people, show little affect, and become pessimistic about life. At the same time, they are likely to experience persistent symptoms of arousal such as difficulty sleeping, irritability, hypervigilance, concentration difficulty, or an exaggerated startle response. In light of this disturbing symptom picture, it is understandable that people who have survived a trauma would go to great lengths to reduce their symptoms and alleviate their profound distress. Preliminary research has pointed to the possibility that the beta-blocker drug propranolol can dampen the memory of trauma, and thereby make life more bearable for some trauma survivors. With the emerging possibility that a drug can dampen the memory of trauma, a controversy has arisen about whether this intervention is really as beneficial as it sounds.

During the past decade in which the U.S. military has been engaged in the wars in Iraq and Afghanistan, the number of combat soldiers suffering from posttraumatic stress disorder has been stunning. Some estimates suggest that as many as 20% of American soldiers serving in these wars have developed PTSD (www.ptsd.va.gov/public/pages/how-common-is-ptsd.asp). In light of the potentially devastating effects on the lives of these veterans, and the lives of their loved ones, researchers and clinicians have devoted tremendous effort to developing interventions that can alleviate the symptoms of PTSD. One area of investigation has focused on the beta-blocker drug propranolol. Assuming that this drug can dampen the memory, and the emotional impact of the trauma, might it serve as a useful component of interventions for combat veterans suffering from PTSD?

Dr. Elise Donovan takes issue with a report published in 2003 by the President's Council on Bioethics, which was critical of this intervention and contended that it disrupts one's sense of self. She asserts that veterans who cannot function in society have essentially lost their sense of self. If we have an intervention that can assist them in their return to healthier functioning, she argues, it would not be justifiable to withhold research and treatment that may alleviate their distressing symptoms. Dr. Donovan notes that individuals taking propranolol will still remember the "facts" of the trauma, but their appraisal of these facts will change. Because propranolol targets fear-based memories, even if the experience of fear is reduced, an individual could still retain other emotional reactions to the event such as disgust or sadness. Dr. Donovan also describes another benefit of propranolol, namely its effect in fostering posttraumatic growth, the beneficial transformations that occur as a result of trauma, including the reevaluation of life goals and feelings of increased self-reliance, empathy, social support, and intimacy.

Although Dr. Donovan argues against administering propranolol prior to combat situations due to possible effects that could impair a soldier's cognitive and physiological functioning, she asserts that we do have a moral and ethical obligation to military service members to maximize efforts to alleviate PTSD symptoms in veterans who have been traumatized by the atrocities of war and combat.

Arguing against the use of memory-dampening drugs for alleviating symptoms of trauma, the Council contends that, as we reminisce from a greater distance and with more life experience, even our most painful experiences can often acquire for us a meaning that we did not foresee when the experiences occurred. The Council asserts that our identities are formed both by what we do and by what we undergo or suffer. Although we may regret the shadows that unchosen memories cast over our pursuit of happiness, we cannot simply escape them while remaining who we really are. Those who endure bad memories should not use the new biotechnical powers to ease the psychic pain of bad memories. Using such medications does not preserve memories' truth, but attempts instead to make the problem go away, and with it the truth of the experience in question.

The Council purports that altering the formation of emotionally powerful memories risks falsifying our perception and understanding of the world, making shameful acts seem less shameful, or terrible acts less terrible. Thus, the inference can be made from the Council's arguments that combat veterans might actually benefit from the experience of dealing with traumatic memories, possibly in the form of posttraumatic growth in which they mature emotionally as a result of surviving traumatic events. Furthermore, the Council contends that these drugs are effective only when administered during or shortly after a traumatic event. Thus, it would be necessary to make a predictive judgment as to which traumatized individuals should be treated with these drugs. Would this be possible in the field of combat?

YES

Elise Donovan

Propranolol Use in the Prevention and Treatment of Posttraumatic Stress Disorder in Military Veterans: Forgetting Therapy Revisited

An Army Ranger medic in Afghanistan fractured several vertebrae in a fall after enemy shrapnel disabled his parachute. He medicated himself and proceeded to treat the other injured soldiers around him. Four years after his return to the United States, he had such a vivid flashback to combat that he physically attacked his own mother and father at a lake house vacation, while his wife watched helplessly. Between 17 and 25% of soldiers returning from Iraq suffer from posttraumatic stress disorder (PTSD). These are documented cases; if unreported cases were included, this number would likely be much higher. Other reports indicate that 20.3% of active soldiers and 42.4% of soldiers who have returned from active service require mental health treatment (Hoge et al. 2004; Milliken, Auchterlonie, and Hoge 2007). During proceedings of a 2008 class-action lawsuit on behalf of nearly 2 million veterans against the Department of Veterans Affairs, it was reported that approximately 1,000 veterans receiving care attempt suicide monthly. Experiences such as that of the Army Ranger accompanied by these alarming statistics demonstrate the severity and prevalence of this problem, but the impact it has on the lives of those afflicted and their loved ones is often unnoticed by those who have not witnessed it firsthand. Exploration of treatments for PTSD is crucial, but because PTSD is a neuropsychological condition and some treatments include possible mindaltering pharmacological agents, ethical issues exist regarding PTSD research and treatment.

During the past decade, research on the use of drugs to prevent and treat PTSD has been accompanied by discussion and argument of the ethical issues surrounding treatments that may alter emotion and memory (Henry, Fishman, and Youngner 2007; President's Council on Bioethics 2003). Recently, however, research has progressed in a new direction. This new research directly impacts the ethical issues and alters the previous arguments, especially with regard to PTSD in military members returning from active combat. This essay will review the scientific research in this area, discuss the previous ethical issues and arguments, and present a new perspective considering the advances in research and the ethical discussion with a focus on use in military veterans.

From *Perspectives in Biology and Medicine*, vol. 53, no. 1, Winter 2010, pp. 61–74. Copyright © 2010 by Johns Hopkins University Press. Reprinted by permission.

Posttraumatic Stress Disorder and Propranolol

Multiple definitions of PTSD exist, but the *Diagnostic and Statistical Manual of Mental Disorders-IV-TR* states:

> The essential feature of Posttraumatic Stress Disorder is the development of characteristic symptoms following exposure to an extreme traumatic stressor involving direct personal experience of an event that involves actual or threatened death or serious injury, or other threat to one's physical integrity . . . or witnessing an event that involves death, injury, or a threat of physical integrity to another person. . . . The person's response to the event must involve intense fear, helplessness or horror. The full symptom picture must be present for more than 1 month. (p. 463)

In veterans, symptoms include disturbing memories and dreams related to stressful military experiences, acting or feeling like a military experience is happening again, having physical and emotional responses to things that remind the veteran of a military experience, loss of interest in things that used to be pleasurable, alcohol abuse, sleep disturbances including both insomnia and excessive sleeping, distancing from loved ones, and many others (McGhee et al. 2009).

While memory is a complex and integrated process, three phases are applicable to this discussion. These include formation, acquisition, and encoding of the memory; emotional response to and consolidation of the memory; and reconsolidation, reinstatement, and retrieval of the memory, which includes recall and the emotional responses triggered by later stimuli. The neuroendocrine involvement in memory formation and response to trauma has been extensively studied and well reviewed, and the role of stress hormones is established (Bremner et al. 2008; Mathew, Price, and Charney 2008; Roozendaal, Barsegyan, and Lee 2008; van Stegeren 2008; Zohar et al. 2008). Adrenal stress hormones, including glucocorticoids and adrenergic signals (epinephrine and norepinephrine), are released in response to stressful or emotionally arousing events and interact to facilitate memory formation and consolidation. Beta-adrenergic stimulation and the subsequent physiological cascade are an integral part of the fight-or-flight response and play a major role in response to trauma in conjunction with glucocorticoids. Not all memories are modulated by stress hormones; rather, there is preferential modulation during consolidation of emotionally arousing memories (Roozendaal, Barsegyan, and Lee 2008). Van Stegeren (2008) has discussed the role of epinephrine and norepinephrine in emotional memory formation:

> Increased noradrenalin levels lead to better memory performance, whereas blocking the noradrenergic receptors with a beta blocker attenuates this enhanced memory for emotional information. Noradrenalin appears to interact with cortisol in emotional memory processes, varying from encoding to consolidation and retrieval. (p. 532)

The primary pharmacological agent that has been examined for treatment of PTSD is propranolol, a beta-adrenergic receptor antagonist, and the

Department of Veterans Affairs is currently recruiting volunteers for clinical trials. While many beta-antagonists exist—including some that are now prescribed more often and are more potent than propranolol—the majority of research in this area has used propranolol, and it will be the focus of discussion. Research has examined propranolol treatment in each of the three phases of memory mentioned above. If it is known an event will be stressful, such as rescuers responding to a disaster, administration of propranolol would influence formation, acquisition, and encoding. Administration immediately after a traumatic event, such as in the emergency room after a rape, would influence response and consolidation. Administration later—for example, during stimulated arousal of PTSD in those who have been diagnosed—may influence the later stage during recall, retrieval, and reconsolidation. The beta-adrenergic system is involved not only with response and memory formation, but also the conditioning of the emotional response associated with the memory, so propranolol may both dampen memory formation and dissociate the memory from the emotional response. Although this treatment has been termed "forgetting therapy," it isn't designed to make individuals forget their physical experiences but rather to dissociate the emotions and fears from the memories.

Because they slow heart rate and inhibit arterial vasoconstriction, beta-blockers have been administered for years to treat hypertension and other cardiovascular diseases. Memory loss is listed as a potential side effect of propranolol use for cardiovascular conditions (Henry, Fishman, and Youngner 2007). Although propranolol can also interfere with hippocampal centers involved in memory storage, including dampening memory of a trauma and enhancing memory of the events preceding the trauma (Bell 2008), there have been no reported cases of severe memory loss due to the use of propranolol for cardiovascular conditions. In addition, in the transcripts from the proceedings of the President's Council on Bioethics (2002), Dr. James McGaugh states: "The clinically used doses, let's say, propranolol, 20 milligrams, is not going to induce retrograde amnesia."

The first paper reporting experimental results of propranolol use in modulation of memory and emotion in humans was published by Cahill et al. in 1994. Subjects received either propranolol or placebo one hour prior to exposure to an emotional arousal or neutral stimulus, and then recall and emotional response were measured. No differences were observed between groups for neutral stimulus, but with an emotional arousal stimulus, recall in the placebo group was significantly higher than in the propranolol group. These data suggest that the beta-adrenergic system is involved in memory formation, particularly when emotional arousal is involved; this system is central to enhanced memory formation.

Other early results are somewhat contradictory. While one study saw no difference in recall response to emotional arousal one week following initial stimuli with or without propranolol administration (van Stegeren, Everaerd, and Gooren 2002), other data do indicate effectiveness of treatment. Propranolol given during contextual fear conditioning was found to decrease emotional arousal upon subsequent exposure to stimulus (Grillon et al. 2004).

Propranolol use in individuals diagnosed with PTSD has also been examined in this context. Propranolol was given during stimuli, and different responses were observed between arousal and neutral stimuli, but no differences were observed between controls and those with PTSD. However, nearly 75% of the PTSD subjects were taking psychotropic medications, which may have altered the observed effects (Reist et al. 2001). Collectively, these data suggest that propranolol use prior to a substantially traumatic exposure may be effective in reducing emotional and fear responses.

Research on the effect of propranolol immediately following trauma or to disrupt formation and consolidation has focused on administration to individuals in the emergency room. Fewer individuals treated with propranolol within six hours following a traumatic event developed PTSD than those receiving placebo. In addition, and when subjected to imagery trials three months later, no individuals who received propranolol experienced physiologic responses, compared to 43% of controls (Pitman et al. 2002). Despite several subjects not returning for follow-up in this study, these are encouraging results. A subsequent study examined a time course treatment with propranolol in individuals reporting to the emergency room after trauma. Follow-up two months after the trauma indicated that PTSD rates were significantly higher in subjects who refused propranolol (Vaiva et al. 2003).

More recently, research has shifted to examine propranolol use during memory reconsolidation after development of PTSD. Individuals with diagnosed PTSD were examined to determine whether reactivation of traumatic event memory would provide an opportunity for propranolol modulation and subsequent weakened emotional association. Subjects diagnosed with PTSD triggered by a variety of events recalled and described their experiences in detail and received either propranolol or placebo immediately and again two hours later. One week later subjects came back and listened to the accounts of their trauma from the previous week, while physiological indicators of stress were recorded. Responses in subjects who received propranolol were significantly lower on all physiological measurements than those who received placebo (Brunet et al. 2008).

Subsequent studies have shown similar results. Possible weakening or alleviation of the fear response, and prevention of its return by propranolol during reconsolidation were examined by treating subjects with propranolol prior to stimulation and reactivation of their fear memory. According to Kindt et al. (2009): "one reactivation trial combined with the administration of propranolol completely eliminated the behavioral expression of the fear memory 24 hours later" (p. 257). The propranolol did not erase the memory; rather, it dampened the emotional response to subsequent stimuli. These results have profound potential for service members with PTSD, whose condition is often triggered by everyday stimuli such as a car backfire.

Because these data indicate an effectiveness of propranolol both immediately after trauma and during reconsolidation, McGhee et al. (2009) performed a retrospective study on burned service members to examine whether those who had received propranolol during treatment of their physical injuries had different rates of PTSD development. Propranolol is given during treatment of some burn victims to decrease the hypermetabolic and cardiovascular effects associated with the autonomic response to severe burns. No difference was seen in PTSD development in those burned service members who received propranolol and those who didn't, but neither the time between the injury and propranolol administration nor the propranolol dose were reported. The soldiers who received propranolol also had significantly higher burn areas, received significantly more morphine, and had significantly more surgeries during treatment, all of which could confound interpretation. These results do not correlate with those showing effectiveness of propranolol use, but this study was retrospective and not well controlled. Clearly, additional well-controlled prospective studies are needed to adequately address dose, timing, optimal safety, and efficacy of propranolol as a treatment for PTSD.

Ethics and Propranolol Use

While research is not conclusive on the most effective timing and use of propranolol in prevention and treatment of PTSD, results are promising and clinical trials are underway. The major ethical opposition to "forgetting therapy" has come from the President's Council on Bioethics report, *Beyond Therapy: Biotechnology and the Pursuit of Happiness* (2003). In addition, the September 2007 edition of the *American Journal of Bioethics* featured a target article followed by commentary responses that filled nearly half the issue and focused on ethical issues surrounding "forgetting therapy." Both of these sources were published prior to much of the research on propranolol use during memory reconsolidation. *Beyond Therapy* cites only the work by Cahill and Pitman described earlier.

I will begin the discussion of the ethical issues surrounding "forgetting therapy" with excerpts from *Beyond Therapy* and the transcripts of the President's Council proceedings. The President's Council places the debate in the setting of the pursuit of happiness and sense of self. *Beyond Therapy* suggests that because we seek happiness for ourselves and "our soul," not for our material body, our happiness is connected to our personhood and identity. We would not seek happiness if achieving it meant we would lose ourselves or our identity in the process, and memory is essential to this process. "If experiencing our happiness depends upon experiencing a stable identity, then our happiness depends also on our memory, on knowing who we are in relation to who we have been" (p. 238).

The Council's primary objection to propranolol therapy is that use for memory alteration disrupts sense of self. *Beyond Therapy* asserts that our memory preserves us and who we are and where we have been, furnishes our sense of self, and is a combination of happy moments and shameful acts. To be ourselves we cannot abandon or forget who we once were: "To alter or numb our remembrance of things past cuts to the heart of what it means to remember in a human way, and it is this biotechnical possibility that we focus on here" (p. 245). It asserts further that if we sacrifice the accuracy of our memories in order to ease pain and suffering and expand control of our lives, we will ultimately sever ourselves from reality and leave our identity or sense of self behind. The Council suggests that if we treat those who suffer bad memories, we will compromise the truthfulness of how they remember and risk having them live falsely, despite the acknowledgment that some memories are so painful and intrusive as to preclude the possibility for normal life and experience.

The Council acknowledges that those who experience events so traumatic as to be debilitating would benefit from this type of treatment. Nonetheless, it expresses concerns, including treatment of criminals or those who intentionally committed "awful deeds" to dull their pain, treating soldiers before battle to turn them into "killing machines" who would have no cares about their actions, or allowing ready access to the drug to persons who may take it any time they think an event will result in painful memory. An additional concern is whether having the power to dull memories of terrible things will render individuals and society unmoved by suffering, wrongdoing, and cruelty: "Armed with new powers to ease the suffering of bad memories, we might come to see all psychic pain as unnecessary and in the process come to pursue a happiness that is less than human: an unmindful happiness, unchanged by time and events, unmoved by life's vicissitudes" (p. 258). These concerns are legitimate, but they are directed more towards use in everyday occasions in the general public, not in military veterans.

Beyond Therapy's closing statement encapsulates the Council's conclusion regarding alteration of memory:

> Nothing would trouble us, but we would probably be shallow people, never falling to the depths of despair because we have little interest in the heights of human happiness or in the complicated lives of those around us. In the end, to have only happy memories is not to be happy in a truly human way. It is simply to be free of misery—an understandable desire given the many troubles of life, but a low aspiration for those who seek a truly human happiness. (p. 264)

Bell (2008) quotes the Council on the issue of our sense of self: "our memories make us who we are and by rewriting memories pharmacologically we might succeed in easing real suffering at the risk of falsifying our perception of the world and undermining our true identity" (p. 3). Bell's response to this statement acknowledges the Council's concern in that memories affect our life in society, and that by altering memories we may desensitize ourselves to our actions and lose empathy for others who have experienced trauma. Bell continues to suggest that individuals taking propranolol will still remember facts and the traumatic effect, but that their evaluation and appraisal will change:

> Patients taking propranolol will still remember the "facts" as it were, of the traumatic effect. Only their appraisal of these facts will change. Furthermore, propranolol is designed to specifically target fear-based memories, so even if the experience of fear was reduced, one could still retain other emotional reactions to the event such as disgust or sadness, which could serve to remind us why certain behaviours are wrong. (p. 3)

The Council report does not address the idea that normal memory evolution includes a certain amount of decay. This was presented, however, by Dr. James McGaugh in the transcripts of the proceedings of the Council (President's Council 2002). As we age we tend to forget or become less aware of our past memories, particularly those from the more distant past. In addition, anesthetics and analgesics are regularly administered to prevent patients from feeling pain during medical procedures. This is not conceptually different from dulling PTSD-associated emotional pain. The Council does acknowledge that self and sense of self naturally evolve and change over time. An individual of 30 is neither physically, emotionally, nor cognitively the same as he or she was at age one. Thus, sense of self is not a static quality that can only be changed by pharmacological intervention.

Additional relevant points for discussion were presented in the commentaries responding to the target article. Overmedication is a problem in our society, as is "disease mongering"—the labeling of normal human behaviors, adaptations, or responses as medical conditions, and then treating those conditions pharmacologically. This issue is an important concern of the Council, who present the scenario of an individual who witnesses a murder and immediately takes propranolol to render the memory less painful (President's Council 2003). While this scenario is worthy of consideration—and I agree that use in this manner is inappropriate—it is also somewhat unrealistic, as these drugs would not be available like aspirin or Tylenol, which people might carry in their pockets for use at any time. However, emotional experience and response is an aspect of human life. By using propranolol to prevent or treat PTSD, are we disease mongering as suggested by the Council? Trachman (2007) discusses the converse side of the argument in detail. A traumatic experience is a causal event outside a person's control. Some people can assimilate these events, come to terms with them, and be strengthened by them. However, not all people react in this manner. Some people are so affected by the painful experience that rational insight and actions may be impaired. For these people, Trachman reasons, "interventions that help control their passions should ultimately result in improved self-understanding, personal behavior, and well being" (p. 22). The key in this argument in support of use is in the triggering of PTSD by events outside of the control of the individual. This is different from behaviors such as cigarette smoking, where the individual knowingly chooses to engage in a behavior that will likely result in the need for treatment. Trachman supports propranolol use but advocates research to better predict individuals who will develop PTSD, so it will be clearer whom to treat in the ER (see also Bell 2007). Consideration of use during reconsolidation would alter this argument.

Beyond Therapy argues not only against the use of memory-altering pharmacotherapy, but also against research into its effectiveness. There is resistance to this stance. For example, Hall and Carter (2007) note that: "[The] President's Council on Bioethics (PCB) involve a series of speculative harms that do not provide good reasons to oppose trials to assess the safety and effectiveness of propranolol. Nor does the PCB make a case for proscribing the clinical use of propranolol if the clinical trials indicate that it is effective" (p. 23). Hall and

Carter also point out that use of propranolol in PTSD patients may reduce their abuse of alcohol and other recreational drugs to self-medicate. Between 35 and 40% of veterans have used alcohol more than they intend to, and nearly 30% of that same cohort report wanting or needing to cut down on alcohol consumption (Hoge et al. 2004). Obviously unreported cases are not included here, which would surely increase the prevalence.

Another argument is that this treatment is still being studied, that ethical content of memories is "highly debatable and contingent on individual valuations," and that ethicists should simply consider relief of human suffering (Rosenberg 2007). Some agree with the Council that grief and stress following a traumatic situation are normal, and that over time these tend to subside (Bell 2007). This line of argument states that the experience of trauma and stress and the subsequent response make us who we are as people and are thus essential to personal growth. However, I contend that the essence of PTSD is these emotions *not* subsiding, and that therefore these arguments don't hold against the idea of using propranolol to dissociate emotional response from memory in individuals diagnosed with PTSD.

Another argument against the use of propranolol is that the effects of propranolol on cognition, or conscious decision-making, are unknown. Would altering memory and emotion have an effect on decision-making? Craigie (2007) reports that propranolol has been shown to influence decision-making in different paradigms, with contradictory results. It would be helpful to determine whether—and how—propranolol may cause this effect. If it does, then the risk/benefit ratio of administering propranolol must be reconsidered.

A topic not discussed in *Beyond Therapy* is the effect of propranolol on posttraumatic growth (PTG). PTG refers to the beneficial transformations that occur as a result of trauma, including the reevaluation of life goals and increased self-reliance, empathy, social support, and levels of intimacy. Warnick (2007) reports that PTG occurs more frequently than PTSD, and that the two can occur concurrently, but states there are no data on the effects of propranolol on PTG: "If propranolol diminishes emotion-laden memory, it thus appears reasonable to assume it could drastically reduce the amount of rumination on an emotional event and prevent the development of PTG" (p. 37). In fact, one therapy for people who have experienced traumatic events is an attempt to induce PTG. If, however, an individual with PTSD is afflicted to the point of functional loss or self-harm, he or she may be incapable of experiencing PTG. Propranolol administration and disruption of reconsolidation may aid in induction of PTG as well as relieve PTSD. Warnick rightly suggests expanding research to include effects on PTG.

Discussion Regarding Propranolol Use

While it is imperative that more research be conducted to determine the efficacy of propranolol use in military members suffering from PTSD, the ethical stance against propranolol use is questionable. We have a moral and ethical obligation to military service members to maximize efforts to alleviate PTSD. The consensus seems to be that the President's Council's arguments are unfounded, and that using propranolol to treat PTSD is not unethical. However, independent of arguments regarding the ethical issues, the timing of propranolol use in military service members warrants discussion and should influence the direction of future research.

Using any beta-blocker prior to combat to prevent PTSD in military personnel should not be considered, as it would likely be more detrimental than beneficial. First, the beta-adrenergic signaling system is mediated by the catecholamines epinephrine and norepinephrine. These hormones are central to the fight-or-flight response, and they trigger the heightened awareness necessary for soldiers to survive in combat situations. Propranolol causes slowed heart rate and impairs the ability of the body to raise heart rate; in addition, it inhibits vasoconstriction (thus its effectiveness in treating high blood pressure). It also inhibits exercise performance, because many of the physiological adaptations that occur during exercise to accommodate the increased demand on body systems are facilitated by epinephrine. Therefore, propranolol administration prior to combat situations would not only dampen soldiers' awareness and fight-or-flight response, but it would also impair their ability to respond physiologically and meet the physical demands of combat. Second, the use of propranolol on soldiers before battle to get them to forget what they are being submitted to, to make them forget what they have done to others, or to make them not care would certainly be morally and ethically wrong (Evars 2007; Henry, Fishman, and Youngner 2007; President's Council 2003). The fact that giving soldiers propranolol prior to battle would inhibit their physiological ability to perform and would be counterproductive renders this ethical argument moot.

Ethical issues surrounding propranolol can be separated into two categories, those related to research, and those related to clinical use. Nearly all publications on this issue state that more research on the effects and efficacy of propranolol use is needed. It has been difficult to decipher the proper time, dose, and administration of propranolol in part because of the different paradigms used to examine it: results don't translate between experiments because conditions differ greatly between them. Furthermore, research into which areas of the brain are involved in traumatic memory formation must rely on models, rather than subjecting animals or individuals to actual trauma. It may therefore be impossible to design experiments that truly test the human response to trauma and the effect of propranolol on that response. In addition, many service members don't develop PTSD for three to five years following return from duty, which presents a difficult timeline for study and decisions as to who should be examined.

Most of the ethical issues presented in the literature are in reference to clinical use. When considering treating people before a potentially traumatic experience, or immediately after trauma, one must consider whether the individual in question will actually develop PTSD. Individuals respond differently to traumatic experiences, and not all subsequently suffer from PTSD. Thus the two following questions are posed. Does the mere possibility of developing PTSD warrant preventive treatment, particularly when data suggest that propranolol can successfully dissociate the emotional response from the memory after development of PTSD? And would individuals be capable of informed consent following a traumatic event?

Because of the current widespread use of propranolol for other conditions and the mildness of its side effects, we can conclude there is no harm in using it for preventative therapy. If propranolol use proves to be effective in treatment of PTSD) during the reconsolidation phase, then the argument against using the drug to prevent PTSD because we don't know who will actually develop it becomes moot, because only those who do develop PTSD would be treated. This would also alleviate the concern about people taking propranolol because they feel bad. Regulation could hinge on the concept presented earlier: that cases in which a causal event outside the person's mind, and outside the realm of normal human adaptation, should be treated. It also seems reasonable that the use of propranol would be inappropriate in less severe cases of PTSD, but this is a judgment best left to the clinicians. While the statement is not included in *Beyond Therapy*, McGaugh states in the transcripts that in circumstances in which an event is "really so horrible, it's going to flash into my head, recur and recur so that it begins to take over my life; then that would be a case, I think, in which a little propranolol, if the studies bear out, might be of value" (President's Council 2002).

The Council's major argument against propranolol use to suppress memory is that this action would violate identity and sense of self, and that altering individual memories would affect society, cause people to lose empathy for fellow sufferers, and desensitize people to their actions. Memory is an intrinsic human quality, so does pharmacologically tampering with memory infringe on basic human qualities? In response to this, I present the following two scenarios. Take first the case of a 30-year-old veteran who has completed a tour in Kosovo in addition to three tours in Iraq. Upon walking past a cemetery on the way to a 4th of July BBQ, he is overtaken by grief at the sight of veterans' graves decorated for the holiday. The grief, guilt, and memories triggered by this sight result in his spending over an hour sobbing uncontrollably in the cemetery on the grave of a deceased veteran, while sounds of civilians enjoying their holiday can be heard in the distance. On this same 4th of July, a Vietnam veteran drives miles into an isolated mountain campground because the sounds of the fireworks set off in celebration trigger his flashbacks to combat experiences. When PTSD has reached the point that it impairs daily function and affects relationships as in these two cases, and when PTG is not possible, affected individuals have already lost their sense of self and identity. Society should feel morally and ethically obligated to assist them to regain "normal" life in society, particularly because their condition was caused by their service to their country.

The President's Council states that if experiencing happiness depends upon experiencing a stable identity, then happiness also depends on memory. Individuals with PTSD are neither stable nor happy, and if the members of society are not affected by the sight or knowledge of these soldiers, they have lost their empathy. Those who have suffered and been helped would have more empathy and support and would relate to those who continue to suffer. The Council asks: "could we be happy in the absence of happy memories?

Conversely, could we be happy in the presence of terrible memories, memories so traumatic and so life-altering that they cast a deep shadow over all that we do, today and tomorrow?" (p. 241) Does knowing that 18 Iraqi war veterans commit suicide every month as a consequence of their service answer these questions? I am not arguing that any memory evoking a challenging or emotional response should be blunted, but that when emotions associated with memories alter and destroy lives, considering treatments is a moral necessity.

While substantive ethical issues attend both research and clinical use of memory-altering therapies, the central consideration is the development of treatments to help PTSD patients live normal, productive lives. Since death associated with war is considered ethically acceptable, and the risk of death in war is outweighed by the benefits of fighting that war, helping those who carried out the agenda, risked death, and suffer with a condition associated with their service should be considered an ethical obligation. In the very least, research into the use and effectiveness of propranolol in treating soldiers who have been diagnosed with PTSD is warranted. If it proves to be ineffective, so be it—but if it does prove to be effective and the benefits outweigh the risks, its use should be encouraged. Hall and Carter (2007) also support this view: "If it is reasonable to ask these individuals to engage in life threatening and emotionally distressing activities, then it would be wrong to deny them access to medications that may reduce their considerable risk of developing PTSD" (p. 24). If propranolol use disrupts our sense of self, why do we prescribe it so widely for cardiovascular disease? One cannot argue that use of a drug in the same dose but for different conditions is ethically acceptable in one case and not the other, when the physiological effects in both cases are the same.

Beyond Therapy argues that propranolol use presents risks to episodic memory, to the memory of actual events, and potentially to emotionally positive memory (Henry, Fishman, and Youngner 2007). "Forgetting therapy" is an inappropriate label, as treatment does not induce memory loss per se; rather, it dissociates emotions from memory. Therefore, arguments that loss of episodic memory of events is a risk become moot. This may also indicate a disconnection between the science and scientific research on the one hand, and the ethics community on the other, in that individuals in different academic and educational fields construe different meanings from the same terms.

I will close with the following excerpt from Kolber's (2007) commentary. Kolber quotes a PTSD victim as saying: "I have severe posttraumatic stress disorder and would sell my soul to the devil himself to be rid of my 24/7 hellish flashbacks and night terrors" (p. 25). We have an ethical and moral obligation to treat PTSD. Opinions on propranolol treatment in military veterans should be revised in light of the recent advances in research and updated discussions of ethical issues.

References

American Psychiatric Association (APA). 2000. *Diagnostic and statistical manual of mental disorders*, 4th ed. text revision (DSM-IV-TR). Washington, DC: APA.

Bell, J. 2007. Preventing post-traumatic stress disorder or pathologizing bad memories? *Am J Bioeth* 7(9):29–30.

Bell, J. 2008. Propranolol, post-traumatic stress disorder and narrative identity. *J Med Ethics* 34(11):e23.

Bremner, J.D., et al. 2008. Structural and functional plasticity of the human brain in post-traumatic stress disorder. *Prog Brain Res* 167:171–83.

Brunet, A., et al. 2008. Effect of post-retrieval propranolol on psychophysiological responding during subsequent script-driven traumatic imagery in post-traumatic stress disorder. *J Psychiatr Res* 42(6):503–6.

Cahill, L., et al. 1994. Beta-adrenergic activation and memory for emotional events. *Nature* 371(6499):702–4.

Craigie, J. 2007. Propranolol, cognitive biases, and practical decision-making. *Am J Bioeth* 7(9) :31–32.

Evars, K. 2007. Perspectives on memory manipulation: Using beta-blockers to cure post-traumatic stress disorder. *Camb Q Healthc Ethics* 16(2):138–46.

Grillon, C., et al. 2004. Effects of the beta-blocker propranolol on cued and contextual fear conditioning in humans. *Psychopharmacology* 175(3):342–32.

Hall, W., and A. Carter. 2007. Debunking alarmist objections to the pharmacological prevention of PTSD. *Am J Bioeth* 7(9):23–25.

Henry, M., J. R. Fishman, and S. J. Youngner. 2007. Propranolol and the prevention of post-traumatic stress disorder: Is it wrong to erase the sting of bad memories? *Am J Bioeth* 7(9):12–20.

Hoge, C. W., et al. 2004. Combat duty in Iraq and Afghanistan, mental health problems, and barriers to care. *N Engl J Med* 351 (l):13–22.

Kindt, M., M. Soeter, and B. Vervliet. 2009. Beyond extinction: Erasing human fear responses and preventing the return of fear. *Nat Neurosci* 12(3):256–58.

Kolber A. 2007. Clarifying the debate over therapeutic forgetting. *Am J Bioeth* 7(9):25–27.

Mathew, S. J., R. B. Price, and D. S. Charney. 2008. Recent advances in the neurobiology of anxiety disorders: Implications for novel therapeutics. *Am J Med Genet C Semin Med Genet* 15:89–98.

McGhee, L. L., et al. 2009. The effect of propranolol on posttraumatic stress disorder in burned service members. *J Burn Care Res* 30(1):92–97.

Milliken, C. S., J. L. Auchterlonie, and C. W Hoge. 2007. Longitudinal assessment of mental health problems among active and reserve component soldiers returning from the Iraq war. *JAMA* 298(18):2141–48.

Pitman, R. K., et al. 2002. Pilot study of secondary prevention of posttraumatic stress disorder with propranolol. *Biol Psychiatry* 51(2):189–92.

President's Council on Bioethics. 2002. Proceedings transcripts. www.bioethics.gov/topics/memory_index.html.

President's Council on Bioethics. 2003. *Beyond therapy: Biotechnology and the pursuit of happiness.* Washington, DC: President's Council on Bioethics; Dana Press.

Reist, C., et al. 2001. Beta-adrenergic blockade and emotional memory in PTSD. *Int J Neuropsychopharmacol* 4 (4):377–83.

Roozendal, B., A. Barsegyan, and S. Lee. 2008. Adrenal stress hormones, amygdala activation, and memory for emotionally arousing experiences. *Prog Brain Res* 167:79–97.

Rosenberg, L. 2007. Necessary forgetting: On the use of propranolol in post-traumatic stress disorder management. *Am J Bioeth* 7(9):27–28.

Trachman, H. 2007. Spinoza's passions. *Am J Bioeth* 7(9):21–23.

Vaiva, G., et al. 2003. Immediate treatment with propranolol decreases posttraumatic stress disorder two months after trauma. *Biol Psychiatry* 54 (12):947–49.

van Stegeren, A. H. 2008. The role of the noradrenergic system in emotional memory. *Acta Physiol* 127:532–41.

van Stegeren, A. H.,W. Everaerd, and L. J. G. Gooren. 2002. The effect of beta-adrenergic blockade after encoding on memory of an emotional event. *Psychopharmacology* 163(2):202–12.

Warnick, J. 2007. Propranolol and its potential inhibition of positive post-traumatic growth. *Am J Bioeth* 7(9):37–38.

Zohar, J., et al. 2008. Post-traumatic stress disorder: Facts and fiction. *Curr Opin Psychiatry* 21:74–77.

Beyond Therapy: Biotechnology and the Pursuit of Happiness

Chapter Five

Who has not wanted to escape the clutches of oppressive and punishing memories? Or to calm the burdensome feelings of anxiety, disappointment, and regret? Or to achieve a psychic state of pure and undivided pleasure and joy? The satisfaction of such desires seems inseparable from our happiness, which we pursue by right and with passion.

In these efforts at peace of mind, human beings have from time immemorial sought help from doctors and drugs. In a famous literary instance, Shakespeare's Macbeth entreats his doctor to free Lady Macbeth from the haunting memory of her own guilty acts:

> *Macbeth.* Canst thou not minister to a mind diseas'd,
> Pluck from the memory a rooted sorrow,
> Raze out the written troubles of the brain,
> And with some sweet oblivious antidote
> Cleanse the stuff'd bosom of that perilous stuff
> Which weighs upon the heart?
>
> *Doctor.* Therein the patient
> Must minister to himself.

Ministering to oneself, however, is easier said than done, and many people have found themselves unequal to the task without some outside assistance. For centuries, they have made use of external agents to drown their sorrows or lift their spirits.

The burgeoning field of neuroscience is providing new, more specific, and safer agents to help us combat all sorts of psychic distress. Soon, doctors may have just the "sweet oblivious antidote" that Macbeth so desired: drugs (such as beta-adrenergic blockers) that numb the emotional sting typically associated with our intensely bad memories[.]

To be sure, these agents—and their better versions, yet to come—are, for now at least, being developed not as means for drug-induced happiness but rather as agents for combating major depression or preventing posttraumatic stress disorder (PTSD). Yet once available for those purposes, they could also be used to ease the soul and enhance the mood of nearly anyone.

From the *President's Council on Bioethics,* October 2003.

By using drugs to satisfy more easily the enduring aspirations to forget what torments us and approach the world with greater peace of mind, what deeper human aspirations might we occlude or frustrate? What qualities of character may become less necessary and, with diminished use, atrophy or become extinct, as we increasingly depend on drugs to cope with misfortune? How will we experience our incompleteness or understand our mortality as our ability grows to medically dissolve all sorts of anxiety? Will the availability of drug-induced conditions of ecstatic pleasure estrange us from the forms of pleasure that depend upon discipline and devotion? And, going beyond the implications for individuals, what kind of a society are we likely to have when the powers to control memory, mood, and mental life through drugs reach their full maturity and are widely used?

I. What Are "Happy Souls"?

Because the happiness we seek we seek for *ourselves*—for *our* self, not for someone else's, and for our *self* or embodied soul, not for our bodies as material stuff—our happiness is bound up with our personhood and our identity. We would not want to attain happiness (or any other object of our desires) if the condition for attaining it required that we become someone else, that we lose our identity in the process.

The importance of identity for happiness implies necessarily the importance of memory. If experiencing our happiness depends on experiencing a stable identity, then our happiness depends also on our memory, on knowing who we are in relation to who we have been.

But if enfeebled memory can cripple identity, selectively altered memory can distort it. Changing the content of our memories or altering their emotional tonalities, however desirable to alleviate guilty or painful consciousness, could subtly reshape who we are, at least to ourselves. With altered memories we might feel better about ourselves, but it is not clear that the better-feeling "we" remains the same as before. Lady Macbeth, cured of her guilty torment, would remain the murderess she was, but not the conscience-stricken being even she could not help but be.

[A]n unchecked power to erase memories, brighten moods, and alter our emotional dispositions could imperil our capacity to form a strong and coherent personal identity. To the extent that our inner life ceases to reflect the ups and downs of daily existence and instead operates independently of them, we dissipate our identity, which is formed through engagement with others and through immersion in the mix of routine and unpredictable events that constitute our lives.

II. Memory and Happiness

Our identity or sense of self emerges, grows, and changes. Yet, despite all the changes, thanks to the integrating powers of memory, our identity also, remarkably, persists *as ours*.

We especially want our memories to be not simply a sequence of discon-nected experiences, but a narrative that seems to contain some unfolding pur-pose, some larger point from beginning to end, some aspiration discovered, pursued, and at least partially fulfilled.

Memory is central to human flourishing, in other words, precisely because we pursue happiness in time, as time-bound beings. We have a past and a future as well as a present, and being happy through time requires that these be connected in a meaningful way. If we are to flourish as ourselves, we must do so without abandoning or forgetting who we are or once were. Yet because our lives are time-bound, our happiness is always incomplete—always not-yet and on-the-way, always here but slipping away, but also always pos-sible again and in the future. Our happiest experiences can be revivified. And, as we reminisce from greater distance and with more experience, even our painful experiences can often acquire for us a meaning not in evidence when they occurred.

The place of memory in the pursuit of happiness also suggests some-thing essential about human identity, a theme raised in various places and in different ways throughout this report: namely, our identities are formed both by what we do and by what we undergo or suffer. We actively choose paths and do deeds fit to be remembered. But we also live through memora-ble experiences that we would never have chosen—experiences we often wish never happened at all. To some extent, these unchosen memories constrain us; though we may regret the shadows they cast over our pursuit of happiness, we cannot simply escape them while remaining who we really are. And yet, through the act of remembering—the act of discerning and giving meaning to the past as it really was—we can shape, to some degree, the meaning of our memories, both good and bad.

The capacity to alter or numb our remembrance of things past cuts to the heart of what it means to remember in a human way, and it is this biotechni-cal possibility that we focus on here. Deciding when or whether to use such biotechnical power will require that we think long and hard about what it means to remember truthfully, to live in time, and to seek happiness without losing or abandoning our identity. The rest of this discussion of "memory and happiness" is an invitation to such reflection.

Good Memories and Bad

[T]he significance of past events often becomes clear to us only after much rumination in light of later experience, and what seems trivial at one time may appear crucial at another. Neither can an excellent memory be one that remembers only what we *want* to remember: sometimes our most valuable memories are of events that were painful when they occurred, but that on reflection teach us vital lessons.

Biotechnology and Memory Alteration

It is a commonplace observation that, while some events fade quickly from the mind, emotionally intense experiences form memories that are peculiarly vivid and long-lasting. Not only do we recall such events long after they happened, but the recollection is often accompanied, in some measure, by a recurrence of the emotions aroused during the original experience.

When a person experiences especially shocking or violent events (such as a plane crash or bloody combat), the release of stress hormones may be so intense that the memory-encoding system is over-activated. The result is a consolidation of memories both far stronger and more persistent than normal and also more apt, upon recollection, to call forth the intense emotional response of the original experience. In such cases, each time the person relives the traumatic memory, a new flood of stress hormones is released, and the experience may be so emotionally intense as to be encoded as a new experience. With time, the memories grow more recurrent and intrusive, and the response—fear, helplessness, horror—more incapacitating. As we shall see, drugs that might prevent or alleviate the symptoms of PTSD are among the chief medical benefits that scientists expect from recent research in the neurochemistry of memory formation.

In fact, the discovery of hormonal regulation of memory formation was quickly followed up by clinical studies on human subjects demonstrating that memory of emotional experiences can be altered pharmacologically. In one particularly interesting series of experiments, Larry Cahill and his colleagues showed that injections of beta-blockers can, by inhibiting the action of stress hormones, suppress the memory-enhancing effects of strong emotional arousal.

[T]aking propranolol appears to have little or no effect on how we remember everyday or emotionally neutral information. But when taken at the time of highly emotional experiences, propranolol appears to suppress the normal memory-enhancing effects of emotional arousal—while leaving the immediate emotional response unaffected. These results suggested the possibility of using beta-blockers to help survivors of traumatic events to reduce their intrusive—and in some cases crippling—memories of those events.

[A]lthough the pharmacology of memory alteration is a science still in its infancy, the significance of this potential new power—to separate the subjective experience of memory from the truth of the experience that is remembered—should not be underestimated. It surely returns us to the large ethical and anthropological questions with which we began—about memory's role in shaping personal identity and the character of human life, and about the meaning of remembering things that we would rather forget and of forgetting things that we perhaps ought to remember.

Memory-Blunting: Ethical Analysis

If we had the power, by promptly taking a memory-altering drug, to dull the emotional impact of what could become very painful memories, when might we be tempted to use it? And for what reasons should we yield to or resist the temptation?

At first glance, such a drug would seem ideally suited for the prevention of PTSD, the complex of debilitating symptoms that sometimes afflict those who have experienced severe trauma. These symptoms—which include persistent reexperiencing of the traumatic event and avoidance of every person, place, or thing that might stimulate the horrid memory's return[1] can so burden mental life as to make normal everyday living extremely difficult, if not impossible.[2] For those suffering these disturbing symptoms, a drug that could separate a painful memory from its powerful emotional component would appear very welcome indeed.

Yet the prospect of preventing (even) PTSD with beta-blockers or other memory-blunting agents seems to be, for several reasons, problematic. First of all, the drugs in question appear to be effective only when administered during or shortly after a traumatic event—and thus well before any symptoms of PTSD would be manifested. How then could we make, and make on the spot, the *prospective* judgment that a particular event is sufficiently terrible to warrant preemptive memory-blunting? Second, how shall we judge *which* participants in the event merit such treatment? After all, not everyone who suffers through painful experiences is destined to have pathological memory effects. Should the drugs in question be given to everyone or only to those with an observed susceptibility to PTSD, and, if the latter, how will we know who these are? Finally, in some cases merely witnessing a disturbing event (for example, a murder, rape, or terrorist attack) is sufficient to cause PTSD-like symptoms long afterwards. Should we then, as soon as disaster strikes, consider giving memory-altering drugs to all the witnesses, in addition to those directly involved?

If the apparent powers of memory-blunting drugs are confirmed, some might be inclined to prescribe them liberally to all who are involved in a sufficiently terrible event. After all, even those not destined to come down with full-blown PTSD are likely to suffer painful recurrent memories of an airplane crash, an incident of terrorism, or a violent combat operation. In the aftermath of such shocking incidents, why not give everyone the chance to remember these events without the added burden of painful emotions? This line of reasoning might, in fact, tempt us to give beta-blockers liberally to soldiers on the eve of combat, to emergency workers en route to a disaster site, or even to individuals requesting prophylaxis against the shame or guilt they might incur from future misdeeds—in general, to anyone facing an experience that is likely to leave lasting intrusive memories.

Yet on further reflection it seems clear that not every intrusive memory is a suitable candidate for prospective pharmacological blunting. As Daniel Schacter has observed, "attempts to avoid traumatic memories often backfire":

> Intrusive memories need to be acknowledged, confronted, and worked through, in order to set them to rest for the long term. Unwelcome memories of trauma are symptoms of a disrupted psyche that requires attention before it can resume healthy functioning. Beta-blockers might make it easier for trauma survivors to face and incorporate traumatic recollections, and in that sense could facilitate long-term adaptation. Yet it is also possible that beta-blockers would work against the normal process of recovery: traumatic memories would not spring to mind with the kind of psychological force that demands attention and perhaps intervention. Prescription of beta-blockers could bring about

an effective trade-off between short-term reductions in the sting of traumatic memories and long-term increases in persistence of related symptoms of a trauma that has not been adequately confronted.[3]

The point can be generalized: in the immediate aftermath of a painful experience, we simply cannot know either the full meaning of the experience in question or the ultimate character and future prospects of the individual who experiences it. We cannot know how this experience will change this person at this time and over time. Will he be cursed forever by unbearable memories that, in retrospect, clearly should have been blunted medically? Or will he succeed, over time, in "redeeming" those painful memories by actively integrating them into the narrative of his life? By "rewriting" memories pharmacologically we might succeed in easing real suffering at the risk of falsifying our perception of the world and undermining our true identity.

Finally, the decision whether or not to use memory-blunting drugs must be made in the absence of clearly diagnosable disease. The drug must be taken right after a traumatic experience has occurred, and thus before the different ways that different individuals handle the same experience has become clear. In some cases, these interventions will turn out to have been preventive medicine, intervening to ward off the onset of PTSD before it arrives—though it is worth noting that we would lack even post hoc knowledge of whether any particular now-unaffected individual, in the absence of using the drug, would have become symptomatic.[4] In other cases, the interventions would not be medicine at all: altering the memory of individuals who could have lived well, even with severely painful memories, without pharmacologically dulling the pain. Worse, in still other cases, the use of such drugs would inoculate individuals in advance against the psychic pain that *should* accompany their commission of cruel, brutal, or shameful deeds. But in all cases, from the defensible to the dubious, the use of such powers changes the character of human memory, by intervening directly in the way individuals "encode," and thus the way they understand, the happenings of their own lives and the realities of the world around them.

Remembering Fitly and Truly
Altering the formation of emotionally powerful memories risks severing what we remember from how we remember it and distorting the link between our perception of significant human events and the significance of the events themselves. It risks, in a word, falsifying our perception and understanding of the world. It risks making shameful acts seem less shameful, or terrible acts less terrible, than they really are.

Imagine the experience of a person who witnesses a shocking murder. Fearing that he will be haunted by images of this event, he immediately takes propranolol (or its more potent successor) to render his memory of the murder less painful and intrusive. Thanks to the drug, his memory of the murder gets encoded as a garden-variety, emotionally neutral experience. But in manipulating his memory in this way, he risks coming to think about the murder as more tolerable than it really is, as an event that should not sting those who witness it. For our opinions about the meaning of our experiences are shaped partly by the feelings evoked when we remember them. If, psychologically, the murder is transformed into an event our witness can recall without pain—or without *any* particular emotion—perhaps its moral significance will also fade from consciousness. If so, he would in a sense have ceased to be a genuine witness of the murder. When asked about it, he might say, "Yes, I was there. But it wasn't so terrible."

This points us to a deeper set of questions about bad memories: Would dulling our memory of terrible things make us too comfortable with the world, unmoved by suffering, wrongdoing, or cruelty? Does not the experience of hard truths—of the unchosen, the inexplicable, the tragic—remind us that we can never be fully at home in the world, especially if we are to take seriously the reality of human evil? Further, by blunting our experience and awareness of shameful, fearful, and hateful things, might we not also risk deadening our response to what is admirable, inspiring, and lovable? Can we become numb to life's sharpest sorrows without also becoming numb to its greatest joys?

There seems to be little doubt that some bitter memories are so painful and intrusive as to ruin the possibility for normal experience of much of life and the world. In such cases the impulse to relieve a crushing burden and restore lost innocence is fully understandable: If there are some things that it is better never to have experienced at all—things we would avoid if we possibly could—why not erase them from the memory of those unfortunate enough to have suffered them? If there are some things it is better never to have known or seen, why not use our power over memory to restore a witness's shattered peace of mind? There is great force in this argument, perhaps especially in cases where children lose prematurely that innocence that is rightfully theirs.

And yet, there may be a great cost to acting compassionately for those who suffer bad memories, if we do so by compromising the truthfulness of how they remember. We risk having them live falsely in order simply to cope, to survive by whatever means possible.

The Obligation to Remember

Having truthful memories is not simply a personal matter. Strange to say, our own memory is not merely our own; it is part of the fabric of the society in which we live. Consider the case of a person who has suffered or witnessed atrocities that occasion unbearable memories: for example, those with firsthand experience of the Holocaust. The life of that individual might well be served by dulling such bitter memories,[5] but such a humanitarian intervention, if widely practiced, would seem deeply troubling: Would the community as a whole—would the human race—be served by such a mass numbing of this terrible but indispensable memory? Do those who suffer evil have a duty to remember and bear witness, lest we all forget the very horrors that haunt them?

Surely, we cannot and should not force those who live through great trauma to endure its painful memory *for the benefit of the rest of us.* But as a community, there are certain events that we have an obligation to remember—an obligation that falls disproportionately, one might even say unfairly, on those who experience such events most directly.[6] What kind of people would we be if we did not "want" to remember the Holocaust, if we sought to make the anguish it caused simply go away? And yet, what kind of people are we, especially those who face such horrors firsthand, that we can endure such awful memories?

The answer, in part, is that those who suffer terrible things cannot or should not have to endure their own bad memories alone. If, as a people, we have an obligation to remember certain terrible events truthfully, surely we ought to help those who suffered through those events to come to terms with their worst memories. Of course, one might see the new biotechnical powers, developed precisely to ease the psychic pain of bad memories, as the mark of such solidarity: perhaps it is our new way of meeting the obligation to aid those who remember the hardest things, those who bear witness to us and for us. But such solidarity may, in the end, prove false: for it exempts us from the duty to suffer-with (literally, to feel *com*-passion for) those who remember; it does not demand that we preserve the truth of their memories; it attempts instead to make the problem go away, and with it the truth of the experience in question.

The Soul of Memory, the Remembering Soul

[W]e might often be tempted to sacrifice the accuracy of our memories for the sake of easing our pain or expanding our control over our own psychic lives. But doing so means, ultimately, severing ourselves from reality and leaving our own identity behind; it risks making us false, small, or capable of great illusions, and thus capable of great decadence or great evil, or perhaps simply willing to accept a phony contentment. We might be tempted to alter our memories to preserve an open future—to live the life we wanted to live before a particular experience happened to us. But in another sense, such interventions assume that our own future is not open—that we cannot and could never redeem the unwanted memory over time, that we cannot and could never integrate the remembered experience with our own truthful pursuit of happiness.

To have only happy memories would be a blessing—and a curse. Nothing would trouble us, but we would probably be shallow people, never falling to the depths of despair because we have little interest in the heights of human happiness or in the complicated lives of those around us. In the end, to have only happy memories is not to be happy in a truly human way. It is simply to be free of misery—an understandable desire given the many troubles of life, but a low aspiration for those who seek a truly human happiness.

Notes

1. These symptoms are observed especially among combat veterans; indeed, PTSD is the modern name for what used to be called "shell shock" or "combat neurosis." Among veterans, PTSD is frequently associated with recurrent nightmares, substance abuse, and delusional outbursts of violence. There is controversy about the prevalence of PTSD, with some studies finding that up to 8 percent of adult Americans have suffered the

disorder as well as a third of all veterans of the Vietnam War. See Kessler, R. C., et al., "Post-Traumatic Stress Disorder in the National Comorbidity Survey," *Archives of General Psychiatry* 52(12): 1048–1060, 1995; Kulka, R. A., et al., *Trauma and the Vietnam War Generation: Report of Findings from the National Vietnam Veterans Readjustment Study*, New York: Brunner/ Mazel, 1990.

2. There is already ongoing controversy about excessive diagnosis of PTSD. Many psychotherapists believe that a patient's psychic troubles are generally based on some earlier (now repressed) traumatic experience which must be unearthed and dealt with if relief is to be found. True PTSD is, however, generally transient, and the search for treatment is directed against the symptoms of its initial (worst) phase—the sleeplessness, the nightmares, the excessive jitteriness.

3. Of course, many Holocaust survivors managed, without pharmacological assistance, to live fulfilling lives while never forgetting what they lived through. At the same time, many survivors would almost certainly have benefited from pharmacological treatment.

4. There is no definitive diagnostic criterion for PTSD, but the core symptoms are thought to include persistent re-experiencing of the traumatic event, avoidance of associated stimuli, and hyperarousal. See *Diagnostic and Statistical Manual of Mental Disorders, Fourth Edition, text revision*, Washington, D.C.: American Psychiatric Association, 2000, pp. 463–486.

5. Schacter, D., *The Seven Sins of Memory: How the Mind Forgets and Remembers*, New York: Houghton Mifflin, 2001, p. 183.

6. For a discussion of memory-altering drugs and the meaning of "bearing witness," see the essay by Cohen, E., "Our Psychotropic Memory," *SEED*, no. 8, Fall 2003, p. 42.

EXPLORING THE ISSUE

Should Memory-Dampening Drugs Be Used to Prevent and Treat Trauma in Combat Soldiers?

Critical Thinking and Reflection

1. Assuming that a medication is effective in alleviating the symptoms of combat-related PTSD, what are some of the risks and costs of using such an intervention?
2. Consider societal responsibility pertaining to the use of memory-dampening drugs in treating combat-related PTSD. Namely, to what extent does society have a responsibility to try to alleviate these symptoms?
3. Some experts assert that for some people, the experience of trauma can lead to posttraumatic growth in which the trauma survivor has a greater appreciation of life and relationships. If memory-dampening drugs are found to reduce the potential for posttraumatic growth, how should that consideration be weighed in determining the appropriateness of these drugs?
4. Assuming that memory-dampening drugs are effective in reducing PTSD symptoms, who should make the decision about their appropriateness in a given case, a physician, the trauma survivor, or a team of experts? Also, when should they be administered to combat soldiers, on the field, back at base, or upon returning home?
5. How should researchers go about studying the effects of memory-dampening drugs on survivors of combat trauma? What are some of the methodological challenges involved in this kind of research? What are some of the ethical considerations that must be weighed?

Is There Common Ground?

Dr. Elise Donovan and the President's Council on Bioethics acknowledge that the experience of trauma can have debilitating effects on people who are exposed to such horrifying experiences. Posttraumatic stress disorder has justifiably received increasing attention in America as a result of the alarming numbers of soldiers diagnosed with this condition who have fought in the wars in Iraq and Afghanistan. American society has a responsibility to respond to the devastating effects of PTSD on combat soldiers, on their loved ones, and on the country as a whole. Dr. Donovan and the Council agree that drugs such as propranolol can be effective in alleviating some of the debilitating symptoms of PTSD. Dr. Donovan contends that it is justifiable and ethical to use these drugs to treat soldiers who have been traumatized by combat. The Council, however, expresses strong reservations about these drugs on ethical grounds, contending that individuals who take these drugs to alleviate symptoms of trauma would possibly be deprived of the opportunity to grow as a result of their traumatic experience. Dr. Donovan is also concerned about ethical and moral issues, but asserts that for those who have risked their lives to serve the country, and who suffer with PTSD as a result, there is an ethical obligation to try to alleviate their psychological distress.

Additional Resources

Chu, J. A. (2011). *Rebuilding shattered lives: Treating complex PTSD and dissociative disorders*. Hoboken, NJ: John Wiley & Sons.

Dent, M. F., & Bremner, J. (2009). Pharmacotherapy for posttraumatic stress disorder and other trauma-related disorders. In M. M. Antony, M. B. Stein (Eds.), *Oxford handbook of anxiety and related disorders* (pp. 405–416). New York: Oxford University Press.

Hurley, E. (2010). Combat trauma and the moral risks of memory manipulating drugs. *Journal of Applied Philosophy, 27*(3), 221–245.

PTSD Alliance. www.ptsdalliance.org/

United States Department of Veterans Affairs National Center for PTSD. www.ptsd.va.gov/

ISSUE 8

Is Addiction a Brain Disease?

YES: National Institute on Drug Abuse, from *Drugs, Brain, and Behavior: The Science of Addiction*, revised ed., Washington, DC: National Institute on Drug Abuse (2007)

NO: Sally Satel and Scott O. Lilienfeld, from "Singing the Brain Disease Blues," *AJOB Neuroscience* (vol. 1, no. 1, pp. 46, 47, January 2010)

Learning Outcomes

After reading this issue, you should be able to:

- Understand the concept of "brain disease" as it applies to behaviors such as addiction.
- Critically evaluate the contrasting view that addiction is a brain disease versus the notion that addictive behavior is a choice.
- Consider the extent to which addiction is influenced by the biological makeup of the individual.
- Understand the bodily systems that are affected by drug abuse, and the ways in which drugs work on the brain to produce feelings of pleasure.
- Discuss the extent to which addiction is influenced by environmental factors.

ISSUE SUMMARY

YES: In the NIDA publication, the argument is made that addiction is indeed a disease, and that scientific information is available about the nature, prevention, and treatment of this disease.

NO: Psychiatrist Sally Satel and psychologist Scott O. Lilienfeld object to the brain disease characterization of drug addiction, asserting that addiction is an activity whose course can be altered by its foreseeable consequences.

$\mathbf{F}$or quite some time, the American people have been given the message that drug addiction is not a moral failing, but rather a medical disease. In other words, it is not the fault of addicts that they are unable to control irresistible urges to consume drugs any more than it is the fault of a person who struggles with the debilitating symptoms of diabetes. This premise has been supported by the American Medical Association, which endorses the ideas that drug dependencies, including alcoholism, are diseases, and that their treatment is a legitimate component of medical practice. Thousands of Web sites that promote treatment programs for substance-dependent individuals characterize addiction as a disease, treated by health professionals.

A common misconception exists that Alcoholics Anonymous (AA) promotes the view that alcoholism is a disease. However, AA has no opinion on controversial issues such as the nature of alcoholism. They state merely that alcoholism "is an illness which only a spiritual experience will conquer." Words such as these would certainly not be applicable to medical diseases such as diabetes or asthma. Interestingly, it seems that the disease model of drug addiction has been promulgated most vehemently by agencies of the U.S. government such as the National Institute on Drug Abuse (NIDA) and the Substance Abuse and Mental Health Services Administration (SAMHSA). Although these agencies provide valuable services, social observers question whether promotion of the disease model is to acquire funding for research.

In the NIDA publication, the argument is made that addiction is indeed a disease, and that scientific information is available about the nature, prevention, and treatment of this disease. NIDA promotes the idea that it is important for scientists to study the effects that drugs have on the brain and on behavior, so that this information can be used to develop drug abuse prevention and treatment programs. NIDA highlights the fact that although the initial decision to take drugs is voluntary, over time drug-addicted individuals show physical changes in areas of the brain that are critical to judgment, decision making, learning and memory, and behavior control.

NIDA views addiction as a chronic, relapsing brain disease that is characterized by compulsive drug seeking and use, despite harmful consequences. Over time, if drug use continues, pleasurable activities become less pleasurable, and drug abuse becomes necessary for abusers to simply feel "normal." Drug abusers reach a point where they seek and take drugs, despite the tremendous problems caused for themselves and their loved ones. Some individuals may start to feel the need to take higher or more frequent doses, even in the early stages of their drug use.

NIDA contends that the initial decision to take drugs is mostly voluntary. However, when drug abuse takes over, a person's ability to exert self-control can become seriously impaired. Brain imaging studies from drug-addicted individuals show physical changes in areas of the brain that are critical to judgment, decision making, learning and memory, and behavior control. The overall risk for addiction is influenced by the biological makeup of the individual. According to NIDA, addiction can even be influenced by gender or ethnicity, a person's developmental stage, and the surrounding social environment. Scientists studying the effects that drugs have on the brain and on people's behavior use this information to develop programs for preventing drug abuse and for helping people recover from addiction.

Psychiatrist Sally Satel and psychologist Scott Lilienfeld object to the brain disease characterization of drug addiction, asserting that addiction is an activity whose course can be altered by its foreseeable consequences. Further, the brain disease model erroneously suggests that the brain is the most useful level of analysis for understanding and treating addiction. These authors point out that repetitive drug use is reduced or stopped altogether when the adverse consequences of drug use exceed its rewards. They also contend that society should view drug users in terms of their capacity for self-governance, rather than as helpless individuals incapable of changing their behavior.

Satel and Lilienfeld state that addiction can be defined in any way the definer thinks fit. However, if one's purpose is providing psychosocial treatment and devising policy, then the "neurocentric" view doesn't help much. Whether powered by changes in meaning or incentives, the capacity for self-governance is the key to the most promising treatments for addiction. This fact is often obscured . . . and the state of "addiction" is taken to mean that the desire to use is unmalleable and beyond the reach of environmental contingencies. In circular fashion, then, addicted individuals are believed to be helpless to change their behavior.

According to authors Satel and Lilienfeld, no amount of reinforcement or punishment can alter the course of an entirely autonomous biological condition. They assert that the mechanical simplicity of the "brain disease" rhetoric has a seductive appeal that obscures the considerable degree of choice in addiction. The brain disease model implies erroneously that the brain is necessarily the most important and useful level of analysis for understanding and treating addiction. In other words, what role does the mind play in influencing a person's choice to use, abuse, and become addicted to drugs?

Drugs, Brain, and Behavior: The Science of Addiction

Drug Abuse and Addiction

What Is Drug Addiction?

Addiction is defined as a chronic, relapsing brain disease that is character-ized by compulsive drug seeking and use, despite harmful consequences. It is considered a brain disease because drugs change the brain—they change its structure and how it works. These brain changes can be long lasting, and can lead to the harmful behaviors seen in people who abuse drugs.

Is Continued Drug Abuse a Voluntary Behavior?

The initial decision to take drugs is mostly voluntary. However, when drug abuse takes over, a person's ability to exert self control can become seriously impaired. Brain imaging studies from drug-addicted individuals show physi-cal changes in areas of the brain that are critical to judgment, decision mak-ing, learning and memory, and behavior control. Scientists believe that these changes alter the way the brain works, and may help explain the compulsive and destructive behaviors of addiction.

Why Do Some People Become Addicted to Drugs, While Others Do Not?

As with any other disease, vulnerability to addiction differs from person to per-son. In general, the more risk factors an individual has, the greater the chance that taking drugs will lead to abuse and addiction. "Protective" factors reduce a person's risk of developing addiction.

What Factors Determine If a Person Will Become Addicted?

No single factor determines whether a person will become addicted to drugs. The overall risk for addiction is impacted by the biological makeup of the individual—it can even be influenced by gender or ethnicity, his or her devel-opmental stage, and the surrounding social environment (e.g., conditions at home, at school, and in the neighborhood).

Published by *National Institutes of Health*, NIH Pub no. 07-5605, April 2007, pp. 5, 7, 8, 10, 15–20.

Which Biological Factors Increase Risk of Addiction?

Scientists estimate that genetic factors account for between 40 and 60 percent of a person's vulnerability to addiction, including the effects of environment on gene expression and function. Adolescents and individuals with mental disorders are at greater risk of drug abuse and addiction than the general population.

The Brain Continues to Develop into Adulthood and Undergoes Dramatic Changes During Adolescence

One of the brain areas still maturing during adolescence is the prefrontal cortex—the part of the brain that enables us to assess situations, make sound decisions, and keep our emotions and desires under control. The fact that this critical part of an adolescent's brain is still a work-in-progress puts them at increased risk for poor decisions (such as trying drugs or continued abuse). Thus, introducing drugs while the brain is still developing may have profound and long-lasting consequences.

Drugs and the Brain

Introducing the Human Brain

The human brain is the most complex organ in the body. This three-pound mass of gray and white matter sits at the center of all human activity—you need it to drive a car, to enjoy a meal, to breathe, to create an artistic masterpiece, and to enjoy everyday activities. In brief, the brain regulates your basic body functions; enables you to interpret and respond to everything you experience, and shapes your thoughts, emotions, and behavior.

The brain is made up of many parts that all work together as a team. Different parts of the brain are responsible for coordinating and performing specific functions. Drugs can alter important brain areas that are necessary for life-sustaining functions and can drive the compulsive drug abuse that marks addiction. Brain areas affected by drug abuse—

- *The brain stem* controls basic functions critical to life, such as heart rate, breathing, and sleeping.
- *The limbic system* contains the brain's reward circuit—it links together a number of brain structures that control and regulate our ability to feel pleasure. Feeling pleasure motivates us to repeat behaviors such as eating—actions that are critical to our existence. The limbic system is activated when we perform these activities—and also by drugs of abuse. In addition, the limbic system is responsible for our perception of other emotions, both positive and negative, which explains the mood-altering properties of many drugs.
- *The cerebral cortex* is divided into areas that control specific functions. Different areas process information from our senses, enabling us to see, feel, hear, and taste. The front part of the cortex, the frontal cortex or forebrain, is the thinking center of the brain; it powers our ability to think, plan, solve problems, and make decisions.

How Does the Brain Communicate?

The brain is a communications center consisting of billions of neurons, or nerve cells. Networks of neurons pass messages back and forth to different structures within the brain, the spinal column, and the peripheral nervous system. These nerve networks coordinate and regulate everything we feel, think, and do.

- *Neuron to Neuron*
  Each nerve cell in the brain sends and receives messages in the form of electrical impulses. Once a cell receives and processes a message, it sends it on to other neurons.
- *Neurotransmitters—The Brain's Chemical Messengers*
  The messages are carried between neurons by chemicals called neurotransmitters. (They transmit messages between neurons.)
- *Receptors—The Brain's Chemical Receivers*
  The neurotransmitter attaches to a specialized site on the receiving cell called a receptor. A neurotransmitter and its receptor operate like a "key and lock," an exquisitely specific mechanism that ensures that each receptor will forward the appropriate message only after interacting with the right kind of neurotransmitter.
- *Transporters—The Brain's Chemical Recyclers*
  Located on the cell that releases the neurotransmitter, transporters recycle these neurotransmitters (i.e., bring them back into the cell that released them), thereby shutting off the signal between neurons.

How Do Drugs Work in the Brain?

Drugs are chemicals. They work in the brain by tapping into the brain's communication system and interfering with the way nerve cells normally send, receive, and process information. Some drugs, such as marijuana and heroin, can activate neurons because their chemical structure mimics that of a natural neurotransmitter. This similarity in structure "fools" receptors and allows the drugs to lock onto and activate the nerve cells. Although these drugs mimic brain chemicals, they don't activate nerve cells in the same way as a natural neurotransmitter, and they lead to abnormal messages being transmitted through the network.

Other drugs, such as amphetamine or cocaine, can cause the nerve cells to release abnormally large amounts of natural neurotransmitters or prevent the normal recycling of these brain chemicals. This disruption produces a greatly amplified message, ultimately disrupting communication channels. The difference in effect can be described as the difference between someone whispering into your ear and someone shouting into a microphone.

How Do Drugs Work in the Brain to Produce Pleasure?

All drugs of abuse directly or indirectly target the brain's reward system by flooding the circuit with dopamine. Dopamine is a neurotransmitter present in regions of the brain that regulate movement, emotion, cognition, motivation, and feelings of pleasure. The overstimulation of this system, which rewards our natural behaviors, produces the euphoric effects sought by people who abuse drugs and teaches them to repeat the behavior.

How Does Stimulation of the Brain's Pleasure Circuit Teach Us to Keep Taking Drugs?

Our brains are wired to ensure that we will repeat life-sustaining activities by associating those activities with pleasure or reward. Whenever this reward circuit is activated, the brain notes that something important is happening that needs to be remembered, and teaches us to do it again and again, without thinking about it. Because drugs of abuse stimulate the same circuit, we learn to abuse drugs in the same way.

Why Are Drugs More Addictive Than Natural Rewards?

When some drugs of abuse are taken, they can release 2 to 10 times the amount of dopamine that natural rewards do. In some cases, this occurs almost immediately (as when drugs are smoked or injected), and the effects can last much longer than those produced by natural rewards. The resulting effects on the brain's pleasure circuit dwarfs those produced by naturally rewarding behaviors such as eating and sex. The effect of such a powerful reward strongly motivates people to take drugs again and again. This is why scientists sometimes say that drug abuse is something we learn to do very, very well.

What Happens to Your Brain If You Keep Taking Drugs?

Just as we turn down the volume on a radio that is too loud, the brain adjusts to the overwhelming surges in dopamine (and other neurotransmitters) by producing less dopamine or by reducing the number of receptors that can receive and transmit signals. As a result, dopamine's impact on the reward circuit of a drug abuser's brain can become abnormally low, and the ability to experience any pleasure is reduced. This is why the abuser eventually feels flat, lifeless, and depressed, and is unable to enjoy things that previously brought them pleasure. Now, they need to take drugs just to bring their dopamine function back up to normal. And, they must take larger amounts of the drug than they first did to create the dopamine high—an effect known as tolerance.

How Does Long-Term Drug Taking Affect Brain Circuits?

We know that the same sort of mechanisms involved in the development of tolerance can eventually lead to profound changes in neurons and brain circuits, with the potential to severely compromise the long-term health of the brain. For example, glutamate is another neurotransmitter that influences the reward circuit and the ability to learn. When the optimal concentration of glutamate is altered by drug abuse, the brain attempts to compensate for this change, which can cause impairment in cognitive function. Similarly, long-term drug abuse can trigger adaptations in habit or nonconscious memory systems.

Conditioning is one example of this type of learning, whereby environmental cues become associated with the drug experience and can trigger uncontrollable cravings if the individual is later exposed to these cues, even without the drug itself being available. This learned "reflex" is extremely robust and can emerge even after many years of abstinence.

What Other Brain Changes Occur with Abuse?

Chronic exposure to drugs of abuse disrupts the way critical brain structures interact to control behavior—behavior specifically related to drug abuse. Just as continued abuse may lead to tolerance or the need for higher drug dosages to produce an effect, it may also lead to addiction, which can drive an abuser to seek out and take drugs compulsively. Drug addiction erodes a person's self-control and ability to make sound decisions, while sending intense impulses to take drugs.

Sally Satel and Scott O. Lilienfeld  **NO**

Singing the Brain Disease Blues

Well over a decade ago, the National Institute on Drug Abuse began advancing the idea that addiction is a "brain disease." Over the years, the concept has become orthodoxy—a dubious achievement that has justifiably prompted Buchman and his colleagues (2010) to call for a more nuanced perspective on addiction. In this peer commentary we challenge the validity of the brain disease model of addiction and discuss its adverse implications for treatment.

Let us begin with the concept of brain disease. "That addiction is tied to changes in brain structure and function is what makes it, fundamentally, a brain disease," wrote a former director of the National Institute on Drug Abuse in a seminal 1997 *Science* article (Leshner 1997). What does this statement really mean? Surely, drugs operate at the level of the brain (Hyman 2007). No dispute there. Regular, heavy use of alcohol, nicotine, heroin, cocaine, and other substances produces brain changes (reward centers are "hijacked," as it is commonly put) that, in turn, influence the urge to use drugs and the struggle to quit. Brain-related differences among users influence the rapidity with which they develop addiction, their subjective experience of the drug, the potency of their craving, and the severity of their withdrawal symptoms.

That said, why should this make addiction a brain disease as opposed to, say, a molecular disease, a psychological disease, or a sociocultural disease? All are equally valid perspectives for different purposes. As psychologist Nick Heather wisely asserted, "Addiction can be defined in any way the definer thinks fit. . . . The crucial issue is how useful the definition is for specific purposes" (Heather 1998). So, for example, if one's purpose is to investigate dopamine circuitry, then viewing addiction as as brain-based phenomenon makes sense. But if one's purpose is providing psychosocial treatment and devising policy, then the "neurocentric" view doesn't help much.

The mechanical simplicity of the "brain disease" rhetoric has a seductive appeal that obscures the considerable degree of choice in addiction, as Buchman and colleagues note. Consider the daily routine of addicts. They rarely spend all of their time in the throes of an intense neurochemical siege. Most heroin addicts, for example, perform some kind of gainful work between administrations of the drug. In the days between binges, cocaine addicts make many decisions that have nothing to do with drug-seeking. Should they try to find a different job? Kick that freeloading cousin off their couch? Attend a Narcotics Anonymous meeting, enter treatment if they have private insurance, or register at a public clinic if they don't? These decisions are often based on personal meaning. Many autobiographical accounts by former addicts reveal that they were startled into quitting by a spasm of self-reproach (Lawford 2008): "My God, I almost robbed someone!" or "What kind of mother am I?"

Most important, knotty philosophical issues of free will versus determinism aside, addiction is an activity whose course can be altered by its foreseeable consequences. No amount of reinforcement or punishment can alter the course of an entirely autonomous biological condition. Imagine bribing an Alzheimer's patient to keep her dementia from worsening, or threatening to impose a penalty on her if it did. It won't work. But incentives do work in addicted patients, as clinical trials of a strategy called "contingency management" show. The standard trial compares addicts who know they will receive a reward for submitting drug-free urines with matched addicts not offered rewards (Silverman et al. 2001). In general, the groups that are eligible to be rewarded with, for example, cash, gift certificates, or services are about two to three times more likely to turn in drug-free urines compared with similar counterparts who were not able to work for such incentives. In drug courts (a jail-diversion treatment program for nonviolent drug offenders), offenders are sanctioned for continued drug use (perhaps a night or two in jail) and rewarded for cooperation with the program. The judge holds the person, not his or her brain, accountable for setbacks and progress.

Even without formal incentives or sanctions, users perform their own mental calculations all the time. Repetitive drug use is reduced or stopped altogether when the adverse consequences of drug use exceed its rewards. An addict might reason, for example, "Heroin quells my psychic pain and soothes withdrawal, but it is costing my family too much." In a choice model, according to psychologist Gene Heyman (2009), addiction is the triumph of feel-good local decisions ("I'll use today") over punishing global anxieties ("I don't want to be an addict tomorrow"). As the relative value of costs and benefits of addiction change over time (yes, benefits: people use drugs and maintain addictions for psychological reasons—a reality obfuscated by the brain disease model), users become less ambivalent about quitting.

Whether powered by changes in meaning or incentives, the capacity for self-governance is the key to the most promising treatments for addiction. This fact is often obscured, however, by a semantic glitch whereby the state of "addiction" is taken to mean that the desire to use is unmalleable and beyond the reach of environmental contingencies. In circular fashion, then, addicted individuals are believed to be helpless to change their behavior. And, if so, it is wrong to expect them to respond to sanctions.

This was the destructive logic employed by the opponents of Proposition 36 in California, a 2001 referendum on the state's jail diversion program for nonviolent drug offenders (Urada et al. 2008). They prevailed and within a few years treatment program staff began clamoring for permission to use modest penalties and incentives—without them, the staff had no leverage. Similarly, drug courts and probationary programs have been hampered by ideological resistance to imposing consequences for positive urine tests because, after all, victims of a brain disease cannot be held accountable for their behavior; what's more, they are "supposed" to relapse.

The brain disease model implies erroneously that the brain is necessarily the most important and useful level of analysis for understanding and treating addiction. Like Buchman and colleagues, we believe that it is far more productive to view addiction as a behavior that operates on several levels, ranging from molecular function and structure to brain physiology to psychology to psychosocial environment and social relations (see also Kendler 2005; Lilienfeld 2007). The lower levels of explanation, particularly the brain, are merely among them—and not necessarily the most informative for practical purposes. Indeed, an "eliminative" or "greedy" (to use philosopher Daniel Dennett's apt term) reductionistic view—which posits that lower levels of analysis render higher levels superfluous—leads to ambivalence about the importance of holding addicts accountable and, in turn, undermines the most effective behavioral treatments available (Dennett 1995). Fortunately for addicts, their behavior can be modified by contingencies. Official rhetoric does them a disservice when it implies they are merely helpless victims of their own hijacked brains.

All **references for articles included in** *Taking Sides: Clashing Views in Abnormal Psychology, 7/e* **can be found on the Web at www.mhhe.com/cls.**

EXPLORING THE ISSUE

Is Addiction a Brain Disease?

Critical Thinking and Reflection

1. Imagine that you are a researcher who initiated a study assessing the relative contributions of biology and personality to the development of drug addiction. How would you go about studying this complex question?
2. Put yourself in the place of a clinician who is beginning to treat a drug-addicted individual. What questions would you ask in order to assess the extent to which the client is taking personal responsibility for the addiction?
3. Imagine that you are an educator with the goal of helping young people understand why drugs can be so addictive. Which points would you emphasize in your lecture?
4. What are the pros and cons of viewing drug addiction as a brain disease?
5. If unlimited funds were available for a program designed to reduce drug addiction, what initiatives would you imagine as the most effective?

Is There Common Ground?

In discussing the phenomenon of addiction, we turn first to accepted definitions of substance dependence, which is defined by behavior consisting of at least three of the following symptoms during a 12-month period: tolerance; symptoms of withdrawal; use of the substance in larger amounts or over a longer period than intended; persistent desire or unsuccessful attempts to cut down or control use; extensive time devoted to activities involved in obtaining, using, or recovering from substance use; a giving up or reduction in important activities because of substance use; and continued use despite knowledge of a substance-caused physical or psychological problem.

Over time, substance dependence evolves into addiction that is chronic and debilitating, and very difficult to shake. Both NIDA and Satel and Lilienfeld understand that addiction becomes an all-consuming aspect of a person's life, and both parties see that the initial decision to take drugs is voluntary. They differ, however, with regard to the individual's capacity for self-control once dependence on the substance develops. NIDA focuses on the brain changes that take place, whereas Satel and Lilienfeld focus on an individual's capacity for self-governance, but do state that addiction is a behavior that operates on several levels, with the brain being merely one of those levels.

Additional Resources

Alcoholics Anonymous. (2012). www.aa.org

Carter, A., & Hall, W. (2012). Addiction may not be a compulsive brain disease, but it is more than purposeful medication of untreated psychiatric disorders. *AJOB Neuroscience, 3*(2), 54–55.

Heyman, G. M. (2009). *Addiction: A disorder of choice.* Cambridge: Harvard University Press.

Hoffman, J. (2007). *Addiction: Why can't they just stop? New knowledge. New treatments. New hope.* Emmaus, PA: Rodale Books.

Mate, G. (2010). *In the realm of hungry ghosts: Close encounters with addiction.* Berkeley, CA: North Atlantic Books.

Nace, E. P., & Tinsley, J. A. (2007). *Patients with substance abuse problems: Effective identification, diagnosis, and treatment.* New York: W. W. Norton.

National Institute on Drug Abuse.(2012). www.drugabuse.gov

Poland, J., & Graham, G. (2011). *Addiction and responsibility.* Cambridge MA: MIT Press.

Vale, P. H. (2010). Addiction—and rational choice theory. *International Journal of Consumer Studies, 34*(1), 38–45.

Internet References . . .

Website of Dr. Ken Pope

This site provides resources on ethical and professional issues, including a section on detainee interrogations.

http://kspope.com/index.php

The Society for the Psychological Study of Social Issues (SPSSI)

This site provides research on the psychological aspects of important social issues and public policy solutions.

www.spssi.org/

The Body Image Program at Rhode Island Hospital

This site provides research and clinical services pertaining to body image disturbances such as body dysmorphic disorder.

www.rhodeislandhospital.org/rih/services/mentalhealth/bodyimage/

Media Psychology Division of the American Psychological Association

This APA division promotes research into the impact of media on human behavior.

www.apa.org/divisions/div46/

Against Pornography

This website aims to raise awareness about the harms of pornography.

https://againstpornography.org/

American Constitution Society for Law and Policy

This nonprofit legal organization focuses on issues of human dignity, equality, individual rights, liberties, and access to justice.

www.acsblog.org

Crime and Consequences

This website is dedicated to ensuring that criminals are punished quickly and in accord with the Constitution.

www.crimeandconsequences.com

American Psychological Association

This website contains information on issues pertaining to the science and practice of psychology, including topics such as the psychological aftereffects of abortion.

www.apa.org

afterabortion.com

This website contains "neutral, nonjudgmental, nonreligion based, nonpolitically affiliated online support, information, help and healing."

www.afterabortion.com/

Social, Ethical, and Legal Issues

*M*any issues in the field of abnormal psychology interface with social issues, ethical concerns, and legal matters, with heated debate emerging about topics pertaining to efforts to protect personal rights while also being responsive to societal concerns. Some of these issues are interesting reflections of changes in social behavior, such as the phenomenal expansion of social network services such as Facebook, and the questions that arise about the psychological characteristics of people who use these services excessively. Other issues are much more serious, and find their way to the judicial system where debates about psychological experiences provide the basis for arguments in court, as has been the case with lawsuits about limiting the sale of violent video games to minors, the acceptability of virtual child pornography, the ability of mentally ill convicts to understand why they are being sentenced to death, the use of aversive treatments for people who engage in self-harming behaviors, or the forced medicating of severely mentally ill individuals. Legal and legislative battles have also raged about abortion, and psychologists have been called upon to present evaluative summaries of research on potential psychological effects on a woman who undergoes an abortion. Debates have also surfaced about the responsibility of health professionals to override an individual's autonomy by forcibly feeding anorexic individuals against their will, or refusing to acquiesce to the bizarre wish of a person who insistently pleads to have a healthy limb amputated.

- Does Research Confirm That Violent Video Games Are Harmful to Minors?
- Would Legalization of Virtual Child Pornography Reduce Sexual Exploitation of Children?
- Must Mentally Ill Murderers Have a Rational Understanding of Why They Are Being Sentenced to Death?
- Does Research Confirm That Abortion Is a Psychologically Benign Experience?
- Should Individuals with Anorexia Nervosa Have the Right to Refuse Life-sustaining Treatment?
- Is the Use of Aversive Treatment an Inhumane Intervention for Psychologically Disordered Individuals?
- Is It Unethical for Psychologists to Be Involved in Coercive Interrogations?
- Is It Ethical to Support the Wish for Healthy Limb Amputation in People with Body Integrity Identity Disorder (BIID)?
- Is Forced Treatment of Seriously Mentally Ill Individuals Justifiable?
- Is Excessive Use of Facebook a Form of Narcissism?

ISSUE 9

Does Research Confirm That Violent Video Games Are Harmful to Minors?

YES: **Leland Y. Yee and Steven F. Gruel,** from "Brief of *Amicus Curiae* in Case of *Brown v. Entertainment Merchants Association*," U.S. Supreme Court, No. 08-1448 (2010)

NO: **Patricia A. Millett,** from "Brief of *Amici Curiae* in *Brown v. Entertainment Merchants Association*," U.S. Supreme Court, No. 08-1448 (2010)

Learning Outcomes

After reading this issue, you should be able to:

- Discuss and critically evaluate the arguments about the strength of scientific evidence that either supports or discredits the relationship between playing violent video games and engaging in aggressive behavior among youth.
- Understand the ways in which playing video games can influence neurological structure and functioning.
- Evaluate the extent to which playing violent video games by young people can lead to academic problems.
- Compare the rationale used by the government to regulate other media such as television and radio and the arguments made for and against the regulation of violent video game sales to children.
- Consider the similarities and differences between passively watching a violent movie and actively participating in a violent video game.

ISSUE SUMMARY

YES: California State Senator Leland Yee and Attorney Steven F. Gruel (Counsel of Record for the professional associations in pediatrics and psychology) contend that substantial research shows that violent video games can cause psychological or neurological harm to minors. Studies have shown that, in addition to fostering aggressive thought and behavior, ultra-violent video games can lead to reduced activity in the frontal lobes of the brain as well as behavioral problems such as antisocial behavior and poor school performance. Senator Yee and Attorney Gruel believe that the government has a duty to protect children, and that the First Amendment of the U.S. Constitution, with regard to free speech, should not be used to place at risk immature children who cannot discern the difference between fantasy and reality.

NO: Attorney Patricia A. Millett (Counsel of Record for the amicus curiae submitted on behalf of the Entertainment Merchants Association) argues that there is insufficient evidence to show that violent video games can cause psychological or neurological harm to minors. Attorney Millett claims that the various studies cited in the opposing amicus curiae are either flawed or have been discredited. She also asserts that studies have shown no compelling causal connections between playing violent video games and aggressive or antisocial behavior in youths.

In recent years, video games have caught the attention of the public because of various reports about violent and sexually explicit imagery contained in products sold to young people. The debate about the potential impact of exposure to aggressive or sexually explicit media has raged for decades, with social critics expressing great concern about the impact on young people who seem to be flooded with images that would have been unimaginable 30 years ago. American society has become increasingly tolerant of violent movies, some of which have developed cult-like followings. Violent movies with scenes of maiming, torture, sexual assault, and murder, which might have been censored in the twentieth century, are now common, and some have even become the basis of cinematic parody.

As society seems to have become desensitized to violence in the movies, shifts have also taken place in the extremity of violence in video games. Social science researchers and neuroscientists have been recruited to study the extent to which playing such games negatively influences behavior and causes changes in the brain. Special concern has focused on the effects on children for whom perceptual experiences influence the development of personality as well as brain functioning. The challenges of conducting such research are understandably formidable. How does a social science researcher determine that Joey's misbehavior in school on Monday is related to his playing a violent video game the day before? How does a neuroscientist assess the relationship between Jane's abnormal brain functioning and her exposure to video game violence? Lacking clear answers to such questions, legislators face a difficult task in any attempt to regulate the sale of violent video games to minors. Critics of such proposed legislation, such as companies that develop and sell these games, are likely to employ two arguments: (1) research cannot demonstrate a causal connection between playing violent video games and aggressive behavior or abnormal brain functioning, and (2) the U.S. Constitution protects the dissemination of media that has not been proven to be harmful.

Senator Leland Yee, who has a doctorate in developmental psychology, has long opposed the sale of violent video games to children. In his role on the San Francisco Board of Education and through his work in various mental health settings, Dr. Yee has had a long history of working on behalf of children and becoming aware of the forces in society that can have detrimental impact on them. Thus, it is not surprising that he would submit a brief reflecting efforts to protect minors from harm that could result from playing violent video games. The argument is made that research demonstrates that participating in the playing of violent video games by children increases aggressive thought and behavior, increases antisocial behavior and delinquency, engenders poor school performance, and desensitizes the game player to violence.

In the brief submitted by Senator Yee, neuroscience research is also cited about brain effects resulting from exposure to violent video games. For example, functional magnetic resonance imaging (fMRI) research points to a relationship between alterations in brain functioning and exposure to media violence. Namely, teenagers who played a violent video game exhibited increased activity in a part of the brain that governs emotional arousal, and decreased activity in the parts of the brain involved in focus, inhibition, and concentration.

One argument against the sale of violent video games to minors highlights the difference between passive exposure to violence, such as watching a movie, and the active engagement involved in playing a video game in which the participant is a shooter who personally decides whether to pull the trigger and whether to kill or not. The implication is that a young person who is "shooting" and "assaulting" via a role play is much more powerfully affected by this behavior than would be a young person watching such behaviors in a movie.

Aside from the debate about the psychological and neurological effects of playing violent video games, there is debate about the legality of restricting their sale to any person, including a minor. Does the U.S. Constitution view the distribution of violent video games as being protected by the First Amendment? Senator Yee points to restrictions on the sale of alcohol, tobacco, and firearms to minors as providing justification for such restrictions on the sale of violent video games to impressionable young people.

The NO side of the argument emerges primarily from the premise that research is seriously deficient in demonstrating a causal relationship between the playing of violent video games and aggressive behavior or brain changes. As any beginning psychology student knows, correlation does not equal causation. In other words, is Joey aggressive because he plays violent video games, or is Joey an aggressive boy by nature who finds that playing violent video games is fun? In the brief submitted by Attorney Millett on behalf of the Entertainment Merchants Association, the argument is made that the courts should reject the studies submitted as evidence of a relationship between violent video games and aggressive behavior, contending that those studies do not even establish correlation, much less causation. Thus, arguers on this side of the debate assert that, in order to demonstrate such a relationship, substantial scientific evidence must be presented in order to validate the claim that violent video games cause psychological harm or neurological effects to minors. Attorney Millett contends that the scientific evidence submitted has failed to substantiate those claims.

In criticizing research pointing to a relationship between violent video games and changes in brain functioning, Attorney Millett asserts that, while fMRI studies may indicate areas of the brain that decrease in activation during a task, it is not yet understood how brain activation is influenced by neural development in children. Furthermore, because fMRI studies depend on statistical analysis, it is possible that errors in the procedure of analysis may undermine the reliability of the results.

YES

Leland Y. Yee and Steven F. Gruel

Brief of *Amicus Curiae* in Case of *Brown v. Entertainment Merchants Association*

Summary of Argument

By any measure, California has a compelling interest in protecting the physical and psychological care of minors. When juxtaposed against the backdrop of protecting the First Amendment, this Court has held that the Constitution does not confer the protection on communication aimed at children as it does for adults. When weighing the conflicting concerns of minors this Court correctly carved a flexible standard of review and not a strict scrutiny approach. We know, of course, that a state can prohibit the sale of sexually-explicit material to minors under a "variable obscenity" or "obscenity as to minors" standard. *Ginsberg v. New York*, 390 U.S. 629 (1968). Just as it was rational for the State to conclude that that type of material was harmful to minors, the restrictions to assist parents in protecting their children's well-being is, in a practical sense, no different than the concerns supporting California's enactment of California Civil Code Sections 1746–1746.5.

Indeed, restricting the sale and rental of extremely violent interactive videos to minors advances the very same societal interests understood in *Ginsberg*. Contrary to the Ninth Circuit's perception, *Ginsberg* was not meant to exclusively apply to sexually explicit materials, but can and should apply to equally harmful materials depicting violence. *Video Software Dealers Association v. Schwarzenegger*, 556 F.3d 950 (9th Cir. 2009).

Needless to say, the world is much different today than it was in 1968 when *Ginsberg* was decided. What *has* remained for the past 40 years, however, is the commonsense understanding that the First Amendment does not protect materials harmful to minors.

In 2006, a Federal Trade Commission study revealed that nearly 70 percent of 13 to 16 year olds are able to successfully purchase Mature or M-rated video games. These M-rated games, labeled by the industry as such in an attempt to voluntarily "police" the distribution of harmful videos, are designed specifically for adults. The content in these types of games enable the user to murder, burn, and maim law enforcement officers, racial minorities, and members of clergy as well as sexually assault women.

U.S. Supreme Court, 2010.

In his March 29, 2006 testimony submitted to the Subcommittee on the Constitution, Civil Rights, and Property Rights of the United States Senate Judiciary Committee, Senator Yee noted that the interactive nature of video games is vastly different than passively listening to music, watching a movie, or reading a book. With interactive video games, the child becomes a part of the action which serves as a potent agent to facilitate violence, and over time learns the destructive behavior. This immersion results in a more powerful experience and potentially dangerous learned behavior in children and youth. In fact, often times it is the same technology that our military and police use to simulate and train for real life battle conditions and violent law enforcement confrontations in the community.

Moreover, there is a practical side in favor of the State's effort to regulate the sale or rental of violent video games to children. Parents can read a book, watch a movie or listen to a CD to discern if it is appropriate for their child. These violent video games, on the other hand, can contain up to 800 hours of footage with the most atrocious content often reserved for the highest levels that can be accessed only by advanced players after hours upon hours of progressive mastery.

Just as the technology of video games improves at astonishing rates, so too does the body of research consistently demonstrate the harmful effects these violent interactive games have on minors. Hundreds of peer-reviewed studies, produced over a period of 30 years documenting the effects of screen violence (including violent video games), have now been published in the professional journals of the American Academy of Pediatrics, American Academy of Child and Adolescent Psychiatry, American Psychological Association, American Medical Association, American Academy of Family Physicians, and the American Psychiatric Association and others.

This *amicus* brief includes some of the most recent research addressing this serious concern including a meta-analysis of approximately 130 studies pertaining to the effects of playing violent video games which was published in March 2010.

These data continually and strongly suggest that participating in the playing of violent video games by children increases aggressive thought and behavior; increases antisocial behavior and delinquency; engenders poor school performance; and desensitizes the game player to violence.

Notably, extended play has been observed to depress activity in the frontal cortex of the brain which controls executive thought and function, produces intentionality and the ability to plan sequences of action, and is the seat of self-reflection, discipline and self-control.

Also, United States Surgeon General David Satcher warned in his Report on Youth Violence (2000) of a demonstrated link between screen violence and subsequent physical aggression in children and adolescents that is stronger than the link between secondhand smoke and cancer.

Finally, new data shows that the intensity of interactive video games may be habituating and that 2 to 3 hour sessions of intense interactions with video games raise adrenaline levels in children and produces extended physiological arousal. In the medical community concern has been raised at prolonged and regularly repeated states of adrenalized arousal and hyper-vigilance involved in children watching violent video games and the possible harmful effects on still developing bodies and brains.

These studies demonstrate that playing ultra-violent games can cause automatic aggressiveness, increase aggressive thoughts and behavior, antisocial behavior, desensitization, poor school performance and reduced activity in the frontal lobes of the brain.

As a society, we understand the clear unequivocal commonsense reasons to prohibit the sale of alcohol, tobacco, firearms, driver's licenses and pornography to minors. That same reasoning applies in the foundation and enactment of California Civil Code Sections 1746—1746.5. Given that the First Amendment does not protect the State's restriction on the sale or rental of harmful violent video games to minors, the Court should reverse the decision of the Ninth Circuit Court of Appeals and uphold the California law as a statutory safeguard necessary in this modern day world.

Argument

I. This Court Has Acknowledged Society's Rational and Compelling Interest in Distinguishing and Limiting the Rights Enjoyed by Minors.

This Court has long agreed that there is an overriding justification in protecting children from conduct pervasive in society. Without question, restricting a minor's access to gambling, smoking and alcohol serve the community's interest in both protecting a minor's development as well as safeguarding against the individual and widespread collateral consequences which flow from a minor's early addiction to these vices.

As a general proposition, many constitutional rights vary in the degree to which the exercise of the right by minors is protected from government abridgment. For example, minors do not have the right to exercise the franchise. Similarly, a minor's right to have an abortion may be subject to regulations that would be rejected as unduly burdensome if they were applied to adult women. Thus, there is a recognized foundation for distinguishing between minors and adults in analyzing the constitutionality of regulations.

This foundation comports with the common sense intuition that, because children lack maturity to make wise judgments, their autonomy deserves less respect from the state than does the autonomy of adults. While paternalistic state regulations are correctly viewed as demeaning when applied to adults, there are considered appropriate, if not necessary, for children.

In *Ginsberg*, of course, this Court concluded that the State had greater authority to limit the exercise of protected freedoms because children were involved and, in relying on its precedents, recognized that "the State has an interest 'to protect the welfare of children' and to see that they are 'safeguarded from abuses' which might prevent 'their growth into free and independent well-developed men and citizens.'"

As it relates to expressive materials, there is no language from this Court suggesting that the State's interest in protecting minors from such material *is limited* to speech with sexual content. In *Erznoznik v. City of Jacksonville,* a case concerning restrictions on films depicting nudity from being shown in drive-in movies, the Court was unwilling to protect minors from brief exposure to such images.

However, the alleged harm caused by the minimal exposure to nude images a child passing by a drive-in theater might witness cannot realistically be compared to harm resulting from repeated and long-term exposure to violent video games. In fact, in *FCC v. Pacifica Foundation,* 438 U.S. 726 (1978), this Court supported an FCC determination that the radio broadcast of a George Carlin monologue containing "filthy words" could be restricted precisely because it was accessible to young children.

Children, this Court has acknowledged, are different in the eyes of the law because of brain development. *Ropers v. Simmons,* 543 U.S. 551 (2005). Under the "evolving standards of decency" test, the *Ropers* Court held that it was cruel and unusual punishment to execute a person who was under the age of 18 at the time of the murder. Writing for the majority, Justice Kennedy cited a body of sociological and scientific research that found that juveniles have a lack of maturity and sense of responsibility compared to adults. Adolescents were found to be over-represented statistically in virtually every category of reckless behavior.

In *Ropers,* the Court noted that in recognition of the comparative immaturity and irresponsibility of juveniles, almost every state prohibited those under age 18 from voting, serving on juries, or marrying without parental consent. The studies also found that juveniles are also more vulnerable to negative influences and outside pressures, including peer pressure. They have less control, or experience with control, over their own environment. More recently, in *Graham v. Florida,* 130 S.Ct. 2011 (2010) this Court used the same rationale in finding that some life sentences without parole for minors were unconstitutional. This unequivocal commonsense approach by the Court to constitutional matters and children should be likewise applied in addressing the deepening dangers to minors from violent video games.

In sum, "[A] state or municipality can adopt more stringent controls on communicative materials available to youths than on those available to adults." *Erznoznik,* at 212.

Here, California's marginal control on the sale or rental of violent video games to minors is within the permissible advancement of a significant, if not compelling, public interest in protecting the development and mental health of minors.

California's concern for its minors in the modern violent video game world is not fanciful or without basis. Science supports the legislative public policy determination.

II. Science Confirms That Violent Video Games Are Harmful to Minors Allowing the State Clear Justification in Regulating Children's Access to These Materials.

1. Overview of Scientific Research Confirms Harmful Effects to Minors from Violent Video Games.

Testimony before Congress has elicited a large body of testimony by national experts, medical and mental health professional associations and others, the gist of which is that there is a significant relationship between exposure to media violence and aggressive behavior, and that repeated exposure leads to general increases in aggressiveness over time. The following testimony is typical:

> "Though there are many complexities in this realm of behavioral research, there is one clear and simple message that parents, educators, and public policy makers such as yourselves need to hear: Playing violent video games can cause increases in aggression and violence."

In October 2009, the American Academy of Pediatrics (AAP) issued its Policy Statement on Media Violence. The AAP, after considering the evidence from the extensive research on the effects of media violence, concluded that exposure to media violence, including playing violent video games, "*represents a significant risk to the health of children and adolescents.*" (emphasis added). Indeed, both before and since California's enactment of the statutes in this case, there have been hundreds of studies in the area of the effects of playing violent video games on children.

In fact, as part of this *amicus* brief, leading researchers, scholars and scientists from around the United States, Germany and Japan, who have studied the harmful effects of violent video game playing on minors, are submitting their Statement on Video Game Violence for this Court's consideration. *See* Appendix. Nearly 100 other leading researchers and scholars from around the globe have endorsed this Statement. *See* Endorsement list in Appendix. These researchers have clearly found harmful effects to minors in playing violent video games.

Repeatedly thinking about violent characters, choosing to be aggressive, enacting that aggressive choice, and being rewarded for it can be conceived as a series of learning trials influencing a variety of types of aggressive knowledge structures. *"Violent Video Games: Specific Effects of Violent Content on Aggressive Thoughts and Behavior,"* Advances in Experimental Social Psychology, Vol. 36 (2004).

The American Academy of Pediatrics also, with numerous others, concludes that exposure to violence in media, including violent video games, can contribute to aggressive behavior, desensitization to violence, nightmares and fear of being harmed. *"Media Violence,"* American Academy of Pediatrics, Volume 108, Number 5 (November 2001). The American Academy of Pediatrics found that American children between 2 and 18 years of age spend an average of 6 hours and 32 minutes each day using media, including video games.

Predicated on years of studies and research, in August 2005, the American Psychological Association formally recognized the serious negative impact of violent video games on this nation's children and passed its Resolution "On Violence in Video Games and Interactive Media."

These prestigious associations of experts concluded not only that there are long-term negative effects on children in playing these violent video games, but that the industry, the public, parents, caregivers and educational organizations had a responsibility to intercede in this epidemic.

The statute authored by Senator Yee which California enacted into law was a direct response to that alarm for state assistance given our children's unfettered access to violent video games. The First Amendment does not preclude the state action carefully crafted in this case.

> 2. A Minor's Exposure to Violent Video Games—More Time Spent Playing Games with Increasing Graphic Violence.

A minor's exposure to the avalanc[h]e of violent video games is staggering. Video games first emerged in the 1970s, but it was during the 1990s that violent games truly came of age. In 1992, *Wolfenstein 3D*, the first major "first-person shooter" game was released. In a first-person shooter, one "sees" the video game world through the eyes of the player, rather than seeing it as if looking on from afar. The player is the one fighting, killing, and being killed. Video game historian Steven Kent noted that "part of *Wolfenstein 3D* popularity sprang from its shock value. In *Wolfenstein 3D*, enemies fell and bled on the floor."

With ever changing advancements in technology, the dramatic increases in speed and graphic capability have resulted in more realistic violence. As an example, in the video game *Soldier of Fortune*, the player/shooter can wound an enemy causing exposed bone and sinew.

As the video games became more graphically violent, the average time children played these games continued to climb. In the book, *Violent Video Game Effects on Children and Adolescents*, the authors note that in the early 1990s, boys averaged 4 hours a week and girls 2 hours a week playing video games. In a few years these averages jumped to 7.1 and 4.5, respectively. In a recent survey of over 600 eighth-and ninth-grade students, children averaged 9 hours per week with boys averaging 13 hours per week and girls averaging 5 hours per week.

In 1993, United States Senators Joseph Lieberman and Herbert Kohl noticed the increasing violence in video games and held hearings to examine the issue. Although there was much less research on the effects of violent video games, the senators put pressure on the video game industry to create a rating system. The goal of the rating system was to provide information to parents about the content of games so that they could make informed decisions about which games their children could play. However, these industry "voluntary" labels rating video games are inherently flawed and have failed due to "invalid assumptions about what is safe versus harmful."

In 2003, more than 239 million computer and video games were sold in the United States; that is almost two games for every household in the United States. More than 90% of all U.S. children and adolescents play video games. The National Youth Violence Prevention Resource Center (2004) has stated that a 2001 review of the 70 top-selling video games found 49% contained serious violence. In 41% of the games, violence was necessary for the protagonists to achieve their goals. There is no doubt, violent video games are among the most popular entertainment products for teens and adolescents, especially for boys.

New generation violent video games contain substantial amounts of increasingly realistic portrayals of violence. Elaborate content analyses revealed that the favored narrative is a "human perpetrator engaging in repeated acts of justified violence involving weapons that results in some bloodshed to the victim."

3. Scientific Studies Confirm That Violent Video Games Have Harmful Effects [on] Minors.

In a nutshell, teens and adolescents play video games frequently, and a significant portion of the games contain increasingly realistic portrayals of violence. Viewing violence increases aggression and greater exposure to media violence is strongly linked to increases in aggression.

Playing a lot of violent games is unlikely to turn a normal youth with zero, one or even two other risk factors into a killer. But regardless of how many other risk factors are present in a youth's life, playing a lot of violent games is likely to increase the frequency and the seriousness of his or her physical aggression, both in the short term and over time as the youth grows up. These long-term effects are a consequence of powerful observational learning and desensitization processes that neuroscientists and psychologists now understand to occur automatically in the human child. Simply stated, "adolescents who expose themselves to greater amounts of video game violence were more hostile, reported getting into arguments with teachers more frequently, were more likely to be involved in physical fights, and performed more poorly in school.

In a recent book, researchers once again concluded that the "active participation" in all aspects of violence: decision-making and carrying out the violent act, result in a greater effect from violent video games than a violent movie. Unlike a passive observer in movie watching, in first-person shooter and third-person shooter games, you're the one who decides whether to pull the trigger or not and whether to kill or not. After conducting three very different kinds of studies (experimental, a cross-sectional correlational study, and a longitudinal study) the results confirmed that violent games contribute to violent behavior.

The relationship between media violence and real-life aggression is nearly as strong as the impact of cigarette smoking and lung cancer: not everyone who smokes will get lung cancer, and not everyone who views media violence will become aggressive themselves. However, the connection is significant.

In an upcoming publication concerning children and violent video games, three complementary theoretical perspectives are discussed when contemplating the effects of playing video games. The *General Aggression Model* and its offshoot the *General Learning Model* describe the basic learning processes and effects involved in both short-term and long-term effects of playing various types of games. The *Five Dimensions of Video Game Effects* perspective describes different aspects of video games and video game play that influence the specific effects likely to occur. The *Risk and Resilience* perspective describes the effects of video game play—prosocial, antisocial, and other—take place within a complex set of social and biological factors, each of which contribute to development of the individual's thoughts, feelings, and behaviors.

The main findings can be succinctly summarized: playing violent video games causes an increase in the likelihood of physically aggressive behavior, aggressive thinking, aggressive affect, physiological arousal, and desensitization/low empathy. It also decreases helpful or prosocial behavior. With the exception of physiological arousal (for which there are no cross-sectional or longitudinal studies), all of the outcome variables showed the same effects in experimental, cross-sectional, and longitudinal studies. The main effects occurred for both males and females, for participants from low-violence collectivistic type Eastern countries (*e.g.*, Japan), and from high-violence individualistic type Western countries (*e.g.*, USA, Europe).

Research also indicates that the aggression carried out by video game characters is usually portrayed as justified, retributional, necessary to complete the game, rewarded and followed by unrealistic consequences. The overall level and realism of violent depictions, use of guns and likelihood of being killed by a gun has risen substantially over time; additionally, female victims and police officer victims rose significantly across time.

Many researchers have begun studying the concept of video game "addiction" and most researchers studying the pathological use of computer or video games have defined it similarly to how pathological gambling is defined—based on damage to family, social, school, occupational, and psychological functioning. The pace of studies has increased greatly in the past decade. In 2007, the American Medical Association released a report on the "addictive potential" of video games. The report concluded with a recommendation that the "AMA strongly encourage the consideration and inclusion of 'Internet/video game addiction' as a formal diagnostic disorder in the upcoming revision of the *Diagnostic and Statistical Manual of Mental Disorders-IV*" (p. 7).

The most comprehensive study to date in the US used a national sample of over 1,100 youth aged 8 to 18, in which 8.5% of video game players were classified as pathological demonstrates that it is not a trivial number of people who are suffering damage to their lives because of their game play.

School Performance

Several studies have documented a negative relation between amount of time playing video games and school performance among children, adolescents, and college students. The displacement hypothesis, that games displace time on other activities, is the most typical explanation for this relation. It could be argued, however, that the relation might be due to the children themselves, rather than to game time. It is highly likely that children who perform more poorly at school are likely to spend more time playing games, where they may feel a sense of mastery that eludes them at school. Nevertheless, each hour a child spends playing entertainment games (in contrast to educational games, which have been demonstrated to have educational benefits) is an hour not spent on homework, reading, exploring, creating, or other things that might have more educational benefit. Some evidence has been found to support the displacement hypothesis. In one nationally representative US sample of 1,491 youth between 10 and 19, gamers spent 30% less time reading and 34% less time doing homework. Therefore, even if poor school performance tends to cause increases in time playing video games, large amounts of video game play are likely to further hurt their school performance.

In short, the recent explosion in research on video game effects has greatly improved our understanding of how this medium affects its consumers. Several conclusions can be drawn without any reasonable doubt. First, there are many different effects of playing video games on the player. Some of these are short term, whereas others are long term. Second, the specific effects depend on a host of factors, including the content, structure, and context of the game. Third, the same game can have multiple effects on the same person, some of which may be generally beneficial whereas others may be detrimental. Fourth, playing violent video games is a causal risk factor for a host of detrimental effects in both the short and the long term, including increasing the likelihood of physically aggressive behavior.

Negative Effects on the Brain

Studies have shown evidence that exposure to violent video games reduces the player's use of some brain areas involved in higher order thought and impulse control.

In addition to behavioral-psychological theories explaining the relationship between media violence exposure and aggressive behavior, recently attention has turned to neuro-psychological theories. These theories attempt to identify areas of brain functioning that may be affected by media violence exposure and that may underlie aggressive behavior.

As recently as June 2010, another study of violent video game effects on frontal lobe activity was published wherein it was concluded that playing a violent video game for only 30 minutes immediately produced lower activity levels (compared to a nonviolent video game) in prefrontal regions thought to be involved in cognitive inhibition. This study shows that playing a violent video game for 30 minutes causes a decrease in brain activity in a region of the frontal lobe that is known to be important in the ability to inhibit impulsive behavior. The study also suggested that that violent games may also impair emotional functioning when it noted that "an impaired role of DLPFC (dorsolateral prefrontal cortex) in inhibition, therefore, may yield impaired emotional functioning following violent video game play."

Other studies of the neurological underpinnings of aggressive behavior, for example, indicate that a neural circuit that includes parts of the frontal cortex, amygdala and temporal lobes is important in emotional regulation and violence. Research strongly suggests an underactivity of brain inhibitory mechanisms in the frontal cortex and striatum, coupled with hyperarousal of the amygdala and temporal lobe regions, is responsible for chronic, explosive and/or severe aggressive behavior.

Research clearly indicates that areas in the frontal lobe and amygdale may be activated by viewing violent television and playing violent video games.

With the use of functional magnetic resonance imaging (fMRI), research has shown a direct alteration in brain functioning from exposure to media violence. Researchers found that teenagers who played a violent video game exhibited increased activity in a part of the brain that governs emotional arousal and the same teenagers showed decreased activity in the parts of the brain involved in focus, inhibition and concentration.

Youth who play a lot of violent video games (but who have not been diagnosed with a behavioral disorder) show a similar pattern of brain activity when doing complex executive control tasks as youth who have been diagnosed with some type of aggression-related behavior disorder. This pattern is very different from control-group youth who do not play a lot of violent games (and who have not been diagnosed with a behavioral disorder).

Youth who play a lot of violent video games show a deficit in a specific type of executive control known as proactive control. Proactive control is seen as necessary to inhibit impulsive reactions. This difference shows up in the brain wave patterns as well as in behavioral reactions.

Additionally, video game violence exposure and aggressive behavior to brain processes have been linked reflecting a desensitization in the aversive motivational system. Repeated exposure to media violence reduces its psychological impact and eventually produced aggressive approach-related motivational states theoretically leading to a stable increase in aggression.

Finally, in a functional magnetic resonance imaging study on players of the first-shooter game *Tactical Ops: Assault on Terror,* the violent portions of a video game activated the regions in the brain known to be active in fight-or-flight situations. In other words, the brain reacted to the fictional violence of a video game in much the same way as it reacts to real violence.

In short, neuroscience research supports a critical link between perpetration of virtual violence with reduced activation of a neural mechanism known to be important for self-control and for evaluation of affect. These findings strongly suggest that focusing on the activity of prefrontal cortical structures important for executive control could provide important mediational links in the relationship between exposure to violent media and increased aggression.

4. Recent Studies and Researchers Continue to Find Harmful Effects to Minors from Playing Violent Video Games

In March 2010, leading researchers in the area of media violence from the United State and Japan worked together to conduct a meta-analytic procedure testing the effects of violent games on aggressive behavior, aggressive cognition, aggressive affect, physiological arousal, empathy/desensitization, and prosocial behavior. In conducting [the] meta-analysis on the effects of video game violence, these researchers retrieved over 130 research reports which entailed scientific tests on over 130,000 participants. This study has been described as "probably about as exhaustive a sampling of the pre-2009 research literature as one could obtain and far more than that used in any other review of violent video game effects."

This extensive meta-analysis of the effects of violent video games confirms what many theories predicted and what prior research about other violent mass media found: that violent video games stimulate aggression in the players in the short run and increase the risk for aggression behaviors by the players later in life. The effects occur for males and females and for children growing up in Eastern and Western cultures. Also, the effects were stronger for more violent than less violent outcomes.

From their overarching analysis, these researchers concluded that the scientific debate should move beyond the simple question whether violent video game play is a causal risk factor for behavior because "scientific literature has effectively and clearly shown the answer to be 'yes.'"

Regardless of research method (experimental, correlational, or longitudinal) and regardless of cultures tested (East and West), the same effects are proven: exposure to violent video games is a causal risk factor for aggressive thoughts and behavior, and decreased empathy and prosocial behavior in youths. In fact, Dr. Anderson, one of three 2010 American Psychological Association Distinguished Scientist Lecturers, has stated that this recent meta-analysis on violent video games may be his last because of its "definitive findings."

5. The Shortcomings of Purported "Research" Contesting the Scientific Studies Showing the Harmful Effects to Minors Playing Violent Video Games

The Video Software Dealers Association and the Entertainment Software Association will likely contest the science showing the harmful effects of violent video games on minors. Apart from the self-serving motive for such opposition, one need only consider a professional organization that clearly does not doubt the serious aggression-teaching abilities of violent video games—the United States Department of Defense. Both the U.S. Army and U.S. Marines have their own video games used to train soldiers as tactical "first-person shooters" leading teams in "close-quarters urban combat." Many of these military combat training videos, such as *Full Spectrum Warrior* and *First To Fight* have been adapted and placed on the commercial market for minors to play.

Also, alleged "scientific" studies may be suggested by Respondents to argue that there are no harmful effects from violent video game playing. These "findings" can be explained by small sample size, poor test conditions and chance. The simple response to these studies is the recent and clear findings of the meta-analysis comprising 130 studies of the effects of violent video games showing the like between violent video games and aggression.

Conclusion

The scientific debate about whether exposure to media violence causes increases in aggressive behavior is over. All major types of research methodologies have been used, including experiments, cross-sectional correlational studies, longitudinal studies, intervention studies and meta-analyses. For each category, exposure to media violence was significantly associated with increased aggressions or violence. Likewise, the harmful effects on minors from playing violent video games are documented and not seriously contested.

Much research over several decades documents how witnessing violence and aggression leads to a range of negative outcomes for children. Negative outcomes result both from witnessing real violence as well as from viewing media violence. The most recent comprehensive review of the media violence literature documents the ". . . unequivocal evidence that media violence increases the likelihood of aggressive and violent behavior in both immediate and long-term contexts."

In the end, we need only to circle back from this rising ocean of research and return to simple commonsense. Society has a direct, rational and compelling reason in marginally restricting a minor's access to violent video games. Indeed, under the statute any parent remains completely free to provide any video game for their children.

Although this Court has never directly dealt with this precise issue, the Court's clear and understandable precedent in protecting children establishes that the lower court should be reversed and given the scientific findings by the community of mental health professions, the California statute upheld.

Respectfully submitted,

Steven F. Gruel
Counsel of Record
July 19, 2010
Counsel for Amicus Curiae

Appendix

Statement on Video Game Violence

"Both the American Psychological Association and the American Academy of Pediatrics have issued formal statements stating that scientific research on violent video games clearly shows that such games are causally related to later aggressive behavior in children and adolescents. Extensive research has been conducted over many years using all three major types of research designs (experimental, cross-sectional, and longitudinal). Numerous original empirical research studies have been conducted on children and adolescents. Overall, the research data conclude that exposure to violent video games causes an increase in the likelihood of aggressive behavior. The effects are both immediate and long term. Violent video games have measurable and statistically significant effects on both males and females. Theoretically important effects of violent video games have been confirmed by many empirical studies. The effects have been replicated by researchers in different settings and in numerous countries. The psychological processes underlying such effects are well understood and include: imitation, observational learning, priming of cognitive, emotional and behavioral scripts, physiological arousal, and emotional desensitization. These are general processes that underlie all types of social behavior, not just aggression and violence; they have been confirmed by countless studies outside of the media violence domain. In addition to causing an increase in the likelihood of aggressive behavior, violent video games have also been found to increase aggressive thinking, aggressive feelings, physiological desensitization to violence, and to decrease pro-social behavior."

Patricia A. Millett  **NO**

Brief of *Amici Curiae* in *Brown v. Entertainment Merchants Association*

Introduction and Summary of Argument

As respondents explain, California's ban on the sale and rental of certain video games to minors is subject to strict scrutiny because it directly regulates video games based on the content of a game, *i.e.,* whether the game is deemed "violent." California asserts that its law is necessary to "prevent psychological or neurological harm to minors who play violent video games." Pet. App. 23a. Under strict scrutiny, California must both provide "substantial evidence" that the video games it regulates cause psychological or neurological harm to minors who play them, and demonstrate that the restriction will "alleviate these harms in a direct and material way." *Turner Broadcasting Sys., Inc. v. FCC,* 512 U.S. 622, 664, 666 (1994). *See Ashcroft v. Free Speech Coalition,* 535 U.S. 234, 253 (2002).

California has done neither. Indeed, California does not offer any reliable evidence, let alone substantial evidence, that playing violent video games causes psychological or neurological harm to minors. California confesses it cannot prove causation, but points to studies that it says show a "correlation" between the two. Pet. Br. 52. But the evidence does not even do that.

California and Senator Yee also cite studies that purport to show a link between the playing of violent video games and violent, aggressive, and antisocial behavior by minors. But in the court of appeals, California expressly disclaimed any interest in regulating video games sales and rentals to minors to prevent such conduct, Pet. App. 23a–24a, and therefore these studies are waived because the argument was waived. The studies are of no help to California in any event because they document neither a causal connection nor a correlation between the playing of violent video games and violent, aggressive, or antisocial behavior.

Indeed, whether attempting to link violent video games with psychological and neurological harm or with violent, aggressive, and antisocial behavior, all of the studies that California and Senator Yee cite suffer from inherent and fundamental methodological flaws.

- *The survey of aggressive behavior.* The courts below carefully considered this survey and correctly discredited it because the questions it posed

U.S. Supreme Court, 2010.

are simply not valid indicators for actual violent or aggressive behavior and because it fails to account or control for other variables that have been proven to affect the behavior of minors.

- *The laboratory experimental study of aggression.* This study, too, was rightly discounted by the courts below because it relies on proxies for aggression that do not correlate with aggressive behavior in the real world.
- *The "meta-analysis" of video game violence research.* A meta-analysis combines the results of many other studies on a particular subject. But the accuracy and utility of any meta-analysis depends on the quality of the underlying studies themselves. Put another way, a meta-analysis of scientifically unreliable studies cannot cure the studies' flaws. Here, the meta-analysis on which Senator Yee relies was compromised because it was based on studies that used invalid measures of aggression.
- *"Longitudinal" studies of aggression.* A longitudinal study analyzes participants on many occasions over an extended period. The studies that Senator Yee cites are not longitudinal because they observed participants on only a few occasions and over just a short period of time. Additionally, those studies both failed to account for other variables that may explain aggressive behavior and used invalid measures of aggression.
- *Neuroscience studies.* These studies supposedly show a connection between playing violent video games and altered brain activity. The courts below properly concluded that they do not. Further, the neuroscience studies are rooted in fundamentally flawed statistical methodologies and do not address the cause of brain activation and deactivation in children.

Methodological flaws are only the beginning of the studies' problems. Both California and Senator Yee repeatedly exaggerate the statistical significance of the studies' findings, failing to inform the Court of express disclaimers and cautionary statements in the studies about the nature of their findings.

Finally, California and Senator Yee ignore a weighty body of scholarship, undertaken with established and reliable scientific methodologies, debunking the claim that the video games California seeks to regulate have harmful effects on minors.

Argument

I. California's Asserted Interest in Preventing Psychological and Neurological Harm to Minors Is Not Supported by Any Reliable, Let Alone, Substantial Evidence.

A. California's Studies Do Not Show a Causal Link, or Even a Correlation, Between Playing Violent Video Games and Psychological or Neurological Harm to Minors.

California's ban on the sale and rental of violent video games to minors rests on the same flawed studies that court after court has rejected. Pet. Br. 52–56; Pet. App. 27a–32a, 63a–64a; *Entertainment Software Ass'n v. Blagojevich,*

404 F. Supp. 2d 1051, 1059–1067 (N.D. Ill. 2005), *aff'd* 469 F.3d 641 (7th Cir. 2006); *Interactive Digital Software Ass'n v. St. Louis County,* 329 F.3d 954, 958–59 (8th Cir. 2003); *American Amusement Machine Ass'n v. Kendrick,* 244 F.3d 572, 578–79 (7th Cir. 2001) ("AAMA"); *Entertainment Software Ass'n v. Foti,* 451 F. Supp. 2d 823, 832 (M.D. La. 2006); *Entertainment Software Ass'n v. Hatch,* 443 F. Supp. 2d 1065, 1069–70 & n.2 (D. Minn. 2006); *Entertainment Software Ass'n v. Granholm,* 426 F. Supp. 2d 646, 652–54 (E.D. Mich. 2006). The courts were right to reject these studies because they do not even establish the "correlation" between violent video games and psychological harm to minors that California says exists, let alone the causation of harm that, as respondent explains, the First Amendment requires. Nor do the studies show a connection between playing violent video games and violent or aggressive behavior of minors, which explains why California disclaimed that interest below.

First, California points to a 2004 study by Douglas Gentile of approximately 600 eighth-and ninth-grade students. Pet. Br. 52–53 (citing JA 600). These students completed surveys that asked questions about the types of video games they preferred and how "violent" they were. (The survey did not provide any definition of "violent.") The survey also recorded how often the students played the games; the students' hostility level; how often they had argued with teachers during the past year; their average grades; and whether they had been in a physical fight in the past year. JA 613–15. From the survey answers, Gentile concluded that "[a]dolescents who expose themselves to greater amounts of video game violence" were more hostile and reported getting into more arguments with teachers and physical fights and performing poorly in school. JA 601.

Although California relies heavily on the Gentile survey, Pet. Br. 52–53, it has absolutely no relevance here. The survey examines only the purported connection between video game violence and "aggressive behavior" or "physical aggression" towards third parties. Pet. Br. 53. It does not study, and says nothing about, the psychological or neurological harm allegedly caused to those who play violent video games, which is the only interest that California defended below and thus is the only interest that is properly before this Court. Pet. App. 24a.

Even if the Gentile survey were relevant, it simply does not say what California says it does. California states that the survey "suggest[s] a causal connection between playing violent video games and aggressive behavior." Pet. Br. 53. It does no such thing. The survey makes absolutely no finding that exposure to violent video games leads to physical aggression. To the contrary, it explicitly cautions against making that inference: "It is important to note . . . that this study is limited by *its correlational nature. Inferences about causal direction should be viewed with caution.*" JA 638 (emphasis added); see also JA 632–33 ("Are young adolescents more hostile and aggressive because they expose themselves to media violence, or do previously hostile adolescents prefer violent media? Due to the correlational nature of this study, we cannot answer this question directly").

Beyond that, the Gentile survey is rife with methodological flaws that undermine even the suggested correlation. For example, the measures of "aggressive behavior" that Gentile employed are highly suspect. Having an argument with a teacher—without any further exploration into the nature of the event—does not even suggest violent or aggressive behavior. And simply asking students whether they had been in a fight—again, without any further analysis of the event—is not a valid indicator for violent or aggressive behavior.

Additionally, there are many factors that may influence youth violence or aggressive behavior, including: family violence, antisocial personality traits, and association with delinquent peers. *See* Herrenkohl et al., *Risk Factors for Violence and Relational Aggression in Adolescence,* 22 Journal of Interpersonal Violence 386 (2007); *see also* Savage, *The Role of Exposure to Media Violence in the Etiology of Violent Behavior: A Criminologist Weighs In,* 51 American Behavioral Scientist 1123, 1127 (2008) ("A focus on media violence literature, where we might find some correlations in a subset of studies, would lead to an exaggerated view of the importance of media violence in the etiology of violent behavior if we ignore the empirical evidence on other individual factors and situational factors."). Because Gentile's survey failed to control for, or even consider, those other variables, its conclusion that there is a correlation between video games and hostility to third parties lacks scientific grounding. In fact, controlling for gender alone removes most of the variance from which Gentile finds a correlation. Ferguson, *Blazing Angels or Resident Evil? Can Violent Video Games Be a Force for Good?,* 14 Review of General Psychology 74–75 (2010). In other words, the correlation Gentile claims to find is equally explainable by the effect of gender: boys tend to play more violent video games and tend to be more aggressive. *Id.*

Second, California points to a 2004 study of 130 college students by Craig Anderson. Pet. Br. 53 (citing JA 479, 493–94). That study measured the blood pressure of students before, during, and after playing selected video games and had students take a "word completion" test after playing selected video games. JA 497. Based on the resulting measurements, Anderson concluded that the students' blood pressure increased while playing certain video games he labeled "violent" and that game play "increase[d] . . . the accessibility of aggressive thoughts." JA 507.

The Anderson study is no help to California, because it does not show that a rise in students' blood pressure has any relationship to whether violent video games cause psychological or neurological harm. Nor does California show how "aggressive thoughts" leads to psychological harm.

Laboratory experiments, like Anderson's, that measure aggression immediately following the playing of a video game are common in the field of media effects research. *See generally* Kutner & Olson, supra, at 73–74. And like Anderson's, these experiments rely on proxies for *real* aggressive or violent behavior, such as the participants' willingness to administer blasts of white noise against an unseen (and non-existent opponent). Freedman, *supra,* at 60–63. The problem is that the proxies bear no relationship to whether someone is going to act aggressively or violently in the real world. Kutner & Olson, *supra,* at 73–74. Similarly, giving participants words with blank spaces and evaluating whether they make "aggressive" or "non-aggressive" words with the letters they fill in (i.e., "explo_e" could be completed as "explore" or "explode"), as Anderson did in his experiment, JA 496, has no known validity for measuring aggressive behavior (or even aggressive thinking).

Third, California points to a 2004 study of fourth- and fifth-grade students by Jeanne Funk, and claims it "found that playing violent video games was correlated with lower empathy as well as stronger pro-violence attitudes." Pet. Br. 53 (citing JA 705–06). But the Funk study specifically disclaimed any proof of causality. JA 730. As Funk admitted, the children in her study whose scores indicated lower empathy or stronger pro-violence attitudes may simply have been drawn to violent video games. *Id.* Moreover, the small sample size—just 150 children—and the failure to control for or consider any other variables undermine even the study's tentative conclusion of a correlation between violent video games and proviolence attitudes.

> B. The Additional Studies Cited by Senator Yee Do Not Support California's Ban on the Sale and Rental of Violent Video Games to Minors.

Senator Yee's brief boldly declares that "science confirms that violent video games are harmful to minors." Yee Br. 10. But the studies he discusses do not show that.

Senator Yee leans heavily on a one-page statement by some researchers, who did not join his amicus brief. Yee Br. 11. That statement focuses on whether violent video games increase the likelihood of "aggressive behavior," which is the interest that California disclaimed below. Pet. App. 24a. With respect to the interest that California defended below—whether violent video games cause psychological or neurological harm to minors—the statement offers only one line at its tail end expressing concern about aggressive "thinking," aggressive "feelings," desensitization, and a decrease in "pro-social" behavior. But if the First Amendment means anything, it means government cannot ban speech to stop thoughts or feelings, and certainly not to promote "pro-social" behavior.

Aside from his reliance on the one-page statement of scholars, Senator Yee refers to "recent research," "new data," and "hundreds of studies" regarding the effects of violent video games. Yee Br. 5, 6. But there rarely are citations in Senator Yee's brief to support these broad assertions.

Read carefully, the "recent research" and "new data" that Senator Yee offers boils down to (1) a meta-analysis conducted by Craig Anderson, (2) a book co-authored by Anderson and Douglas Gentile, (3) certain purported "longitudinal studies," (4) broad policy statements of the American Academy of Pediatrics and the American Psychological Association, and (5) a few neuroscience studies. None of these sources provides substantial evidence that violent video games cause psychological or neurological harm to minors or lead to violent, aggressive, or antisocial behavior in minors.

1. *Anderson Meta-analysis.* This recent study is labeled a "meta-analysis" of video game violence research. Anderson et al., *Violent Video Game Effects on Aggression, Empathy and Prosocial Behavior in Eastern and Western Countries: A Meta-Analytic Review*, 136 Psychological Bulletin 151 (2010). "Meta-analysis"

is a research technique that merges the results of many studies on a particular topic using statistical analysis.

The accuracy and usefulness of this tool necessarily depends, however, on the choice and quality of the studies that are merged for analysis, and the "end-product will never be better than the individual studies that make up the meta-analysis." Anderson's study is an example of how a meta-analysis can simply compound the methodological flaws in the underlying studies.

For example, Anderson's meta-analysis combines studies that used methods for measuring aggression that have not been proven to be valid. Ferguson & Kilburn, *Much Ado About Nothing: The Misestimation and Overinterpretation of Violent Video Game Effects in Eastern and Western Nations: Comment on Anderson et al.,* 136 Psychological Bulletin 174, 175–76 (2010). By incorporating those studies into his analysis, Anderson replicated their methodological flaws in his meta-analysis, severely eroding the reliability of its findings.

Additionally, the process by which Anderson selected the studies for inclusion in the meta-analysis casts serious doubt on the results. Anderson reasonably included some unpublished studies in his meta-analysis given the risk of publication bias in the field of violent video game effects research. But the process by which Anderson selected unpublished studies—he included his own unpublished work and the work of others whose conclusions mirror his, and excluded a wealth of unpublished studies from a contrary perspective—injected more, not less, bias into the analysis. Ferguson & Kilburn, *supra,* at 175.

Notably, Senator Yee fails to mention that the methodology of Anderson's meta-analysis was resoundingly criticized in the very same issue of the journal in which the meta-analysis was first published. Ferguson & Kilburn, *supra.*

Leaving the methodological flaws aside, Anderson's meta-analysis does not support Senator Yee's sweeping claims that it contains "definitive findings" and "unequivocal evidence" that "prove[s]" playing violent video games increases aggressive thoughts and behavior. Yee Br. 26, 28. That is because the estimated "effect size" between playing violent video games, on the one hand, and aggressive behavior, on the other, that Anderson identified is minimal. Anderson et al., *supra,* at 170. An "effect size" estimate represents the proportion of shared variance between two variables. It is, roughly speaking, the degree to which one variable can predict the other improving upon chance alone. For example, an effect size of 1% means that knowing variable x (playing violent video games) for an individual would be 1% better than chance alone in predicting whether that individual was likely to engage in aggressive or violent behavior. In contrast, an effect size of 100% means that the variable is a fully accurate predictor.

In his meta-analysis, Anderson concedes that the estimated effect size between playing violent video games and aggressive behavior is "small," specifically, 0.152 or 2.31%. Anderson et al., *supra,* at 170. Thus, the effect size that Anderson himself calculates—far from being a significant "causal risk factor," Yee Br. 26—means that playing violent video games is only 2.31% better than chance alone at predicting whether that individual will engage in aggressive behavior. And even that insignificant effect size is likely inflated because

Anderson's study did not control for well-accepted risk factors for aggressive behavior, such as the influence of peers and family. Ferguson & Kilburn, *supra,* at 177.

Finally, other meta-analytic research that incorporated studies with valid and reliable methodologies, properly accounted for publication bias, and controlled for "third" variables have found little evidence that violent video games cause psychological harm (or any other harm) to minors.

For example, in a 2009 study published in the Journal of Pediatrics, Dr. Christopher Ferguson and Dr. John Kilburn conducted a meta-analytic review of studies that considered the impact of violent media on aggressive behavior. They relied on studies that used well-validated measures for assessing aggressive behavior, properly corrected for publication bias, and controlled for well-accepted risk factors for aggressive behavior. Ferguson & Kilburn, *Public Health Risks, supra,* at 759–60. The results suggest that the overall effect for exposure to media violence (both television and video game violence) was less than 1%. *Id.* at 761. Thus, the authors concluded that the results of their study "do not support the conclusion that media violence leads to aggressive behavior." *Id.* at 759.

In another recent meta-analytic study, Dr. John Sherry concluded that while there are researchers in the field who "are committed to the notion of powerful effects," they have been unable to prove such effects; that studies exist that seem to support a relationship between violent video games and aggression but other studies show no such relationship; and that research in this area has employed varying methodologies, thus "obscuring clear conclusions." Sherry, *Violent Video Games and Aggression: Why Can't We Find Effects?,* Mass Media Effects Research: Advances Through Meta-Analysis 231, 232 (2007); see also Sherry, *The Effects of Violent Video Games on Aggression: A Meta-Analysis,* 27 Human Communication Research 409–31 (2001). Although Dr. Sherry "expected to find fairly clear, compelling, and powerful effects," based on assumptions he had formed regarding video game violence, he did not find them. Sherry, *Violent Video Games, supra,* at 231, 245. Instead, he found only a small relationship between playing violent video games and short-term arousal or aggression and further found that this effect lessened the longer one spent playing video games. *Id.* at 243–45.

Such small and inconclusive results prompted Dr. Sherry to ask: "[W]hy do some researchers continue to argue that video games are dangerous despite evidence to the contrary?" *Id.* at 244. Dr. Sherry further noted that if violent video games posed such a threat, then the increased popularity of the games would lead to an increase in violent crime. *Id.* But that has not happened. Quite the opposite, during the same period that video game sales, including sales of violent video games, have risen, youth violence has dramatically declined.

2. *Anderson and Gentile Book.* Senator Yee touts a "recent book" (Yee Br. 16–17), co-authored by Anderson and Gentile, that asserts there are "reasons to expect" larger effects from exposure to violent video games because of their interactive nature. Anderson, Gentile, & Buckley, *Violent Video Game Effects on Children and Adolescents: Theory, Research, and Public Policy* 135 (Oxford Univ.

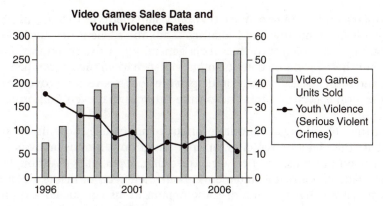

(Source: Ferguson & Olson et al., *Violent Video Games, Catharsis Seeking, Bullying, and Delinquency: A Multivariate Analysis of Effects*, Crime & Delinquency 5 (2010))

Press 2006). But that assertion rests on the same old research of Anderson and Gentile that has been rejected as fundamentally flawed by every court that has considered it. Pet. App. 29a, 64a; *see, e.g., Blagojevich*, 404 F. Supp. 2d at 1063 ("Dr. Anderson also has not provided evidence to show that video games. . . are any more harmful than violent television, movies, Internet sites or other speech-related exposure.").

3. *Longitudinal Studies.* A longitudinal study examines a subject on several occasions over an extended period of time. *See* Kutner & Olson, *supra*, at 68–69. Both Anderson and Gentile (the main proponents of the idea that violent video games have harmful effects on minors) acknowledged in the record below that "there is a 'glaring empirical gap' in video game violence research due to 'the lack of longitudinal studies'" (Anderson) and that therefore "longitudinal research is needed" (Gentile). Pet. App. 28a, 30a.

Senator Yee claims that this gap has now been closed: according to Senator Yee, longitudinal studies of violent video games have been done and have proven harmful effects. Yee Br. 26. But Senator Yee provides no citations to support this proposition.

Amici are aware of one recent study of students in the United States and Japan that Anderson has described as "longitudinal" data that "confirm[s]" that playing violent video games is an "important causal risk factor for youth aggression." Anderson et al., *Longitudinal Effects of Violent Video Games in Aggression in Japan and the United States,* 122 Pediatrics 1067 (2008). But there is nothing "longitudinal" about this study. Rather than studying participants multiple times over extended periods, it surveyed participants only twice and with only a few months lag in between. Additionally, the flaws that taint Anderson's other research (*e.g.*, failing to control for "third" variables and using measures of aggression that have not been proven reliable) recur in this study. Finally, Anderson's sweeping assertion of a causal connection is belied by the study's insignificant effect sizes (between .152 and .075, or 0.5% and 2.3%).

4. *Policy Statements.*   Senator Yee cites policy statements of two organizations, the American Academy of Pediatrics and the American Psychological Association, that violence in the media generally is a risk to minors. Yee Br. 10–12. But these pronouncements indict violence in *all* media, not just video games, and thus, if acted upon, would open the door to sweeping governmental restrictions on speech in films and on the Internet that even California does not propone.

Further, broad organizational pronouncements, like those in the policy statements that Senator Yee cites, are not based on a serious analysis of the relevant scientific evidence. See, e.g., Freedman, *supra*, at 9 ("Although they have all made unequivocal statements about the effects of media violence, it is almost certain that not one of these organizations conducted a thorough review of the research. They have surely not published or made available any such review."). The lack of any detailed analysis underpinning the statements is illustrated by (a) the American Academy of Pediatrics' assertion that *"[m]ore than 3500 research studies* have examined the association between media violence and violent behavior; all but 18 have shown a positive relationship," American Academy of Pediatrics, *Media Violence,* 108 Pediatrics 1222 (2001), emphasis added (cited at Yee Br. 11), and (b) an assertion in a 2000 joint statement of medical and psychological groups that *"well over 1000 studies . . .* point overwhelmingly to a causal connection between media violence and aggressive behavior in some children," JA 378, emphasis added (quoted at Pet. Br. 44). The rub is that there have not been over 3500—or even over 1000—scientific studies done on this topic. And the studies that have been conducted do not reach the uniform or "overwhelming" conclusion that the organizations claim they do. Freedman, *supra,* at 9; *see also* Kutner & Olson, *supra,* at 78. Finally, it is telling that the citations in the policy statements on which Senator Yee relies are to the flawed studies that were incorporated into Anderson's meta-analysis.

5. *Neuroscience Research.*   California's ban on the sale and rental of violent video games to minors is based on an assumption that "[e]xposing minors to depictions of violence in video games . . . makes those minors more likely . . . to experience a reduction of activity in the frontal lobes of the brain." Pet. App. 8a. In both the trial court and the court of appeals, California relied on research by William Kronenberger that purported to identify a connection between violent video games and altered brain activity using functional magnetic resonance imaging ("fMRI") technology. Pet. App. 3la. But every single court to review Kronenberger's fMRI research, including the courts below, have found no such connection. *Id.; See, e.g., Blagojevich,* 404 F. Supp. 2d at 1063–65; *Granholm,* 426 F. Supp. 2d at 653. California has now abandoned all reliance on Kronenberger's fMRI research or any other fMRI study.

Senator Yee, however, invokes Kronenberger's fMRI research, as well as a handful of other neuroscience articles, claiming that they show "a critical link" between virtual violence and altered brain functioning Yee Br. 24. They do no such thing.

To begin with, Senator Yee fails to acknowledge the intense debate in the scientific community, widely reported in both the academic and popular press, regarding whether fMRI technology is being misused and its results being exaggerated. *See, e.g.,* Lehrer, *Picturing Our Thoughts,* The Boston Globe, Aug. 17, 2008; Vul et al., *Puzzlingly High Correlations in fMRI Studies of Emotion, Personality, and Social Cognition,* 4 Perspectives on Psychological Science 274 (2009); *see also* Hotz, *The Brain, Your Honor, Will Take the Witness Stand,* The Wall Street Journal, Jan. 15, 2009 (reporting scholars' criticism that fMRI brain scans cannot be used as legal evidence because they are "easily manipulated" and "can't be trusted yet"); Begley, *Of Voodoo and the Brain,* Newsweek, Jan. 31, 2009 (reporting scholars' claim that many published fMRI studies show "voo-doo correlations," methods and analysis so poor that they must be redone); Begley, *Brain Imaging and (More) Voodoo, But Politer,* Newsweek, April 27, 2009 (asking "isn't it time the fMRI community came to grips with the growing criticism of its methods"); Hamilton, *False Signals Cause Misleading Brain Scans,* National Public Radio, July 7, 2009 (reporting "furious debate" as to whether flaws in statistical analysis have made fMRI results "appear stronger than they really are" and that "even the strongest defenders of fMRI acknowledge that there are problems"); Sanders, *Trawling the Brain,* ScienceNews, Dec. 19, 2009 (describing growing concern in scientific community as to fMRI's reliability and warning that "the singing of fMRI's praises ought to be accompanied by a chorus of caveats"); Logothetis, *What We Can Do and What We Cannot Do with fMRI,* Nature, June 2008 ("[F]undamental questions concerning the interpreta-tion of fMRI data abound, as the conclusions drawn often ignore the actual limitations of the methodology.").

As many scholars have cautioned, fMRI studies of brain activation have inherent methodological issues that make them difficult to understand and interpret. In a typical fMRI experiment, a subject is placed in a tube-shaped machine (just like the one used for an ordinary MRI test), told to lie perfectly still and then to perform some experimental task, such as looking at an image and making a decision. Magnets detect the ratio of the change between oxygen-ated and deoxygenated blood in a specific region of the brain. A complicated statistical analysis is then used to turn that signal into an "activation" in the brain. The underlying assumption is that active neurons require more oxygen to work and, therefore, more oxygen means greater neuronal activity.

A central problem, however, is that while fMRI studies may indicate areas of the brain that decrease in activation during a task, deactivations that may occur simultaneously are not well understood and, thus, are only tenta-tively discussed in published fMRI studies. *See, e.g.,* Kalbfleish, *Getting to the Heart of the Brain: Using Cognitive Neuroscience to Explore the Nature of Human Ability and Performance,* 30 Roeper Review 165 (2007). Additionally, it is not yet understood how brain activation is influenced by neural development in children. *Id.*

Further, because fMRI studies depend on statistical analysis, errors in the method or procedure of that analysis may undermine the reliability of the results. *See* Vul et al., *supra.* A recent study surveyed 55 fMRI studies on brain activation and emotion, personality, and social cognition and found that, in about half of these studies, the methods and analysis were so flawed that the results were "entirely spurious correlations." *Id.* at 274.

On top of the inherent limitations of fMRI research generally, the particular fMRI studies that Senator Yee cites—three studies conducted in part by Kronenberger and one study conducted by Rene Weber—have their own specific flaws and their results are so inconclusive that they do not remotely support the asserted link between playing video games and altered brain functioning.

The Kronenberger articles—each of which expressly states that it was funded by a grant from the anti-media violence Center for Successful Parenting—set forth findings that are so qualified as to render them meaningless.

In the most recent Kronenberger study, *see* Yee Br. 21 (citing Hummer et al., *Short-Term Violent Video Game Play by Adolescents Alters Prefontal Activity During Cognitive Inhibition,* 13 Media Psychology 136 (2010)), forty-five adolescents were divided into two groups, with one group playing a car racing video game and the other group playing a shooting game. After thirty minutes of play, each participant was subjected to an fMRI scan, during which they were required to press a button for each letter that was displayed, except for the letter x, for which there was no response. Looking at the resulting data, Kronenberger and his co-authors made the broad conclusion that there were lower activity levels for the shooting game in regions of the brain *"thought to be involved* in cognitive inhibition." *Id.* at 147 (emphasis added).

As a threshold matter, this study cannot possibly support California's claim that violent video game cause harm to minors because a decrease in activity in an area of the brain is not necessarily a negative effect and, instead, may indicate nothing more than expertise in a practiced task. *See, e.g.,* Poldrack et al., *The Neural Correlates of Motor Skill Automaticity,* 25 Journal of Neuroscience 5356 (2005). The mere fact that the brain changes as it responds to stimuli does not prove that the stimuli are harmful.

Additionally, the study's own express qualifications undercut its findings. The authors admitted that the two video games chosen differed in ways other than the presence or absence of violent content and thus created "potential confounds" for the results. Hummer et al., *supra,* at 149.

The two other studies conducted in part by Kronenberger did not consider exposure to video games specifically, just "media violence" generally, and thus do not support California's claim that violent *video games* cause harm to minors. See Kronenberger et al., *Media Violence Exposure and Executive Functioning in Aggressive and Control Adolescents,* 61 Journal of Clinical Psychology 725, 726 (2005) (cited at Yee Br. 21); Mathews et al., *Media Violence Exposure and Frontal Lobe Activation Measured by Functional Magnetic Resonance Imaging in Aggressive and Nonaggressive Adolescents,* 29 Journal of Computer Assisted Tomography 287 (2005) (cited at Yee Br. 22). More importantly, each study is expressly announced to be inconclusive. For example, in their study of media violence and "executive functioning," Kronenberger and his colleagues explicitly warn that the results are only "preliminary" and "should be viewed with caution." Kronenberger et al., *supra,* at 726," *see also* Mathews et al., *supra,* at 291–92 (explaining study's "limitation" is that it "did not evaluate other brain regions involved in emotional control"; authors recommended "further study" to evaluate "the entire system involved in aggressive behavior").

Senator Yee fares no better in his reliance on the Weber fMRI study. Yee Br. 24 (citing Weber et al., *Does Playing Violent Video Games Induce Aggression? Empirical Evidence of a Functional Magnetic Resonance Imaging Study,* 8 Media Psychology 39 (2006)). The Weber study involved thirteen adult men who were observed playing a supposedly violent video game for an hour. The study examined brain activity patterns that were similar to those seen in a previous study of individuals "imagin[ing] scenarios involving aggressive behavior." *Id.* at 42–43, 53. What those patterns mean, however, is not explained by the science. Nor do the patterns demonstrate any real-world connection between the "imagin[ings]" and violence or harmful neurological effect. And Senator Yee fails to explain how this limited study of a small pool of adult men substantiates the sweeping assertions about minors' neurological functioning on which California's law depends.

C. California and Senator Yee Ignore the Large Body of Empirical Evidence That Shows No Causal Connection, or Even a Correlation, Between Violent Video Games and Harm to Minors.

California and Senator Yee ignore a wealth of recent empirical evidence disabusing the notion that violent video games are harmful to minors. Here is just a snapshot of that body of scholarship:

- A study of 603 Hispanic youths (ages ten to fourteen), recently published in The Journal of Pediatrics, examined various risk factors for youth violence, including video game violence, delinquent peer association, family conflict, depression, and others. Ferguson et al., *A Multivariate Analysis of Youth Violence and Aggression: The Influence of Family, Peers, Depression, and Media Violence,* 155 Journal of Pediatrics 904 (2009). The children listed television shows and video games and rated how often they viewed or played the media— a reliable and valid method of evaluating violent media exposure. *Id.* at 905. The children were then evaluated using the Child Behavior Checklist, a well-researched and well-validated tool for measuring behavioral problems in children and adolescents. *Id.* A statistical analysis of the results revealed that exposure to video games had a negligible effect size and was not predictive of youth violence and aggression. *Id.* at 906.
- A study of 1,254 seventh- and eighth-grade students examined the influence of exposure to violent video games on delinquency and bullying behavior. Ferguson & Olson et al., *supra*. The Entertainment Software Ratings Board ratings were employed as a standardized measure of participants' exposure to violence in video games. *Id.* at 8. The study applied a multivariate statistical method that considered other factors that might be predictive of aggressive behavior (such as level of parental involvement, support from others, and stress). *Id.* at 7–8. This study did not use abstract measures of aggression, but instead focused on specific negative behaviors such as delinquency and bullying. *Id.* at 8, 9. A statistical analysis

revealed insignificant effect sizes between exposure to violent video games and delinquency or bullying. *Id.* at 11, 12. The authors accordingly concluded that exposure to such games was not predictive of delinquency or bullying. *Id.*

- A study of 213 participants examined the influence of violent video game play on aggressive behavior. Williams & Skoric, *Internet Fantasy Violence,* 72 Communication Monographs 217 (2005). The 213 participants were divided into a 75-person treatment group that played a single game, Asheron's Call 2, a type of "massively multiplayer online role-playing game" that is "highly violent" and has "a sustained pattern of violence," for at least five hours over a one-month period, and a 138-person control group that did not play the game. *Id.* at 221, 224. Participants then completed self-reported questionnaires that included a range of demographic, behavioral, and personality variables. *Id.* at 225. Aggression-related beliefs were measured according to the Normative Beliefs in Aggression general scale, a well-validated scale for measuring beliefs about the acceptability of aggression, and aggressive social interactions were measured using specific behavioral questions. Both measurement techniques had been successfully used in previous studies of violent television and video game effects. *Id.* The results of this study found no effects associated with aggression caused by playing violent video games. *Id.* at 228.

These studies are just the tip of the iceberg. They rate barely a mention in Senator Yee's brief, which disparages them as "alleged 'scientific studies'" that involved "small sample size, poor test conditions and chance." Yee Br. 27. That is wrong. The studies employed large sample sizes, long-standing and validated measures of aggression, and superior statistical controls. Ironically, the studies also include the work of researchers whom California and Senator Yee cite favorably. For example, as noted above, California relies on the research of Jeanne Funk. Pet Br. 53 (citing JA 705–06). But, in a separate study that California does not mention, Funk "fail[ed] to find" even a correlation between violent video games and aggressive emotions and behavior. *See* Funk et al., *Aggression and Psychopathology in Adolescents With a Preference for Violent Electronic Games,* 28 Aggressive Behavior 134 (2002). Notably, this second Funk study employed the Child Behavior Checklist, which is a better validated measure of aggression than measures utilized in the studies on which California and Senator Yee rely.

At minimum, the scholarship that California and Senator Yee ignore belies the notion that the "substantial evidence of causation" standard imposes an "insurmountable hurdle" on science or legislatures. Pet. Br. 52. These studies show unequivocally that the causation research can be done, and, indeed, has been done. The problem confronting California and Senator Yee thus is not the constitutional standard; it is simply their inability to meet that standard in this case because validated scientific studies prove the opposite, leaving no empirical foundation for the assertion that playing violent video games causes harm to minors.

Conclusion

For the foregoing reasons, the judgment of the court of appeals should be affirmed.

Respectfully submitted.

Michael C. Small
Katharine J. Galston
AKIN, GUMP, STRAUSS,
HAUER & FELD LLP

Patricia A. Millett
Counsel of Record
AKIN, GUMP, STRAUSS,
HAUER & FELD LLP

Attorneys for Amici Curiae

September 17, 2010

EXPLORING THE ISSUE

Does Research Confirm That Violent Video Games Are Harmful to Minors?

Critical Thinking and Reflection

1. The U.S. Constitution's First Amendment prohibits making any law that infringes on freedom of speech. What are your thoughts about video games being viewed as a form of free speech?
2. In light of the fact that government controls the sale of alcohol and tobacco to minors, what are the arguments for and against similar governmental control of the sale of violent video games to minors?
3. In what ways is the practice of playing violent video games similar to and different from watching violent movies? What are your thoughts about the possibility that exposure to violence can lead to desensitization to violence?
4. How would you go about designing a research project to study the effects of playing violent video games on minors? How you would go about determining causality, rather than correlation?
5. After reading the criticisms of the research studies cited in these briefs, what are some of the methodological limitations evident in the studies cited? If you were conducting such research, how would you try to overcome these limitations?

Is There Common Ground?

It would seem safe to offer the conjecture that adults as a rule do not want to put children in harm's way. As a society we strive to project humans from birth from being exposed to dangerous threats in the environment. Laws dictate that children must be protected in car seats, that house paint must be lead-free to prevent brain damage from accidental ingestion, and that tobacco and alcohol sales to children are prohibited. Thus, the argument could be made that if violent video games have a detrimental effect on children, efforts should be made by society to keep minors away from these media. But how do we go about determining that these video games are indeed detrimental to a child's development?

The authors of the brief pointing to the detrimental effects on children of violent video games believe that they have summarized compelling evidence that unwanted behavioral and neurological changes result from playing these games. However, in light of the great methodological challenges involved in studying this issue, is the research cited all that convincing? Has sufficient research been conducted to assess the extent to which there might be a differential impact between watching violent movies and playing violent video games? What about the effect on a child of seeing graphic images of war on the news in which real people are being blown to pieces in war zones? Do such images lead these impressionable children toward being more aggressive themselves?

The author of the brief on the opposing side of the argument pokes holes in the research positing a connection between playing violent video games and engaging in aggressive behavior. She raises some compelling arguments about the limitations of these research studies, and contests the extent to which such research should be the basis for drawing conclusions about speculative causality. What is not addressed in this brief, however, is the question "how violent is too violent?" Perhaps "shooting" an alien is acceptable, but what about raping an innocent victim? Most people would be critical of video games in which horrifying acts of torture and assault are glorified, but what is the threshold of violent acts that should be kept out of the games played by children?

Additional Resources

Kutner, L., & Olson, C. K. (2011). *Grand theft childhood: The surprising truth about violent video games and what parents can do.* New York: Simon & Schuster.

Nije Bijvank, M., Konijn, E. A., & Bushman, B. J. (2012). "We don't need no education": Video game preferences, video game motivations, and aggressiveness among adolescent boys of different educational ability levels. *Journal of Adolescence, 35*(1), 153–162. doi:10.1016/j.adolescence.2011.04.001

Polman, H., de Castro, B., & van Aken, M. G. (2008). Experimental study of the differential effects of playing versus watching violent video games on children's aggressive behavior. *Aggressive Behavior, 34*(3), 256–264. Retrieved from

web.ebscohost.com.silk. library. umass.edu/ehost/detail?vid=7&hid=7&sid=0e2bl9af-8751-4d92-826d-07fc8403f873%40sessionmgrl5&bdata=JnNpdGU9ZWhvc3OtbG12 ZSZzY29wZTlzaXRl#db=a ph&AN=31875598

Quarterly Newsletter of the Entertainment Merchants Association. Retrieved from www.entmerch.org/government-relations/ema-v-schwarzenegger-faqs.html

Sacks, D. P., Bushman, B. J., & Anderson, C. A. (2011). Do violent video games harm children? Comparing the scientific amicus curiae "experts" in *Brown v. Entertainment Merchants Association, Northwestern Law Review,* 106, 1–12.

ISSUE 10

Would Legalization of Virtual Child Pornography Reduce Sexual Exploitation of Children?

YES: Arnold H. Loewy, from "Taking Free Speech Seriously: The United States Supreme Court and Virtual Child Pornography," *UNC Public Law Research Paper No. 02-17* (November 2002)

NO: Diana E. H. Russell and Natalie J. Purcell, from "Exposure to Pornography as a Cause of Child Sexual Victimization," in Nancy E. Dowd, Dorothy G. Singer, and Robin Fretwell Wilson, *Handbook of Children, Culture, and Violence* (Sage Publications, 2006)

Learning Outcomes

After reading this issue, you should be able to:

- Understand the legal standard of free speech and how it applies to the distribution and use of materials that are considered socially offensive by many people.
- Discuss the difference between virtual and real child pornography.
- Debate the notion that the distribution of virtual child pornography should be considered as constitutionally protected forms of free speech.
- Discuss the question of whether virtual sexual images involving children set the stage for real-life exploitation of children.
- Evaluate the argument that child pornography in any form undermines the social prohibition against adult-child sex.

ISSUE SUMMARY

YES: Professor of law Arnold H. Loewy views the issue of virtual child pornography from a legal perspective, asserting that such material is a form of free speech that ought to be constitutionally protected. He also contends that legalizing virtual child pornography would reduce the extent to which real children would be exploited.

NO: Authors Diana E. H. Russell and Natalie J. Purcell express vehement objections to any forms of pornography involving images of children, asserting that Internet users with no previous sexual interest in children may find themselves drawn into a world in which the societal prohibition against adult–child sex is undermined.

Since the introduction of the Internet into homes and offices all over the world, the number of sites devoted to pornography has expanded exponentially, and the pornography industry has become a multi-billion dollar enterprise. In addition to the innumerable commercial sites offering pornography, the amateur segment of the pornographic Internet world now addresses any imaginable fetishistic fantasy. Within a span of only a few years, taboos have faded, and more and more people have become addicted to Internet pornography. Along with their addictive craving, many consumers of Internet pornography have pushed the limits farther and farther in their pursuit of images that will excite, and possibly shock their sensibilities. The ultimate taboo, sadly, involves pornography involving children. Some individuals who seek out child pornography have pedophilic tendencies, while others seem to be excited also by the absolutely forbidden nature of the content of child pornography. Few, if any, sane people would defend the exploitation of real children in order to serve the masturbatory fantasies of pornography consumers. However, some have argued that virtual forms of pornography might actually protect real children by accommodating the fantasies of adults who crave sexual images of children. The debate heats up, however, when critics of child pornography in any form argue that permitting even virtual images of children in sexual situations violates a societal boundary and puts children at great risk of being victimized in real life.

In recent years judicial decisions have come down on the side of the legality of virtual child pornography. For example, in 2002 the U.S. Supreme Court (*Ashcroft v. The Free Speech Coalition*) ruled that virtual child pornography is speech that is protected under the First Amendment, and cannot be banned by child-pornography laws. Rulings on the state level have followed suit, with decisions such as that of the Ohio Supreme Court in 2007 which ruled that pornographic images that are wholly faked, no matter how realistic, are legal.

Professor of law Arnold Loewy takes a stand that rests on legal and pragmatic arguments. In the legal realm he argues that pornography is a form of free speech that is constitutionally protected. In his view, unless all speech is free, no speech is free. It is better to deny government the power to suppress "bad speech" than it would be to allow it to suppress speech that may turn out to be valuable. He asserts that virtual child pornography is speech that ought to be constitutionally protected. Loewy contends that, even if it could be proven that virtual child pornography causes significant net harm, it would not follow that the law should permit its suppression.

Pragmatically speaking, Loewy acknowledges that child pornography is a reality that is here to stay; he believes that legalizing virtual child pornography may actually reduce the number of children who are currently being exploited by what he calls a "perverted industry." According to Attorney Loewy, pedophiles most likely obtain child pornography because they are attracted to children, rather than becoming attracted to children by looking at the child pornography they already possess. He states that it is neither intuitively obvious, nor has it been proven, that eliminating all virtual pornography from the face of the earth would significantly reduce the incidents of pedophilia.

According to Loewy, if virtual child pornography is (or can be made) nearly identical to real child pornography, and only real pornography is unlawful, why wouldn't pornographers and consumers view the virtual content? Thus, there is good reason to believe that legalizing virtual child pornography may actually reduce the number of children that are currently exploited by this perverted industry.

Authors Diana Russell and Natalie Purcell sound the alarm bell regarding child pornography in any form. They advocate the implementation of legal sanctions against child pornography as critically important deterrents to the exploitation of children. Russell and Purcell believe that allowing sexual images in any form that involve children undermines the prohibition against adult–child sex, and facilitates the proliferation of Internet sites on which such behaviors or desires are not considered deviant and where pedophiles and others interested in child pornography can feel more normal. The ultimate risk in their view is that more and more children will be put at risk of sexual victimization.

According to Russell and Purcell, Internet users with no previous sexual interest in children may find themselves aroused by child pornography, which transforms children into sexual objects, often acting as mini-adults engaging in sexual intercourse, masturbation, and various sexual poses. They assert that fear of legal sanctions is the most important factor in restraining potential and active molesters from abusing children. The more effective molesters perceive the social sanctions to be, the less likely they are to become perpetrators.

Russell and Purcell contend that some males who have never acted on their desire to have sex with a child may be ignorant or anxious about how to proceed with this. While such concerns could inhibit them from perpetrating such an act, child pornography removes this impediment by providing instructions for the sexual abuse of children. In addition, many pedophiles and child molesters show pornography to children in order to arouse their sexual curiosity or desire and thereby undermine the children's abilities to avoid, resist, or escape being sexually abused, to persuade children that they would enjoy certain sexual acts, and to convince them that what they are being asked to do is alright.

The inclusion of child pornography cartoons in mainstream men's magazines such as *Playboy* and *Penthouse* communicates its social acceptability, and the boards of various sites allowing visitors to form communities in which such behaviors or desires are not considered deviant, and where pedophiles and others interested in child pornography can feel more normal, merely encourage child sexual victimization.

YES

Arnold H. Loewy[1]

Taking Free Speech Seriously: The United States Supreme Court and Virtual Child Pornography

I. The Importance of Protecting Bad Speech

Few liberal democracies challenge freedom of speech in the abstract. Specific applications, however, are different. Many, who would never challenge freedom of speech in the abstract, balk at extending such protection to flag burners,[2] and Nazis.[3] Yet, the slightest reflection should reveal that unless all speech is free, no speech is free. No sensible government, including the most dictatorial, will ever prosecute good speech or even neutral speech.[4] Indeed, no democracy would even think of prosecuting ordinarily bad speech (*e.g.,* vote Republican).[5] It is only when we get to very bad speech that the government even thinks about prosecution. Thus, it is in those situations in which free speech is needed most. Hence, protection for Nazis, flag burners, and virtual child pornographers logically follows if we want to take free speech seriously.

But should we want to take it seriously if the cost of doing so is to give added protection for speech that we would all be better off without? One's first intuition is to say "no," and indeed that is the result regularly reached in European courts[6] and too frequently in American courts.[7] The reason that this should bother us is that it gives government the power to decide which speech can compete in the marketplace and which speech is dead on arrival.

While some of us might be happy to relegate flag burning, Nazis, and virtual pornography to the scrapheap of dead on arrival speech, few would say that about speech urging racial integration. Yet speech urging racial integration fifty years ago would have been thought highly offensive to much of the citizenry of a large number of communities (including Charleston, South Carolina) and would have been subject to prohibition under a standard that protects the dignitary interest of some against the speech of others. Thus, even though government may be correct about some types of speech it is better to deny government the power to suppress that speech than it would be to allow it to suppress speech that may turn out to be valuable (such as civil rights speech).[8] . . .

UNC Public Law Research Paper No. 02-17, November 2002. First published in the *First Amendment Law Review.* Copyright © 2002 by Arnold H. Loewy. Reprinted by permission.

II. Distinguishing Real Child Pornography

Real child pornography is rightly subject to prosecution. But the reason that it is so treated has nothing to do with the abhorrent nature, or intrinsic worthlessness, of the material. It can be prosecuted for the same reason that employment of child labor can be prosecuted. Just as child labor harms the children that manufacture the goods to be sold, so does child pornography. It would not be a defense to a child labor prosecution that employment of children was necessary to enhance the quantity or quality of the product produced. Similarly, it should be no defense that the finished product had some kind of literary or artistic merit. It is the use of a child in an explicit sexual performance that is rightly forbidden.[9]

Similarly, as the United States Supreme Court has suggested, morphed child pornography, that is images of a real child morphed to appear to be engaging in sexual activity, is enough like real child pornography that it should be treated as though it were real.[10] A morphed image does not harm a real child by making the picture, but it does harm the child by providing an unauthorized permanent and false record of the child's engaging in sexual activity.[11]

Apart from pornography that displays the image of a real child, actual or morphed, the objections to the material are similar to the objections to any kind of distasteful speech and should be subject to the same kind of scrutiny. In the remainder of this paper, I shall explain why none of the justifications generally advanced against virtual child pornography warrant its prohibition.

III. Virtual Pornography's Capacity to Harm Real Children

Proponents of criminalizing virtual pornography argue that there are two ways in which the material can harm real children. First, they argue that virtual child pornography can whet a pedophile's appetite, making it more likely that he will abuse real children. Second, it is argued that a pedophile can use a picture of what appears to be a real child enjoying her sexuality as a visual aid to persuade an innocent victim to engage in similar activity. I will treat these arguments separately.

As to the first argument, I question both its factual accuracy and its legal significance. As to its accuracy, it is undoubtedly true that many, if not most, pedophiles possess child pornography. It is quite another thing to assume that the pornography caused the pedophilia. More likely, it was the perpetrator's attraction to children that caused him to possess the pornography rather than vice versa.[12] Indeed, one does not have to approach a "Clockwork Orange"[13] scenario to find behavioralists employing child pornography for the purpose of curing pedophiles?[14]

I do not mean to argue that there has never been a pedophile who but for the pornography would not have committed his crime. But, that can hardly be the relevant standard. For one to sustain this justification, it would be necessary to establish that virtual child pornography (as opposed to real child pornography) has significantly increased pedophilia. To prove that five people who viewed virtual pornography committed an act of pedophilia that they otherwise would not have committed (assuming one could establish causation, which I doubt) would only tell half of the story. We would also have to know how many potential pedophiles had their appetites satiated by virtual child pornography, and therefore left real children alone.

To illustrate, three of the most heinous crimes in history were inspired respectively by the holy Bible[15], an Anglican High Church Service[16], and the movie the Ten Commandments.[17] Obviously nobody measures the worth of these sources by the worst thing that they inspired. To be sure, child pornography, virtual or otherwise, has undoubtedly done far more harm and far less good than the aforementioned sources. Nevertheless, it is neither intuitively obvious, nor has it been proven, that eliminating all virtual pornography from the face of the earth would significantly reduce the incidents of pedophilia.

More importantly, even if it could be proven that virtual child pornography caused significant net harm, it would not follow that the law should permit its suppression. One of the costs of free speech is the recognition that sometimes speech will do more harm than good. Even so, for the reasons already given,[18] it is better to allow it to cause whatever harm it may rather than allow the government the power to decide whether the book can be published at all. For example, the Turner Diaries were said to have been the inspiration for Timothy McVeigh's massacre at Oklahoma City. It would not be hard for a court to conclude that on a cost/benefit basis that book should be condemned. Indeed, it is hard for me to believe that the Turner Diaries did not do significantly more harm than good. Yet, I would vehemently oppose the government's power to remove it from the marketplace of ideas.

To further illustrate the wrongness of allowing judges (or legislators) to condemn a book based on its net harm, imagine a claim in the United States that the Qur'an should be banned because it was said to inspire the 9/11 terrorists. Would anybody feel comfortable leaving a good versus harm standard to American judges, most of whom are Christian, in regard to Islam's holiest book? I certainly would not, and thus conclude that even if virtual child pornography were conclusively shown to do more harm than good, the Supreme Court was correct in not allowing it to be eliminated.[19]

As to the argument that virtual pornography can be used to seduce children, Justice Kennedy, for the Supreme Court, got it exactly right when he noted that if virtual pornography is to be suppressed because of its capacity to seduce children, we might as well suppress "cartoons, video games, and candy."[20] And, I might add that he could have included bicycles, puppy dogs, and vans. The point, of course, is that many things, including but not limited to literature, can be misused. But, as the Court once succinctly put it: "We cannot reduce the entire adult population to reading only that which is fit for children."[21]

IV. Distinguishing Virtual from Real Child Pornography

By far the most powerful argument for punishing virtual child pornography is the difficulty of distinguishing it from the real thing. The argument is that virtual and real pictures look so indistinguishable that a person marketing real child pornography might argue either that the material is virtual (and you can't prove beyond a reasonable doubt that it isn't) or at least that the defendant believed that it was virtual. To the extent that this argument rests on a factually sound premise, it presents a very serious problem. If real child pornography is punishable, but virtual isn't, and you can't tell the difference, what's a government to do?

The good news is that, at least for now, that does not seem to be an insurmountable problem. Although defendants have argued that the material was virtual, it has never been a successful defense.[22] Furthermore, there is technology available that allows the government to take a picture apart, pixel by pixel, to determine its origin.[23] Thus, as with the erstwhile nuclear arms race, detection appears to be keeping up with technology.

To the extent that technology outstrips detection and one really cannot tell the difference, some type of burden of proof shifting device might be appropriate. Surely, the government should be able to argue that a picture that appears real can be treated as real in the absence of evidence that it isn't. Such a rule would differ from the one at issue in *Ashcroft,* where the statute allowed punishment even when it was clear that the picture was virtual.

As for the *scienter* issue, presumably it would take more than the defendant's word that he intended to transmit virtual pictures to create a reasonable doubt. If the Government proves that the pictures are real, a simple statement from the defendant that he thought they were virtual would be very unlikely to create a reasonable doubt.

V. Decriminalizing Virtual Pornography May Protect Real Children

It is certainly not immediately obvious that real children would be *better* off by allowing the sale of virtual pornography, yet that may in fact be the case. In an ideal world, nobody would want child pornography, real or virtual. Unfortunately, the world we live in is not ideal. Despite the efforts of all civilized governments to suppress child pornography, it is still with us. Why? Simply because the demand is there. If one accepts the unfortunate truth that the demand for child pornography exists despite these governmental efforts, there is little reason to believe that we will totally stamp it out.

On the other hand, if virtual child pornography is (or can be made) nearly identical to real child pornography and only the latter is unlawful, why wouldn't the pornographer sell only the former? Certainly most pornographers would love to avoid the risk of prison if their anticipated profit would not be compromised. And, from the consumer's perspective, a virtual picture would also shield him from prosecution.[24] Thus, there is good reason to believe that legalizing virtual child pornography may reduce the number of children that are currently exploited by this perverted industry. And so, the United States Supreme Court may well have rendered a decision that will ultimately protect children as well as it protects freedom of speech.

Notes

1. Graham Kenan Professor of Law: University of North Carolina School of Law.

2. See Chief Justice Rehnquist's impassioned dissent (joined by Justices White and O'Connor) in Texas v. Johnson 491 U.S. 397 at 421 (1989). See also Justice Stevens' dissent at 436. After *Johnson,* Congress and the President again attempted to ban flag burning with the "Flag Protection Act of 1989" which the Supreme Court again overturned by a bare 5–4 majority in U.S. v. Eichman 496 U.S. 310 (1990).

3. See dissenting opinion of Judge Sprecher in Collin v. Smith 578 F. 2d 1197 at 1210 (1978). A recent European example with strong ramifications in the United States has been the case of La Ligue Contra Le Racisme et L'Antisemitisme v. Yahoo (tried in America as Yahoo v. LICRA. 169 F. Supp. 2d 1181 N.D. Cal. 2001). Here a French judge held that the act of displaying Nazi memorabilia itself violated French law (Article R645-1 Penal Code) and that the American web site Yahoo must comply with French law and not display Nazi memorabilia on its own, American site. Also see David Kretzmer, *Free Speech and Racism,* 8 Cardozo L. Rev. 445 (1987).

4. For example, "Blue is prettier then green." See Arnold H. Loewy, *Criminal Speech: Should Free Trade in Ideas be Absolute?,* 2 Crim. L. F. 117, 118 (1990).

5. Or if you don't like that one, try "Vote Democrat."

6. See, for example, Gay News, Ltd. v. United Kingdom 5 E. H. R. R. 123 (1982). Cf Jeremy Jones v. Fredrick Toben (No H97/120) dealing with section 18C of Australia's Racial Discrimination Act of 1975 that makes it a crime "to offend, insult, humiliate, or intimidate another person or group of people" based on "race, colour or national or ethnic origin."

7. See, e.g., the Supreme Court's willingness to uphold obscenity laws such as in Miller v. California 413 U.S. 15 (1973). See Loewy, *Obscenity, Pornography, and First Amendment Theory, supra* at note 2. See also the four justice dissent in Texas v. Johnson, *supra* at note 9. As I have said elsewhere "It is understandable that our President, Congress, legislators, and general populace who do not regularly study the First Amendment would initially condemn the *Johnson* decision. It is more difficult to rationalize the opinions of the Supreme Court dissenters who really ought to know better." Arnold H. Loewy, *The Flag-Burning Case: Freedom of Speech When We Need It Most,* 68 N.C. L. Rev. 165 at 172–173 (1989).

8. For a more detailed development of this point, see Arnold H. Loewy, *Freedom of Speech as a Product of Democracy,* 27 U. Rich. L. Rev. 427 (1993).

9. I put to one side the issue of whether the jurisdiction punishing the dissemination of child pornography is the one in which the pornography was made. I deal with the resolution of that issue elsewhere. See Arnold H. Loewy, *Obscenity, Pornography, and First Amendment Theory,* 2 Wm. & Mary Bill Rts. J. 471 at 480–482 (1993). Cited *supra* at note 2.

10. But did not hold. Justice Kennedy wrote that "Although morphed images may fall within the definition of virtual child pornography, they implicate the interests of real children and are in that sense closer to the images in *Ferber."* Ashcroft v. Free Speech Coalition 122 S. Ct. at 1397.

11. Any doubt that such pictures can be harmful, sometimes when least expected, was dispelled by the recent Miss North Carolina dispute in the

Miss America contest. The winner's picture was taken unauthorizedly while she was changing clothes. The suggested presence of those pictures was enough to disqualify her.

12. See Eberhard Kronhausen & Phyllis Kronhausen, *Pornography and the Law,* (1959 and 1964 update). Also see studies done in Denmark, Sweden and the former West Germany concluding that the availability of sexually explicit material leads to less crime, not more. Reprinted in Marcia Pally, Sense and Censorship: The Vanity of Bonfires (Americans for Constitutonal Freedom 1991, vol. 2). Even opponents of pornography have long had to concede that there is "no substantial basis for the belief that erotic materials constitute a primary or significant cause or development of character defects or that they operate as a significant determanitive factor in causing crime and delinquency." President's Commission on Obscenity and Pornography (Bantam 1970) p. 243. See a similar concession in Lydia W. Lee, *Child Pornography Prevention Act of 1996: Confronting the Challenges of Virtual Reality,* 8 S. Cal. Interdisc. L. J. 639 (1999).

13. A Clockwork Orange (Warner Brothers 1972). In this film, a criminal is repeatedly shown images of horrific violence and given a drug that makes him associate it with strong feelings of nausea. The character is released into the world unable to commit any violent acts or even to think violent thoughts.

14. See Lobitz, W.C. and LoPiccolo, J., *New Methods in Behavioral Treatment of Sexual Dysfunction,* J. Behav. Ther. & Exp. Psychiat. Vol. 3 pp. 265–71. See generally, Patricia Gillan, *Therapeutic Uses of Obscenity,* reprinted in Dhavan and Davies, Censorship and Obscenity (Martin and Robertson 1978).

15. Albert Fish was inspired to castrate and 'sacrifice' young boys by reading about sacrifices in the Bible. See Earl Finbar Murphy, *The Value of Pornography,* 10 Wayne L. Rev. 655,668 (1964).

16. John George Haigh was inspired by the procedures of the Anglican High Church Service to drink his victims' blood through straws and dissolve their bodies in acid baths. *Id.*

17. Heinrich Pommerenke was prompted by Cecil B. DeMille's film The Ten Commandments to rape, abuse, and slay women. *Id.*

18. *Supra,* section I.

19. Anybody who doubts this would do well to see the Hollywood satire "Pleasantville," which recounts the story of a town from the fifties where only sweetness and light is allowed. Anybody who dares to deviate from the approved "everything is perfect" mantra is dealt with harshly.

20. 122 S. Ct. at 1402.

21. Butler v. Michigan 352 U.S. 380 at 384.

22. At least as of April 16, 2002 when *Ashcroft* was decided. See 122 S. Ct. at 1406 citing Brief for Petitioners 37.

23. The technique is called "digital pixel examination." Reported in ABC News "Detecting Real Child Porn: New software tools spot doctored pictures." (April 22, 2002) Available at. . . .

24. The only reason that this might not happen is the dollar cost of producing virtual child pronography. This, of course, is a reason for the law to keep the cost of exploiting real children high. It is also a reason to decriminalize virtual pornography as the Supreme Court has done.

**Diana E. H. Russell and
Natalie J. Purcell**

Exposure to Pornography as a Cause of Child Sexual Victimization

Researchers almost universally agree that photographing children for child pornography constitutes child sexual victimization. We will argue in this chapter that a causal relationship exists between adult and juvenile males' exposure to child pornography—including computer-generated, written, and oral forms of pornography—and their perpetration of child sexual victimization. Because the theoretical work behind this model comes from the work of Diana Russell over decades, we describe this as "Russell's theory."

Because child pornography does not negatively affect all viewers to the same degree, some researchers conclude that mere exposure to this material cannot play a causal role in child sexual victimization. This is analogous to the tobacco industry's faulty claim that, since many smokers do not die of lung cancer, smoking does not cause lung cancer. Such reasoning is faulty. When there are multiple causes for a phenomenon, any one of them "may be a sufficient but not necessary condition for the occurrence of the effect or a necessary but not sufficient condition" (Theodorson & Theodorson, 1979, p. 40). In this sense of the term, we argue that exposure to child pornography causes child sexual victimization.

Although women have been known to sexually abuse both male and female children, males form the overwhelming majority of child pornography consumers and perpetrators of child sexual victimization. Therefore, Russell's three-factor causal theory focuses on male perpetrators. (The terms "man," "men," "male," or "males" in this chapter should be understood to include juvenile and adult males.)

Catharsis vs. Intensified Desire

According to the catharsis theory, the repeated exposure of males to pornography "leads to a steadily decreasing interest" in the material (Bart & Jozsa, 1980, p. 210). This exposure is frequently described as a "safety valve." As applied to child pornography, this theory assumes that repeated viewing of child pornography decreases viewers' desire for sex with children. Hence, according to this

From *Handbook of Children, Culture, and Violence*, 2006, pp. 59–84. Copyright © 2006 by Sage Publications. Reprinted by permission.

theory, viewers of child pornography should be less likely to sexually victimize children.

Zillmann and Bryant (1986) conducted an experiment based on 160 subjects.

These researchers found that the subjects' boredom after repeatedly viewing the same pornographic material motivated them to switch to viewing different and more extreme pornography, such as material involving the infliction of pain, violent pornography, and "uncommon or unusual sexual practices," including bondage, sadomasochism and bestiality (Zillmann & Bryant, 1986, p. 577).

Research aside, common sense and rationality unequivocally challenge the catharsis theory. Very few people would likely support a proposal to solve the problem of parents physically beating their children by having them watch movies that show parents battering and torturing their children. Why is it only in the case of misogynistic pornography that so many individuals—including a handful of researchers—believe that exposure dissipates the problem? The plain inconsistency and irrationality of the catharsis theory suffice to dismiss the notion that pornography serves as a "safety valve."

Pornography as a Cause of Child Sexual Victimization

The major objective of this chapter is to challenge the belief that exposure to child pornography is harmless and to demonstrate that exposure to child pornography can cause child sexual victimization in societies where this is proscribed.

Causal Factor IA: Viewing Child Pornography Predisposes Some Males, Not Previously So Disposed, to Sexually Desire Children

It is commonly believed that exposure to child pornography cannot create a desire for sexual contact with children in males for whom it did not previously exist. Most people prefer to believe that any man who becomes sexually interested in children must have been predisposed to this interest. The following . . . points present ways in which exposure to child pornography can cause sexual arousal in some males who were not previously sexually interested in children. These points demonstrate that "normal" heterosexual males can become sexually aroused by depictions of children.

By Sexualizing/Sexually Objectifying Children

Child pornography transforms children into sexual objects designed to appeal to pedophiles and non-pedophilic child molesters.

Child pornographers often direct the girls they photograph to get into sexual poses or to engage in masturbation or sexual intercourse like women in adult pornography. These sexualized pictures of girls (often acting as mini-adults) evoke a sexual response in some males who previously had no interest in sex with girls.

By Application of the Laws of Learning

While some may believe that only males who are sexually aroused by child pornography would search for it, O'Connell (2001) maintains that "All the evidence is that many people [males] at least browse in this area [of child pornography], if not actively downloading" Web site pictures (p. 7).

A classic experiment by Rachman and Hodgson (1968) demonstrates that male subjects can learn to become sexually aroused by seeing a picture of a woman's boot after repeatedly seeing women's boots in association with sexually arousing slides of nude females. The laws of learning that created the boot fetish can also presumably teach males who previously were not sexually aroused by depictions of adult–child sex, to become aroused after exposure to child pornography.

Masturbation to child pornography during or following exposure to it, reinforces the association between these images and sexual gratification. This constitutes what McGuire, Carlisle, and Young (1965) refer to as "masturbatory conditioning" (p. 185). These researchers hypothesized that "an individual's arousal pattern can be altered by directly changing his masturbatory fantasies" (Abel, Blanchard, & Becker, 1978, p. 192). Abel et al. (1978) have treated violent sexual perpetrators by conditioning them to masturbate and ejaculate to nonviolent consensual portrayals of sex.

Presumably, it is equally possible to change males' non-deviant sexual fantasies and behavior to deviant ones. Hence, when male Internet users with no previous sexual interest in children inadvertently find themselves looking at child pornography, or when curiosity prompts such males to deliberately search out child pornography, they may be surprised to find themselves aroused by sexualized pictures of children. If these male viewers masturbate while viewing sexual pictures of children, this presumably can be the beginning of a growing interest in sex with children. For example, Jenkins (2001) notes that some posts on the Web "suggest that individuals were 'converted' after discovering the material [child pornography]" (p. 106). Furthermore, repeated masturbation to these portrayals may result in increased arousal. The pleasurable experience of orgasm is an exceptionally potent reinforcer. Adult and child pornography are widely used by males as ejaculation material and thus are effective at constructing or reconstructing viewers' patterns of sexual arousal and expression.

By Males Who Have Become Habituated to Adult Pornography Seeking Different or More Extreme Forms of Pornography

It is important to recognize that males who frequently view adult pornography, persons Russell describes as pornophiles, can also become interested and sexually aroused by child pornography.

It seems reasonable to suppose that some of the males who become bored with ordinary adult pornography would opt to view child pornography since it qualifies as a "less commonly practiced sexual activity."

Causal Factor IB: Viewing Child Pornography Intensifies the Desire of Some Males Who Are Already Sexually Aroused by Children

By Increasing Males' Masturbatory Activity Thereby Reinforcing Their Desires for Sex with Children

When pedophiles and other males who desire sex with children are exposed to child pornography that corresponds to their specific preferences (e.g., the gender and age of the child), their sexual arousal intensifies.

Many males with a sexual interest in children deliberately use child pornography to intensify their sexual desire as a prelude to masturbation or the sexual abuse of children. Silbert and Pines (1993) report that a father in their study used to show "his friends pornographic movies to get them sexually aroused before they would rape" his 9-year-old daughter (p. 117–118).

In sum, the more pedophiles and child molesters masturbate to child pornography, the stronger their arousal to this material, and the more it reinforces the association between their fantasies and their desire to have sex with or sexually abuse children.

By Suggesting Exciting New Ideas for Having Sex with/Sexually Abusing Children

Jenkins (2001) notes that most pedophiles consider the old child pornography pictures still circulating on the Internet (which he refers to as "oldies") to be boring (p. 84). Consequently, "[a] common theme on the pedo boards is requests for material that is not readily available,"—that is, novel kinds of child pornography (p. 84). "The range of requests is bewilderingly perverse," according to Jenkins. "A few themes recur often and arouse real enthusiasm. By far the most common include calls for 'Black loli,' African or African American subjects. . . . Also in demand are incest pictures" (p. 85).

With regard to incestuous abuse, every conceivable relationship is portrayed in pictorial and written forms on the Internet—especially fathers having sex with their daughters. Rare forms of incestuous abuse are greatly overrepresented, including mother–son incest and female-on-female incestuous abuse. Many of the acts demonstrated or described in Internet pornography are portrayed as exciting and unconventional, providing viewers with new ideas for having sex with children.

By Providing Images and Models of Adult–Child Sex/Abuse for Males to Imitate

Child pornography provides models for males who already have a sexual interest in children. By seeing the different acts perpetrated on children (many of which elicit no negative responses and some of which appear to elicit positive responses or enjoyment), these "newbies" (a term used by many pedophiles) are provided with models that can shape and intensify their desires. Portrayals of child pornography showing only positive consequences for the perpetrators and the victims are particularly conducive to imitation. (However, for males who are sadistic, child pornography showing negative consequences for the victim is more likely to intensify sexual arousal and serve as a model to imitate.)

Several examples illustrate the use of pornography as a model for imitation.

Consider also the young girl who testified in the 1985 Government Commission on Pornography:

> My father had an easel that he put by the bed. He'd pin a picture on the easel and like a teacher he would tell me this is what you're going to learn today. He would then act out the pictures on me. (Attorney General's Commission on Pornography: Final Report, Vol. 1, 1986, p. 782)

Tim Tate (1990) provides another example, quoting Len, a pedophile who had molested several hundred young boys during his lifetime:

> Child pornography became important to me because I enjoyed it, fantasized and masturbated to it. It wasn't a safety valve, though. At the time I was looking at the magazine it was OK, I was fine . . . but you're not going to look at a magazine all day. So when I went out in the open I would see another pretty boy and find myself chatting him up. In the end I would put into practice what I had seen in the magazines. (p. 110)

By Creating a Desire for Increasingly More Extreme Forms of Child Pornography

Jenkins (2001) maintains that some viewers of child pornography become addicted, with an increasing "hunger for ever more illegal material" (p. 109). Newcomers to child pornography on the Internet may be "amazed and stimulated by the first few softcore pornographic images" they see (p. 109). However, these images "are all too likely to become routine," motivating the more frequent downloaders to turn "avidly to the harder-core sites" (p. 109).

Habituation is clearly an intrinsic feature in the escalation described by viewers of child pornography. Some child pornography users acknowledge that "involvement thus becomes a cumulative process" (Jenkins, 2001, p. 109). For example, one pedophile explained, "With this hobby we get bored after a while with the usual and we risk a bit to get new stuff or get actual experience. It's a natural progression" (p. 109).

In conclusion, it seems clear that exposure to child pornography often becomes an escalating problem; what may have begun as observation of seemingly nonviolent images of adult–child sexual abuse can lead to sexual interest in increasingly more hardcore and violent images of child sexual victimization.

Causal Factor II: Viewing Child Pornography Undermines Some Males' Internal Inhibitions Against Acting Out Their Desires to Have Sex with/Sexually Victimize Children

Each component of Causal Factor II contributes to the undermining of moral beliefs that inhibit some males with a sexual interest in children from acting out their sexual desires.

By Sexualizing/Sexually Objectifying and/or Depersonalizing Girls

Exposure to child pornography plays a vital role in both creating a sexual interest in children in some males not previously so disposed and undermining some males' internal inhibitions against acting out their desire to have sex with children. Child pornography portraying girls in sexually provocative poses or happily engaged in sexual acts with other children or with adult men or women can convince those exposed to it that some children want and enjoy sex with adult males.

By Undermining the Prohibition Against Adult–Child Sex/Victimization

Although legal ages of consent vary in different countries, adult–child sex is proscribed in most countries today.

Despite the prohibition in the United States, there are massive numbers of child pornography Web sites that promote adult–child sexual victimization through photographs, videos, or written stories. For example, an incest Web site titled "Golden Incest Sites!" lists 50 titles. . . . The pictures, stories, videos, and other material it makes accessible to interested Internet surfers can serve as highly suggestive models for viewers who may never before have thought of their daughters, sons, nieces, nephews, and other younger relatives in a sexual way. The ubiquity of incest pornography also conveys the popularity of such images, suggesting that large numbers of men must experience such desires.

The prevalence of child pornography sites, their content, and their positive portrayals of adult–child sexual abuse all serve to diminish the deviant nature of incestuous and extrafamilial child sexual abuse. This in turn enhances the likelihood that some men's internal inhibitions against acting out incestuous and extrafamilial child sexual victimization will be undermined.

It is also important to note two other ways in which the prohibition against adult–child sex is undermined by child pornography. First, the inclusion of many child pornography cartoons in mainstream men's magazines like Playboy and Penthouse communicates its social acceptability. Second, the boards on various sites allow visitors to form their own subcultural communities in which such behaviors or desires are not considered deviant and where pedophiles and others interested in child pornography can feel more normal. . . .

By Advocating, Legitimizing, and/or Normalizing Adult–Child Sex/ Victimization

The legitimatizing and normalizing of adults' sexual victimization of children in child pornography are two of the most frequently cited ways in which this material undermines some viewers' internal inhibitions. As Tate (1990) points out,

> All paedophiles need to reassure themselves that what they are doing or want to do is OK. It [child pornography] validates their feelings, lowers their inhibitions and makes them feel that their behaviour is pretty normal in the context of this pornography—they see other people doing it in the videos or the magazines and it reassures them. (p. 24)

Clearly, child pornography has the power "to reinforce both the paedophile's attraction to children and his self-justification process" (Tate, 1990, p. 110). Pedophiles also "use porn to convince themselves that their behavior is not abnormal, but is shared by others" (Calcetas-Santos, 2001, p. 59).

By Providing Specific Instructions on How to Sexually Victimize a Child

Some males who have never acted on their desire to have sex with a child may be ignorant or anxious about how to proceed with this. Such concerns can inhibit them from perpetrating such an act. Child pornography removes this impediment by providing instructions for the sexual abuse of children. Tyler, a detective sergeant in the San Bernardino, California, Sheriff's Department, testified in hearings on child pornography and pedophilia conducted by Senator Arlen Specter about a child pornography magazine that described "how to have sex with prepubescent children" (Child Pornography and Pedophilia, 1984, p. 33). During these hearings, Senator Specter also discussed a book titled How to Have Sex With Kids that described "how to meet children, how to entice them, how to develop a relationship with them, and how to have sex with them" (p. 30). Sexually explicit illegal material presumably demonstrates at what ages it is possible for adult males to penetrate young children anally and vaginally.

Presumably, pedophiles and child molesters in general find such instructions useful. Even when explicit instructions on how to sexually victimize a child are not provided in child pornography, this material always provides models that viewers may learn from and attempt to emulate.

Causal Factor III: Viewing Child Pornography Undermines Some Males' Social Inhibitions Against Acting Out Their Desires to Have Sex with/Sexually Victimize Children

Child pornography undermines viewers' social inhibitions against sexually victimizing children. It does so in three distinct ways.

By Diminishing Fear of Disapproval

Potential or actual child molesters who look at or download child pornography on the Internet will quickly become cognizant of the enormous number of child pornography Web sites, videos, and chat rooms. This material makes it abundantly clear that there are many other viewers and collectors of child pornography as well as many others who act out their sexual attraction to children. As Jenkins (2001) states it, "He [the pedophile viewer] finds that he is not alone in his deviant interests" (p. 106). This revelation "helps support the notion that the boards [where individuals post messages] are safe space that one can visit at will, [and] where like-minded friends can reliably be found," thereby diminishing viewers' fear of universal disapproval for their sexual interest in children (p. 108).

Crimmins (1995) testified at the Senate Judiciary Committee Hearings on Child Pornography on the Internet that, "People who may have never acted on such impulses before, are emboldened when they see that there are so many other individuals who have similar interests" (p. 2). Furthermore, Jenkins (2001) argues that, "The more pedophiles and pornographers are attacked by law enforcement agencies, mass media, and anti-pedos, the greater the sense of community against common enemies" (p. 114). The knowledge that they have a support group of like-minded colleagues contributes to undermining the fear of disapproval for sexually victimizing children.

By Diminishing Fear of Legal and Social Sanctions

Fear of legal sanctions is the most important factor in restraining potential molesters from abusing children. The more effective potential molesters perceive the social sanctions to be, the less likely they are to become perpetrators. Fear of legal sanctions also serves to restrain active child molesters.

However, child pornography consistently communicates the false message that those who violate children are in no danger of being apprehended or facing other negative consequences. We have not seen any pictorial child pornography that shows a sexual predator being apprehended by the police or ending up in prison. The same applies to written child pornography stories, fantasies, lists of Web sites and videos, as well as child pornography in men's magazines. The outcomes of child sexual abuse are always positive for the perpetrators. Hence, exposure to child pornography gives would-be child molesters a false sense of immunity from legal sanctions, thereby undermining their social inhibitions against acting out their desires.

Contributory Factor IV: Viewing Pornography Undermines Some Children's Abilities to Avoid, Resist, or Escape Sexual Victimization

Some perpetrators use force to accomplish their acts of child sexual victimization. In these cases, children's abilities to avoid, resist, or escape sexual victimization are irrelevant. There are, however, cases where children's exposure to pornography undermines these abilities and permits sexual abuse to occur where it otherwise would not.

By Arousing Children's Sexual Curiosity and/or Desire

Showing pornography to boys and girls is a common seduction strategy of pedophiles who hope thereby to arouse children's sexual curiosity or sexual desire.

Pedophiles posing as young teenagers in Internet teen chat groups often send pornographic pictures or e-mail messages containing pornographic language to children. These predators use pornographic pictures to arouse the children's curiosity or sexual interest and manipulate them into meeting. These meetings typically culminate in the sexual victimization of the child or children.

Thus we conclude that exposure to child or adult pornography can arouse children's sexual curiosity or desire and thereby undermine their abilities to avoid, resist, or escape being sexually abused.

By Legitimizing and/or Normalizing Child Sexual Victimization for Children

Many pedophiles and child molesters show pornography to children "in order to persuade them that they would enjoy certain sexual acts" (Kelly, 1992, p. 119). Another motive is "to convince them that what they are being asked to do is alright." Showing them a picture "legitimizes the abuser's requests" (p. 119).

In the following example, an incestuous father's attempts to use pornography to normalize and legitimize having sex with his daughter were unusually persistent.

> The incest started at the age of eight. I did not understand any of it and did not feel that it was right. My dad would try to convince me that it was ok. He would find magazines articles or pictures that would show fathers and daughters or mothers, brothers and sisters having sexual intercourse. (Mostly fathers and daughters.) He would say that if it was published in magazines that it had to be all right because magazines could not publish lies. . . . He would say, "See it's okay to do because it's published in magazines." (Attorney General's Commission on Pornography: Final Report, Vol. 1, 1986, p. 786)

Child molesters also send pornography to the children they have targeted for sexual victimization to convince them "that other children are sexually active" (Hughes, 1999, p. 28). Showing children child pornography thus normalizes and legitimatizes adult–child sexual encounters in the minds of some children.

By Desensitizing or Disinhibiting Children

A child molester's step-by-step "grooming" of a child serves to gradually desensitize her or him to the culminating act of sexual abuse, which is his goal. He moves from befriending a child, to touching her or him, to introducing her or him to an X-rated video, slowly showing more of it "until the child is able to sit and watch the videos without becoming too uncomfortable" (Whetsell-Mitchell, 1995, p. 201). Juliann Whetsell-Mitchell concludes, "Variations on the grooming ['seduction'] process are many but the end result is desensitizing the child to engaging in sexual acts with the perpetrator, other children, or other adults" (p. 201).

By Creating Feelings of Guilt and Complicity, Thereby Silencing Children

When child molesters expose targeted children to pornography, the children often feel guilty and complicit, particularly if they found the material sexually exciting or masturbated to it. According to Scotland Yard, one of the five major ways that pedophiles use pornography is to "ensure the secrecy of any sexual activity with a child who has already been seduced" (Tate, 1990, p. 24). Child molesters can often silence their victims by telling them that their parents would be very upset to learn that they had watched pornography. Even without such warnings, children often fear that their parents will blame and punish them for having looked at this material. Children who are sexually abused following the exposure may feel complicit in the abuse and thus become even more motivated to remain silent. Ultimately, this reduces the likelihood that abused children will disclose the sexual abuse to their parents or others.

Conclusion

Despite the relative dearth of research, we believe we have provided sufficient evidence to substantiate Russell's theory. This theory explains how exposure to child pornography can create a sexual interest in children in some males who previously had no such interest. When sexual interest in children exists, exposure to child pornography can intensify sexual desires and undermine internal and social inhibitions against acting them out. Thus, exposure to pornography induces some men, who otherwise would not sexually abuse children, to become child molesters.

All references for articles included in *Taking Sides: Clashing Views in Abnormal Psychology, 7/e* **can be found on the Web at www.mhhe.com/cls.**

EXPLORING THE ISSUE

Would Legalization of Virtual Child Pornography Reduce Sexual Exploitation of Children?

Critical Thinking and Reflection

1. For decades the United States Supreme Court has debated the definition of pornography. In light of dramatic changes in public attitudes during the past two decades, what would be a reasonable definition of pornography in contemporary American society?
2. Federal and state laws regard the production and procuring of pornography involving children as criminal. Should other groups of people be added to the category of individuals who should be protected from exploitation for the purposes of pornography (e.g., developmentally disabled people, psychiatrically disturbed individuals, senile or demented persons)?
3. Debate has arisen regarding the extent to which pedophiles should be viewed as criminals or as psychologically disturbed individuals. How might this same debate apply to adults who claim that they are addicted to child pornography?
4. What kind of research study could be developed to assess the extent to which virtual child pornography increases or reduces the likelihood of sexual victimization of children?
5. The treatment of pedophiles occasionally involves an aversive therapy in which shock is applied when the adult becomes sexually aroused at the sight of an inappropriate image involving a child. What are the pros and cons of using virtual images in such an intervention?

Is There Common Ground?

The legality of sexually explicit graphic content has been debated for most of the past century, with increasing acceptance of material that would have been viewed as obscene a few decades ago. Nevertheless, the use of children for pornography has been regarded throughout the world as an absolutely unacceptable form of exploitation that is as heinous a crime as rape. Despite international efforts to apprehend purveyors and consumers of child pornography, the exploitation of children for sexual purposes continues. For various reasons, some people who are presumably stunted in their psychological development find sexual gratification in viewing images of children engaging in sexual acts. Can the sexual wants of these individuals be satisfied by viewing virtual images of such behavior in which no real children are being harmed? Questions certainly arise about whether this is a slippery slope that would eventually lead some to believe that adult–child sex is acceptable.

In the articles in this chapter, both parties would concur with the premise that children must be protected at all costs from exploitation and abuse. Attorney Loewy is not advocating the exploitation of children, but seems to believe that real children can be protected from predators whose wants could be served through gratification derived from viewing virtual images. He is arguing his points primarily from a legal vantage point in which free speech is protected, and without risk of children being exploited. Authors Russell and Purcell respect the constitutional right of free speech, but certainly do not consider child pornography in any form to be constitutionally protected.

Additional Resources

Anti-Child Porn.org. Retrieved from www.antichildporn.org/index.html

Antiporn Feminists. Retrieved from http://antipornfeminists.wordpress.com/

Carr, J. (2003). *Child abuse, child pornography, and the Internet.* London: NCH.

Graf, M., & Dittmann, V. (2011). Forensic-psychiatric treatment for internet sex offenders: Ten years of experience. In D. P. Boer, R. Eher, L. A. Craig, M. H. Miner, & F. Pfäfflin (Eds), *International perspectives on the assessment and treatment of sexual offenders: Theory, practice, and research* (pp. 479–488). Boston: Wiley-Blackwell.

Kleinhans, C. (2004). Virtual child porn: The law and the semiotics of the image. *Journal of Visual Culture, 3*(1), 17–34.

Luck, M. (2009). The gamer's dilemma: An analysis of the arguments for the moral distinction between virtual murder and virtual paedophilia. *Ethics and Information Technology, 11*(1), 31–36.

NewSafeKids. Retrieved from www.nap.edu/netsafekids/pp_li_pfa.html

Peters, R. (March, 2004). *The link between pornography and violent sex crimes.* From www.moralityinmedia.org/.

Quayle, E. (2011). Pedophilia, child porn, and cyberpredators. In C. D. Bryant (Ed.), *The Routledge handbook of deviant behavior* (pp. 390–396). New York: Routledge/Taylor & Francis Group.

Seto, M. C., & Eke, A. W. (2005). The criminal histories and later offending of child pornography offenders. *Sexual Abuse: A Journal of Research and Treatment, 17*(2), 201–210.

Wolak, J., Finkelhor, D., & Mitchell, K. (2011). Child pornography possessors: Trends in offender and case characteristics. *Sexual Abuse, 23*(1), 22–42.

ISSUE 11

Must Mentally Ill Murderers Have a Rational Understanding of Why They Are Being Sentenced to Death?

YES: American Psychological Association, American Psychiatric Association, and National Alliance on Mental Illness, from "Brief for *Amici Curiae* American Psychological Association, American Psychiatric Association, and National Alliance on Mental Illness in Support of Petitioner," *Scott Louis Panetti v. Nathaniel Quarterman,* U.S. Supreme Court, No. 06-6407 (2007)

NO: Greg Abbott et al., from "On Writ of Certiorari to the United States Court of Appeals for the Fifth Circuit: Brief for the Respondent," *Scott Louis Panetti v. Nathaniel Quaterman,* U.S. Supreme Court, No. 06-6407 (2007)

Learning Outcomes

After reading this issue, you should be able to:

- Understand the concept of "rational understanding" as it is used in the American legal system.
- Discuss the ways in which mental illness can impair an individual's ability to understand right from wrong, as well as the rationale for being punished following wrongful behavior.
- Understand the meaning and purpose of retribution as it is used in the American legal system.
- Discuss the reasons why professional associations (e.g., the American Psychological Association and American Psychiatric Association) would submit an *amicus curiae* brief to the Court.
- Critically evaluate the extent to which it is possible to accurately assess malingering in the case of an accused murderer.

ISSUE SUMMARY

YES: The American Psychological Association, the American Psychiatric Association, and the National Alliance on Mental Illness collaborated in the preparation of an *amici curiae* brief pertaining to the case of Scott Panetti, who was sentenced to death for murder. In this brief, The argument is made that mentally ill convicts should not be executed if their disability significantly impairs their capacity to understand the nature and purpose of their punishment or to appreciate why the punishment is being imposed on them.

NO: In his position as Attorney General of Texas, Greg Abbott argued the case of *"Scott Louis Panetti, Petitioner v. Nathaniel Quarterman,* Director, Texas Department of Criminal Justice, Correctional Institutions Division, Respondent."* Attorney General Abbott asserts that punishment for murder does not depend on the rational understanding of the convicted individual, but rather on the convict's moral culpability at the time the crime was committed.

For hundreds of years, debate has raged about how to respond as a society to criminal acts committed by mentally ill individuals. Within the American legal system much of the discussion has focused on the insanity defense, with the debate intensifying in the 1980s following John Hinckley's attempt to assassinate President Ronald Reagan. Hinckley, who was obsessed with the actress Jodie Foster, believed that if he killed the president, Jodie Foster would be so impressed that she would fall in love and marry him. When the case went to trial, Hinckley was ruled insane and was sent to a psychiatric hospital rather than to prison. Subsequent to this case, Congress passed the Insanity Defense Reform Act of 1984, which made it much more difficult for a defendant to be acquitted on the basis of the insanity plea. Concurrently, there was a sea change in America, at least in certain states, regarding the appropriateness of the death penalty for horrific acts such as murder. With the reduced likelihood of being acquitted on the basis of insanity, questions emerged about the ethics of executing individuals who lack an understanding of their criminal act or a realization that they are being sentenced to death because of this act.

The complexity of the issue of executing the mentally ill received special scrutiny as a result of the case of Scott Panetti that was heard by the U.S. Supreme Court in 2007. In 1992, Panetti murdered his mother-in-law and father-in-law while his wife and his daughter watched. Panetti, who had a lengthy history of mental illness and psychiatric hospitalizations during which he was treated for intense delusions and hallucinations, was nevertheless sentenced to death in Texas. In 2003, Panetti petitioned the Texas state court to determine his competency for execution, but this court ruled him competent. When Panetti brought his case to a higher level, the federal district court found fault with the earlier ruling and summoned three psychologists and a psychiatrist, all of whom concurred that Panetti suffered from mental illness characterized by impaired cognitive process and delusions consistent with schizoaffective disorder. Even with this startling evidence of disturbance, the court ruled that Panetti was competent to be executed. Panetti's case then went to the Fifth Circuit, and the argument was put forth that a previous U.S. Supreme Court ruling (*Ford v. Wainwright*) required that Panetti not only be aware of the fact that he would be executed, but also that he have a rational understanding of *why*. Panetti asserted that he was being executed because he preached the gospel, not because of his murders.

The American Psychological Association, the American Psychiatric Association, and the National Alliance on Mental Illness collaborated on the submission to the Supreme Court of an *amicus curiae* (a document submitted by an uninvolved party in which opinion or advice is offered to the court). This brief provided information to the court about serious mental illness and the nature of symptoms in some individuals, namely that individuals with psychotic conditions such as that of Panetti may experience delusions and a disrupted understanding of reality; also, they may be unable to connect events or understand cause and effect (i.e., the connection between murder and punishment).

According to the *amicus* brief, mentally ill convicts are not competent to be executed if they have a disability that significantly impairs their capacity to understand the nature and purpose of their punishment, or to appreciate why the punishment is being imposed on them. People with schizophrenia and schizoaffective disorder may not be able to rationally understand the reasons for their execution sentence. Convinced of the reality of their delusions, they cannot grasp the essential truth: that their impending execution is retribution for their crimes. Executing a prisoner who cannot appreciate why he or she is being executed does not further the retributive purpose of the death penalty.

In the *amicus* brief it is argued that the Eighth Amendment forbids the execution of individuals who are unaware of the punishment they are about to suffer *and why they are to suffer it*. The Constitution requires that, before a prisoner is deemed competent to be executed, the prisoner must be aware of (1) the fact that he or she will be put to death, and (2) the reason for that sentence, namely society's retribution for the prisoner's criminal acts.

The brief contends that Scott Panetti belongs to the class of mentally ill persons who suffer from severe psychotic disorders that impede cognitive functioning in some respects, while leaving other aspects relatively unimpaired. Such individuals suffer from delusions: false beliefs that cannot be corrected by reasoning and that usually involve a misinterpretation of perceptions or experiences. Such people may possess the ability to comprehend and understand facts about the subject of their delusions, but they are often unable to appreciate the personal significance of those facts or to reason about them in a logical way. Psychotic disorders such as schizophrenia distort the mind in certain ways while leaving other functions generally intact. While the *process* of the person's thinking appears normal, the *content* of the thoughts defies accepted reality. The Fifth Circuit's approach permits the execution of severely delusional individuals even though they believe they are to be executed *for something other than their crimes*, notwithstanding the State's assertions to the contrary.

On the other side of the argument are the points raised by Attorney General Abbott, including the assertion that the court should reject the proposition that a murderer must possess a rational understanding of the reasons for execution, to render death an acceptable punishment under the Eighth Amendment to the Constitution (cruel and unusual punishment). Mr. Abbott argued that capital punishment in such cases should not rest on whether or not a convict has rational understanding, but rather on the convict's moral culpability at the time the crime was committed by this person.

Mr. Abbott argues that the viability of retribution as a permissible theory of punishment depends not on the rational understanding that a convict may or may not have, but rather on the convict's moral culpability at the time he or she committed the crime. He therefore contends that the Court should reject the proposition that a capital convict must possess a "rational understanding" of the reasons for execution to render death an acceptable punishment under the Eighth Amendment. Such a standard is not tailored to the particular interests at stake in the post-sentencing phase of capital proceedings, it invites malingering and abuse, and it is not necessary to advance the retributive and deterrent justifications for the death penalty.

According to Abbott, given the high rate of serious mental illness among homicide defendants, granting psychiatric exemptions could leave very few individuals eligible for the death penalty. The conceded objective of the submitted brief, Abbott states, is not simply avoiding the inhumanity of executing a person who is truly insane, but rather removing from death row as large a class of capital convicts as reasonably possible, and thus exempting vast numbers of convicted murderers from execution. Requiring a "deep" or "meaningful" appreciation of the State's reasons for imposing the death penalty would create an even greater risk that the Court's test could be circumvented through malingering or abuse.

In the U.S. Supreme Court ruling on this case, a split court overturned the death sentence. In a sharp rebuke to lower courts, the justices ruled 5 to 4 that Panetti was not shown to possess sufficient understanding of why he was to be put to death for murdering his wife's parents in 1992. Justice Clarence Thomas was joined by Justices Roberts, Scalia, and Alito in dissent, calling the ruling a "half-baked holding that leaves the details of the insanity standard for the District Court to work out."

YES ⬅ American Psychological Association, American Psychiatric Association, and National Alliance on Mental Health

Brief for *Amici Curiae* American Psychological Association, American Psychiatric Association, and National Alliance on Mental Illness in Support of Petitioner

The American Psychological Association is a voluntary, nonprofit, scientific and professional organization with more than 155,000 members and affiliates, and is the major association of psychologists in the nation.

The American Psychiatric Association, with more than 36,000 members, is the nation's leading organization of physicians who specialize in psychiatry.

The National Alliance on Mental Illness was founded in 1979 and is the nation's largest grassroots organization dedicated to improving the quality of life of persons living with serious mental illness and their families.

Members of *amici* are regularly called before courts to participate in competency hearings. *Amici* therefore have both pertinent expertise and a strong interest in the establishment of legal competency standards consistent with the best scientific knowledge about individuals suffering from mental illness.

In 2003, the American Bar Association established a Task Force on Mental Disability and the Death Penalty, which included mental health professionals who are members and representatives of *amici*. The Task Force was convened in light of this Court's decision in *Atkins* to address unresolved issues concerning application of the death penalty to persons suffering from impaired mental conditions. In 2005, the Task Force presented a series of recommendations.

[T]he Task Force identified several situations in which the death penalty should not be applied to individuals with mental illness. One category encompasses individuals who, though having been determined competent to stand trial and sentenced to death, suffer from a severe mental disorder or disability that renders them incompetent to understand the nature and purpose of the death penalty. This category would include, for example, individuals whose mental illness worsens in material respects after imposition of valid sentences.[1] Based on the Task Force Report *amici* and the American Bar Association recommended, in substantially similar form, that the death penalty should not be applied to such persons.[2]

Supreme Court, 2007.

Introduction and Summary of Argument

The Fifth Circuit, in this case and in *Barnard v. Collins*, 13 F.3d 871 (5th Cir. 1994), has adopted a very narrow construction of this Court's decision in *Ford*, a construction that permits the execution of individuals whose severe mental illness precludes them from understanding that the State is putting them to death as retribution for their crimes. The Fifth Circuit recognized that Scott Panetti suffers from schizoaffective disorder, a severe form of psychosis, and that as a direct result he "suffer[s] from paranoid delusions that his [sentence of] execution was the result of a conspiracy against him and not his crimes." *Panetti v. Dretke*, 448 F.3d 815, 819 (5th Cir. 2006). The court of appeals nevertheless deemed Panetti competent to be executed under *Ford*.

Amici respectfully submit that the Fifth Circuit's approach is inconsistent with the reasoning of the controlling opinions in *Ford*. Scientific knowledge about schizophrenia and schizoaffective disorder supports the conclusion that persons in Panetti's condition cannot rationally understand the reasons for their execution. Convinced of the reality of their delusions, they simply cannot grasp the essential truth: that their impending execution is retribution for their crimes. Where the prisoner cannot appreciate the reason, his execution cannot further the retributive purpose of the death penalty any more than if the prisoner, as in *Ford*, suffers delusions that he can never be executed at all. As explained further in this brief, for these reasons *amici* American Psychological Association, American Psychiatric Association, and the National Alliance on Mental Illness each has resolved that a prisoner is not competent to be executed if he "has a mental disorder or disability that significantly impairs his or her capacity to understand the nature and purpose of the punishment, or to appreciate the reason for its imposition in the prisoner's own case." *See, e.g.*, American Psychological Association Council of Representatives, APA Policy Manual: N. Public Interest (2001) (incorporating policy adopted by the Council of Representatives in February 2006), *available at*. . . . *Amici*'s approach, which is consistent with *Ford*, requires reversal of the Fifth Circuit here.

In Part I of this brief, *amici* explain that individuals who, like Panetti, suffer from severe psychotic disorders such as schizophrenia or schizoaffective disorder, frequently suffer from bizarre delusions that disrupt their understanding of reality. These delusional beliefs are genuine and often unshakeable, withstanding all attempts to introduce logic or contrary evidence. When they attach to the State's reasons for carrying out the mentally ill prisoner's execution, such delusions can deny the prisoner all rational understanding about "why" he is to be executed. In such a circumstance, proceeding with the execution would not further the purposes of the death penalty. In Part II, *amici* explain that mental health experts can assist the courts in identifying prisoners with mental illness who suffer delusions that preclude them from understanding the actual reasons for their execution. Mental health professionals routinely evaluate patients for the presence of delusional beliefs and generate reliable conclusions as to how those delusions impact the patients' ability to rationally understand information.

Argument

I. The Fifth Circuit's Interpretation of *Ford v. Wainwright* Fails to Protect a Class of Severely Mentally Ill Prisoners, in Contravention of the Purposes That Animated *Ford*

A. *In* Panetti *and* Barnard, *the Fifth Circuit Has Interpreted and Applied* Ford *Very Narrowly*

In 1986, this Court held that the Eighth Amendment forbids the execution of individuals suffering from mental illness that renders them incompetent. *Ford v. Wainwright*, 477 U.S. 399 (1986). The Court relied on common law to support its interpretation of the Eighth Amendment and identified several reasons why the execution of the insane is unacceptable in a civilized society. *Id.* at 409–410.[3] As one justification, the Court "seriously question[ed] the retributive value of executing a person who has no comprehension of why he has been singled out and stripped of his fundamental right to life." *Id.* at 409. Yet, while suggesting that the Constitution prevents the execution of a prisoner who lacks "comprehension of why he has been singled out" for death, the Court did not provide a substantive test for defining insanity in this context. Justice Powell attempted to do so, in a separate concurring opinion largely devoted to explaining his disagreements with the procedural protections set forth by the four-justice plurality. Justice Powell noted that "today, as at common law, one of the death penalty's critical justifications, its retributive force, depends on the defendant's awareness of the penalty's existence and purpose." *Id.* at 421 (Powell, J., concurring). Accordingly, he concluded that "the Eighth Amendment forbids the execution . . . of those who are unaware of the punishment they are about to suffer *and why they are to suffer it.*" *Id.* at 422 (emphasis added). Justice Powell recognized that the Constitution requires, as a minimum before a prisoner may be deemed competent to be executed, that the prisoner be aware of both the fact that he will be put to death and the reason for that: society's retribution for his criminal acts.

In the case at bar, the Fifth Circuit . . . has ruled that the Constitution permits the execution of a severely delusional man who has no awareness of the true reason for his execution. In upholding Panetti's death sentence, the court of appeals expressly ruled that the Constitution does not bar the execution of an individual "suffer[ing] from paranoid delusions that his execution was the result of a conspiracy against him *and not his crimes.*" *Panetti v. Dretke*, 448 F.3d 815, 819 (5th Cir. 2006) (emphasis added). Panetti understands that he has been found guilty of murder and faces execution, but holds the unequivocal and delusional belief that the State is using his crimes as a pretext, and that its real motivation is "to prevent him from preaching the Gospel." *Id.* at 816 (citing *Panetti v. Dretke*, 401 F. Supp. 2d 702, 709 (W.D. Tex. 2004)). Relying on *Barnard*, the court of appeals found Panetti's recognition of the State's *articulated* reason for his execution adequate to satisfy the standard set forth in Justice Powell's *Ford* concurrence, despite the court's recognition that Panetti's delusional thinking denies him awareness that the stated rationale is genuine. *Panetti*, 448 F.3d at 819 (noting that "Justice Powell did not state that a prisoner must 'rationally understand' the reason for his execution, only that he must be 'aware' of it").

B. Panetti Is Readily Identifiable as Suffering from Delusions
That Commonly Accompany Schizophrenia and Schizoaffective Disorder

Scott Panetti is not an anomaly who by some odd quirk can correctly comprehend the fact of his execution and the State's explanation for it yet who breaks with reality when he ascribes the State's true motivation to a fantastical conspiracy or bizarre purpose. Rather, he is readily recognizable as belonging to the class of mentally ill persons who suffer from severe psychotic disorders that impede their cognitive functioning in some respects while leaving other aspects relatively unimpaired.[4] Such people may possess the ability to comprehend and understand facts about the subject of their delusions, but they are often unable to appreciate the personal significance of those facts or to reason about them in a logical way.

1. Individuals who suffer from delusions firmly hold false, illogical beliefs that cannot be corrected with reason and that interfere with their ability to interpret ordinary experiences.   In the scientific literature, individuals such as Panetti are commonly described as suffering from delusions: false beliefs that cannot be corrected by reasoning and that usually involve a misinterpretation of perceptions or experiences. Such delusions are often characterized by flaws in logical thinking that prevent those who suffer from them from making the right connections between ideas and from testing their beliefs about the world in ways that would enable them to determine the veracity of those beliefs.

Delusional thinking forms part of various psychotic disorders. A delusion has been defined as:

> A false belief based on incorrect inference about external reality that is firmly sustained despite what almost everyone else believes and despite what constitutes incontrovertible and obvious proof or evidence to the contrary. The belief is not one ordinarily accepted by other members of the person's culture or subculture (e.g., it is not an article of religious faith). When a false belief involves a value judgment, it is regarded as a delusion only when the judgment is so extreme as to defy credibility.

American Psychiatric Association, *Diagnostic and Statistical Manual of Mental Disorders* 821 (4th ed. text rev. 2000) (hereinafter DSM-IV-TR).

Delusional thinking is a hallmark symptom of schizophrenia[5] and of related psychotic disorders, such as schizoaffective disorder.[6] It may also occur as a symptom of mood disorders such as depressive disorders or bipolar disorders.[7] It is particularly pronounced in what is known as the Paranoid Type of Schizophrenia. DSM-IV-TR 313-314. The essential feature of this type of schizophrenia is "the presence of prominent delusions or auditory hallucinations in the content of a relative preservation of cognitive functioning and affect." *Id.* at 313. Typically, persons with this condition suffer from delusions that are categorized as *persecutory* and/or *grandiose*. *Id*. A persecutory delusion, generally speaking, is a delusion whose theme involves a conspiracy or other form of malicious obstruction to thwart the individual's goals. *Id*. at 325. A grandiose delusion is one whose central theme involves the patient possessing a great yet unrecognized talent, sometimes accompanied by the belief that the patient has a special relationship with a prominent person or bears a special message from a deity. *Id*. The two types of delusions are often intertwined: persons experiencing persecutory delusions may reason that, as one textbook puts it, "they must be very important if so much effort is spent on their persecution." Robert Cancro & Heinz E. Lehmann, *Schizophrenia: Clinical Features*, in *Kaplan & Sadock's Comprehensive Textbook of Psychiatry* 1187 (7th ed. 2000).[8]

Psychotic disorders such as schizophrenia distort the mind in certain ways while leaving other functions generally intact. As noted above, an individual with paranoid schizophrenia may possess "a relative preservation of cognitive functioning." DSM-IV-TR 313. Yet such a person, plagued by a delusional psychotic disorder, may have no ability to apply his cognitive functions to test the veracity of the conclusions that he draws; while the *process* of a person's thinking appears normal, the *content* of the thoughts defies accepted reality. For example, a person who is under the delusion that he is the basketball player Michael Jordan may be unable to "test reality" in a way that would disprove his belief. Michael Jordan is tall, athletically gifted, widely recognized, and wealthy. Even after it is pointed out to the delusional person that he possesses none of these characteristics "and even if the person *agrees* that he does not" he may persist in his belief that he is in fact Michael Jordan.

Such persons may understand much of the world around them and have real intelligence. Yet their delusional thought process may consistently lead them to wildly incorrect results. As one psychiatry textbook explains:

> Disturbances of thinking and conceptualization are one of the most characteristic features of schizophrenia. The feature common to all manifestations of schizophreni[c] thought disorder is that patients think and reason . . . according to their own intricate private rules of logic. Schizophrenic patients may be highly intelligent, certainly not confused, and they may be painstaking in their abstractions and deductions. But their thought processes are strange and do not lead to conclusions based on reality or universal logic.

Cancro & Lehmann, *supra*, at 1189. Thus, a person suffering from schizophreniaor schizoaffective disorder may know that he has committed a crime; tha the death penalty is imposed on persons who commit such crimes; and that the State has asserted he will be put to death because he committed that crime; and yet be absolutely and unwaveringly certain that his execution is not in fact a response to his crime but is instead an effort to prevent him from preaching the Gospel.

2. Panetti suffers from grandiose, persecutory delusions that disrupt his understanding of the purpose of his execution.   Based upon the record and findings in this case, Panetti clearly falls into this framework. He is not incoherent: the district court found that "at least some of the time, Panetti is capable of communicating, and apparently understanding, in a coherent fashion." *Panetti*, 401 F. Supp. 2d at 708. As one of the State's experts concluded, Panetti possessed a "capacity to understand the Bible, to understand history, movies." *Id.* Indeed, he represented himself at trial, cross-examined witnesses, and applied for subpoenas.

Yet, in the decade preceding his crime, Panetti was hospitalized with diagnoses that included schizophrenia, schizoaffective disorder, and bipolar disorder—all serious mental disorders that, in his case, were accompanied by psychotic symptoms such as auditory hallucinations and delusions of persecution and grandiosity. Pet. 3. While defending himself at trial, he exhibited a wide array of delusional behaviors. His cross-examination tended to be rambling and illogical, and he attempted to subpoena John F. Kennedy, Pope John Paul II, and Jesus Christ. Although Panetti knows that the State claims it intends to execute him for the murders that he committed, he believes in the words of one of the experts who examined him that "God had nullified it, God had forgiven him, God had wiped the slate clean." *Panetti*, 401 F. Supp. 2d at 707. And the district court credited testimony from one of the State's experts who concluded that:

> Panetti does not even understand that the State of Texas is a lawfully constituted authority, but rather, he believes the State is in league with the forces of evil that have conspired against him. [That expert's] testimony is consistent with that of Dr. Conroy, Dr. Rosin, and Dr. Silverman, each of whom testified Panetti believes the real reason he is to be executed is for preaching the Gospel.

Id. at 712; *see also id.* at 707 (Panetti suffers from "grandiosity and a delusional belief system in which he believes himself to be persecuted for his religious activities and beliefs"). As reflected in the findings and the testimony below, therefore, Panetti is able to draw some logical connections but suffers from textbook persecutory and grandiose delusions centered around religion that render him deeply disturbed and deny him any genuine understanding of the reason for his execution.

Although the record does not reflect the methods employed by the doctors who examined Panetti, it is likely that his delusional belief withstood all attempts to "test reality" by confronting him with contrary evidence. A person who is captive to such a delusion would likely be unconvinced by evidence that, for example (1) the State does not, in fact, seek to execute people for preaching the Gospel and (2) the State has certainly not sought to execute others whose preaching is heard by many more than Panetti's.[9]

C. Contrary to the Rationale of Ford, by Permitting the Execution of Prisoners Who Suffer from Psychotic Delusions, the Fifth Circuit's Approach Permits Executions That Do Not Further the Death Penalty's Retributive Purpose

Insisting that the death penalty must serve its core retributive purpose in every case, Justice Powell wrote in *Ford* that "the Eighth Amendment forbids the execution . . . of those who are unaware of the punishment they are about to suffer and why they are to suffer it." 477 U.S. at 422. In *Panetti*, the Fifth Circuit held that "'awareness,' as that term is used in *Ford*, is not necessarily synonymous with 'rational understanding.'" *Panetti*, 448 F.3d at 821. Accordingly, the court of appeals allowed the execution of an individual who believes that the State's expressed reason for his execution is merely a pretext for the true reason: to stop him from preaching Gospel. The Fifth Circuit's approach fails to recognize the force of the delusions that characterize psychotic disorders such as Panetti's, and thus, contrary to *Ford*, permits executions where the retributive purpose of the death penalty is not served.

As a simple linguistic matter, "awareness of why" a person is to suffer the death penalty might arguably be construed to include mere "awareness of *what the State has claimed as a reason*." But that circumscription of Justice Powell's test otherwise makes little sense. There are individuals, like Panetti, who know what the State says but believe just as surely that the State's claim is not true. The Fifth Circuit's approach permits the execution of such severely delusional individuals even though they believe they are to be executed for *something other than their crimes*, notwithstanding the State's assertions to the contrary.

The Fifth Circuit's standard makes some forms of severe delusion about one's impending execution matter, while others do not. For example, an individual capable of repeating back the State's stated reasons for the execution may not be executed if he believes that his execution is impossible (as in *Ford*), but may be executed if he considers it possible or certain but entirely misapprehends why the death penalty is actually being applied to him. Yet both individuals suffer from debilitating delusional thinking about their forthcoming execution and therefore the retributive purpose of the death penalty is not served in either circumstance. Indeed, Justice Powell plainly recognized that the prisoner's awareness of the "why" was as important to the legitimacy of the execution as his awareness of the "whether." Nor does it appear that the retributive purpose is served more fully when the State executes a person whose delusions cause him entirely to disbelieve the State's asserted rationale than when it executes one who cannot comprehend that rationale in the first place.

Indeed, of the various grounds articulated by the *Ford* majority, none supports privileging one sort of fundamental delusion about an impending execution over another. Whether the ground is that "the execution of an insane person simply offends humanity," 477 U.S. at 407, or that such an execution "provides no example to others," *id.*, or that "it is uncharitable to dispatch an offender into another world, when he is not of a capacity to fit himself for it," *id.*, or that "madness is its own punishment," *id.*, or that executing an insane person serves no retributive purpose, *id.*; *see also id.* at 422 (Powell, J., concurring), there is no reason to spare one individual beset by a delusion regarding whether death awaits or the State's purported reasons for imposing the penalty, yet to execute another individual plagued by a different yet equally irrational delusion regarding the same subject.

D. All Three *Amici* Have Adopted a Common Position on This Issue

For these reasons, with respect to competency to be executed, *amici* and the American Bar Association have respectively adopted substantively identical versions of a recommendation proposed by the Task Force on Mental Disability and the Death Penalty:

> If, after challenges to the validity of the conviction and death sentence have been exhausted and execution has been scheduled, a court finds that a prisoner has a mental disorder or disability that significantly impairs his or her capacity to understand the nature and purpose of the punishment, or to appreciate the reason for its imposition in the prisoner's own case, the sentence of death should be reduced to a lesser punishment.[10]

This recommendation, *amici* submit, draws the proper line between individuals who are competent to be executed and those who are not. The recommendation recognizes that it is impossible to draw a meaningful line among the myriad delusions that may fog an individual's understanding of his pending execution, or the reasons for it.

Specifically, under the recommendation, awareness of the "why" of an execution necessarily includes understanding the reason the death penalty is being applied in one's own case. The Report of the Task Force, which explains the reasoning that underlies each recommendation, stated that an offender who has been sentenced to die

> must "appreciate" its personal application in the offender's own case— that is, why it is being imposed *on the offender*. This formulation is analogous to the distinction often drawn between a "factual understanding" and a "rational understanding" of the reason for the execution. If, as is generally assumed, the primary purpose of the competence-to-be-executed requirement is to vindicate the retributive aim of punishment, then offenders should have more than a shallow understanding of why they are being executed.

Recommendation and Report on the Death Penalty and Persons with Mental Disabilities, 30 Mental & Physical Disability L. Rep. 668, 675 (2006). In short, it does not fulfill the retributive purpose of the death penalty to execute an individual, like Panetti, who has no rational understanding as to why the punishment is being imposed on him. For that reason, the Fifth Circuit's ruling should be reversed.[11]

II. Mental Health Professionals Can Reliably Identify the Nature and Extent of an Individual's Rational Understanding of an Impending Execution and Routinely Make Similar Assessments in Other Judicial Contexts

In the case at bar, the experts for the State and for the defense largely concurred in the most important aspects of their assessments. *Panetti v. Dretke*, 401 F. Supp. 2d 702, 707–708, 712 (W.D. Tex. 2004) (all experts testified that Panetti possesses cognitive functionality with respect to certain topics and communications, yet suffers delusions, including the belief that he will be executed for preaching the Gospel). Disagreements were limited to the degree, and not existence, of Panetti's delusions pertaining to the reason for his impending execution, *Panetti v. Dretke*, 448 F.3d 815, 817 (5th Cir. 2006), and thus the parties' dispute has focused on the impact of Panetti's functional deficiencies on the ultimate question of "competence to be executed," which is a legal, not a scientific or medical, question.

Expert agreement in this area can be attributed to two factors: first, the underlying scientific and clinical concepts, the nature of psychotic delusions, and the concept of "rational understanding" are well established; second, when the diagnosis is made through an evaluation of the prisoner's currently presenting condition, no extrapolation is needed to assess the prisoner's condition at a remote time in the past.[12] Indeed, the expert consensus on Panetti's diagnosis is consistent with studies showing that mental health professionals using structured interviews and assessing present-oriented functional capacities typically have very high levels of agreement. *See, e.g.*, Gary B. Melton, *et al., Psychological Evaluations for the Courts: A Handbook for Mental Health Professionals and Lawyers* 138 (2d ed. 1997). Thus, mental health experts can provide testimony that can meaningfully inform judicial decisions about competency to be executed with established procedures that have a record of producing reliable, consistent results.

Conclusion

Amici submit that the Fifth Circuit's competence for execution standard permits the execution of individuals who lack any meaningful understanding of the nature and purpose of their punishment, contrary to this Court's decision in *Ford*. *Amici* urge this Court to reverse the judgment of the Fifth Circuit.

Notes

1. Both parties have consented to the filing of this brief. No counsel for a party authored any part of this brief. No person or entity other than *amici* and their counsel made any monetary contribution to the preparation or submission of this brief.
2. In addition to the recommendation discussed in text, the Task Force presented, and *amici* and the ABA adopted, recommendations relating to persons with mental retardation and equivalent impairments of intellectual and adaptive functioning, persons who were mentally ill at the time of the offense, and persons not competent to seek or assist counsel in post-conviction proceedings. *See Recommendation and Report on the Death Penalty and Persons with Mental Disabilities*, 30 Mental & Physical Disability L. Rep. 668, 668 (2006).
3. *Amici* gratefully acknowledge the assistance of Richard J. Bonnie, J.D., Joel A. Dvoskin, Ph.D., Kirk S. Heilbrun, Ph.D., and Diane T. Marsh, Ph.D., in the preparation of this brief.
4. The term "appreciate" approximates the term "rationally understand." *See* Norman G. Poythress, *et al., Adjudicative Competence: The MacArthur Studies* 112 (2002); *see also Martin v. Dugger*, 686 F. Supp. 1523, 1569–1573 (S.D. Fla. 1988).

5. Justice Powell concurred in parts one and two of Justice Marshall's opinion, 477 U.S. at 418, creating a majority for the holding that "the Eighth Amendment prohibits a State from carrying out a sentence of death upon a prisoner who is insane." *Id.* at 409.

6. *Amici* of course have not examined Panetti in person; rather, *amici* rely upon the facts as set forth in the record and on Panetti's prior mental health evaluations.

7. Schizophrenia is typically defined as encompassing two or more of the following five symptoms: (1) delusions; (2) hallucinations; (3) disorganized speech; (4) grossly disorganized or catatonic behavior; and (5) negative symptoms, *i.e.*, affective flattening (diminished emotional expressiveness), alogia (poverty of speech), or avolition (inability to initiate and persist in goal-oriented activities). DSM-IV-TR 299–301, 312.

8. Schizoaffective disorder essentially consists of schizophrenic symptoms coupled with, at some point, either a major depressive episode, a manic episode, or a mixed episode (*i.e.*, an episode in which the individual alternates between major depressive and manic symptoms). DSM-IV-TR 319–323.

9. *See generally* DSM-IV-TR 345–428; *see also id.* at 327 (discussing Mood Disorders With Psychotic Features).

10. It is important to distinguish delusional beliefs from beliefs that are merely wrong. An individual who believes that her husband is cheating on her may be mistaken, but her view may not be delusional, depending upon the facts that she adduces to support her belief. But, the individual who, in one reported case, based such a belief solely on the presence of a red car outside of her apartment, is clearly delusional. *See* Adolfo Pazzagli, *Delusion, Narrative, and Affects*, 34 J. of the Am. Acad. of Psychoanalysis & Dynamic Psychiatry 367, 370 (2006).

11. The record in *Barnard* is much more sparse than in *Panetti*; accordingly, it is difficult to assess the true nature of Barnard's delusions. Because the state court found that Barnard tended to blame his conviction on "a conspiracy of Asians, Jews, Blacks, homosexuals, and the Mafia," 13 F.3d at 876, it is likely that his beliefs would have withstood efforts to test reality by presenting him with evidence that (1) those five groups do not, in fact, work in concert, (2) there is no reason why those groups would have any motive to do him harm, and (3) most fundamentally, those groups do not control the judicial system, and thus did not bring about his conviction.

12. American Psychological Association Council of Representatives, APA Policy Manual: N. Public Interest (2001) (incorporating policy adopted by the Council of Representatives in February 2006), *available at . . . Mentally Ill Prisoners on Death Row: Position Statement*, American Psychiatric Association (2005), *available at . . .* The National Alliance on Mental Illness adopted an earlier version of this language. *Public Policy Platform of the National Alliance on Mental Illness* 50 (8th ed. 2006), *available at . . .* The ABA adopted a later version of this proposal with a different final clause. *Recommendation and Report on the Death Penalty and Persons with Mental Disabilities*, 30 Mental & Physical Disability L. Rep. 668, 668 (2006).

Greg Abbott et al.

 **NO**

On Writ of Certiorari to the United States Court of Appeals for the Fifth Circuit: Brief for the Respondent

Statement of the Case

A. The Crime

Scott Louis Panetti has led a troubled and violent life. Between 1981 and 1992, Panetti was hospitalized on multiple occasions and variously diagnosed with substance abuse and dependence, personality disorders, depression, chronic undifferentiated schizophrenia, and schizoaffective disorder. JA 339–41;1 Federal Petition for Writ of Habeas Corpus, No. 1:99-CV-00260 (W.D. Tex. Sept. 7, 1999) (hereinafter "Federal Petition") (Ex. 14). Although his doctors initially treated him only with therapy, they later placed him on medication, which proved effective in controlling his mental illness. *Id.*, at 462–63 (noting in 1986 that, while taking medication, Panetti "shows no evidence of thought disorder" and "was not paranoid in his attitude"), 466 (observing in 1990 that, after Panetti was stabilized on his medication, he displayed no evidence of "any delusions or any psychotic thinking, or any suicidal or homicidal ideations").

Panetti married his second wife, Sonja, in 1988, and they had a daughter the following year. 31.RR.61. In August 1992, Sonja separated from Panetti because of his drinking and physical threats. 31.RR.62. She took their daughter, then three years old, to live with her parents, Amanda and Joe Alvarado. 31.RR.60-61. Panetti later called to threaten Sonja and his in-laws, saying he would kill both her and the Alvarados or burn down their house. 31.RR.64. On September 2, 1992, in response to these threats, Sonja obtained a protective order against Panetti. 31.RR.65-66; 41.RR (SX 91).

Six days later, Panetti awoke before dawn, 33.RR.695, shaved his head, 31.RR.95-96, and dressed himself in camouflage, 33.RR.679. Arming himself with a rifle, a sawed-off shotgun, 33.RR.696, and several knives, 33.RR.706-07, Panetti drove to the Alvarados' house, 33.RR.696. When he arrived, Panetti broke his shotgun trying to shatter a sliding glass door near Sonja's bed. 31.RR.69; 33.RR.717. He chased Sonja out of the house and confronted her in the front yard, 33.RR.704, hitting her face with the butt of his rifle, 31.RR.73.

Although Sonja managed to retreat into the house and lock the front door, Panetti shot the lock off and cornered Joe and Amanda Alvarado in the

Supreme Court, 2007.

kitchen. 31.RR.42-43; 33.RR.705. He asked Sonja, who was standing in the adjoining hallway, who she would like to see die first. 31.RR.84. Using his rifle, Panetti then shot and killed Joe Alvarado. 31.RR.84. Sonja begged Panetti not to kill her mother, 31.RR.91, but Panetti pressed the rifle against Amanda Alvarado's chest and pulled the trigger, 32.RR.417-18, killing her and spraying Sonja and their daughter with blood, 31.RR.91. Then his rifle jammed. 31.RR.92.

Panetti grabbed Sonja and their daughter and walked them out to his Jeep. 31.RR.92-93. He drove them back to his bunkhouse, 31.RR.94, where he had them wash off the blood, 31.RR.96. When Sonja asked if she could go check on her parents, he responded: "I just shot your parents. No more mommy, no more daddy; get that through your head." 31.RR.96-97. He then forced Sonja to read the protective order aloud. 31.RR.97-98. Sonja asked Panetti if he planned to shoot her and her daughter. 31.RR.98. He replied that he had not yet decided. 31.RR.98.

At dawn, Panetti allowed both Sonja and their daughter to leave the bunkhouse, telling Sonja that he planned to stay there and "shoot two or three policemen" before taking his own life. 31.RR.101. Panetti surrendered to police that afternoon. 31.RR.241. Later the same day, Panetti confessed to the murders, recounting the details of the crime to police. 33.RR.692-737. When asked if he thought that his mental condition excused his behavior, Panetti replied, "it doesn't excuse me from any of that. You know, I made my bed and I'm going to lie in it. . . . I f***ed up. I feel a lot of remorse." 33.RR.734-35; see also JA 208.

Dr. Michael Lennhoff, a psychiatrist, interviewed Panetti several times at the local jail. Panetti stated that he had followed his drug regimen over the preceding year, but he later confessed that he had not taken his medication for one week before the murders. Federal Petition Ex. 14, at 431, 436. Although Dr. Lennhoff noted that Panetti exhibited genuine mental illness, he also concluded that "Panetti may have wanted to impress me with how mentally disturbed he is, perhaps in an exaggerated way." *Id.*, at 434. After a later meeting, Dr. Lennhoff felt that Panetti was "still trying to impress me as not having committed a deliberate crime." *Id.*, at 436.

B. Panetti's Exhaustively Affirmed Conviction and Sentence and the Rejection of His Alleged Incompetence to Stand Trial and to Waive Counsel

Panetti was charged with capital murder. 1.CR.8. The trial court appointed Dr. E. Lee Simes, a psychiatrist, to evaluate Panetti's competence for trial. JA 9. Dr. Simes noted that, despite Panetti's delusional thinking, "his overall story was quite consistent and insightful." JA 13. In particular, Dr. Simes observed that Panetti understood why he was facing capital-murder charges, the significance of those charges, and the significance of the punishment he might receive. JA 13. Panetti also displayed ability to process questions and information and to assist in his defense. JA 13. Dr. Simes concluded that Panetti was competent to stand trial. JA 13.

In April 1994, Panetti moved for a competence hearing. 2.CR.236-41. In the first trial-competence hearing, the jury deadlocked at four for incompetent, three for competent, and five undecided. 3.CR.295-96; 10.RR.379.2. At the second trial-competence hearing, the jury found Panetti competent to stand trial. 13.RR.206-07.

Eight months later, Panetti sent the trial judge a letter explaining that he had stopped taking all medication and, as a result, was "restored to sanity"; he had dismissed his attorneys; he felt competent to represent himself; he did not intend to "act like a lawyer" in his trial; and he would be able to prove that he was insane at the time of the murders. 3.CR.360. Panetti's attorneys then moved to withdraw as his counsel. 3.CR.363–64.

The trial court called a pretrial hearing to inquire further into Panetti's expressed desire to represent himself. 15.RR.5. The judge told Panetti that he personally did not want Panetti to represent himself, 15.RR.10, and asked Panetti's attorneys to confer privately with Panetti about waiving counsel, 15.RR.11. After this consultation, Panetti's attorneys reported that they did not think Panetti should represent himself, but that was his "clear intent." 15.RR.12–13. Panetti confirmed that he wanted to represent himself because he had the right to do so under Texas law and the United States Constitution, and that he was "fully aware" of the penalty for the charges against him. 15.RR.18. Panetti then executed a voluntary waiver of counsel. 3.CR.369. The district attorney informed the court that, because the State was "concerned about protecting the Defendant's rights," he did not want Panetti's attorneys to withdraw. 15.RR.24. When the court reexamined Panetti about his decision, Panetti replied, "I understand everything that's been going on today, sir. I do, however, feel a little bit insulted that I have been asked the same question so many times, Your Honor." 15.RR.25–28. The court held that Panetti had voluntarily and intelligently exercised his right to represent himself and then appointed standby counsel for Panetti. 15.RR.29–30.

At trial, Panetti entered a plea of not guilty by reason of insanity. 31.RR.24. In his rambling opening statement, Panetti informed the jury that he had been diagnosed with paranoid schizophrenia and manic depression in 1986, and that he believed only an insane person could prove the insanity defense. 31.RR.28–29. As Panetti explains in his brief, he exhibited bizarre and incoherent behavior throughout his trial. Panetti Br. 11–15. He did call as witnesses two psychiatrists who had previously treated him, 38.RR.1567–1616, and endeavored to establish through one that, when he did not take his medication, his mental illness could prevent him from distinguishing right and wrong, 38.RR.1574–75. The jury nonetheless found Panetti guilty of capital murder and sentenced him to death. 7.CR.1041–44; 38.RR.1685; 39.RR.102. The Texas Court of Criminal Appeals (CCA) affirmed Panetti's conviction and sentence, *Panetti v. Texas*, No. 72,230 (Tex. Crim. App. Dec. 3, 1997) (unpublished), and the Court denied certiorari, 525 U.S. 848 (1998) (Mem.). Panetti then filed a state habeas petition raising fourteen claims, including whether he was competent to stand trial and competent to waive counsel. State Petition for Writ of Habeas Corpus, No. 3310-A, at 3–4 (Tex. Crim. App. June 19, 1997). The CCA denied relief. (pp. 1–5)

In sum, one jury and four courts rejected Panetti's trial-incompetence claim; one court found him competent to waive counsel and four courts rejected his collateral challenge to that determination; and another jury and two courts rejected his insanity defense. No judge or jury has ever found him incompetent.

C. Panetti's Efforts to Prove Incompetence to Be Executed in State and Federal Court

Once an execution date was set, Panetti filed a motion in the state trial court under Texas Code of Criminal Procedure Article 46.05 asserting incompetence to be executed. JA 355. After concluding that Panetti had failed to make a substantial showing of incompetence, the state court denied his Article 46.05 motion, JA 355, and the CCA dismissed his appeal, *Ex parte Panetti*, No. 74,868 (Tex. Crim. App. Jan. 28, 2004) (*per curiam*) (unpublished).

Panetti then filed a habeas petition in federal district court, asserting that *Ford v. Wainwright*, 477 U.S. 399 (1986), prohibited his execution. JA 355–56. The district court granted a stay of execution and allowed Panetti an opportunity to present his renewed allegations to the state trial court. JA 357.

In response to Panetti's second Article 46.05 motion, the state court appointed two neutral experts, Dr. George Parker and Dr. Mary Anderson, to assess Panetti's competence to be executed. JA 59. After conducting a joint interview of Panetti, Drs. Parker and Anderson filed a report documenting their observations and conclusions. JA 70–76. This report reflects Panetti's hostility to Drs. Parker's and Anderson's questions, his tendency toward religious conversation, his attempted manipulation of the interview process, and his general refusal to cooperate with the court-appointed experts. JA 70–73, 75.

Because of Panetti's refusal to cooperate, Drs. Parker and Anderson also relied on several sources of collateral data—including prison records; letters that Panetti had recently written to friends and family; court documents, including documents relating to other competence determinations; discussions with prison staff; and another expert evaluation of Panetti—to help form their relevant opinions. JA 73–75. Based on these data and their personal observations, Drs. Parker and Anderson concluded that Panetti (1) "knows that he is to be executed, and that his execution will result in his death" and (2) "has the ability to understand the reason he is to be executed." JA 75.

In response, Panetti filed a detailed submission criticizing Drs. Parker and Anderson's methodology and contrasting their conclusions with those in a psychiatric evaluation that Panetti had previously presented to the court. JA 79–98. After considering that submission, the state court again denied relief under Article 46.05. JA 99.

Panetti then sought habeas relief in the federal district court, JA 375, which concluded that the state court's determination of Panetti's competence to be executed was not entitled to AEDPA deference because Panetti allegedly failed to receive constitutionally sufficient process, JA 359–61. After granting Panetti's motions for appointment of counsel, discovery, and funds for expert and investigative assistance, JA 358, the district court held an evidentiary hearing on competence, JA 362. At the hearing, Panetti presented expert testimony[.]" (pp. 5–7)

"All of the expert witnesses agreed that Panetti suffers from some degree of mental illness." Although some of the experts labeled this illness schizophrenia or schizoaffective disorder, *e.g.*, JA 144–45, 205, they were collectively unable to agree on a single diagnosis, see JA 239, 313.[1]

The experts did agree, however, that Panetti has the capacity to—and does, in fact—understand that he will be executed. JA 147–48, 207, 236, 243, 245.[2]

Further expert testimony established Panetti's specific understanding that he committed the murders. Indeed, Dr. Rosin testified that Panetti recounted details of his activity on the day of the murders and expressed sorrow for having committed the crime. JA 208; see also JA 148–49 (Dr. Conroy's testimony that Panetti believed that God had forgiven him for killing the Alvarados and had "wiped the slate clean"). Dr. Silverman testified to uncertainty about whether Panetti knows that he killed the Alvarados, but only because Panetti steadfastly refused to answer his questions on this topic. JA 221.

Several experts also concluded that Panetti's delusions created a false sense of the true reason for his execution. *E.g.*, JA 149, 156, 202, 209 (testimony from Drs. Conroy and Rosin that Panetti believes his execution was ordered to prevent him from preaching the Gospel). Importantly, however, these same experts testified that Panetti understands that the State's stated reason for his execution is punishment for capital murder. JA 157, 214.

Dr. Parker testified that portions of Panetti's responses to the experts execution-competence examinations could be attributed to malingering, see JA 241–43; see also, *e.g.*, JA 174, 177, 181 (noting additional reports of Panetti's suspected malingering in the past), and Drs. Parker and Anderson each specifically testified that Panetti has the capacity to understand the reason for his execution, JA 245, 247, 303–04. Both Dr. Parker and Dr. Anderson emphasized that Panetti was deliberately manipulative and uncooperative during his interview with them. JA 239–40, 244–46, 271, 300, 303, 312–14; accord JA 75. They based their ultimate conclusions on Panetti's overall cognitive functionality, as demonstrated through letters he wrote to friends and family, his logical responses to interview questions, and his ability to understand such things as history and movies. JA 242–43, 302–04.

Dr. Parker's suspicions of malingering were corroborated by evidence of psychiatric evaluations conducted in the two years following Panetti's capital trial. For example, Dr. Michael Gilhousen noted that loosening of Panetti's thought processes "appeared to be intentional on his part to create the impression of mental illness." JA 167, II-30. After another interview, Dr. Gilhousen described Panetti's behavior as "obviously manipulative and theatrical." JA 171-72, II-20. Another doctor expressed the belief that Panetti's switching among different voices was "contrived . . . to impress us or lead us to believe that he did have alter personalities." JA 170, II-41.

After hearing all the evidence, the federal district court made three factual findings. First, based on the expert's agreement, the court concluded that Panetti is aware that he will be executed. JA 372.

Second, the district court found that Panetti is aware that he committed both murders. JA 372. The court based this conclusion on Dr. Conroy's and Dr. Rosin's testimony that Panetti knows that he murdered the Alvarados. JA 372. Although the court recognized that Dr. Silverman's testimony cast doubt on this conclusion, the court discounted that testimony, noting that it was based on Panetti's limited responses during his interview with Dr. Silverman. JA 372.

Third, the district court found that Panetti understands the State's stated reason for execution. JA 372. The court based this finding on the testimony of Drs. Conroy and Rosin, and discounted Dr. Silverman's contrary testimony for the same reason. JA 372–73.

Additionally, the district court recounted Dr. Parker's and Dr. Anderson's assessments that "some portion of Panetti's behavior could be attributed to malingering," and it expressly concluded that, although all of the experts had agreed Panetti had "some degree" of mental illness, their testimony collectively "casts doubt on the extent of Panetti's mental illness and symptoms." JA 363.

Finally, the district court noted Dr. Cunningham's testimony that "suggests" that Panetti's delusions prevent him from understanding that Texas is a lawfully constituted authority and lead him to believe that the State "is in league with the forces of evil that have conspired against him," and it observed that this testimony was consistent with the testimony of Panetti's other experts. JA 373. The court made no finding, however, whether these delusions were genuine or the partial product of malingering, because the court deemed it irrelevant to the question of whether Panetti "knows the reason for his execution" within the meaning of the court of appeals's execution-competence test. JA 373.

Based on these factual findings, the district court concluded that Panetti is competent to be executed. JA 373. Although the court denied Panetti's habeas petition, it stayed his execution pending appeal, JA 373, and granted a certificate of appealability, *Panetti v. Dretke*, No. 04-CA- 042 (W.D. Tex. Nov. 4, 2004). The court of appeals affirmed the district court's denial of habeas relief, *Panetti v. Dretke*, 448 F.3d 815 (CA5 2006); JA 374–84, and the Court granted certiorari, JA 387.

Summary of the Argument

In devoting fully half of his brief to his statement of the case, Panetti endeavors to focus the Court's attention on his lengthy mental-health history, explaining that "incompetency runs like a fissure through every proceeding in this case." Panetti Br. 6. But that fissure has been mostly sealed once and for all by the conclusive determinations of state and federal courts repeatedly rejecting Panetti's direct and collateral challenges to adverse rulings on his insanity defense, his competence to stand trial, and his competence to waive counsel. For that reason, Panetti correctly concedes that, as a matter of law, he is now presumed competent to be executed. *Ibid.*

The state court, the district court, and the court of appeals have all concluded that Panetti has failed to overcome that presumption. The district court found as a factual matter that Panetti knows that he murdered the Alvarados, that he will be executed, and that the State's stated reason for executing him is that he committed two murders. Panetti has not challenged those factual findings on appeal. (pp. 7–11)

"Both Panetti's and his *amici's* proposed standards, which require that a convict rationally understand" the reasons for his execution, are fundamentally flawed. Given the inherent subjectivity and manipulability of such a standard, capital murderers could as a routine matter claim a lack of "rational understanding" through malingering or refusing to cooperate with experts. (p. 12) . . . "Finally, the retributive and deterrent interests served by the death penalty—focused primarily as they are on society at large rather than the capital murderer—do not demand the "rational understanding" that Panetti urges.

The Court should instead adopt a clear and objective test for execution competence. Specifically, the Court should hold that a mentally ill capital convict is incompetent to be executed only if, because of his illness, he lacks the *capacity* to recognize that his punishment (1) is the result of his being convicted of capital murder and (2) will cause his death. This standard controls for the malingering or uncooperative convict, is appropriately tailored to the execution stage of capital proceedings, and serves the twin goals of retribution and deterrence that justify capital punishment. Applying this standard, the Court should hold that Panetti is competent to be executed. (pp. 12–13)

Argument

II. Even if AEDPA Deference Does Not Apply, Panetti's Execution Does Not Violate the Eighth Amendment

Only if the Court concludes that the AEDPA does not bar habeas review should it reach Panettis claim that the court of appeals employed the wrong legal standard for execution competence. Although *Ford* held that the Eighth Amendment proscribes execution of the "insane," 477 U.S., at 409–10, the Court did not define "insanity" or otherwise delineate the constitutional threshold of competence to be executed, *id.*, at 418 (Powell, J., concurring in the judgment), a question which remains unresolved.

Before turning to the merits of that claim, two issues bear emphasis. **First,** there is no dispute that, under *Ford*, executing the insane violates the Eighth Amendment. Executing the insane was forbidden at common law, and it is forbidden today." (p. 19) . . . "And **second,** there is no dispute that, like many capital defendants, Panetti suffers from some degree of mental illness." (p. 19)

"The only legal question before the Court on the merits of this case is what is the definition of "insanity"—that is, what must a court find to conclude that a capital murderer is constitutionally incompetent to be executed." (p. 19)

Although execution of the "insane" was deemed cruel and unusual in 1971, *Ford*, 477 U.S., at 406–08, the common law did not then draw fine distinctions in mental ability, and thus did not delineate any precise competence standard. Consequently, the standards of the common law are, at best, inconclusive. Likewise, a survey of modern state legislation offers indefinite guidance, as it yields no consensus at all on the mental faculty a capital murderer must possess at the time of his execution. Finally, in the exercise of its independent judgment, the Court should reject the proposition that a capital convict must possess a "rational understanding" of the reasons for his execution to render death an acceptable punishment under the Eighth Amendment. Such a standard is not tailored to the particular interests at stake in the postsentencing phase of capital proceedings, invites malingering and abuse, and is not necessary to advance the retributive and deterrent justifications for the death penalty.

For all of these reasons, the Court should reject Panetti's and his *amici's* proposed execution-competence standards." (pp. 20–21)

C. The Court Should Hold That the Appropriate Constitutional Standard for Competence to Be Executed is Whether a Defendant Has the Capacity to Recognize That His Punishment Is the Result of His Being Convicted of Capital Murder and Will Cause His Death. (p. 33)

"Both Panetti's and his *amici's* proposed execution-competence standards are deeply flawed. The State urges the Court to reject those proposals and instead adopt a clearer and more objective test. Specifically, the Court should hold that a mentally ill capital convict is incompetent to be executed only if, because of his illness, he lacks the *capacity* to recognize that his punishment (1) is the result of his being convicted of capital murder and (2) will cause his death.

The State's proposed standard—derived from *Ford* and the Court's Eighth Amendment jurisprudence—prevents the execution of the truly incompetent, while at the same time (1) incorporating essential safeguards against malingering and noncooperation with psychological examiners, (2) being specifically tailored to the postsentencing phase of capital proceedings, and (3) effectively advancing the modern penological interests behind the death penalty.

   1. **Because of the inherent uncertainties and subjectivity of psychiatric testing, and the risks of malingering and abuse, any standard for competence to be executed should be rigorous and clear."** (pp. 33–34)

"The Court has often noted the difficulties that attend even the most skilled psychiatric diagnoses. "[P]sychiatrists disagree widely and frequently on what constitutes mental illness [and] on the appropriate diagnosis to be attached to given behavior and symptoms." *Ake v. Oklahoma*, 470 U.S. 68, 81 (1985). For that reason, "a particularly acute need for guarding against error inheres in a determination that 'in the present state of the mental sciences is at best a hazardous guess however conscientious.'" *Ford*, 477 U.S., at 412 (plurality op.) (quoting *Solesbee v. Balkcom*, 339 U.S. 9, 23 (1950) (Frankfurter, J., dissenting)). As Justice Powell explained,

   "Unlike issues of historical fact, the question of petitioner's sanity calls for a basically subjective judgment. And unlike a determination of whether the death penalty is appropriate in a particular case, the competency determination depends substantially on expert analysis in a discipline fraught with 'subtleties and nuances.'" *Id.*, at 426 (Powell, J., concurring in the judgment) (quoting *Addington v. Texas*, 441 U.S. 418, 430 (1979)) (citations omitted).

Just last Term, the Court observed that the medical definitions of mental illness "are subject to flux and disagreement," and that such diagnoses "may mask vigorous debate within the profession about the very contours of the mental disease itself." *Clark v. Arizona*, 126 S.Ct. 2709, 2722, 2734 (2006). "[T]he consequence of this professional ferment," the Court noted, "is a general caution in treating psychological classifications as predicates for excusing otherwise criminal conduct." *Id.*, at 2734.

Not only are psychiatric diagnoses subjective and frequently conflicting, they are by their nature subject to change. *Atkins* and *Roper* were predicated on constant variables: if a defendant is fifteen or seventeen or twenty at the time of the crime, that age at that instant is fixed and unchanging; likewise, if an individual is of normal intelligence throughout his or her life, that person cannot be expected later to become mentally retarded. In contrast, if a person is sane yesterday and today, that does not mean he or she will be sane tomorrow. As Justice O'Connor cautioned in *Ford*, that mutability carries with it serious risks of malingering:

> "[T]he *potential for false claims and deliberate delay* in this context is *obviously enormous*. This potential is exacerbated by a unique feature of the prisoner's protected interest in suspending the execution of a death sentence during incompetency. By definition, this interest can *never* be conclusively and finally determined: Regardless of the number of prior adjudications of the issue, until the very moment of execution the prisoner can claim that he has become insane sometime after the previous determination to the contrary." 477 U.S., at 429 (O'Connor, J., concurring in part and dissenting in part) (citations omitted) (first two emphases added).[3]

Finally, unlike with age or retardation, capital murderers facing execution may have some ability to voluntarily choose to render themselves incompetent to be executed simply by ceasing to take their medication. Indeed, in the case at bar, the evidence indicates that Panetti's medication had been largely successful in controlling his mental illness, Federal Petition Ex. 14, at 462–63, but that he willingly chose to stop taking it, *id.*, at 431, 436; 3.CR.360.

Panetti's proposed "rational understanding" standard has no basis in the Court's precedent and would invite abuse. (pp. 34–36)

a. **A "rational understanding" inquiry would engraft Fifth and Sixth Amendment concerns on an Eighth Amendment test.**

Although Panetti uses the phrase loosely, "rational understanding" is a specific term of art; it describes the core of several pre-sentencing competence tests. "Rational understanding" was introduced in *Dusky*, in which the Court defined the test for competence to stand trial as whether the defendant has "sufficient present ability to consult with his lawyer with a reasonable degree of rational understanding" and has "a rational as well as factual understanding of the proceedings against him." 362 U.S., at 402 (quotation marks omitted); see also *Godinez v. Moran*, 509 U.S. 389, 398 (1993) (concluding that the "rational understanding" test should also be used to measure a defendant's competence to plead guilty and to waive the right to counsel). (p. 37)

"[A] "rational understanding" is necessary to ensure that defendants do not foolishly or mistakenly relinquish valuable constitutional rights. A defendant faced with such choices must be able to "understand the nature and object of the proceedings against him, to consult with counsel, and to assist in preparing his defense." *Drope*, 420 U.S., at 171.

But a capital convict, unlike a capital defendant, has substantially fewer rights, and there are no significant strategic choices left for him to make. See *Herrera v. Collins*, 506 U.S. 390, 399 (1993) (explaining that the presumption of innocence disappears after conviction and listing numerous constitutional rights that defendants enjoy but that convicts do not); *Barefoot v. Estelle*, 463 U.S. 880, 887–88 (1983) (discussing the "secondary and limited" nature of federal habeas proceedings); see also *Ford*, 477 U.S., at 421 (Powell, J., concurring in the judgment) (noting that, because the Court's decisions already recognize . . . that a defendant must be competent to stand trial, . . . the notion that a defendant must be able to assist in his defense is largely provided for"). Assuming that a convict is competent to be executed, only the remote possibilities of clemency or commutation—processes that call for no significant strategic decisions by a convict—can prevent the sentence from being carried out.

b. Panetti's conception of "rational understanding" is far too expansive.

Panetti's argument is, in fact, even more aggressive than one for inclusion of only a pure "rational understanding" component. Although he invokes that phrase throughout his brief, the substantive requirement that Panetti asks the Court to incorporate is actually a version of the heightened "knowing and voluntary" requirement that the Court has held applicable, over and above the "rational understanding" competence component, with respect to a defendant's decision to plead guilty or to waive his right to counsel. *Godinez*, 509 U.S., at 400–01 & n.12; *Faretta v. California*, 422 U.S. 806, 835 (1975).

As *Godinez* explained, "knowing and voluntary" is not part of any competence test; it is an additional safeguard designed to ensure not merely that a defendant has the *capacity* to understand trial proceedings, but rather that he "*actually does* understand the significance and consequences of a particular decision and whether the decision is uncoerced." 509 U.S., at 401, n.12 (emphasis added). (pp. 38–39)

"[R]equiring a "deep" or "meaningful" appreciation of the State's reasons for imposing the death penalty would create an even greater risk that the Court's test could be circumvented through malingering or abuse. See *supra* Part II.C.1." (p. 39)

When viewed in light of the overall death-row population, Panetti's proposal is especially problematic. As a matter of common understanding, most individuals who commit heinous murders are, almost by definition, not entirely sane. Although estimates vary, some sources indicate that as many as 70 percent of death-row inmates suffer from some form of schizophrenia or psychosis. Nancy S. Horton, Restoration of Competency for Execution: Furiosus Solo Furore Punitur, 44 Sw. L.J. 1191, 1204 (1990) (citing Amnesty International, United States of America: the Death Penalty 108–09 (1987)); see JA 142 (expert testimony that most of the convicts in federal Bureau of Prisons hospitals are schizophrenic). Many, if not most, schizophrenics exhibit the type of delusional thinking that Panetti has been observed to exhibit. See Douglas Mossman, *Atkins v. Virginia: A Psychiatric Can of Worms,* 33 N.M. L. Rev. 255, 280 (2003); APA Br. 8 (noting that "[d]elusional thinking is a hallmark symptom of schizophrenia" (citing DSM-IV-TR 299–301, 312)).[4] Accordingly, Panetti's "rational understanding" requirement would be applied to a population that is, in significant part, delusional—and thus necessarily *irrational.* See APA Br. 9, n.11." (p. 40)

[T]he introduction of Panetti's ill-defined—and inherently indefinite—"rational understanding" component would render the execution-competence standard substantially overinclusive. See Mossman, *supra,* at 289 ("Given the high rate of serious mental illness among homicide defendants, granting psychiatric exemptions could leave very few individuals eligible for the death penalty.").

Nor is this potential for exempting vast numbers of convicted murderers from execution an unintended consequence of Panetti's and his *amici*'s proposed test. Indeed, *amicus* APA is nothing if not candid, explaining that both its own position and the ABA's is that "an individual who is found incompetent to face the death penalty" should not have his sentence "merely suspended," but should "have his sentence *permanently commuted* to a non-capital punishment." APA Br. 17, n.15 (emphasis added). Thus, the conceded objective of these *amici* (and the predictable consequence of their proposed test) is not simply avoiding the inhumanity of executing a person who is truly insane, but rather removing from death row as large a class of capital convicts as reasonably possible.[5] (pp. 40–41)

Application of the State's proposed test will advance the modern penological interests behind the death penalty.

The Court has recently confirmed that retribution and deterrence are capital punishment's two predominant social purposes. *Roper,* 543 U.S., at 571 (citing *Gregg v. Georgia,* 428 U.S. 153, 183 (1976) (joint opinion of Stewart, Powell, and Stevens, JJ.)); accord *Atkins,* 536 U.S., at 318–19. As shown below, application of the State's proposed test will advance each of those interests.[6]

a.   The State's test will further the retributive purpose of punishment.

Retribution aims either "to express the community's moral outrage or . . . to right the balance for the wrong to the victim." *Roper,* 543 U.S., at 571; see

Atkins, 536 U.S., at 319 (explaining that retribution is "the interest in seeing that the offender gets his 'just deserts' "). The Court has repeatedly emphasized the societal focus of retribution. See, *e.g.*, *Thompson v. Oklahoma*, 487 U.S. 815, 836 (1988); see also *Schriro v. Summerlin*, 542 U.S. 348, 360 (2004) (Breyer, J., dissenting); *Gregg*, 428 U.S., at 183–84 (joint opinion of Stewart, Powell, and Stevens, JJ.). Panetti misunderstands the societal nature of retribution, erroneously equating it with vengeance. Panetti Br. 46 & n.33. (p. 43)

i.   **The retributive justification for punishment necessarily precedes any execution-competence analysis.**

The viability of retribution as a permissible theory of punishment depends not on the "rational understanding" that a convict may or may not have, see *supra* Part II.C.2; cf. Panetti Br. 46, but rather on the convict's moral culpability at the time he committed his crime, *Enmund v. Florida*, 458 U.S. 782, 800–01 (1982) (reflecting that "personal responsibility and moral guilt" define a criminal's level of culpability and concluding that execution of one convict for murders that he did not personally commit failed to serve the retributive goal of punishment). (p. 44)

[I]n the present context the question of culpability will already have been conclusively—and affirmatively—resolved. The issue is not whether the Constitution permits society to *impose* the death penalty on a criminal who was, for some reason, less culpable at the time of his crime, cf. *Roper*, 543 U.S., at 556, 578; *Atkins*, 536 U.S., at 306–08, 321, but rather whether an unquestionably valid death sentence may be *carried out* against a criminal who has subsequently become mentally ill, see *Ford*, 477 U.S., at 425 (Powell, J., concurring in the judgment). This is so because any convict to whom the execution-competence test is applied will necessarily have been adjudicated both sane at the time of his offense and competent to stand trial, removing any doubts about culpability that might in some cases arise from mental illness.

ii. **There are substantial problems with the wholly personal view of retribution that Panetti advances.** (pp. 44–45)

"Relying heavily on nonjudicial sources, Panetti asserts that retribution requires a condemned prisoner to have a subjective appreciation of the moral impropriety of his criminal conduct and to "suffer the anguish" of knowing the reason for his fate. Panetti Br. 45. (p. 45)

Putting aside its lack of support in case law, there are significant problems with Panetti's mind-of-the-criminal approach. First, tailoring the execution competence test to the innermost thoughts of capital convicts would present substantial practical problems. It is difficult to imagine how anyone other than the convict himself could accurately assess whether he truly appreciates the magnitude of his moral wrong—at least with respect to a convict who is willing to lie about such things. And under Panetti's proposed test, it would be remarkably easy for a convict to feign his way out of a death sentence.

Second, allowing the execution-competence test to be shaped primarily by a personal, subjective view of the retributive rationale would prevent the execution of convicts who genuinely lack moral qualms about their crimes. It cannot be that amoral capital convicts should be excused from death sentences based on amorality alone. Yet Panetti's proposed standard would yield that result. (p. 46)

D. Under Both the State's Proposed Test and the Test That the Court of Appeals Applied, Panetti Is Competent to Be Executed. (p. 48)

Under the State's proposed test, Panetti could properly be held incompetent to be executed only if, because of mental illness, he lacked the capacity to recognize that his punishment (1) is the result of his being convicted of capital murder and (2) will cause his death. To the extent, this test varies from that applied by the court of appeals, any such variances are immaterial to the result because, as shown below, the record establishes that Panetti is competent to be executed under either standard.

First of all, it is undisputed that Panetti has the capacity to recognize that the punishment he faces is death. Indeed, the experts all agreed and the district court expressly found that, as a factual matter, "Panetti is aware he is to be executed," JA 363, 372; accord JA 373. Panetti did not oppose this conclusion in the district court, see JA 367, 372, did not challenge it in the court of appeals, and does not challenge it here. Therefore, Panetti is unquestionably "[]aware of the punishment [he is] about to suffer," JA 379 (quoting *Ford*, 477 U.S., at 422 (Powell, J., concurring in the judgment))" (p. 48–49).

The only question that remains is whether Panetti has the capacity to recognize that his punishment is the result of his being convicted of capital murder, or, under the court of appeals's analysis, whether he is aware of why he is to be executed, JA 379. The record establishes that Panetti passes each of these prongs as well.

Dr. Parker and Dr. Anderson each testified that Panetti has the capacity to understand that he is being executed for the murders of which he was convicted. JA 245, 247 (testimony of Dr. Parker), 303–04 (testimony of Dr. Anderson); accord JA 75 (joint report of Drs. Parker and Anderson), and the district court explicitly concluded that "[t]here is evidence in the record to support a finding that Panetti is *capable* of understanding the reason for his execution," JA 367. Again, Panetti does not challenge this conclusion. And under the State's proposed test, it is irrelevant that these witnesses "were unable to reach a formal conclusion that [Panetti] did, in fact, understand" the reason for his execution. JA 364. For the reasons already noted, it is the *capacity* to understand—rather than actual demonstration of understanding—that defines the minimal level of competence needed to satisfy this prong of the State's proposed test. See *supra* Part II.C.3.

And with respect to the court of appeals's test, the district court accurately noted that two of Panetti's own execution-competence experts testified that, "despite his delusions, Panetti understands [that] the State's stated reason for seeking his execution is for his murders." JA 366; see also JA 157 (testimony of Dr. Conroy); JA 214 (testimony of Dr. Rosin). Thus, not only did the district court explicitly find that "Panetti is aware he committed the murders that serve as the basis for his execution," JA 372, but the court further found that "Panetti understands the State's stated reason for executing him is that he committed two murders," JA 372.

The district court also correctly concluded that the alternative sense of "understand" embodied in Panetti's proposal did not match the court of appeals's standard. JA 369 (p. 49–50).

In sum, the record establishes that Panetti: (1) has the capacity to recognize that his punishment will cause his death (and does in fact does recognize this), and (2) has the capacity to recognize that his punishment is the result of his being convicted of capital murder (or, within the meaning of the court of appeals's test, is aware of why he is to be executed). Taken together, these facts conclusively establish Panetti's competence to be executed under both the court of appeals's test and the State's proposed test.

Conclusion

The judgment of the court of appeals should be affirmed. (p. 50)

Notes

1. Citations to the transcript of Panetti's capital-murder trial are noted as "RR" ("Reporters Record"). Citations to the States exhibits admitted into evidence during those proceedings are noted as "SX" ("State Exhibit"). Citations to the pleadings, orders, and motions filed in the trial court are noted as "CR" ("Clerk's Record"). Citations to the federal district court's hearing on execution competence are noted as "FH" ("Federal Hearing"). Citations to the joint appendix filed in this Court are noted as "JA."

2. Panetti incorrectly reports the final vote as nine-to-three in favor of incompetence. Panetti Br. 8, n.6. That vote occurred earlier in the deliberations. 3.CR.290.

3. Dr. Conroy noted that "the major portion of our population in our inpatient units in federal Bureau of Prisons hospitals are diagnosed with some form of schizophrenia," JA 142, and Dr. Silverman opined that most schizophrenics are competent to be executed, JA 227.

4. Lay testimony corroborated this point. Major Miller testified that Panetti cooperated with him in going over the State's pre-execution forms, JA 281, II-42–53, and demonstrated his understanding of the forms' questions about disposition of assets, choice of last meal, and the like. JA 287–88. Additional lay testimony reflected Panetti's demonstrated ability to communicate coherently—and politely—with prison staff. *E.g.*, 1 FH 193–96 (testimony of Terri Hill); 1 FH 200 (testimony of Victoria Williams).

5. In so noting, Justice O'Connor echoed the concerns of Hale, who, some three centuries earlier, likewise urged courts to guard against the potential for "great fraud" concerning those claiming incompetence. 1 Hale, *supra*, at 35; Legal Historians Br. 15, n.8.

6. Indeed, one death-row study of a limited population noted that half of the profiled inmates exhibited delusional tendencies, which included persecutory delusions (*e.g.*, inmate's belief that he was target of a Jewish conspiracy). Barbara A. Ward, Competency for Execution: Problems in Law and Psychiatry, 14 Fla. St. U. L. Rev. 35, 39–40 & n.26 (1986) (citing Bluestone & McGahee, Reaction to Extreme Stress: Impending Death by Execution, 119 Am. J. Psychiatry 393, 393 (1962)). Other inmates in the study coped with their predicament through obsessive rumination, "thinking furiously about other things, such as appeals, religion, or philosophy." *Ibid.*

EXPLORING THE ISSUE

Must Mentally Ill Murderers Have a Rational Understanding of Why They Are Being Sentenced to Death?

Critical Thinking and Reflection

1. In murder cases in which the assertion is made that an individual's crime was attributable to mental illness, complex questions arise about how to assess the legitimacy of the accused person's psychiatric symptoms. If you were a member of a jury in such a case, what kind of evidence would you deem necessary so that a determination could be made about the accused person's psychological functioning?

2. In criminal cases involving mentally ill individuals, several debates have emerged about the condition of the accused within the context of the trial. A particularly thorny issue pertains to whether the accused should be taken off all antipsychotic medication for the trial, so that the court can see this individual in a nonmedicated state (possibly similar to the functional level at the time of the crime). Discuss the benefits and problems of this option.

3. Some proponents of the death penalty would argue that people who engage in violent murder should be executed, regardless of whether they are mentally ill, if for no reason other than ridding society of such people. Discuss the moral implications of this stance.

4. Forensic specialists have worked diligently for years to develop assessment measures to determine whether people accused of a crime are malingering (faking symptoms for an ulterior motive). If you were given the task of developing such an instrument, what kind of data would you look for?

5. Discuss the hypothetical situation in which a convicted murderer understands the nature of his crime but has no understanding of what the death penalty means or why it would be associated with the crime he had committed. Discuss the moral dilemmas inherent in a decision to execute such an individual.

Is There Common Ground?

Related to the debate under consideration in these two selections is the legal concept of insanity, and the defense that is sometimes invoked to defend an accused murderer. The insanity defense refers to the argument presented by a lawyer acting on behalf of the client that, because of a mental disorder, the client should not be held legally responsible for criminal actions. In an attempt to develop uniform standards for the insanity defense, the American Law Institute published guidelines in 1962 stating that people are not responsible for criminal behavior if at the time of the crime their mental disorder prevented them from appreciating the wrongfulness of their behavior or from exerting the necessary willpower to control an irresistible impulse.

In the case of Panetti, the heart of the debate was not so much whether he was insane at the time he committed the murders, but whether he understood why he had been sentenced to execution. He asserted that he was being executed because he preached the gospel, not because of the murders. Thus, even though both sides of the debate respect the insanity defense, they disagree with the notion that the convicted murderer must have a rational understanding of his sentence to death.

Additional Resources

Ackerson, K. S., Brodsky, S. L., & Zapf, P. A. (2005). Judges' and psychologists' assessments of legal and clinical factors in competence for execution. *Psychology, Public Policy, & Law, 11*, 164–193.

American Constitution Society for Law and Policy. Retrieved from www.acsblog.org

American Psychological Association. Retrieved from www.apa.org

Crime and Consequences (Criminal Justice Legal Foundation). Retrieved from www.crimeandconsequences.com

Dahl, R. J. (2011). Barring the mentally ill from the death penalty: A national survey. *Dissertation Abstracts International, 71.*

Denney, R. L. (2012). Criminal responsibility and other criminal forensic issues. In G. J. Larrabee (Ed.), *Forensic neuropsychology: A scientific approach,* 2nd ed. (pp. 473–500). New York: Oxford University Press.

Mason, T. (2011). The insanity defence and diminished responsibility. In P. Barker (Ed.), *Mental health ethics: The human context* (pp. 317–324). New York: Routledge/Taylor & Francis Group.

National Alliance on Mental Illness. Retrieved from www.nami.org

Saks, E. R., & Jeste, D. V. (2006). Capacity to consent to or refuse treatment and/or research: Theoretical considerations. *Behavioral Sciences & the Law, 24*(4), 411–429.

Shapiro, D. L. (2005). Ethical dilemmas in competency for execution evaluations. *Journal of Forensic Psychology Practice, 5*(4), 75–82.

Slobogin, C. (2006). *Minding justice: Laws that deprive people with mental disability of life and liberty.* Cambridge, MA: Harvard University Press.

ISSUE 12

Does Research Confirm That Abortion Is a Psychologically Benign Experience?

YES: APA Task Force on Mental Health and Abortion (**Brenda Major, Mark Appelbaum, Linda Beckman, Mary Ann Dutton, Nancy Felipe Russo, Carolyn West**), from *Report of the APA Task Force on Mental Health and Abortion* (American Psychological Association, 2008)

NO: Priscilla K. Coleman, from "Critique of the APA Task Force on Abortion and Mental Health" (2008), http://aaplog.octoberblue.com/wp-content/uploads/2010/02/Coleman-Critiqueof-APA-Report.pdf

---

Learning Outcomes

After reading this issue, you should be able to:

- Understand the methodology used by the Task Force of the American Psychological Association to review published studies on the mental health of women who had undergone abortions.
- Critically evaluate the conclusions drawn regarding the mental health of women post-abortion, giving consideration to the strengths and limitations of the studies reviewed.
- Discuss the role of political ideology that might be reflected on both sides of the debate regarding the psychological effects of abortion.
- Consider the methodological challenges involved in conducting research on possible psychological effects of abortion.
- Discuss the ways in which cultural factors might influence the psychological impact of abortion.

ISSUE SUMMARY

YES: The APA Task Force (TFMHA) reviewed the empirical literature and concluded that for women who have an unplanned pregnancy, the risk of mental health problems is no greater than the risk for women who deliver an unplanned pregnancy.

NO: Professor Priscilla K. Coleman contends that the TFMHA analysis of the evidence reflects politically motivated bias in the selection of studies, analysis of the literature, and the conclusions derived.

Perhaps no other issue in American judicial history has sparked as much debate and controversy as the Supreme Court decision in 1973 in the case of *Roe v. Wade* in which the Court determined a woman's right to abortion. This decision, based on the constitutional right to privacy, sparked an uproar of dissension that has continued for four decades, and has involved several spheres of American society including religion, politics, health care, and economics. Proponents of a woman's right to choose have ardently sought to fend off efforts to reduce or eradicate access to abortion. Opponents of abortion have engaged in a wide range of activities aimed at convincing Americans that abortion is not only morally wrong, but psychologically hazardous to the women who undergo this procedure. The term postabortion syndrome emerged in the 1980s to characterize detrimental psychological symptoms that may follow the experience of abortion. Over the past few decades, several studies have been conducted in an effort to assess the psychological effects of undergoing an abortion. Periodically, reviews of these research studies have been conducted. For example, in 1987 President Reagan instructed Surgeon General C. Everett Koop to issue a report on the health effects of abortion. Although the report lacked compelling conclusions one way or the other, controversy and political positioning escalated as a result. The American Psychological Association then stepped in to summarize the research, which culminated in a 1990 article in *Science* concluding that scientific studies did not point to adverse psychological effects from abortion. Nevertheless, the controversy refused to go away, and in 2007 the American Psychological Association appointed yet another task force to review the literature.

In an effort to assess the psychological effects of abortion on women, the American Psychological Association commissioned a task force to review all research on this topic. The 2008 APA Task Force on Mental Health and Abortion was chaired by Brenda Major, Ph.D., Professor of Psychology at UC Santa Barbara. Dr. Major was one of the co-authors of the 1990 *Science* article, and the first author of a 2000 article in the prestigious *Archives of General Psychiatry*, which examined women's psychological responses following abortion. In the 2008 report, the TFMHA reviewed the empirical literature and concluded that for women who have an unplanned pregnancy, the risk of mental health problems is no greater than the risk for women who deliver an unplanned pregnancy. In drawing this conclusion from the research, they highlight methodological problems inherent in the research that pointed to detrimental psychological effects following abortion.

The TFMHA evaluated all empirical studies published in English in peer-reviewed journals post-1989 that compared the mental health of women who had an induced abortion to the mental health of comparison groups of women ($N = 50$) or that examined factors that predict mental health among women who have had an elective abortion in the United States ($N = 23$). The Task Force urged caution in drawing conclusions from research pointing to psychiatric disorders in women who had abortions. In pointing out methodological problems, for example, it is noted that Fergusson et al. (2008) (1) did not measure wantedness of pregnancy, (2) used a comparison group of women who had never been pregnant, (3) used a very small sample of 48, (4) did not control for number of prior abortions or births, and (5) conducted the study in New Zealand. Also, a study by Gilchrist et al. (1995), which stood out for its methodological rigor, concluded that once psychiatric disorders prior to pregnancy were taken into account, the rate of total psychiatric disorder was no higher after termination of an unplanned pregnancy than after childbirth. The most methodologically strong studies showed that interpersonal concerns, including feelings of stigma, perceived need for secrecy, exposure to antiabortion picketing, and the perception or anticipation of low social support for the abortion decision, negatively affected women's postabortion psychological experiences.

Dr. Priscilla Coleman, Associate Professor of Human Development and Family Studies at Bowling Green State University, takes aim at the TFMHA report, asserting that it reflects an extensive, politically motivated bias in the selection of studies reviewed, analysis of the literature, and conclusions drawn. Dr. Coleman contends that bias is evident even in the choice of Task Force members, and she contends that the conclusion drawn in the report does not follow from the literature reviewed.

According to Dr. Coleman, the TFMHA conveniently restricts its review to studies conducted in the United States, thereby eliminating at least 40 studies, including a large Swedish study of 854 women in which rates of negative experiences were considerably higher than in previously published studies using more superficial assessments. Furthermore, Dr. Coleman asserts, the TFMHA fails to highlight methodological strengths of research pointing to adverse psychological effects of abortion. For example, the study by Fergusson et al. (2008) (1) was longitudinal, (2) included comprehensive mental health assessments, (3) had lower estimated abortion concealment rates than previous studies, (4) used a sample representing 80–83 percent of a group of 630 subjects, and (5) used extensive controls. She goes on to state that TFMHA essentially bases the final conclusion of the report on a study by Gilchrist et al. (1995) which has a number of ignored flaws: (1) the response rate is not reported; (2) there are very few controls for confounding variables; (3) the study had a problematically high attrition rate; and (4) no standardized measures of mental health diagnoses were used, and the diagnoses were reported by general physicians, not psychiatrists. Dr. Coleman concludes that the power attributed to cultural stigmatization of women's abortion-related stress is unsupported, as there have been few well-designed studies that support this claim.

YES ⤴   APA Task Force on Mental Health and Abortion (Brenda Major et al.)

Mental Health and Abortion

Executive Summary

The Council of Representatives of the American Psychological Association charged the Task Force on Mental Health and Abortion (TFMHA) with "collecting, examining, and summarizing the scientific research addressing the mental health factors associated with abortion, including the psychological responses following abortion, and producing a report based upon a review of the most current research." In considering the psychological implications of abortion, the TFMHA recognized that abortion encompasses a diversity of experiences. Women obtain abortions for different reasons; at different times of gestation; via differing medical procedures; and within different personal, social, economic, and cultural contexts. All of these may lead to variability in women's psychological reactions following abortion. Consequently, global statements about the psychological impact of abortion on women can be misleading.

The TFMHA evaluated all empirical studies published in English in peer-reviewed journals post-1989 that compared the mental health of women who had an induced abortion to the mental health of comparison groups of women (*N*-50) or that examined factors that predict mental health among women who have had an elective abortion in the United States (*N*-23). This literature was reviewed and evaluated with respect to its ability to address four primary questions: (1) Does abortion cause harm to women's mental health? (2) How prevalent are mental health problems among women in the United States who have had an abortion? (3) What is the relative risk of mental health problems associated with abortion compared to its alternatives (other courses of action that might be taken by a pregnant woman in similar circumstances)? and (4) What predicts individual variation in women's psychological experiences following abortion?

A critical evaluation of the published literature revealed that the majority of studies suffered from methodological problems, often severe in nature. Given the state of the literature, a simple calculation of effect sizes or count of the number of studies that showed an effect in one direction versus another was considered inappropriate. The quality of the evidence that produced those effects must be considered to avoid misleading conclusions. Accordingly, the TFMHA emphasized the studies it judged to be most methodologically rigorous to arrive at its conclusions.

The best scientific evidence published indicates that among adult women who have an *unplanned pregnancy* the relative risk of mental health problems is no greater if they have a single elective first-trimester abortion than if they deliver that pregnancy. The evidence regarding the relative mental health risks associated with multiple abortions is more equivocal. Positive associations observed between multiple abortions and poorer mental health may be linked to co-occurring risks that predispose a woman to both multiple unwanted pregnancies and mental health problems.

The few published studies that examined women's responses following an induced abortion due to fetal abnormality suggest that terminating a wanted pregnancy late in pregnancy due to fetal abnormality appears to be associated with negative psychological reactions equivalent to those experienced by women who miscarry a wanted pregnancy or who experience a stillbirth or death of a newborn, but less than those who deliver a child with life-threatening abnormalities.

The differing patterns of psychological experiences observed among women who terminate an unplanned pregnancy versus those who terminate a planned and wanted pregnancy highlight the importance of taking pregnancy intendedness and wantedness into account when seeking to understand psychological reactions to abortion.

None of the literature reviewed adequately addressed the prevalence of mental health problems among women in the United States who have had an abortion. In general, however, the prevalence of mental health problems observed among women in the United States who had a single, legal, first-trimester abortion for nontherapeutic reasons was consistent with normative rates of comparable mental health problems in the general population of women in the United States.

Nonetheless, it is clear that some women do experience sadness, grief, and feelings of loss following termination of a pregnancy, and some experience clinically significant disorders, including depression and anxiety. However, the TFMHA reviewed no evidence sufficient to support the claim that an observed association between abortion history and mental health was caused by the abortion per se, as opposed to other factors.

This review identified several factors that are predictive of more negative psychological responses following first-trimester abortion among women in the United States. Those factors included perceptions of stigma, need for secrecy, and low or anticipated social support for the abortion decision; a prior history of mental health problems; personality factors such as low self-esteem and use of avoidance and denial coping strategies; and characteristics of the particular pregnancy, including the extent to which the woman wanted and felt committed to it. Across studies, prior mental health emerged as the strongest predictor of postabortion mental health. Many of these same factors also predict negative psychological reactions to other types of stressful life events, including childbirth, and, hence, are not uniquely predictive of psychological responses following abortion.

Well-designed, rigorously conducted scientific research would help disentangle confounding factors and establish relative risks of abortion compared to its alternatives as well as factors associated with variation among women in their responses following abortion. Even so, there is unlikely to be a single definitive research study that will determine the mental health implications of abortion "once and for all" given the diversity and complexity of women and their circumstances. . . .

Summary and Conclusions

The empirical literature on the association between abortion and mental health has been asked to address four primary questions: (1) Does abortion cause harm to women's mental health? (2) How prevalent are mental health problems among women in the United States who have had an abortion? (3) What is the relative risk of mental health problems associated with abortion compared to its alternatives (other courses of action that might be taken by a pregnant woman in similar circumstances)? and (4) What predicts individual variation in women's psychological experiences following abortion? As discussed above, the first question is not scientifically testable from an ethical or practical perspective. The second and third questions obscure the important point that abortion is not a unitary event, but encompasses a diversity of experiences. That said, in the following section we address what the literature reviewed has to say with respect to the last three questions.

The Relative Risks of Abortion Compared to Its Alternatives

The TFMHA identified 50 papers published in peer-reviewed journals between 1990 and 2007 that analyzed empirical data of a quantitative nature on psychological experiences associated with induced abortion, compared to an alternative. These included 10 papers based on secondary analyses of two medical record data sets, 15 papers based on secondary analyses of nine public data sets, 19 papers based on 17 studies conducted for the primary purpose of comparing women who had first-trimester abortions (or an abortion in which the trimester was unspecified) with a comparison group, and 6 studies that compared women's responses following an induced abortion for fetal abnormality to women's responses following other reproductive events. These studies were evaluated with respect to their ability to draw sound conclusions about the relative mental health risks associated with abortion compared to alternative courses of action that can be pursued by a woman facing a similar circumstance (e.g., an unwanted or unintended pregnancy).

A careful evaluation of these studies revealed that the majority suffered from methodological problems, sometimes severely so. Problems of sampling, measurement, design, and analyses cloud interpretation. Abortion was often underreported and underspecified and in the majority of studies, wantedness of pregnancy was not considered. Rarely did research designs include a comparison group that was otherwise equivalent to women who had an elective abortion, impairing the ability to draw conclusions about relative risks. Furthermore, because of the absence of adequate controls for co-occurring risks, including systemic factors (e.g., violence exposure, poverty), prior mental health (including prior substance abuse), and personality (e.g., avoidance coping style), in almost all of these studies, it was impossible to determine whether any observed differences between abortion groups and comparison groups reflected consequences of pregnancy resolution, preexisting differences between groups, or artifacts of methodology. Given this state of the literature, what can be concluded about relative risks from this body of research?

One approach would be to simply calculate effect sizes or count the number of published papers that suggest adverse effects of abortion and those that show no adverse effects (or even positive effects) of abortion when compared to an alternative course of action (e.g., delivery). Although tempting, such approaches would be misleading and irresponsible, given the numerous methodological problems that characterize this literature, the many papers that were based on the same data sets, and the inadequacy of the comparison groups typically used. Given this state of the literature, the TFMHA judged that the best course of action was to base conclusions on the findings of the studies identified as most methodologically rigorous and sound.

Of the studies based on medical records, the most methodologically rigorous studies were conducted in Finland. The largest and strongest of these examined the relative risk of death within a year of end of pregnancy associated with abortion versus delivery (Gissler et al., 2004b). It demonstrated that the relative risk differs depending on how cause of death is coded. Compared to women who delivered, women who had an abortion had lower rates of direct pregnancy-related deaths (cause of death was directly related to or aggravated by the pregnancy or its management, but not from accidental or incidental causes) but higher rates of pregnancy-associated deaths (deaths occurring within one year from end of pregnancy, regardless of whether deaths are pregnancy-related). When therapeutic abortions were excluded from the category of pregnancy-associated deaths, however, this latter difference was not significant. Across both the Medi-Cal and Finland record-based studies, a higher rate of violent death (including accidents, homicide, and suicide) was observed among women who had an abortion compared to women who delivered. This correlational finding is consistent with other evidence indicating that risk for violence is higher in the lives of women who have abortions and underscores the importance of controlling for violence exposure in studies of mental health associated with pregnancy outcome.

With respect to the studies based on secondary analyses of survey data, the conclusions regarding relative risk varied depending on the data set, the approach to the design of the study, the covariates used in analyses, the comparison group selected, and the outcome variables assessed. Analyses of the same data set (the NLSY) with respect to the same outcome variable (depression) revealed that conclusions regarding relative risk differed dramatically depending on the sampling and exclusion criteria applied.

The strongest of the secondary analyses studies was conducted by Fergusson et al. (2006). This study was based on a representative sample of young women in Christchurch, NZ, was longitudinal (although Fergusson also reported concurrent analyses), measured postpregnancy/abortion psychiatric morbidity using established diagnostic categories, and controlled for mental health prior to the pregnancy in prospective analyses. Fergusson et al. compared women who terminated a pregnancy to women who delivered or had not been pregnant. The prospective analyses reported by Fergusson et al. are most informative. These analyses compared number of total psychiatric disorders among women who had an abortion prior to age 21 to number of total psychiatric disorders among women who had delivered a child by age 21 or among women who had never been pregnant by age 21, controlling for pre-pregnancy mental health and other variables that differed initially among the three groups. In these analyses, women who had one or more abortions prior to age 21 had a significantly higher number of total psychiatric disorders by age 25 than women who had delivered or had never been pregnant by age 21. This study thus suggests that women who have one or more abortions at a young age (<21) are at greater relative risk for psychiatric disorder compared to women who deliver a child at a young age or women who do not get pregnant at a young age.

There are several reasons why caution should be used in drawing the above conclusion from this study. First and most importantly, Fergusson et al. (2006) did not assess the *intendedness or wantedness* of the pregnancy. As noted earlier, approximately 90% of pregnancies that are aborted are unintended, compared to only 31% of those that are delivered (Henshaw, 1998). Thus, although these were young women, it is reasonable to assume that at least some of the women in the delivery group were delivering a planned and wanted child. Delivery of a planned and wanted child would be expected to be associated with positive outcomes and is not a viable option for women facing an unintended pregnancy. Second, the other comparison group used by Fergusson et al.—women who had never been pregnant—is not a viable option for women already facing an unintended pregnancy. Third, the prospective analyses were based on only 48 women who had abortions, an extremely small sample. Fourth, the study did not control for number of prior abortions or births. Fifth, the study focused on women who had one or more abortions at a young age (<21 years), limiting its generalizability to younger women; younger age has been linked in some studies to more negative psychological experiences following abortion (e.g., Major et al., 2000). Finally, this study was conducted in New Zealand, a country with more restrictive abortion regulations than those in the United States. Because the focus of APA is on mental health in the United States, it may thus be less useful as a basis for drawing conclusions about relative risks of abortion for US. women.

The TFMHA also reviewed and evaluated 19 papers based on 17 studies conducted tor the primary purpose of comparing women who had first-trimester abortions (or an abortion in which trimester was unspecified) with a comparison group on a mental health relevant variable. These studies varied widely in methodological quality and cultural context. Although most of the studies showed no significant differences between the psychological experiences of women who had an induced first-trimester abortion and women in a variety of comparison groups once important covariates (e.g., marital status, age) were controlled, most also were characterized by methodological deficiencies. These included problems of sampling, measurement, design, analyses, and inappropriate comparison groups. Thus, as a group, these studies also do not provide good answers to questions of relative risk or prevalence.

One study, however, stood out from the rest in terms of its methodological rigor. This study was conducted in the United Kingdom by the Royal College of General Practitioners and the Royal College of Obstetricians and Gynecologists (Gilchrist et al., 1995). It was longitudinal, based on a representative sample, measured postpregnancy/abortion psychiatric morbidity using established diagnostic categories, controlled for mental health prior to the pregnancy as well as other relevant covariates, and compared women who terminated an unplanned pregnancy to women who pursued alternative courses of action. In prospective analyses, Gilchrist et al. compared postpregnancy psychiatric morbidity (stratified by prepregnancy psychiatric status) of four groups of women, all of whom were faced with an unplanned pregnancy: women who obtained abortions, who did not seek abortion, who requested abortion but were denied, and who initially requested abortion but changed their mind. The researchers concluded that once psychiatric disorders prior to the pregnancy were taken into account, the rate of total reported psychiatric disorder was no higher after termination of an unplanned pregnancy than after childbirth.

This study provides high-quality evidence that among women faced with an unplanned pregnancy, the relative risks of psychiatric disorder among women who terminate the pregnancy are no greater than the risks among women who pursue alternative courses of action. What appears to be a discrepancy between the conclusions of this study and those of Fergusson et al. (2006) is likely due to differences in sampling and study design. First and most importantly, Gilchrist et al. (1995) restricted their study to women identified by their family doctor as having an "unplanned" pregnancy, whereas Fergusson et al. did not assess the intendedness of the pregnancy, as noted above.

Consequently, the comparison groups used by Gilchrist et al. are more appropriate for addressing the question of relative risk of negative psychological experiences following elective abortion *compared to other courses of action women in similar circumstances (i.e., facing an unplanned pregnancy) might take.* Second, the Gilchrist et al. study was not restricted to women who became pregnant at a young age; hence the sample is more representative of women who seek abortion. Third, differences in abortion sample size were dramatic. The prospective analyses by Gilchrist et al. were based on an abortion sample of 6,410 women, as compared to 48 in the Fergusson et al. study. Fourth, unlike the study by Fergusson et al., the Gilchrist et al. study controlled for number of prior abortions and births. For these reasons, the TFMHA had more confidence in arriving at conclusions about relative risk based on the findings of Gilchrist et al. Nonetheless, it should be noted that the abortion context in the United Kingdom may differ from that in the United States, weakening generalization to the U.S. context.

The TFMHA reviewed six studies that compared women's responses following an induced abortion for fetal abnormality to women's responses following other reproductive events. These studies were based on extremely small samples often characterized by high attrition rates and low response rates.

Nonetheless, these studies suggest that terminating a wanted pregnancy, especially late in pregnancy, can be associated with negative psychological experiences comparable to those experienced by women who miscarry a wanted pregnancy or experience a stillbirth or death of a newborn, but less severe than those experienced by women who deliver a child with a severe abnormality. At least one study also suggests that the majority of women who make this difficult choice do not regret their decision (e.g., Kersting et al., 2005). As a group, these studies of responses to termination of a wanted pregnancy for fetal abnormality underscore the importance of considering the wantedness of the pregnancy, as well as the reason for and timing of the abortion, in studying its psychological implications. Interpretation of prevalence of psychological distress and relative risk is clouded when researchers lump together under the category of "abortion" women who abort a wanted pregnancy for reasons of fetal anomaly with women who have an elective abortion of an unplanned and unwanted pregnancy.

In summary, although numerous methodological flaws prevent the published literature from providing unequivocal evidence regarding the relative mental health risks associated with abortion per se compared to its alternatives (childbirth of an unplanned pregnancy), in the view of the TFMHA, the best scientific evidence indicates that the relative risk of mental health problems among adult women who have an unplanned pregnancy is no greater if they have an elective first-trimester abortion than if they deliver that pregnancy (Gilchrist et al., 1995).

The evidence regarding the relative mental health risks associated with multiple abortions is more equivocal. One source of inconsistencies in the literature may be methodological, such as differences in sample size or age ranges among samples. Positive associations observed between multiple abortions and poorer mental health (e.g., Harlow et al., 2004) also may be due to co-occurring risks that predispose a woman to both unwanted pregnancies and mental health problems.

Terminating a wanted pregnancy late in pregnancy due to fetal abnormality appears to be associated with negative psychological experiences equivalent to those experienced by women who miscarry a wanted pregnancy or experience a stillbirth or the death of a newborn.

Prevalence of Mental Health Problems Among U.S. Women Who Have an Abortion

A second question this literature has been used to address concerns the prevalence of mental health problems among women in the United States who have had an abortion. As noted at the outset of this report, research capable of adequately addressing this question requires at minimum: (1) a clearly defined, agreed upon, and appropriately measured mental health problem (e.g., a clinically significant disorder, assessed via validated criteria); (2) a sample representative of the population to which one wants to generalize (e.g., women in the United States); and (3) knowledge of the prevalence of the same mental health problem in the general population, equated with the abortion group with respect to potentially confounding factors. None of the studies reviewed met all these criteria and hence provided sound evidence regarding prevalence. Few of the U.S. studies assessed clinically significant disorders with valid and reliable measures or physician diagnosis. In those studies that did use clinically relevant outcome measures, sampling strategies were inadequate to address the question of prevalence in the larger U.S. population either because the samples were biased, highly selected, geographically restricted or failed to use appropriate sampling weights. Furthermore, because of the lack of adequate control for co-occurring risks, the extent to which the incidence of mental health problems associated with abortion was due to the procedure versus to potentially confounding factors, such as poverty, poorer prior mental health, etc., was impossible to establish.

Given these caveats, however, the prevalence of mental health problems observed among women in the United States who had a single, legal, first-trimester abortion for nontherapeutic reasons appeared to be consistent with normative rates of comparable mental health problems in the general population of women in the United States. Consider, for example, the overall prevalence of depression among women in the NLSY, a longitudinal national survey of a cohort of men and women aged 14–21 years in 1979. Among *all* women in the NLSY, irrespective of reproductive history and without controlling for any covariates, 22% met criteria for depression in 1992 (i.e., scored above the clinical cutoff on the CES-D). Among women who reported one abortion, the corresponding percentage was 23%. Among women who reported multiple abortions, however, the percentage was higher; 31% met criteria for depression (see Table). A similar pattern was reported by Harlow et al. (2004) in their study of a representative sample of women in the Boston metropolitan area.

To say that women *in general* do not show an increased incidence of mental health problems following a single abortion, however, does not mean that no women experience such problems. Abortion is an experience often hallmarked by ambivalence and a mix of positive and negative emotions is to be expected (Adler et al., 1990; Dagg, 1991). Some women experience beneficial outcomes, whereas others experience sadness, grief, and feelings of loss following the elective termination of a pregnancy. Some women experience clinically significant outcomes, such as depression or anxiety. However, the TFMHA reviewed no evidence sufficient to support the claim that an observed association between abortion history and a mental health problem was caused by the abortion per se, as opposed to other factors. As observed throughout this report, unwanted pregnancy and abortion are correlated with preexisting conditions (e.g., poverty), life circumstances (e.g., exposure to violence, sexual abuse), problem behaviors (e.g., drug use), and personality characteristics (e.g., avoidance style of coping with negative emotion) that can have profound and long-lasting negative effects on mental health. Differences in prevalence of mental health problems or problem behaviors observed between women who have had an abortion and women who have not may be primarily accounted for by these preexisting and ongoing differences among groups.

Population estimates of proportion of all women and women identified as having been pregnant exceeding CES-D clinical cutoff score, National Longitudinal Survey of Youth: 1992.

Group (N)	CES-D>15
All women (unweighted N = 4401)	22%
No abortion ever	21%
Ever abortion	25%
One abortion	23%
Multiple abortions	31%
All women ever pregnant + (unweighted N = 3503)	23%
No abortion ever	23%
Ever abortion	25%
One abortion	22%
Multiple abortions	31%

Notes: + Includes pregnancies ending in miscarriages.
No covariates are controlled.

Predictors of Individual Variation in Responses Following Abortion

A third issue addressed in the literature on abortion and mental health concerns individual variation in women's psychological experiences following abortion. The TFMHA reviewed 23 papers based on 15 data sets that were based solely on samples of women who had abortions in the United States, but that otherwise met inclusion criteria. These noncomparison group studies typically focused on predictors of individual variation in response. They were of two major types: (1) prospective or concurrent studies that usually included preabortion measures of psychological adjustment and risk factors and one or more postabortion assessments of adjustment and (2) retrospective studies that assessed women's perceived reactions to the event and current level of psychological functioning several years after the abortion. The retrospective studies had serious methodological problems that made interpretation of their findings difficult. The prospective studies, despite limitations of high attrition, geographically limited samples, and potential confounds that were not measured, provided valuable information about sources of variation in individual women's psychological experiences and, to a more limited extent, mental health problems subsequent to abortion.

The most methodologically strong studies in this group showed that interpersonal concerns, including feelings of stigma, perceived need for secrecy, exposure to antiabortion picketing, and low perceived or anticipated social support for the abortion decision, negatively affected women's postabortion psychological experiences. Characteristics of the woman also predicted more negative psychological experiences after first-trimester abortion, including a prior history of mental health problems, personality factors such as low self-esteem and low perceived control over her life, and use of avoidance and denial coping strategies. Feelings of commitment to the pregnancy, ambivalence about the abortion decision, and low perceived ability to cope with the abortion prior to its occurrence also predicted more negative postabortion responses. Across studies, prior mental health emerged as the strongest predictor of postabortion mental health (Major et al., 2000). Type of abortion procedures, at least those used in the first trimester, did not appear to be related to postabortion psychological well-being or mental health.

In considering these risk factors, it is important to recognize that many of the same factors shown to be associated with more negative postabortion psychological experiences also predict more negative reactions to other types of stressful life events, including childbirth (e.g., low perceived social support, low self-esteem, low self-efficacy, avoidance coping). For instance, low perceived social support and low self-esteem also are risk factors for postpartum depression (Beck, 2001; Logsdon & Usui, 2001). Most risk factors are not uniquely predictive of psychological experiences following abortion. Women characterized by one or more such risk factors might be equally (or more) likely to experience negative psychological reactions if they pursued an alternative course of action (motherhood or adoption).

Conclusions and Future Research

Based on our comprehensive review and evaluation of the empirical literature published in peer-reviewed journals since 1989, this Task Force on Mental Health and Abortion concludes that the most methodologically sound research indicates that among women who have a single, legal, first-trimester abortion of an unplanned pregnancy for nontherapeutic reasons, the relative risks of mental health problems are no greater than the risks among women who deliver an unplanned pregnancy. This conclusion is generally consistent with that reached by the first APA task force (Adler et al., 1990).

This report has highlighted the methodological failings that are pervasive in the literature on abortion and mental health. This focus on methodological limitations raises the question of whether empirical science is capable of informing understanding of the mental health implications of and public policy related to abortion. Some policy questions cannot be definitively answered through empirical research because they are not pragmatically or ethically possible.

Other questions, however, are amenable to the methods of well-designed, rigorously conducted scientific research. For example, empirical research can identify those women who might be more or less likely than others to show adverse or positive psychological outcomes following an abortion. Well-designed research can also answer questions of relative risk and prevalence. What would this research look like?

Such research would use methods that are prospective and longitudinal and employ exacting sampling methods (including the use of sampling weights that allow proper generalization back to the populations to whom the conclusions are being applied). Careful attention would be paid to adequately assessing preexisting and co-occurring conditions such as marital status, domestic violence, age, socioeconomic status, parity, prior mental health, and prior problem behaviors as well as other situations that are known to be associated with both differential utilization of abortion and mental health problems. Importantly, comparison groups would be selected so as to be equivalent to the abortion group on all variables other than abortion history. Critical variables such as intendedness and wantedness of the pregnancy would be assessed, and abortion status verified objectively (not only through self-report). Careful use of covariance or similar adjustment techniques (applied to pre-defined covariates) would be employed. Precision of measurement (both in terms of specification of outcome measure and psychometric adequacy of the measurements) would also be guaranteed. Positive psychological responses and experiences as well as negative mental health would be assessed. Repeated assessment of responses over time would be made to assess relevant changes, positive and negative, in the trajectory of responses following abortion. Samples sufficiently large to guarantee adequate power to detect effects that are present would be used, and attention would be paid to effect-size estimation in addition to the simple reliance on null hypothesis statistical testing.

Research that met the above scientific standards would help to disentangle confounding factors and establish relative risks of abortion compared to its alternatives. Even so, there is unlikely to be a single definitive research study that will determine the mental health implications of abortion "once and for all" as there is no "all," given the diversity and complexity of women and their circumstances. Important agendas for future research are to further understand and alleviate the conditions that lead to unwanted pregnancy and abortion and to understand the conditions that shape how women respond to these life events, with the ultimate goal of improving women's lives and well-being.

Priscilla K. Coleman

 **NO**

Critique of the APA Task Force on Abortion and Mental Health

The charge of the APA Task Force on Abortion and Mental Health was to collect, examine, and summarize peer-reviewed research published over the last 17 years pertaining to outcomes associated with abortion.

Evidence described below indicates an extensive, politically motivated bias in the selection of studies, analysis of the literature, and in the conclusions derived by the Task Force. As opposed to bringing light to a complex literature, the misleading report carries enormous potential to hinder scientific understanding of the meaning of abortion in women's lives. The report should be recalled and at a minimum, the conclusion changed. There is sufficient data in the world's published literature to conclude that abortion increases risk of anxiety, depression, substance use, and suicide. At this juncture, the APA cannot be trusted to provide accurate assimilation of information.

Problematic Features of the Report Substantiated in This Critique
The conclusion DOES NOT follow from the literature reviewed
    When comparing reviews of the literature there is selective reporting
    Avoidance of quantification
    Biased selection of Task Force members and possibly reviewers
    Power attributed to cultural stigmatization in women's abortion-related stress is unsupported
    Selection criteria resulted in dozens of studies indicating negative effects being ignored
    Methodologically based selection criteria as opposed to geographic locale should have been employed and consistently applied
    Shifting standards of evaluation of studies presented based on the conclusion's fit with a pro-choice agenda

The Conclusion (in Italics Below) Does Not Follow from the Literature Reviewed

"The best scientific evidence published indicates that among adult women who have an unplanned pregnancy the relative risk of mental health problems is no greater if they have a single elective first-trimester abortion than if they deliver that pregnancy."

From Priscilla K. Coleman (August 13, 2008).

They also note "Rarely did research designs include a comparison group that was otherwise equivalent to women who had an elective abortion, impairing the ability to draw conclusions about relative risks."

They are essentially basing the final conclusion of the entire report on one study by Gilchrist et al. (1995), which has a number of ignored flaws. The three studies that I authored or co-authored with unintended pregnancy delivered as a comparison group indicated that abortion was associated with more mental health problems. A few flaws of the Gilchrist study are highlighted below:

1. The response rate was not even provided.
2. Very few controls for confounding third variables. The comparison groups may very well have differed systematically with regard to income, relationship quality including exposure to domestic violence, social support, and other potentially critical factors.
3. On page 247, the authors report retaining only 34.4% of the termination group and only 43.4% of the group that did not request a termination at the end of the study. The attrition rate is highly problematic as are the differential rates of attrition across the comparison groups. Logically, those traumatized are less likely to continue in a study.
4. No standardized measures for mental health diagnoses were employed and evaluation of the psychological state of patients was reported by general practitioners, not psychiatrists. The GPs were volunteers and no attempt was made to control for selection bias.

When Comparing Reviews of the Literature There Is Selective Reporting

A review of Bradshaw and Slade (2003) in the report ignores this statement from the abstract: "Following discovery of pregnancy and prior to abortion, 40–45% of women experience significant levels of anxiety and around 20% experience significant levels of depressive symptoms. Distress reduces following abortion, but up to around 30% of women are still experiencing emotional problem after a month."

Also ignored from Bradshaw and Slade (2003) is the following: "The proportion of women with high levels of anxiety in the month following abortion ranged from 19% [to] 27%, with 3–9% reporting high levels of depression. The better quality studies suggested that 8–32% of women were experiencing high levels of distress."

Coleman is quoted from a testimony given in South Dakota rather than quoting from the two reviews she has published in prestigious peer-reviewed journals.

There is a claim that other reviews such as those of Coleman and a very strong quantitatively based one by Thorp et al. (2003) are incorporated, but the conclusions of these reviews are avoided entirely.

Avoidance of Quantification

The authors of this report avoid quantification of the numbers of women likely to be adversely affected by abortion. This seems like an odd omission of potentially very useful, summary information. There is consensus among most social and medical science scholars that a minimum of 10% to 30% of women who abort suffer from serious, prolonged negative psychological consequences (Adler et al., 1992; Bradshaw & Slade, 2003; Major & Cozzarelli, 1992; Zolese & Blacker 1992). With nearly 1.3 million U.S. abortions each year in the U.S. (Boonstra et al., 2006), the conservative 10% figure yields approximately 130,000 new cases of mental health problems each year.

In the report, the authors note "Given the state of the literature, a simple calculation of effect sizes or count of the number of studies that showed an effect in one direction versus another was considered inappropriate." What??? Too few studies to quantify, but a sweeping conclusion can be made?

Biased Selection of Task Force Members and Reviewers

No information whatsoever is provided in the report regarding how the Task Force members were selected. What was done to assure that the representatives do not all hold similar ideological biases? What was the process for selecting and securing reviewers? How many were offered the opportunity? Did any decline? How was reviewer feedback incorporated into revising the document? . . . very minimally from this reviewer's vantage point. Disclosure of this information is vital for credibility and accountability purposes.

Power Attributed to Cultural Stigmatization in Women's Abortion-Related Stress Is Unsupported

There are few well-designed studies that have been conducted to support this claim. In fact, many studies indicate that internalized beliefs regarding the humanity of the fetus, moral, religious, and ethical objections to abortion, and feelings of bereavement/loss often distinguish between those who suffer and those who do not (see Coleman et al., 2005 for a review).

Selection Criteria Resulted in Dozens of Studies Indicating Negative Effects Being Ignored

According to the report "The TFMHA evaluated all empirical studies published in English in peer-reviewed journals post-1989 that compared the mental health of women who had an induced abortion to the mental health of comparison groups of women ($N=50$) or that examined factors that predict mental health among women who have had an elective abortion in the United States ($N=23$)."

Note the second type of study is conveniently restricted to the U.S. resulting in elimination of at least 40 studies. As a reviewer, I summarized these and sent them to the APA. There is an insufficient rationale (cultural variation) for exclusively focusing on U.S. studies when it comes to this type of study.

Introduction of this exception allowed the Task Force to ignore studies like a large Swedish study of 854 women one year after an abortion, which incorporated a semi-structured interview methodology requiring 45–75 minutes to administer (Soderberg et al., 1998). Rates of negative experiences were considerably higher than in previously published studies relying on more superficial assessments. Specifically, 50–60% of the women experienced emotional distress of some form (e.g., mild depression, remorse or guilt feelings, a tendency to cry without cause, discomfort upon meeting children), 16.1% experienced serious emotional distress (needing help from a psychiatrist or psychologist or being unable to work because of depression), and 76.1% said that they would not consider abortion again (suggesting indirectly that it was not a very positive experience).

Methodologically Based Selection Criteria as Opposed to Geographic Locale Should Have Been Employed and Consistently Applied

If the Task Force members were interested in providing an evaluation of the strongest evidence, why weren't more stringent criteria employed than simply publication of empirical data related to induced abortion, with at least one mental health measure in peer-reviewed journals in English on U.S. and non-U.S. samples (for one type of study)? Employment of methodological criteria in selection would certainly have simplified the task of evaluation as well. Sample size/characteristics/representativeness, type of design, employment of control techniques, discipline published in, etc. are logical places to begin. I am shocked to not see the development of criteria that reflect knowledge of this literature.

Shifting Standards of Evaluation of Studies Presented Based on the Conclusion's Fit with a Pro-Choice Agenda

There are numerous examples of studies with results suggesting no negative effects of abortion being reviewed less extensively and stringently than studies indicating adverse effects. Further the positive features of the studies suggesting abortion is a benign experience for most women are highlighted while the positive features of the studies revealing adverse outcomes are downplayed or ignored. All the studies showing adverse effects were published in peer-reviewed journals, many in very prestigious journals with low acceptance rates. Clearly then, the studies have many strengths, which outweigh the limitations.

The same standards and criteria are simply not applied uniformly and objectively in the text, and I could literally write pages and pages pointing out examples of this blatantly biased survey of the literature. A few examples are provided below:

a. The Medi-Cal studies are sharply criticized for insufficient controls; however with the use of a large socio-demographically homogeneous sample many differences are likely distributed across the groups. Moreover, the strengths of the study include use of actual claims data (diagnostic codes assigned by trained professionals), which eliminate the problems of simplistic measurement, concealment, recruitment, and retention, which all are serious shortcomings of many post-abortion studies. The authors of the Medi-Cal Studies also removed all cases with previous psychological claims and analyzed data using an extended time frame, with repeated measurements enabling more confidence in the causal question. . . .

b. Results of the Schmiege and Russo (2005) study are presented as a superior revision of the Reardon and Cougle (2002) study, yet none of the criticism that was publicly leveled against the former study on the BMJ website is described. I contributed to this Rapid Response dialogue, and I reiterate a few of my comments here: "The analyses presented in Table 3 of the article do not incorporate controls for variables identified as significant predictors of abortion (higher education and income and smaller family size). These associations between pregnancy outcome and depression are troubling since lower education and income and larger family size predicted depression (see Table 4). Without the controls, the delivery group, which is associated with lower education and income and larger families, will have more depression variance erroneously attributed to pregnancy resolution. Among the unmarried, white women, 30% of those in the abortion group had scores exceeding the clinical cut-off for depression, compared to 16% of the delivery group. Statistical significance is likely to have been achieved with the controls instituted. This group is important to focus on as unmarried, white women represent the segment of the U.S. population obtaining the majority of abortions. Failure to convey the most scientifically defensible information is inexcusable when the data set contains the necessary variables. I strongly urge the authors to run these analyses. Curiously, in all the comparisons throughout the article, the authors neglect to control for family size without any explanation."

c. Fergusson and colleagues' (2006) study had numerous positive methodological features: (1) longitudinal in design, following women over several years; (2) comprehensive mental health assessments employing standardized diagnostic criteria of DSM III-R disorders; (3) considerably lower estimated abortion concealment rates than found in previously published studies; (4) the sample represented between 80% [and] 83% of the original cohort of 630 females; and (5) the study used extensive controls. Variables that were statistically controlled in the primary analyses included maternal education, childhood sexual abuse, physical abuse, child neuroticism, self-esteem, grade point average, child smoking, history of depression, anxiety, and suicidal ideation, living with parents, and living with a partner. Very little discussion in the report is devoted to the positive features of this study and the limitations, which are few compared to most published studies on the topic, are emphasized.

d. Attrition as a methodological weakness is downplayed because the studies with the highest attrition rates (those by Major et al.) are also the ones that provide little evidence of negative effects and are embraced despite attrition as high as 60%. Common sense suggests that those who are most adversely affected are the least likely to want to think about the experience and respond to a questionnaire. Research indicates that women who decline to participate or neglect to provide follow-up data are more likely to be negatively impacted by an abortion than women who continue participating (Soderberg, Anderson, Janzon, & Sjoberg, 1997).

Suffice to say, there is clear evidence of bias in reporting and in keeping with the rather transparent agenda of discrediting studies showing negative effects regardless of their true methodological rigor.

I strongly recommended evaluating only studies that met stringent inclusion criteria and then summarizing the studies in table format in such a way that the reader can quickly note the strengths and limitations of every study in a non-biased manner. Picking and choosing particular criteria from a large assortment of methodological criteria to evaluate various studies is inappropriate, suggestive of bias, and obfuscates the informative literature that is currently available. Lack of uniform application of evaluation standards creates a warped perception of the relative contributions of the studies.

The following quote by the editors of the *Canadian Medical Association Journal* (CMAJ) would have been insightful to the Task Force members as they incorporated feedback and endeavored to produce a report in keeping with their charge of objective assessment: "The abortion debate is so highly charged that a state of respectful listening on either side is almost impossible to achieve. This debate is conducted publicly in religious, ideological and political terms: forms of discourse in which detachment is rare. But we do seem to have the idea in medicine that science offers us a more dispassionate means of analysis. To consider abortion as a health issue, indeed as a medical 'procedure,' is to remove it from metaphysical and moral argument and to place it in a pragmatic realm where one deals in terms such as safety, equity of access, outcomes and risk–benefit ratios, and where the prevailing ethical discourse, when it is evoked, uses secular words like autonomy and patient choice." (CMAJ, 2003. p. 93)

EXPLORING THE ISSUE

Does Research Confirm That Abortion Is a Psychologically Benign Experience?

Critical Thinking and Reflection

1. Reviews of the literature on psychological consequences of abortion, and critiques of these reviews, are labeled by many as politically biased. What steps would you recommend for assembling a task force that would be free from bias on this topic?
2. Imagine that you are a researcher with a large grant to study the psychological experiences of women following abortion. What variables would be especially important to consider in the design of such a study?
3. Imagine that you are a clinician who is consulting with a woman who is considering an elective abortion and asks for reading recommendations on the topic of what she might experience after going through the procedure. What considerations would influence the publications that you recommend?
4. Priscilla K. Coleman criticizes the TFMHA on the basis that the review was restricted to studies conducted in the United States. What are the pros and cons of covering research studies on this topic that were conducted in non-U.S. countries?
5. The TFMHA report contends that negative postabortion psychological experiences are more likely attributable to interpersonal concerns such as feelings of stigma and low perceived or anticipated social support for the abortion decision. How would you go about assessing the extent to which psychological difficulties following abortion are due to concerns about stigma rather than due to emotional distress about the experience itself?

Is There Common Ground?

The issue of abortion has been one of the most hotly debated topics of the past half century and has been addressed from many vantage points, including legal, psychological, medical, political, and human rights perspectives. Political campaigns at all levels of government have been influenced by a candidate's stance on the abortion issue, with vehement assertions on both sides of the debate about the ethics and impact of abortion.

In the field of psychology, a major focus has been placed on understanding the emotional impact of abortion on a woman. Studying this variable is understandably challenging because researchers face the difficult task of inquiring about a very personal issue, and they realize that even asking questions about a woman's attitude about the experience and the psychological impact of abortion can in itself be emotionally provocative. The APA Task Force reviewed research studies published post-1989 in peer-reviewed journals and concluded that for women who have an unplanned pregnancy, the risk of mental health problems is no greater than the risk for women who deliver an unplanned pregnancy. The Task Force was critical of the methodology of some studies that pointed in the other direction. Contesting the conclusions of the Task Force, Dr. Coleman also zeroes in on methodological limitations of the published studies. We can predict that controversy regarding the psychological impact of abortion will not abate. Thus, the door remains open for the development of methodologically rigorous studies to assess the various ways in which women respond psychologically to abortion.

Additional Resources

Afterarbortion.com. Retrieved from www.afteraborton.com

American Psychological Association. Retrieved from www.apa.org

Bazelon, E. (2007, January 21). Is there a post-abortion syndrome? *New York Times Magazine, 40–47,* 62, 66, 70.

Charles, V. E., Polis, C. B., Sridhara, S. K., & Blum, R. W. (2008). Abortion and long-term mental health outcomes: A systematic review of the evidence. *Contraception, 79,* 436–450.

Coyle, C. T., Coleman, P. K., & Rue, V. M. (2010). Preabortion counseling and decision conflict as predictors of subsequent relationship difficulties and psychological stress in men and women. *Traumatology, 16,* 16–30.

Fergusson, D. M., Horwood, L. J., & Boden, J. M. (2008). Abortion and mental health disorders: Evidence from a 30-year longitudinal study. *British Journal of Psychiatry, 193,* 444–451.

Gilchrist, A., Hannaford, P., Frank, P. & Kay, C. (1995). Termination of pregnancy and psychiatric morbidity. The British Journal of Psychiatry, 167(2), 243–248.

Grote, N. K., & Bledsoe, S. (2007). Predicting postpartum depressive symptoms in new mothers: The role of optimism and stress frequency during pregnancy. *Health and Social Work, 32,* 107–118.

Hess, R. F. (2006). Postabortion research: Methodological and ethical issues. *Qualitative Health Research, 16,* 580–587.

Kimport, K., Foster, K., & Weitz, T. A. (2011). Social sources of women's emotional difficulty after abortion: Lessons from women's abortion narratives. *Perspectives on Sexual and Reproductive Health, 43*(2), 103–109.

Macleod, C. (2011). *"Adolescence," pregnancy and abortion: Constructing a threat of degeneration.* New York, NY: Routledge/Taylor & Francis Group.

MacNair, R. M. (2008). Understanding how killing traumatizes the killer. In R. M. MacNair & S. Zunes (Eds.), *Consistently opposing killing: From abortion to assisted suicide, the death penalty, and war* (pp. 39–46). Westport, CT: Praeger Publishers/Greenwood Publishing Group.

Major, B., Appelbaum, M., Beckman, L., Dutton, M., Russo, N., & West, C. (2009). Abortion and mental health: Evaluating the evidence. *American Psychologist, 64*(9), 863–890. doi:10.1037/a0017497.

National Abortion Foundation. Retrieved from www.prochoice.org/about_abortion/myths/post_abortion_syndrome.html

Pedersen, W. (2008). Abortion and depression: A population-based longitudinal study of young women. *Scandinavian Journal of Public Health, 36,* 424–428.

Russo, N. (2008). Understanding emotional responses after abortion. In J. C. Chrisler, C. Golden, & P. D. Rozee (Eds.), *Lectures on the psychology of women* (4th ed.) (pp. 173–189). New York, NY: McGraw-Hill.

Sit, D., Rothschild, A. J., Creinin, M. D., Hanusa, B. H., & Wisner, K. L. (2007). Psychiatric outcomes following medical and surgical abortion. *Human Reproduction, 22,* 878–884.

Steinberg, J., & Russo, N. F. (2008). Abortion and anxiety: What's the relationship? *Social Science and Medicine, 67,* 238–252.

Wright, A. A., & Katz, I. T. (2006). Roe versus reality—Abortion and women's mental health. *The New England Journal of Medicine, 355*(1), 1–9.

ISSUE 13

Should Individuals with Anorexia Nervosa Have the Right to Refuse Life-sustaining Treatment?

YES: Campbell, A.T., and Aulisio, M.P. (2012), from "The Stigma of 'Mental' Illness: End Stage Anorexia and Treatment Refusal," *International Journal of Eating Disorders*. {in press}

NO: Tan, J.O., Stewart, A., Fitzpatrick, R., and Hope, T. (2010), from "Attitudes of Patients with Anorexia Nervosa to Compulsory Treatment and Coercion," *International Journal of Law and Psychiatry, 33*, 13–19.

Learning Outcomes

After reading this issue, you should be able to:

- Critically evaluate the criteria that should be involved in declaring a person as mentally competent to make decisions regarding treatment.
- Discuss the impact of severe anorexia nervosa on a person's cognitive functioning and ability to make informed decisions about treatment.
- Consider the extent to which the concept of *stigma* applies to compulsory treatment for a life-threatening condition.
- Debate whether respect for an individual's decision to refuse life-sustaining intervention represents a form of assisted suicide.
- Discuss the role of society, particularly the legal system, in defining limits on a person's autonomy regarding the right to refuse treatment.

ISSUE SUMMARY

YES: Dr. Campbell and Dr. Aulisio argue that anorexia patients should be allowed to refuse treatment so long as they are competent and capable of understanding the implications of their actions.

NO: Drs. Tan, Stewart, Fitzpatrick, and Hope assert that anorexia nervosa profoundly affects individuals with this condition in a variety of ways which could make them incompetent.

Health practitioners have long debated the ethics of treating individuals against their will. When an individual engages in behavior that may lead to self-harm, and possible death, it is assumed that professionals have an obligation to intervene. In the case of suicidal behavior, most would support hospitalization, with or without the person's consent. However, consider instances in which the individual may lack the competence to evaluate the extent to which a behavior is life-threatening, or instances in which the individual may reject medical assistance, regardless of medical recommendations. Some people with severe anorexia nervosa fall into this category.

Anorexia nervosa occurs in two forms: restricting type and binge eating/purging type. People with anorexia nervosa refuse to maintain body weight at or above minimally normal weight for their age and height; they have an intense fear of gaining weight or becoming fat, even though they are underweight; they have disturbances in the way they experience body weight, or their self-evaluation is unduly influenced by body weight or shape, or they deny the seriousness of their deficient weight; and for females beyond puberty, they miss at least three consecutive menstrual cycles. For some, the medical problems that result from malnutrition, binging, and purging are so extreme that they result in death.

It is unclear whether a person in the throes of malnutrition can make a competent decision about feeding and nutrition, even though this individual seems to demonstrate competence in other areas of life. Professionals trying to treat such individuals face an ethical dilemma about a "duty to protect." In other words, they confront decisions about whether to take actions to protect a patient, regardless of the patient's preference to be left to his or her own choices.

Some health professionals treating patients who refuse life-sustaining treatment question whether permitting the patient autonomy regarding this decision is actually a form of "assisted suicide." In other words, health professionals who step aside in an effort to respect the patient's freedom of choice regarding death might be seen as colluding in a decision made by people who may not be competent to understand their medical/psychiatric condition, realize the consequences of their choice, or come to a rational decision.

The issue of coercive intervention in the fields of medicine and psychiatry is complex and continuously evolving. For example, the practice of commitment to a psychiatric institution is an emergency procedure for the involuntary hospitalization of a person who, if not hospitalized, is deemed likely to create harm to self or other people as a result of mental illness. The government vests in various professionals such as psychologists and physicians the authority to protect individuals who are deemed incapable of protecting themselves. The law also recognizes and respects the individual's right to refuse treatment if the individual is deemed competent to make a rational choice. In the case of severe anorexia nervosa in which malnutrition may impair cognitive functioning, how can a decision be made between protecting the patient from death on the one hand, and respecting the individual's autonomy on the other hand?

Drs. Campbell and Aulisio build their argument for autonomous choice on well-established laws that support the right of competent adults to refuse treatment, including life-sustaining treatment. For example, it is widely accepted that a terminally ill patient has the right to refuse medical care and opt instead for comfort care such as that provided by hospice. In parallel fashion, some individuals with chronic anorexia nervosa have developed what might be viewed as intractable psychiatric conditions such as potentially lethal potassium imbalance resulting from severe and chronic anorexia. For what might be viewed as an "end stage psychiatric disorder" these authors question what the conditions are, if any, under which an individual might legally and ethically choose to refuse further treatment, and opt instead for comfort care.

According to Drs. Campbell and Aulisio, the argument for autonomous decision making regarding such self-determination rests on an assessment of the individual's mental capacity to make such a decision. This capacity assessment should evaluate the individual's ability to (1) understand the information provided, (2) appreciate the consequences of the decision, (3) reason through the information to make a decision, and (4) communicate this choice. These authors criticize the presumption of incapacity for persons with psychiatric illness, or the view that they are so vulnerable that they need to be overprotected. They argue that capacity should be presumed, and respected, for all patients, no matter the diagnosis, to the fullest extent possible, and this should not stop at the psychiatric diagnosis or the life-sustaining door. They raise the possibility that there may be a psychiatric disorder for which all has been tried and which has truly entered an "end stage-like" state for the sufferer. These individuals may be at a point of saying "enough," and should be respected for their wish for comfort care rather than unwanted medical intervention.

Dr. Tan and her colleagues present arguments justifying compulsory treatment and coercion for individuals with severe anorexia nervosa. They base their arguments on a qualitative interview study of 29 young women who generally supported the use of compulsory and coercive intervention where the condition was life-threatening. Dr. Tan and her colleagues define *compulsion* as a restriction or removal of free choice with regard to treatment; *formal compulsion* as involving legal treatment orders; and *coercion* as indicating a negative perception of a loss of choice or freedom.

The participants in this study agreed that overriding treatment refusal by employing compulsion, including formal compulsory treatment if required, is necessary in order to save life. Many participants spoke about how they had resisted or disagreed with treatment under compulsion at the time, but were grateful for it in hindsight. Although Dr. Tan and her colleagues make an argument that compulsory treatment should be used to save a life, they note that there is less consensus concerning the use of compulsory measures for the treatment of anorexia nervosa in the absence of immediate risk to life. They also address the notion of "perceived coercion" in which some psychiatric patients experience coercion even if legal means are not. For example, a patient may be "encouraged" to behave in a certain way in response to a threat of the use of more formal coercion or the loss of some benefit. Although the use of such leverage can be an effective and flexible way of enabling acceptance of treatment while avoiding the stigma and trauma of formal legal compulsion, there are concerns about the ethics of such an approach.

YES

**Amy T. Campbell and
Mark P. Aulisio**

The Stigma of "Mental" Illness: End Stage Anorexia and Treatment Refusal

Introduction

It is well-settled law that competent adults have the right to refuse treatment, including life-sustaining treatment.[1, 2] Too, persons with mental health conditions should not be automatically presumed incompetent. Although their status might cause one to question decision-making capacity, there is typically a presumption of competence and a more functional versus global determination of one's capacity to make decisions, including health care decisions.[3] Moreover, most would agree that an individual or surrogate may refuse life sustaining treatments in favor of comfort care when well-accepted terminal dignoses are given such as end stage metastatic lung cancer; however, what if the diagnosis is primarily driven by an intractable psychiatric condition such as a potentially lethal potassium imbalance which is a direct result of severe, chronic, and intractable anorexia? That is, is there such a thing as an "end stage psychiatric disorder" and if so, what are the conditions, if any, under which an individual might be able to legally and ethically choose to refuse further treatment for this disorder and opt for comfort care?[I]

In this article, we explore these issues through analysis of two cases that draw out key considerations related to capacity and end-of-life decision making in the patient with anorexia. We consider the rights of competent persons to refuse treatment, even life-sustaining treatment, the ability of persons with psychiatric disorders to make decisions about treatment, and whether for the latter this too can include refusals of life-sustaining treatment and the accessing of comfort care (e.g., palliative or hospice care). We end with recommended next steps to support development of a framework to guide systematic analysis of issues raised by this article.

Grounding the Issues: Anorexia Case Studies[II]

Eating disorders are among the most intractable, and potentially life threatening, of all psychiatric disorders.[4, 5] As with other psychiatric disorders, there is a continuum of severity and chronicity among eating disorder sufferers, with some facing the illness for decades. It is this latter population—the most chronic—who typically also face the most serious physical repercussions (e.g., cardiac arrhythmia) of the disorder, as might be expected. Unfortunately, for anorexia in particular, evidence for effective interventions is generally weak.[6]

The complex interrelationship of the mental and the physical in eating disorders raises a host of important ethical, legal, and psychiatric questions. Our focus here is to question if patients with these disorders, specifically anorexia, might ever be able to refuse aggressive treatment where such refusal is likely to end in death.

"Alison"

Alison was a 55-year-old female patient with 40+year history of anorexia. She had no history of suicide attempts. Alison had been to several eating disorders programs across the nation for intensive multimonth treatment, with numerous recent medical admissions and/or emergency room (ER) visits. She has also been on several antidepressant and anti-anxiety medications, but an underlying personality disorder complicated treatment.

In the past year, Alison experienced significant weight loss; however, she refused to be admitted to an inpatient eating disorder unit. At every outpatient visit, a capacity evaluation was performed, and Alison was found to be competent. As part of this assessment, she was found to be alert, able to process information (critical given concerns related to hypoglycemia and an electrolyte imbalance), and able to engage in conversation. Others in the clinic, who would see her on occasion, also attested to her capacity. Throughout this time, she repeatedly expressed her understanding that her low potassium could cause death as she was choosing not to treat it.

During her most recent hospitalization, she signed herself out against medical advice, telling the team she "does not want to do this anymore." For years, she had expressed a deep desire to get better, but now said that all medical treatment attempts had failed her. Her treating team was in agreement with the decision after Alison's primary care physician confirmed the years of treatment of Alison's disorder, countless treatment attempts, and repeated capacity assessments—including confirmation she was not clinically depressed at that time. Referral to hospice was made to assist with end of life care. Her immediate family was supportive of this decision; however, Alison's psychiatrist was resistant to this shift, viewing acquiescence to Alison's wishes as paramount to assisting a "suicide." After prodding, he did agree however to supply a letter to the hospice director indicating that Alison was capable of making this decision and that he could not think of any other treatment options at this point.

"Emily"

Emily was a 40-year-old female with a 25+year history of anorexia nervosa. Emily had a long history of psychiatry involvement and had attended several treatment centers. She was given the diagnoses of "failure to thrive" a few days before the ethics consultation and was discharged home to receive hospice care. Emily stated that she wanted to live and that she understood what was needed to improve her condition; however, she also stated that she was not willing to take those steps. At the time of the consult request, Emily was deemed to have decision-making capacity.

The central issue in the case was deemed to be Emily's ability to make decisions for herself, i.e., her decisional capacity and her understanding of her options and consequences of a decision to refuse aggressive treatment in favor of hospice. It was agreed that provided she had decisional capacity Emily should be allowed to refuse hospice or any other medical interventions. Ultimately, Emily was deemed to have capacity and, therefore, to be capable of exercising a right to refuse aggressive treatment in favor of comfort measures.

General Decision-Making Authority

Informed Consent and the Right to Refuse Treatment

Creating an Obligation to Obtain informed Consent.

Law and ethics have evolved to support a competent individual's right to decide the course of her treatment. This arose in law from tort concepts, which view treatment without consent as an unlawful touching (battery).[7] Over time, this legal understanding became more nuanced, and connected to an emerging ethical vision, wherein true consent must be informed. Essentially, this means that certain pieces of information (e.g., diagnosis and prognosis, proposed treatment, alternatives, risks, and benefits of all) should be discussed to ensure consent is legally, and ethically, valid.[8] Ethically, we may say that this supports an individual's right to self-determination, and respects her autonomy to make treatment decisions that fit within her larger vision of her life plan and values. We presume adults are capable of making informed decisions. If clinical facts make clear that the patient has capacity to make decisions and the patient is adequately informed, she gets to decide. Moreover, an individual does not lack capacity simply because that person is believed to be making a mistake or a "bad decision."

Capacity Assessment Briefly.

The process of information disclosure and sharing might reveal concerns about the ability of the individual to make reasoned choices. In this event, capacity assessments can and should be made, particularly as the risks of certain decisions rises. When a patient's capacity to make a decision is of concern, a clinician will look to the individual's ability to understand the information that was shared, appreciate her situation and consequences of any decisions made, reason through the information to make a decision, and then communicate this choice.[9] If the criteria are met, the decision rests with that patient. (This does not obviate the fact that patients often consult with providers and family members to help make decisions.) The default is that a patient can, with information, consent to treatment and also refuse that treatment. That is, if someone has the right of informed consent, for it to be meaningful, that should include a right of informed refusal.

Does the Right to Refuse Treatment Also Extend to the Right to Refuse Life-Sustaining Treatment?

Law and ethics also support an individual's right to refuse life-sustaining treatment.[1, 2] That is, decisional authority of competent individuals extends to a decision to stop aggressive treatment. Although we clinically might wish to set a higher capacity bar for these decisions, fundamentally, we support reasoned decisions of such nature. This might be seen as the ultimate example of one determining one's own life course. Too, surrogates can make these decisions for individuals who have lost capacity, or potentially have never even been competent.[1, 10, 11] While debate over assisted suicide and futility legislation raise new and vexing issues, these core considerations are fairly well-settled for persons with physical disorders.

What about, however, persons with psychiatric disorders? There is some literature expressing the importance of end of life planning for patients with a psychiatric disorder.[12, 13] To our knowledge, however, there is little to help clinicians analyze these issues when the primary diagnosis driving a treatment refusal decision is a psychiatric one.[14–16] Before we consider decision-making authority in the context of end of life care, it may be helpful to step back to the more general issues around a psychiatric patient's decision-making authority (and its limits).

Decision-Making Authority When Capacity Is a Potential Issue

Informed Consent and the Right to Refuse Treatment for the Person with a Psychiatric Disorder

Clinical and ethical insights suggest that we should not simply presume incapacity for persons with psychiatric illness.[3] While law may be more black/white vis-à-vis "competence," it too is accepting of shades of gray to the extent that it supports psychiatric patients' decision making in some regards, for example, a potential right to refuse certain treatments even when involuntarily committed.[17] Of course, a psychiatric disorder may be evidence to suggest a reason to question someone's capacity, particularly as the stakes of the decision rise. For end of life decision making, in particular, there is hesitance to appear to be complicit in a patient's "suicide." Yet, as in all ethical decision making, context, here, should matter.

Psychiatric Disorders and Life-Sustaining Treatment

Do Persons with Psychiatric Disorders Ever Get to Make Decisions to Refuse (Further) Life-Sustaining Treatment?

There is little to be found explicitly addressing rights of persons with serious mental disorders to refuse life-sustaining treatments. Yet, depression is recognized as having potential impact on a patient's decision to refuse life-sustaining treatment and may impact a team's willingness to acquiesce to a patient's wishes. Numerous studies illustrate ways to mitigate the impact of depression or other capacity-decreasing impairments to allow for patient decision making,[18, 19] or even support clinician decision making when patients lack capacity.[20] Thus, in the literature and from anecdotal experience, there are many instances when those with a psychiatric condition, albeit most commonly described as secondary to an underlying physical condition, may decide, or have a surrogate decide, to withdraw or withhold life-sustaining treatment. This potentially opens the door to allowing persons with serious mental illnesses to make certain end-of-life decisions: the issue becomes how wide the door should be opened and by whom.

Why Might We Worry About This? The Pendulum Swings Between Abuse and Victimhood.

History of Abuse and Legal Response.   Much has been written about the history of abuse in psychiatry in the United States and elsewhere.[21] For centuries, persons with psychiatric disorders have been segregated, their individual rights usurped, and their conditions labeled in stigmatizing ways[21, 22]—even by leading authoritative bodies like the U.S. Supreme Court.[23] During the latter part of the 20th century, however, as abuses came to light,[24] and medical advancements led to greater understanding of psychiatric disorders,[25] the experience of abuse and stigma lessened a bit with a medicalization of mental disorder. (This shift has its own weaknesses, but is beyond the scope of this paper.) When joined with a disability rights discourse—within a climate of "rights" movements—this led to historic legislative accomplishments advancing the interests of persons with psychiatric disorders.[26, 27]

And yet, the "abuse" narrative that has painted persons with psychiatric disorders as vulnerable persists and today ironically may lead to potential overprotection by the law, at least as interpreted, applied, or "felt" by these individuals, irrespective of evidence of the many capacities of these persons to the contrary.[28] Researchers may overemphasize vulnerability and thus disallow participation in certain studies or seek surrogate (vs. individual) decision-making authority.[29] Clinicians may see the mental health diagnosis as subsuming all clinical encounters, potentially limiting an ability to listen to the consumer's nonmental diagnosis related concerns.[30] Beyond health care, courts may siphon cases into special problem-solving courts specifically for persons with mental health issues, potentially creating psychiatric disorder as a "separate class" of offender with its own set of penalties.[31]

History, therefore, has encrusted in legal and social institutions a mindset of mind/body dualism, wherein mental health continues to exist within its own silo.[32] Emblematic of this dualism are arguments over mental health insurance parity. Rather than frame the issue more broadly as what and how insurance should cover "health" conditions, policymakers grapple with how to fashion a "mental health benefit" in a similar manner (e.g., what is covered and reimbursed) as one would a "physical health" benefit.

Why Might We Challenge a "Stigma" Defense? Mind/Body Dualism and Mental Health Exceptionalism.

A regime of "separate but equal" often falls down on the latter point (i.e., equal). More fundamentally, the former (i.e., separate) belies the reality that the mind and body are integrally connected. Studies increasingly show how so-called physical health conditions (e.g., diabetes) may lead to psychiatric ailments (e.g., depression). In addition, the literature highlights co-morbidities associated with mental health conditions[33-35] and includes examples of how patients may somatize disorders or how serious illness may bring with it emotional consequences.[36, 37] This leads us to question whether one can be truly "well" without an integrated state of mind/body connection and stability.

The past few years have witnessed a push toward integrated medicine to break down the boundaries between physical and mental health.[30,38] Although primary care has been a focus of these efforts,[38] integrated thinking is called for at the end of life as well. That is, rather than focus on what sort of disorder is "primary" driver of the "end stage" situation, with subsequent silo'ing of psychiatric disorders, our cases suggest we would do better to integrate our thinking and approach—to worry less about the primary diagnosis and more about the context of decision making and the supports needed as tied to end of life planning. Diagnosis is not meaningless, but it should not create artificial boundaries that lead to disparate treatment. Contextual sensitivity should be our chosen approach whether the disorder originally derived in the kidney, stomach, heart, or brain. Often, the ultimate effects of the disorder transcend the mind/body distinction; so, too, should our ethical analysis and decision making.

Unfortunately, dualism contributes to a state of mental health exceptionalism: A psychiatric label separates one's situation into an entirely separate class. Thus, do we have the psychiatric hospital/unit, the mental health insurance benefit, and the mental health court. Thus, may we see patients under or overtreated. The latter suggests some persons with psychiatric disorders may be burdened with too much treatment at the end of life. In turn, this idea leads us to ask whether there is such a thing as a psychiatric disorder for which all has been tried and which has truly entered a "end stage-like" state for the psychiatric sufferer: Is there ever a "rational" decision to refuse further treatment of an eating disorder (as distinguished from arguments over a "rational suicide"[39]). Our cases consider these points, and after ethical reflection, posit there just might be.

So Might We Allow Some Decisions Even When About Life-Sustaining Treatment?

How.   If we accept, as we do, that persons with mental health concerns do not always lack global competence to make decisions, and also recognize that this means that at certain times, these persons may hold capacity to make treatment decisions, we suggest that these decisions should include, as they do with all other patients, potential life-sustaining treatment decisions. Of course, as with all patients, we would still want to assess capacity. This could involve querying individuals to walk us through their understanding of the benefits and burdens of different treatment options, their perspective on their quality of life, and why they might now be saying "enough."[14, 15] And yes, this also involves to some extent recognizing that at some level suffering of the mind might be as real and painful as that of the physical body. Critically, however, we argue that capacity should be presumed—and respected—for all patients, no matter the diagnosis, to the fullest extent possible (i.e., unless obviously incapacitated, e.g., in a coma, profoundly cognitively impaired); and this should not stop at the psychiatric diagnosis or life-sustaining treatment door.

When.   As part of this, we should also consider where the patient is within a historical context of the disorder. That is, a new diagnosis or few attempts at treatment might lead us to query the patient's true capacity. However, as we recognize that certain minors might have capacity built from years of experience with a disorder to make decisions given their experience-built maturity,[40] so too should we also consider that a history of chronic treatment attempt and relapse might result in a much greater understanding of the benefits and burdens of an experience of an eating disorder that milder, earlier course, or non-eating disordered patients might simply not understand. In sum, we argue it is critical to recognize that decisions are made within a patient's life context—one that may involve years of experience that informs a rich perspective that should not be lightly brushed aside to project a health care professional's decision on a (potentially) capable-in-context patient.

Procedural Safeguards.   Of course, this does not mean that it is unreasonable to query a bit more the person with an eating disorder, all the more so if the given treatment refusal integrally connects with that disorder (e.g., a refusal of food), and if such decisions have life-or-death implications. Our proposals on this topic are not blind to the concerns over possible "suicidal" ideation masking as a treatment decision, or a delusional or incapacitated type of decision. We simply ask that a sliding scale approach to capacity assessment be used as it is with other patients, whereas also recognizing that the bar may justifiably be a bit higher (or scrutinized perhaps a bit more closely or procedurally more slowly) for decisions by persons with psychiatric disorders, especially those with life consequences. A balance should be sought that respects individual decision making and abilities, but also recognizes the legacy of discrimination against persons with mental health disorders. Thus, assessments should build in certain "safeguards" to test capacity in contextual ways[15]; however, such safeguards should not set the bar so high that all requests to stop life-sustaining treatment be seen as suicide requests for psychiatric patients, whereas (often) reasonable requests for (most) others.

Anorexia Nervosa and Refusal of Life-Sustaining Treatment

Our Cases

Ethical Analysis.
Ethical analysis is in many ways primarily a guide to clinical decision making in complex situations. As analytic guide, clinical ethics follows a fairly consistent pattern: review of facts and the range of clinical options available, meeting with key players, consideration of ethical approaches (e.g., principles) to frame

decision making, and recommendations (but not ultimate decision-making authority).[41-43] Applying this approach to our cases, we see a long history of chronic eating disorder, multiple treatment attempts, and failures, a feeling among treatment providers that there were no good treatment options left, and a general consensus that the patient in each case had at least had some capacity to make certain critical decisions.

Consider our approach if we stepped back and removed the primary-psychiatric disorder status: If we had a patient with assessed capacity, a limited ability to treat, highly burdensome treatment options, notable suffering, and likely death within months (if not weeks) with no treatment, a discussion of shifting to palliative care only would seem likely, and ethically sound. The critical element, thus, in our cases, was the primary psychiatric disorder designation driving the discussion (vs. a cancer patient who also happens to have depression). That is, the crux of the ethical analysis in these two cases hinged on whether end of life care was appropriate, and at a broader philosophical level, the nature of suffering and possibility of end stage psychiatric illness.

Applying a Framework for End of Life Decision-Making to "Alison" and "Emily."

A standard framework for end of life decision making, however well-established, cannot be applied to any case without careful attention to the context in which the case emerges. The context for both Alison and Emily was not one in which the patients were new and relatively unknown to care providers; nor was it one in which patients—early in their eating disorder trajectory and with limited treatment to date—were asking to be left to die. To the contrary, both Alison and Emily were well-known to care providers and had received an exhaustive battery of treatment interventions with only modest success over a period of many years. In addition, each patient suffered from severe sequelae secondary to their eating disorders (e.g., kidney failure).

Given the intractable and chronic history of the disorder and the physical condition of each, Alison and Emily could plausibly said to have a severe life-threatening illness. Thus, context helped paint a full picture of the integrated mental/physical status of each patient, and potential capacity with the facts given for each to decide that treatment was no longer working. Within this context, as one might for any patient facing such a dilemma, a shift to end of life planning might fully be appropriate—clinically, ethically, and legally.[16] Importantly, there was no search for a magic number (e.g., number of times hospitalized, number of years with disorder, number of medications tried, or the expected number of days until death); rather, the totality of circumstances and treatment history, and abilities of each respective patient to make decisions within such, helped guide the analysis.

In Broader Context: An "End Stage" Eating Disorder?

In both of our cases, there was reluctance, especially among the psychiatrists, to consider an eating disorder as conceivably "end stage." On the one hand, taken in a more limited sense, the term referred to the clinical picture wherein all that could be thought of had been tried, often on multiple occasions and in different combinations (e.g., psychotherapy, medication, and hospitalization). Both clinical teams, including the psychiatrists, felt there were no good treatment options left. But for the psychiatric diagnosis, this would have been an obvious time to engage more fully in end of life planning: so why does that psychiatric diagnosis matter, and should it?

As explicated during a conversation with R. W. Pies, MD, on July 22, 2010, we recognize the concern raised by different understandings of labeling a disorder as "end stage": What should we make of a distinction between cases where the pathological progression inexorably leads to death no matter what treatment is tried versus those situations, closer to our own, where "we have tried all we can think of doing." For a psychiatric disorder, the suffering is often internalized—and science is seen as being able to stop a physical decline. The taboo (legally and ethically) around "suicide," and physician complicity in such, further complicates the matter. Few physicians want to see their patients die because there is little they can do; when that death comes at the hand of something so mysterious as a disorder marked by restricted eating (where treatment could forcibly feed someone and keep him/her alive), it is much more difficult a transition.

We contend that rather than blanket condemnation or acceptance, it would be good to see more nuanced and reflective consideration of the possibility of end stage psychiatric disorder (more specifically here, eating disorder) on a case-by-case basis. That is, is there ever a time when medical (psychiatric) treatment has done pretty much all it can (at this time)?[16] Is mental suffering any less real than physical (and are the two all that separate)? We leave it to others to debate if there is such a thing as a "rational suicide"; we ask merely if there is such a thing as a rational treatment refusal decision in a psychiatric patient for what appears to be an intractable psychiatric illness.

In our cases, we concluded that each represented an "end stage eating disorder" (even if not termed such). Critical to the decision was the context: decades of treatment, a wide range of treatment option attempts with little success, physical decline, and repeated clinical assessments of capacity for decision making with ethical consultation (akin to earlier discussion of procedural safeguards). We are not dissuaded from this course by "slippery slope" arguments that this creates a new class of end stage illness. Certainly, it is right to question any hint of abandonment of the "difficult patient" by moving too quickly to acquiesce to a patient's wish to be left to die. Frustration or a knee-jerk allegiance to "rights" discourse should not lead us blindly to accept blanket pronouncements about when/how psychiatric disorders may be labeled end stage.

We also recognize that to focus on the weakened physical state (and likelihood of irreversible organ damage)—which was emphasized by certain clinicians in both of our cases—as driving the decision making potentially reinforces an approach grounded in mind/body dualism. One may rightly question whether decades of psychic suffering are any less real than a physical sort (e.g., from cancer or amyotrophic lateral sclerosis (ALS)). It is outside the context of this article to look at the issues more broadly and address the rights of those with psychiatric disorders to avail themselves of "death with dignity" laws, but we do consider such questions critical for review to better globally approach the nature of suffering, and its integrated mind/ body aspects.[III]

Ultimately, although cognizant of such preceding caveats, when limited to our presenting case facts and context, we were convinced that end of life planning including hospice and comfort care measures was the clinically, ethically, and legally appropriate path for Alison and Emily.

Discussion

In sum, we believe that the hesitancy among many—especially psychiatric professionals—to support certain individual psychiatric-driven life-sustaining treatment decision making potentially perpetuates the stigma directed toward persons with psychiatric disorders as well as the historical tendency to see the mind as distinct from the body. Rather than reinforce (even implicitly) stigma or mind/body dualism from which it partially stems, we would argue that health care professionals more holistically address persons with a long-standing history of psychiatric struggle, and be contextually sensitive to the range of decision-making abilities—and targets of those decisions (e.g., extension to end of life decisions).

Just as the ethical consultation in both cases aimed to educate providers about the potential ethical propriety of considering an eating disorder case to be "end stage," we hope that this article provides food for thought for other providers in similar situations in the future to ethically analyze each case to consider whether it too might be appropriate for a shift to comfort care. Especially for psychiatrists, we recommend fuller contemplation of the limits of medicine, the nature of suffering, and the potentiality that a patient with an eating disorder may at some point make a rational decision to end aggressive treatment (which we very much distinguish from suicide).

Our analytic, process-oriented (question generating) framework would start first with case facts, and then use capacity assessment wherein cognitive and emotional understandings are gauged. We would urge that health care professionals recognize capacity may extend to life-sustaining treatment decisions, even extending to when the life-threatening condition is brought about by the underlying psychiatric disorder. We would situate this in an ethics-driven process over a legalistic (check the boxes/more proscriptive) approach. Although we may not be able to create good judgment via a process, we can use this framework to enhance ability of clinicians to more sensitively address needs and wishes of all patients, regardless of diagnosis; that is, we can make it easier to exercise good judgment via framing questions and a more systematic process. Moreover, we would encourage our law partners to create space for this more nuanced approach. Too, we encourage policymakers to consider the consequences of policy decisions that create rights and obligations around end of life planning and access to palliative and hospice services, and how such policies might enhance, or at least not frustrate, equivalent access among persons with psychiatric disorders such as our patients.

And so, our call is not so much for a new model of care than an expansion of the model of end of life care and palliative care to include patients with psychiatric-driven disorders, and an expansion of the model of integrated primary physical/behavioral health to end of life care. That is, capacity assessment processes and the decisions to which they apply should not maintain false dichotomies between the physical and the mental. Blurring the boundaries might make decisions less clear-cut, but life is complex. And patients with psychiatric disorders deserve no less (or more).

Notes

I. We also recognize that perhaps a more common concern with psychiatric illness would be the boundaries of surrogate decision making; future work will explore this set of issues more fully. Our current paper focuses on patients who are clinically deemed as having capacity, at least for some decisions. We also do not focus in this article on the specific issues related to access to palliative care for this population of patients, but recognize this too is worthy of future investigation.

II. The two cases are based on real-world cases confronted by the authors, but modified to remove identifying information and also for authors' purposes for their use: to ground the paper's discussion (vs. use as exhaustive case reports).

III. A forthcoming paper will apply the preceding analysis to how arguably a surrogate might be able to make life-sustaining treatment decisions were the psychiatric patient assessed as lacking (most) treatment decision making. For our purposes here, we posit that a best interest test that looks to benefits and burdens and likelihood of treatment success could conceivably, at times, lean in favor of discontinuing treatment. We recognize the importance, too, of education among psychiatrists, palliative care specialists, and hospice providers to facilitate palliative care and "comfort only" care among this population. Although not our given focus here, full discussion of these issues in the future is warranted.

References

1. Cruzan v. Director, Missouri Department of Health, 110 S. Ct. 2841, 1990.

2. Meisel A. The legal consensus about forgoing life-sustaining treatment: Its status and its prospects. Kennedy Inst Ethics J 1992;2:309–345.

3. Ganzini L, Volicer L, Nelson WA, Fox E, Derse AR. Ten myths about decision-making capacity. J Am Med Dir Assoc 2005;6(Suppl 3):S100–S104.

4. Kaye W. Eating disorders: Hope despite mortal risk. Am J Psychiatry 2009;166:1309–1311.

5. Berkman ND, Lohr KN, Bulik CM. Outcomes of eating disorders: A systematic review of the literature. Int J Eat Disord 2007;40:293–309.

6. Bulik CM, Berkman ND, Brownley KA, Sedway JA, Lohr KN. Anorexia nervosa treatment: A systematic review of randomized controlled trials. Int J Eat Disord 2007;40:310–320.

7. Schloendorff v. Society of New York Hospital, 211 N. Y. 125, 1914 (establishing the legal basis for patients to consent to healthcare treatment, reasoning that without consent, treatment would constitute a Tort).

8. Meisel A. Roth LH, Lidz CW. Toward a model of the legal doctrine of informed consent. Am J Psychiatry 1977;134:285–289.

9. Appelbaum PS, Grisso T. Assessing patients' capacities to consent to treatment. N Engl J Med 1988;319:1635–1638.

10. Superintendent of Belchertown State School v. Saikewicz, 370 N.E.2d 417, 1977.

11. Annas GJ. Reconciling Quinlan and Saikewicz: Decision making for the terminally ill incompetent. Am J Law Med 1979;4:367–396.

12. Foti ME. "Do it your way": A demonstration project on end-of-life care for persons with serious mental illness. J Palliat Med 2003;6:661–669.

13. Foti ME, Bartels SJ, Merriman MP, Fletcher KE, Van Citters AD. Medical advance care planning for persons with serious mental illness. Psychiatr Serv 2005;56:576–584.

14. Draper H. Anorexia nervosa and respecting a refusal of life-prolonging therapy: A limited justification. Bioethics 2000;14:120–133.

15. Gans M, Gunn WB. End stage anorexia nervosa: Criteria for competence to refuse treatment. Int J Law Psychiatry 2003;26:677–695.

16. Lopez A, Yager J. Feinstein RE. Medical futility and psychiatry: Palliative care and hospice are as a last resort in the treatment of refractory anorexia nervosa. Int J Eat Disord 2010;43:372–377.

17. Rivers V. Katz 67, N.Y.2d 485, 1986 (extending the right to refuse treatment and make medical decisions to persons who are mentally ill and involuntarily committed).

18. Sullivan MD, Younger SJ. Depression, competence, and the right to refuse lifesaving medical treatment. Am J Psychiatry 1994;151:971–978.

19. Ganzini L, Lee MA, Heintz RT, Bloom JD, Fenn DS. The effect of depression treatment on elderly patients' preferences for life-sustaining medical therapy. Am J Psychiatry 1994;151:1631–1636.

20. White DB. Curtis JR, Lo B, Luce JM. Decisions to limit life-sustaining treatment for critically ill patients who lack both decision-making capacity and surrogate decision-makers. Crit Care Med 2006;34:2053–2059.

21. Whitaker R. Mad in America: Bad Science, Bad Medicine, and the Enduring Mistreatment of the Mentally Ill. New York: Basic Books, 2010.

22. Fink PJ, Tasman A, editors. Stigma and Mental Illness. Washington, DC: American Psychiatric Press, 1992.

23. Buck v. Bell, 274 U.S. 200, 1927 ("It is better for all the world, if instead of waiting to execute degenerate offspring for crime, or to let them starve for their imbecility, society can prevent those who are manifestly unfit from continuing their kind.").

24. Moreno JD. Regulation of research on the decisionally impaired: History and gaps in the current regulatory system. J Health Care Law Policy 1998;1:1–21.

25. Shorter E. A History of Psychiatry: From the Era of the Asylum to the Age of Prozac. Hoboken: Wiley, 1997.

26. Americans with Disabilities Act. Americans with Disabilities Act (ADA) of 2010, 42 USCA Section 12101, 2010.

27. Olmstead v. L.C. ex rel. Zimring, 527 U.S. 581, 1999.

28. Winick BJ. The MacArthur treatment competence study: Legal and therapeutic implications. Psychol Public Pol L 1996;2:137–166.

29. Dunn LB, Candilis PJ, Roberts LW. Emerging empirical evidence on the ethics of schizophrenia research. Schizophr Bull 2006;32:47–68.

30. Boardman JB. Health access and integration for adults with serious and persistent mental illness. Fam Syst Health 2006;24:3–18.

31. Erickson SK, Campbell A, Lamberti JS. Variations in mental health courts: Challenges, opportunities, and a call for caution. Community Ment Health J 2006;42:335–344.

32. Corrigan PW, Markowitz FE, Watson AC. Structural levels of mental illness stigma and discrimination. Schizophr Bull 2004;30:481–191.

33. Carney CP, Jones LE. Medical comorbidity in women and men with bipolar disorders: A population-based controlled study. Psychosom Med 2006;68:684–691.

34. Carney CP, Jones L, Woolson RF. Medical comorbidity in women and men with schizophrenia: A population-based controlled study. J Gen Intern Med 2006;21:1133–1137.

35. Felker B, Yazel JJ. Short D. Mortality and medical comorbidity among psychiatric patients: A review. Psychiatr Serv 1996;47:1356–1363.

36. Ford CV. The somatizing disorders. Psychosomatics 1986;27:327–337.

37. Juergens MC, Seekatz B, Moosdorf RG, Petrie KJ, Riel W. Illness beliefs before cardiac surgery predict disability, quality of life, and depression 3 months later. J Psychosomatic Res 2010;68:553–560.

38. Blount A. Integrated primary care: Organizing the evidence. Fam Syst Health 2003;21:121–133.

39. Leeman CP, Distinguishing among irrational suicide and other forms of hastened death: Implications for clinical practice. Psychosomatics 2009;50:185–191.

40. Freyer DR. Care of the dying adolescent: Special considerations. Pediatrics 2004;113:381–388.

41. Aulisio MP, Arnold RM, Younger SJ. Ethics Consultation: From Theory to Practice. Baltimore: Johns Hopkins University Press, 2003.

42. Jonsen AR, Siegler M, Winslade WJ. Clinical Ethics: Approach to Ethical Decisions in Clinical Medicine, 4th ed. New York: McGraw-Hill, Inc., 1998.

43. Fletcher JC, Lombardo PA, Marshall MF, Miller FJ, editors. Introduction to Clinical Ethics, 2nd ed. Hagerstown: University Publishing Group, 1997.

Jacinta O.A. Tan, Anne Stewart,
Raymond Fitzpatrick, and Tony Hope

 **NO**

Attitudes of Patients with Anorexia Nervosa to Compulsory Treatment and Coercion

Background

Anorexia nervosa is a mental disorder which often leads to serious risk of physical harm or even death to the individual, through self-imposed dietary or other behavioural strategies aimed at losing weight and self harm (Harris & Barraclough, 1997, 1998). However, there is controversy over whether compulsory treatment for anorexia nervosa is appropriate (Draper, 2000; Giordano, 2003; Tiller, Schmidt, & Treasure, 1993).

Compulsion is not solely achieved through legal measures. Some mental health professionals use not only formal legal powers to compel patients to have treatment, but also the threat of legal orders or other powers as 'leverage' to obtain agreement to treatment (Appelbaum & Redlich, 2006; Carney, Tait, Richardson, & Touyz, 2008; Carney, Wakefield, Tait, & Touyz, 2006). In cases where patients are legal minors, it is common to use other means of compulsion such as parental consent (Ayton, Keen, & Lask, 2009). Psychiatric patients' perceptions of coercion are complex and not directly correlated with the use of compulsory legal orders (Bindman et al., 2005; Rajkumar, Saravanan, & Jacob, 2006; Salize & Dressing, 2005; Watson, Bowers, & Andersen, 2000). One study found that patients with anorexia nervosa experience high levels of 'perceived coercion'—that is, the perception that they are being coerced whether or not formal mechanisms are used. Some of these patients changed their views in hindsight about the coercion that they had received (Guarda et al., 2007). Most research in this area has focussed on using quantitative measures of perception of coercion. There have been few in-depth studies exploring the views of patients who suffer or have suffered from anorexia nervosa, about their experiences of coercion and compulsory treatment.

Tan, Jacina; Stewart, Anne; Fitzpatrick, Raymond; Hope, Tony. From *International Journal of Law and Psychiatry,* January/February 2010, pp. 13–19. Copyright © 2010 by Elsevier Health Sciences. Reprinted by permission via Rightslink.

Method

A qualitative interview study was carried out to determine the views of people with anorexia nervosa as well as their parents with respect to compulsory treatment, treatment decision-making and competence. In this article we report the patient participants' views concerning compulsory treatment.

The qualitative interviews were semi-structured and the interview was conducted using a topic guide, which served as a springboard for wider, more flexible and unstructured narratives and discussions. Participants were asked to talk about their own experiences of treatment, and the interviewer encouraged elaboration of experiences relating to the three main foci of the study given above. Questions in the topic guide relating specifically to compulsory treatment are listed in Box 1. As will be seen the questions ask about whether it is acceptable to 'make people have treatment' or 'to be treated even if they don't agree.' The concept of coercion and compulsory treatment was thus left to participants to interpret as they saw fit and was not defined in terms of legal processes.

Box 1

EXCERPT FROM TOPIC GUIDE FOR PATIENT PARTICIPANTS

Attitudes to use of compulsion

1. *Attitudes to compulsory treatment of any kind*—Do you think it's ever acceptable to make people have treatment when they don't want it or agree to it?
2. *Attitudes to compulsory treatment of mental disorders in general*—Do you think people with mental illnesses like schizophrenia should, under some circumstances, be treated even if they don't agree with the treatment? Why?
3. *Attitudes to compulsory treatment of anorexia nervosa in particular*—Do you think there are some circumstances under which people with anorexia nervosa should be treated even if they don't agree with the treatment? If so, what are these circumstances?
- *when is it justified?*
- *when is it effective?*

The interviews were audio-taped and transcribed, with names and places removed. The coding framework categorising the broad issues discussed in the interviews was developed through repeated readings of the transcripts, followed by trials of application to transcripts and discussions between two coders who coded some transcripts independently. Each transcript was then coded using the final coding framework. Common emergent themes as well as divergent themes within each category of the frame were further analysed. The N6 qualitative software programme was used to assist the coding process and collation of themes and subthemes (QSR International, 2005).

Participants

Twenty-nine patients with current or recent anorexia nervosa were recruited from four different treatment centres in southern England, which covered a range of characteristics: private and National Health Service, adolescent and adult treatment services, specialist eating disorder centres and general mental health units. The patients' ages ranged from 15 years 10 months to 26 years 2 months (median 17 years 0 months, mean 18 years 1 month). Note that in England the age of legal majority is 18 years, which is also usually the age at which patients move from adolescent to adult mental health services. Although one of the treatment centres did allow goals of 'maintenance' for certain adult patients not yet ready to accept treatment, for all the participants in this study the treatment from the mental health services consisted of a combination of a weight restoration as well as psychological therapies. Agreement to treatment therefore meant accepting both weight restoration and psychological treatment.

Patient records were not accessed, so all information was obtained from the participants themselves. Participants' self-reported Body Mass Indices (BMI) ranged from 12.4 (dangerously underweight) to 28.4 (overweight, technically 'pre-obese'), with a mean body mass index of 17.7 (below normal range) and a median BMI of 17.65. By their own accounts, the participants were at various stages of illness, treatment and recovery at the time of interview.

Of the 29 participants, eight were inpatients in mental health units although at the time of interview none was detained under the Mental Health Act 1983.[1] Eighteen participants were either day patients or outpatients utilising mental health services at the time of interview. One participant was waiting to have treatment. One participant had been discharged by the eating disorder service after declining an offer of inpatient treatment for low weight. One participant had chosen not to accept treatment as she had a previous aversive experience of inpatient treatment.

Of the eight inpatient participants, five described themselves as having been admitted without free choice, either owing to parental pressure or under the implied or overt threat from the meatal health professionals of a Mental Health Act 1983 'section' (compulsory detention order for the purposes of assessment or treatment) if they did not comply. Two of these had subsequently been placed on a Mental Health Act 1983 Section 3 (a compulsory detention order for treatment of a mental disorder) during the course of their admission and both had been recently discharged from the Section 3 order at the time of interview. One of these two patients had also experienced being detained using the Mental Health Act 1983 during a previous admission. Only three of the eight inpatients, therefore, described themselves as having made a free choice to be admitted to hospital for the current admission, and one of these three participants described a previous inpatient admission to a different unit to which she had not given consent.

Only three of the 18 day patient and outpatient participants said they had made a choice to enter and remain in treatment on their own. Six participants described being coerced into having treatment against their will. A further nine described either shared decisions concerning treatment made together with doctors and parents (with varying degrees of pressure from professionals and parents ranging from encouragement to ultimatums), or decisions about treatment made by doctors and relatives on their behalves with their tacit agreement. It is important to note that the Mental Health Act 1983 did not enable compulsory outpatient or day patient treatment, so no formal compulsory treatment under mental health legislation would have been possible.

Only two out of the 29 participants (6.9%) had ever experienced formal compulsory treatment, both under the Mental Health Act 1983; but 15 of the 29 participants (51.7%) gave accounts of having experienced loss of freedom of choice regarding treatment either during their current treatment or in the past. Types of loss of freedom of choice included 'leverage' in the form of threats (overt or implied) of compulsory admission, other types of compulsion such as parental consent for treatment, or restriction of choices such as only being allowed to choose between types of treatment (for example, inpatient or outpatient) but not whether to have treatment. These figures are consistent with the published literature. This literature shows that a relatively low proportion of inpatients with anorexia nervosa are placed on formal compulsory treatment orders, with reports ranging from 9% to 28% (Carney et al., 2008; Ramsay, Ward, Treasure, & Russell, 1999; Royal College of Psychiatrists, 1992; Watson et al., 2000). A user survey, however, suggests that a much higher proportion of patients perceive a lack of choice regarding treatment (Newton, Robinson, & Hartley, 1993), and some studies suggest that 'leverage' is commonly used by psychiatrists with a significant minority of psychiatric patients in order to increase compliance with treatment without resorting to legal compulsion (Appelbaum & Redlich, 2006; Bindman et al., 2005).

Results

Experiences of Compulsion in 'Voluntary' Treatment

In this article, we will use the term 'compulsion' to indicate a restriction or removal of free choice with regard to having treatment; 'formal compulsion' to indicate compulsion using legal treatment orders; and 'coercion' to indicate a negative perception of a loss of choice or freedom. Participants described many pressures to accept 'voluntary' treatment without the use of legal powers and experienced these as restricting their freedom of choice with regard to treatment. Box 2 gives four examples.

Box 2

EXPERIENCES OF COMPULSION IN 'VOLUNTARY' TREATMENT

My dad was very heavily involved and V and Dr. P have been involved in it quite a lot, (3 seconds) but (4 seconds) I mean I came, technically I came in here voluntarily, and technically I suppose it was my decision . . . but it doesn't always feel like that when there's a lot of pressure and a lot of guilt, that's played a big part in it. And personally I was just left feeling that . . . . there really was no other choice.

Continued

I was meant to go as an inpatient at the P [adolescent general psychiatric unit] about two years ago, but I didn't want to, and so I did the treatment at home. And I didn't really think I had a choice [about whether to have treatment], looking back on it now I think: 'Well, why didn't I just not eat?' And I didn't want to, but I still did it because I thought I didn't have a choice. So in a way that was sort of forced upon me, I didn't want to get better then.

Well, I was given two options really. Either I refused, and they said 'if you refuse to put on weight we're taking you straight up to the hospital and you're on tubes and drips and everything and, you know, you're going to have to gain weight or, and you'll be made an inpatient.' So they said they'd put me in a hospital first to get me up [in weight], just on kind of whatever and then I'd become an in-patient. And, or I was an outpatient but I gained weight. So I chose the outpatient version because if I went, if I had to become an inpatient I would be in there for five or six months, they told me, with the amount of weight gain I had to have. And I wouldn't want to be in a mental institution for six months, that sounds kind of incredibly depressing to me.

I was desperate, I didn't want to do it, I did want a way out but I also didn't, if you know what I mean. It comforted, it made me feel *disgusting* but it comforted me in a way, and so I didn't want to give it up and the only reason that I came to X [adolescent treatment centre] was because they said that if I didn't come voluntarily I'd be Sectioned and I didn't want that on my record.

Attitudes to the Use of Formal Compulsion for Mental Disorders

All participants thought that formal compulsory treatment under the Mental Health Act 1983 was justified for some individuals. Indeed, participants thought that mentally disordered patients, for example those with schizophrenia, have a right to be treated, compulsorily if necessary, in order to protect themselves and others from harm. Participants viewed such compulsion as supportive and helpful. Many participants justified such compulsory treatment in terms of the effect of mental disorders in limiting the ability to understand and decide on the need to have treatment (see Box 3).

Box 3

ATTITUDES TO THE USE OF FORMAL COMPULSORY TREATMENT IN MENTAL DISORDERS

I don't know much about schizophrenia, but like I said, if they're a danger to themselves or other people or even sometimes if they're living alone. Then yeah, I'd say they need support, they need help.

I suppose in a way, yes, if it's going to cause harm to someone else. So schizophrenia, if they're causing, yeah if they're going to cause harm to other people then yes, I think it's right that you know like: murder, death, which you do hear about, so at that stage yes I think we should be [treating them against their will], and I suppose if they are really at risk of death to themselves.

I suppose a *mental* disorder though, the thing is they might have a mental problem which is screwing up their view of whether they need it or not, they have it, like in anorexia. So physically they do need it.

I think that when one is in the hands of mental illness and there are times when you're aware you're thinking in ways which really aren't natural to you, there are moments, I think, of lucidity when you crave for help and I don't see that a schizophrenic is any less needy [of help] in those terms.

Attitudes to the Use of Compulsion in Anorexia Nervosa in Order to Save Life

With respect to anorexia nervosa, the participants all agreed that overriding treatment refusal using compulsion, including formal compulsory treatment (e.g. under the Mental health Act 1983) if required, was necessary in order to save life (See Box 4). This was generally seen as self-evidently the right thing to do because no one should be allowed to die from the consequences of having anorexia nervosa. This view was often based on personal experiences of compulsion and risk to self. Many participants spoke about how they had resisted or disagreed with treatment under compulsion at the time, but were grateful for it in hindsight.

Some participants considered that informal compulsion from professionals and families was also acceptable to save life. The central reason that participants gave to justify compulsory treatment was that no one should die from a treatable disorder as such a death would be a waste of life. Several participants also argued that the acceptance of a high risk of death was not usually the true or fixed view of people with anorexia nervosa but rather a result of the disorder. Furthermore, at the extremely low weights and poor physical condition where people are at risk of death, participants felt that patients suffering from anorexia nervosa are unable to make their own decisions. Participants saw saving patients' lives as having the effect of saving them to think about accepting treatment another day. In these dire circumstances, the views of patients were thought to be suspect or even irrelevant, as the disorder would be dominant and would be driving the wishes and behaviour of the person with respect to treatment.

Participants did not universally view 'leverage' and other non-legal forms of restriction of choice as negative or unethical; indeed, formal compulsion through legal means was generally seen as a worse option than these more informal means of compulsion. There was a view that being placed on a compulsory detention order would be highly stigmatizing and would affect their future, particularly with regard to their careers (see last quotes in Boxes 2 and 4). Some participants also had a perception of greater restriction with formal compulsory treatment orders, mainly through the perceived losses of personal freedom and the ability to negotiate terms of their treatment.

Box 4

ATTITUDES TO THE USE OF COMPULSION IN ANOREXIA NERVOSA

Justification for Formal Compulsory Treatment Is to Save Life

I meant the taking charge, is when basically when someone's at the point where they just collapse and you need to put them on drips and that sort taking charge. But I mean I don't think with anorexia there's going to be any other point where you really need to completely take charge with them. 16P

I think if somebody's life is in danger and is threatened and they have to go into hospital then yes it's very important to obviously re-feed them and to get them to a stage where they're not, where they're medically stable, but you can't enter anybody into treatment if they're not willing to. 36P

Approval of the Use of Compulsion (with Gratitude in Hindsight)

I think other people should be made to have treatment because you do get to the point where you don't know what's right for you. I know last year when I was ill there was no way I would have let anybody do anything to treat me, like for my own choice I would have just carried on losing weight, I know I would have done until I didn't live anymore, but now I hate to think that just because I said 'no' I would have been left. 30P

If I had been left without somebody forcing treatment upon me I would have just starved myself to death. So, you know, I wouldn't have got to my target weight and got happy and have things that I'll have in the future. 21P

So then although when I was back there [i.e., very ill] I'd say 'no, that's a stupid idea,' now being *here* I look back on it, I think 'hell yeah, you can't *not* treat someone who's going to die because they're starving themselves.' 20P

Need for Compulsion Because of Inability to Make Decisions

I suppose if you just let people carry on losing weight then they can die of a heart attack, and they might in the future have wanted to get better; so you've got to, if people are in danger, you've got to get them to that stage where they want to get better. 19P

I think ultimately beating anorexia has to be a decision that you make yourself. But if your health is so bad that you're dying or you're at risk of very, very severe illness, then I think you should be treated until you can make the decision. Because I think if you're ill enough you can't make that kind of decision. 22P

Perceptions of Mental Health Act 1983 Treatment Orders

I don't really know what a [Mental Health Act 1983] Section 3 entails. I mean for me I thought it was, well for one, it makes you look mental. And it doesn't look good when you're looking for a job, on your CV, and it's written down, you were on Section 3 or I've had you know and it plays an effect on going abroad I think, someone said to me. So I don't really know a lot about it but I mean if that's what's going to happen for this poor girl or, or boy of, you know 11, 12, 13, 14, 15, 16, 17, that's really horrible. They don't want that put on their lives at such a young age. So if that entails the parents [use of parental consent] I would definitely go with the parents' point of view. 18P

Attitudes to the Use of Compulsion in Anorexia Nervosa in Order to Treat the Disorder

In contrast with the universally held view that formal compulsion through legal procedures was justified to save life, there was a spectrum of views concerning the use of compulsion to treat the disorder itself (see Box 4). Two participants felt that formal compulsory treatment could be useful in an early stage because the disorder would be relatively easy to treat and timely treatment could prevent a great deal of future suffering. The general view, however, was that formal compulsory treatment in the absence of life-threatening illness was neither desirable nor helpful in terms of achieving true recovery. The arguments against the use of compulsory treatment were both its inefficacy and unfeasibility. Most participants thought that going through treatment and achieving recovery required some degree of consent and cooperation from the person herself. Indeed, there was a commonly held view that the inappropriate use of compulsion could be harmful in itself.

Participants' views about the use of informal means of compulsion, coercion and pressure to comply with treatment were more complex. Many participants held the view that people with anorexia can become less able to make treatment decisions because of four distinct problems: a sense of anorexia nervosa being a part of their personal identity, the issue of control and loss of control, changes in values due to the disorder itself, and difficulties and thinking about the risks involved. This result validates the findings of a previous smaller study reported elsewhere (Tan, Hope, & Stewart, 2003a,b; Tan, Hope, Stewart, & Fitzpatrick, 2003c; Tan, Hope, Stewart, & Fitzpatrick, 2006). These issues provide grounds for doctors and nurses to use some pressure or restriction of choice in order to deal with refusal or reluctance to engage with treatment. Participants also described how the context and relationships within which treatment decisions were made were crucial to the participants' perceptions of compulsion or choice. This is taken up in the next section.

The Context of Treatment Decisions and How They Affect the Experience of Compulsion

A major emergent set of themes concerned context and relationships. Having freedom of choice was often less important to participants than their relationships with, and the attitudes of, those around them and treating them. Many described decisions made on the basis of trust and good relationships rather than on the basis of the elements highlighted by most theoretical, clinical and legal descriptions of capacity such as understanding treatment information, retaining it, reasoning and weighing it up, and communicating a choice (Grisso & Appelbaum, 1998; Roth, Meisel, & Lidz, 1977).[2]

Some participants who had not been given free choice did not appear to resent their experiences nor perceive them as coercive. Instead, they viewed the strong influence, pressure, supervision or restrictions imposed by parents and professionals as helpful, caring and supportive (see Box 5). In some cases, this was to the extent that they felt it would be inappropriate for parents or professionals to place the sole responsibility of making a decision on the patient herself.

Some participants did resent the supervision and restrictions imposed on them and viewed these restrictions as having been unhelpful in the process of recovery (see Box 6). For these participants the key reason for this resentment and sense of coercion was the feeling that they had been dismissed,

---

Box 5

EXPERIENCE OF THE RESTRICTIONS OF CHOICE IN TREATMENT AS HELPFUL AND SUPPORTIVE

I think it [the treatment] is really good, really appropriate for me, anyway. I think they're quite good at getting the balance between giving you responsibility and freedom without giving you too much. (Laughs) Giving you more than you can cope with. Like they don't sort of, the freedom they give you doesn't jeopardise your recovery, it sort of makes it more bearable. 19P

Do, you need help, you need treatment, you need to come into a place where you can get extra support, extra external help, you need to hand over the controls because you're not in control anymore, it deludes you in thinking you are in control but you have to, that's where you have to stand back or somebody else has to stand back for you and say look you are not in control, it is completely controlling you. 36P

---

belittled, or punitively treated in the process of receiving treatment rather than the nature and extent of the restrictions themselves. These participants described feelings of being stripped of their individuality and having had their wishes ignored within overly restrictive regimes which felt inappropriate to their requirements for consultation or personal choice.

The participants' relationships with parents and professionals emerged as an important factor in decision-making. To some participants, the issue central to the decision was not whether treatment was perceived by them as being the best course, but whether they were able to trust their parents and professionals enough to overcome their own ambivalence and reservations. It was also their relationships with these people that helped them to decide to engage with and

Box 6

EXPERIENCE OF THE RESTRICTIONS OF CHOICE IN TREATMENT AS UNHELPFUL AND COERCIVE

If I refuse some food because I just don't want it, everyone's thinking 'oh she's not having that, why is she not having that, she should be having that!' and then the feeling of being watched over; and [I would like them instead to be] kind of letting me get on with it myself, but knowing that I could go and talk to them and it wouldn't affect them, they wouldn't suddenly run round and say 'have this, do this, do that!' but at the same time it's being able to speak to someone and to say to me 'yes, you know you can,' that's good. 26P

And also that's something I find it very hard to talk about, it's very hard to just say [to the psychiatrist] you know 'well actually, you know, you've pushed me too far and I'm now throwing up after every meal.' I mean you can't really say that to someone, it's very hard to say that, you know. And also I reckon that obviously if I did say that, I just didn't want to just have to think about the restrictions that would then be placed on me. I'd just be even more restricted. But you know I wouldn't have been pushed to that [i.e., becoming bulimic] if I'd been given more choice about [how slowly I gained weight] perhaps you know, because I was gaining weight, it wasn't as if there was an issue with me gaining weight, I was just doing it more slowly. And I was doing it in a way that I was comfortable with. 16P

---

accept treatment, which was often restrictive in terms of diet plans, regimentation of their lives and strict supervision (see Box 7). Two participants stated how they decided to have treatment not because they wished to recover, but because having anorexia nervosa was causing their parents distress.

Participants described how a poor relationship with either parents or professionals resulted more from punitive, dismissive or disrespectful behaviour and failure to listen carefully and respectfully to their feelings and wishes, than from

---

Box 7

TRUST AND RELATIONSHIPS AND THEIR IMPACT ON ACCEPTANCE OF RESTRICTIONS OF CHOICE

I mean trust was definitely the *key* issue with me. Because if you don't trust your doctors or you don't trust your parents to be doing what they think is best, then you're not going to do it. So yeah, I think that I had

Continued

good doctors, because they really understood. And they all, it was always sort of, from my, it didn't feel like they were all ganging against me, it felt like they were coming from my point of view. Which made it much easier to trust them. And, yeah, I feel, I feel that it's been done well. 14P

I think that (3 seconds) again from just a very personal point of view I know that there was a time when I *couldn't* eat enough to make me live or whatever and therefore I had, I was put in a position where I still accepted although I resisted, but where I was told I had to, black or white. I think physically you reach a stage where yes, you need that, psychologically it can be quite damaging. But I do think that in the most extreme initial phases, that yes, maybe it [i.e., use of compulsion] is necessary but always, *always* listening and even when a patient resists to listen to why they are resisting, not to assume you know why they are resisting. Because then that's how you best help them. 24P

---

compulsion or the restriction of choice itself (see Box 6). However, several voiced the opinion that it was better for compulsion to be exerted by professionals than by parents; as parental coercion could result in resentment and damaged personal relationships. Compulsion from professionals, by contrast, was perceived as part of the professionals' job even when participants did not agree with it.

Discussion

Whatever their views about the use of compulsion in anorexia nervosa in general, or on issues of competence and capacity, all participants thought that it is right to impose treatment in order to save life. No participant supported the view that it is right to allow a person with anorexia nervosa to die as a result of respecting their refusal of treatment.

A concept that is receiving increasing research attention is that of 'perceived coercion' (Bindman et al., 2005; Guarda et al., 2007). This is the idea that psychiatric patients often experience coercion whether or not formal legal means are used. Such coercion includes 'leverage' when a patient may be 'encouraged' to behave in a certain way through a threat of the use of more formal coercion or the loss of some benefit (Appelbaum & Redlich, 2006). The participants in this study described such perceived coercion. Indeed their experience of formal legal compulsion was much less frequent than that of other forms of compulsion.

The participants' frequent accounts of experiences of lack of choice and the use of leverage are ethically problematic when contrasted with the relative infrequency of legal compulsion they experienced. On the one hand, the use of leverage can be an effective and flexible way of enabling acceptance of treatment while avoiding the stigmatizing and potentially traumatic experience of formal legal compulsion, and may not be experienced negatively; on the other hand, the use of leverage and other non-legal forms of coercion leave already vulnerable patients at risk of unethical treatment and loss of autonomy and rights without the protection of legal procedure, advocacy and right of appeal that formal legal compulsion brings. It has been argued that it is unethical and discriminatory towards those with mental disorders to use any form of coercion or act in a patient's best interests without consent unless he or she clearly lacks capacity (Szmukler, 2001); and furthermore, that coercion is counterproductive in anorexia nervosa (Rathner, 1998). Studies suggest that patient perception of 'coercion' or experience of formal legal compulsion is not subsequently associated with a poorer engagement with treatment or poorer therapeutic relationship with mental health professionals (Ayton et al., 2009; Bindman et al., 2005; Greenberg, Mazar, Brom, & Barer, 2005). The limited research also does not clearly show that formal compulsory treatment is associated with poorer short or longer term clinical outcome (Ayton et al., 2009; Carney et al., 2008; Ramsay et al., 1999; Watson et al., 2000). Even if there is no clinical harm, however, the issue of compulsion in treatment for anorexia nervosa is still ethically problematic. From the ethical point of view, a traditional stance is that patient autonomy should be respected even if unwise or foolish decisions are made, and the justification for acting in a patient's best interests instead of according to his or her wishes is the pivotal issue of capacity (Buchanan & Brock, 1989).

What is striking from this study is that the issue of capacity was not the central one for participants in the context of compulsory treatment. It is true that many participants did view treatment refusal by people with anorexia nervosa as problematic because the anorexia compromises decision-making. But this was not the main issue in their consideration of the rights and wrongs of compulsion. The main issues centred on their relationships with those involved in the treatment: health professionals and sometimes parents. The participants did not appear to resent leverage or 'informal' compulsion if it is carried out in the context of a trusting relationship and perceived as care and help, and may not even experience it as coercive.

These results have implications for the ethical analysis of compulsory treatment in the context of anorexia. One approach, we suggest, is that, on the accounts of those with anorexia, the central issue is not the question of whether and when a person lacks capacity to consent to, or refuse, treatment. Instead the central issue concerns the context and relationships involved in good and compassionate psychiatric care. A greater objective restriction of choice may be experienced as less negative, and indeed ultimately as good care, if conducted within a trusting and supportive relationship and environment. Such an approach might be seen as a 'virtue ethics approach' in which the focus is on how carers can act with compassion. It is also consistent with recent trends in bioethics that highlight the importance of trust in decision-making (O'Neill, 2002).

An alternative response to the accounts reported here is to retain the emphasis on autonomy and capacity in thinking about the ethics of compulsion but to suggest that more subtle and broader difficulties in making treatment decisions may need to be considered (Charland, 1998). Key questions are: when and why a patient may fail to make autonomous decisions because of the influence of the mental disorder, and whether help and even coercion to engage in treatment might increase autonomy (Charland, 2002; Tan & Hope, 2006; Tan et al., 2006). Conversely, a patient may technically lack capacity, for example being impaired in his or her ability to retain information, but broader factor, such as an ability to express underlying values may enable him or her to continue to make valid choices with the appropriate support (Department of Constitutional Affairs, 2007; Tan et al., 2006).[3]

These two approaches are not mutually exclusive, as poor relationships and difficult or hostile settings tend to disempower patients with respect to whether they feel able to make decisions for themselves and can also cause them to resist or refuse help; while strong, trusting relationships and supportive treatment settings tend to facilitate patients in making their own decisions and help them to feel more actively involved in their care. Indeed, the ethical justifications voiced in these results suggest that it is a complex mix of a virtue ethics and nuanced capacity approach that is used by patients in thinking of their experiences of, and attitudes to, compulsory treatment and coercion. The analysis of this study and results of a previous study suggest that in anorexia nervosa issues of control and choice can have a strong influence on whether patients are able to make decisions. This is because patients suffering from anorexia nervosa often struggle to remain in control of themselves and their lives and, as a result, resist help, while at the same time feeling out of control with respect to their eating behaviour and wishing to have help (Tan et al., 2003c).

In conclusion, in this qualitative interview study, patients with anorexia nervosa reported considerable experience of compulsion and restriction of choice despite a relative lack of the use of formal compulsory treatment. Nevertheless, there is strong consensus that compulsory treatment should be used if needed to save life in anorexia nervosa. There was less consensus concerning the use of compulsory measures for the treatment of anorexia nervosa in the absence of immediate risk to life. A striking result was that what mattered most to participants was not whether they were compelled to have treatment but the nature of their relationships with parents and mental health professionals. Indeed, within a trusting relationship compulsion may be experienced as care.

Ethics Approval: This study was conducted with multi-centre research ethics approval from the South East MREC number 01/1/65.

Notes

1. Note that the research interviews were conducted from 2002 to 2006, before the Mental Health Act 2007 amendment to the Mental Health Act 1983 became law.

2 In England and Wales the relevant legislation is The Mental Capacity Act 2005, which has the following definition of (in)capacity: 'a person is unable to make a decision for himself if he is unable (a) to understand the information relevant to the decision, (b) to retain that information, (c) to use or weigh that information as part of the process of making the decision, or (d) to communicate his decision (whether by talking, using sign language or any other means).'

3 The Mental Capacity Act 2005: Part 1, 1: The Principles (3) A person is not to be treated as unable to make a decision unless all practicable steps to help him to do so have been taken without success.

References

Appelbaum, P. S., & Redlich, A. (2006). Use of leverage over patients' money to promote adherence to psychiatric treatment. *Journal of Nervous and Mental Disorders, 194*(4), 294–302.

Ayton, A., Keen, C., & Lask, B. (2009), Pros and cons of using the Mental Health Act for severe eating disorders in adolescents. *European Eating Disorders Review, 17*(1), 14–23.

Bindman, J., Reid, Y., Szmukler, C., Tiller, J., Thornicroft, G., & Leese, M. (2005). Perceived coercion at admission to psychiatric hospital and engagement with follow-up—a cohort study. *Social Psychiatry and Psychiatric Epidemiology, 40*(2), 160–166.

Buchanan, A. E., & Brock, D. W. (1989). Chapter 1: Competence and incompetence. *Deciding for others: The ethics of surrogate decision making* (pp. 17–86). Cambridge: Cambridge University Press.

Carney, T., Wakefield, A., Tait, D., & Touyz, S. (2006). Reflections on coercion in the treatment of severe anorexia nervosa. *Israel Journal of Psychiatry and Related Sciences, 43*(3), 159–165.

Carney, T., Tait, D., Richardson, A., &; Touyz, S. (2008). Why (and when) clinicians compel treatment of anorexia nervosa patients. *European Eating Disorders Review, 16*(3), 199–206.

Charland, L. C. (1998). Appreciation and emotion: Theoretical reflections on the MacArthur Treatment Competence Study. *Kennedy Institute Ethics Journal, 8*(4), 359–376.

Charland, L. C. (2002). Cynthia's dilemma: Consenting to heroin prescription. *American Journal of Bioethics, 2*(2), 37–47.

Department of Constitutional Affairs. (2007). Chapter 3: How should people be helped to make their own decisions? *Mental Capacity Act 2005 Code of Practice* (pp. 29–39). TSO.

Draper, H. (2000). Anorexia nervosa and respecting a refusal of life-prolonging therapy: A limited justification. *Bioethics, 14*(2), 120–133.

Giordano, S. (2003). Anorexia nervosa and refusal of naso-gastric treatment: A response to Heather Draper. *Bioethics, 17*(3), 261–278.

Greenberg, D., Mazar, J., Brom, D., & Barer, Y. C. (2005). Involuntary outpatient commitment: A naturalistic study of its use and a consumer survey at one community mental health center in Israel. *Medicine and law, 24*(1), 95–110.

Grisso, T., & Appelbaum, P. S. (1998). Chapter 3: Abilities related to competence. *Assessing competence to consent to treatment: A guide for physicians and other health professionals* (pp. 31–60). London: Oxford University Press.

Guarda, A. S., Pinto, A. M., Coughlin, J. W., Hussain, S., Haug, N. A., & Heinberg, L. J. (2007). Perceived coercion and change in perceived need for admission in patients hospitalized for eating disorders. *American Journal of Psychiatry, 164*(1), 108–114.

Harris, E. C., & Barraclough, B. (1997). Suicide as an outcome for mental disorders. A meta-analysis. *British Journal of Psychiatry, 170,* 205–228.

Harris, E. C., &: Barraclough, B. (1998). Excess mortality of mental disorder. *British. Journal of Psychiatry, 173,* 11–53.

Newton, J. T., Robinson, P. H., & Hartley, P. (1993). Treatment for eating disorders in the United Kingdom. Part II. Experiences of treatment: A survey of members of the eating disorders association. *Eating Disorders Review, 1*(1), 10–21.

O'Neill, O. (2002). *Autonomy and trust in bioethics.* Cambridge: Cambridge University Press.

QSR International. (2005). NG. Retrieved 19 August 2005, from http:/www.qsrintemational.com/produtts/productoview/product_overview.htm

Rajkumar, A. P., Saravanan, B., & Jacob, K. S. (2006). Perspectives of patients and relatives about electroconvulsive therapy: A qualitative study from Vellore, India. *Journal of ECT, 22*(4), 253–258.

Ramsay, R., Ward, A., Treasure, J., & Russell, G. F. M. (1999). Compulsory treatment in anorexia nervosa. *British Journal of Psychiatry, 175,* 147–153.

Rathner, G. (1998). A plea against compulsory treatment of anorexia nervosa. In W. Vandereycken & P. J. Beumont (Eds.). *Treating eating disorders: Ethical, legal and personal Issues* (pp. 179–215). London, UK: The Athlone Press.

Roth, L. H., Meisel, A., & Lidz, C. W. (1977). Tests of competency to consent to treatment. *American Journal of Psychiatry, 134*(3), 279–284.

Royal College of Psychiatrists. (1992). *Report to the College Section of General Psychiatry by the Eating Disorders Working Group.* London: Royal College of Psychiatrists.

Salize, H. J., & Dressing, H. (2005). Coercion, involuntary treatment and quality of mental health care: Is there any link? *Current Opinion in Psychiatry, 18*(5), 576–584.

Szmukler, G. (2001). Double standard on capacity and consent? *American Journal of Psychiatry, 158*(1), 148–149.

Tan, J. O., & Hope, T. (2006). Mental health legislation and decision making capacity: Capacity is more complex than it looks. *British Medical Journal, 332*(7533), 119.

Tan, J., Hope, T., & Stewart, A. (2003a). Competence to refuse treatment in anorexia nervosa. *International Journal of Law and Psychiatry, 26*(6), 697–707.

Tan, J. O., Hope, T., & Stewart. A. (2003b). Anorexia nervosa and personal identity: The accounts of patients and their parents. *International Journal of Law and Psychiatry, 26*(5), 533–548.

Tan, J. O., Hope, T., Stewart, A., & Fitzpatrick, R. (2003c). Control and compulsory treatment in anorexia nervosa: The views of patients and parents, *International Journal of Law and Psychiatry, 26*(6), 627–645.

Tan, J. O. A., Hope, T., Stewart. A., & Fitzpatrick, R. (2006). Competence to make treatment decisions in anorexia nervosa: Thinking processes and values. *Philosophy, Psychology, and Psychiatry, 13*(4), 267–282.

Tiller, J., Schmidt, U., & Treasure, J. (1993). Compulsory treatment for anorexia nervosa: Compassion or coercion? *British Journal of Psychiatry, 162,* 679–680.

Watson, T. L., Bowers, W. A., & Andersen, A, E. (2000). Involuntary treatment of eating disorders. *American Journal of Psychiatry, 157*(11), 1806–1810.

EXPLORING THE ISSUE

Should Individuals with Anorexia Nervosa Have the Right to Refuse Life-Sustaining Treatment?

Critical Thinking and Reflection

1. To what extent should anorexia nervosa be viewed as a medical disorder vs. a psychiatric disorder, and how should this determination influence legal arguments pertaining to coercive treatment?
2. What are the arguments pro and con pertaining to the notion that permitting a person to have autonomy to refuse life-sustaining treatment is a form of assisted suicide?
3. Imagine that you are a clinician treating a patient who states that she has had "enough" treatments for her intractable anorexia over several decades, and she now wants to refuse any and all interventions. How would you respond, and on what basis would you make your response?
4. What criteria should be used in determining competence on the part of a severely anorexic patient who wants to refuse life-sustaining treatment?
5. What criteria should be specified in legislation pertaining to the well-established precedent that individuals have the legal right to refuse treatment? In other words, what kinds of clinical cases should be excluded from this legal right?

Is There Common Ground?

In both articles, we read about the importance of respect for human rights and autonomy, and both sets of authors emphasize the importance of being watchful for any procedures that might result in the loss of personal freedom or a reduction in a person's ability to negotiate the terms of treatment. Both sets of authors also see the issue of control as playing a central role in the personality and symptom picture of people with anorexia nervosa. Dr. Tan and her colleagues view people with anorexia as less able to make treatment decisions because they fear losing control, whereas Drs. Campbell and Aulisio emphasize the importance of respecting the right of these individuals to exercise autonomous choice. Common ground can be found in the wish of both sets of authors to approach the care of people with severe anorexia with respect for their human abilities, attention to their legal rights, and dedication to the best medical and psychological care.

Additional Resources

National Institute of Mental Health. *Eating Disorders.* Retrieved from www
.nimh.nih.gov/health/publications/eating-disorders/complete-index.shtml

PsychRights: Law Project for Psychiatric Rights. Retrieved from http://
psychrights.org/articles/rightorefuse.htm

Rumney, A. (2009). *Dying to please: Anorexia, treatment and recovery* (2nd ed.).
Jefferson, NC: McFarland & Company, Inc., Publishers.

Shepphird, S. F. (2010). *100 questions & answers about anorexia nervosa.
Burlington, MA:* Jones & Bartlett Publishers.

ISSUE 14

Is the Use of Aversive Treatment an Inhumane Intervention for Psychologically Disordered Individuals?

YES: **Laurie Ahern and Eric Rosenthal**, from *Torture Not Treatment: Electric Shock and Long-Term Restraint in the United States on Children and Adults with Disabilities at the Judge Rotenberg Center* (Mental Disability Rights International, 2010)

NO: **Matthew L. Israel**, from *Aversives at JRC: A Better Alternative to the Use of Drugs, Restraint, Isolation, Warehousing, or Expulsion in the Treatment of Severe Behavior Disorders* (Judge Rotenberg Center, 2010)

Learning Outcomes

After reading this issue, you should be able to:

- Critically evaluate the pros and cons of using aversive treatments such as the Graduated Electronic Decelerator (GED) device on individuals with severe behavioral disorders.
- Discuss the argument that aversive treatments are forms of torture.
- Understand the debate about whether withholding aversive treatments from disabled individuals is a form of discrimination, because they would be deprived access to interventions which might help them control their behavior.
- Consider whether the infliction of pain can be justified on moral grounds as a form of psychological intervention.
- Consider the threshold for determining a possible justification for administering aversive treatments (e.g., head banging, eye gouging, interpersonal assault, etc.).

ISSUE SUMMARY

YES: Laurie Ahern and Eric Rosenthal, writing on behalf of Mental Disability Rights International (MDRI), characterize the intentional infliction of pain at JRC as human rights abuses.

NO: Psychologist Matthew Israel, director of the Judge Rotenberg Center (JRC), responds to the MDRI with insistence that JRC is using behavioral methods to save individuals from their treatment-resistant, life-threatening disorders.

One of the most heartbreaking experiences for parents of emotionally disordered children is to see these fragile youngsters engage in self-injurious and even self-mutilating behaviors such as head banging, self-punching, and even manually pulling out teeth. Many of these children are also aggressive, sometimes to the point of life-threatening violence. In these extreme cases, parents desperately seek out solutions so that the well-being of these troubled children can be protected. Traditional therapeutic interventions are customarily the first line of treatment, as parents turn to mental health professionals for therapy for themselves and their children. When talking approaches prove to be of limited value, medications are likely to be recommended. For some children, however, even the most potent of antipsychotic medications may be ineffective in reducing self-destructive behaviors. Feeling exhausted, bewildered, and frightened, the guardians of these very disturbed individuals seek out the options of last resort, which sometimes involve behavioral interventions involving the use of physical restraints and aversive conditioning. A leader in the application of such procedures is the Judge Rotenberg Center (JRC) in Canton, MA, which has been at the center of controversy for the four decades that it has been in operation.

On behalf of Mental Disability Rights International (MDRI), human rights activists Laurie Ahern and Eric Rosenthal prepared a scathing critique of the behavioral techniques used at JRC, which they label "torture" rather than treatment. This report was submitted to the United Nations along with a request that the UN initiate an inquiry into what are described as "abusive practices perpetrated against residents of JRC." MDRI contends that the severe pain and suffering perpetrated against children and adults with disabilities violates the UN Convention Against Torture.

MDRI asserts that no population is more vulnerable to abuse than children with disabilities detained in an institution. For this population, the use of electric shock in the form of the Graduated Electronic Decelerator (GED), long-term restraint, and other aversives used by JRC constitute human rights violations that are even more serious than corporal punishment in a school. They assert that the GED is used to administer shock for behaviors that are not problematic, such as getting out of one's seat or nagging other students. According to MDRI, aversive interventions such as the GED device are used with children with all kinds of disabilities, many without self-injurious behaviors.

MDRI contends that behavioral programming at JRC is not sufficiently monitored by appropriate professionals at the school, and in many cases the level of background and preparation of staff are not sufficient for overseeing the intensive treatment of children with challenging emotional and behavioral disorders. While the infliction of pain may stop a person from engaging in a specific behavior while being subject to a course of aversive treatment, aversive treatment cannot treat an underlying emotional disorder or intellectual disability.

Dr. Matthew Israel, founding director of JRC, expresses strong objection to the MDRI claims, citing the fact that for the last four decades JRC has used safe intensive behavioral therapy to treat the most severe forms of behavior disorders, and has freed hundreds of individuals from disturbing alternatives such as excessive sedation, restraint, seclusion, and institutional warehousing. The claim is made that JRC's 24-hour behavioral system works effectively for individuals for whom every other treatment has failed. In these individuals, positive behaviors replace the prior behaviors of self-abuse, aggression, and destruction.

According to Dr. Israel, under state and federal law, nondisabled individuals have the right to choose aversive therapy to treat behavioral problems such as smoking and drinking. To deny persons with developmental or behavioral/psychiatric disabilities the same right to treat their behavior problems with aversives would be to impose an invidious form of discrimination against those unfortunate enough to suffer from such disabilities. Instead of using problematic interventions (e.g., cocktails of mind-numbing drugs, restraint, take-downs, isolation, warehousing, expulsion), Dr. Israel explains that JRC employs a corrective consequence in the form of a 2-second shock to the skin. This treatment, which feels like a hard pinch, Dr. Israel notes, has been validated in the scientific literature, is extremely effective, and has no significant adverse side effects.

Dr. Israel contends that all of the students at JRC have at least one thing in common—they suffer from severe behavior disorders that could not be effectively treated by the many other treatment programs and psychiatric hospitals they had been in prior to coming to JRC. JRC uses extraordinary safeguards. Each individual's treatment program that includes the use of skin shock must be preapproved by a physician and by the parent, must be included in the student's Individualized Education Program or Individual Health Plan, must be approved by a human rights committee and a peer review committee, and must be individually preapproved and reviewed at regular intervals by a Massachusetts Probate Court Judge. Techniques of behavior modification and applied behavior analysis involve analyzing the causes of problematic behaviors, eliminating triggering events, rewarding desired behaviors, and applying corrective consequences for undesired behaviors.

YES

**Laurie Ahern and
Eric Rosenthal**

Torture Not Treatment: Electric Shock and Long-Term Restraint in the United States on Children and Adults with Disabilities at the Judge Rotenberg Center

Introduction

The Judge Rotenberg Center (JRC) was founded by psychologist Matthew Israel almost 40 years ago in California when it was known then as the Behavior Research Institute (BRI). According to Israel, the school's philosophy is based on the work of renowned behaviorist B.F. Skinner.[2] In the 1950s, Israel was a student of Skinner's at Harvard University, and today he is a self-proclaimed devotee of radical behaviorism.

In 1981, a 14 year old boy died face down, tied to his bed. JRC (then known as BRI) was not held responsible for the boy's death, but the death resulted in an investigation by California's Department of Social Services. California issued a critical report the following year, citing widespread abuse of children at the facility and the state of California greatly limited the use of punishment as treatment.[3] The facility was then moved to Rhode Island and then again to Canton, Massachusetts, where it is located today.

Today, JRC boasts a main campus with a school and offsite residential apartments with 24 hour staffing. The facility serves as a residential school for children with disabilities, as well as a residential facility for adults. There are approximately 200 children and adults at JRC at any given time,[4] with costs paid for by state and local school districts and state agencies serving adults with disabilities at approximately $220,000 per year, per person. People with disabilities living at the JRC residential center mostly come from New York and Massachusetts, and seven other states.

The Judge Rotenberg Center program

The program of "behavior modification" and "aversive treatment" and the rationale for its use is spelled out on JRC's website. The theory of behavior modification is that every human being responds to positive rewards or negative

From *Mental Disability Rights International* by Laurie Ahern and Eric Rosenthal (Mental Disability Rights International (MDRI), 2010). Copyright © 2010 by Mental Disability Rights International (MDRI). Reprinted by permission.

punishments and that all behavior can be manipulated through a combination of rewards and punishments. Using this approach, "rewards" and "punishments" constitute treatment.[5] Treatment entails the infliction of pain. JRC is clear that this approach "differs markedly" from "traditional approaches" to mental health care.[6] The website boasts that "JRC is probably the most consistently behavioral treatment program in existence."

JRC maintains that the same form of reward and punishment works for anyone, justifying a "near-zero rejection policy" for admission.[7] As a result:

> . . . we really pay relatively little attention to psychiatric diagnosis which are essentially labels for groups of behaviors. . . . Of the first two students we worked with, one was labeled autistic and one was labeled schizophrenic.[8]

The implication of this approach is a highly unorthodox program for treatment and education. All residents, regardless of diagnosis or history, are subjected to the same behavior modification techniques of reward and punishment. The use of traditional psychological therapies and/or medication is virtually non-existent at JRC.[9] Psychotropic medications are rarely used.[10] According to JRC, seventy percent of educational instruction in the school consists of solitary work on a computer referred to by JRC as "self-paced programmed instruction."[11] . . .

Early on, punishments—known as aversives—were used to control the behavior of people who were called severely "mentally retarded" and children with autism. Punishments included pinching, spatula spankings, water sprays, muscle squeezes, forced inhalation of ammonia and helmets which battered the brain with inescapable white noise.[24]

In the late 1980s, JRC began using SIBIS (Self-Injurious Behavior Inhibiting System) machines on students, as an alternative to spanking, squeezing and pinching. The machine, developed in 1985, produced a 0.2 second shock of 2.02 milliamps on the arms or legs of the recipient, with the intention of stopping self-injurious behaviors in children with autism and other developmental disabilities. Controversial from the outset and shunned by advocates, the use of SIBIS was largely abandoned in the 1990s in favor of "positive-based" practices.[25]

Over the years, JRC has found that an individual who responds to low levels of electricity may become "adapted" to pain and "needs a stronger stimulation."[26] The 12 year old nephew of Massachusetts State Representative Jeffrey Sanchez was diagnosed with autism and was a student at JRC in 1989 when JRC began using the SIBIS machine. As described in testimony before the Massachusetts legislature,[27] one day he received more than 5,000 shocks to stop his behaviors—to no avail. When the manufacturer of SIBIS refused JRC's request to provide them with a stronger and more painful shock machine, JRC developed its own mechanism for administering shock, the Graduated Electronic Decelerator (GED). The GED is a remotely controlled device that can be strapped to an individual's back or another part of the body with electrodes attached to the torso, arms, legs, hands and feet. The

GED administers 15.5 milliamps of electricity. A stronger version, the GED-4, subjects an individual to a shock of 45.5 milliamps. Both may be used up to 2.0 seconds. The director of JRC, Matthew Israel, describes the shock as "very painful."[28] Sanchez's nephew is now 31 years old and remains at JRC. According to testimony before the Massachusetts Legislature in November 2009, he is still tethered to the GED shock machine.[29]

JRC also uses physical restraints as a form of aversive treatment, some-times simultaneously with electric shock.[30] The GED and restraints are sometimes combined because it is necessary to stop a person from ripping the GED pack off his or her body. Other times, physical restraints may be added to the use of the GED when the aversive power of electricity alone is not sufficient. As described on the JRC website, "[T]he safest way to do this is to use mechanical restraint to contain the student, in a prone position, on a flexible plastic restraint platform that has been specially designed for the purpose."[31] It is worth noting that, outside JRC, the use of any "prone" (face down) restraints are widely considered to be inherently dangerous, and many states have banned any form of prone restraints in the mental health context.[32] . . .

Critique of Aversive Treatment from Research and Policy

What's wrong with punishments is that they work immediately, but give no long-term results. The responses to punishment are either the urge to escape, to counterattack or a stubborn apathy.

—B.F. Skinner interview, *The New York Times*, 1987[36]

. . . The NY Psychological Association Task Force, which reviewed NYSED's report, raised particular concerns about the use of aversives at JRC without careful attention to the patients' diagnosis. They point out that for certain children—in particular abuse or trauma survivors—aversives can be particu-larly dangerous.[45] Other researchers have warned that "restraints and seclusion should never be used with children who present with certain psychological or medical characteristics. . . . Contraindications for the use of seclusion and restraints with children include a history of sexual abuse, physical abuse, or neglect and abandonment."[46]

. . . While the infliction of pain may stop a person from engaging in a specific behavior while being subject to a course of aversive treatment, aversive treatment cannot treat an underlying emotional disorder or intel-lectual disability. A review of the research found that "the implementation of punishment-based procedures, including those that incorporate noxious stimulation, do not guarantee long-term reductive effects in the treatment of severe disorders."[48] The alleviation of symptoms only takes place while aver-sives are in place, leaving a person subject to this painful treatment over a long period of time. This is why JRC has had to create increasingly strong systems for administering pain and shock. JRC's website candidly acknowledges that aversives only bring about the temporary alleviation of symptoms. . . .

Findings: The Use of Aversives at JRC

Electric Shock

As described above, JRC's stated reason for the use of electric shocks is behavior modification and punishment.[57] Children and adults at JRC are routinely subject to electric shock, receiving multiple skin shocks on their legs, arms, hands, feet, fingers and torsos for behaviors such as getting out of their seats, making noises, swearing or not following staff directions.[58] The homemade shock devices, invented by the school's founder, Matthew Israel, and manufactured at the school, are carried by students in backpacks with electrodes attached to their skin.[59] The shock is administered remotely by minimally trained staff— some with only two weeks of training.[60] Students never know when they will receive a jolt or where on their body they will be shocked. Some children are subjected to dozens of shocks over the course of a day. The April 2009 report by the Massachusetts Department of Mental Retardation (DMR), found that of the 109 children subjected to electric skin shocks, 48 had been receiving the shocks for 5 years or more.[61] . . .

Restraints

> Some problem behaviors can be controlled and prevented by putting the student into continual manual or mechanical restraint. To manually restrain a vigorous young man can take the efforts of many staff members and is inevitably a dangerous exercise. Putting a student in continuing restraints is much more cruel than changing his/her behavior quickly with a powerful positive reward program that is supplemented with occasional two-second skin shocks.
>
> —JRC website, Frequently Asked Questions

JRC refers to physical restraints as "limitation of movement" (LOM), and this is a core part of its aversive treatment program. According to the JRC website, some students receive shocks while strapped prone to a platform board in 4-point mechanical restraints.[75] Restraints are used in combination with the GED to stop a person from ripping off the GED pack while receiving painful electrical impulses.[76] Restraints may also be used to increase the level of pain and discomfort when electric shock alone is not adequate to produce the behavior changes sought by JRC.[77]

A nurse at the facility is responsible for monitoring abrasions due to restraints, according to the NYSED. Depending on the recommendations of the nurse, "a student may be restrained in a prone, seated, or upright position."[78] As described by the NYSED investigators:

> With mechanical movement limitation the student is strapped into/ onto some form of physical apparatus. For example, a four-point platform board designed specifically for this purpose; or a helmet with thick padding and facial grid that reduces sensory stimuli to the ears and eyes. Another form of mechanical restraint occurs when the student

is in a five-point restraint in a chair. **Students may be restrained for extensive periods of time (e.g. hours or intermittently for days)** [emphasis added] when restraint is used as a punishing consequence. Many students are required to carry their own "restraint bag" in which the restraint straps are contained.[79]

MDRI's investigation suggests that restraints may last even longer than reported by the NYSED team. A former patient, a mother, a former teacher at JRC, and an attorney who represented clients at JRC all informed MDRI that children are restrained for weeks and months at a time. . . .

MDRI interviews indicate that students are likely to be restrained after they are admitted and before they go before a court to determine whether they can be subject to Level III aversive treatment. These findings are supported by the findings of the New York State and Massachusetts evaluation teams.[90] These findings raise concerns that restraints may used to pressure or coerce individuals into consenting to the GED. . . .

According to the NYSED evaluation team:

It is during this initial restrictive placement at JRC that the frequency of behaviors is documented for purposes of obtaining a substituted judgment for the use of Level III aversive procedures. . . . In this setting, interactions with students involved little to no instruction; staff primarily attended to students' negative behaviors and employed the use of physical and mechanical restraints at a high frequency and for extended periods of time.[91]

The Massachusetts Certification Team found that restraints were used without being included in treatment plans.[92] According to one observer from the Massachusetts team, "the more JRC used these interventions, the more aggressive the students became."[93] . . .

Provocation of Bad Behavior

One component of treatment at JRC is referred to as the behavioral rehearsal lesson (BRL).[95] Students are restrained and GED administered as the student is forcibly challenged to do the behavior the punishment seeks to eliminate. JRC students are sometimes induced to exhibit a behavior for which they will receive a shock punishment. Students endure surprise mock attacks and threatened stabbings by staff, which compel them to react with aggression, fear or screaming—deemed unacceptable or inappropriate behavior—for which they are subject to more shock for their reactions.

Former students report BRLs as particularly terrifying and some staff describe BRLs as "difficult to participate in and dramatic to watch."[96]

It was reported by a JRC staff member that one of the BRL episodes involved holding a student's face still while a staff person went for his mouth with a pen or pencil threatening to stab him in the mouth while repeatedly yelling "You want to eat this?"

—June 2006 report on JRC by New York State Education Department[97]

The worst thing ever was the BRLs. They try and make you do a bad behavior and then they punish you. The first time I had a BRL, two guys came in the room and grabbed me—I had no idea what was going on. They held a knife to my throat and I started to scream and I got shocked. I had BRL's three times a week for stuff I didn't even do. It went on for about six months or more. I was in a constant state of paranoia and fear. I never knew if a door opened if I would get one. It was more stress than I could ever imagine. Horror.

—MDRI interview with former JRC student[98]

Food Deprivation

In addition to the use of electric shock, restraints, mock stabbings and assaults as a means of punishment, JRC uses dangerous food deprivation techniques to further abuse children, adding to the environment of fear, pain, punishment and control. Collectively known as "Loss of Privileges" or "LOPs," the abuses are masked in clinical sounding terminology. The "Contingent Food Program" (CFP) and the "Specialized Food Program" (SFP) include the systematic withholding of food as a form of punishment.[99] The CFP "is widely applied and designed to motivate students to be compliant."[100] If children or adolescents exhibit any behaviors not tolerated by JRC staff, a portion of food is withheld during the day. **Food not earned during the day is then given to the child in the evening, "which consists of mashed food sprinkled with liver powder."**[101] The SFP is "more restrictive" for those whose behavior does not improve—there is no make-up food given at the end of the day.[102] . . .

Other LOPs include limitations and restrictions with regard to visits to the school's store, television viewing, bedtime, and permission to talk with other students. And some LOPs result in even harsher consequences. One former student reported that she was forced to eat her dinner tied to a chair, alone in her room, for almost a month—LOPs she earned for talking in class without raising her hand.[105]

When we first visited JRC, she had a beautiful room with a TV and stereo. Within one month, she only had a mattress on the floor.

—MDRI interview with mother of a former JRC student[106]

Stopping work for more than 5 seconds and you would lose points and get LOPs. I sat in front of the computer all day, other than lunch. And we couldn't have a social conversation with any staff member.

—MDRI interview with former JRC student[107]

Creating Social Isolation

To further maintain strict control, socialization among students, between students and staff, and among staff, is also extremely limited.[108] For students, socialization with other peers must be earned. Children spend their school days in classrooms facing the walls and staring at a computer screen. Using self-teaching software, conversations and discussions are virtually non-existent and getting up from a chair or attempting to leave the classroom without permission could result in a shock or other form of punishment. . . .

Additionally, staff is not allowed to carry on any personal conversations with the students and all are under 24 hour video surveillance. Employees must also sign a confidentiality agreement at the beginning of their tenure with JRC, effectively barring them from ever talking about what they observe or participate in at the school—including the use of GEDs—or face legal action against them by the school.[111]

> *You are sworn to secrecy. It is like a secret society. We had to sign a paper that if we said anything that would harm their reputation, they would prosecute you. If you talked bad about the school, everything is taped. If we needed to talk, we had to go outside.*

> —MDRI interview with former JRC employee[112]

Aversives for Harmless Behavior

One of the critiques of the GED identified by the NYSED evaluation team is that it is used on behaviors that "the district did not consider problematic for a student that they had placed at JRC (i.e. getting out of seat, nagging)."[113] Indeed, the NYSED evaluators found that:

> *Many of the students observed at JRC were <u>not</u> exhibiting self-abusive/mutilating behaviors, and their IEP's had no indication that these behaviors existed. However, they were still subject to Level III aversive interventions, including the use of the GED device. The review of the NYS students' records revealed that Level III interventions are used for behaviors including 'refuse to follow staff directions'; 'failure to maintain a neat appearance', 'stopping work for more than 10 seconds', interrupting others', 'nagging', 'whispering and/or moving conversation away from staff', 'slouch in chair'. . . .*[114]

The observations of the NYSED evaluators were mirrored by a former teacher at JRC.[115] According to this teacher, children are routinely given shock for behaviors as normal or innocuous as reacting in fear when witnessing other students getting shocked; attempting to remove electrodes from their skin; tearing a paper cup; blowing bubbles with saliva; standing up out of a seat without permission; going to the bathroom in one's pants; or asking to go to the bathroom more than five times, which is considered an inappropriate verbal behavior.[116] MDRI interviewed a teacher and a former JRC student who told similar stories:

> *One girl who was blind, deaf and non-verbal was moaning and rocking. Her moaning was like a cry. The staff shocked her for moaning. Turned out she had broken a tooth. Another child had an accident in the bathroom and was shocked.*

> —MDRI interview with former JRC teacher.[117]

I felt terrible for the kids with autism getting shocked. This one 13 year old girl with autism kept getting the GED. They get it for verbal inappropriate behaviors. They made noises, that's how they communicate. They are non-verbal but they would get more shocks. The poor girl would hurt herself a lot.

—MDRI interview with former JRC student
who was also getting shocked[118]. . .

Deaths and Subsequent Legal Challenges

From the outset, Israel's treatment for children with disabilities was controversial and the focus of much media attention. This was especially true when the magnitude and severity of punishments being perpetrated against children came to light or when an unexplained death occurred at the facility, of which there have been six. As previously described, it was a death at the facility in 1980 that resulted in the virtual ban on the use of aversives in California.

In 1990, the Massachusetts DMR conducted an exhaustive investigation on the horrific death of a 19 year old, a young woman diagnosed with severe mental retardation, who also died at the facility. The report states that the staff and administration committed acts against her that were "egregious" and "inhumane beyond all reason" and violated "universal standards of human decency."[196] The young woman, who was unable to speak, became ill and refused to eat, attempted to vomit and made sounds and noises that were not usual for her. For this she was punished repeatedly as the staff translated her actions as misbehaviors. In the hours leading up to her death from a perforated stomach and ulcers, the investigation found that she endured "8 spankings, 27 finger pinches, 14 muscle squeezes" and was forced to smell ammonia and eat "either vinegar mix, or jalapeno peppers or hot sauce."[197]

Prior to her death, she had been subjected to the school's punishment of withholding food for being unable to do school work on the computer or getting wrong answers, despite having the mental capacity of a pre-schooler. At times she was limited to 300 calories per day.

In the end, DMR concluded that there was not enough evidence to link the punishments to her death.

The Massachusetts Office for Children (OFC) ordered the closure of JRC. The school and its parents sued the OFC and appealed the closure. A state administrative law judge ruled that the school could remain open but limited the use of aversives during the litigation.[198]

In 1986, in the midst of the OFC litigation, JRC (then called the Behavior Research Institute) brought one of its most self-abusive students before the Bristol County Probate Court (MA) and Chief Judge Ernest Rotenberg (for whom the school is now named) for a substituted judgment hearing to allow JRC to use aversive treatments on the student. Judge Rotenberg found in JRC's favor and JRC began to bring each student they felt needed aversives before Judge Rotenberg for approval.

Despite the objections of the OFC, Judge Rotenberg was eventually given judicial authority over all pending legal actions between the OFC, JRC and parents of students and a settlement was reached. In the December 1986 agreement, aversives were permitted with a court-ordered treatment plan, and a monitor must report to the court on the clients' treatment.[199]. . .

New York's Attempts to Limit Use of Aversives

New York State sends more of its children to JRC than any other state. As a result of questions and concerns by NY lawmakers regarding the use of punishment at JRC, specifically electric shock and restraint, the NYSED sent a review team to JRC in April and May 2006. The team included NYSED staff and three behavioral psychologists. One visit was announced; the other was unannounced. The NYSED review team reported a litany of abuses involving the most painful of punishments used by JRC. Following the publication of the NYSED report, New York held public hearings. As a result, NYSED adopted restrictive new regulations that would phase out new cases where aversive treatment would be approved.[206] Before New York could implement these new regulations, parents representing children at the school challenged the regulations in federal court, claiming they have a right to subject their children to Level III aversives. They claim that such treatment is necessary for their children to receive an appropriate education as required by IDEA. The federal court has ordered a stay on the implementation of New York's regulations until the substantive issues under IDEA are heard.[207]

A summary of the NYSED review team findings include:

- Level III punishments are given to children with all kinds of disabilities, many without self-injurious behaviors;
- Level III punishments are given for swearing, nagging and failure to maintain a neat appearance;
- The use of electric shock skin devices raises health and safety concerns;
- The withholding of food as punishment could pose risks affecting growth and development;
- Delayed punishment practices are used so that subjects may not be able to comprehend any relationship between a punishment and a behavior;
- The JRC setting discourages social interactions;
- There is insufficient academic and special education instruction;
- JRC compromises the privacy and dignity of students.[208]

Ultimately, the NYSED's review team concluded that the effects of the punishment on children at JRC are increased fear, anxiety or agression.[209]

One of the findings of the NYSED review team was that "behavioral programming at JRC is not sufficiently monitored by appropriate professionals at the school and in many cases the level of background and preparation of staff is not sufficient to oversee the intensive treatment of children with challenging emotional and behavioral disorders.[210]

The reality is that JRC staff may have had even less training than was represented to the NYSED review team. In May 2006, the Massachusetts Division of Professional Licensure found that JRC had improperly claimed that fourteen JRC clinicians were trained as licensed psychologists. In a consent agreement with the Board of Registration of Psychologists, JRC paid $43,000 in fines.[211] Dr. Matthew Israel, the Director of JRC, was personally fined $29,600 and was reprimanded by the Board.[212]

Recent Incidents of Abuse

In August 2007, an investigation of JRC was conducted by the Massachusetts Department of Early Education and Care (EEC)—the licensing agency for JRC residences—following the unauthorized administering of shock to two boys at their JRC residence. According to the report, one boy received 29 electric shocks, and the other received 77 shocks within a three hour time period.[213] The incident occurred when a former JRC student phoned the residence in the middle of the night, pretending to be a staff person, and ordered the residence staff to use shocks on the sleeping adolescents. EEC investigators interviewed the boys and staff and reviewed video footage and found that both boys had been awoken from their sleep when they received the shock; both boys had additional shocks when they were strapped to a 4-point restraint board; both were in transport restraints (legs and waist) while they were in their beds; and one of the boys did not have the required Level III court approval for restraints in his record. Neither boy was evaluated by any medical staff until the following day after the incident, despite asking for a nurse and complaining of pain.

> Staff reported that it is not atypical for a resident to say that they have injuries following a GED application. It was reported that typically staff would not call a nurse when a resident voices that he is in pain from a GED application and described it as a pinch.

The EEC report stated that staff observed that the "skin was off" and there were "fresh marks" on the calf of one of the boys, who complained of leg pain. It was later diagnosed as a stage two ulcer. These wounds were located at the same site that the resident had received the shock.

The EEC investigation further concluded that:

- staff was physically abusive toward the residents;
- the staff was unable to provide for the safety and well being of a child;
- staff lacked necessary training and experience;
- staff used poor judgment;
- staff failed to provide a safe environment;
- staff failed to follow policies regarding medical treatment;
- staff were neglectful in the care of residents.

The incidents of unlawful restraint of the boys at the JRC residence would never have been discovered had EEC not been investigating the unauthorized shock "prank.". . .

Conclusions and Recommendations

. . . No population is more vulnerable to abuse than children with disabilities detained in an institution. This population needs the strongest level of international protection to protect them against abuse. For this population, the use of electric shock, long-term restraint, and other aversives used by JRC constitutes human rights violations that are even more serious than corporal punishment in a school, where children eventually go home to friends and family in the community. The UN Special Rapporteur on Torture has stated that corporal punishment constitutes inhuman and degrading treatment. For a population detained in an institution, such as JRC, the vulnerability is much greater—and the experience of pain and suffering is likely more extreme. Thus, severe pain perpetrated against this population should be viewed as fully tantamount to torture. According to Nowak, "[t]he powerlessness of the victim is the essential criterion which the drafters of the Convention had in mind when they introduced the legal distinction between torture and other forms of ill-treatment."[225] . . .

A flat ban on the use of electricity or long-term use of restraints to treat or modify behavior would be the best way to prevent future abuse. Such a ban would be consistent with federal policy and best practice in the field of behavior modification that strongly supports positive behavioral supports instead of painful aversives. Such a ban would be consistent with what CAT has called for to protect people in custody in a law enforcement context. In 2000, as described above, CAT recommended that the United States "abolish electro-shock stun belts and restraint chairs as methods of restraining those in custody since 'their use almost invariably leads to breaches of article 16 of the Convention [defining inhumane and degrading treatment].'"[226]

This year, CAT will be conducting its fifth periodic review and report of the United States of America and its compliance with the UN Convention against Torture. In its last review of the US in 2006, CAT's report made a number of recommendations to the US government with regard to torture, including a concern they voiced over the use of electro-shock devices: "*restricting it to substitution for lethal weapons and eliminate the use of these devices to restrain persons in custody. . . .*"[227] In this year's review by CAT, in their list of issues of concern, they again bring up the use of electro-shock devices and ask the government if they have restricted its use as a substitution for lethal weapons only, as recommended in CAT's previous observations. And they ask point blank, "Are such devices still used to restrain persons in custody?"[228] CAT has also asked for updated information on steps taken to "address the concern about the conditions of detention of children" with a particular emphasis on the use of excessive force.[229] And finally CAT asks:

> Please describe steps taken to end the practice of corporal punishment in schools, in particular of mentally and/or physically disabled students.[230]

This year, the United States human rights record is being scrutinized by the United Nations as part of a process known as "universal periodic review" under all the human rights conventions the United States has ratified. The

United States report to the United Nations should include detailed information on the use of force against children with disabilities at JRC.

Since the United States legal system has failed to protect children and adults with disabilities, **MDRI brings this urgent appeal to the UN Special Rapporteur on Torture and recommends:**

- The UN Special Rapporteur on Torture should demand a full international accounting by the United States government of the abusive practices being perpetrated at the facility;
- The use of electric shock and long-term restraints should be brought to an immediate halt as a form of behavior modification or treatment;
- New federal law should be adopted to completely ban the infliction of severe pain for so-called therapeutic purposes in any context;
- Torture as treatment should be banned and prosecuted under criminal law. . . .

Notes

2. Matthew L. Israel, History of JRC, 1971–1985: Beginnings, Philosophy and Early Growth, *available at* http://www.judgerc.org/history.html (last visited April 8, 2010).

3. Jennifer Gonnerman, *School of Shock,* 32 Mother Jones, 36,41 (Sept.–Oct. 2007).

4. The number of students is an average taken from a legislative hearing.

5. Matthew L. Israel, Frequently Asked Questions, "Supplementary aversives at JRC—13. How is an aversive defined and which aversives are considered acceptable?" Judge Rotenberg Center, *available at* http://www.judgerc.org/ (last visited April 8, 2010).

6. Matthew L. Israel, *supra* note 2, at 1971–1985: Beginnings, Philosophy and Early Growth.

7. *Id.*

8. *Id.*

9. *Id.*

10. *Id.,* at 1971–1985: Beginnings, Philosophy and Early Growth—No or minimal use of psychotropic medication.

11. Matthew L. Israel, Distinguishing Features of the Judge Rotenberg Center, Judge Rotenberg Center, *available at* http://www/judgerc.org/ (last visited April 20, 2010).

24. Matthew L. Israel, *supra* note 2.

25. Sharon Lohrmann-O'Rourke and Perry A. Zirkel, *The Case Law on Aversive Interventions for Students with Disabilities,* 65 Exceptional Children 101 (Fall 1998).

26. Matthew L. Israel, *supra* note 5, at "Is it true that one of the consequences JRC uses is to administer several GED applications, over a half-hour period during which a student may be restrained on a restraint board?"

27. Patricia Wen, *Showdown over shock therapy testimony moves some critics; new bill would limit, not ban, treatment,* The Boston Globe 1 (Jan. 17, 2008), *available at* http://www.boston.com/news/local/articles/2008/01/17/showdown_over_shock_therapy/.

28. Paul Kix, *The Shocking Truth,* Boston Magazine Online 3 (2008), *available at* http://www.bostonmagazine.com/articles/the_shocking_truth/.

29. Patricia Wen (2008), *supra* note 27, at 1.

30. Matthew L. Israel, *supra* note 5, at "The use of restraint as an aversive consequence."

31. Matthew L. Israel, *supra* note 5, at "Multiple Applications of GED Combined with Restraint as an Aversive."

32. Gregory D. Kutz, Seclusions and Restraints: Selected Cases of Death and Abuse at Public and Private Schools and Treatment Centers, US Government Accountability Office, GAO-09-719T 4 (2009).

36. Daniel Goleman, *Embattled Giant of Psychology Speaks His Mind,* N.Y. Times, Aug. 25, 1987, at C1 and C3.

45. NY Psychological Association Task Force (2006), *supra* note 37, at 13.

46. *1d*. at 11, *quoting* D. Day, "A review of the literature on restraints and seclusion with children and youth: toward the development of a perspective in practice" (2000), *available at* http://rccp.connell.edu/pdfs/Day.pdf (retrieved July 26, 2006).

48. Frank L. Bird & James K. Luiselli, "Positive behavioral support of adults with developmental disabilities: assessment of long-term adjustment and habilitation following restrictive treatment histories," 31 Journal of Behavior Therapy and Experimental Psychiatry 5, 7 (2000).

57. Matthew L. Israel., Use of Skin Shock as a Supplementary Aversive, Judge Rotenberg Center, para. 1 (2002), *available at* http://www.judgerc.org/ (last visited April 21, 2010).

58. Matthew L. Israel (2002), *supra* note 57, at 1990-date: Development of the GED and GED-4 Devices.

59. *Id.*

60. Certification Team, *Report of the Certification Team on the Application of the Judge Rotenberg Education Center for Level II Behavior Modification Certification,* Commonwealth of Massachusetts, Executive Office of Health & Human Services, Department of Mental Retardation 10 (April 27, 2009) (on file with author).

61. *Id.*

75. Matthew L. Israel, *supra* note 5, at "Is it true that one of the consequences JRC uses is to administer several GED applications, over a half-hour period during which a student may be restrained on a restraint board?" See also, Jennifer Gonnerman (2007), *supra* note 3, at 38.

76. Matthew L. Israel, *supra* note 5, at "Multiple applications of the GED skin shock."

77. Matthew L. Israel, *supra* note 5.

78. NYSED Review Team (2006), *supra* note 17, at 8.

79. *Id.*

90. Certification Team (2009), *supra* note 60, at 32. *See* also, NYSED Review Team (2006), *supra* note 17, at 5.

91. NYSED Review Team (2006), *supra* note 17, at 6.

92. Certification Team (2009), *supra* note 60, at 32.

93. *Id.*

95. Matthew L. Israel, *supra* note 5, at "1. Is it true that at JRC a staff member will sometimes prompt a student to begin to engage in a problem behavior and then arrange an aversive for that? 2. Is there any professional support in the literature for that procedure?"

96. NYSED Review Team (2006), *supra* note 17, at 19.

97. *Id.*

98. MDRI Interview (2009).

99. NYSED Review Team (2006), *supra* note 17, at 10.

100. *Id.*

101. *Id.*

102. *Id.*

105. MDRI Interview (2009).

106. MDRI Interview (2009).

107. MDRI Interview (2009).

108. NYSED Review Team (2006), *supra* note 17, at 24.

111. Jennifer Gonnerman (2007), *supra* note 62, at 46–47.

112. MDRI Interview (2009).

113. NYSED Review Team (2006), *supra* note 17, at 14.

114. *Id.*

115. Greg Miller, *Response to Dr. Matthew Israel's letter entitled "Outrage Over Jennifer Gonnerman's Article, 'School of Shock"* (Sept. 4, 2007) (posted on Mother Jones comment blog for "School of Shock" article) *available at* http://motherjones.com/politics/2007/08/school-shock?page=4.

116. *Id.*

117. MDRI Interview (2009).

118. MDRI Interview (2009).

196. Letter from Disability Advocates, Addendum to A Call to Action to Eliminate the Use of Aversive Procedures and Other Inhumane Practices, 6 (Sept. 2009), *citing* Coalition for the Legal Rights of People with Disabilities, 6 The Communicator 1 (1995).

197. *Id.*

198. Matthew L. Israel, *supra* note 2, at "1985–1987 Failed Attempt by Office for Children to close JRC."

199. *Behavior Research Institute v. Mary Kay Leonard,* Sup. Ct. Dept. of the Trial Ct., and Prob. and Fam. Ct. of the Dept. of the Trial Ct., Docket No. 86E-0018-GI, Settlement Agreement (December 12, 1986). Under the settlement agreement, aversive procedures are only permitted with a court-ordered "substituted judgment" treatment plan. In presenting requesting a court-ordered "substituted judgment" treatment plan, the petitioner must show (1) the client's inability to provide informed consent and (2) "target behaviors" to be treated; what procedures will be used to treat the target behaviors; foreseeable adverse side-effects; professional discipline of staff members; prognosis should the procedures be implements; opinions of the client's family; client's previous treatment at BRI or elsewhere; description of appropriate

behaviors; client's IEP. The settlement agreement requires a monitor to report to the court on the client's treatment. The court will also appoint a doctor to oversee BRI's compliance.

206. Rick Karlin, *Regents set to reject use of electric shock,* Albany Times Union, January 9, 2007.

207. *Jeanette Alleyne v. N. Y. State Educ. Dep't,* No. 1:06-cv-00994-GLS (N.D.N.Y 2010) (memorandum-decision and order to the parties).

208. NYSED Review Team (2006), *supra* note 17, at 2–3.

209. *Id.*

210. NYSED Review Team (2006), *supra* note 17, at 11.

211. Massachusetts Office of Consumer Affairs and Business Regulation, "Judge Rotenberg Center clinicians fined $43,000, Consent agreement with Board of Psychologists Reached," Oct. 9, 2006, *available at* http://www.arcmass.org/AversivesPress/tabid/592/Default.aspx#JRCfine

212. Abbie Ruzicka, *Rotenberg Center director fined over clinicians' titles,* The Boston Globe, October 7, 2009.

213. Investigation Report, Massachusetts Department of Early Education and Care 4, November 1, 2007.

225. Nowak & MacArthur (2008), *supra* note 124, at 76–77.

226. Committee Against Torture, Conclusions and Recommendations of the Committee against Torture: United States of America, 15 May 2000, A/55/44, para. 180(c).

227. Committee Against Torture, Conclusions and Recommendations of the Committee Against Torture: United States of America, 18 May 2006, CAT/C/USA/CO/2, para. 35.

228. Committee Against Torture, List of issues prior to the submission of the fifth periodic report of UNITED STATES OF AMERICA 9,20 Jan. 2010, CAT/C/USA/Q/5.

229. *Id.*

230. *Id.*

Matthew L. Israel    **NO**

Aversives at JRC: A Better Alternative to the Use of Drugs, Restraint, Isolation, Warehousing, or Expulsion in the Treatment of Severe Behavior Disorders[1]

Why Behavior Modification Treatment, Including Aversives in Some Cases, Is Needed

The Judge Rotenberg Educational Center (JRC)[2,3,4], founded in 1971, is a residential education and treatment program in Canton, MA that provides behavior modification therapy, essentially without the use of psychotropic drugs, for 215 special needs children and adults from 7 different states. All of the students have at least one thing in common—they suffer from severe behavior disorders that could not be effectively treated by the many previous treatment programs and psychiatric hospitals they had been in prior to coming to JRC. Because of its zero-rejection, zero-expulsion policy, JRC serves the largest collection of individuals with difficult-to-treat self-abusive, aggressive and severely harmful behaviors in the country. JRC saves individuals from the mental and emotional pain, crippling disabilities, permanent injuries and even death caused by their otherwise untreatable behavior disorders. Before coming to JRC, many students were confined for years in psychiatric or correctional facilities or were living on the streets.

The students who are treated at JRC have shown, prior to admission to JRC, self-abusive behaviors such as: gouging out their eyes, causing near-blindness; smearing feces; head-banging to the point of causing detached retinas and blindness[5] or even stroke[6]; skin scratching to the point of fatal blood and bone infection; pulling out their own adult teeth[7]; running into a street filled with moving cars; or suicidal actions such as attempting to hang oneself, swallowing razor blades, taking a drug overdose, and jumping out of a moving vehicle or off of a building. Some students have shown violent aggression such as biting, hitting, kicking, punching, and head butting others. Some have pushed a parent down a flight of stairs, raped someone, tried to strangle a parent while the parent was driving, and beat a peer so severely that plastic surgery was required. Some have attempted to injure or kill others—for example, by pushing a child into oncoming traffic, smothering a sibling, stabbing a teacher, or slicing a peer's throat. Some have attacked police and therapists. Some have set their homes on fire, lit a fire in school, and lit themselves or family members on fire. Some have engaged in prostitution, been involved in gangs, and assaulted others with weapons such as a machete and chainsaw.

The following letter, which was written by the parents of a student who, prior to her treatment at JRC, had detached both of her retinas through self-abusive head-poking, illustrates what such behavior problems mean to a family. This letter was sent to legislators who were considering a proposed bill in the Massachusetts legislature to ban the use of aversives:

To Whom it May Concern:

We would like to tell you about our daughter, Samantha, and how the Judge Rotenberg School in Canton Massachusetts has saved her life.

We first discovered Samantha was different when she was about 2 years old. She would not relate well to others, had very little speech, and would stare at her hands or small objects for hours at a time. She also had frequent tantrums, and cried often. She began with early intervention, and over the next ten years, she went to four specialized schools for autistic children. In addition to her schooling, numerous therapists, and teachers came to our house to work with Samantha after hours, most of which was paid for out of our own funds. All these schools worked closely with her in small groups, and on a one to one basis, using learning trials, and positive reinforcement. In addition to this, Samantha was under the care of a psychiatrist, and given several different psychotropic medications.

Despite, all these well caring professionals working with our daughter, Samantha progressively deteriorated. Over the years, she became more violent. She would attack us, other children, and her teachers. She would bite, scratch, kick, hit, pinch, and head-butt. In addition she became more self-abusive. She would throw herself on the floor, hit herself, and throw herself against hard objects. She constantly had marks, and bruises on her from her own self abuse. We were also prisoners in our own home, as we could not take her anywhere, due to her behaviors; this had an impact on our other children as well. The final straw came when she hit herself in her head with such force, that she detached both retinas of her eyes, and was virtually blind. This has subsequently required 6 eye surgeries to repair, and her vision is still far from normal. The Anderson School, where she was at the time, told us they could not handle her, and asked us to find another school. This is when we learned about the Judge Rotenberg School (JRC), and the GED device.

Within several weeks of getting treated with the GED device, a miracle happened; Samantha stopped hitting herself, and stopped her violent behavior. She appeared much happier. She was able to be weaned off all of her psychotropic medications.

There was a period of deterioration. In June 2006, aversive treatment became a big issue in New York State. A law was passed prohibiting

*the use of the GED for antecedent behaviors, leading up to more aggres-
sive behaviors. Samantha became more aggressive, and angry. Some of
her old behaviors returned. An injunction to this law was obtained several months later, and the GED was then able to be applied as indicated
in the JRC program. Samantha improved, and was happier, and no longer
aggressive towards herself or others. This was proof that she needs an
ongoing program that includes the GED.*

*Recently, Samantha had another challenge. Due to a congenital
condition, she had to undergo complex orthopedic surgery on both legs
to correct a balance problem, and prevent future arthritis. JRC was absolutely wonderful. They accompanied her to all her appointments at the
Boston Children's Hospital. She remained in the hospital for 6 days after
her surgery. JRC had staff members in her room 24 hours a day, during
her entire stay in the hospital. In her post operative period, the staff was
with her in her residence at all times, and met her every need. She had
to be non-weight bearing for 6 weeks post op, and the JRC staff helped
her and transported her to school, and to all her post operative doctor's
appointments. One of the most remarkable things about her surgical
experience, is through all her pain and all her frustration of not being
able to walk, she remained calm, and pleasant. This proves the durability
of this program at JRC. If she was anywhere else, surely her old behaviors
would have returned, and may have affected her post operative outcome.*

*Sometimes, we feel that JRC is the most misunderstood place in
the world. Samantha has now been at JRC for over 5 years, and we have
seen nothing but love and affection for her on the part of the entire staff.
They appear to have the same love for all the students at the school. The
GED is given only after the failure of positive reinforcement programs,
and only after the approval of a judge. It is given carefully, and under
strict protocols. Everything done at this school and in the residences is
video monitored. The program is 100 percent transparent, and has nothing to hide.*

*The bottom line is that this program helped, and continues to help
our daughter where all other programs have failed. Our daughter is a
different person than 5 years ago. She is happy, able to concentrate and
learn, and fun to be with. She is on no psychotropic medications.*

*JRC takes only the most difficult kids that have failed at other pro-
grams, and make successes of a large number of them. Many of these
children have life threatening behaviors, before arriving at JRC. Everything there is done out of love, not cruelty. We believe our daughter would
be dead, or in an institution heavily sedated if it were not for this wonderful school, and caring staff. Many other parents feel the same.*

Sincerely,
Mitchell Shear, MD, and Marcia Shear[8]

Fortunately, behavioral psychology has developed a treatment for problematic behaviors such as Samantha's self-abuse. The treatment is called

"behavior modification" or "applied behavior analysis." Simply put, this involves analyzing the causes of the problematic behaviors, eliminating events that "trigger" the occurrence of the behaviors, arranging rewards for desired behaviors, and applying corrective consequences (consequences designed to decrease problem behaviors, or *aversives)* for undesired behaviors.

JRC's treatment relies overwhelmingly on the use of positive procedures such as rewards and educational procedures. In fact, JRC has created a unique Yellow Brick Road Reward Area[9] for its students that is found in no other program. However, in the case of 22% of its school-age population (and 41% of its total population), these procedures are not sufficiently effective to treat severe problem behaviors. JRC's experience in this respect is fairly consistent with the scientific literature. Thee major literature reviews show that positive-only procedures are effective in only 50–60% of the cases[10] (JRC's positive programming is able to achieve better results than the literature reports because of JRC's cutting edge reward programs.)

For individuals who do not respond to positive-only procedures, most treatment facilities do the following: administer a cocktail of mind-numbing, sometimes addicting, dangerous, and often ineffective psychotropic drugs; use restraint, take-downs, isolation rooms, and/or warehousing (doing nothing); or expel the student, leaving the parent with no options at all[11]. Instead of using these alternatives, all of which are problematic, JRC employs a corrective consequence ("aversive") in the form of a 2-second shock to the surface of the skin, typically of an arm or leg. This treatment, which feels like a hard pinch, has been extensively validated in the scientific literature (113 published papers since the 1960s[12]), is extremely effective[13], and has no significant adverse side effects[14]. For some individuals it is only required at the beginning of their treatment and can be faded out gradually as their behaviors improve. Even in the minority of cases where it is necessary, it is used rarely (the median number of applications per week at JRC is 0 and the mean is 3), and its use is initiated only after trying positive-only procedures for an average of 11 months. JRC uses this procedure only with an extensive and extraordinary list of safeguards[15]. For example, each individual's treatment program that includes the use of skin shock must be pre-approved by a physician, the parent (who can revoke this consent at any time), included in the student's IEP or IHP, approved by a human rights committee and a peer review committee. It also must be individually pre-approved and reviewed at regular intervals by a Massachusetts Probate Court Judge.[16,17]

JRC has been licensed or approved continuously, throughout its 39-year history, by the state education, developmental disabilities and child care departments of Rhode Island and Massachusetts. The Massachusetts Department of Developmental Services ("DDS") has granted and renewed, ever since 1986, JRC's special certification to use aversive behavioral procedures. More than 15 different judges of the Massachusetts Probate and Family Court have, during the last 25 years, approved individual petitions, by guardians on behalf of incompetent children and adults at JRC, to allow the use of aversive therapy in individual behavior modification treatment programs[18]. Thousands of loving parents—including professors at Harvard and NYU, as well as psychiatrists and pediatricians—have entrusted the care and habilitation of their children to JRC.[19] Former JRC students have voluntarily come before legislative committees to testify that JRC saved their lives.[20]

Certain well-intentioned, but ill-informed advocates object to JRC's use of skin shock and are constantly seeking regulations and legislation to ban the use of aversives. Because JRC is the leading example of a program willing to supplement positive behavioral supports, such as rewards, with skin shock as an aversive, in cases where the person cannot be effectively treated without them, JRC has become the focus of attacks by anti-aversive advocates. Characteristically, these persons are unwilling to rationally weigh the risks or intrusiveness of skin shock aversives against the benefits, and to consider whether using such aversives might be a better choice than the alternatives. They simply ignore the small population of people who cannot be effectively treated with psychotropic drugs and positive behavioral supports alone, and who are being warehoused and drugged into submission. In some cases, these anti-aversives advocates have been so dogmatic that they have contributed to a child's death through self-abuse rather than allow him to receive life-saving therapy that includes aversives[21].

Under state and federal law, non-disabled individuals have the right to choose aversive therapy to treat behavioral problems such as smoking and drinking. To deny persons with developmental or behavior/psychiatric disabilities the same right to treat their behavior problems with aversives would be to impose an invidious form of discrimination against those unfortunate enough to suffer from such disabilities.

The Mental Disabilities Rights International (MDRI) Report

The authors of the MDRI Report have a strong philosophical opposition to aversives. Like other anti-aversive advocates, they are unwilling to use a rational risks-versus-benefits analysis in evaluating the use of aversives. Presumably, even if treatment with behavioral skin shock were the only treatment that could save a child from maiming or killing himself or herself, they would oppose its use. Indeed, Dr. Fredda Brown, one of the key persons who provided information to the authors of the MDRI Report was involved in just such a case.[22] In that case, a young man who was maiming himself through self-abusive scratching until he received effective treatment with behavioral skin shock at JRC. Unfortunately, anti-aversive advocates persuaded his parents that he no longer needed that treatment and could live in a supported apartment where aversives would no longer be available. Without aversives, however, his self-abusive scratching (causing blood and bone infection and eventual paralysis) resumed and caused him a painful and premature death at the age of 25.

Almost all of the persons listed as sources for the information for the MDRI Report have testified in Massachusetts for bills that would, if passed, ban the use of aversives. After trying, unsuccessfully to pass such bills for 24 years, the proponents of these bills now are looking to the United Nations Rapporteur on Torture for help with their political cause.

Because of the authors' strong philosophical opposition to aversives, what they refer to as an "investigation" was simply not that. They never visited

JRC, never sought to discuss their concerns with JRC's clinicians or staff, never spoke to the hundreds of parents who are pleased with what JRC has been able to accomplish for their children, never advised JRC of their investigation or invited JRC to respond to their concerns, and never interviewed current or former students who have been pleased with the results of their treatment at JRC, including the use of aversives.

MDRI's "investigation" consisted largely of the following: finding and using unverified negative accusations available on the internet; taking selective quotations from the JRC website given by parents and students in *support* of JRC's use of aversives, and fraudulently revising those portions to make up false or misleading statements designed to make the authors appear to be *negative* toward JRC's treatment; soliciting information from an individual who, according to an August 29, 2006 police report, claimed to have placed a "whistle blower" inside JRC;[23] soliciting as many negative quotes as possible from persons who are opposed to JRC; accepting and publishing anonymous accusations without researching whether there was any truth to them; taking selective quotations from reports by a state agency that has a philosophical opposition to aversives (and that is currently being sued by a group of JRC parents in the Federal District Court of Northern New York) without any reference to JRC's responses to those accusations, all of which are available on JRC's website; and presenting as facts, outdated, re-hashed, and long-since refuted accusations, some of which are now as much as 30–40 years old.

Here are a few examples of the poorly researched, false and misleading statements in the MDRI Report. More can be found in JRC's full response to the MDRI Report.

1. **"The Judge Rotenberg Center (JRC) was founded . . . in California . . . was then moved to Rhode Island." (p. 6)** This is an example of the shoddiness of the MDRI authors' research, even in simply reporting what they found in JRC's publicly available website. JRC's website clearly states that JRC was started in Cranston, Rhode Island.[24]

2. **"in 1981 [in California], a 14 year-old boy died face down . . ." [bracketed material supplied] (p. 6)** JRC was not operating a program in California in 1981 and was not responsible for this boy's care and treatment.

3. **"What's wrong with punishments is that they work immediately, but give no long-term results . . ." B.F. Skinner interview The New York Times, 1987. (p. 10)** This is another example of MDRI's misleading the reader by providing incomplete misinformation. Subsequent to the interview referred to, Skinner issued a statement on punishment that clarified his position regarding the usefulness of punishment in the treatment of certain behaviors. In this statement he wrote:

   > [s]ome autistic children, for example, will seriously injure themselves or engage in other excessive behavior unless drugged or restrained, and other treatment is then virtually impossible. If brief and harmless aversive stimuli, made precisely contingent on self-destructive or other excessive behavior, suppress the behavior and leave the children free to develop in other ways, I believe it can be justified.[25]

4. **"I would be frequently restrained and placed in a small room . . ."** **(p. 17 of the full MDRI Report)** Again, MDRI has fraudulently taken out of context a small part of a longer statement that is very supportive toward JRC and toward the use of the GED skin shock.[26] By selecting and rearranging words, MDRI makes it seem like a critical statement. The words as quoted were not what the student actually said. Notably absent from the words that MDRI chose to quote are the following words, *"About the GED, it saved my life,"* which appear as the first sentence in the final paragraph of the letter. The full statement, a letter from a former JRC student, Brian Avery, is re-printed below. The words taken out of context are indicated by bold font.

> *My name is Brian Avery and I was a student at JRC from September 1998 to January 2004. Prior to me entering JRC at age 12, I was in and out of several psychiatric hospitals and failed in two alternative educational settings.*
>
> *My behavioral problems really began to escalate when I was 8 or 9 years old. I was on several medications including Tegretol, Haldol, Ritalin, Risperdal, Depekote, Prozac and Paxil. At age 10, my behavior become dangerously out of control. While in school, I would climb on furniture, climb under furniture, mouth off at the teacher, run out of the classroom and would have to be chased down by school staff. I would disrespect authority figures, yell, swear, exhibit inappropriate sexual behaviors in school. I would even try to stab myself with a pencil. I would become physically aggressive with my teachers and would have to be confined in a small padded room. In December of 1996 I was moved from a co-ed class with a 10:2 student/teacher ratio to another elementary school a few towns over and placed in a all male class with a 6:2 student/teacher ratio. That change delivered little improvement in my behavior and academic progress. At home, I spent most of my time sleeping or being a couch potato, a debilitating side effect of all the medication I was taking. During the time that I was awake, I would disrespect my parents, be aggressive towards my parents and siblings, throw tantrums, destroy property, and would spend hours on end crying. In November of 1996, I spend three weeks in a psychiatric hospital. In February of 1998, and also in May of that year, I spent another three weeks in a psychiatric hospital. After my third hospitalization, my parents and school district finally came to the conclusion that I needed to be placed in a residential school. After visiting numerous schools in New York, Pennsylvania, New Jersey, and Massachusetts, my parents chose JRC.*
>
> *In September of 1998, I was placed at JRC. Within three months of being at JRC, I was taken off all of my medication. My first few months at JRC were very depressing. For the first month or so of being at JRC, my behavior was much more under control than it had been for a very long time. However, once I became acclimated to the program, my behavior began to deteriorate. I would once again display the same inappropriate behaviors that I did in*

*public school. **I would be** frequently **restrained and placed in a small room.** JRC would employ an elaborate scheme of behavior contracts and punishments (not the temporary skin shock). Such contracts included earning a small snack and 10 minutes of free time for going an hour without exhibiting inappropriate behaviors, earning a preferred breakfast for completing my morning routine without incident, being able to order take out for going a full day without displaying inappropriate behavior, being able to attend the weekly BBQ and go on field trips for going a week without displaying inappropriate behavior, and so on. Punishments that JRC would employ involve me spending the day in a small room with a staff person whom I was forbidden from socializing with, going to bed at 7 pm, having to do schoolwork or chores on the weekend without being able to socialize with my housemates. Other punishments included being deprived of foods that were rewards. For example, if everyone else were having pizza, I would be served peanut butter and jelly. I would also be put through a ball task, which involved me needing to place 250 foam balls, one at a time, into a trash can while wearing mitts, a task that is very unpleasant. Although I would have occasional bouts of progress (staying on contract for two months at one point), I made no sustainable progress in 1998 through most of 1999. In the fall of 1999, JRC and my parents had decided that it was time to give the GED a try. I reluctantly agreed to the GED and decided not to fight JRC's attempt to place me on the device. I figured that although unpleasant, the GED would deter me from displaying behaviors that would result in me being restrained and losing out on the rewards that came with the program.*

In December of 1999, I was placed on the GED. For the first month or so that I was on the GED, I displayed few inappropriate behaviors, however, once I became acclimated to the fact that I was on the device and was aware of what the GED felt like, I would start displaying lots of more minor behaviors that were not treated with the GED. Once on the GED, instances of me acting out became fewer and more far in between. Although when my contract was broken, I would display lots of inappropriate behaviors, but I would be selective as to not exhibit GED behaviors, although I would occasionally slip up and receive a GED application. By the spring of 2001, it had been several months since my previous major behavioral incident. JRC then began to rapidly fade me off the GED (although the fading process started nearly a year prior, bouts of behavioral episodes impeded the fading process). In July of 2001, I was completely faded from the GED and was moved into a less restrictive residence (apartment), with a student/staff ratio of 4:1. In the apartment, I enjoyed many privileges, such as grocery shopping, going on weekly field trips to the movies, to the arcade, YMCA, local parks etc. I even attended a few sporting events, including the Providence Bruins, Harlem Globetrotters, and even a Red Sox-Yankees game at Fenway Park. I was also given independence to move about the residence and school unsupervised. All of these were privileges I could not even dream of prior to being placed on the GED. From September 2001–September 2002, I would have a few bouts of behavioral incidents and was placed on and off the GED. However, in October of 2002, I was faded from the GED for good. In the fall of 2002, I attended a culinary class at Blue Hills Technical school, and in November I worked in the computer department as an in school job. Also, I began preparing for the New York Regents exams, and in 2003 I began taking the Regents exams. In the fall of 2003, it became clear to JRC, my parents, and school district that I had accomplished all I could while at JRC and in January 2004 I was transitioned back to public school in New York and mainstreamed.

I moved to Florida in August of 2004 and graduated from high school with honors in May 2005. Since then, I took and passed a couple of college courses and had a few jobs, including a seasonal position working for a bank as a data capture specialist, a job that I obtained because of my quick typing skills that I acquired while at JRC.

About the GED, it saved my life. There are lots of opponents to this controversial, yet potentially life-saving treatment, and under-standably so. For someone who has never had the kind of problems I had nor has dealt with anyone who has my kind of problems, when hearing about the GED for the first time, it is only natural to cry torture. However, in reality, being on the GED is a much nicer alternative than being warehoused in a hospital, incarcerated, or being doped up on psychotropic drugs to the point of oblivion. A brief 2-second shock to the surface of the skin sure beats out spend-ing my days restrained and drugged up on drugs and not making any academic progress. I did not like being on the GED when I felt like acting up because it prevented me from being able to do so. But in the end, I'm thankful for the GED because of the enormous progress I made with it and have continued to make once I no longer needed it.

Some people may wind up spending the majority of their life at JRC while being able to enjoy the benefits and privileges the pro-gram has while others, like myself, are able to go on to live an independent life. The bottom line is, if those who opposed the GED had their way, I would currently be locked up and heavily medicate at a hospital or in jail or possibly even dead. So for those who have set out to ban the GED please don't.

Thank you very much

Sincerely,

Brian Avery

5. **"I refused to allow the GED . . ." (p. 18 of the full MDRI Report)**
   This is another example of MDRI fraudulently taking a very positive and supportive statement off of JRC's website and editing it to make it appear to be saying something negative about JRC. This statement

comes from the testimony of Ricardo Mesa, the father of a current JRC student. Mr. Mesa's full testimony is given below.[27] To illustrate how blatantly out of context this quote is, the full testimony is reproduced here and the words taken out of context are shown in bold font. Notably absent from the words that the MDRI Report chose to quote are the words, *"What means something is that I have a daughter who has a life now . . . and is happy."*

> *I have a daughter, Nicole, who went to JRC in 2004. She's still at JRC in the adult services and she was diagnosed with autism and later Landau-Kleffner Syndrom. As the years went by she got progressively worse. She had brain surgery to remove the epilepsy, which helped with her receptive language. But her behavior continued to be extremely severe. To the point that she would constantly punch her eyes like this {demonstrates} constantly. And I used to be a martial Arts instructor and I used to block and there was no way you could block those punches. Those were hard punches to the eyes. She was doing about a thousand a week. We had to pad the entire room, in her bedroom, she lived with us, she still lives with us. We had to, um, we couldn't go anywhere, we couldn't go on vacation, we couldn't. . . . At nights we would hear her banging her head constantly, all night long. She would run out, pinching constantly, her face, her body her breasts, black and blue. You get the picture. She went to the May Center, she went to the LCDC Center, she went to Lighthouse, she went to Perkins School for the Blind, she went to the behavioral program, the neuro-behavioral program at the May Center. These are all excellent programs with very devoted teachers and excellent staff. They couldn't help her. They couldn't stop her. Finally, the Boston School District, the ETL suggested JRC because of some of the progress she had seen from some of the children and I went to see it. We decided to send her over there. And I refused to allow the GED. Because it just, it's so counter-intuitive, I love my daughter, so **I refused to allow it.** And they were fine with it. They allowed me to keep her in the school. They used other methods to try to keep her safe, the restraints, the arm splints and so forth. But Nicole was not making any progress. When she'd come home it was the same story. I agreed after a long time and the hardest day of my life was going before Judge Souten (sp) and asking for them to allow her to use the GED. I told my wife, "We will give them one month. If I don't see immediate progress, she's off it." They put her on the GED, she had a few applications the first day. A few days went by and she had one more. And from that point on she's had an application once every three months, two months and they were usually for very severe behaviors. I don't allow them to use it for any other type of behavior. That contradicts prior testimony {gesturing about someone behind him.} They are fine with it. They have not asked me to take her out of there. Because of that, now she gets one maybe once every year, six months. I mean it's been a long, long time. I can't even recall. She lives at home with us. At home she doesn't wear the GED. It's there in the house and I remind her, that if I see the antecedents, I tell her, "You're going to have to wear*

the GED." She's fine with it. She has to dress well to go to school. She takes really good care of herself. The staff is extremely loving to her. Always has been, that's one of the things I love. I know them well. My wife knows them very well. We've been able to go to a vacation to Florida every year and Virginia Beach, we are able to go to the movies, we are able to go to dinner together, we have a life. And she lives with us. And that's the way I want it. My biggest fear is that we'll lose all of this ground we've made. That she might return to those horrible days, when she was hurting herself so badly. She knocked out my wife a couple of times with headbutts, this was before the GED. And if she were to go back to that stage, it would be just a matter of time before we would have to put her in an institution, or, she wouldn't be able to live with us. So, you know, I really, I know there's a lot of emotion in all of this. A lot of these are articles that have been written, I spoke one time to a reporter all about my daughter and the Boston Globe and the only thing they did, was post "Torture Versus Love." Not one word about what I told them about my daughter was in that article. You can't believe everything you read. And there's a public outcry, against this and exaggerations about what they are doing at the school. I can't speak for anybody else, but I can speak for my daughter and for my life. And I am not a crazy person, or an uninformed person. I am an accountant and I am also an ordained permanent Deacon with the Archdiocese of Boston. I work very closely with Cardinal Law, I mean Cardinal Sean O'Malley. I studied psychology when I was in school. All of that doesn't mean anything. What means something is that I have a daughter who has a life now. I taught her how to ride a bicycle, who can go swimming, who can go on vacation, who goes to school and comes home and is happy.

Particularly disturbing is the authors' willingness to distort testimonial material from JRC's own website, as shown in items 4 and 5 above. The authors took words out of context, made up statements that were not made by the persons who gave the testimonials, and represented the material to be negative comments about JRC and/or skin shock aversives. If the authors were so willing to falsify statements that can be so easily checked—just by going to the JRC website—how much have they distorted the many other accusations in the MDRI Report that were made anonymously and whose accuracy cannot be checked?

In summary, the MDRI Report is a false, misleading, sensationalized, and one-sided account of JRC that is worthy only of a tabloid. It is not a serious or accurate piece of reporting or investigation. One fervently hopes that this Report is an aberration, and not representative of the standards used by MDRI for its other work on both the national and international fronts.

Notes

1. For a more detailed presentation of the material in this document, see pp. 1–50 of JRC's complete Reply to MDRI Report, available at www.judgerc .org/MDRIReportResponse.pdf.

2. JRC's website, at www.judgerc.org, contains a wealth of information. Additional information about aversives can be found at www.effectivetreatment.org.

3. See http://judgerc.org/parents_journey.wmv ("Parents' Journey") for film clips showing some of these types of behavior problems, and giving an overview of how JRC uses positive reward and educational procedures, supplemented with aversives when necessary, in treating these behaviors.

4. JRC's Board of Directors contains five Ph.D. level behavioral psychologists, three of whom are college professors, and one of whom is the President-elect of the Association for Behavior Analysis International, the leading professional organization of behavioral psychologists.

5. JRC currently has such a student who at one point, prior to attending JRC, had detached both retinas due to head-hitting and knee-to-head. Her previous placement, a program that used positive-only treatment procedures, was unable to stop the behavior. Supplementary skin shock at JRC was successful in treating the behavior and thereby enabling the retinas to be re-attached. The young lady is now thriving. See below for photos of this student before and after her treatment at JRC, and for a letter from her parents.

6. JRC currently has a student who is only 16 years old, but who has engaged in head-hitting so forcefully that he has caused himself to have a stroke. His physician has advised JRC that in all probability continued head-banging will cause a fatal brain hemorrhage.

7. JRC currently has a student who has pulled out all but 14 of his adult teeth.

8. This and other letters from JRC parents may be found on the JRC website at http://www.judgerc.org/parentletters.html#letter66.

9. See http://judgerc.org/yellowbrickroad.html.

10. Carr, E. G., Robinson, F., Taylor, J. & Carlson, J. (1990). Positive approaches to the treatment of severe behavior problems in persons with developmental disabilities. In: *National Institute of Mental Health Consensus Development Conference* (pp. 231–341). NIH Publication No. 91-2410. And see Carr, E. G., Horner, R. H., Turnbull, A. P., Marquis, J. G., Magito McLaughlin, D., McAtee, M. L., Smith, C. E., Anderson Ryan, K., Ruef, M. B., & Doolabh, A. (1999). *Positive behavior support for people with developmental disabilities: A research synthesis.* Washington, D.C.: American Association of Mental Retardation. Full text available at http://www.judgerc.org/PositiveBehaviorSupport.pdf. And see Horner, R. H., Carr, E. G., Strain, P. S., Todd, A .W., and Reed, H. K. (2002). Problem behavior interventions for young children with autism: A research synthesis. *Journal of Autism and Developmental Disorders, 32,* 423–445.

11. Israel, M. L., Blenkush, N. A., von Heyn, R. E., and Sands, C. C. Seven Case studies of individuals expelled from positive-only programs (2010). *The Journal of Behavior Analysis of Offender and Victim Treatment and Prevention, 2* (1), 20–36. Full text available at http://www.judgerc.org/SevenCaseStudies.pdf. See also http://www.judgerc.org/posonlyprograms.pdf (contains documentary proof of the assertion that well-known positive-only programs expel students whose behaviors prove to be too severe to be treated with positive-only treatment procedures).

12. See http://www.effectivetreatment.org/bibliography.html.

13. Israel, M. L., Blenkush, N. A., von Heyn, R. E., & Rivera, P. M. (2008). Treatment of aggression with behavioral programming that includes supplementary skin-shock. *The Journal of Behavior Analysis of Offender and Victim Treatment and Prevention, 1* (4), 119–166. Full text available at http://www.judgerc.org/AggressionPaper.pdf.

14. van Oorsouw, W. M. W. J., Israel, M. L., von Heyn, R. E., & Duker, P. C. (2008). Side effects of contingent shock treatment. *Research in Developmental Disabilities, 29*, 513–523. Full text available at http://www.judgerc.org/SideEffectsContingent.pdf.

15. See "Safeguards for the Use of Aversives with Students at JRC," a paper that may be found in Appendix F in JRC's full response to the MDRI Report, at http://www.judgerc.org/MDRIReportResponse.pdf.

16. In these adversarial hearings, the judge appoints an independent attorney to represent the interests of the student, as distinct from the interests of the parent or JRC. That attorney is given funds to hire an expert who evaluates the student and his/her treatment needs and advises the attorney as to JRC's proposed treatment program. At the hearing, the judge decides whether the student is competent to make his/her own treatment decisions, and whether, if incompetent, he/she would have chosen to use aversives to treat the problem behavior.

17. All programs that educate children with difficult behaviors use aversives but either hide them or give them different names (e.g., "emergency procedures" or "reactive procedures"). If a program administers a "take-down" every time a child is aggressive, this may function as an aversive. The same applies to "time-out" procedures or seclusion procedures that are administered as consistent consequences for certain behaviors. Holding a young autistic child still for 30–60 seconds against his/her will is a frequently used aversive. Physical "redirection" procedures or physical "prompts" that are accompanied with a hard squeeze on the shoulder or arm can also function as "hidden" aversives. A loud shouted "NO!" can be a terrifying aversive for young child. A spank on the buttocks is a common aversive that parents sometimes use. Monetary fines, bad grades, point losses, losses of privileges, ignoring, and signs of disapproval can also function as aversives. It is not the case that JRC uses aversives and other programs do not. Rather, JRC chooses to use a safer and more effective aversive (skin shock) than these other procedures, and is willing to label it for what it really is—an aversive. For an explanation of what aversives are, how and why they are used and the reasons why skin shock is so much more effective than, and preferable to, other aversives, *see* Israel, M. L. (2008). *Primer on Aversives.* Full text available at www.judgerc.org/aversivesprimer.pdf.

18. A brief summary of the legal status of aversives at JRC may be found at http://judgerc.org/LegalBasisAversives.pdf.

19. *See* http://www.judgerc.org/intensivetreatment.html#State_House_Testimonies,_November_2009 and http://www.judgerc.org/Comments/parents_AV.html.

20. *Id.*

21. A young man from New York had been maiming himself through self-abusive scratching until he was placed at JRC where he received effective treatment with behavioral skin shock. Unfortunately, anti-aversive advocates persuaded his parents that he no longer needed that treatment and

could live in a supported apartment where aversives would no longer be available. Without aversives, however, his self-abusive scratching (causing blood and bone infection and eventual paralysis) resumed and caused him a painful and premature death at the age of 25. See Note 5 in JRC's Response to MDRI Report at *persons already enjoy when they use aversives to treat behaviors such as excessive smoking or drinking* http://www.judgerc.org/MDRIReportResponse.pdf.

22. Dr. Brown, a zealous advocate of deinstitutionalization and an anti-aversive supporter, was instrumental in the removal from JRC in the late 1990s of a student named James Velez. James suffered from a debilitating compulsion to scratch and gouge his skin with his fingernails—a behavior that caused serious blood and bone infections and caused him to require a wheelchair. At JRC his behavior improved sufficiently to enable him to get out of the wheelchair. His self-mutilation was drastically reduced, his skin bone infections cleared to the point where he could have some skin grafts, and he was even able to attend classes at a local public high school with having to wear his GED skin shock device. Unfortunately the anti-aversive advocates, advised by Dr. Brown persuaded James' parents that he no longer needed the behavioral structure or aversives of JRC.

James was then removed from JRC against JRC's advice. The advocates who removed him were so hostile to JRC that they refused to even communicate with JRC's medical director about what James' medical needs were, and refused to discuss with JRC's clinicians what his treatment needs were. JRC was unable to even find out where James was living. The anti-aversive advocates were so eager to remove him from JRC that they removed him even before there was a group home or supported apartment ready for him in New York, his home state. As a result he spent 2 years in a ward for developmentally disabled persons at the Brooklyn Development Center.

Eventually James was moved into a supported apartment in Brooklyn operated by an agency that was opposed to the use of aversives. After moving into his apartment, James was invited by the anti-aversive advocates to tell his story at a Boston conference of TASH, an advocacy organization that is strongly opposed to aversives. (Jan Nisbet, one of the other persons providing information for the MDRI Report is a former President of TASH.) James' life story to this point was chronicled in a manner quite sympathetic to the anti-aversive advocates, in four front page articles that ran in the *New York Times* in June and December 1997. Copies of the four *New York Times* articles, James' obituary, and a proposed OpEd piece about James by Dr. Israel are attached hereto in Appendix J. (This Appendix may be found in JRC's full response to the MDRI Report, at www.judgerc.org/MDRIReportResponse.pdf.)

At his shared apartment James' behavioral consultant was Dr. Brown. Devoid of the behavioral structure and aversives that had served him at JRC, James resumed his scratching, had to use a wheelchair once again, and within about 13 months was hospitalized and nearly died from a leg infection. By February, 1999 he was paralyzed and by October 1999 he was dead at the age of 25, due to infections of the blood and spine caused by the very behaviors JRC had been able to successfully control through the use of skin shock. Characteristically, the anti-aversive advocates showed no remorse over his death or second thoughts as to the wisdom of removing from JRC the one program that had gotten him out of a wheelchair, made him healthy again, and kept him alive. The director of the supervised apartment program in which he died is quoted in his obituary as saying, "Things turned out not to be so simple as we first thought. For the last few years, though, I think that James had the best life that he could have. If that's what this experiment proves, that's a lot. . . . He had the life he wanted . . . James paved the way."

After James' death, when Dr. Brown came to JRC to testify against the use of aversives in the treatment program of another student, Dr. Israel invited her to his office to discuss the case. She refused and marched out of his office when the subject was raised.

23. A copy of the police report may be found in Appendix A of JRC's full response to the MDRI Report, at www.judgerc.org/MDRIReportResponse .pdf. Note that even a fellow JRC-accuser admitted, "I guess we know the whistle blower is not reliable."

24. *See* http://judgerc.org/history.html.

25. Skinner, B. F. A Statement on Punishment. *APA Monitor*, June 1988, p. 22. Full text available at http://www.judgerc.org/Griffin1988Skinner-punishmentstatementAJMR.pdf.

26. Letter from former JRC Student Brian Avery, received June 7, 2009. This statement in its entirety appears on JRC's website at http://judgerc.org/Comments/stultr15.html.

27. Testimony of Father of a JRC Student to Massachusetts Legislative Committee, October 27, 2009. Available in its entirety testimony at: http://judgerc.org/StateHouseTestimonies/42.%20Ricardo%20Mesa%20State%20House%20Testimony%2011.4.09.wmv.

EXPLORING THE ISSUE

Is the Use of Aversive Treatment an Inhumane Intervention for Psychologically Disordered Individuals?

Critical Thinking and Reflection

1. In cases in which traditional interventions such as counseling and medication have been ineffective, what options would you recommend to the parents of children who engage in dangerous aggression toward themselves or others?
2. What considerations should be given to the question of how much is too much when it comes to the use of aversive techniques?
3. Imagine that you have been appointed by the governor to conduct an objective evaluation of the ethics of techniques such as those used at JRC. What factors would you include in your evaluation?
4. Assume that you've been awarded a large grant to compare the effectiveness of the JRC techniques to other interventions. What kind of study would you design?
5. What are your thoughts about the emotional effects on the clinicians who administer the aversive techniques to clients?

Is There Common Ground?

When considering the almost unimaginable behaviors of some profoundly disturbed people, one's heart goes out to the family members whose loved one engages in acts that are dangerous to the body, and possibly fatal. Seemingly uncontrollable impulses to gouge out an eye, yank out a tooth, bite through one's skin, or assault another person are horrifying to observe. For individuals with profound intellectual disability or extreme forms of psychological disturbance, traditional forms of behavior therapy may be ineffective. Both MDRI and Dr. Israel would certainly support any intervention that can effectively control such behaviors, and both parties would support using the least intrusive and restrictive procedures possible. The goal of individuals on both sides of this argument is to protect human beings from harm. MDRI believes that aversives such as the GED go too far, and deprive humans of their basic rights. Dr. Israel contends that thoughtful policies and careful procedures have been established to protect the rights of these disabled individuals, and he cites the pleas of family members to help their loved ones acquire the skills they need to refrain from engaging in self-injurious behaviors.

Additional Resources

Altiere, M. J., & von Kluge, S. (2009). Searching for acceptance: Challenges encountered while raising a child with autism. *Journal of Intellectual and Developmental Disability, 34*(2), 142–152.

Coalition Against Institutionalized Child Abuse. Retrieved from www.caica.org

Farrell, J. J. (2009). Protecting the legal interests of children when shocking, restraining, and secluding are the means to an educational end. *St. John's Law Review, 83*(1), 395–426.

Howlin, P. (2010). Evaluating psychological treatments for children with autism-spectrum disorders. *Advances in Psychiatric Treatment, 16*, 133–140.

Matson, J. L. (Ed.) (2009). *Applied behavior analysis for children with autism spectrum disorders.* New York, NY: Springer.

Sailor, W., Dunlap, G., Sugai, G., & Horner, R. (Eds.) (2009). *Handbook of positive behavior support.* New York, NY: Springer.

Wang, P., Baker, L. A., Gao, Y., Raine, A., & Lozano, D. I. (2012). Psychopathic traits and physiological responses to aversive stimuli in children aged 9–11 years. *Journal of Abnormal Child Psychology, 40,* 1–11. www.springerlink.com.silk.library.umass.edu/content/0091-0627/

Weiss, N. R., & Knoster, T. (2008). It may be nonaversive, but is it a positive approach? Relevant questions to ask throughout the process of behavioral assessment and intervention. *Journal of Positive Behavior Interventions, 10*(1), 72–78.

Wood, J., Drahota, A., Sze, K., Har, K., Chiu, A., & Langer, D. (2009). Cognitive behavioral therapy for anxiety in children with autism spectrum disorders: A randomized, controlled trial. *Journal of Child Psychology and Psychiatry, 50*(3), 224–234.

ISSUE 15

Is It Unethical for Psychologists to Be Involved in Coercive Interrogations?

YES: Mark Costanzo, Ellen Gerrity, and M. Brinton Lykes, from "Psychologists and the Use of Torture in Interrogations," *Analyses of Social Issues and Public Policy (ASAP)* (December 2007)

NO: Kirk M. Hubbard, from "Psychologists and Interrogations: What's Torture Got to Do with It?" *Analyses of Social Issues and Public Policy (ASAP)* (December 2007)

Learning Outcomes

After reading this issue, you should be able to:

- Understand the role of a professional organization such as the American Psychological Association in defining behaviors that the organization views as unethical.
- Discuss the pros and cons of using coercive interrogation procedures to obtain actionable intelligence from suspected terrorists.
- Critically evaluate the criteria delineating effective questioning from coercive interrogation.
- Discuss ways in which psychologists have an opportunity to use their scientific knowledge to develop and implement effective questioning techniques which stop short of coercion.
- Consider the impact on the individuals who conduct coercive interrogations as well as the captives who are coercively interrogated.

ISSUE SUMMARY

YES: Psychologists Mark Costanzo, Ellen Gerrity, and M. Brinton Lykes assert that the involvement of psychologists in enhanced interrogations is a violation of fundamental ethical principles.

NO: Psychologist and intelligence expert Kirk M. Hubbard asserts that psychologists can assist in developing effective, lawful ways to obtain actionable intelligence in fighting terrorism and can bring a wealth of knowledge to the administration of interrogations.

Since the September 11 terrorist attacks, many Americans fear that other assaults could happen at any time. On the international scene, the "war against terror" escalated, as potential terrorists were tracked down, apprehended, and held in various places around the globe and were interrogated, at times through means that many would regard as inhumane violations of the Geneva Convention. These "enhanced interrogation techniques" were designed to extract information from detainees and included procedures such as forced nudity, painful stress positions, sleep deprivation, and waterboarding (provokes the sensation of being drowned).

Psychologists were called upon by various sectors of the U.S. government to develop effective techniques for eliciting information from detainees. Some of these techniques were based on the "learned helplessness" theory of the prominent research psychologist Martin Seligman. For much of the decade, the American Psychological Association (APA) debated whether it was unethical for psychologists to use their scientific knowledge and clinical expertise for the development and implementation of enhanced interrogation techniques. Although many vocal critics argued that such participation was tantamount to participating in torture, opponents of this view saw the potential for psychologists to play a major role in protecting national security by assisting government personnel in obtaining information about potential threats.

The debate about the involvement of psychologists in controversial activities such as enhanced interrogation techniques culminated in a 2010 decision by the APA to amend its Ethics Code to address potential conflicts among professional ethics, legal authority, and organizational demands. Previously, the Ethics Code implied that if psychologists could not resolve such conflicts, they could adhere to the law or to demands of an organization without further consideration. The 2010 amendments to the Ethics Code were intended to affirm APA's long-standing policy that psychologists may never violate human rights, regardless of demands placed upon them.

Psychologists Mark Costanzo, Ellen Gerrity, and M. Britton Lykes argue strongly that psychologists should not be involved in interrogations that involve torture or other forms of cruel, inhumane, or degrading treatment. They assert that the involvement of psychologists in designing, assisting with, or participating in such interrogations is a violation of fundamental ethical principles. These psychologists also contend that torture produces severe and lasting trauma for the individuals who experience it, and for the societies that support such acts.

Dr. Costanzo and his colleagues state that psychologists should be expressly forbidden from engaging in activities associated with interrogations that involve the use of torture and any form of cruel, inhuman, or degrading treatment of human beings. Furthermore, they contend that coercive interrogations are ineffective in extracting reliable information, and that there is irrefutable evidence that techniques *less coercive* than torture have produced verifiably false confessions. Many survivors of torture report that they would have said anything to "make the torture stop."

Psychologist and intelligence expert Kirk M. Hubbard asserts that psychologists from various subdisciplines can bring a wealth of knowledge to the administration of legal interrogations. Dr. Hubbard asks whether psychology should withhold information about ways in which to protect the country or to influence terrorists to disclose information. He contends that, if the psychological profession does not like the use of coercion to obtain actionable information, then the profession should step up and suggest effective alternatives.

Dr. Hubbard finds it objectionable to think that it is unfair to use what is known about psychological science to protect American families and to defend American lives and culture. He criticizes Dr. Costanzo and his colleagues for creating an argument that is not grounded in current knowledge of terrorism, as they attempt to "(mis)lead" readers into thinking that legal interrogations do not yield actionable intelligence.

According to Dr. Hubbard, the assertion that rapport and liking are the keys to obtaining information ignores the coercive pressures inherent in the circumstances. For terrorists who do not care if they live or die, there is little or no incentive to work with interrogators. He asserts that there is no reason why psychologists cannot assist in developing effective, lawful ways to obtain actionable intelligence in fighting terrorism. In fact, Dr. Hubbard argues that the case of Jose Padilla (who was planning to destroy apartment buildings and detonate a "dirty bomb") is a prime example of how a legal interrogation of a known terrorist led to the prevention of an attack.

YES

Mark Costanzo, Ellen Gerrity, and M. Brinton Lykes

Psychologists and the Use of Torture in Interrogations

This article argues that psychologists should not be involved in interrogations that make use of torture or other forms of cruel, inhumane, or degrading treatment. The use of torture is first evaluated in light of professional ethics codes and international law. Next, research on interrogations and false confessions is reviewed and its relevance for torture-based interrogations is explored. Finally, research on the negative mental health consequences of torture for survivors and perpetrators is summarized. Based on our review, we conclude that psychologists' involvement in designing, assisting with, or participating in interrogations that make use of torture or other forms of cruel, inhumane, or degrading treatment is a violation of fundamental ethical principles, a violation of international and domestic law, and an ineffective means of extracting reliable information. Torture produces severe and lasting trauma as well as other negative consequences for individuals and for the societies that support it. The article concludes with several recommendations about how APA and other professional organizations should respond to the involvement of psychologists in interrogations that make use of torture or other forms of cruel, inhumane, or degrading treatment.

The United States and its military should immediately ban the use of torture, and psychologists should be expressly prohibited from using their expertise to plan, design, assist, or participate in interrogations that make use of torture and other forms of cruel, inhumane, or degrading treatment. The use of torture as an interrogation device is contrary to ethical standards of conduct for psychologists and is in violation of international law. Torture is ineffective as a means of extracting reliable information, and likely leads to faulty intelligence. Torture has long-term negative consequences for the mental health of both survivors and perpetrators of torture. The use of torture has far-reaching consequences for American citizens: it damages the reputation of the United States, creates hostility toward our troops, provides a pretext for cruelty against U.S. soldiers and citizens, places the United States in the company of some of the most oppressive regimes in the world, and undermines the credibility of the United States when it argues for international human rights.

From *Analyses of Social Issues and Public Policy*, 7(1), pp. 7–16, December 2007. Copyright © 2007 by The Society for the Psychological Study of Social Issues. Reprinted by permission of Wiley-Blackwell.

1. Torture as a Violation of Professional Codes of Conduct

The American Psychological Association's *Ethical Principles of Psychologists and Code of Conduct* encourages psychologists to, " . . . strive to benefit those with whom they work and take care to do no harm." These guidelines incorporate basic *principles* or *moral imperatives* that guide behavior as well as specific *codes of conduct* describing what psychologists *can* or *cannot* do and are, therefore, directly applicable to the participation of psychologists in torture or in interrogation situations involving harm. Psychologists, physicians, and other health and mental health professionals are also guided by international and inter-professional codes of ethics and organizational resolutions, such as the 1985 joint statement against torture issued by the American Psychiatric Association and the American Psychological Association. In 1986, the American Psychological Association passed a *Resolution against Torture and Other Cruel, Inhuman, or Degrading Treatment*. Both statements "condemn torture wherever it occurs."

The International Union of Psychological Science (IUPsyS), the International Association of Applied Psychology (IAAP), and the International Association for Cross-Cultural Psychology (IACCP) are collaborating in the development of a Universal Declaration of Ethical Principles for Psychologists. They have identified "principles and values that provide a common moral framework . . . [to] "guide the development of differing standards as appropriate for differing cultural contexts." . . . An analysis of eight current ethical codes identified across multiple continents revealed five cross-cutting principles: (1) respect for the dignity and rights of persons, (2) caring for others and concern for their welfare, (3) competence, (4) integrity, and (5) professional, scientific, and social responsibility. Sinclair traced the origins of these eight codes to 12 documents including the Code of Hammurabi (Babylon, circa 1795–1750 BC), the Ayurvedic Instruction (India, circa 500–300 BC), the Hippocratic Oath (Greece, circa 400 BC), the (First) American Medical Association Code of Ethics (1847 AD), and the Nuremberg Code of Ethics in Medical Research (1948 AD). Among the ethical principles proposed as universal for all psychologists is that they "uphold the value of taking care to do no harm to individuals, families, groups, and communities."

A wide range of declarations, conventions, and principles govern the conduct of doctors and all health professionals in the context of torture (e.g., the World Medical Association's (1975) Tokyo Declaration), including the establishment of international standards for medical assessments of allegations of torture (e.g., the *Manual on the Effective Investigation and Documentation of Torture and Other Cruel, Inhuman or Degrading Treatment or Punishment (Istanbul Protocol,* United Nations, 1999). Specific restrictions prohibiting the participation of medical personnel in torture and degrading interrogation practices were established in the 1982 United Nations' *Principles of Medical Ethics* (United Nations, 1982). The World Medical Association has also established that it is not ethically appropriate for physicians or other health professionals to serve as consultants or advisors in interrogation.

Psychologists can find themselves in contexts where expected professional and ethical conduct and the protection of human rights conflict with compliance with government policies and practices. A 2002 report of Physicians for Human Rights described this "dual loyalty" now confronting a growing number of health professionals within and outside of the Armed Forces. This tension is particularly acute when such policies and practices run counter to international declarations, laws, and conventions that protect human rights (see, for example, the report of Army Regulation-15, 2005).

2. Torture as a Violation of Law

As citizens, psychologists in the United States are required to observe a wide range of international and national treaties, conventions, and laws that prohibit torture. The *Universal Declaration of Human Rights* (United Nations, 1948) and the *International Covenant on Civil and Political Rights* (United Nations, adopted in 1966, entered into force, 1976), alongside six other core international human rights treaties, constitute an international "bill of human rights" that guarantees freedom from torture and cruel, inhuman, or degrading treatment (see Article 5 of the Universal Declaration on Human Rights).

Article 1 of the UN *Convention against Torture and other Cruel, Inhuman or Degrading Treatment (CAT),* (United Nations, 1984, 1987), which was signed by the United States in 1988 and ratified in 1994, defines torture during interrogation as:

> Any act by which severe pain or suffering, whether physical or mental, is intentionally inflicted on a person for such purposes as obtaining from him or a third person information or a confession . . . when such pain or suffering is inflicted by or at the instigation of or with the consent or acquiescence of a public official or other person acting in an official capacity.

Article 2 (2) of the Convention outlines specific additional prohibitions and obligations of states that: "No exceptional circumstances whatsoever, whether a state of war or a threat of war, internal political instability or any other public emergency, may be invoked as a justification of torture." . . .

Multiple U.S. laws and resolutions, including the U.S. Bill of Rights, the U.S. Constitution, and the joint congressional resolution opposing torture that was signed into law by President Reagan on October 4, 1984 (United States Congress, 1984), prohibit cruel, inhuman, or degrading treatment or torture. Other conventions to which the United States subscribes prohibit any form of torture as a means of gathering information in times of war (see, for example, the *Geneva Conventions* (1949) and the *European Convention* (1989)) relative to the treatment of prisoners of war and to the prevention of torture. In this tradition, Senator John McCain's Amendment (section 1403 of H.R. 1815), approved by the U.S. Congress and signed by President Bush at the end of 2005, prohibits torture and cruel, inhumane, and degrading treatment. However, President Bush's less widely publicized accompanying "signing statement" indicated that he would interpret the law in a manner consistent with his presidential powers, re-igniting debate in many circles within and beyond government. The inconclusiveness of debates among branches of government, and the condemnation of the United States's treatment of prisoners at Guantánamo and Abu Ghraib by foreign governments as well as the UN Committee Against Torture, underscore the urgent need to clarify ethical guidelines for psychologists.

3. Research on Interrogations and the Utility of Torture as an Interrogation Tool

Although the primary purpose of torture is to terrorize a group and break the resistance of an enemy, the use of torture is frequently justified as an interrogation device. However, there is no evidence that torture is an effective means of gathering reliable information. Many survivors of torture report they that would have said anything to "make the torture stop." Those who make the claim that "torture works" offer as evidence only unverifiable anecdotal accounts. Even if there are cases where torture may have preceded the disclosure of useful information, it is impossible to know whether less coercive forms of interrogation might have yielded the same or even better results.

Because torture-based interrogations are generally conducted in secret, there is no systematic research on the relationship between torture and false confessions. However, there is irrefutable evidence from the civilian criminal justice system that techniques *less coercive* than torture have produced verifiably false confessions in a surprising number of cases. An analysis of DNA exonerations of innocent but wrongly convicted criminal suspects revealed that false confessions are the second most frequent cause of wrongful convictions, accounting for 24% of the total. . . . In a recent large-scale study, Drizin and Leo identified 125 proven false confessions over a 30-year period. Two characteristics of these known false confessions are notable. First, they tended to occur in the most serious cases—81% confessed to the crime of murder, and another 9% confessed to the crime of rape. Second, because only *proven* false confessions were included (e.g., cases where the confessor was exonerated by DNA evidence or cases where the alleged crime never occurred), the actual number of false confessions is likely to be substantially higher. Military action based on false information extracted through the use of torture has the potential to jeopardize the lives of military personnel and civilians.

The defining feature of an interrogation is the presumption that a suspect is lying or withholding vital information. If torture is an available option, interrogators are likely to resort to torture when they believe a suspect is lying about what he or she knows or does not know. However, there is no reason to believe that interrogators are able to tell whether or not a suspect is lying. Indeed, there is considerable research demonstrating that trained interrogators are *not* accurate in judging the truthfulness of the suspects they interrogate. Overall, people with relevant professional training (e.g., interrogators, polygraphers, customs officers) are able to detect deception at a level only slightly above chance. Moreover, some researchers have identified a troubling perceptual bias among people who have received interrogation training—an increased tendency to believe that others are lying to them. In addition, although specialized training in interrogation techniques does not improve the ability to discern lying, it does increase the confidence of interrogators in their ability to tell whether a suspect is lying or withholding information. The presumption that a suspect is lying, in combination with the overconfidence produced by interrogation training, leads to a biased style of questioning which seeks to confirm guilt while ignoring or discounting information that suggests that a suspect is being truthful. There is also evidence that interrogators become most coercive when questioning innocent suspects, because truthful suspects are regarded as resistant and defiant. Thus, interrogators may be especially likely to resort to torture when faced with persistent denials by innocent suspects. Under such conditions, torture may be used to punish a suspect or as an expression of frustration and desperation on the part of the interrogator. More broadly, there is substantial evidence that judgments about others are influenced by conscious and nonconscious stereotyping and prejudice. Prejudice may lead interrogators to target suspects for torture based on physical appearance, ethnicity, or erroneous stereotypes about behavioral cues.

Unless local authorities (e.g., commanders in charge of a military detention facility) explicitly prohibit the use of torture in interrogations, the risk of torture will be unacceptably high. Decades of research by social psychologists has demonstrated that strong situational forces can overwhelm people's better impulses and cause good people to treat others cruelly. These forces include the presence of an authority figure who appears to sanction the use of cruelty, and a large power disparity between groups, such as the disparity that exists between prisoners and guards. In addition, the dehumanization and demonization of the enemy that occurs during times of intense group conflict—particularly during times of war—reduce inhibitions against cruelty. All of these conditions, combined with the stresses of long-term confinement, appear to have been present at Abu Ghraib. The well-documented reports of torture at the Abu Ghraib and Guantanamo Bay facilities serve as disturbing reminders that it is essential for military authorities to issue clear directives about unacceptable practices in the interrogation of prisoners. These directives need to be combined with effective monitoring of military detention facilities, especially during times of war.

In an effort to circumvent ethical concerns and the lack of evidence about the effectiveness of torture, advocates of the use of torture often resort to hypothetical arguments such as the "ticking time bomb scenario." This frequently used justification for the use of torture as an interrogation tactic presupposes that the United States has in its custody a terrorist who has knowledge of the location of a time bomb that will soon explode and kill thousands of innocent people. Embedded in this implausible scenario are several questionable assumptions: that it is known for certain that the suspect possesses specific "actionable" knowledge that would avert the disaster; that the threat is imminent; that only torture would lead to the disclosure of the information; and that torture is the fastest means of extracting valid, actionable information. Of course, this scenario also recasts the person who tortures as a principled, heroic figure who reluctantly uses torture to save innocent lives. While this scenario might provide a useful stimulus for discussion in college ethics courses, or an interesting plot device for a television drama, we can find no evidence that it has ever occurred and it appears highly improbable.

4. The Effects of Torture on Survivors and Perpetrators

Torture is one of the most extreme forms of human violence, resulting in both physical and psychological consequences. It is also widespread and occurs throughout much of the world. Despite potentially confounding variables, including related stressors (such as refugee experiences or traumatic bereavement), and comorbid conditions (such as anxiety, depression, or physical injury), torture itself has been shown to be directly linked to posttraumatic stress disorder (PTSD) and other symptoms and disabilities. The findings from both uncontrolled and controlled studies have produced substantial evidence that for some individuals, torture has serious and long-lasting psychological consequences.

Most trauma experts—including survivors of torture, mental health researchers, and therapists—agree that the psychiatric diagnosis of PTSD is relevant for torture survivors. However, these same experts emphasize that the consequences of torture go beyond psychiatric diagnoses. Turner and Gorst-Unsworth highlighted four common themes in the complex picture of torture and its consequences: (1) PTSD as a result of specific torture experiences; (2) depression as a result of multiple losses associated with torture; (3) physical symptoms resulting from the specific forms of torture; and (4) the "existential dilemma" of surviving in a world in which torture is a reality. The 10th revision of the *International Classification of Diseases* includes a diagnosis of "Enduring Personality Change after Catastrophic Experience" as one effort to capture the long-term existential consequences of the tearing up of a social world caused by torture. The profound psychological and physical consequences of torture are also evident in several carefully written personal accounts of the experience of torture.

Comprehensive reviews of the psychological effects of torture have systematically evaluated research with torture survivors, examining the unique consequences associated with torture and the complex interaction of social, environmental, and justice-related issues. As noted in these reviews, the psychological problems most commonly reported by torture survivors in research studies include (a) psychological symptoms (anxiety, depression, irritability or aggressiveness, emotional instability, self-isolation or social withdrawal); (b) cognitive symptoms (confusion or disorientation, impaired memory and concentration); and (c) neurovegetative symptoms (insomnia, nightmares, sexual dysfunction). Other findings reported in studies of torture survivors include abnormal sleep patterns, brain damage, and personality changes. The effects of torture can extend throughout the life of the survivor affecting his or her psychological, familial, and economic functioning. Such consequences have also been shown to be transmitted across generations in studies of various victim/survivor populations and across trauma types.

Studies conducted over the past 15 years strongly suggest that people who develop PTSD may also experience serious neurobiological changes, including changes in the body's ability to respond to stress (through alterations in stress hormones), and changes in the hippocampus, an area in the brain related to contextual memory. Thus, the development of PTSD has direct and long-term implications for the functioning of numerous biological systems essential to human functioning.

For survivors, having "healers" participating in their torture by supporting interrogators or providing medical treatment in order to prolong torture can erode future recovery by damaging the legitimate role that physicians or therapists could provide in offering treatment or social support, essential components in the recovery of trauma survivors. For these reasons, numerous medical associations, including the American Psychiatric Association and the World Medical Association, include as part of their ethical and professional standards a complete prohibition against participation of their members in interrogation, torture, or other forms of ill treatment. Similarly, the South African Truth and Reconciliation Commission documented how health providers were at times complicit in human rights abuses under apartheid, and through their report, hoped to shed light on this worldwide phenomenon and work toward an international effort to prevent such abuses from occurring.

Research that focuses directly on the participation of health professionals in torture and interrogation has documented important contextual issues for understanding how such participation can occur. Robert Lifton interviewed Nazi doctors who participated in human experimentation and killings, and found them to be "normal professionals" who offered medical justifications for their actions. In studies of physicians and other health providers who are involved in forms of military interrogation, Lifton elaborates on "atrocity-producing" environments in which normal individuals may forsake personal or professional values in an environment where torture is the norm. Furthermore, these same health care professionals may, through their actions, transfer legitimacy to a situation, supporting an illusion for all participants that some form of therapy or medical purpose is involved.

Other studies of those who torture have provided details about the step-by-step training that can transform ordinary people into people who can and will torture others, by systematically providing justifications for actions, professional or role authority, and secrecy. Participation in torture and other atrocities has been shown to have long-term negative psychological consequences for perpetrators, even in situations where professional or environmental justifications were offered to them in the context of their actions. . . .

Therefore, we urge APA and other scholarly and professional associations of psychologists to:

1. Unambiguously condemn the use of torture and other forms of cruel, inhuman, or degrading treatment as interrogation devices and call upon the U.S. government and its military to explicitly ban the use of such treatment and enforce all laws and regulations prohibiting its use.

2. Conduct an independent investigation of the extent to which psychologists have been involved in using torture or other cruel, inhuman, or degrading treatment as interrogation tools. If psychologists are found to have participated in the design or conduct of interrogations that have made use of torture, they should be appropriately sanctioned by APA and other professional organizations.
3. Expressly forbid psychologists from planning, designing, assisting, or participating in interrogations that involve the use of torture and any form of cruel, inhuman, or degrading treatment of human beings.
4. Develop specific guidelines and explicit codes of conduct for psychologists working in contexts of war and imprisonment. These guidelines should be consistent with international treaties and human rights covenants as well as guidelines developed for health professionals. Such guidelines should include meaningful enforcement, processes for the investigation of violations, and professional and legal consequences for violations.

Kirk M. Hubbard

 **NO**

Psychologists and Interrogations: What's Torture Got to Do with It?

In an article that has been endorsed by SPSSI, Costanzo, Gerrity, and Lykes (2007) argue that "psychologists should not be involved in interrogations that make use of torture or other forms of cruel, inhumane, or degrading treatment" (doi:10.1111/j.1530-2415.2007.00118.x). Their statement is ironic, for torture is illegal in the United States. But even more importantly, it seems to come from and apply to a world that no longer exists, and that simplifies issues so that they can be as one might like them to be. As recent events in England illustrate (August 2006), Islamic militants seek to kill us and undermine if not destroy our way of life. We have only to listen to what they say and watch their actions in order to know that regardless of how we would like things to be, they mean us harm. We also know from findings of the 9/11 commission that this problem did not start, nor will it likely finish, with the current presidential administration. An important point that is illustrated is that we no longer live in a world where people agree on what is ethical or even acceptable, and where concern for other humans transcends familial ties. When adolescents carry bombs on their bodies and plan suicides that will kill others, we know that shared values no longer exist. In the words of Scottish comedian Billy Connolly, "It seems to me that Islam and Christianity and Judaism all have the same god, and he's telling them all different things."

A prominent challenge for psychologists is determining how narrowly or broadly the field should prescribe what is acceptable behavior for professionals working with diverse populations, for increasingly psychologists come from differing backgrounds and hold varying beliefs. Effective practice with one population may be totally ineffective with another; we as a profession have not yet thoughtfully addressed how we balance what one culture defines as ethical against what another could view as necessary to be successful. The comment by Costanzo et al., and its rejoinders, provide a good illustration, namely, how does one balance standards of behaviors against results. What if, hypothetically, Middle Eastern psychologists told us that in order to successfully obtain information from suspected terrorists we would have to use approaches that we found inappropriate or unethical? I reject the idea that it is somehow unfair to use what we know about psychological science to protect our families and defend our lives and culture. Many areas of psychology

From *Analyses of Social Issues and Public Policy*, 7(1), pp. 29–33, December 2007. Copyright © 2007 by The Society for the Psychological Study of Social Issues. Reprinted by permission of Wiley-Blackwell.

owe their advancement in large part to research conducted under the auspices of the military and supported by it. Clinical psychology has roots in the military and the OSS, and many psychologists have proudly defended their country with honor. In this context, the SPSSI policy statement by Costanzo et al. is both unnecessary and gratuitous. It is unnecessary because torture is already illegal in the United States. It is gratuitous because it feeds the egos of those who endorse it. It gives the illusion of possessing a higher moral ground, when in fact what is left unsaid and readable between the lines reveals it to be ideological and political. As parallels, SPSSI might put out policy statements against rape and murder, for those also are illegal, and we would not want our members participating in such behaviors. But murder and rape occur despite being illegal, and similarly, behaviors that are classified as torture may periodically occur. But that does not mean that torture is a government-sanctioned tool for conducting interrogations or even acceptable to use. There are specific and strict federal guidelines regarding what constitutes a legal and acceptable interrogation. I submit that there is no evidence that psychologists were involved in cases of torture—certainly not at Abu Ghraib prison.

A second issue of import is whether or not psychologists should be involved in legal interrogations. Again, the position of the authors is too simplistic. I take exception to the suggestion that all psychologists should be banned from assisting in legal interrogations. It is one thing to "ban" psychologists who are members of APA from engaging in torture, but quite another to prohibit them from consulting or advising during legal interrogations. First, there are many types of psychologists (social psychologist, industrial/organizational psychologists, and experimental psychologists, for example) who are not licensed mental health professionals and therefore should not be bound by the doctor/patient relationship code of ethics. Yet they bring information from their fields that help exert influence. Second, I object to the "psychocentric" and seemingly arrogant position that receiving training in psychology trumps all other roles a person may choose to pursue, or because of circumstances, are obliged to fulfill. Is it not possible for someone to receive training in psychology and then decide to pursue a career in law enforcement and engage in legal interrogations? Should being a psychologist as well as a law enforcement agent prohibit their participation if psychologists are prohibited? And, third, how is psychology accountable to society—should it withhold information about ways in which to protect our population or to influence terrorists to disclose information? What does psychology owe society? Should we focus exclusively on individuals with whom psychologists come in contact? What about helping to protect communities from terrorism? I simply do not believe that at a policy level we should decide that the "rights" of an individual count more than the rights and safety of society. APA and SPSSI should do something positive to fight terrorism rather than merely sit on the sidelines and criticize others who are trying to protect the United States from another senseless 9/11 attack. Honorable men and women are at war with those who seek to harm us, and the rest of us are at risk from terrorists. If psychology wants to make a positive contribution, the profession should accept that it is sometimes necessary to get information from those who would harm us and are intentionally withholding information that could stop attacks. If we as a profession do not like the use of coercion to obtain actionable information, then we as a profession should be willing to step up to the plate and suggest reliable and effective alternatives that do not rely on psychological or physical coercion. Have we as professional organizations of psychologists committed resources to develop ethical, nonpunishing approaches that improve the quality of information that we can extract from individuals who are not willing to share it?

I also find it ironic that SPSSI can so readily become exercised about cruel and degrading treatment of suspected terrorists, yet conduct only limited research on similar behaviors that are manifested all too frequently in military boot camps, in legal police interrogations, in U.S. prisons, and government psychiatric hospitals. Indeed, even college fraternities and schoolyard bullies engage in cruel and degrading behavior. Why is it so easy for SPSSI to react so adamantly about illegal interrogations, yet do so little about domestic kinds of cruel and degrading treatment?

I also wonder how Costanzo et al. would feel if the "ticking time bomb scenario" that they attempt to render as "implausible" were to occur. Would they feel responsible for telling U.S. citizens that it won't ever happen? The "ticking bomb" scenario may be implausible for many APA members, but it was very real for those individuals interrogating Khalid Sheik Mohammed or Abu Zubaydah. Instead of focusing on decades old research that may no longer be relevant, Constanzo et al. might have cited the Jose Padilla case that was covered by the press. As readers may recall, Jose Padilla was a trained al Qaeda operative who was arrested as he tried to enter the United States in Chicago on May 8, 2002. He had accepted an assignment to destroy apartment buildings and had planned to detonate a radiological device commonly referred to as a "dirty bomb." As reported by CNN (June 11, 2002) and *Time* (June 16, 2002), Padilla was arrested directly as a result of an interrogation of captured senior al Qaeda member Abu Zubaydah. The Padilla case is a prime example of how a legal interrogation of a known terrorist led to the prevention of another terrorist attack.

Similarly, imagine that al Qaeda leader Abu Mussib al Zarqawri has been captured alive in Iraq rather than killed by bombings. Is there anyone who believes that he would have no potentially worthwhile knowledge of attacks planned to occur in the days following his capture? Costanzo et al. create a scenario that is not grounded in current knowledge of terrorism in general and terrorists in particular when they attempt to (mis)lead us into thinking legal interrogations do not yield actionable intelligence.

The prototypical "expert" on interrogation asserts that information is more reliable when voluntarily given rather than coerced. Well, of course it is. The expert then may assert that the way to elicit voluntary provision of information is to build a relationship with the terrorist so that the terrorist likes you or to appeal to common values so the terrorist sees your interests as converging with his/hers, and then the terrorist will tell you what you need to know. Such reasoning ignores the demand characteristics of both the prototypical law enforcement interrogation and the terrorist's values and operational intent. Are we to think the terrorist has the following thoughts: "You know, nobody has ever been as nice to me as these people—I'm going to turn my back on my God and my life's work and tell them what they what to know." Alternatively, maybe the terrorist will think "What a clever way of asking that question. Now that they put it that way, I have no choice but to tell them what they need to know to disrupt my plans." Unfortunately, it is difficult to envision scenarios where useful information will be forthcoming.

For many Westerners caught after committing a crime, the psychological pressure of trying to influence whether or not they are charged, what they are charged with, and the kind of punishment they are likely to receive coerces them into working with the person who seems to understand them to make the best deal in a bad set of circumstances. The "experts'" assertion that rapport and liking are the keys to obtaining information, ignore the coercive pressures inherent in the circumstances. To pretend that these coercive pressures are not present does not make them go away. For terrorists who do not care if they live or die and have no fear of prison, there is little or no incentive to work with interrogators. And, to our discredit, we as psychologists have contributed little to increasing our understanding of circumstances like these and techniques of persuasion that might be effective.

Lastly, I found the call for an independent investigation of the extent to which psychologists have been involved in using torture or other cruel, inhuman, or degrading treatment during an interrogation unwarranted. Costanzo et al. present virtually no evidence that psychologists have been involved in even a single case. APA/SPSSI has no authority by which to sanction nonmembers. Many psychologists are choosing not to join APA or to allow their memberships to lapse, believing that it does not represent their interests and values. In my opinion, APA and some of its divisions have drifted from a being a professional organization advancing the science of psychology and translating research to action and policy, to a point where they are promoting a social and political agenda.

I am opposed to torture. But I endorse the use of interrogation when used consistently with current federal law and conducted by trained interrogators. And I certainly see no reason why psychologists cannot assist in developing effective, lawful ways to obtain actionable intelligence in fighting terrorism. If the information can be obtained noncoercively, all the better. Social psychology taught us how to use social influence in getting people to do things they ordinarily would not do and buy things they often do not need or want. In my view, it is common sense that you would want psychologists involved in the interrogation of known terrorists. As psychologists, rather than decrying illegal use of cruel and inhumane treatment to obtain information, we should work to develop reliable noncoercive ways to get people to tell us about terrorist activity of which they have knowledge and are attempting to withhold. We need to take a proactive stance in saving lives and preventing acts of terror. The Costanzo et al. article does not appreciably help psychology to move forward, for it limits opportunities for psychologists to gain first-hand knowledge of the nature of the challenges interrogators face, and focuses on current approaches rather than on developing new ones that apply and improve current psychological knowledge.

EXPLORING THE ISSUE

Is It Unethical for Psychologists to Be Involved in Coercive Interrogations?

Critical Thinking and Reflection

1. What variables should be considered in drawing the line between interrogation techniques that are inhumane and those that are effective, but not cruel?
2. How might participation in enhanced interrogation techniques affect the psychological well-being and functioning of the interrogators?
3. Imagine that you are a psychologist who is being hired to develop effective techniques for extracting critical information from suspected terrorists. With whom would you consult to ensure that the techniques are not in violation of human rights?
4. What kind of responsibility does society have for detainees who have been coercively interrogated, but then released when it becomes apparent that they lack useful information?
5. Some social observers contend that as the years have passed since the 9/11 attacks, feelings of vulnerability among Americans have lessened, while critiques of government efforts to protect national security have escalated. What are your thoughts on this observation?

Is There Common Ground?

Spokespersons on both sides of the debate regarding interrogations would concur that thoughtful and effective methods must be used to protect national security. The trauma of the September 11 terrorists attacks will remain in the minds of every American who was alive on that tragic day and was able to process the horror of that event. Since that fateful day, countless reports have appeared in the news about attempts on the part of potential terrorists to engage in acts that would take the lives of innocent people. When such plots are detected, the government faces the challenge of collecting information from the potential terrorist, which can be used to track down the behind-the-scenes perpetrators, so that subsequent efforts can be thwarted.

Dr. Constanzo and his colleagues would concur with Dr. Hubbard that psychologists can play an instrumental role in developing and implementing interrogation techniques that are effective in obtaining actionable intelligence. The field of psychology is devoted to the understanding of human behavior and motivations. Thus, many psychologists have the knowledge to formulate procedures that can effectively motivate terror suspects to provide information that can avert a tragedy. The challenge they face, however, is the task of coming up with procedures that are effective, yet do not cross the line into the realm of what is considered inhumane and torturous behavior. Psychologists will certainly be called upon to assist in the development and evaluation of these procedures.

Additional Resources

Davis, D., & Leo, R. A. (2012). The problem of interrogation-induced false confession: Sources of failure in prevention and detection. *The handbook of forensic sociology and psychology,* Stephen Morewitz & Mark Goldstein, eds., (Springer, 2013 Forthcoming) (pp. 1–59).

De Vos, J. (2011). Depsychologizing torture. *Critical Inquiry, 37*(2), 286–314.

Ethics Website of Dr. Ken Pope: www.kspope.com

Freedman, A. M. (2009). The work of psychologists in the U.S. intelligence community. *Consulting Psychology Journal: Practice and Research, 61*(1), 68–83.

Halpern, A. L., Halpern, J. H., & Doherty, S. B. (2008). "Enhanced" interrogation of detainees: Do psychologist and psychiatrists participate? *Philosophy, Ethics, and Humanities in Medicine, 3,* 21.

Kalbeitzer, R. (2009). Psychologists and interrogations: Ethical dilemmas in times of war. *Ethics and Behavior, 19*(2), 156–168.

Pope, K. S., & Gutheil, T. G. (2009). Contrasting ethical principles of physicians and psychologists concerning interrogation of detainees. *British Medical Journal, 338,* b1653.

Society for the Psychological Study of Social Issues (SPSSI). Retrieved from www.spssi.org

Soldz, S. (2008). Healers or interrogators: Psychology and the United States torture regime. *Psychoanalytic Dialogues, 18*(5), 592–613.

ISSUE 16

Is It Ethical to Support the Wish for Healthy Limb Amputation in People with Body Integrity Identity Disorder (BIID)?

YES: Tim Bayne and Neil Levy, from "Amputees by Choice: Body Integrity Identity Disorder and the Ethics of Amputation," *Journal of Applied Philosophy* (vol. 22, no. 1, 2005)

NO: Wesley J. Smith, from "Secondhand Smoke: Blog of Wesley J. Smith" (2007)

Learning Outcomes

After reading this issue, you should be able to:

- Discuss the thinking and motivations of people who pursue the amputation of a healthy limb.
- Debate the extent to which physicians have a responsibility to persuade would-be amputees from taking action to alter their bodily structure.
- Discuss the question of whether body integrity identity disorder (BIID) should be considered a form of mental illness.
- Understand arguments that assert that the wish for limb amputation is markedly different from the wish for elective cosmetic surgery.
- Critically evaluate the argument that a person has a moral right to alter his or her body in any way desired.

ISSUE SUMMARY

YES: Authors Tim Bayne and Neil Levy argue that people with body integrity identity disorder are in emotional pain because of their experience of incongruity between their body image and their actual body. Such individuals should be accorded with their prerogative to have a healthy limb amputated.

NO: Author Wesley J. Smith objects to the notion of acquiescing to the wishes for healthy limb amputation in people whom he views as severely mentally disturbed. Smith asserts that these people need treatment, not amputation.

Body modification is a phenomenon that has been prevalent throughout recorded history. In contemporary society plastic surgery and cosmetic surgery procedures are common, with large numbers of people seeking to have their appearance changed to change a body part to look better. Plastic surgery is usually performed to treat birth defects or to remove skin blemishes such as scars, birthmarks, warts, or acne. Cosmetic surgery procedures are much more elective, in that they are done less for the purpose of correcting an obvious anomaly, and more for the purpose of helping a person modify appearance for the sake of looking younger or more attractive. Commonly performed elective cosmetic procedures include breast augmentation, buttock augmentation, abdominoplasty ("tummy tuck"), rhinoplasty (reshaping of the nose), otoplasty (reshaping of the ear), rhytidectomy ("face lift"), suction-assisted lipectomy (removal of fat from the body), as well as procedures performed on the genitals (e.g., surgical reshaping or the labia).

With millions of people undergoing such elective procedures each year, very little controversy has arisen about the ethics. Nor, for that matter, has there been an uproar about the remarkable surge in recent years of body tattooing and extreme forms of body piercing. In contrast, a very different response emerges when the topic turns to elective amputation of healthy limbs. People with body integrity identity disorder (BIID) have a form of body dysmorphic disorder so extreme that they feel compelled to seek amputation of a healthy body part. Individuals with this condition claim that they are so psychologically pained by the discrepancy between their actual body and their body image that they live a life of torment. The emotional pain that they report is not unlike that described by preoperative transsexuals. The question arises, then, about whether it is appropriate for health professionals to acquiesce to the wishes of people with BIID (who refer to themselves as "wannabes") to amputate a healthy limb, with the aim of satisfying the wish of these individuals to enhance psychological well-being.

Authors Bayne and Levy argue that surgeons should accede to the requests of people with BIID who ask for healthy limb amputation. Seeing no compelling moral arguments against such surgery, these authors sympathize with the plight of people who have spent much of their lives with a nonstandard sense of embodiment. Just as physicians respect the autonomy of patients seeking elective cosmetic surgery, so also should they respect the right of people seeking limb amputation to determine the structure of their own bodies.

Bayne and Levy assert that people with BIID have spent many years (often since childhood) with a nonstandard sense of embodiment, and their experience of themselves has been built around this sense. Whether would-be amputees (or "wannabes," as they refer to themselves) are correct in thinking that their disorder requires surgery or not, these authors assert that we must recognize that many of them will persist in their desire for amputation, and will take matters into their own hands, risking extensive injury or death in doing so. Surgery may be the least of all evils. Furthermore, autonomy demands only that one have an adequate understanding of the likely consequences of an action, and a would-be amputee can have a reasonable understanding of what life as an amputee would be like before becoming an amputee.

Authors Bayne and Levy contend that an individual's conception of his or her own good should be respected in medical decision-making contexts. When a would-be amputee has a longstanding and informed request for amputation, it seems permissible for a surgeon to act on this request. In the case of at least some would-be amputees the limb in question is not as healthy as it might appear: in an important sense, a limb that is not experienced as one's own is not in fact one's own. Disorders of depersonalization are not observable from the third-person perspective in the way that most other disorders are, but the fact that they are inaccessible should not lead us to dismiss the suffering they might cause.

Wesley Smith views would-be amputees as severely mentally disturbed individuals who need treatment, not amputation. Only a severely mentally disturbed person would want a healthy leg, arm, hand, or foot cut off. Such people need treatment, not amputation. In light of the fact that amputation is an irreversible procedure, insufficient thought is given to the likelihood of post-amputation regret. Once a limb is gone, it is gone for good. What if the patient has regrets? Smith contends that these individuals should be protected from harming themselves, and he critiques the notion of "choice" in such matters.

Smith asserts that physicians are duty-bound to "do no harm," and thus should refuse to provide harmful medical services to patients—no matter how earnest the request. A physician who accedes to a patient's request to be mutilated would essentially be abandoning the patient. If we allow doctors to remove healthy limbs, what is next? Helping people who want to cut themselves, slice themselves repeatedly? Or helping people who want to burn themselves do so safely? He also states that "choice" is becoming a voracious monster. Would-be amputees need to be protected from harming themselves. As Smith states, we once had the basic humanity and decency to understand that, but we have become so consumed by radical individualism that we no longer seem to possess such qualities.

YES    Tim Bayne and Neil Levy

Amputees by Choice: Body Integrity Identity Disorder and the Ethics of Amputation

In 1997, a Scottish surgeon by the name of Robert Smith was approached by a man with an unusual request: he wanted his apparently healthy lower left leg amputated. Although details about the case are sketchy, the would-be amputee appears to have desired the amputation on the grounds that his left foot wasn't part of him—it felt alien. After consultation with psychiatrists, Smith performed the amputation. Two and a half years later, the patient reported that his life had been transformed for the better by the operation.[1] A second patient was also reported as having been satisfied with his amputation.[2]

Smith was scheduled to perform further amputations of healthy limbs when the story broke in the media. Predictably, there was a public outcry, and Smith's hospital instructed him to cease performing such operations. At present, no hospital offers healthy limb amputations. Would-be amputees—or 'wannabes', as they refer to themselves—would appear to number in the thousands. They have their own websites and are the subject of a recent documentary.[3]

In this paper, we are concerned with two basic questions. First, what would motivate someone to have an apparently healthy limb amputated? Second, under what conditions is it reasonable for doctors to accede to such requests? We believe that the first question can shed significant light on the second, showing that, on the evidence available today, such amputations may be morally permissible.

What Is It Like to Be a Wannabe?

What motivates someone to desire the amputation of a healthy limb? One possibility is that wannabes suffer from Body Dysmorphic Disorder (BDD), a condition in which the individual believes, incorrectly, that a part of their body is diseased or exceedingly ugly.[4] This belief can be a matter of intense concern for the individual and is resistant to evidence against it. BDD appears to be closely akin to anorexia nervosa, in that both appear to be monothematic delusions that are sustained by misperceptions of one's own body.[5] Perhaps wannabes desire amputation in order to rid themselves of a limb that they believe to be diseased or ugly.

From *Journal of Applied Philosophy,* vol. 22, no. 1, 2005. Copyright © 2005 by Blackwell Publishing, Ltd. Reprinted by permission.

A second explanation is that wannabes have a sexual attraction to amputees or to being an amputee.[6] On this account, the desire for amputation would stem from apotemnophilia, which is a kind of paraphilia—a psychosexual disorder. Apotemnophiles are sexually attracted to amputees, and sexually excited by the notion that they might become amputees themselves.

A third explanation is that there is a mismatch between the wannabe's experience of their body and the actual structure of their body. On this view, there is a mismatch between their body and their body as they experience it—what we might call their phenomenal (or subjective) body. On this view, which is increasingly gaining favour, wannabes suffer from Body Integrity Identity Disorder (BIID), also known as Amputee Identity Disorder (AID).[7]

The BIID account can be developed in different ways depending on the type of bodily representation that is thought to be involved. On the one hand, one could conceive of BIID in terms of a mismatch between the patient's body and their body *schema*. The body schema is a representation of one's body that is used in the automatic regulation of posture and movement.[8] It operates subpersonally and sub-consciously, guiding the parts of one's body to successful performance of action. The body schema is a dynamic structure, providing a moment-by-moment sense of how one's body parts are articulated.

Mismatches between a person's body schema and their actual body are not uncommon. Individuals who lose (or have never had) a limb often experience a phantom limb: they feel as though the limb is still there, and in some cases attempt to employ it in order to carry out actions—such as answering the telephone. Whereas the body schema of individuals with phantom limbs includes body parts that they lack, other patients have no body schema for body parts they have. Patients who have undergone deafferentation from the neck down lose any proprioceptive sense of how their limbs are currently positioned, and rely on visual cues to control action.[9]

Perhaps wannabes also have a body schema that fails to incorporate the full extent of their bodies. Although we do not want to dismiss this suggestion, the evidence we have to date weighs against this account. As far as we know, wannabes do not exhibit any of the impairments in control of movement that one would expect in a person with a distorted or incomplete body schema. Further, wannabes who have had the amputation they desire seem, as far as we can tell, to be content to use a prosthesis. This suggests that the problem they suffer from is not primarily a conflict between their body and their body schema.

A more plausible possibility is that BIID involves a mismatch between the wannabe's body and their body *image*. One's body image is a consciously accessible representation of the general shape and structure of one's body. The body image is derived from a number of sources, including visual experience, proprioceptive experience, and tactile experience. It structures one's bodily sensations (aches, pains, tickles, and so on), and forms the basis of one's beliefs about oneself.[10]

Discrepancies between a person's body and their body image occur in a wide range of cases, known as asomatognosias. Asomatognosia can occur as a result of the loss of proprioception, in post-stroke neglect, and in the context of depersonalisation.[11] In many of these cases, the patient in question has become delusional and denies either the existence of the affected limb or their ownership of it. In a condition known as somatoparaphrenia, patients will even ascribe ownership of their limbs to another person.[12]

Other forms of asomatognosia concern only the patient's perception of their body and leave the doxastic component of their body image intact. Oliver Sacks eloquently describes his own experience of this condition:

> In that instant, that very first encounter, *I knew not my leg*. It was utterly strange, not-mine, unfamiliar. I gazed upon it with absolute non-recognition. . . . The more I gazed at that cylinder of chalk, the more alien and incomprehensible it appeared to me. I could no longer feel it as mine, as part of me. It seemed to bear no relation whatever to me. It was absolutely not-me—and yet, impossibly, it was attached to me—and even more impossibly, continuous with me.[13]

Sacks did not become delusional—he knew that the leg in question was his—but he no longer experienced it as his own. Perhaps BIID involves a similar form of nondelusional somatic alienation. If so, then there might be a very real sense in which the limb in question—or at least, the neuronal representation of it—is not healthy.

It is also tempting to draw parallels between BIID and the discrepancy between body image and the person's actual body that characterizes anorexia nervosa and bulimia nervosa.[14] Of course, there are also important differences between these conditions: Whereas the person with anorexia or bulimia fails to (fully) recognize the discrepancy between her body and her body image, the wannabe is all too aware of this discrepancy.

None of the three explanations of the desire for amputation that we have outlined attempts to provide *complete* models of the phenomenon: the BDD model does not attempt to explain why wannabes might regard the limb in question as diseased or ugly; the apotemnophilia model does not attempt to explain why wannabes might be sexually attracted to a conception of themselves as amputees; and the BIID model does not attempt to explain why wannabes might fail to incorporate the limb into their body image. Clearly these models can, at best, provide only a first step in understanding why someone might become a wannabe. Nevertheless, even though these models are incomplete, we can make some progress in evaluating them.

A first point to make is that these models may not be exclusive. It could be that there are two or three bases for the desire for amputation, with some patients suffering from BDD, others suffering from a paraphilia, and others suffering from a form of BIID. Some individuals might even suffer from a combination of these disorders. Perhaps, for example, the sexual element is better conceived of as a common, though not inevitable, element of asomatognosia. Sexuality is, after all, an essential ingredient in most people's sense of identity. Elliott reports that at least one wannabe (who is also a psychologist) characterizes their desire for amputation as indissolubly a matter of sex *and* identity.[15] Like Gender Identity Disorder, BIID might be importantly sexual without ceasing to be essentially concerned with identity.

However, although each of the three models might play some role in accounting for the desire for healthy limb amputation, we can also ask which model best fits most wannabes. The initial media stories and a subsequent BBC documentary, *Complete Obsession*, identified Robert Smith's patients as suffering from BDD. However, there seems good reason to doubt whether any of these individuals suffered from BDD, strictly speaking. Neither of the two individuals featured in *Complete Obsession* appears to find their limbs diseased or ugly. Instead, they feel in some way alienated from them. Further evidence against the BDD hypothesis is provided by recent research by Michael First.[16] First conducted in-depth anonymous interviews with 52 wannabes, nine of whom had either amputated one of their limbs themselves or had enlisted a surgeon to amputate it. Only one of the 52 individuals interviewed cited the ugliness of the limb as a reason for wanting the amputation.

What about the suggestion that the desire for amputation stems from apotemphilia? First's study provides limited grounds for thinking that the desire for amputation might have a sexual basis in some cases. 15% (n = 8) of First's interviewees cited feelings of sexual arousal as their primary reason for desiring amputation, and 52% cited it as their secondary reason. Further, 87% of his subjects reported being sexually attracted to amputees. Additional support for the apotemenophilia hypothesis stems from the fact that there is a large overlap between the classes of devotees (acrotomophiles: people sexually attracted to amputees), pretenders (people who consciously fake a disability) and wannabes. More than 50% of devotees are also pretenders and wannabes, suggesting a common cause for all three syndromes.[17] Because of this overlap, the data researchers have gathered on devotees may be relevant to the desire for amputation.

Devotees are apparently more sexually attracted to the *idea* of amputation than to amputees themselves. Though many have had sexual relations with amputees, few go on to establish long-term relationships with particular individuals. As Riddle puts it, for the acrotomophile, 'No amputee is the right amputee'.[18] Bruno suggests that this fact is evidence that acrotomophilia essentially involves projection: the wannabe imagines themselves in place of the amputee. Acrotomophilia is apotemnophilia displaced, projected onto others. If apotemnophilia is essentially a body integrity disorder, Bruno seems to think, it could not be displaced so easily. But it seems just as plausible to interpret the acrotomophile's lack of interest in the individual amputee as evidence that it is a concern with his *own* body that motivates the devotee.

In any case, although First's study provides some support for thinking that the desire for amputation can have a sexual component in some instances, it offers little support for the paraphilia hypothesis as the best explanation of the disorder. After all, only 15% of wannabes identified sexual arousal as the primary motivation for amputation: this leaves 85% unaccounted for.

First's data provides equivocal support for the third model, on which the desire for amputation derives from the experience of a gulf between one's actual body and one's subjective or lived body. The leading primary reason First's subjects gave for wanting an amputation was to restore them to their true identity (63%, n = 33). Participants said such things as, 'I feel like an amputee with natural prostheses—they're my legs, but I want to get rid of them—they don't fit my body image', and, 'I felt like I was in the wrong body; that I am only complete with both my arm and leg off on the right side'. First suggests that this data supports the view that most wannabes suffer from BIID, which he considers akin to Gender Identity Disorder.

There is reason for caution here. For one thing, only 37% (n = 19) of First's participants said that the limb in question felt different in some way, and only 13% (n = 7) said that the limb felt like it was not their own. In addition, we know of no evidence that wannabes suffer from the kinds of sensory and attentional impairments—such as neglect—that tend to accompany, and perhaps underlie, standard forms of asomatognosia.

Perhaps the notion of body image that First's subjects have in mind is closer to that of the self-image of the person who wants cosmetic surgery, say, for breast enlargement. She knows that she has small breasts, but her idealised image of herself is of someone with large breasts. She does not feel comfortable—at home—in her own body.

Although more research needs to be done about the nature and aetiology of the desire for amputation of a healthy limb, the foregoing suffices to put us in a position to make an initial foray into the ethical issues raised by such requests. We turn now to an examination of three arguments in favour of performing the requested amputations.

Harm Minimization

The first and perhaps weakest of the three arguments is familiar from other contexts. Whether wannabes are correct in thinking that their disorder requires surgery or not, we must recognize that a significant proportion of them will persist in their desire for amputation, even in the face of repeated refusals, and will go on to take matters into their own hands. The Internet sites run by wannabes often discuss relatively painless and safe ways of amputating limbs, or damaging them sufficiently to ensure that surgeons have no choice but to amputate. Six of the 52 participants in First's study had amputated a limb themselves, utilizing dangerous means including a shotgun, a chainsaw and a wood chipper. Other patients have turned to incompetent surgeons after competent doctors refused to treat them. In 1998, a seventy-nine year old man died of gangrene after paying $10,000 for a black-market amputation.[19]

Given that many patients will go ahead with amputations in any case, and risk extensive injury or death in doing so, it might be argued that surgeons should accede to the requests, at least of those patients who they (or a competent authority) judge are likely to take matters into their own hands. At least so long as no other treatments are available, surgery might be the least of all evils. This raises familiar practical and ethical issues to do with participation in a practice of which we might disapprove and our inability to confidently distinguish those patients for whom the desire for an amputation might be transient from those who will persist in their demand. Because these issues are familiar and have been extensively treated elsewhere, we will not dwell on them here.

Autonomy

It is well-entrenched maxim of medical ethics that informed, autonomous desires ought to be given serious weight. An individual's conception of his or her good should be respected in medical decision-making contexts. Where a wannabe has a long-standing and informed request for amputation, it therefore seems permissible for a surgeon to act on this request.

As an analogy, consider the refusal of life-saving treatment on religious grounds. Although such decisions might result in the death of the patient, they are accorded significant weight in the context of medical decision making. If we ignore the informed and repeated wishes of the Jehovah's Witness who refuses the blood-transfusion needed to save her life, we fail to respect her as an autonomous moral agent who is living her life according to her conception of the good. If it is permissible (or even obligatory) to respect informed and autonomous rejections of life-saving treatment, it is also permissible to act on informed and autonomous requests for the amputation of a healthy limb.

Of course, the parallel between the Jehovah's Witness who refuses life-saving treatment and the wannabe who requests the amputation of a limb is not exact: the first case involves an omission but the second case involves an action. This is a difference, but whether or not it is morally relevant depends on what one makes of the act/omission distinction. We are doubtful that the distinction can do much moral work in this context, but to make the case for this position would take us too far away from our present concerns.

We shall consider two objections to the argument from autonomy. The first is that wannabes are not fully rational, and that therefore their requests should not be regarded as autonomous. As Arthur Caplan put it: 'It's absolute, utter lunacy to go along with a request to maim somebody', because there is a real question whether sufferers 'are competent to make a decision when they're running around saying, "Chop my leg off".'[20]

It is clear that some individuals who might request the amputation of healthy limbs are not rational. Neither the schizophrenic patient who believes that God is telling her to amputate her leg nor the patient with somatoparaphrenia who attempts to throw his leg out of bed because he thinks it is not his own is rational. To what extent wannabes are also incompetent depends on what kinds of wannabes they are.

There is a prima facie case to be made for thinking that wannabes suffering from BDD are not competent to request surgery. There are grounds for regarding BDD as a monothematic delusion, akin to, say, Capgras' delusion (the delusion that a close relative has been replaced by an impostor) or Cotard's delusion (the delusion that one is dead). After all, individuals with BDD appear to satisfy the DSM definition of a delusion: they have beliefs that are firmly sustained despite what almost everyone else believes and despite incontrovertible and obvious proof or evidence to the contrary.[21]

Of course, the circumscribed and monothematic nature of this delusion problematizes the charge of incompetence. These patients are not globally irrational. One might argue that despite the fact that their beliefs about the affected limb have been arrived at irrationally, their deliberations concerning what to do in the light of these beliefs are rational, and hence ought to be respected. One might draw a parallel between the position of the person who requests amputation as a result of BDD and the person who refuses life-saving treatment on the grounds of strange religious beliefs. One might argue that in both cases the agent has arrived at their beliefs irrationally, but they may have chosen a reasonable course of action given their beliefs. And—so the argument continues—one might argue that competence is undermined only by unreasonable practical reasoning, not by impaired belief-fixation or theoretical reasoning.

There is obviously much more that could be said about whether or not individuals with BDD are competent to request surgery, but we will not pursue these issues, for—as we have already pointed out—First's data suggest that few wannabes are motivated by the belief that their healthy limb is diseased or exceedingly ugly. Instead, most wannabes appear to have some form of BIID: they appear to be motivated to achieve a fit between their body and their body image. Are wannabes with BIID delusional?

We have already suggested that they are not. Although wannabes seem not to experience parts of their body as their own, they do not go on to form the corresponding belief that it is alien. The wannabe with BIID clearly recognizes that the leg is hers: she does not identify it as someone else's leg, nor does she attempt to throw it out of bed, in the way that patients with somatoparaphrenia sometimes do.

One might argue that the wannabe's response to her somatic alienation demonstrates a form of irrationality. One might think that the rational response to a conflict between one's subjective experience of embodiment and one's body would be to change one's experience of embodiment rather than change the structure of one's body. The claim is correct but irrelevant: the wannabe's desire for amputation appears to be born out of an inability to change the way in which she experiences her body. Of course, it may be that some wannabes would rather change their actual body to fit their experienced body than vice versa. Is someone with such a desire set competent to make a request for amputation? They certainly challenge our notions of autonomy and competency, but it is far from obvious that they ought to be regarded as incompetent. It is important to bear in mind that they have spent many years—perhaps even decades—with a non-standard sense of embodiment. (Most wannabes report having had a feeling of somatic alienation since childhood.) Their experience of themselves has been built around this sense, and to require them to change it is, to some extent, to require them to change who they are. The case is not dissimilar to a situation in which an elderly person, blind from an early age, is suddenly presented with the opportunity to regain her sight. The decision to decline such an offer can be understood as an exercise of rational agency.

A useful angle on the question of whether the requests of wannabes could be competent is provided by contrasting wannabes with people who desire cosmetic surgery (where the surgery is not for the treatment of disfigurement). While one can certainly argue on feminist grounds that such people are not fully competent, these arguments have left many people unmoved.[22] We allow individuals to mould their body to an idealized body type, even when we recognize that this body image has been formed under the pressure of non-rational considerations, such as advertising, gender norms, and the like. If this holds for the individual seeking cosmetic surgery, what reason is there to resist a parallel line of argument for those seeking amputation? Of course, the latter individual is seeking to mould their body to an ideal that few of us aspire to, and one that has been formed under conditions that are far from perfect, but why should these facts cut any moral ice? In fact, one might think that the desire for cosmetic surgery (and gender-reassignment surgery) is *more* problematic than the desire for amputation. Men who believe that they are really women 'trapped in a man's body'—and the overwhelming majority of transsexuals are male-to-female—typically reinforce a stereotyped view of femininity, and contribute, however unwittingly and obliquely, to gender inequality.[23] The essential woman they seek to be is weak and helpless, obsessed by appearance, and so on.[24] There are related feminist grounds (and not only feminist grounds) on which to criticize cosmetic surgery: it reinforces a very unfortunate emphasis on appearance over substance. It is hard to see that the desire for amputation could be criticized upon grounds of these kinds, since it goes against the grain of our culturally endorsed ideals of the body.

A second objection to the argument from autonomy is that the wannabe is not in a position to give informed consent to the surgery, for he or she does not—and cannot—know what it is like to be an amputee without first becoming an amputee.

We think that this objection is weak. First, it is not at all obvious that the wannabe cannot know what it will be like to be an amputee without becoming an amputee. Arguably, there is a sense in which the wannabe *already* knows what it is like to be an amputee. We might also note that at least some wannabes pretend to be amputees—they spend their weekends in a wheelchair, and so on. To some degree, it seems that a wannabe can know what it is like to be an amputee.

But a more important point to be made here is that the objection appears to set the bar for autonomy too high.[25] Autonomy demands only that one have an adequate understanding of the likely consequences of an action, and one can have a reasonable understanding of what life as an amputee would be like without first becoming an amputee. Arguably, the wannabe is in a better position to appreciate the consequences of the desired surgery than is the person who seeks cosmetic surgery, the would-be surrogate mother, or the person desiring gender reassignment surgery.

Therapy

A third argument in favour of operating appeals to the therapeutic effects promised by such operations. The argument rests on four premises: (i) wannabes endure serious suffering as a result of their condition; (ii) amputation will—or is likely to—secure relief from this suffering; (iii) this relief cannot be secured by less drastic means; (iv) securing relief from this suffering is worth the cost of amputation. This argument parallels the justification for conventional amputations.

There is some reason to endorse (i). First, the lengths to which wannabes go in an effort to amputate their own limbs suggest that their desires are strong and unrelenting. Even when wannabes do not take active steps to secure an amputation, their feeling of bodily alienation seems to cause severe disruption to their everyday lives. 44% of First's subjects reported that their desire interfered with social functioning, occupational functioning, or leisure activities.

Some writers suggest that (ii) is problematic. Bruno and Riddle claim that the desire for amputation has its origins in attention-seeking sparked by the deprivation of parental love.[26] On this hypothesis, though it is *possible* that satisfying their wish for an amputation might give the wannabe the attention and kindness they seek, it is unlikely. Though amputees are treated with a certain degree of solicitude in many situations, the daily frustrations and difficulties caused by their condition almost certainly more than overbalance this care. Moreover, it is quite likely that the wannabe will not be satisfied with the solicitude of strangers. Instead she will seek ongoing commitment from particular individuals, and there is little reason to think that she is more likely to get this than are non-amputees. Finally, it might be that even the love of particular others will not suffice: it may be that literally nothing can stand in for the love of which she was deprived as a child. Bruno suggests that psychotherapy is the appropriate response to the disorder, not surgery. The patient needs to develop insight into the real source of her problems before she can solve them.

Bruno's proposal is empirically testable: we can evaluate whether the desire for amputation responds to psychotherapy, and whether amputation simply leads to the displacement of the patient's symptoms. What little data we have to date suggests that Bruno is wrong on both counts. We know of no systematic study of the effects of psychotherapy on the desire for amputation, but First's study suggests that it is not particularly effective. Of the 52 individuals he interviewed, 18 had told their psychotherapist about their desire for amputation, and none reported a reduction in the intensity of the desire following psychotherapy.

On the other hand, on the scant evidence available, wannabes who succeed in procuring an amputation seem to experience a significant and lasting increase in well-being. Both of Robert Smith's patients were reported as having been very happy with their operations, and the nine subjects in First's study who had had an amputation also expressed satisfaction with the results.[27] As far as we can tell, such individuals do not develop the desire for additional amputations (in contrast to individuals who have had cosmetic surgery). Nor, as far as we know, do such patients develop (unwanted) phantom limbs. Of course, it may be that the sample to which researchers have had access is self-selecting: adherents of the BIID account are motivated to come forward to adduce evidence in favour of their theory, while those who have had more unhappy experiences simply lose interest in the debate, or are too depressed to motivate themselves to take any further part. In any case, the sample sizes are too small to be statistically significant. Unfortunately, it is hard to see how it will be possible to collect sufficient data of the required sort. We can of course follow the fortunes of those who have arranged non-medical amputations for themselves, but a controlled study would presumably require medical amputations, and ethical approval for performing such operations is unlikely to be forthcoming without this very data.[28]

We turn now to (iii): can the wannabe secure relief from their suffering by less drastic means than amputation? Again, the jury is out on this. First's study suggests that psychotherapy is not a particularly effective form of treatment, but psychotherapy is not the only alternative to amputation. Some form of cognitive behavioural therapy might prove effective, perhaps in combination with psychotropic drugs. But it might also be that some wannabes cannot be helped by available drugs or talking therapy whatever the aetiology of the disorder. After all, the phantom limb phenomenon is resistant to these forms of treatment. For at least some patients, there may be no treatment available other than amputation.

Finally, we turn to (iv): is securing relief from this suffering worth the cost of amputation? This, of course, will depend on the degree of suffering in question and the costs of amputation. We have already noted that there is reason to think that wannabes often experience significant misery from their condition. But what should we say about the costs of amputation? These, of course, will vary from case to case, depending on the financial and social circumstances of the individual, and the nature of the amputation itself. The costs might be offset by the benefits of amputation in some cases but not in others. It is interesting to note that of the two would-be amputees featured in the *Complete Obsession* documentary, the person seeking amputation of a single leg was given psychiatric approval, while the person seeking to have both her legs amputated was denied psychiatric approval. And of course the costs are not always borne just by the patient; they are often also borne by the patient's family and by society as a whole.

There is ample room here for false consciousness. On the one hand, one can argue that wannabes have an overly rosy image of what life as an amputee involves. And certainly those wannabes who have become amputees have a motivation for thinking that their life is better than it really is. On the other hand, one could also argue that those of us who are able bodied have an overly pessimistic image of the lives of the disabled. As able-bodied individuals, we might be tempted to dwell on the harm that accompanies amputation and minimize what is gained by way of identification. Perhaps we are tempted to think that the effects of the surgery are worse than they are.

Repugnance

We believe that the arguments canvassed above establish a *prima facie* case for thinking that wannabes should have access to amputation, at least in those instances in which they suffer from BIID. However, we recognize that many people will continue to find the idea of voluntary amputation of a healthy limb objectionable, even when they acknowledge the force of these arguments. What motivates such reactions?

We suspect that much of this hostility derives from the sense of repugnance that is evoked by the idea that a person might wish to rid themselves of an apparently healthy limb. Dennis Canavan, the Scottish member of parliament who campaigned to prevent Robert Smith from carrying out such operations was quoted as saying: 'The whole thing is repugnant and legislation needs to be brought in now to outlaw this'.[29] Mr Canavan is surely not alone in having such a reaction. Wannabes evoke an affective response not dissimilar to that evoked by the prospect of kidney sales, bestiality, or various forms of genetic engineering. Even when a limb is severely diseased and must be removed in order to save the patient's life, the thought of amputation strikes many as distasteful at best.

Although they should not be dismissed, we think that such responses should be treated with a great deal of caution. A large number of morally benign practices—such as masturbation, inter-racial marriage, burial (and cremation) of the dead, organ selling, artificial insemination, tattooing and body piercing—have the ability to elicit disgust responses. Disgust responses can alert us to the possibility that the practices in question *might* be morally problematic, but they do not seem to be reliable indicators of moral transgression.[30]

Indirect Effects

We have explored three arguments for allowing self-demand amputation of healthy limbs: the argument from harm minimization, the autonomy argument and the therapeutic argument. We have suggested that these arguments have some force. But even if we are right about that, it does not follow that we ought to allow self-demand amputation of healthy limbs. One might hold that although these arguments are strong, their force is outweighed by reasons for not allowing such surgery.

In our view, the strongest such argument concerns the possible effects of legitimising BIID as a disorder. The worry is that giving official sanction to a diagnosis of BIID makes it available as a possible identity for people. To use Ian Hacking's term, psychiatric categories have a "looping" effect: once in play, people use them to construct their identities, and this in turn reinforces their reality as medical conditions.[31] Arguably, something like this has occurred in the case of Dissociative Identity Disorder (formerly multiple personality disorder): the explosion of diagnoses of DID might be due in part to the fact that people regard DID as a culturally sanctioned disorder. The very awareness of a disorder can contribute to its proliferation.

Could a similar effect occur for BIID? Is it likely that the inclusion of the disorder in the forthcoming DSM-V will generate an explosion of cases on the order of that seen in the study of dissociation? Perhaps, but there is reason to think that such fears are unwarranted. The desire for amputation of a healthy limb is at odds with current conceptions of the ideal body image. The preference for bodily integrity is deep-seated in normal human beings, and advertising does much to reinforce such norms. We therefore think it unlikely that the desire for amputation will proliferate.

Conclusion

In a world in which many are born without limbs, or lose their limbs to poisons, landmines, and other acts of man and God, it might seem obscene to legitimise the desire for the amputation of healthy limbs. But we have argued that, in the case of at least some wannabes, the limb in question is not as healthy as it might appear: in an important sense, a limb that is not experienced as one's own is not in fact one's own. Disorders of depersonalisation are invisible to the outside world: they are not observable from the third-person perspective in the way that most other disorders are. But the fact that they are inaccessible should not lead us to dismiss the suffering they might cause. Whether amputation is an appropriate response to this suffering is a difficult question, but we believe that in some cases it might be.[32]

Notes

1. K. SCOTT (2000) Voluntary amputee ran disability site. *The Guardian*, February 7.

2. G. FURTH and R. SMITH (2002) *Amputee Identity Disorder: Information, Questions, Answers, and Recommendations about Self-Demand Amputation* (Bloomington, IN, 1st Books).

3. M. GILBERT (2003) *Whole* U.S.A.

4. K. PHILLIPS (1996) *The Broken Mirror: Understanding and Treating Body Dysmorphic Disorder* (Oxford, Oxford University Press).

5. D. M. GARNER (2002) Body image and anorexia nervosa in T. F. CASH and T. PRUZINSKY (eds) *Body Image: A Handbook of Theory, Research, and Clinical Practice* (New York, The Guilford Press).

6. J. MONEY, R. JOBARIS, and G. FURTH (1977) Apotemnophilia: Two cases of self-demand amputation as paraphilia. *The Journal of Sex Research*, 13, 2, 115–125.

7. Furth & Smith op. cit.

8. The term 'body schema' is used in different ways by different authors. We are following Shaun Gallagher's usage. See S. GALLAGHER (1995) Body schema and intentionality in J. BERMÚDEZ, N. EILAN and J. MARCEL (eds) *The Body and the Self.* (Cambridge MA, M.I.T. Press) pp. 225–44 and S. GALLAGHER (2001) Dimensions of embodiment: Body image and body schema in medical contexts in S. K. TOOMBS (ed) *Handbook of Phenomenology and Medicine* (Dordrecht, Kluwer Academic Publishers) pp. 147–75.

9. S. GALLAGHER and J. COLE 1995 Body schema and body image in a deafferented subject, *Journal of Mind and Behavior*, 16, 369–90.

10. The term 'body image' is also used in different ways by different authors. Again, we follow Shaun Gallagher's usage of the term. See reference [8].

11. T. E. FEINBERG, L. D. HABER, and N. E. LEEDS (1990) Verbal asomatognosia, *Neurology*, 40, 1391–4; J. A. M. FREDERIKS (1985) Disorders of the body schema. In Clinical Neuropsychology in J. A. M. FREDERIKS (ed) *Handbook of Clinical Neurology*, rev. Series, No. 1 (Amsterdam, Elsevier); M. SIERRA and G. E. BERRIOS (2001) The phenomenological stability of depersonalization: Comparing the old with the new, *The Journal of Nervous and Mental Disorders*, 189, 629–636.

12. An account of such a case is described in O. SACKS (1985) The man who fell out of bed, in *The Man Who Mistook His Wife for a Hat* (New York, Touchstone).

13. O. SACKS (1991) *A Leg to Stand On* (London, Picador).

14. R. M. GARDNER and C. MONCRIEFF (1988) Body image distortion in ano-rexics as a non-sensory phenomenon: A signal detection approach, *Journal of Clinical Psychology*, 44, 101–107 and T. F. CASH and T. A. BROWN (1987) Body image in anorexia nervosa and bulimia nervosa: A Review of the literature, *Behavior Modification*, 11, 487–521.

15. C. ELLIOTT (2003) *Better Than Well: American Medicine Meets the American Dream* (New York, W.W. Norton & Company).

16. M. B. FIRST (unpublished) Desire for amputation of a limb: Paraphilia, psychosis, or a new type of identity disorder? Submitted.

17. R. BRUNO (1997) Devotees, pretenders and wannabes: Two cases of facti-tious disability disorder, *Journal of Sexuality and Disability*, 15, 243–260.

18. G. C. RIDDLE (1988) *Amputees and Devotees: Made for Each Other?* (New York, Irvington Publishers).

19. C. E. ELLIOTT (2000) A new way to be mad, *The Atlantic Monthly*, 286, 6, December.

20. Quoted in R. DOTINGA (2000) Out on a limb, *Salon*, August 29, 1.

21. AMERICAN PSYCHIATRIC ASSOCIATION (2000) *Diagnostic and Statisti-cal Manual of Mental Disorders, Text Revision*. Fourth Edition (Washington D.C., American Psychiatric Association).

22. For a feminist argument against the permissibility of cosmetic surgery see K. P. MORGAN (1991) Women and the knife: Cosmetic surgery and the colonization of women's bodies, *Hypatia* 6, 3, 25–53.

23. H. BOWER (2001) The gender identity disorder in the DSM-IV classifica-tion: a critical evaluation, *Australian and New Zealand Journal of Psychiatry*, 35, 1–8.

24. M. GARBER (1993) *Vested Interests: Cross-Dressing & Cultural Anxiety* (London, Penguin).

25. See J. OAKLEY (1992) Altruistic surrogacy and informed consent, *Bioethics*, 6, 4, 269–287.

26. Bruno op. cit. and Riddle op. cit.

27. See also ELLIOTT (2000) and (2003) op. cit. and F. Horn (2003) A life for a limb: Body integrity identity disorder, *Social Work Today*, Feb 24.

28. R. SMITHAND and K. FISHER (2003) Healthy limb amputation: ethical and legal aspects (letter), *Clinical Medicine*, 3, 2, March/April, 188.

29. Quoted in Dotinga op. cit.

30. See J. R. RICHARDS (1996) Nefarious goings on, *The Journal of Medicine and Philosophy*, 21, 375–416.

31. I. HACKING (1995) *Rewriting the Soul: Multiple Personality and the Sciences of Memory* (Princeton, Princeton University Press).

32. We are very grateful to Shaun Gallagher, Jonathan Cole, Michael First and an anonymous reviewer for their very useful comments on a previous ver-sion of this paper. We also thank Suzy Bliss for her valuable help.

Wesley J. Smith

 **NO**

Should Doctors Be Allowed to Amputate Healthy Limbs?

If you want to see why Western culture is going badly off the rails, just read the drivel that passes for learned discourse in many of our professional journals. The most recent example is "Amputees by Choice: Body Integrity Identity Disorder and the Ethics of Amputation," published in the current issue of the *Journal of Applied Philosophy* (Vol. 22, No. 1, 2005).

The question posed by the authors, Tim Bayne and Neil Levy, both Australian philosophy professors, is whether physicians should be permitted to amputate a patient's healthy limb because the patient is obsessed with becoming an amputee, an apparently newly discovered mental disorder that has been given the name "Body Integrity Identity Disorder" (BIID).

For people of common sense, the answer is obvious: NO! First, who but a severely mentally disturbed person would want a healthy leg, arm, hand, or foot cut off? Such people need treatment, not amputation. Second, physicians are duty bound to "do no harm," that is, they should refuse to provide harmful medical services to patients—no matter how earnestly requested. (Thus, if I were convinced that my appendix was actually a cancerous tumor, that would not justify my doctor acquiescing to my request for an appendectomy.) Finally, once the limb is gone, it is gone for good. Acceding to a request to be mutilated would amount to abandoning the patient.

But according to Bayne and Levy, and a minority of other voices in bioethics and medicine, the need to respect personal autonomy is so near-absolute that it should even permit doctors to cut off the healthy limbs of "amputee wannabes." After all, the authors write, "we allow individuals to mould their body to an idealized body type" in plastic surgery—a desire that is "more problematic than the desire for amputation" since cosmetic surgery "reinforces a very unfortunate emphasis on appearance over substance." Moreover, the authors claim in full postmodernist mode, just because a limb is biologically healthy, does not mean that the leg is real. Indeed, they argue, "a limb that is not experienced as one's own is not in fact one's own."

That this kind of article is published in a respectable philosophical journal tells us how very radical and pathologically nonjudgmental the bioethics movement is becoming. And lest you believe that such advocacy could never reach the clinical setting: Think again. Such surgeries have already been performed in the United Kingdom with no adverse professional consequence to the amputating physicians.

Even more worrisome, the current trends in American jurisprudence could one day legalize amputation as treatment for BIID. For example, in 1999, the Montana Supreme Court invalidated a law that required abortions to be performed in hospitals. But rather than limit the decision to that issue, the 6-2 majority opinion in James H. Armstrong, M.D. v. The State of Montana, imposed a radical and audacious medical ethic on the people of Montana, ruling: "The Montana Constitution broadly guarantees each individual the right to make medical judgments affecting her or his bodily integrity and health in partnership with a chosen health care provider free from government interference."

If indeed almost anything goes medically in Montana—so long as a patient wants it and a health care professional is willing to provide it—then it would seem that a physician could legally amputate a patient's healthy limbs upon request to satisfy a neurotic BIID obsession.

⌖

Yours Truly Taken to Task for Allegedly Inaccurate Article

I have heard from one of the authors of the journal article supporting the right of doctors to amputate healthy limbs for sufferers of a new mental health disorder known as Body Integrity Identity Disorder (BIID). He is unhappy with me. Neil Levy claims I misrepresented his and co-author Tim Bayne's work.

Levy wrote: "You write that we advocate 'abandoning the patient' by acceding to their request to amputate a healthy limb. First, as you fail to mention, we conclude that the question is difficult, but we think that 'in some cases' it 'might' be acceptable to accede. Second, you misrepresent our views by taking them out of context. You say that we write, 'in full postmodernist mode, just because a limb is biologically healthy, does not mean that the leg is real.'" (Indeed, they argue, "a limb that is not experienced as one's own is not in fact one's own.") "If we had implied any such thing, we would deserve your mockery. But it should be clear, from even a cursory reading, that we intended to claim not that if the patient believes the limb is not theirs, it is not. We couldn't be claiming any such thing, because we distinguish between somatoparaphrenia, which is a delusion in which the patient denies ownership of the limb, and BIID, in which there are no false beliefs. The claim, rather, is that acknowledging ownership is normally a necesary condition for full ownership. Think of disowning a child. This is an act which does not alter the biological relationship, but alters the lived relationship. There is nothing 'postmodernist' about this. If you were familiar with norms in analytic philosophy you would hesitate to make such an accusation: no one is more vocal in denouncing facile relativism about truth. Third, we do not advocate abandoning the patient. Once again, a careful reading of the article would indicate that amputation is recommended only as a last resort: so long as there is genuine and significant suffering and there is no alternative treatment that is effective. If there is such an affective treatment developed, then it is obviously preferable."

My response was as follows:

"Thank you for writing.

It was a 550 word opinion piece. It is very clear that the term abandonment was mine and not yours, as was the opinion and interpretation that cutting off a healthy limb would be an act of abandonment. I never claimed you believed in abandoning a patient.

I quoted you accurately about the healthy limb not being the patient's, an amazing statement in my view. Whether or not a patient "owns" the limb, does not make it any less real. And the point I was making is that autonomy is getting recklessly out of control in bioethics advocacy, and in jurisprudence as well, ergo the quoting of the Montana court case. I probably should have said that "as a last resort," you would permit amputation. But you would still allow amputation.

I certainly had no intention of misrepresenting your article. I don't believe I did. I believe the essence of what I wrote is true."

(I would also note that the abstract of the article, which the authors wrote, states that they argue, "BIID sufferers meet reasonable standards for rationality and autonomy: so as long as no other effective treatment for their disorder is available, surgeons ought to be allowed to accede to their requests," in other words, cut off healthy limbs.)

⚬◆⚬

"Choice" Gone Mad: Amputee Wannabes

We are witnessing the beginning of the public normalization of the profound mental illness known as Body Integrity Identity Disorder (BIID)—also known as "amputee wannabe" because its sufferers become obsessed with losing one or more limbs. A column published in *The Guardian* is an example: Susan Smith (not her real name) writes about wanting to have both legs amputated because **"the image I have of myself has always been one without legs."**

To achieve these ends, Susan harmed herself so that one leg would have to be removed. And now, she plans to do it again: **"Removing the next leg will not be any easier than the first; the pain will be horrendous. But I have no regrets about the path I have chosen. In fact, if I regret anything,** it is that I didn't do this sooner. For the first time in my life, I can get on with being the real me."

And here's the normalizing part: "I think BIID will stay taboo until people get together and bring it out. A hundred years ago, it was taboo to be gay in many societies, and 50 years ago the idea of transsexuals was abhorrent to most. I have tried to make the condition more understood but it is difficult to get a case out in the open by yourself. My psychiatrist went to a meeting last year in Paris, and many doctors there told her that they had operated on people who needed an amputation under mysterious circumstances, and how happy the person was when they woke up. It led them to believe that perhaps BIID is more prevalent than people think."

Something has gone terribly wrong with us at a profound and fundamental level. And deeper minds than mine need to figure out precisely what it is. Because, in the name of "being myself" we are moving toward normalizing mutilating surgery. Indeed, I have already attended a transhumanist conference where two Ph.D.s advocated that doctors be allowed to remove healthy limbs. And it has been suggested as worth considering in a professional journal article by Tim Bayne and Neil Levy. What next? Help people who want to cut themselves, slice themselves repeatedly? Or burn themselves, do it safely? Or what about kill themselves? Oh, that's right. It is already explicitly legal to help do that in Oregon, the Netherlands, Belgium, and Switzerland.

People like Susan need to be protected from harming themselves. We used to have the basic humanity and decency to understand that. But we have become so in the thrall of radical individualism, I wonder whether we still do. "Choice" is becoming a voracious monster.

EXPLORING THE ISSUE

Is It Ethical to Support the Wish for Healthy Limb Amputation in People with Body Integrity Identity Disorder (BIID)?

Critical Thinking and Reflection

1. Tattooing and body piercing are regarded by some people not as forms of bodily degradation, but rather as artistic personal expressions. What differentiates these procedures from the choice to undergo limb amputation in order to enhance one's sense of self and emotional well-being?
2. In some extreme cases of body integrity identity disorders, individuals have attempted to sever their own limbs. When such procedures fail, and the individual is left with a badly damaged limb, and a possibly medically dangerous condition, how should physicians respond?
3. Some would argue that a person has the moral right to alter his or her body in any way desired. What are the arguments for and against this notion?
4. What kind of psychological assessment and intervention would you recommend for a person requesting limb amputation?
5. Assuming that a surgeon agrees to amputate a limb of a person with BIID, should health insurance cover this operation? Why or why not?

Is There Common Ground?

Both sets of articles include arguments supportive of the premise that human beings have the moral right to make choices about their body. They also concur in their understanding of the fact that some people feel intense distress about their appearance and their experience of their body. Authors Bayne and Levy argue that people wishing limb amputation experience a mismatch between their body and their body image that is so disturbing that they will go to great lengths to resolve this mismatch. They may go so far as to risk severe injury or death in their pursuit, and should therefore be accommodated by physicians who will acquiesce to their surgical request. Smith would certainly not want such individuals to engage in life-threatening behaviors, but believes that they are mentally ill and need professional help, but not in the form of limb amputation.

Physicians as well as mental health professionals face considerable challenges when dealing with individuals who pursue irreversible elective surgery. In cases as extreme as those involving body integrity identity disorder, the task becomes one of determining whether the individual's request for limb amputation is an expression of mental disorder, or an extreme variation of the request for elective cosmetic surgery. Health professionals must then determine whether their support for such surgery involves a collusion with a delusional person, or a statement of respect for an individual's right to make choices about bodily structure. In any of these situations, professionals are expected to proceed with great caution, and to consult with professional colleagues about the ethical, medical, and psychological issues involved.

Additional Resources

Elliott, C., & Kramer, P. D. (2004). Amputees by choice. In *Better than well: American medicine meets the American dream* (pp. 208–236). New York, NY: W. W. Norton.

First, M. B. (2005). Desire for amputation of a limb: Paraphilia, psychosis, or a new type of identity disorder. *Psychological Medicine, 35*(6), 919–928.

First, M. B., & Fisher, C. E. (2012). Body integrity identity disorder: The persistent desire to acquire a physical disability. *Psychopathology, 45*(1), 3–14.

Henig, S. S. (2005, March 22). At war with their bodies, they seek to sever limbs. *The New York Times.*

Schramme, T. (2007). Should we prevent non-therapeutic mutilation and extreme body modification? *Bioethics.* Retrieved from www.blackwell-synergy.com/toc/biot/0/0

Small, G., & Vorgan, G. (2011). *The other side of the couch: A psychiatrist solves his most unusual cases.* New York, NY: William Morrow.

The Body Dysmorphic Disorder Program at Rhode Island Hospital. Retrieved from www.rhodeislandhospital.org/psychiatry/body-image-program

ISSUE 17

Is Forced Treatment of Seriously Mentally Ill Individuals Justifiable?

YES: Samuel J. Brakel and John M. Davis, from "Overriding Mental Health Treatment Refusals: How Much Process Is 'Due'?" *Saint Louis University Law Journal* (2007)

NO: James B. Gottstein, from "How the Legal System Can Help Create a Recovery Culture in Mental Health Systems," *Leading the Transformation to Recovery* (2005)

Learning Outcomes

After reading this issue, you should be able to:

- Discuss the role of the law in determining whether mentally ill individuals can be treated against their will, with particular attention to constitutional limits on involuntary commitment and forced drugging.
- Critically evaluate the benefits and risks known to be associated with antipsychotic medications.
- Discuss the history of treatment for mentally ill individuals in the United States during the past half century, with particular consideration of the move away from approaches that were inhumane.
- Understand the meaning of civil commitment and the procedures associated with this process.
- Consider alternative options to involuntary treatment that would be viewed as humane as well as effective.

ISSUE SUMMARY

YES: Attorney Samuel J. Brakel and psychiatrist John M. Davis assert that society has a responsibility to take care of seriously mentally ill individuals who are incapable of making an informed decision about their need for care and treatment.

NO: Attorney James B. Gottstein contends that forced treatment of mentally ill citizens represents a curtailment of liberty which leads many people down a road of permanent disability and poverty.

The deinstitutionalization movement that began in the final quarter of the twentieth century was regarded as an important positive trend in the treatment of seriously mentally ill people. Although some patients who were transferred to community programs and halfway houses thrived in a less restrictive environment, other patients became lost in the maze, with many becoming homeless and destitute. In response to the social crisis following deinstitutionalization, some social critics have called for more aggressive efforts to reach out to seriously mentally ill people so that they can be provided with badly needed care, even if these individuals resist such solicitous efforts. A controversy has raged about whether therapeutic treatment should be forced upon seriously mentally ill people.

In the first reading, attorney Samuel Brakel argues that many citizens with profound mental illness are incapable of caring for themselves, and will resist treatment because they do not view themselves as mentally ill. According to Brakel, interventions such as psychiatric medication can have a markedly beneficial impact on the lives of mentally ill people; without such treatment, many individuals will not only be at risk, but will also be deprived of experiencing a better quality of life. Attorney Brakel believes that mental health professionals should be allowed to initiate treatment over a patient's objection in instances involving seriously ill individuals who cannot be convinced to accept treatment voluntarily.

According to Brakel, what unknowing critics see as an "orgy of pill pushing" is no more than a reflection of the reality that, without drugs as the base treatment for schizophrenia and other psychotic disorders, there is no hope for improvement. Talk and behavior therapy, by themselves, are useless treatment methods for schizophrenia, and may be harmful if used to the exclusion of needed pharmacology. Many people suffering from psychosis have a neurological inability to appreciate that they are sick and need treatment (a condition called anosognosia). These people will resist treatment because they do not view themselves as mentally ill.

Brakel asserts that, if a patient cannot be convinced to accept prescribed treatment, the physician should be allowed to initiate treatment over the patient's objection with minimal legal interference. Studies show that patients who adhere to *continued* drug treatment benefit on virtually all important personal and social measures. Both the old and new antipsychotic drugs used in treatment are highly efficacious and without the purported negative side effects portrayed by anti-psychiatry alarmists. Individuals who are appropriately treated have lower rates of rehospitalization, criminal recidivism, and violent behavior. Also, they experience improved quality of life because of a reduction in symptoms, an improvement in functioning, more appropriate use of the mental health system, and a reduced likelihood of homelessness.

In the second reading, Attorney James B. Gottstein argues vehemently against the idea of forcing treatment upon unwilling citizens. He argues that myths about mental illness need to be debunked, while efforts are made to provide more humane, effective, recovery-oriented, and noncoercive interventions. Gottstein contends that it is easier for the system to lock people up and drug them into submission than it is to engage them in a much more humane process of recovery. He advocates spending time with them to develop a therapeutic relationship, and thus being able to engage troubled individuals with voluntary humane alternatives leading to recovery. He asserts that forced drugging simply cannot be scientifically proven to be in a person's best interest. Furthermore, information is lacking about the long-term effectiveness or the possible harm associated with these drugs.

According to Gottstein, mental patients are not by definition incapable of making rational decisions; nor are they necessarily less competent than non-mentally ill medical patients. As posited by the United States Supreme Court, involuntary commitment does nothing to enhance autonomy, but rather represents a "massive curtailment of liberty." Rather than providing remarkable opportunities for growth and autonomy, the system of forced psychiatry leads a tremendous number of people down a road to permanent disability and poverty.

YES  Samuel J. Brakel and John M. Davis

Overriding Mental Health Treatment Refusals: How Much Process Is "Due"?

Abstract

Getting mental health treatment to patients who need it is today a much belegaled enterprise. This is in part because law makers have a skewed view of the enterprise, in particular the treatment of patients with antipsychotic medications. The properties and uses of these medications are misunderstood by many in the legal community, while the drugs' undesirable side-effects are typically overstated and the remedial effects undersold when not outright ignored. One specific legal effect has been to accord to mental patients a substantively outsized right to refuse treatment that comes with a correspondingly action-stifling dose of procedural safegxuards, this despite the patients' frequent lack of capacity to exercise the right wisely and the bad personal and systemic consequences that flow from that. The purpose of this article is to provide better balanced and accurate evidence of the properties of antipsychotic drugs so as to convince law makers and advocates for the mentally disabled that it is safe to roll back some of the more counterproductive legal strictures on the effort to provide mental health treatment. . . .

I. Introduction

In 1991 the above listed authors published an article in the *Indiana Law Review* titled "Taking Harms Seriously: Involuntary Mental Patients and the Right to Refuse Treatment."[1] In it we argued that the extension to involuntarily committed mental health patients of a legal right to refuse mental health treatment (at least in the sense of its being protected by potentially multiple judicial hearings), was a legal/logical anomaly and one that had bad consequences for those patients who exercised the right, not to mention their fellow patients, the hospital doctors and the institutions in which the patients were (ware) housed. We felt, somewhat naively perhaps, that the reason the law was askew stemmed from the lack of good medical information on the part of lawyers, judges and legislators and that rectifying the situation required the presentation in an appropriate legal forum of such information. Everyone's eyes would be opened and the law would change in the direction warranted

From *bepress Legal Series*, Year 2007 Paper 1964, 2007. Reprinted with permission of the Saint Louis University Law Journal © 2008 St. Louis University School of Law, St. Louis, Missouri.

by our confidence in the medical facts—*i.e.*, that the antipsychotic drugs predominantly used in treatment were highly efficacious and without anywhere near the negative side-effects profiles portrayed by antipsychiatric alarmists. There has been some success in the realization of this hope, though pinning much or any of it on the publication/dissemination of a legal academic article would be presumptuous.[2] There has been progress in the law in the sense that the cases and statutes today are somewhat more likely than a decade or so ago to reflect an appropriate appreciation of what the medications can do (and what they won't do), in multiple contexts. Whether the issue is civil commitment and treatment (inpatient or outpatient), or treatment in the criminal justice-mandated context of competency commitments (whether pretrial or presentence) or post-conviction treatment in the prison setting, medical authority to medicate unwilling patients has overall expanded while judicial review has been relegated to a lesser and later ("postdeprivation") role—a realignment of power that one would surmise has much to do with better knowledge of the (large) benefits vs. (relatively small) costs in potential negative consequences of the medications.

At the same time, however, there has been some jurisprudential backsliding as well, including at the U.S. Supreme Court level, (p. 5) . . . where a small number of decisions have been handed down and some language articulated that seems to give new life to what one had hoped was the moribund view of psychotropic drugs as predominantly harmful and the accompanying disbelief in the competence and integrity of doctors to appropriately prescribe them.

Given the thus still uneven, not to say precarious, lay of the legal landscape on treatment refusals, we feel it is timely to do a reprise of sorts of our 1991 article and to present once again what we believe is a true picture of the risks and benefits of antipsychotic medications. It is a picture that in many respects is and can be more optimistic than before, consistent with another set of major advances over the last 10–15 years in psychiatric medicine (in particular, the development of the so-called atypicals, a new line of antipsychotic drugs with higher benefit potential and fewer risks than the "old" medications, and continuing improvement in their usage). . . .

We will begin by presenting the new medical data because (1) it is the most significant (new) element in the debate on the matter of treatment rights, including the right to refuse it and (2) it immediately makes more intelligible what that debate is about as well as what our preferences/biases as authors are and from where these derive. We will present the research and anecdotal results documenting the heightened efficacy and the reduced possibility of untoward effects of the new antipsychotic drugs. This section of the paper will include information, new information to the extent it has been developed, on the harms, both personal and institutional, that result from withholding for legal reasons treatment that is medically indicated—in short we will present some indication at least of the costs of an inefficient legal treatment refusal regime, one that makes any conscientious and medically justified attempt to override the patient's resistance to treatment cumbersome to the point of impractical, if not impossible. . . .

II. Of Typicals and Atypicals: The Old and New Medical Data

We begin this section on the new medical data by summarizing what we said in the old article. Under the heading "Separating Myth from Reality" we first reported on a review we conducted of the legal literature on the use of psychotropic drugs—law journals as well as judicial opinions—concluding that the vast bulk of it was woefully, even willfully, misinformed about the both the drugs' risks and benefits.[3] The prevalence and severity of negative (side-) effects were almost uniformly overstated, alleged misuse of "drugging" by state physicians was played up as rampant if not the norm (embellishments/ inventions ranging from the charge that drugs were administered mostly for administrative convenience or punishment to the suggestion by analogy that it might be or at least risked being done to suppress political dissent), while the huge health benefits of proper drug usage for people with serious mental illness got no play at all (the whole helping rationale behind psychiatric treatment being simply ignored).[4] We wrote of the characteristic internal referencing aspect of this legal literature where reliance for authority was not on original medical publications but almost exclusively on a few biased analyses written by non-physicians or one or two radical antipsychiatry doctors, leading to an inevitable repetition of false information and myth or even, as in the legal cases ruled by common law precedent, the outright transformation of medical myth into legal fact.[5] . . .

One area where the law needs to adjust is the treatment of patients with antipsychotic drugs. When these drugs were first discovered in the early 1950's they were referred to as tranquilizers. The first antipsychotic drug, chlorpromazine, did have considerable sedative properties. Thence came the charge that the drugs "dulled the senses" or that they were a convenient chemical straightjacket. But even the early drugs did not act by sedation. Like the newer drugs their action is to counteract psychosis by blocking excessive dopamine in the brain, a hormone-like substance whose release in abnormal quantities is associated with "positive" psychiatric symptoms such as hallucinations and delusions.[6] While the drugs may quiet a highly agitated and excited patient, they also help restore apathetic, affect-less patients.[7] The restoration is in the nature of a regaining of cognitive skills, ideally as close as possible to normal premorbid thinking and functioning. . . .

Treatment with antipsychotic drugs is the hallmark of psychiatric treatment of patients suffering from schizophrenia and other major mental disorders. In no institution today, whether the remaining state facilities, private general hospitals or specialized facilities, the medical schools, or for that matter in the doctor's office, is psychological or psychosocial treatment alone provided. Treatment is always given with drugs. It is not true that wealthy patients get verbal psychotherapy while poor patients are drugged. The wealthy get drugs *plus* psychotherapy. Medication dispensation and management have become primary aspects of psychiatric treatment for mentally ill patients of all classes and cultures. What is seen by unknowing critics as an orgy of pill pushing is no more than a reflection of the reality that without drugs as the base treatment for schizophrenia and other psychotic disorders there is no hope for improvement. Talk and behavior therapy are still provided, but such therapy builds on the substantial degree of cognitive and emotional restoration that can be achieved with medication. Often its focus is on developing the patient's and even the family's coping skills, to sharpen recognition of the onset of an episode of the conditions, stresses that signal vulnerability, and what to do in the face of them. . . . By themselves however these treatment methods are useless for schizophrenia, potentially harmful even, particularly if used to the exclusion of needed pharmacology.[8]

Prior to the early 1950s most schizophrenic patients spent much of their life in state insane asylums. Since schizophrenia's onset is typically in adolescence, the illness took away most of the patients' normal lives. In the early 1950s, 50% of the hospital beds in the country were in massive state mental facilities located in rural areas.[9] Up to half a million mental patients filled these beds.[10] When chlorpromazine was discovered in 1953 its use spread quickly throughout the world in two or three years. Violence in state hospitals in the United States dropped by 90% almost overnight.[11] The number of patients in hospitals began to drop year by year with comparable alacrity. Today the total [number] of patients in state mental hospitals throughout the United States is less than 10% of what it was in the mid-1950s and the facilities themselves have almost completely disappeared, been restructured for new use or torn down.[12]

When good care is available and patients take their medication the majority of them can return to work or school and be productive members of society. Unfortunately, many schizophrenic patients do not have access to high quality care. The emptying of the state hospitals was accompanied by the realization that much of the treatment burden would now fall on community, mostly outpatient, programs. But the will or wherewithal to create a community treatment system equal to the task never materialized. The result is that the hope of full social rehabilitation, a theoretical possibility for many schizophrenic patients, is realized in all too few cases. For other patients it is worse than that. They may get brief treatment in a hospital or, more likely today, in a jail but they will stop taking their medication once released. Their lives will spiral downward to where episodes of active schizophrenia grow more frequent and worse and recovery is less complete with each episode. Eventually the disease process may flatten out but by then too often alcoholism, drug abuse and homelessness will have become dominant if not permanent features of the patient's existence.[13] What used to be the back wards of hospitals for these patients have today become the back streets and jails. As presently structured, the law and the courts provide little in the way of relief from this pattern.

Schizophrenia is not normally thought of as a fatal illness. The average life expectancy of schizophrenic patients is lower than that of the normal population, but many live into old age. Much of the shorter life span is attributable to a high suicide rate among people suffering from schizophrenia, as well as accidental death and the negative lifestyle effects of those who are not well cared for. In that respect, it is relevant to note that schizophrenic patients not receiving drugs die at a rate ten times higher than patients on medication.[14] . . .

[T]here is today a great deal more documented evidence of the concept of anosognosia.[15] More than just an assertion that mentally ill people sometimes lack full awareness of or adequate insight into their illness and distinct from denial as a psychologically-based defense tactic, the term is meant to describe a "biologically-based" or even "neurological" inability on the part of the sick person to appreciate that he/she is sick and needs treatment, which is a characteristic of the illness itself. It is said to afflict some 47%–57% of schizophrenic patients[16] with implications not just for health and behavior (as mentioned, untreated mental illness is strongly related to psychiatric deterioration and violence) but of course also the law's assessment of a treatment refuser's 'competence' and the desirability/wisdom of honoring his or her wishes. . . .

We also wrote of the costs of treatment delayed or denied because of the law's overprotections: individual clinical costs such as mental deterioration and the inability to recapture such psychiatric loss; institutional costs and harms on the order of increased violence in hospitals on the part of untreated patients and its effect on compliant patients and care givers; and the direct financial costs of warehousing patients before they can be treated, as well as legal process expenditures in judicially or administratively resolving treatment refusal disputes.[17]

Finally, we wrote of the "true risks of side effects" of the antipsychotic drugs (the first-generation drugs of that time), noting that on the one hand all drugs have side effects, and on the other, that as measured by both their efficacy (high but underappreciated) and their asserted bad effects (grossly overstated as to seriousness, general prevalence and particular risk to the patient or patient class) the antipsychotics predominantly used were relatively benign.[18] (p. 13) . . . [T]he risk of death from untreated psychosis, drawn from hospital studies documenting large numbers of deaths from lethal catatonia, suicide, accidents, infection and other harms that used to befall chronically psychotic patients in predrug days, was infinitely larger than from the antipsychotic drugs, a situation we analogized to the benefits of penicillin which exponentially increased medical survival rates in homes, hospitals and on the battle fields despite the fact that an allergic reaction to the drug can on occasion be fatal.[19] (p. 13) . . . To anticipate arguments about autonomy or (even) free speech, we emphasized, as we do today, the restorative properties of the drugs; that the evidence of cognitive/perceptual restoration to premorbid "normal" mental processing was substantial for many patients treated with the drugs; and the bearing this in turn should have on which of the patient's choices in what mental state to honor.[20]

This was the state of the medication treatment art in regard to what have since been called the "typicals" (*i.e.*, haloperidol, chlorpromazine, thioridazine, fluphenazine, perphenazine), the "old," "conventional" antipsychotic drugs that in the early 1990s began to be replaced by a newer line of pharmaceuticals called (of course) the "atypicals" (the forerunner clozapine and later olanzapine, quetiapine, risperidone, ziprasidone, and aripiprazole). Trials and other research on the atypicals tended to show substantial efficacy gains as well as a marked reduction in the prevalence and seriousness of undesirable side effects. . . .

The evidence also continues to accumulate and solidify that all drugs, old or new, produce major gains and help safeguard against psychiatric loss which occurs in the absence of treatment and cannot be recouped even after treatment is initiated. Recent studies document disturbingly high percentages of untreated mental illness or treatment that is interrupted against medical advice (this, in a context where the law's preoccupation continues, anachronistically, to be with alleged unneeded and unwanted treatment). A 2001 report of a National Comorbidity Survey conducted between 1990 and 1992 found that fewer than 40% of a cohort of seriously mentally ill patients received stable treatment, with the primary reason for failure to seek treatment or failing to continue being the subjects' unwillingness or inability to see the need.[21] The prognosis for these patients is a diminishing chance of amelioration or recovery as relapses mount and symptoms increase in acuity, severity (negative symptoms in particular) and resistance to remediation.[22] At the same time, studies on adherence to drug treatment, many conducted in the context of attempts to evaluate the merits of so-called outpatient commitment (OPC),[23] show the benefits of treatment and especially *continued* treatment (even for the minimally symptomatic) on virtually all important personal and social measures: *i.e.,* reduced hospital recidivism and reduced criminal recidivism/violent behavior,[24] as well as reduced victimization;[25] quality of life improvements such as measured by reduced psychiatric symptomatology and better functioning;[26] and systemic gains in terms of less discordant and more appropriate use of the mental health and correctional systems, respectively, for mentally ill people who come into contact with the law as well as appreciable gains in housing situations (reductions in homelessness).[27]

Finally, as mentioned, new findings and confirmation of older study results on anognosia, which document the relationship between schizophrenia and lack of insight as one of the latter being a neurological function/symptom of the former,[28] provide strengthening support for a best-medical-interests decision making model in mental health matters. The implications of the concept of anognosia for treatment adherence/compliance are self-evident. A person who believes he is not sick will resist treatment at all stages and levels. To the extent the implications for the person's mental health (negative, as they would be for most any untreated somatic illness) are not equally self-evident, they have been described and documented in studies such as those cited in the preceding paragraph. Last, while the details may ultimately bedevil some or many, we believe no spelling out is required of anognosia's implication *in principle* regarding the need for and propriety of the option of (legal) coercion in mental health treatment. Much as we might want, desirable as it may seem, we cannot afford to limit mental health treatment to its entirely voluntary provision and acceptance.

These then are the contemporary medical facts against whose backdrop we proceed with the analysis in the remainder of the paper.

III. Once Again: What Is the Legal Debate About?

. . . All patients have a legally, even constitutionally, protected right to refuse treatment. There is no disagreement on this and need not be. Nor, despite its constitutionally protected status, is there any doubt that this right of a patient

(p. 17) . . . in some situations must yield to superior interests, in particular the interests of treating doctors and/or those they represent. The "issue" is how much/what kind of process must be observed to override the patient's refusal, should that be considered medically necessary. This is where opinions, both legal and lay, diverge. And the legal/medical context in which the refusal is asserted will have everything to do with what the answer is or, better, as there is no consensus here, what we think the answer ought to be. This is the crux of the matter. . . .

VI. Legislative Process and Progress

Reports by groups favoring psychiatric intervention when needed such as the Treatment Advocacy Center (TAC)[29] suggest that in regard to inpatient commitment observable strides have been made nationally—*i.e.*, jurisdiction by jurisdiction—to impart a more medically-oriented/*parens patriae* perspective and, if not replace, to at least supplement the danger-to-others/police power focus of the earlier statutes. This has been accomplished via a revival of the need for treatment standard to suffice for commitment and an accompanying refocus of the legal lens on indicators such as psychiatric treatment history, recent decompensation, deterioration or destabilization, or even mere risk of such—all of which avoid, conceptually, the implicit emergency/police power strictures that dominate the dangerousness formulation, and should help us move away in practice from the consequent futile pattern of repetitive one-at-a-time, typically post-crisis, interventions.

As for outpatient commitment statutes, the concept underlying them is not new, but they have over the past few years swept the country in terms of increased visibility and use.[30] The objective of these laws, at least partly met according to early studies,[31] is to ensure treatment for those who otherwise resist, avoid, stop, slip-through-the-cracks-of, and "recycle" through the mental health and criminal justice systems, to their own as well as their fellow citizens' detriment. More, and especially earlier, treatment for more people who need it is the aspiration here, as is the continuation of treatment already begun given the proven benefits of adherence/compliance and the well-documented negatives associated with the interruption or cessation of the treatment regimen. The concept's ancillary virtue . . . "is that it is and has been correctly perceived by many as a lesser infringement on patients' liberty than having the treatment need met by inpatient hospitalization (or the 'police need' for segregation met by incarceration)." In other words, it is a concept on which people of differing political/philosophical persuasion and orientation—*i.e.*, those on opposite sides of the traditional advocacy divide—should be able to agree.[32] . . .

A. Increased Treatment Focus in Commitment Statutes

1. Persistence of Dangerousness as the Sole Commitment Criterion (and Four Deviations)

It is the view, correct in our opinion, that for determining the need for psychiatric intervention it is both apposite and sufficient to use psychiatric standards and terms, and not those of law enforcement. The law is not asking a secondary question here such as it does in the context of, say, the insanity defense, where the psychiatric input is meant to address cognitive or volitional capacity so as to help resolve the ultimate legal issue of accountability/culpability, or any of a number of issues where the law seeks psychiatric consultation as it were via testimony on so-called penultimate issues.[33] This is direct and ultimate: it is about treatment and treatability. The question can both be posed and answered directly, in medical terms.[34] . . .

[A] growing number of states are passing statutory provisions that premise involuntary hospitalization on a finding by the committing court that the individual proposed therefore lacks capacity to make treatment decisions. . . . Such laws collapse the inquiry into need for hospitalization with the (to us, self-evident) need to be treated once hospitalized and thereby avoid the anomaly of legally sustainable treatment refusals. . . .

B. Outpatient "Commitment" Laws

The judicial power to order treatment outside the institutional context has today been formalized in the laws of all but eight states in the U.S. with the passages of what are generally, if oxymoronically, known as outpatient commitment statutes.

VII. The ADA, *Olmstead* and the "Conversion" of Justice Kennedy

It must be remembered that for the person with severe mental illness who has no treatment, the most dreaded of confinements can be the imprisonment inflicted by his own mind, which shuts reality out and subjects him to the torment of voices and images beyond our powers to describe. . . . It is a common phenomenon that a patient functions well with medication, yet, because of the mental illness itself, lacks discipline or capacity to follow the regime the medication requires.[35] . . .

Conclusions

We believe that for civil commitment . . . and commitment for restoration to trial competence both the substantive standards and procedures can and should be medical. As we said at the outset, every patient or proposed patient has a right to refuse treatment if he/she does not want it. That is to say, patients as other citizens should be able to articulate their objection to prescribed treatment and that objection, if made, should be heard. Moreover, the physician who is responsible for treating the patient should try to convince the patient that the course prescribed is best for him/her or propose another course or courses that the patient finds more palatable but that, despite perhaps being suboptimal, still work(s). In short, we support the kind of therapist/patient dialogue about therapy that we will presume takes place in any hospital, community treatment center or doctor's office to the extent the patient's mental condition permits.[36]

However, if the patient cannot be convinced to accept the prescribed treatment, rejecting it and any plausible alternative courses (including trial and error), the physician should be allowed to initiate treatment over the patient's objection with minimal legal interference. That is, the only substantive criterion that need or should inform the physician's decision to proceed to treat is medical need/propriety. Inquiries into the patient's dangerousness, the government's (compelling) interest in prosecuting or any similarly diversionary issues should not be required. Procedurally, in-house medical review of the initial treatment decision should suffice to allow the primary physician to go ahead. The purpose after all of each of these commitments, simply stated even if not always simple to achieve, is to restore mental health and functioning as much and as quickly as possible. . . .

Judges cannot be and should not be the baseline decision makers in any of these institutional (or non-institutional), post-legal judgment phases of the treatment process. Forced treatment can begin once the medical reviewer has approved the treating physician's recommendation. Post-deprivation judicial review, after treatment has been initiated and limited by the professional judgment rule, is all the law should call for at this juncture.[37]

Notes

1. Samuel J. Brakel & John M. Davis, *Taking Harms Seriously: Involuntary Mental Patients and the Right to Refuse Treatment*, 25 IND. L. REV. 429 (1991).

2. Indeed, it would be demonstrably wrong. (1) What success there is has been slow in coming and uneven. (2) The article has not been cited with great frequency, its appeal apparently being limited mostly to the already converted. And (3) the achievement of significant legal change tends to require a combination of many factors and forces, among which academic writings may play a role but not usually a prominent one. . . .

3. Brakel & Davis, *supra*, note 1, at 437–438 and notes.

4. *Ibid.*

5. *Id.* at 438–440, especially note 33, citing *In re* the Mental Commitment of M.P., 510 N.E. 2d 645 (IN 1987) and *In re* Orr, 531 N.E. 2d 64 (IL 1988) as textbook examples. The earlier Indiana case had made reference to a "virtually undisputed allegation that a person medicated with antipsychotic drugs has a 50% risk of contracting tardive dyskinesia." This in fact highly disputable, if not plain erroneous (the much less alarming facts were not widely known at the time), allegation was then cited by the Illinois court in a subsequent decision as a "fact" "found" by the Indiana Supreme Court. . . .

6. There are imaging data today from living schizophrenic patients that show excessive dopamine release in the brain when the patient is having hallucinations and delusions, as well as of the blocking effect on dopamine receptors when antipsychotics are administered. *See* A. Abi-Dargam, R. Gil, J. Krystal *et al.*, *Increased Striatal Dopamine Transmission in Schizophrenia: Confirmation in a Second Cohort*, 155 AM. J. PSYCHIATRY 761 (1998); A. Bartolomeis, D.R. Weinberger, N. Weisenfeld *et al.*, *Schizophrenia Is Associated with Elevated Amphetamine-Induced Synaptic Dopamine Concentrations: Evidence from a Novel Positron Emission Tomography Method*, 94 PROC. NAT'L. ACAD. SCI. U.S.A. 2569 (1997).

7. The amotivational, apathetic, poor social skills aspects of schizophrenia are its so-called negative symptoms. Combined with cognitive/executive defects, these deficits contribute greatly to poor social and vocational functioning among people with the illness. But today's drugs can go a long way toward remedying these deficits and we have an under-standing, albeit imperfect, of how they work. S. R. Marder, J. M. Davis & G. Chouinard, *The Effects of Risperidone on the Five Dimensions of Schizophrenia Derived by Factor Analysis: Combined Results of the North American Trial,* 58 *J. CLIN. PSYCHIATRY* 538 (1997); J.M. Davis & N. Chen, *Clinical Profile of an Atypical Antipsychotic: Risperidone,* 28 *SCHIZOPHRENIA BULLETIN* 43 (2002). . . .

8. It is less a matter of psychosocial treatments having no place or a lesser place in the treatment of severe mental illness today than that the treatments are entirely different. They *capitalize* today on the gains in thinking and func-tioning that can be achieved by the medications, as distinct from trying the impossible, which is to achieve these gains directly through verbal or behavioral therapy. *See Osherhoff v. Chestnut Lodge, Inc.* 62 Md. App. 519, 490 A.2d 720 (1985) for an early case—the reported court case merely affirms an arbitration award for allegedly negligent treatment that took place in 1979—involving the recognition that verbal therapy as such is ineffective in treating mental illness with substantial biological components, in this instance a psychotic depressive reaction, and that the failure on the part of the defendant to initiate psychopharmacologic treatments may consti-tute negligence. The defendant institution, Chestnut Lodge, was a facility famous for furthering psychoanalytic theory and practice, having trained a number of prominent American psychiatrists of this school, a fact which seems to have influenced the diagnosis its staff made of the plaintiff's men-tal health problems as much as the treatment course that was pursued in the face of unmistakable evidence that the patient was getting worse rather than better.

9. E. Fuller Torrey, *OUT OF THE SHADOWS* (1997).

10. *Ibid. See* also, H. Brill & R.E. Patton, *Population Fall in New York State Mental Hospitals in First Year of a Large-Scale Use of Tranquilizing Drugs,* 114 *AM. J. PSYCHIATRY* 509 (1957).

11. See Brill & Patton, *supra,* note 28.

12. *See OUT OF THE SHADOWS, supra,* note 27. The lawyer author of this paper conducted social/legal research in the early 1970's at Kankakee State Hospital 30 miles south of Chicago at a time when it housed some 4,000 patients. Within a few years the hospital was a relic, empty of mentally ill patients and in the process of being converted, to the extent possible, to other uses.

13. The neuropsychological deficits and the loss of grey matter seem to get worse after the patient's first psychotic episode and there is strong evi-dence that failure to treat the first episode with antipsychotic drugs leads to substantially worse outcome, in terms of repeat episodes and recovery there-from, in the following five years. There is beginning evidence that at least some of the second-generation drugs in particular are effective in block-ing the progression of these deficits and losses. K. Kasai, M.E. Shenton *et al., Progressive Decrease of Left Superior Temporal Gyrus Grey Matter Volume in Patients with First-Episode Schizophrenia,* 160 *AM. J. PSYCHIATRY* 156

(2003); W. Cahn, H.E. Hulshoff Poll *et al.*, *Brain Volume Changes in First-Episode Schizophrenia: A One-Year Follow-Up Study*, 59 ARCH. GEN. PSYCHIATRY 1002 (2002). Moreover, a large study carried out in Finland, based on that country's central register, found that the risk of untreated schizophrenic patients dying was 10 times higher than that of patients on medication. J. Tiihonen, K. Wahlbeck *et al.*, *Effectiveness of Antipsychotic Treatments in a Nationwide Cohort of Patients in Community Care after First Hospitalization Due to Schizophrenia and Schizoaffective Disorder: Observational Follow-Up Study*, 333 BRITISH MED. J. 224 (2006).

14. *Ibid.* . . .

15. Researchers most prominently identified with the concept of anosognosia, through studies conducted in the early 1990s, are psychologist Xavier Amador at Columbia University in New York and psychiatrist Anthony David at the Institute of Psychiatry in London (UK). Psychiatrist Joseph McEvoy of the University of Pittsburgh however first explicitly linked the characteristic to the illness in the 1980s. Joseph P. McEvoy *et al.*, *Why Must Some Schizophrenic Patients Be Involuntarily Committed? The Role of Insight*, 30 COMPR. PSYCHIATRY 13 (1989); Joseph P. McEvoy *et al.*, *Measuring Chronic Schizophrenic Patients' Attitudes Toward Their Illness and Treatment*, 32 HOSP. COMMUNITY PSYCHIATRY 856 (1981).

16. Xavier Amador *et al.*, *Awareness of Illness in Schizophrenia and Schizoaffective and Mood Disorders*, 51 ARCHIVES GEN. PSYCHIATRY 826 (1994); Xavier Amador *et al.*, *Awareness Deficits in Neurological Disorders and Schizophrenia* (abstract), 24 SCHIZOPHRENIA RES. 96 (1997). . . .

17. *Id.* at 453–461, under "Research Findings on the Harms Resulting from Delayed Treatment."

18. *Id.* at 461–467. . . .

19. *Ibid.* . . .

20. *Id.* at 465. . . .

21. Ronald C. Kessler, Patricia A. Berglund, Martha L. Bruce *et al.*, *The Prevalence and Correlates of Untreated Serious Mental Illness*, 36 HEALTH SERVICES RESEARCH 978 (2001).

22. *E.g.*, Diana O. Perkins, Hongbin Gu, Kalina Boteva & Jeffrey A. Lieberman, *Relationships Between Duration of Untreated Psychosis and Outcome in First-Episode Schizophrenia: A Critical Review and Meta Analysis*, 162 AM. J. PSYCHIATRY 1785 (2005); D.A.W. Johnson, G. Pasterski, L. Ludlow *et al.*, *The Discontinuance of Maintenance Neuroleptic Therapy in Chronic Schizophrenic Patients: Drug and Social Consequences*, 67 ACTA PSYCHIATR. SCAND. 339 (1983); Charles M. Beasley, Jr., Virginia K. Sutton, Cindy C. Taylor *et al.*, *Is Quality of Life Among Minimally Symptomatic Patients with Schizophrenia Better Following Withdrawal or Continuation of Antipsychotic Treatment?* 26 J. OF CLINICAL PSYCHOPHARMACOLOGY 40 (2006).

23. See section on this topic *infra*. . . .

24. Jeffrey W. Swanson, Randy Borum, Marvin S. Swartz, Virginia A. Hiday *et al.*, *Can Involuntary Outpatient Commitment Reduce Arrests Among Persons with Severe Mental Illness?* 28 CRIM. JUSTICE AND BEHAVIOR 156 (2001); Jeffrey W. Swanson, Marvin S. Swartz, Randy Borum, Virginia A. Hiday *et al.*, *Involuntary Outpatient Commitment and Reduction of Violent Behaviour in*

Persons with Severe Mental Illness, 176 *BRITISH J. OF PSYCHIATRY* 324 (2000); Marvin S. Swartz, Jeffrey W. Swanson, H. Ryan Wagner, Barbara J. Burns *et al., Can Involuntary Outpatient Commitment Reduce Hospital Recidivism?: Findings from a Randomized Trial with Severely Mentally Ill Individuals*, 156 *AM. J. PSYCHIATRY* 1968 (1999).

25. Virginia A. Hiday, Marvin S. Swartz, Jeffrey W. Swanson, Randy Borum & H. Ryan Wagner, *Impact of Outpatient Commitment on Victimization of People with Severe Mental Illness*, 159 *AM. J. PSYCHIATRY* 1403 (2002).

26. Jeffrey W. Swanson, Marvin S. Swartz, Eric B. Elbogen *et al., Effects of Involuntary Outpatient Commitment on Subjective Quality of Life in Persons with Severe Mental Illness*, 21 *BEHAV. SCIENCES AND THE LAW* 473 (2003).

27. Haya Ascher-Svanum, Douglas E. Faries, Baojin Zhu *et al., Medication Adherence and Long-Term Functional Outcomes in the Treatment of Schizophrenia in Usual Care*, 67 *J. OF CLINICAL PSYCHIATRY* 453 (2006).

28. See Amador and McEvoy articles, *supra.* Also, Joseph P. McEvoy, Paul S. Appelbaum, L. Joy Apperson *et al., Why Must Some Schizophrenic Patients Be Involuntarily Committed? The Role of Insight*, 30 *COMPR. PSYCHIATRY* 13 (1989); Anthony S. David, *Insight and Psychosis*, 156 *BRITISH J. OF PSYCHIATRY* 798 (1990); Xavier F. Amador, David H. Strauss, Scott A. Yale & Jack M. Gorman, *Awareness of Illness in Schizophrenia*, 17 *SCHIZOPHRENIA BULLETIN* 113 (1991); Faith B. Dickerson, John J. Boronow, Norman Ringel & Frederick Parente, *Lack of Insight Among Outpatients with Schizophrenia*, 48 *PSYCHIATRIC SERVICES* 195 (1997); Xavier F. Amador & Regina A. Seckinger, *The Assessment of Insight: A Methodological Review*, 27 *PSYCHIATRIC ANNALS* 798 (1997); Graig Goodman, Gabriella Knoll, Victoria Isakov & Henry Silver, *Insight into Illness in Schizophrenia*, 46 *COMPR. PSYCHIATRY* 284 (2005).

29. See the *CATALYST* (Newsletter of the Treatment Advocacy Center) Spring/Summer 2004. TAC also maintains a website, www.psychlaws.org, on which it provides, *e.g.,* updates on the latest legislative reforms. TAC advocates refer to the process as "assisted outpatient treatment" (AOT) which apart from deemphasizing the nonconsensual aspects of "outpatient commitment" also has the advantage of avoiding its oxymoronic quality, the term commitment being associated with confinement in an institution, *i.e.,* being an *in*patient.

30. *Ibid.*

31. *CATALYST,* Spring/Summer 2005 at 7 and 15. The latter page presents "real-world results" on New York's Kendra's law under the title "Kendra's Law families and participants laud program: Report shows sharp reductions in hospitalizations, incarcerations, homelessness." The TAC group points to a number of other studies supporting the notion that the outpatient commitment laws have achieved their intended effects: Guido Zanni & Leslie deVeau, *Inpatient Stays Before and After Outpatient Commitment*, 37 *HOSP. & CMTY PSYCHIATRY* 941 (1986); M.R. Munetz *et al., The Effectiveness of Outpatient Civil Commitment*, 47 *Psychiatric Services* 1251 (1996); B.M. Rohland, *The Role of Outpatient Commitment in the Management of Persons with Schizophrenia*, IOWA CONSORTIUM FOR MENTAL HEALTH SERVICES, TRAINING, AND RESEARCH (1998); and Gustavo A. Fernandez & Sylvia Nygard, *Impact of Involuntary Outpatient Commitment on the Revolving-Door*

Syndrome in North Carolina, 41 *HOSP. & CMTY PSYCHIATRY* 1001 (1990). Later studies in North Carolina have been especially persuasive in documenting positive effects of mandated outpatient treatment in various respects. *See* (the titles are indicative) Marvin S. Swartz, Jeffrey W. Swanson, H. Ryan Wagner *et al., Can Involuntary Outpatient Commitment Reduce Hospital Recidivism?* 156 *AM. J. PSYCHIATRY* 1986 (1999); Jeffrey W. Swanson, Marvin S. Swartz, R. Borum *et al., Involuntary Outpatient Commitment and Reduction in Violent Behaviour in Persons with Severe Mental Illness,* 176 *BRIT. J. PSYCHIAT.* 224 (2000); Jeffrey W. Swanson, R. Borum, Marvin S. Swartz *et al., Can Involuntary Outpatient Commitment Reduce Arrests among Persons with Severe Mental Illness?* 28 *CRIM. JUSTICE & BEHAVIOR* 156 (2001); Virginia A. Hiday, Marvin S. Swartz, Jeffrey W. Swanson *et al., Impact of Outpatient Commitment on Victimization of People with Severe Mental Illness,* 159 *AM. J. PSYCHIAT.* 1403 (2002). . . .

32. In theory at least. A recent article by Richard J. Bonnie and John Monahan, *From Coercion to Contract: Reframing the Debate on Mandated Community Treatment for People with Mental Disorders,* 29 *LAW AND HUMAN BEHAVIOR* 485 (2005), confirms (by the title alone) that there is much less agreement on the value of the concept than its proponents once optimistically believed. See also note 277, *supra.* . . .

33. The law has gone back and forth on whether it is appropriate for mental health experts to offer testimony on ultimate legal issues, with the post-Hinckley reforms following the acquittal by reason of insanity of President Reagan's would-be assassin, enacted in 1984 for the federal courts, leading the way toward the currently dominant position of disallowing it.

34. It has been pointed out innumerable times by both judges and legal commentators that commitment is a social/legal decision rather than a medical one, but this does not alter the fact that medical criteria and medical facts are what that social/legal decision should be heavily based on. . . .

35. *Id.* at 609–610.

36. The law is allowed to, should in fact, assume basic medical/institutional realities including such that there ordinarily is communication about treatment prospects and plans between therapist and patient. As distinct from case law drawn from litigation where worst-case evidence is introduced, the statutory or regulatory law ordinarily need not and should not be written based on worst-case scenarios. *Cf.* the discussion of *Rennie v. Klein* in the text, *supra,* . . . where we reproduce the administrative regulation—presumptively a codification of practices—guiding doctors in New Jersey on how to approach patients who resist prescribed treatment. Substantively, the regulation in fact incorporates the least intrusive/least restrictive principle and its procedural mandates suggest abundant deference to the patient's preferences via the physician's stated obligation to discuss alternatives with the patient, to try make the patient understand and to encourage voluntary acceptance (with the help of relatives and friends if so indicated) before seeking approval from the hospital medical director to proceed over the patient's objections. . . .

37. Postdeprivation judicial review should suffice because (1) judges have no expertise in medical matters and therefore should not be baseline (first-instance) decision makers and (2) the costs in time and treatment foregone, deflection of resources, and institutional bad effects of the judiciary's failing to show proper deference to medical professionals are large.

James B. Gottstein

NO

How the Legal System Can Help Create a Recovery Culture in Mental Health Systems

Summary

The purpose of this paper is to show how strategic litigation can and should be a part of efforts to transform mental health systems to a culture of recovery. Currently, involuntary commitment and forced drugging are by far the "path of least resistance" when society is faced with someone who is disturbing and their thinking does not conform to society's norms.[1] In other words, it is far easier for the system to lock people up and drug them into submission, than it is to spend the time with them to develop a therapeutic relationship and thus able to engage the person with voluntary humane alternatives leading to recovery.[2] I estimate that 10% of involuntary commitments in the United States and none of the forced drugging under the *parens patriae* doctrine[3] are legally justified. This presents a tremendous opportunity to use litigation to "encourage" the creation of voluntary, recovery-oriented services.[4]

In my view, though, in order to be successful various myths of mental illness need to be debunked among the general public and humane, effective recovery oriented, noncoercive alternatives must be made available. . . . The thesis of this paper is that strategic litigation (and public education) are likely essential to transforming the mental health system to one of a recovery culture. . . .

For example, debunking the myth among the general public that people do not recover from a diagnosis of serious mental health illness can encourage the willingness to invest in recovery-oriented alternatives. Similarly, having successful, recovery-oriented alternatives will help in debunking the myth that people don't recover from serious mental illness. In like fashion, judges and even counsel appointed to represent psychiatric defendants believe the myth "if this person wasn't crazy, she would know these drugs are good for her" and therefore don't let her pesky rights get in the way of doing the "right thing," i.e., forced drugging. The myth of dangerousness results in people being locked up. In other words, the judges and lawyers reflect society's views and to the extent that society's views change, the judges and lawyers' responses will change to suit. That leads to taking people's rights more seriously. The converse is true as well. Legal cases can have a big impact on public views. *Brown v. Board of Education*,[5] which resulted in outlawing segregation is a classic example of this. Finally, the involuntary mental illness system[6] operates largely illegally, including through its failure to offer less restrictive alternatives.[7] Thus, litigation can force the creation of such alternatives. At the same time, as a practical matter, the availability of acceptable (to the person) recovery-oriented alternatives are necessary for anyone to actually be able to get such services when faced with involuntary commitment and forced drugging.

The Involuntary Mental Illness System Operates Largely Illegally

Involuntary "treatment"[8] in the United States largely operates illegally in that court orders for forced treatment are obtained without actual compliance with statutory and constitutional requirements. One of the fundamental constitutional rights that is ignored in practice is that of a "less restrictive alternative."[9] Thus, enforcement of this right through the courts can be instrumental in bringing about change. First, I will discuss the key constitutional principles. . . .

Constitutional Limits on Involuntary Commitment

The United States Supreme Court has recognized for a long time that involuntary civil commitment is a "massive curtailment of liberty"[10] requiring substantive due process protection:

> Freedom from bodily restraint has always been at the core of the liberty protected by the Due Process Clause from arbitrary governmental action. "It is clear that commitment for any purpose constitutes a significant deprivation of liberty that requires due process protection."[11]

Constitutional Limits on Forced Drugging

The United States Supreme Court has also held a number of times that being free of unwanted psychiatric medication is a fundamental constitutional right.[15] In the most recent case, *Sell*, the United States Supreme Court reiterated:

> [A]n individual has a "significant" constitutionally protected "liberty interest" in "avoiding the unwanted administration of antipsychotic drugs."[16] . . .

The Massachusetts Supreme Judicial Court has held people have the absolute right to decline medication unless they are incompetent to make such a decision and if they are incompetent they cannot be medicated against their will except by a court made Substituted Judgment Decision that includes the following factors:

1. The patient's expressed preferences regarding treatment.
2. The strength of the incompetent patient's religious convictions, to the extent that they may contribute to his refusal of treatment.

3. The impact of the decision on the ward's family—this factor being primarily relevant when the patient is part of a closely knit family.
4. The probability of adverse side effects.
5. The prognosis without treatment.
6. The prognosis with treatment.
7. Any other factors which appear relevant. . . .

[I]n *Rivers v. Katz,*[24] decided strictly on common law and constitutional due process grounds, New York's highest court held a person's right to be free from unwanted antipsychotic medication is a constitutionally protected liberty interest:

> [I]f the law recognizes the right of an individual to make decisions about . . . life out of respect for the dignity and autonomy of the individual, that interest is no less significant when the individual is mentally or physically ill.

> We reject any argument that the mere fact that appellants are mentally ill reduces in any manner their fundamental liberty interest to reject antipsychotic medication. We likewise reject any argument that involuntarily committed patients lose their liberty interest in avoiding the unwanted administration of antipsychotic medication.

> If . . . the court determines that the patient has the capability to make his own treatment decisions, the State shall be precluded from administering antipsychotic drugs. If, however, the court concludes that the patient lacks the capacity to determine the course of his own treatment, the court must determine whether the proposed treatment is narrowly tailored to give substantive effect to the patient's liberty interest, taking into consideration all relevant circumstances, including the patient's best interests, the benefits to be gained from the treatment, the adverse side effects associated with the treatment and any less intrusive alternative treatments. The State would bear the burden to establish by clear and convincing evidence that the proposed treatment meets these criteria. . . .

[I]n practice, people's rights are not being honored.[25] There are other states which have just as good legal rights and some that don't under state law, but the common denominator in all of them is whatever rights people have, they are uniformly ignored. . . .

In *Sell*, decided in 2003, the United States Supreme Court held someone could not be force drugged to make them competent to stand trial unless:

1. The court finds that *important* governmental interests are at stake.

2. The court must conclude that involuntary medication will *significantly further* those concomitant state interests.
3. The court must conclude that involuntary medication is *necessary* to further those interests. The court must find that any alternative, less intrusive treatments are unlikely to achieve substantially the same results.
4. The court must conclude that administration of the drugs is *medically appropriate*, i.e., in the patient's best medical interest in light of his medical condition. The specific kinds of drugs at issue may matter here as elsewhere. Different kinds of antipsychotic drugs may produce different side effects and enjoy different levels of success.

(italics in original) These are general constitutional principles and should apply in the civil context. Thus, for example, while in *Sell*, the "*important* governmental interest" is in bringing a criminal defendant to trial, the governmental interest in the civil context is (supposedly) the person's best interest, i.e., the *parens patriae* doctrine.[26]

With respect to the second requirement that the forced drugging "will *significantly further*" those interests, the question in the competence to stand trial context is whether the forced drugging is likely to make the person competent to stand trial, while in the civil context, the question is whether it is in the person's best interest or is the decision the person would make if he or she were competent.

The third requirement that the forced drugging must be *necessary* and there is no less restrictive alternative is hugely important in the civil context because it is a potential lever to require less restrictive (i.e., nondrug, recovery-oriented alternatives). It is important to note here that failure to find these alternatives does not give the government the right to force drug someone. If a less restrictive alternative could be made available, the forced drugging is unconstitutional.[27] . . .

The fourth requirement is also very important because it essentially requires the state to prove the drugging is in the person's best interest and not merely recite "professional judgment."

The take-away message is, in my view, people are constitutionally entitled to noncoercive, nondrugging, recovery-oriented alternatives before involuntary commitment and forced drugging can occur and even then forced drugging can only constitutionally occur if it is in the person's best interest. There are a couple of ways to look at this since the reality is so far from what the law requires. One is to see it as a tremendous opportunity to improve the situation. The other is that there are forces operating to totally defeat people's rights. Both are true and this paper suggests there are actions that can be taken to have people's rights honored that can play a crucial part in transforming the mental health system to one of a recovery culture.

Proper Procedures and Evidentiary Standards

Mentioned above are the United States Supreme Court rulings that involuntary commitment can occur only pursuant to proper procedures and evidentiary standards. In contrast to this legal requirement, involuntary commitment and forced drugging proceedings can quite fairly be characterized as a sham, a farce, Kangaroo Courts, etc., in the vast majority of cases.[29] . . .

Proper Procedures . . .

Proper evidentiary standards.   . . . [I]involuntary commitment is constitutionally permissible only if the person is a harm to self or others as a result of a "mental illness." In *Addington v. Texas*[33] the United States held that this has to be proven by "clear and convincing evidence," which is less than "'beyond a reasonable doubt,'" but more than the normal "preponderance of the evidence"[34] standard in most civil cases. . . .

The truth is psychiatric testimony as to a person's dangerousness is highly unreliable with a high likelihood of overestimating dangerousness.

> The voluminous literature as to the ability of psychiatrists (or other mental health professionals) to testify reliably as to an individual's dangerousness in the indeterminate future had been virtually unanimous: "psychiatrists have absolutely no expertise in predicting dangerous behavior—indeed, they may be less accurate predictors than laymen—and that they usually err by overpredicting violence."[37]

This is the primary reason why I estimate only 10% of involuntary commitments are legally justified. If people were only involuntarily committed when it can be shown, by clear and convincing evidence, under scientifically reliable methods of predicting the requisite harm to self or others, my view is 90% of current commitments would not be granted.

With respect to forced drugging, one of the prerequisites is the person must be found to be incompetent to decline the drug(s). Here, too, psychiatrists, to be kind, overestimate incompetence.

> [M]ental patients are not always incompetent to make rational decisions and are not inherently more incompetent than nonmentally ill medical patients.[38] . . .

The reason why I believe no forced drugging in the civil context is legally justified is it simply cannot be scientifically proven it is in a person's best interest.[40] It would make this paper even more too long than it already is to fully support this assertion, but some will be presented. First, there is really no doubt the current overreliance on the drugs is at least doubling the number of people becoming defined by the system as chronically mentally ill with it recently being estimated it has increased the rate of disability due to "mental Illness" six-fold.[41] In the case where we litigated the issue in Alaska, the trial court found:

> The relevant conclusion that I draw from [the evidence presented by the Respondent's experts] is that there is a real and viable debate among

qualified experts in the psychiatric community regarding whether the standard of care for treating schizophrenic patients should be the administration of antipsychotic medication.

⚹

[T]here is a viable debate in the psychiatric community regarding whether administration of this type of medication might actually cause damage to her or ultimately worsen her condition.[42]

A recent study in Ireland concluded the already elevated risk for death in schizophrenia due to the older neuroleptics was doubled with the newer, so-called "atypical" neuroleptics, such as Zyprexa and Risperdal.[43] More information on these drugs can be found on PsychRights' website. . . .

In sum, my view is the state can never (or virtually never) actually meet its burden of proving forced drugging is in a person's best interest (assuming that is required) because of the lack of long-term effectiveness and great harm they cause. Again, this raises the question of why forced drugging is so pervasive and what might be done about it. In other words, it is an opportunity for strategic litigation playing a key role in a transformation to a recovery-oriented system.

Corrupt Involuntary Mental "Treatment" System

As set forth above, people are locked up under judicial findings of dangerousness and force drugged based on it being in their best interests without any legitimate scientific evidence of either dangerousness or the drugs being in a person's best interests. As Professor Michael Perlin has noted:

[C]ourts accept . . . testimonial dishonesty, . . . specifically where witnesses, especially expert witnesses, show a "high propensity to purposely distort their testimony in order to achieve desired ends." . . .

Experts frequently . . . and openly subvert statutory and case law criteria that impose rigorous behavioral standards as predicates for commitment. . . .

This combination . . . helps define a system in which (1) dishonest testimony is often regularly (and unthinkingly) accepted; (2) statutory and case law standards are frequently subverted; and (3) insurmountable barriers are raised to insure that the allegedly "therapeutically correct" social end is met. . . . In short, the mental disability law system often deprives individuals of liberty disingenuously and upon bases that have no relationship to case law or to statutes.[44]

In other words, testifying psychiatrists lie,[45] the trial (but generally not appellate) courts don't care, and lawyers assigned to represent defendants in these cases, are "woefully inadequate—disinterested, uninformed, roleless, and often hostile. A model of "'paternalism/best interests'" is substituted for a traditional legal advocacy position, and this substitution is rarely questioned."[46]

Counsel appointed to represent psychiatric defendants is more often than not, actually working for the other side, or barely put up even a token defense, which amounts to the same thing.[47]

No one in the legal system is taking psychiatric defendants' rights seriously, including the lawyer appointed to represent the person. There are two reasons for this: The first is the belief that "if this person wasn't crazy, she'd know this is good for her." The second is the system is driven by irrational fear. All the evidence shows people who end up with psychiatric labels are no more likely to be dangerous than the general population and that medications increase the overall relapse rate, yet society's response has been to lock people up, and whether locked up or not, force them to take these drugs.[48] . . .

The Requirement and Necessity of Alternatives

Hopefully it is apparent from the foregoing that people should be allowed (less restrictive) alternatives when they are faced with forced drugging. The same is basically true of involuntary commitment.[55] These alternatives, I suggest, should primarily include noncoercive, for sure, and nondrug alternatives that are known to lead to recovery for many people.[56] The reality is likely a "which came first, the chicken or the egg?" situation, because judges will be reluctant to deny petitions for forced drugging on the basis that a less restrictive alternative could be made available, but in fact is not available. Thus, the actual availability of alternatives is important. However, where sufficient legal pressure is applied, the courts will simply not be able to order forced drugging. I know these are contradictory statements, but that is why they reinforce each other as set forth above (and below).

[A]s set forth above, everyone has the absolute constitutional right to decline psychiatric drugs, with one exception, which is if they are incompetent to do so. Currently, the competency determinations are not legitimate and Advance Directives are ignored. One reason I would posit, is that the system simply does not know what else to do with people so the system deals with it by finding people incompetent when they are not. . . .

The Importance of Public Opinion

It is perhaps easier to see how Public Education and the Availability of Alternatives reinforce each other. Alternatives to the hopelessness driven, medication only, stabilization-oriented system are not available because our society believes it is the only possibility, in spite of all kinds of evidence to the contrary. Thus, to the extent effective alternatives become known to society in general, these alternatives will become desired by society because they produce much more desired outcomes. Not only do people get better, but huge amounts of money will be saved by more than halving the number of people who become a permanent ward of government. At the same time, having successful Alternatives will show society that they are viable. Thus, as with the Availability of Alternatives and Honoring Legal Rights, they reinforce each other. . . .

Interplay Between Public Education and Honoring Legal Rights

As set forth above, the judges and even the lawyers representing people facing forced psychiatry accept the current societal view that people need to be locked up and forcibly drugged for society's and the person's own safety and best interests. To the extent society becomes aware this is not true, the judicial system will reflect that and be much more willing to honor people's rights. . . .

Requirements for Successful Litigation— Attorneys & Expert Witnesses

The building blocks for mounting successful strategic litigation are recruiting attorneys who will put forth a serious effort to discharge their ethical duties to their clients and expert witnesses who can prove the junk science behind current "treatment" and the effectiveness of recovery-oriented alternatives.

Types of Legal Actions . . .

Establishing the Right to Effective Assistance of Counsel

If people's rights were being honored, the problem of forced psychiatry would be mostly solved and this would absolutely force society to come up with alternatives—hopefully recovery oriented. Thus, challenges to the effectiveness of counsel should be made. In light of the current state of affairs, there seems little downside to trying to get the United States Supreme Court to hold it is a right under the United States Constitution. I also believe that ethics complaints should be brought against the attorneys who do not discharge their duty to zealously represent their clients. If every involuntary commitment and forced drugging hearing were zealously represented, each case should take at least half a day. In my view it takes that long to fully challenge the state's case and present the patient's. This, in itself, would encourage the system to look for alternatives (the "path of least resistance" principle).

Challenges to State Proceedings

States that proceed under the "professional judgment" rule should be challenged. The right to state paid expert witnesses should be pursued. The right to less restrictive alternatives should be pursued. Challenges to "expert witness" opinion testimony regarding dangerousness and competence should be made. Challenges to *ex parté* proceedings should be made. There are a myriad of challenges that can be made in the various states, depending on the statutes and procedures utilized in them.[58]. . .

Public Attitudes

Even though this paper is about the court's potential role in transforming mental health systems to a recovery culture, it seems worthwhile to also make a few comments about changing public attitudes. There is an historic opportunity right now to make substantial inroads against the Psychopharmacology/Psychiatric hegemony because of the revelations in the media regarding dangerous, ineffective drugs, but this must be seized or it will be lost. **A serious public education program must be mounted.**

An Effective Public Relations Campaign

In the main, perhaps unduplicated for any other issue, the power of the Psychopharmacology/Psychiatric hegemony has so controlled the message that the media tends not to even acknowledge there is another side. For most issues, the media will present at least one spokesperson from each side. However, when the latest questionable breakthrough in mental illness research or "treatment" is announced, the other side is not even presented. One might want to pass this off as Big Pharma advertising money infecting the news departments, but I think that is way too simplistic and perhaps even largely untrue. . . .

Alternatives

It also seems worthwhile to spend a little bit of space here on creating alternatives. Ultimately, in order to be successful, alternatives need to be funded by the public system.[75] One argument in its favor that should be attractive to government (but has not heretofore been) in the current system is breaking the bank. As Whitaker has shown, the disability rate for mental illness has increased six-fold since the introduction of Thorazine.[76] Making so many people permanently disabled and financially supported by the government, rather than working and supporting the government, is not only a huge human tragedy, but is also a massive, unnecessary governmental expense.

One of the simplest, but very important things that should be done is to compile a readily accessible, accurate, list of existing alternatives and efforts to get them going. I have seen lists of alternatives, but then I hear that this program or that is really not a true nondrugging and/or noncoercive alternative. It would be extremely helpful for there to be a description of each such program with enough investigation to know what is really happening. . . .

Conclusion

A final word about the importance of the potential role of the courts and the forced psychiatry issue. While it is true that many, even maybe most, people in the system are not under court orders at any given time, it is my view that the forced psychiatry system is what starts a tremendous number of people on the road to permanent disability (and poverty) and drives the whole public system. Of course, coercion to take the drugs is pervasive outside of court orders too, but again I see the legal coercion as a key element. If people who are now being dragged into forced psychiatry were given noncoercive, recovery-oriented options, they would also become available for the people who are not subject to forced psychiatry. I hope this paper has conveyed the role that strategic litigation can play in transforming mental health systems to a culture of recovery.

Notes

1. By phrasing it this way, I am not disputing that people become psychotic. I have been there. . . . However, there are lots of degrees—a continuum, if you will—and there are different ways of looking at these unaccepted ways of thinking, or altered states of consciousness. So, what I mean by this terminology is that people are faced with involuntary commitment and forced drugging when two conditions exist: One, they are bothering another person(s), including concern about the risk of suicide or other self-harm, and two, they are expressing thoughts that do not conform to those accepted "normal" by society. Of course, this ignores the reality that a lot of both are often trumped up, especially against people who have previously been subjected to the system.

2. The system believes it is also less expensive, but the opposite is actually true. The overreliance on neuroleptics and, increasingly, polypharmacy, has at least doubled the number of people who become permanently reliant on government transfer payments. In *Anatomy of an Epidemic: Psychiatric Drugs and the Astonishing Rise of Mental Illness in America,* which is available at . . . Robert Whitaker demonstrates the rate of disability has increased six-fold since the introduction of Thorazine in the mid '50s. The Michigan State Psychotherapy Project demonstrated extremely more favorable long-term outcomes for those receiving psychotherapy alone from psychotherapists with *relevant* training and experience. The short-term costs were comparable to the standard treatment and the long-term savings were tremendous. This study can be found at. . . .

3. "Parens Patriae" is legal Latin, literally meaning "parent of his or her country." *Black's Law Dictionary,* seventh edition defines it as "the state in its capacity as provider of protection to those unable to care for themselves." It is invoked with respect to minors and adults who are deemed incompetent to make their own decisions. In the context of forced drugging under the *parens patriae* doctrine, it basically is based on the notion, "If you weren't crazy, you'd know this was good for you."

4. At the same time there are impediments to doing so, primarily the lack of legal resources.

5. U.S. 294, 75 S.Ct. 753, 99 L.Ed. 1083 (1955).

6. In light of the system basically creating massive numbers of people who become categorized as chronically mentally ill, I call it the mental illness system, rather than the mental health system.

7. By saying the mental illness system operates largely illegally I mean that to the extent people are locked up and forcibly drugged when the statutory and constitutional requirements are not being met, that is illegal. Of course, this is done by filing paperwork and getting court orders, which looked at another way, makes it legal.

8. "Treatment" is in quotes because it is both (1) pretty clear the current, virtually exclusive reliance on psychiatric drugs by the public mental illness system hinders recovery for the vast majority of people, and (2) if it isn't voluntary, it isn't treatment.

9. *See*, e.g., *Sell v. United States*, 539 U.S. 166 (2003). However, not everyone agrees with my legal analysis of the right to the least restrictive alternative.

10. *Humphrey v. Cady*, 405 U.S. 504 (1972).

11. *Addington v. Texas*, 441 U.S. 418 (1979).

15. *Mills v. Rogers*, 457 U.S. 291 (1982); *Washington v. Harper*, 494 U.S. 210 (1990; *Riggins v. Nevada*, 504 U.S. 127 (1992); and *Sell v. United States*, 539 U.S. 166 (2003).

16. *Sell v. United States*, 539 U.S. 166, 177-8 (2003), citing to the Due Process Clause, U.S. Const., amend. 5, and *Washington v. Harper*, 494 U.S. 210, 110 S.Ct. 1028 (1990).

24. *Rivers v. Katz*, 495 N.E.2d 337, 341-3 (NY 1986).

25. *See*, Mental Hygiene Law Court Monitoring Project: Part 1 of Report: Do Psychiatric Inmates in New York Have the Right to Refuse Drugs? An Examination of Rivers Hearings in the Brooklyn Court, which can be accessed on the Internet at. . . .

26. I say, "supposedly," because in truth, controlling the person's behavior is a primary interest. "Police power" justification, which actually is based on controlling dangerous behavior, has also been used to justify forced drugging. *See*, *Rivers v. Katz*, 495 N.E.2d 337, 343 (NY 1986). However, the behavior presumably has to be very extreme to invoke "police power" and is not normally the stated basis for seeking forced drugging orders. It has been suggested there is an important government interest in ending indeterminate commitment and returning the individual to society, which can be done most effectively if the person is required to take the prescribed drugs. However, this is not the basis normally asserted and I would argue it is not a sufficient interest to override a person's rights to decline the drugs, particularly in light of the physical harms they cause.

27. There are likely limits on this, such as there being no requirement for Herculean efforts or where the cost is prohibitive. *See*, e.g., *Mathews v. Eldridge*, 424 U.S. 319, 334–35 (1976). . . .

29. An example is described in the recent Alaska Supreme Court brief we filed in *Wetherhorn v. Alaska Psychiatric Institute*, which can be found on the Internet at. . . .

33. 441 U.S. 418 (1979).

34. "Preponderance of the evidence," means more likely than not or, put another way, it only requires the balance to be slightly more on one side than the other. Yet another way to look at it is it just has to be more than 50% likely. . . .

37. Michael L. Perlin, *Mental Disability Law: Civil and Criminal*, §2A-4.3c, p. 109 (2d. Ed. 1998), footnotes omitted. *See*, also, Morris, Pursuing Justice for the Mentally Disabled, 42 San Diego L. Rev. 757, 764 (2005) ("Recent studies confirm . . . that psychotic symptoms, such as delusions or hallucinations, currently being experienced by a person, do not elevate his or her risk of violence.")

38. Perlin, "And My Best Friend, My Doctor/Won't Even Say What It Is I've Got: The Role And Significance Of Counsel In Right To Refuse Treatment Cases," 42 *San Diego Law Review* 735, 746–7 (2005), citing to Thomas Grisso & Paul S. Appelbaum, *The MacArthur Treatment Competence Study. III: Abilities of Patients to Consent to Psychiatric and Medical Treatments*, 19 *Law & Hum. Behav.* 149 (1995). . . .

40. While I believe this is true in the forced drugging context in terms of meeting the legal burden of justifying overriding a person's right to decline the medications, and I know this paper comes off as a polemic against psychiatric drugs, I absolutely believe people also have the right to choose to take them. I do think people should be fully informed about them, of course, which is normally not done, but that is a different issue. Not surprisingly, in a study of people who have recovered after being diagnosed with serious mental illness, those who felt the drugs helped them, used them in their recovery and those that didn't find them helpful, didn't use the drugs in their recovery. "How do We Recover? An Analysis of Psychiatric Survivor Oral Histories," by Oryx Cohen, in *Journal of Humanistic Psychology*, Vol. 45, No. 3, Summer 2005, 333–35, which is available on the Internet at. . . .

41. Anatomy of an Epidemic: Psychiatric Drugs and the Astonishing Rise of Mental Illness in America, by Robert Whitaker, *Ethical Human Psychology and Psychiatry*, Volume 7, Number I: 23–35 Spring 2005, which can be accessed on the Internet at. . . .

42. Order, in *In the Matter of the Hospitalization of Faith Myers,* Anchorage Superior Court, Third Judicial District, State of Alaska, Case No. 3AN-03-277 PR, March 14, 2003, pp. 8, 13, which can be accessed on the Internet at. . . .

43. Prospective analysis of premature mortality in schizophrenia in relation to health service engagement: a 7.5-year study within an epidemiologically complete, homogeneous population in rural Ireland, by Maria G. Morgan, Paul J. Scully, Hanafy A. Youssef, Anthony Kinsellac, John M. Owensa, and John L. Waddingtona, *Psychiatry Research* 117 (2003) 127–135, which can be found on the Internet at. . . .

44. *The ADA and Persons with Mental Disabilities: Can Sanist Attitudes Be Undone? Journal of Law and Health,* 1993/1994, 8 *JLHEALTH* 15, 33–34.

45. "It would probably be difficult to find any American Psychiatrist working with the mentally ill who has not, at a minimum, exaggerated the dangerousness of a mentally ill person's behavior to obtain a judicial order for commitment." Torrey, E. Fuller. 1997. *Out of the Shadows: Confronting America's Mental Illness Crisis*, New York: John Wiley and Sons, page 152. Dr. Torrey goes on to say this lying to the courts is a good thing. Of course, lying in court is perjury. Dr. Torrey also quotes psychiatrist Paul Applebaum as saying when "confronted with psychotic persons who might well benefit from treatment, and who would certainly suffer without it, mental health professionals and judges alike were reluctant to comply with the law," noting that in "'the dominance of the commonsense model,' the laws are sometimes simply disregarded."

46. Perlin, *"And My Best Friend, My Doctor/Won't Even Say What It Is I've Got": The Role And Significance Of Counsel In Right To Refuse Treatment Cases, 42 San Diego Law Review* 735, 738 (2005).

47. This is a violation of professional ethics. For example, the Comment to the Model Rules of Professional Conduct for attorneys, Rule 1.3, includes, "A lawyer should pursue a matter on behalf of a client despite opposition, obstruction or personal inconvenience to the lawyer, and take whatever lawful and ethical measures are required to vindicate a client's cause or endeavor. A lawyer must also act with commitment and dedication to the interests of the client and with zeal in advocacy upon the client's behalf."

48. "Kendra's Law" in New York is a classic example of this. There a person who had been denied numerous attempts to obtain mental health services pushed Kendra in front of a moving subway and when he was grabbed, said something like "now maybe I will get some help." The response was to pass an outpatient commitment law requiring people to take psychiatric drugs or be locked up in the hospital. This is a characterization, but when this was challenged, New York's high court ruled Kendra's Law didn't require people to take the drugs; that all it did was subject people to "heightened scrutiny" for involuntary commitment if they didn't. *See, In the Matter of K.L.*, 806 N.E.2d 480(NY 2004). . . .

55. Many state statutes certainly require it, and I would suggest it is constitutionally required as well.

56. *See,* Effective Non-Drug Treatments, which can be found on the Internet at. . . .

58. For example, I have identified a lot of things under Alaska law where I think valid challenges to what is going on can and should be made. . . .

75. However, I am also in favor of non-system alternatives.

76. *See,* Anatomy of an Epidemic: Psychiatric Drugs and the Astonishing Rise of Mental Illness in America, which is available at. . . .

EXPLORING THE ISSUE

Is Forced Treatment of Seriously Mentally Ill Individuals Justifiable?

Critical Thinking and Reflection

1. What legal protections can be put in place, and what specific procedures followed, to protect the right of individuals to make choices affecting their psychological and physical well-being?
2. What arguments can be made to support the idea that mental health professionals should be accorded the legal right to administer treatments against the will of a mentally ill person?
3. To what extent should family members of a seriously mentally ill individual be given the right to approve treatment for a loved one who is resisting such intervention?
4. In cases in which an involuntarily treated patient begins to recover from symptoms, how should decisions be made by mental health professionals to respect the prerogative of the patient to stop the treatment?
5. How would you go about designing a study to evaluate the psychological impact on individuals for whom treatment has been involuntarily administered?

Is There Common Ground?

In both articles the authors are advocating on behalf of humane care of severely mentally ill individuals. There is agreement about the fact that American history is tainted by horrifying inhumane treatments in mental hospitals up until the second half of the twentieth century. As mentioned by attorneys Brakel and Davis, prior to the 1950s most people with schizophrenia spent much of their life in state insane asylums, with close to a half-million individuals filling these beds. The introduction of antipsychotic medications such as chlorpromazine brought with it optimism that psychotically disturbed patients could be effectively treated, but this hope was naïve. These drugs were seen as an easy solution to the centuries-old problem of how to control the harmful and bizarre behaviors of psychotically disturbed individuals. The initial hope for these drugs was simplistic, in that no one realized that these medications could cause harmful physical side effects, some of which would involve irreversible neurological damage. Fortunately, over the course of the past several decades, considerable advances have been made in the development of medications with less severe side effects.

The deinstitutionalization movement that was active in the 1970s had a profound effect on moving psychologically disturbed individuals out of mental hospitals and into community settings where they could be treated and supported in less restrictive and more humane contexts. However, many of these individuals fell through the cracks, becoming homeless, malnourished, and psychotically disturbed once again. In consideration of these realities, both articles struggle with the question of how to take care of psychologically disturbed individuals who are incapable of self-care. To what extent should their rights to autonomy be respected, particularly when their life may be at risk? These are thorny questions that professionals in the fields of law and mental health continue to address.

Additional Resources

Bassman, R. (2005). Mental illness and the freedom to refuse treatment: Privilege or right. *Professional Psychology: Research and Practice, 36*(5), 488–497.

Chu, J. P., Emmons, L., Wong, J., Goldblum, P., Reiser, R., Barrera, A. Z., & Byrd-Olmstead, J. (2012). Public psychology: A competency model for professional psychologists in community mental health. *Professional Psychology: Research and Practice, 43*(1), 39–49.

Eno Louden, J., & Skeem, J. L. (2012). How do probation officers assess and manage recidivism and violence risk for probationers with mental disorder? An experimental investigation. *Law and Human Behavior.* doi:10.1037/h0093991

Fritz, M. (2006, February 1). A doctor's fight: More forced care for the mentally ill. *The Wall Street Journal*, p. A1.

Morgan, B., & Remington, R. (2012). Nursing educational needs for caring for people with serious mental illness (SMI) at end of life. *The Journal of American Psychiatric Nurses Association, 18,* 55.

Torrey, E. F. (2007, April 27). Commitment phobia. *The Wall Street Journal*, p. A17.

Treatment Advocacy Center (Eliminating Barriers to Mental Illness). Retrieved from www.treatmentadvocacycenter.org

Treatment Advocacy Center (Spring, 2006). *Catalyst.* Arlington, VA: Treatment Advocacy Center.

ISSUE 18

Is Excessive Use of Facebook a Form of Narcissism?

YES: Christopher J. Carpenter, from "Narcissism on Facebook: Self-Promotion and Anti-social Behavior," *Personality and Individual Differences* (vol. 52, 2012)

NO: Bruce C. McKinney, Lynne Kelly, and Robert L. Duran, from "Narcissism or Openness?: College Students' Use of Facebook and Twitter," *Communication Research Reports* (vol. 29, no. 2, 2012)

Learning Outcomes

After reading this issue, you should be able to:

- Describe the narcissistic traits of someone who uses Facebook in excess.
- Discuss the extent to which the extensive use of Facebook and other social networking services represents new ways to communicate, rather than a reflection of narcissism.
- Critically evaluate the research methods used to study the relationship between Facebook usage and personality characteristics.
- Understand the concepts of "grandiose exhibitionism" (GE) and "entitlement/exploitativeness" (EE) as they might apply to Facebook usage.
- Understand the difference between trait narcissism and positive self-presentation.

ISSUE SUMMARY

YES: Communication Professor Christopher J. Carpenter asserts that there is a relationship between the frequency of Facebook use and narcissistic traits. While maintaining that Facebook provides opportunities for positive social interaction, Professor Carpenter argues that some users abuse the affordances and behave in anti-social ways on Facebook. Looking at two characteristics of narcissism, "grandiose exhibitionism" (GE) and "entitlement/exploitativeness"

(EE), GE is related to extensive self-presentation to as large an audience as possible via status updates, photos, and acquiring large numbers of friends. EE is related to anti-social behaviors such as retaliating against negative comments, reading others' status updates for references to self, and seeking more social support than one provides.

NO: Communication Professors Bruce C. McKinney, Lynne Kelly, and Robert L. Duran argue that narcissism is unrelated to the frequency of using Facebook to post about oneself (i.e., status updates and photos), although it is related to number of Facebook friends. They conclude, however, that Facebook is not dominated by narcissistic Millennials, but by people who are oriented toward openness with regard to their daily lives, and who believe that it is appropriate and enjoyable to share information with a wide circle of friends.

***

Facebook, which was launched in 2004, is a social networking service (SNS) which has attracted close to a billion active users. They are required to register in order to use the site, after which they can create a personal profile, add other users as friends, exchange messages, post photos, and so on. In addition to Facebook facilitating personal communications among individuals, this service has also been a boon to corporations and businesses that have tapped into this powerful tool for marketing, sales, and communication. The name of the service dates back to the colloquial term used to describe the directory distributed to incoming first-year students at many colleges containing photos of students as well as basic information such as hometown and the name of the high school from which the student graduated. As a student at Harvard, Mark Zuckerberg collaborated with a few fellow students to develop the Web site as a service to Harvard students, and then to other colleges in the Boston area, and eventually to schools throughout the country. With lightning speed, Facebook membership and usage became an international phenomenon accessed by people all over the world. In May 2012, Facebook made an initial public offering (IPO) at $38 a share, giving the world's number one SNS a $104 billion valuation, the third largest in U.S. history.

Within the course of a decade, Facebook provided users with communication opportunities that had previously been unimaginable. At first, the service was used just by college students eager to share information about friends and acquaintances, perhaps about upcoming parties or last night's celebration. In time, however, grandparents were using the service to view photos of their grandchildren, entrepreneurs were using it to promote their new business ideas, and unfortunately, sinister types were using it to gather personal information about users for illegal purposes. Professionals in the mental health, particularly those treating young people, were hearing more about Facebook insults, hurts, and heartbreaks. Sometimes, the hurt stems from seeing photos of one's "ex," or even current partner, in someone else's arms. Sometimes, it is a posting that contains cruel words, real or imagined. Sometimes, it is the shock of being inexplicably "unfriended."

Some Facebook users take pride in their extensive list of Facebook "friends," which can include hundreds, and even thousands of individuals who range from the intimacy of closest friends to the most random and distant of acquaintances. The question arises about the reason for accumulating a large number of friends, and the motivation for sharing information, sometimes of a very personal nature, with hundreds of people, some of whom the individual has never met. Is such a person a narcissist, or simply an open and spontaneously self-disclosing individual?

The trait of narcissism is characterized by a personality style in which individuals have a grandiose sense of self-importance, difficulty accepting criticism, and a sense of entitlement. In its most extreme form, narcissism can be viewed as a diagnosable condition, narcissistic personality disorder, which has been standard in previous editions of the diagnostic manual, and is included in *DSM-5*. Individuals with narcissistic personality disorder show a range of behaviors such as excessive reliance on others for self-esteem, a desperate need for approval, impaired capacity for empathy, superficiality of relationships, grandiosity, and excessive attempts to be the focus of attention.

In proposing a correlation between narcissism and excessive Facebook usage, Professor Carpenter focuses on two aspects of the trait of narcissism: "grandiose exhibitionism" (GE) and "entitlement/exploitativeness" (EE). People who are grandiosely exhibitionistic tend to be self-absorbed and vain, show off excessively, and act with an air of superiority. They feel a need to be the center of attention, and go to lengths in an attempt to achieve this. They may make shocking statements, self-disclose inappropriately, and take any opportunity to promote themselves. People with the narcissistic characteristic of EE feel that they deserve attention and respect, and are likely to manipulate and take advantage of others.

To study the relationship between narcissism and Facebook usage, Professor Carpenter conducted a study of 294 users ranging in age from 18 to 65 (mean age of 23), and found that GE was related to Facebook behaviors that afforded extensive self-presentation to as large an audience as possible via status updates, photos, and acquiring a large number of friends. EE was related to anti-social behaviors such as retaliating against negative comments about oneself, reading others' status updates for comments about oneself, and seeking more social support than that offered to others. Furthermore, such behaviors tended to be negatively correlated with self-esteem.

Professors McKinney, Kelly, and Duran take a sharply contrasting view, viewing extensive use of Facebook as more reflective of a person's openness about sharing information about oneself with others to facilitate communication and maintain relationships with friends and acquaintances. These researchers conducted a study of 233 university students, and did in fact find a significant but small correlation between narcissism and number of Facebook friends. However, they found that narcissism was unrelated to the frequency of using Facebook to post about oneself with status updates or photos. These researchers conclude that posting about oneself may be better explained by the attitude that it is appropriate and enjoyable to share personal information with a wide circle of friends. These authors mention the changing social mores in which people, especially from the younger generation, feel comfortable disclosing personal information that previously would have been regarded as very private.

YES

Christopher J. Carpenter

Narcissism on Facebook: Self-Promotional and Anti-social Behavior

Introduction

Facebook is one of the most popular websites in the world with over 600 million users (Ahmad, 2011). Those who use Facebook enjoy many benefits. Some college students use Facebook to seek and receive social support when they feel upset (Park, Kee, & Valenzuela, 2009; Wright, Craig, Cunningham, & Igiel, 2007). Toma and Hancock's (2011) recent experiments found when individuals are feeling distressed, they turn to Facebook to feel better. On the other hand, DeAndrea, Tong, and Walther (2011) argue that although online interaction provides opportunities for positive social interaction, some users abuse the affordances of social networking sites like Facebook to behave in anti-social ways. They argue that researchers need to move past seeking to determine if computer-mediated communication (CMC) has positive or negative effects as a whole but to determine why people use websites like Facebook in ways that promote or harm interpersonal relationships.

This study sought to take a step in that direction by examining one possible predictor of anti-social Facebook use: trait narcissism. The narcissistic personality type will first be briefly explicated. Then the existing research on the relationship between narcissism and Facebook use will be explored to develop hypotheses.

Investigating the relationship between narcissism and Facebook behavior is important because Facebook is becoming an increasingly important part of people's lives. Several researchers have found a relationship between narcissism and frequency of using Facebook (Buffardi & Campbell, 2008; Mehdizadeh, 2010; Ong et al., 2011). Other researchers found that narcissism is associated with the number of friends their participants have on Facebook (Bergman, Fearrington, Davenport, & Bergman, 2011). If these findings are accurate, it suggests that when people are interacting with others on Facebook, they are more likely to be interacting with individuals who are high in trait narcissism than in other contexts. If Facebook users are likely to be engaging in negative behaviors, the quality of the interpersonal interactions

Carpenter, Christopher J. From *Personality and Individual Differences*, 2012, pp. 482–486. Copyright © 2012 by Elsevier Health Sciences. Reprinted by permission.

people experience on Facebook will be reduced. Furthermore, some research suggests that people are evaluated not just by their own profiles but by the comments others make on their profiles (Walther, Van Der Heide, Kim, Westerman, & Tong, 2008). The negative behavior of narcissists on Facebook may reflect poorly on the innocent friends of those narcissists. If the relationship between narcissism and various kinds of behaviors can be uncovered, perhaps interventions can be designed to improve the Facebook social skills of trait narcissists.

Narcissism

When they developed the narcissistic personality inventory (NPI) Raskin and Terry (1988) found a great deal of ambiguity in the personality literature concerning the primary aspects of narcissism. They therefore included a variety of heterogeneous traits in their conceptualization of narcissism. These included aspects such as "a grandiose sense of self-importance or uniqueness," "an inability to tolerate criticism," and "entitlement or the expectation of special favors without assuming reciprocal responsibilities" (p. 891).

This definition covers a constellation of concepts and the NPI sought to measure all of them as aspects of a single personality trait.

In contrast, Ackerman et al. (2011) argue that the NPI is really measuring three different traits. They claim that one of the aspects of narcissism measured by the NPI is leadership ability and that aspect is often associated with positive interpersonal outcomes. The leadership aspects of narcissism were not the focus of this investigation as they are associated with pro-social behavior. On the other hand, they argue that the NPI also includes two other aspects of narcissism that they discovered drive the relationship between narcissism and anti-social behavior. These traits were the focus of this investigation.

Ackerman et al. (2011) labeled the first socially toxic element, "Grandiose Exhibitionism" (GE). This aspect of narcissism includes "self-absorption, vanity, superiority, and exhibitionistic tendencies" (p. 6). People who score high on this aspect of narcissism need to constantly be at the center of attention. They say shocking things and inappropriately self-disclose because they cannot stand to be ignored. They will take any opportunity to promote themselves. Simply gaining the interest and attention of others satisfies them.

Attention is not enough for those who posses the other negative aspect of narcissism labeled, "Entitlement/Exploitativeness" (EE). Ackerman et al. (2011) argue this aspect includes "a sense of deserving respect and a willingness to manipulate and take advantage of others" (p. 6). This tendency goes beyond the need for attention associated with GE as people high in this trait are those who will feel they deserve everything. More importantly, these people do not let the feelings and needs of others impede their goals. Ackerman et al. (2011) found that participants with higher EE scores were increasingly likely to have negative interactions reported by their roommate and their roommate was more likely to be dissatisfied with their relationship.

Narcissism and Facebook

Examination of the interpersonal possibilities offered by Facebook as well as the limited extant research suggests several tentative hypotheses about Facebook behaviors and the two aspects of narcissism under investigation. Initially, individuals who are high in GE will want to gain the attention of the widest audience possible (Ackerman et al., 2011). Therefore, they are predicted to have a high friend count given their drive to seek attention from as many people as possible. If they are seeking a wider audience, they are also predicted to accept friend requests from strangers because they would be seeking an audience rather than using Facebook to engage in social interaction with existing friends. They may also attempt to gain the attention of their audience by frequently offering new content. Posting status updates, posting pictures of themselves, and changing their profile are all methods or using Facebook to focus attention on the self. These different aspects of providing content will be labeled self-promotion and as a group they are predicted to be positively associated with GE.

On the other hand, Ackerman et al. (2011) found that EE tended to be associated with anti-social behaviors that indicate that others should cater to the narcissist's needs without any expectation of reciprocity. In the offline world, people high in EE might expect favors such as time, money, social support, and indications of respect from others. Although time and money might be harder to demand on Facebook, those high in EE should expect social support and respect. Some research suggests that many individuals who gain social support on Facebook feel less stress (Wright et al., 2007). Facebook users who are high in EE would be predicted to demand social support but be unlikely to provide it to others. They feel that others should support them when they are distressed, but they feel no duty to reciprocate.

There are several ways that those high in EE might expect to receive respect from their social network on Facebook. Those high on EE would be likely to use Facebook to determine what others are saying about them. They would be more likely to focus on the status updates from their network for the purpose of determining if their network is speaking as well of them as their inflated sense of self-importance would demand. Some research suggests that when someone high in trait narcissism is slighted, they aggressively retaliate (Bushman & Baumeister, 1998; Twenge & Campbell, 2003). Ackerman et al. (2011) argue that EE is the subscale is the aspect of narcissism most associated with socially disruptive behaviors such as aggression. Therefore, EE is predicted to be associated with responding to negative comments from others with verbally aggressive responses. Finally, if the EE subscale is tapping into a trait that demands respect from others, they would also be predicted to become angry when they do not get the respect they feel they deserve. One way this might be expressed on Facebook would be becoming angry when others do not comment on their status updates. When people post status updates on Facebook, others have the opportunity to indicate agreement or praise their comments. Someone high in EE would become angry when they did not get this attention. These hypotheses were tested using a survey of Facebook users.

Method

Sample

There were 294 participants in the survey whose ages ranged from 18 to 65 years ($M = 23.26$, $SD = 7.30$). Of this sample, 74.1% were college students and 68% were female. The sample was a convenience sample recruited by the members of an undergraduate research methods course in a medium sized Midwestern, American university. They contacted their social network and solicited volunteers to complete the survey. Participations were uncompensated. All participants were Facebook users.

Procedure

Participants were given a link to the online consent form that described their rights as research participants. If they indicated that they agreed to participate, an online survey appeared. The online survey began with the questions regarding Facebook use, and then they were asked the GE, and EE subscales of the NPI using the items identified by Ackerman et al. (2011). After the NPI subscales was the Rosenberg (1965) self-esteem scale and then basic demographic items.

Instruments

The items for all the original scales are contained in Appendix A. Table 1 contains means, standard deviations, number of items, and reliability estimates for all of the focal constructs. The first set of items concerned the

Table 1

Means, standard deviations, scale reliability, and number of items for constructs

Measure	M	SD	Reliability	Number of items
GE	3.14	2.18	0.83	9
EE	0.89	1.04	0.68	4
Self-esteem	3.16	0.50	0.87	10
Self-promotion	3.23	1.01	0.84	5
Accept strangers' friend requests	1.98	1.34	—	1
Retaliate against mean comments	1.64	1.14	—	1
Seeking support from others	2.71	1.56	0.95	5
Providing support to others	4.21	1.64	0.92	4
Anger at lack of comments	1.43	1.93	0.96	4
Looking to see if others comment about the self	2.85	1.48	0.87	4
Number of friends	652.58	473.36	—	1
Difference between seeking and providing social support	−1.50	1.60	0.87	

frequency with which the participants engaged in particular Facebook behaviors on a 6-point scale ranging from "never" to "all the time." These include the self-promotion behaviors, accepting strangers as friends, and retaliating against mean comments. The participants were next asked the items from Dillard and Shen (2005) felt anger scale by instructing participants to "Please use the following scale to respond to how you feel when people do not comment as much as you would like on your status updates on Facebook." For each of the four emotions listed (irritated, angry, annoyed, aggravated) they were asked to respond using an 11-point scale ranging from "I feel none of this emotion" to "I feel a great deal of this emotion." Most of the remaining Facebook questions utilized a 7-point Likert scale ranging from "strongly disagree" to "strongly agree." The variable representing the difference between the amount of social support they provide and the amount they seek was calculated by subtracting the amount they provide from how much they seek. Finally, the participants were asked how many friends they had on Facebook (range: 12–4655).

In order to determine the construct validity of the new multi-item measures, a confirmatory factor analysis was conducted. AMOS 18.0 was used to estimate the fit of the four factor model containing the items for self-promotion, checking for comments about the self by others, providing social support, and seeking social support. The data were adequately consistent with the model (*CFI* = .93, *RMSEA* = .09).

The participants responded to the items identified by Ackerman et al. (2011) for the two subscales of interest from the NPI. Their scores were calculated by summing the number of narcissism items they chose on the forced-choice NPI items for each subscale. They also responded to the Rosenberg self-esteem scale. The self-esteem scores were calculated by calculating the average score for each participant such that higher scores indicated greater self-esteem. Table 2 contains a correlation matrix of all the measured constructs.

Results

Statistical Analysis

Initially, the results concerning self-promotion will be examined. Then the results concerning anti-social behaviors will be discussed. All hypotheses were tested by regressing each Facebook behavior onto GE, EE, and self-esteem, with ordinary least squares estimates. Rhodewalt and Morf (1995) argued that including self-esteem in the regression equation controls for the overlap between healthy self-esteem and narcissism. There is conceptually some overlap between self-esteem and narcissism in that GE is driven partially by the narcissist's belief that he or she is due attention because they are such a valuable person. Similarly EE is partially driven by the narcissist's belief that she or he is entitled to anything she or he wants because they perceive themselves to be a valuable person, Regression analysis partials out the healthy parts of self-regard from the unhealthy aspects that drive GE and EE.

Table 2

Correlation matrix of measured constructs

	1	2	3	4	5	6	7	8	9	10	11	12	13	14
1. GE														
2. EE	0.36													
3. SE	0.28	-0.09												
4. Self promotion	0.27	0.07	0.04											
5. Number of friends	0.17	-0.01	0.04	0.33										
6. Accept strangers	0.25	0.31	-0.16	0.26	0.21									
7. Seek support	0.14	0.19	-0.22	0.39	0.13	0.28								
8. Provide support	-0.01	-0.03	-0.10	0.33	0.11	0.10	0.50							
9. Difference in social support	0.14	0.21	-0.11	0.03	0.02	0.17	0.46	-0.54						
10. Anger	0.23	0.20	-0.28	0.08	0.02	0.27	0.23	0.06	0.16					
11. Check for comments	0.14	0.30	-0.16	0.21	0.16	0.30	0.31	0.30	-0.01	0.32				
12. Retaliate with mean comments	0.25	0.36	-0.13	0.32	0.17	0.41	0.34	0.10	0.23	0.30	0.38			
13. Sex	-0.13	-0.10	-0.06	0.26	0.06	-0.14	0.03	0.19	-0.17	-0.08	-0.08	-0.04		
14. Age	-0.21	-0.19	-0.02	-0.22	-0.28	-0.13	-0.10	0.02	-0.12	-0.06	-0.19	-0.16	0.06	
15. College student	-0.11	-0.10	-0.04	-0.19	-0.20	-0.04	-0.12	0.03	-0.15	-0.05	-0.13	-0.15	0.01	0.46

Note: Correlations such that $r > .11$ are $p < .05$, $r > .14$ are $p < .05$, and $r > .18$ are $p < .001$. Sex is coded male = 0 and female = 1. College student status is coded non-college students = 0 and college students = 1.

Table 3

Results of regressing GE, EE, and self-esteem on Facebook behavior with standardized beta weights and R^2 values

Facebook behavior	β			R^2
	GE	EE	SE	
Self promoting behavior	**.28	−.05	−.03	.07
Number of FB friends	**.21	−.09	−.02	.04
Frequency of accepting stranger as friends	**.23	**.21	**−.20	.16
Retaliate against mean comments	**.19	**.28	**−.15	.17
Seek social support	**.18	.10	**−.26	.10
Provide social support	.04	−.06	−.11	.01
Seek more social support than provide	*.13	*.16	*−.14	.07
See if others are talking about me	.09	**.26	**−.16	.12
Get angry at lack of status comments	*.31	.05	*−.36	.18

*Statistically significant at $p < .05$.
**Statistically significant at $p < .01$.

Self-Promotion

Recall that it was predicted that GE would be related positively to self-promoting Facebook behaviors that allow one to present an inflated sense of self to as many people as possible. Examination of Table 3 shows the standardized regression coefficients for the regression of the self-promoting Facebook behavior factor on GE, EE, and self-esteem. GE was the only substantial predictor of the self-promoting Facebook behaviors. Also, it was predicted that GE would be associated with a higher friend count as those high in GE would be seeking a large audience to provide attention. GE was again the only substantial predictor of friend count. Finally, GE was predicted to be positively associated with the frequency with which the participants accept strangers as friends to again expand their audience. GE was positively associated with accepting strangers but surprisingly, EE was a substantial predictor as well.

Anti-Social Behavior

It was also predicted that EE would be positively related to several anti-social behaviors associated with their sense of entitlement to non-reciprocated social support and positive regard. Examination of Table 3 shows the standardized regression coefficients for the regression of each anti-social Facebook behavior on GE, EE, and self-esteem. The regression models showed that EE was a substantial predictor of retaliating against mean comments, seeking more social support than one provides, and checking Facebook to see what others are saying about one. These relationships are consistent with the predicted pattern of a positive association between EE and anti-social behavior. On the other hand, EE did not predict getting angry when people do not comment on one's status. This latter finding was inconsistent with the hypothesis. In general, the data were consistent with the expectation that EE would be associated with behaviors that demonstrated a focus on one's own needs without regard for those of others.

There were also unexpected relationships between GE and anti-social behaviors. In particular, GE was substantially associated with an increased likelihood of retaliating against mean comments about oneself, though the relationship was weaker than the relationship of this behavior with EE. Additionally, GE was predictive of seeking more social support than one provides. Surprisingly, although EE was not a substantial predictor of getting angry about the lack of comments on one's status by others, GE was positively associated with this response.

Self-Esteem

Although self-esteem was not the focus of this investigation, self-esteem tended to be negatively predictive of some of the same behaviors that the two narcissism scales were positively related to. Examination of Table 3 show[s] that self-esteem was not substantially related to the self-promotion behaviors. On the other hand, it was negatively predictive of many of the anti-social behaviors.

Discussion

This study sought to test the prediction that the two socially disruptive elements of narcissism would each predict a particular pattern of Facebook behaviors. Grandiose exhibitionism was predicted to be related to Facebook behaviors that afforded extensive self-presentation to as large an audience as possible via status updates, photos, and attaining large numbers of friends. Entitlement/exhibitionism was predicted to be related to anti-social behaviors such as retaliating against negative comments about oneself, reading others status updates to see if they are talking about oneself, and seeking more social support than one provides. With few exceptions, the data were consistent with these hypotheses. Additionally, in some cases, self-esteem was negatively related to these narcissistic Facebook behaviors.

The anti-social behaviors were predicted to be primarily associated with EE but both aspects of narcissism were predictive of some of these behaviors. Both subscales were related positively to retaliating against mean comments as well as seeking more social support than one provides. Despite EE being identified as the more socially disruptive aspect of narcissism (Ackerman et al., 2011), only GE was related to angry responses to perceived social neglect. Perhaps this finding occurred because people who are seeking attention are more likely to be angered about not getting attention paid to their status updates. This finding suggests that in particular cases, it is GE, not EE that is more strongly anti-social aspect of narcissism. Both GE and EE were associated with angrily retaliating against negative comments about the self. In general, the relationships with both of these two narcissism subscales is consistent with previous research finding that narcissism is negatively predictive of communal orientations to social interaction (Bradlee & Emmons, 1992) and positively predictive of interpersonal deviance (Ackerman et al., 2011).

This study also provided some support for Ackerman et al.'s (2011) contention that these two subscales of the NPI are measuring different constructs. The differential pattern of relationships with the self-promotional behaviors shows that the nomological network of each subscale differs in substantial ways from the other. On the other hand there were several cases in which both subscales were related in the same way to some of the anti-social Facebook behaviors. These findings suggest that although EE does not tap into the desire to self-promote, GE may include some of the aspects of entitlement that Ackerman et al. (2011) predicted would be more associated with the EE trait. Future researchers examining narcissism would be advised to consider each subscale of the NPI both separately and as a whole to further examine the factor structure of the NPI.

Limitations

The generalizability of the findings in this study is limited because the sample was not representative. Although it was not composed entirely of college students, about three fourths of the participants were college students. Given that Facebook is reaching all over the world and across all demographics (Ahmad, 2011) it is important to replicate this study with a broader sample in order to determine if these relationships can be found with other groups. Perhaps in other cultures, narcissism expresses differently on Facebook.

Additionally, the relationships uncovered in this study may have been inflated by several sources of method bias (Podsakoff, MacKenzie, Lee, & Podsakoff, 2003). It is possible that a consistency motif was operating to inflate the relationship among the Facebook behaviors. Item context effects may also have caused some participants to interpret the NPI items based on their Facebook behavior and hypothesis guessing may have encouraged some participants to intentionally inflate those relationships. Additional research should measure individuals' NPI scores and then have independent coders record many of the Facebook behaviors measured in this study by examining the participants' Facebook accounts.

Future Research

More research is needed on socially disruptive Facebook communication. Additional socially disruptive communication patterns should be uncovered and examined. Furthermore, the effects of anti-social behavior on other users is an important and untapped area of research. In general, the "dark side" of Facebook (DeAndrea et al., 2011) requires more research in order to better understand Facebook's socially beneficial and harmful aspects in order to enhance the former and curtail the latter.

Conclusion

Given the explosion in Facebook's popularity (Ahmad, 2011), this article took a significant first step towards identifying the kinds of people who may create a socially disruptive atmosphere on Facebook. If Facebook is to be a place where people go to repair their damaged ego (Toma & Hancock, 2011) and seek social support (Wright et al., 2007) it is vitally important to discover the potentially negative communication one might find on Facebook and the kinds of people likely to engage in them. Ideally, people will engage in pro-social Facebooking rather than anti-social mebooking.

Appendix A

Self-promotion questions

> How often do you post status updates to Facebook?
> How often do you post photographs of yourself on Facebook?
> How often do you update your profile information on Facebook?
> How often do you change your profile picture on Facebook?
> How often do you tag pictures of yourself on Facebook?

Accept friend requests from strangers

> How often do you accept a friend request from a total stranger on Facebook (assuming they do not appear to be a fake profile)?

Retaliate against negative comments

> How often do you make mean comments on someone's status if they said something negative about you on Facebook?

Checking for comments about the self

> I use Facebook to see what people are saying about me.
> I like to read my Facebook newsfeed to see if my friends have mentioned me.
> It is important to me to know if anyone is saying anything bad about me on Facebook.
> I usually know what people are saying about me on Facebook.

Offer social support

> I use Facebook to offer emotional support to people I know when they are feeling upset about something.
> If I see someone post a Facebook status update that indicates they are upset, I try to post a comforting comment on their status.
> It is important to me to try to cheer up my friends by commenting on their Facebook status updates when it appears that they feel distressed.
> I try to make people feel better by commenting on their Facebook status when I can tell they are having a bad day.

Seek self support

> Whenever I am upset I usually post a status update about what is bothering me.

If something made me sad, I usually post a comment about it on Facebook.

Posting a status update to Facebook is a good way to vent when something is bugging me.

If I post a Facebook status update about something that is bothering me, it makes me feel better.

I use Facebook to let people know that I am upset about something.

Number of friends

How many friends do you have on Facebook (total number of people in your "Friends").

References

Ackerman, R. A., Witt, E. A., Donnellan, M. B., Trzesniewski, K. H., Robins, R. W., & Kashy, D. A. (2011). What does the narcissistic personality inventory really measure? *Assessment, 18,* 67–87.

Ahmad, A. (2011). Social network sites and its popularity. *International Journal of Research and Reviews in Computer Science, 2,* 522–526.

Bergman, S. M., Fearrington, M. E., Davenport, S. W., & Bergman, J. Z. (2011). Millennials, narcissism, and social networking: What narcissists do on social networking sites and why. *Personality and Individual Differences, 50*(5), 706–711. doi:10.1016/j.paid.2010.12.022.

Bradlee, P. M., & Emmons, R. A. (1992). Locating narcissism within the interpersonal circumplex and the five-factor model. *Personality and Individual Differences, 13,* 821–830.

Buffardi, L. E., & Campbell, W. K. (2008). Narcissism and social networking web sites. *Personality and Social Psychology Bulleting, 34,* 1303–1314.

Bushman, B. J., & Baumeister, R. F. (1998). Threatened egotism, narcissism, self-esteem, and direct and displaced aggression: Does self-love or self-hate lead to violence? *Journal of Personality and Social Psychology, 75,* 219–229.

DeAndrea, D. C., Tong, S. T., & Walther, J. B. (2011). Dark sides of computer-mediated communication. In W. R. Cupach & B. H. Spitzberg (Eds.), *The dark side of close relationships II* (pp. 95–118). New York. New York: Routledge.

Dillard, J. P., & Shen, L. (2005). On the nature of reactance and its role in persuasive health communication. *Communication Monographs, 72,* 144–168.

Mehdizadeh, S. (2010). Self-presentation 2.0: Narcissism and self-esteem on Facebook. *Cyberpsychology, Behavior, and Social Networking, 13,* 357–364.

Ong, E. Y. L., Ang, R. P., Ho, J. C. M., Lim, J. C. Y., Goh, D. H., Lee, C. S., et al. (2011). Narcissism, extraversion, and adolescents' self-presentation on Facebook. *Personality and Individual Differences, 50,* 180–185.

Park, N., Kee, K. F., & Valenzuela, S. (2009). Being immersed in social networking environment: Facebook groups, uses and gratifications, and social outcomes. *Cyberpsychology & Behavior, 12,* 729–733.

Podsakoff, P. M., MacKenzie, S. M., Lee, J., & Podsakoff, N. P. (2003). Common method variance in behavioral research: A critical review of the literature and recommended remedies. *Journal of Applied Psychology, 88,* 879–903.

Raskin, R. N., & Terry, H. (1988). A principal-components analysis of the narcissistic personality inventory and further evidence of its construct validity. *Journal of Personality and Social Psychology, 54,* 890–902.

Rhodewalt, F., & Morf, C. C. (1995). Self and interpersonal correlates of the narcissistic personality inventory: A review and new findings. *Journal of Research in Personality, 29,* 1–23.

Rosenberg, M. (1965). *Society and the adolescent self-image.* Princeton, NJ: Princeton University Press.

Toma, C. L., & Hancock, J. (2011). *Affirming the self online: Motives and benefits of Facebook use.* Boston, MA: Paper presented at the annual meeting of the International Communication Association.

Twenge, J. M., & Campbell, W. K. (2003). "Isn't it fun to get the respect that we're going to deserve?" Narcissism, social rejection, and aggression. *Personality and Social Psychology Bulletin, 29,* 261–272.

Walther, J. B., Van Der Heide, B., Kim, S. Y., Westerman, D., & Tong, S. T. (2008). The role of friends' appearance and behavior on evaluations of individuals on Facebook: Are we known by the company we keep? *Human Communication Research, 34,* 28–49.

Wright, K. B., Craig, E. A., Cunningham, C. B., & Igiel, M. (2007). *Emotional support and perceived stress among college students using Facebook.com: An exploration of the relationship between source perceptions and emotional support.* Chicago, IL: Paper presented at the annual meeting of the National Communication Association.

Bruce C. McKinney, Lynne Kelly, and Robert L. Duran

NO

Narcissism or Openness?: College Students' Use of Facebook and Twitter

With 845,000,000 + Facebook® users worldwide (see http://www.facebook.com/press/info.php?statistics), it is a popular means by which people stay connected to their social network (Ellison, Steinfield, & Lampe, 2007; Hampton, Goulet, Rainie, & Purcell, 2011). Scholars in psychology have studied personality variables of users of social networking sites (SNSs; e.g., Ryan & Xenos, 2011; Wilson, Fornasier, & White, 2010). Perhaps because these sites have features enabling individuals to share information about themselves, some scholars (e.g., Buffardi & Campbell, 2008; Mehdizadeh, 2010) have focused on narcissism. Despite the limitations of these studies and some inconsistent findings, popular press articles (e.g., Jayson, 2009; O'Dell, 2010; Rosen, 2007) have proclaimed that SNSs breed narcissism among users.

Critiques of SNSs and branding of users as narcissistic are based on limited empirical evidence, and fail to consider that such sites are inherently communication tools. Hampton et al. (2011) found that Facebook users have more close social ties; that most of what they "do" on Facebook, besides provide status updates about themselves, is comment on others' posts, updates, and photos; and that "Facebook use seems to support intimacy rather than undermine it" (p. 25). These and other study results (e.g., Stern & Taylor, 2007; Urista, Dong, & Day, 2009) calls into question the conclusion that activity on an SNS is narcissistic, and raises the possibility that active self-presentation on an SNS reflects an openness about sharing information about one-self with others to facilitate communication and maintain relationships with one's wide circle of friends and acquaintances. This study investigated whether a communication perspective better explains individuals' activities on SNSs than narcissism does. With so many SNS users, it is important to determine whether their behavior is aberrant (i.e., narcissistic) or appropriate for the relationship maintenance purpose of these sites.

Narcissism and Social Networking

Several studies have examined the association between the usage of SNSs—in particular, Facebook—and narcissism. According to Buffardi and Campbell (2008), "Narcissism refers to a personality trait reflecting a grandiose and

Bruce C. McKinney, Lynne Kelly, & Robert L. Duran. From *Communication Research*, 2012, pp. 108–118. Copyright © 2012 by Sage Publications—JOURNALS. Reprinted by permission via Rightslink.

inflated self-concept" (p. 1304). The narcissist tends to view him- or herself as intelligent, powerful, physically attractive, unique, and entitled (Buffardi & Campbell, 2008). Some researchers (e.g., Twenge & Foster, 2010; Twenge, Konrath, Foster, Campbell, & Bushman, 2008a, 2008b) have claimed that there has been a significant increase in narcissism among "generation Ys" or "millennials" over the last 2 decades, although others dispute this (Trzesniewski, Donnellan, & Robbins, 2008a, 2008b).

Research studying the association of narcissism with usage of an SNS has generally concluded that there is a positive relationship (e.g., Buffardi & Campbell, 2008; Mehdizadeh, 2010; Ryan & Xenos, 2011), but a closer look reveals limitations and inconsistent findings. Buffardi and Campbell, using the Narcissistic Personality Inventory (NPI; Raskin & Terry, 1988) and coding, had raters examine individuals' Facebook pages. They found that higher scores on the NPI were related to more interactions on Facebook (specifically, number of friends and wall posts); there was no relation between page owners' narcissism and quantity of information they posted about themselves, as had been expected. Narcissism was positively related to coder ratings of self-promoting information, as well as "main photograph attractiveness, self-promotion, and sexiness" (Buffardi & Campbell, 2008, p. 1310).

Consistent with Buffardi and Campbell (2008), Mehdizadeh (2010) found that narcissism scores were positively correlated with the time spent on Facebook and the number of times Facebook was checked per day. Results provided partial support for the hypothesis that narcissism scores are related to self-promoting content, although the study author did the ratings of self-promoting content; thus, the findings are potentially biased and, therefore, suspect.

In contrast to results obtained by Buffardi and Campbell (2008) and Mehdizadeh (2010), Bergman, Fearrington, Davenport, and Bergman (2011) found narcissism was unrelated to the amount of time spent on SNSs or the frequency of status updates. It also was not related to types of SNS activities, with the exception of more posting of self-focused pictures. However, results indicated that narcissism was positively related to the number of, and desire to have, many SNS friends, as well to the belief that others are interested in one's activities and a desire to let others know what one is doing. Ong et al. (2011) found that over and above extraversion, narcissism was positively related to self-ratings of the attractiveness of Facebook profile pictures and to the frequency of status updates (in contrast to Bergman et al.'s, 2011, findings). However, narcissism was unrelated to social network size (also in contrast to Bergman et al.'s, 2011, findings) and number of photos posted, once extraversion was taken into account. Finally, Ryan and Xenos (2011) reported that, although Facebook users were higher on overall narcissism than non-users, narcissism was unrelated to the amount of time spent on Facebook (consistent with Bergman et al., 2011). This study also found that narcissism was associated with a preference for the "photos" feature, and that the exhibitionism dimension, but not the overall NPI score, was related to a preference for the "status updates" feature. However, the study did not distinguish between photos about oneself or viewing others' photos, or between posting status updates or viewing others' updates.

SNS Tools for Communication and Relationship Maintenance

Research by communication scholars on SNSs is limited, and has focused on how such sites form and maintain social capital (e.g., Ellison et al., 2007; Valenzuela, Park, & Kee, 2009) or on why in individuals are drawn to such sites (e.g., Stern & Taylor, 2007; Urista et al., 2009) and how they use them (e.g., Mansson & Myers, 2011). Findings have been consistent that individuals use these sites, particularly Facebook, largely to maintain existing relationships and stay connected to people in their lives (Ellison et al., 2007; Hampton et al., 2011; Stern & Taylor, 2007; Urista et al., 2009). Mannson and Myers focused on how users expressed affection to maintain relationships, finding that many forms of expressed affection transpired on Facebook. Results of these studies, thus, suggest that users view these sites as enabling communication and the sharing of information about one another.

Rationales and Research Questions

The purposes of this study were twofold. First, because studies of narcissism and SNS usage have produced mixed results, additional research is warranted. This study overcame a limitation of published research by distinguishing between self-focused and other-focused SNS activity. Second, this study offered an alternative to narcissism as the motivator of self-focused SNS activity by viewing SNSs as tools for communication and maintaining relationships. From this perspective, self-focused information may be motivated by a positive attitude about sharing such information to stay connected to one's social network.

To the first purpose, studies have produced mixed results pertaining to the relationship between SNS usage and narcissism. Given these conflicting findings and the lack of research differentiating the focus of Facebook activity (i.e., to promote oneself or check out others), the following research questions were addressed:

> *RQ1: Are there positive relationships between narcissism and both the frequency of using Facebook to provide information about oneself and the number of Facebook friends?*
>
> *RQ2: Is there a negative relationship between narcissism and frequency of using Facebook to find out about others?*

All SNSs are not necessarily used in the same ways; previous research has not distinguished among SNSs or only examined Facebook. One other popular site, Twitter, described as an "information network" (www.twitter.com), has not been studied with respect to narcissism. Twitter would seem to be a perfect venue for narcissists because it allows individuals to answer the question, "What are you doing?," via messages of 140 characters or less. The belief that there is an audience interested in following one's moment-to-moment postings suggests egocentrism, self-aggrandizement, and self-importance—the very characteristics of narcissistic individuals. That one can tweet or follow others' tweets suggests two possible relationships with narcissism. Therefore, we addressed the following research questions:

> RQ3: Is there a positive relationship between narcissism and both the frequency of using Twitter to provide information about oneself and the number of Twitter followers?
>
> RQ4: Is there a negative relationship between narcissism and frequency of using Twitter to follow others?

Although a "New Narcissism" (Rosen, 2007) may, in part, account for the popularity of SNSs, it is also likely that SNSs are simply one way young adults communicate. Bergman et al. (2011), in explaining their unexpected result that narcissism was unrelated to the amount of time on SNSs and the frequency of status updates, concluded the following: "This suggests that Millennials' SNS usage is not solely about attention—seeking . . . but is also a means of staying connected and communication" (p. 709). In addition, the prevalence, ease, norm, and structure of SNSs may foster a positive attitude about being open about oneself. Providing information about oneself is normal and expected behavior on these sites. Acquisti and Gross (2006) concluded that "Respondents are fully aware that a social network is based on information sharing" (p. 18). Indeed, that is what Twitter is intended for, and the structure of Facebook, with user profiles, status updates, and so forth encourages such sharing. Thus, SNS users likely share information about themselves not because they are narcissistic, but because they have a positive attitude about sharing such information—an attitude consistent with viewing SNSs as means to communicate and stay connected. Therefore, the following research questions were addressed:

> RQ5: Are there positive relationships between attitudes about being open in sharing information about oneself and both the frequency of usage of Facebook overall and the frequency of usage of Facebook to inform friends about oneself?
>
> RQ6: Are there positive relationships between attitudes about being open in sharing information about oneself and both the frequency of usage of Twitter overall and the frequency of usage of Twitter to inform friends about oneself?

Method

Participants

Undergraduate students ($N = 233$) in communication classes at a medium-sized, Southern university and at a medium-sized, Northeastern university were administered an anonymous survey. The sample consisted of 144 women (62%) and 89 men (38%), with an average age of 19.77 years ($SD = 1.55$). Of the respondents, 86.6% were White, 5.2% were Hispanic, 4.7% were African American, 0.4% were Asian, and 3% were "other." There were no significant differences on any variables between the two universities.

Measures

Attitude Toward Being Open

This measure consisted of 20 Likert-type items, with response options ranging from 1 (*strongly disagree*) to 5 (*strongly agree*). The items, which we generated, were designed to tap participants' attitudes about how open they are in sharing information about themselves with others in their social circles (e.g., "I share information about myself with only a few close friends," and "I enjoy letting people know things about me"). Existing measures of self-disclosure did not capture the concept of attitude toward being open in sharing information about oneself with the wider social network. For instance, the Wheeless (1978) Revised Self-Disclosure Scale was designed for respondents to focus on a "specific target individual," and all items tap behavior, whereas the measure we developed incorporated items focused on attitudes. However, the Wheeless *amount* and *valence* dimensions were useful in helping us generate items.

Items were factor analyzed using principal components with varimax rotation, producing a three-factor solution accounting for 54.68% of the variance (see Table 1).[1] The first factor, *reveal,* had six items, and tapped participants' willingness to be open and the enjoyment of sharing information about themselves

Table 1

Principal Components Factor Analysis of the Attitude Toward Openness Scale

Items	Factor 1: Reveal	Factor 2: Privacy	Factor 3: Valence
1. I let a wide circle of friends know a lot about me.	.79	.10	.04
2. I share information about myself with only a few close friends. (R)	−.68	−.22	−.05
3. I like letting people know a lot about me.	.72	.20	.05
4. I let very few people know what I've been up to lately. (R)	−.66	−.12	−.08
5. I don't hide much about myself with my wide circle of friends.	.71	.13	.15
6. I enjoy letting people know things about me.	.63	.18	.15
7. Keeping information about myself private is very important to me. (R)	−.29	−.67	−.09
8. People worry too much about their privacy.	.18	.73	−.02
9. I don't worry about how much information people have about me.	.16	.66	.26
10. People today need to be more concerned about their privacy. (R)	−.13	−.79	.00
11. I generally let people know only good things about me. (R)	−.03	−.02	−.73
12. It is okay if people know bad things about me.	.18	.25	.66
13. It is best to let people know only things that make me look good. (R)	−.01	.04	−.76
14. I let people know good and bad things about me.	.21	.10	.74
Eigenvalue	4.40	1.86	1.39
Portion of variance	31.46	13.32	9.91
Cronbach's alpha	.82	.73	.71

Note: N = 233. R in parentheses refers to reflected items.

with a wide circle of friends ($M = 3.03$, $SD = 0.73$). *Privacy,* the second dimension, was defined by four items that referred to a lack of concern for privacy (e.g., "People worry too much about their privacy"; $M = 2.52$, $SD = 0.70$). The final factor, *valence,* consisted of four items focused on willingness to share both positive and negative information about oneself ($M = 3.35$, $SD = 0.64$).

Usage of SNSs.

To measure how frequently participants use Twitter and Facebook, 13 items were generated. Response options for 11 of the items were as follows: 0 (*never*), 1 (*less than a few times a month*), 2 (*a few times a month*), 3 (*a couple of times in a week*), 4 (*1 or 2 times a day*), and 5 (*many times a day*). These items measured the frequency of using Twitter overall and sending tweets about oneself, following others' tweets, and updating one's profile photo and profile information; and the frequency of using Facebook overall and letting friends know what one is doing, finding out about friends, updating one's profile and profile photo, and posting photos of oneself. The other two items asked participants to indicate how many Twitter followers and Facebook friends they have. Table 2 presents descriptive statistics for all variables.

Measure of Narcissism

To assess narcissism, the NPI (Raskin & Terry, 1988) was used. Evidence for construct validity of the NPI is reported by Raskin and Terry and Watson, Grisham, Trotter, and Biderman (1984). The NPI is a 40-item measure in which respondents must choose between two options for each item: an option that is indicative of narcissism (e.g., "I like to be the center of attention") and an option that is not (e.g., "I prefer to blend in with the crowd"). Items were summed to produce a score ($M = 17.74$, $SD = 6.42$); reliability was good ($\alpha = .81$), and the mean was comparable to that obtained by Buffardi and Campbell (2008).

Table 2

Descriptive Statistics

Variable	n	M	SD
Frequency of Twitter use	77	3.10	1.35
Frequency of sending tweets	72	2.71	1.39
Frequency of following tweets	72	3.56	1.42
Number of followers on Twitter	68	72.50	168.49
Frequency of FB use	227	4.41	1.01
Frequency of FB use to tell friends about oneself	210	2.79	1.00
Frequency of FB use to find out about friends	224	3.81	1.06
Frequency of posting photos about oneself on FB	200	1.69	0.71
Narcissism	180	17.74	6.42
Attitude toward openness about sharing information about oneself			
Reveal dimension	229	3.03	0.73
Privacy dimension	232	2.52	0.70
Valence dimension	233	3.35	0.64

Note: N = 233. FB = Facebook®.

Results

Table 2 presents descriptive statistics. Large variation was reported in the number of Twitter followers and Facebook friends; the medians were 38 and 700, respectively. Whereas 227 (97.4%) participants use Facebook, only one-third use Twitter.

The first two research questions focused on the relationships between narcissism and the use of Facebook to provide information about oneself (*RQ1*) and to find out about others (*RQ2*). Bivariate correlations revealed no significant relationships (see Table 3). However, narcissism was significantly and positively related to the number of Facebook friends ($r = .16$, $p < .05$), although the correlation was small.

RQ3 and *RQ4* focused on relationships between narcissism and the frequency of using Twitter and the number of Twitter followers. Narcissism had a significant, positive relationship with the use [of] Twitter to send tweets about oneself ($r = .26$, $p = .05$), but not with the number of Twitter followers or the use of Twitter to follow others (see Table 3).

RQ5 and *RQ6* addressed the relationships between attitude toward being open in sharing information about oneself and both Facebook and Twitter use. The *reveal* dimension of attitude toward openness (i.e., willingness to be open and enjoyment of sharing information about oneself with a wide circle of friends) was significantly and positively related to the frequency of Facebook use to tell friends about oneself ($r = .30$, $p < .01$) and the frequency of sending tweets about oneself ($r = .24$, $p < .05$). The *privacy* dimension (i.e., a lack of concern for privacy) obtained a significant, positive relationship with the number of Twitter followers ($r = .27$, $p < .05$; see Table 3).

Discussion

Results of this study indicated that narcissism is unrelated to the frequency of using Facebook to post about oneself (i.e., status updates or photos) but, consistent with two studies (Bergman et al., 2011; Buffardi & Campbell, 2008), is related to the self-reported number of Facebook friends. However, narcissism was significantly related to using Twitter to send tweets about oneself. Finally, attitude toward being open about sharing information about oneself was significantly related to the frequency of using Facebook and Twitter to provide self-focused updates and photos of oneself.

These findings suggest that Facebook is not dominated by narcissistic millennials, as some have proposed (Jayson, 2009; Rosen, 2007), although, consistent with previous research, those higher on narcissism appear to be driven to amass a larger number of Facebook friends. A contribution of this study is that it examined the attitude toward being open about sharing self-focused information that reflects the communicative and relationship mainte-nance functions of SNSs. The behavior of posting about oneself on Facebook may be better explained by the attitude that it is appropriate and enjoyable to share information with a wide circle of friends. One study found that par-ticipants reported a greater likelihood of disclosing personal information on

Table 3

Correlation Matrix

Variable	(2)	(3)	(4)	(5)	(6)	(7)	(8)	(9)	(10)	(11)	(12)	(13)
(1) Narcissism	.13	.09	-.02	.15	.26*	.07	.04	.04	.06	.05	.12	.16*
(2) Reveal		.47**	.27**	.19	.24*	.01	-.06	.11	.30**	.05	.19**	-.01
(3) Privacy			.24**	.03	.10	-.11	.27*	-.02	.13	.01	.14	.04
(4) Valence				.17	.12	.06	.10	-.08	.04	.00	-.01	.00
(5) Use Twitter					.81**	.85**	.24*	.10	.34**	.15	.32**	.05
(6) Send tweets						.64**	.31*	.09	.45**	.14	.26*	.12
(7) Follow tweets							.18	.04	.11	.07	.24	-.05
(8) Number Twitter followers								-.09	-.08	-.14	-.06	-.02
(9) Use FB									.31**	.61**	.23**	.03
(10) FB about self										.56**	.26**	-.04
(11) FB to find out about friends											.26**	-.06
(12) Post pics about self on FB												.04
(13) Number FB friends												—

Note: $N = 233$. FB = Facebook®.

$*p = .05.$ $**p = .01.$

Facebook than face to face (Christofides, Muise, & Desmarais, 2009), leading the authors to conclude that there is "something different" about the interaction on Facebook, perhaps because it "creates norms regarding what specific information to disclose based on what others have disclosed" (p. 343). Anderson and Raine (2010) stated that "A solid majority of technology experts and stakeholders said the Millennial generation will lead society into a new world of personal disclosure and information sharing using new media" (p. 2). Indeed, as Livingstone (2008) stated, "[S]ocial networking sites typically display as standard precisely the personal information that previous generations often have regarded as private" (p. 404). In sum, our study suggests that the posting of self-focused information and photos on Facebook reflects a positive attitude about such information sharing, not narcissism. This attitude may result from disclosure norms on Facebook, as well as its primary function to connect with one's social network.

An additional contributor is that this study is the first to examine the relationship between narcissism and Twitter usage. Results suggest that Twitter may be the network of choice for narcissists, which may, in part, account for the substantially lower number of Twitter users, as compared to Facebook users. Respondents with significantly higher scores on the NPI also reported sending more tweets about themselves, but narcissism was not related to the number of Twitter followers (which is not in the user's control) or using Twitter to follow others. Whether Twitter is the preferred tool for narcissists requires future research, but this study suggests that it may be.

A limitation of this study is the use of self-reports to assess the frequency of using SNSs to share information and view others' information, as well as self-reports of the frequency of sending tweets about oneself. Actual usage may differ from self-reported usage. A final limitation is that the attitude toward openness measure was author generated, and has not been systematically tested for validity. However, it has face validity, its dimensional structure was solid, and reliabilities were good. Future research should assess the construct validity of the measure.

Results of this study suggest that the use of SNSs by college students is not evidence of narcissism. It appears that the posting of photos of oneself and updating of one's status on Facebook is more a reflection of young adults' orientation to openness with regard to their daily lives. However, the usage of Twitter does appear to be somewhat narcissistically driven. Thus, it appears that it is not the technology that creates narcissism as much as it is the narcissistic personality that seeks a form of technology allowing one to be the center of attention.

Note

1. An earlier factor analysis revealed weak communalities for six items, which were subsequently dropped; many of the items were negatively worded and, thus, potentially confusing to respondents (i.e., 2 items were dropped from each factor—specifically, "I don't like to reveal much about myself," "It is fine if people I'm not close to know what I've been up to

lately," "I don't keep many secrets about myself," "People are too open about themselves with others," "I don't mind revealing things about me that might be embarrassing," and "I don't worry about what others might think about what I say about myself").

References

Acquisti, A. A., & Gross, R. (2006). Imagined communities: Awareness, information sharing, and privacy on the Facebook. *Privacy Enhancing Technologies, 4258,* 1–22. doi:10.1007/11957454_3

Anderson, J., & Raine, L. (2010, July 9). *Millennials will make online sharing in networks a lifelong habit* (Report No.). Retrieved from Pew Internet & American Life Project website: http://www.pewinternet.org/Reports/2010/Future-of-Millennials/Overview.aspx

Bergman, S. M., Fearrington, M. E., Davenport, S. W., & Bergman, J. Z. (2011). Millennials, narcissism, and social networking: What narcissists do on social networking sites and why. *Personality and Individual Differences, 50,* 706–711. doi:10.1016/j.paid.2010.12.022

Buffardi, L. E., & Campbell, W. K. (2008). Narcissism and social networking Web sites. *Personality and Social Psychology Bulletin, 34,* 1303–1314.

Christofides, E., Muise, A., & Desmarais, S. (2009). Information disclosure and control on Facebook: Are they two sides of the same coin or two different processes? *CyberPsychology & Behavior, 12,* 341–345. doi:10.1089/cpb.2008.0226

Ellison, N. B., Steinfield, C., & Lampe, C. (2007). The benefits of Facebook "friends": Social capital and college students' use of online social network sites. *Journal of Computer-Mediated Communication, 12,* 1143–1168.

Hampton, K., Goulet, L. S., Rainie, L., & Purcell, K. (2011, June 16). *Social networking sites and our lives* (Report No.). Retrieved from Pew Internet & American Life Project website: http://www.pewinternet.org/Reports12011/Technology-and-social-networks.aspx

Jayson, S. (2009, August 25). Are social networks making students more narcissistic? *USA Today.* Retrieved from http://www.usatoday.com/news/education/2009-08-24-narcissism-young_N.htm

Livingstone, S. (2008). Taking risky opportunities in youthful content creation: Teenagers' use of social networking sites for intimacy, privacy and self-expression. *New Media & Society, 10,* 393–411. doi:10.1177 /1461444808089415

Mansson, D. H., & Myers, S. A. (2011). An initial examination of college students' expressions of affection through Facebook. *Southern Communication Journal, 76,* 155–168.

Mehdizadeh, S. (2010). Self-presentation 2.0: Narcissism and self-esteem on Facebook. *Cyberpsychology, Behavior, and Social Networking, 13,* 357–364.

O'Dell, J. (2010, August 30). Facebook feeds narcissism, survey says. CNN.com. Retrieved from www.cnn.com/2010/TECH/social.media/08/30/facebook.narcissism.mashable/index.html

Ong, E. Y. L., Ang, R. P., Ho, J. C. M., Lim, J. C. Y., Goh, D. H., Lee, C. S., & Chua, A. Y. K. (2011). Narcissism, extraversion and adolescents' self-presentation on Facebook. *Personality and Individual Differences, 50,* 180–185.

Raskin, R., & Terry, H. (1988). A principal-components analysis of the Narcissistic Personality Inventory and further evidence of its construct validity. *Journal of Personality and Social Psychology, 54,* 890–902.

Rosen, C. (2007). Virtual friendship and the new narcissism. *The New Atlantis, 17,* 15–31. Retrieved from http://www.thenewatlantis.com/docLib/TNA17-Rosen.pdf

Ryan, T., & Xenos, S. (2011). Who uses Facebook? An investigation into the relationship between the Big Five, shyness, narcissism, loneliness, and Facebook usage. *Computers in Human Behavior, 27,* 1658–1664. doi:10.1016/chb.2011.02.004

Stern, L. A., & Taylor, K. (2007). Social networking and Facebook. *Journal of the Communication, Speech & Theatre Association of North Dakota, 20,* 9–20.

Twenge, J. M., & Foster, J. D. (2010). Birth cohort increases in narcissistic personality traits among American college students, 1982–2009. *Social Psychological Personality Science, 1,* 99–106.

Twenge, J. M., Konrath, S., Foster, J. D., Campbell, W. K., & Bushman, B. J. (2008a). Egos inflating over time: A cross-temporal meta-analysis of the narcissistic personality disorder. *Journal of Personality, 76,* 875–901.

Twenge, J. M., Konrath, S., Foster, J. D., Campbell, W. K., & Bushman, B. J. (2008b). Further evidence of an increase of narcissism among college students. *Journal of Personality, 76,* 919–927.

Trzesniewski, K H., Donnellan, M. B., & Robins, W. (2008a). Do today's young people really think they are so extraordinary? An examination of secular trends in narcissism. *Psychological Science, 19,* 181–188.

Trzesniewski, K. H., Donnellan, M. B., & Robins, W. (2008b). Is "generation me" really more narcissistic than previous generations? *Journal of Personality, 76,* 903–918.

Urista, M. A., Dong, Q., & Day, K. D. (2009). Explaining why young adults use MySpace and Facebook through Uses and Gratifications Theory. *Human Communication, 12,* 215–229.

Valenzuela, S., Park, N., & Kee, K. F. (2009). Is there social capital in a social network site?: Facebook use and college students' life satisfaction, trust, and participation. *Journal of Computer-Mediated Communication, 14,* 875–901.

Watson, P. J., Grisham, S. O., Trotter, M. V., & Biderman, M. D. (1984). Narcissism and empathy: Validity evidence for the Narcissistic Personality Inventory. *Journal of Personality Assessment, 48,* 301–304.

Wheeless, L. R. (1978). A follow-up study of the relationships among trust, disclosure, and interpersonal solidarity. *Human Communication Research, 4,* 143–157.

Wilson, K., Fornasier, S., & White, K. M. (2010). Psychological predictors of young adults' use of social networking sites. *CyberPsychology, Behavior, and Social Networking, 13,* 173–176. doi:10.1089/cyber.2009.0094

EXPLORING THE ISSUE

Is Excessive Use of Facebook a Form of Narcissism?

Critical Thinking and Reflection

1. Consider the fact that both articles agree with the idea that there is a positive correlation between the trait of narcissism and the number of Facebook friends of users. What are some methodological problems in studying a relationship such as this?

2. The argument has been made that the Millennial generation is leading society to a new world of personal disclosure and information sharing via new media. To what extent is this evidence of a new standard for openness, or a representation of a failure to understand the value of privacy?

3. What are some factors that may contribute to the fact that Facebook has more users than Twitter? Also, what are your thoughts about the statement that Twitter may be the network of choice for narcissists?

4. How would you explain the fact that very few scholarly articles have been published which report positive psychological benefits derived from Facebook use?

5. If you were awarded a large grant to study the beneficial versus the detrimental personal impact of Facebook, what variables would you study, and why?

Is There Common Ground?

Both sets of authors would concur with the fact that Facebook and other social networking services have changed communication among people during the past decade. Several benefits have been derived as a result of the advances in sharing personal information, photos, and the stories of people's lives. Although for most people Facebook is a convenient means of communicating with a circle of close friends and relatives, for some this service is a vehicle for self-promotion and possible hurt and exploitation of other people. Both articles agree that an unusually high number of Facebook friends corresponds with the trait of narcissism. Professor Carpenter focuses on particularly negative aspects of narcissism such as grandiosity, entitlement, and exploitativeness. Professor McKinney and his colleagues concur with the correlation between narcissism and number of Facebook friends, but they assert that narcissism is unrelated to the frequency of using Facebook to post about oneself.

Additional Resources

Facebook Statistics and News. Retrieved from www.facebook.com/press/info.php?statistics

Kirkpatrick, D. (2011) *The Facebook effect: The inside story of the company that is connecting the world.* New York, NY: Simon & Schuster.

Nadkarni, A., & Hofmann, S. G. (2012). Why do people use Facebook? *Personality and Individual Differences, 52*(3), 243–249. doi:10.1016/j.paid.2011.11.007

Psychology Today's Webpage about Narcissistic Personality Disorder. Retrieved from www.psychologytoday.com/conditions/narcissistic-personality-disorderv

Contributors to This Volume

EDITOR

RICHARD P. HALGIN is a professor of psychology in the Clinical Psychology Program at the University of Massachusetts–Amherst. He is coauthor, with Susan Krauss Whitbourne, of *Abnormal Psychology: Clinical Perspectives on Psychological Disorders*, 6th edition (McGraw-Hill, 2010); and coeditor, with Whitbourne, of *A Casebook in Abnormal Psychology: From the Files of Experts* (Oxford University Press, 1998). His list of publications also includes more than 50 articles and book chapters in the fields of psychotherapy, clinical supervision, and professional issues in psychology. He is a board-certified clinical psychologist, and he has over three decades of clinical, supervisory, and consulting experience. At the University of Massachusetts, his course in abnormal psychology is one of the most popular offerings on campus, attracting more than 500 students each semester. He has also taught the course on a regular basis at Amherst College. His teaching has been recognized at the university and national level: he was honored with the University of Massachusetts Distinguished Teaching Award and the Alumni Association's Distinguished Faculty Award and was also recognized by the Society for the Teaching of Psychology of the American Psychological Association. Upon appointment by the Governor, he serves on the Board of Registration of Psychologists in Massachusetts.

AUTHORS

GREG ABBOTT was reelected as the 50th attorney general of Texas on November 7, 2006. Prior to his election as attorney general, Greg Abbott served as a justice on the Texas Supreme Court and as a state district judge in Harris County.

LAURIE AHERN is the president of Mental Disabilities Rights International (MDRI). She worked for 10 years as a newspaper editor and investigative reporter. Ms. Ahern is the former cofounder and codirector of the federally funded National Empowerment Center, and former vice president of the U.S. National Association of Rights Protection and Advocacy. She has written and lectured extensively on psychiatric recovery and self-determination, and has won several awards and honors for her efforts to improve conditions for, and attitudes toward, people with psychiatric disabilities.

AMERICAN PSYCHIATRIC ASSOCIATION (APA) is an international society working to ensure that all persons with mental disorders receive humane care and effective, accessible psychiatric diagnosis and treatment. In addition to supporting the prevention, diagnosis, and treatment of mental illness and working toward greater funding for education and psychiatric research, the APA educates lawmakers about a variety of issues, including the insanity defense. www.psych.org/

AMERICAN PSYCHOLOGICAL ASSOCIATION (APA) aims to improve psychology as a science and as a profession. As the United States' representative of psychology, the APA aspires to advance education, health, and human welfare by liberally supporting all branches of psychology and psychological research, advancing research methods, and improving psychologists' conduct, education, and ethics standards. The APA also advocates for psychology at the federal level through three directorates: education, public interest, and science. The APA works with federal agencies when they reformulate legislation and regulations of psychological interest. www.apa.org

APA TASK FORCE ON MENTAL HEALTH AND ABORTION consisted of Brenda Major (Chair), Mark Appelbaum, Linda Beckman, Mary Ann Dutton, Nancy Felipe Russo, and Carolyn West. The American Psychological Association (APA) is a 150,000-member scientific and professional organization that represents psychology in the United States. The mission of the APA is to advance the creation, communication, and application of psychological knowledge to benefit society and improve people's lives.

MARK P. AULISIO is the director of the Center for Biomedical Ethics at Metro-Health, the Bioethics Educational Programs, and the Bioethics PhD Program at Case Western Reserve University as well as an associate professor of bioethics at the university. He has taken part as the executive director of the national task force that issued the American Society of Bioethics and Humanities (ASBH) report *Core Competencies for Health Care Ethics Consultation;* and he has chaired the ASBH national task force. He has international experience in ethics consultation and clinical ethics and has authored over 50 publications in these and related areas

STEVEN BALT is a researcher, working psychiatrist, and editor-in-chief of the online newsletter, *The Carlat Psychiatry Report: An Unbiased Monthly Covering All Things Psychiatric.* He is a practicing psychiatrist at North Bay Psychiatric Associates in San Rafael, California. He is experienced in psychopharmacology, cognitive-behavior therapy, dialectical behavior therapy, and community psychiatry, with a special interest in addiction psychiatry and process addictions such as eating disorders.

TIM BAYNE is currently a university lecturer in the philosophy of mind at the University of Oxford and a fellow of St. Catherine's College. Bayne is interested in applied ethics, the philosophy of religion, and especially the philosophy of cognitive science. Some of Bayne's more recent works include *Delusions and Self-Deception: Affective Influences on Belief Formation* (2007), *Hypnosis and the Unity of Consciousness* (2006/7), and *Phenomenology and the Feeling of Doing: Wegner on the Conscious Will* (2006). www.philosophy.ox.ac.uk/members/timothy_bayne

SAMUEL J. BRAKEL is the CEO and education director for the Isaac Ray Forensic Group, a group that provides psychological and forensic psychiatric services in its mission to attain justice and public safety. Attorney Brakel, author of *Law and Psychiatry in the Criminal Justice System* (2001), has faculty appointments at Rush Medical College and DePaul University College of Law and continues to publish widely in the area of mental health law.

AMY T. CAMPBELL is an assistant professor of bioethics and humanities at the State University of New York. She also teaches at Syracuse University College of Law and is associate faculty in the bioethics program of Union Graduate College, Mount Sinai School of Medicine. Her research interests include how to inform bioethicists' role on a global policy stage, better meet legal training needs in medical education, and develop a health policy from a therapeutic and ethical perspective.

CHRISTOPHER J. CARPENTER is a professor in the Department of Communication at Western Illinois University. His teaching interests focus on social influence, interpersonal, and quantitative research and method statistics, and his research interests include cognitive processing of persuasive messages, compliance gaining, power in relationships, and meta-analysis.

PRISCILLA K. COLEMAN is an associate professor of human development and family studies at Bowling Green State University. Her research interests focus on socioemotional development in early childhood, parenting issues, and the psychological effects of the abortion experience.

MARK COSTANZO is a professor of psychology and codirector of the Center for Applied Psychological Research at Claremont McKenna College. He has conducted research on various issues pertaining to the application of psychological science to the legal system. He is the author of *Just Revenge: Costs and Consequences of the Death Penalty.*

PETER COTTON, a clinical and organizational psychologist, is an honorary research fellow at the University of Melbourne, Australia. Cotton has worked as a workplace mental health specialist with the National Occupational Health and Safety Commission in Australia and has published widely in the field of occupational health and well-being.

JOHN M. DAVIS is Gillman Professor of Psychiatry and Research Professor of Medicine at the University of Illinois, Chicago. His research focuses on schizophrenic spectrum disorders, mood disorders, obsessive-compulsive disorder, premenstrual dysphoric disorder, and the biology of major mental illnesses.

GRANT J. DEVILLY is a professorial fellow at the University of Australia, Melbourne and president of the Australasian Society for Traumatic Stress. Devilly's current research focuses on the causes and treatment of posttraumatic stress disorder, and he has also conducted extensive research in the field of criminology, in which he has published extensively on the topics of sex-offending and crime victimization.

ELISE DONOVAN began a postdoctoral fellowship at the Liggins Institute in Auckland, New Zealand, following completion of her PhD in health and exercise science at Colorado State University in 2011. At Colorado State, she studied obesity-associated coronary artery disease under the mentorship of Benjamin Miller and Karyn Hamilton, and also explored issues in philosophy under the direction of Distinguished Professor Bernie Rollin. At the Liggins Institute, she has been studying the developmental origins of chronic disease and evolutionary medicine.

ROBERT L. DURAN is a professor in the School of Communication at the University of Hartford. He teaches courses in small group communication, interpersonal communication, nonverbal communication, and research methodology. His research focuses on social communication competence, technology and interpersonal relationships, media portrayals of relational issues, and teacher–student interaction. He serves on the editorial boards of *Journal of Communication, Communication Quarterly,* and *Communication Reports.*

RAYMOND FITZPATRICK is a professor of public health and primary care at University of Oxford and fellow, Nuffield College, Oxford. He is chair of a National Health Service Research and Development Unit in Oxford and directs the Patient Health Instruments program for the Department of Health. His research focuses on evaluation of health services, particularly interventions of chronic diseases.

ELLEN GERRITY is an assistant professor of psychiatry at Duke University and coeditor of *The Mental Health Consequences of Torture.* She is the associate director of the UCLA-Duke University National Center for Child Traumatic Stress, and has focused her professional work for many years on topics pertaining to trauma and violence.

JAMES B. GOTTSTEIN is a psychiatric rights lawyer from Anchorage, Alaska, where he has practiced law for over 25 years. Gottstein is the president of numerous organizations, including the Law Project for Psychiatric Rights (PsychRights), which he cofounded in 2002; Peer Properties, Inc., which he cofounded in 2002 to offer peer-run housing for mentally ill people in bad living situations; Soteria-Alaska, Inc., an organization that offers noncoercive and mostly nondrug alternatives to psychiatric hospitalization, which he cofounded in 2003; and CHOICES, Inc., which he also cofounded in 2003 to make available peer-run services that particularly support the right of people to choose whether or not to take psychiatric drugs. Gottstein has also been a member of the board of directors for the National Association for Rights Protection and Advocacy since 2005, acting as president in 2006, and he has been on the board of directors of the International Center for the Study of Psychiatry and Psychology since 2006. http://psychrights.org/about/Gottstein.htm

STEVEN F. GRUEL is a high-profile defense attorney in California. He runs a private law firm in San Francisco, where he specializes in criminal defense law. Attorney Gruel is the counsel of record for the amicus brief of Senator Leland Yee.

TONY HOPE is a fellow of St. Cross College in Oxford, a professor of medical ethics, and a founding member of the Oxford Centre for Ethics and Communication in Health Care Practice (Ethox). His research interests include basic neuroscience and Alzheimer's disease, as well as clinical ethics. He has written over 100 academic articles and several books.

KIRK M. HUBBARD has served in administrative and clinical positions in the Veterans Administration Hospital in Hampton, VA, and has held adjunct faculty positions at Eastern Virginia Medical School and the College of William and Mary. Dr. Hubbard served as a psychologist supporting field operations and as director of behavioral sciences research for the CIA.

Helia Garrido Hull is an associate professor of law and the associate dean for student affairs at Barry University in Miami Shores, Florida. She also practices law at Disability Rights Florida, a statewide, not-for-profit corporation that is the designated protection and advocacy system for individuals with disabilities in Florida.

MATTHEW L. ISRAEL is a psychologist who currently serves as director of the Judge Rotenberg Center (JRC), which he founded in 1971 as the Behavior Research Institute. Dr. Israel studied psychology under the late B. F. Skinner as an undergraduate, graduate student, and a postdoctoral fellow at Harvard University. In the 1960s, he was involved in several initiatives using behavioral interventions with disturbed children. JRC is a special needs school in Canton, Massachusetts, serving individuals from the age of 3 through adulthood. For nearly four decades, JRC has provided education and treatment to emotionally disturbed individuals with conduct, behavioral, emotional, and/or psychiatric problems, as well as to individuals with developmental delays and autistic-like behaviors.

LYNNE KELLY is a professor and director of the School of Communication at the University of Hartford, where she teaches courses in group, organizational, and interpersonal communication; communication technologies and relationships; research methods; and a special communication course for shy and apprehensive students. Her research interests include communication technologies like e-mail, cell phones, and instant messaging, and their role in developing and maintaining relationships as well as her career-long focus on the nature and treatment of communication reticence and speech anxiety. She has coauthored four books, has published or presented over a hundred papers on communication topics, and has served on the editorial boards of several communication journals.

NEIL LEVY is a principal research fellow at the University of Melbourne's Australian Research Council Special Research Centre for Applied and Public Ethics. Levy's numerous writings include *On the Competence of Substance Users to Consent to Treatment Programs* (2006), *Autonomy and Addiction* (2006), *Cognitive Scientific Challenges to Morality* (2006), and *The Case for Physician-Assisted Suicide: How Can It Possibly Be Proven?* (2006). www.onlineopinion.com.au/author.asp?id=1414; www.findanexpert.unimelb.edu.au/researcher/person8720.html

SCOTT O. LILIENFELD is a professor of psychology at Emory University and a clinical psychologist. He conducts research on the causes and assessment of personality disorders (especially psychopathic personality), scientific thinking and its application to psychology, and philosophical psychology.

ARNOLD H. LOEWY is a professor of criminal and constitutional law at the Texas Tech University School of Law. Loewy graduated first in his class at Boston University, where he received his bachelor's degree in 1961 and his doctor of jurisprudence degree in 1963. After earning his master of laws degree from Harvard University in 1964, Loewy went on to teach at the University of North Carolina School of Law for 38 years, and then at the University of Connecticut School of Law for 4 years, before joining the Texas Tech University School of Law faculty in 2006. Loewy chaired the criminal justice section of the Association of American Law Schools in 1993, and has spoken to the International Society for the Reform of Criminal Law on the topics of criminal speech (1990), virtual child pornography (2002), and "Systematic Changes to Reduce the Conviction of the Innocent" (2006). www.law.ttu.edu/lawWeb/faculty/bios/Loewy.shtm

M. BRINTON LYKES is a professor of community-cultural psychology at Boston College and the associate director of the Boston College Center for Human Rights and International Justice. Her scholarly activities have focused on a range of social issues such as political violence, humanitarian aid, reparations, and mental health.

BRUCE C. McKINNEY is a professor of communication studies at the University of North Carolina Wilmington. Professor McKinney teaches courses in concepts in communication studies, mediation, communication theory, and negotiation. His research includes studying Vietnamese perceptions of communication, education, public relations, and conflict management.

PATRICIA A. MILLETT is an attorney in Washington, DC, at the law firm of Akin Gump Strauss Hauer & Feld LLP, where she heads the firm's Supreme Court practice and co-heads the firm's national appellate practice. She has argued a total of 31 cases before the U.S. Supreme Court (the most of any woman in history) and approximately 35 in the courts of appeals. She has briefed scores of cases in the Supreme Court and appellate courts across the nation.

JEFFREY T. MITCHELL earned his PhD in human development from the University of Maryland, where he is currently a clinical associate professor of emergency health services. He is also president emeritus of the International Critical Incident Stress Foundation (ICISF). He developed critical incident stress management after serving several years as a firefighter/paramedic. Mitchell has written or coauthored a number of books, including *Critical Incident Stress Debriefing: An Operations Manual for CISD, Defusing and Other Group Crisis Intervention Services,* and many articles about crisis intervention.

STEVEN MOFFIC is a professor in the Department of Psychiatry and Behavioral Medicine as well as the Department of Family and Community Medicine at the Medical College of Wisconsin. He is interested in psychiatric ethics, cultural psychiatry, ecopsychiatry, prison psychiatry, and the nature of evil. He has devoted considerable attention during his career to exploring ethics within the practice of psychiatry.

SHARON MOREIN-ZAMIR is a research associate in the Department of Psychiatry at the University of Cambridge School of Clinical Medicine in England. She is interested in action control and executive function and in the different facets of compulsivity as instances in which control may be impaired. Recently she has become interested in the social and ethical considerations that result from neuroscience research, such as the debate surrounding the use of cognitive enhancing drugs.

NATIONAL ALLIANCE ON MENTAL ILLNESS (NAMI) is dedicated to eliminating mental illness and improving the lives of mentally ill persons and their families. NAMI takes a strong stance on public policy issues that affect the mentally ill and their loved ones. The alliance supports the insanity defense, favoring both volitional and cognitive standards. www.nami.org/

NATIONAL INSTITUTE OF MENTAL HEALTH (NIMH) is one of the 27 constituents that comprise the National Institutes of Health (NIH). The NIH is part of the U.S. Department of Health and Human Services, as well as the federal government's primary organization for behavioral and biomedical research. The NIMH is the lead government research agency for behavioral and mental disorders. www.nimh.nih.gov/index.shtml

NATIONAL INSTITUTE ON DRUG ABUSE (NIDA) was established in 1974 and became part of the National Institutes of Health, Department of Health and Human Services in October 1992. Since then it has been a federal focal point for research on drug abuse and addiction. NIDA's aim is to use the power of science to analyze drug abuse and addiction. NIDA addresses the most fundamental and essential questions about drug abuse, from detecting and responding to emerging drug abuse trends, and understanding how drugs work in the brain and body, to developing and testing new treatment and prevention approaches.

THE PRESIDENT'S COUNCIL ON BIOETHICS was a group of individuals appointed by President George W. Bush in November 2001 to advise his administration on bioethical issues that may emerge as a consequence of advances in biomedical science and technology.

NATALIE J. PURCELL, who holds a master's in public administration, works as a professional in the nonprofit sector, and as a sociopolitical activist associated with Amnesty International. www.amazon.com/Death-Metal-Music-Politics-Subculture/dp/0786415851

ERIC ROSENTHAL is the founder and executive director of Mental Disabilities Rights International (MDRI), and is also vice president of the United States International Council on Disability. He has served as a consultant to the World Health Organization, UNICEF, and the U.S. National Council on Disability. Rosenthal has won awards for his human advocacy efforts on behalf of people with disabilities.

DIANA E. H. RUSSELL, who holds a PhD in social psychology from Harvard, has spent the last 25 years exploring the topic of sexual violence against women and girls. She is a leading expert in her field, having written many books and articles on the topics of pornography, rape, the misogynist murder of women, and incest. Her writings include *The Epidemic of Rape and Child Sexual Abuse in the United States* (2000) and *The Trials and Tribulations of Publishing a Book Attacking Porn* (1999). Russell has won numerous awards, being named to the Veteran Feminists of America's Honor Roll for American Writers in 2002, and receiving the American Humanist Association's "Humanist Heroine" award in 2001. Russell has spoken publicly on television and radio shows, including Oprah Winfrey and National Public Radio. www.dianarussell.com/

BARBARA J. SAHAKIAN is a professor in the Department of Psychiatry at the University of Cambridge School of Clinical Medicine in England. Her research is aimed at understanding the neural basis of cognitive, emotional, and behavioral dysfunction in order to develop more effective pharmacological and psychological treatments. Her lab focuses on early detection, differential diagnosis, and proof of concept studies using cognitive enhancing drugs.

SALLY SATEL is a practicing psychiatrist and lecturer at the Yale University School of Medicine as well as a resident scholar for the American Enterprise Institute for Public Policy Research. She examines mental health policy as well as political trends in medicine. Some of her publications include *The Health Disparities Myth, and One Nation under Therapy,* which she coauthored with Christina Hoff Sommers.

WESLEY J. SMITH left his full-time law practice in 1985 to work in public advocacy and pursue a writing career, and was named one of the nation's top professional thinkers in bioengineering by the *National Journal* in 2004. Smith is an award-winning author, having written or coauthored 11 books, including *Culture of Death: The Assault on Medical Ethics in America,* which was named the 2001 Best Health Book of the Year, a *Consumer Guide to a Brave New World* (2005), and his recently updated *Forced Exit: Euthanasia, Assisted Suicide, and the New Duty to Die* (2006). Smith works as a special consultant for the Center for Bioethics and Culture and as an attorney for the International Task Force on Euthanasia and Assisted Suicide; he is also a senior fellow at the Discovery Institute. Smith runs a well-read Web log titled "Secondhand Smoke," a blog defending the importance and exceptional moral value of human life. www.wesleyjsmith.com/blog/

ANNE STEWART is a consultant adolescent psychiatrist in the Oxford City Child and Adolescent Mental Health Service. She is chair of the Oxfordshire and Buckinghamshire Mental Health Partnership Foundation NHS Trust in the United Kingdom and was an honorary senior clinical lecturer at the University of Oxford. She is a leader in the Oxford City community eating disorder team and is actively involved in assessment, treatment, and consultation regarding adolescent eating disorders. Her research interests include prevention of eating disorders, self-harm in adolescence, cognitions in adolescent depression, and treatment decision making in anorexia nervosa.

JACINTA O. A. TAN is a consultant child and adolescent psychiatrist who is also an empirical medical ethics researcher. She has worked at the University of Oxford, UK, in the Ethox Centre as part of the Department of Public Health and Primary Care. Her research interests are the ethics and law of capacity, the development of autonomy, treatment decision-making models, the ethics of research, and treatment decision-making in anorexia nervosa.

TRADITIONAL VALUES COALITION (TVS), founded in 1980 by Reverend Louis P. Sheldon, is "the largest nondenominational, grassroots church lobby in America." TVC focuses on issues such as marriage, religious liberties, pornography, education, family tax relief, and what the Coalition calls "the right to life" and "the homosexual agenda." The organization emphasizes "the restoration of the values needed to maintain strong, unified families," providing information on these topics to Christians and pastors.

KELLEY WINTERS is the founder of GID Reform Advocates as well as a writer on issues of transgender medical policy. Winters is the author of *Gender Madness in American Psychiatry: Essays from the Struggle for Dignity* (2008), and her articles have appeared in a number of books and journals. She is also on the advisory board for TransYouth Family Advocates and the Matthew Shepard Foundation.

ROGERS H. WRIGHT is a past president of the Division of Clinical Psychology of the American Psychological Association, and cofounded the Council for the Advancement of the Psychological Professions and Sciences (CAPPS). Wright is a fellow of the American Psychological Association.

LELAND Y. YEE is a member of the California State Senate. He earned a doctorate in developmental psychology from the University of Hawaii, and then worked in various educational and mental health settings. As a former member and president of the San Francisco Unified School District Board of Education and as a therapist in the Mental Health Department of San Francisco, he has long opposed the sale of violent video games to children. During his tenure as a member of the state senate, Yee has fought for, among many other things, children and mental health services. Yee authored a statute that prohibited stores in California from selling violent or M-rated video games to minors based on the potential psychological harm they might cause. His statute was eventually overturned by the Supreme Court of the United States in 2011.